PLAYFAIR
CRICKET ANNUAL

EDIT

All statistic

PREFACE

None of my two score of summers on the professional circuit has inspired stronger hopes of a feast of rich entertainment than the one almost upon us. The excitement inspired by the imminent arrival of the outstanding Australian team led by Ricky Ponting has been heightened by the recent success of Michael Vaughan's England side. Victorious in their last four series and having sustained just one defeat in their last 16 encounters, the hosts can realistically expect to give their oldest enemy the real contest craved by even the most ardent antipodean fan. That they are deemed to have even the slightest chance of regaining the Ashes surrendered in 1989 is due in no small measure to the expertise and foresight of their coach, Duncan Fletcher. First with Nasser Hussain and now with Vaughan, he has moved England steadily up the Test match Championship ladder on to the penultimate rung. A continuity of selection, enhanced by central contracts and emphasis on teamwork and fitness, has been crucial in this development. Gradually key pieces have been added to the jigsaw, none more vital than the genuine all-rounder that Andrew Flintoff now is. Accurate fast bowling and superb fielding are now allied to a new-found ability to build an innings before launching into the most brutal hitting seen since Ian Botham left the arena. There is every chance that the dynamic Kevin Pietersen, scorer of England's fastest limited-overs hundred, will be batting alongside him before the summer ends. Then, as Vaughan has suggested, it will be the spectators who may require helmets.

England's upsurge has owed much to some outstanding fast bowling by Steve Harmison and it was with some trepidation that I chose him for the cover of this edition. The curse of *Playfair* has affected most of the players depicted on its recent covers, none more dramatically than Darren Gough. His first delivery of an international at Melbourne on 10 January 1995 coincided with my opening an envelope containing a proof of that year's cover. As I admired Graham Morris's shot of a gleeful 'Goughie' saluting the demise of another victim, his subject collapsed in mid-approach with a stress fracture of his left foot. Last year someone at Headline deliberately tried to protect Vaughan (front cover) by switching his caption with that of Brian Lara (back), a cunning ploy that fooled those who were not aware that Lara is left-handed. Prior to the Curse, Harmison took 67 wickets at 23.92 in 13 Tests. Since his cover proof emerged he has managed nine at 73.22 in five matches. Fortunately for England, Matthew Hoggard (26 wickets) and the astonishing Andrew Strauss (656 runs) were able to paper over some considerable cracks to scramble a 2-1 victory in South Africa.

This season, exceeding last year's by one day, will be the longest professional one ever. It will be in its 15th week when the Ashes campaign gets underway. Sadly it will be the last home series to be broadcast live on terrestrial television for at least four summers; good news for *Test Match Special*, which has had its exclusive mandate extended, but desperate news for those without access to Pay TV, particularly youngsters eager to watch their heroes.

Serious chroniclers of the game have been appalled by the abuse of Test match records engendered by the continuing participation of Zimbabwe and Bangladesh at the highest level. South Africa's recent horrific two-day annihilation of the former produced the fastest fifty and greatest first-day lead in history. The ICC must not further delay removing those countries from the top echelon until their domestic first-class structure is greatly improved. That they are proposing to confuse matters further by giving Test match status to a 'super test' between Australia and the Rest later this year beggars belief. For a decade after the 1970 England v Rest of the World series '*Wisden*'s' records bore a grumbling appendix of those five games – and that rubber at least had the excuse of replacing a series cancelled for political reasons. Logic dictates that 'international' records should be exactly that – 'contests between nations'. Perhaps a compromise would be to segregate matches involving conglomerate teams into a separate Super Test compartment. For the same reasons, the recent Tsunami Appeal game between Asian and World XIs in Melbourne should not be included in the annals of Limited-Overs Internationals – and is excluded from records in this publication. Exceptionally admirable though it was in conception, the game was little more than an exhibition match. While enjoying the occasion hugely, none of the participants, and there were rather too many, seemed to care a hoot about the result. Another piece of gross meddling produced the crass decision to regard the toss as the start of a match. This is contrary to Law 16, which clearly states that the umpire's call of play heralds the start.

BILL FRINDALL
Urchfont, Wiltshire, *7 March 2005*

ACKNOWLEDGEMENTS AND THANKS

Headline
Juliana Foster (Editor)
David Mitchell (proofs)
Letterpart
Chris Leggett
Caroline Leggett
Lorraine Byfield
Career Records
Philip Bailey
Robin Abrahams
Ron Nuttall
Debbie Frindall
Tastats
Ric Finlay
David Fitzgerald
ECB
Alan Fordham
Andy Smith
County Scorer/Statisticians
John Brown (Derbyshire)
Brian Hunt (Durham)
David Norris (Essex)
Andrew Hignell (Glamorgan)
Keith Gerrish Gloucestershire)
Vic Isaacs (Hampshire)
Jack Foley (Kent)
Alan West (Lancashire)
Graham York (Leicestershire)
David Kendix (Middlesex)
Tony Kingston (Northamptonshire)
Gordon Stringfellow (Nottinghamshire)
Gerry Stickley (Somerset)

Keith Booth (Surrey)
John Hartridge (Sussex)
David Wainwright (Warwickshire)
Neil Smith (Worcestershire)
Roy Wilkinson (Yorkshire)
Overseas
Rajneesh Gupta (India)
Rajesh Kumar (India)
Francis Payne (New Zealand)
Andrew Samson (South Africa)
John Ward (Zimbabwe)
Charlie Wat (Australia)
County Administrations
John Smedley (Derbyshire)
Pat Walton (Durham)
Nancy Fuller (Essex)
Caryl Watkin (Glamorgan)
Tom Richardson (Gloucestershire)
Tim Tremlett (Hampshire)
Ross Franklin (Kent)
Diana Lloyd (Lancashire)
James Whittaker (Leicestershire)
Emma Channon (Middlesex)
Lyndsey Hutchings (Northamptonshire)
Mick Newell (Nottinghamshire)
Sally Donoghue (Somerset)
Steve Howes (Surrey)
Francesca Watson (Sussex)
Keith Cook (Warwickshire)
Mark Newton (Worcestershire)
Rachel O'Halloran (Yorkshire)

ENGLAND v BANGLADESH

SERIES RECORDS

2003-04

HIGHEST INNINGS TOTALS

England	in Bangladesh	326	Chittagong	2003-04
Bangladesh	in Bangladesh	255	Dhaka	2003-04

LOWEST INNINGS TOTALS

England	in Bangladesh	295	Dhaka	2003-04
Bangladesh	in Bangladesh	138	Chittagong	2003-04
HIGHEST MATCH AGGREGATE	917 for 33 wickets		Dhaka	2003-04
LOWEST MATCH AGGREGATE	909 for 34 wickets		Chittagong	2003-04

HIGHEST INDIVIDUAL INNINGS

England	in Bangladesh	113	M.E.Trescothick	Dhaka	2003-04
Bangladesh	in Bangladesh	59	Hannan Sarkar	Dhaka	2003-04

HIGHEST AGGREGATE OF RUNS IN A SERIES

England	in Bangladesh	208	(av 69.33)	M.P.Vaughan	2003-04
Bangladesh	in Bangladesh	114	(av 38.00)	Mushfiqur Rahman	2003-04

RECORD WICKET PARTNERSHIPS – ENGLAND

1st	137	M.E.Trescothick (113)/M.P.Vaughan (48)	Dhaka	2003-04
2nd	22	M.P.Vaughan (81*)/M.A.Butcher (8)	Dhaka	2003-04
3rd	138	N.Hussain (95)/G.P.Thorpe (54)	Chittagong	2003-04
4th	36*	M.P.Vaughan (81*)/G.P.Thorpe (18*)	Dhaka	2003-04
5th	116	N.Hussain (76)/R.Clarke (55)	Chittagong	2003-04
6th	63	N.Hussain (76)/C.M.W.Read (37)	Chittagong	2003-04
7th	41	G.P.Thorpe (64)/G.J.Batty (19)	Dhaka	2003-04
8th	8	A.F.Giles (6)/R.L.Johnson (6)	Chittagong	2003-04
9th	5	A.F.Giles (6)/M.J.Saggers (1)	Chittagong	2003-04
10th	28	A.F.Giles (19)/M.J.Hoggard (6*)	Chittagong	2003-04

RECORD WICKET PARTNERSHIPS – BANGLADESH

1st	12	Hannan Sarkar (20)/Javed Omar (3)	Dhaka	2003-04
	12	Hannan Sarkar (59)/Rajin Saleh (8)	Dhaka	2003-04
2nd	108	Hannan Sarkar (59)/Habibul Bashar (58)	Dhaka	2003-04
3rd	20	Hannan Sarkar (59)/Alok Kapali (12)	Dhaka	2003-04
4th	8	Hannan Sarkar (59)/Mushfiqur Rahman (46*)	Dhaka	2003-04
5th	44	Rajin Saleh (32)/Mushfiqur Rahman (46*)	Chittagong	2003-04
6th	60	Mushfiqur Rahman (34)/Khaled Masud (51)	Dhaka	2003-04
7th	29	Mushfiqur Rahman (46*)/Khaled Mahmud (18)	Dhaka	2003-04
8th	34	Khaled Masud (51)/Mohammad Rafique (32)	Dhaka	2003-04
9th	16	Mohammad Rafique (32)/Mashrafe Mortaza (11)	Dhaka	2003-04
10th	13	Mohammad Rafique (12*)/Enamul Haque II (9)	Chittagong	2003-04

BEST INNINGS BOWLING ANALYSIS

England	in Bangladesh	5-35	S.J.Harmison	Dhaka	2003-04
Bangladesh	in Bangladesh	4-60	Mashrafe Mortaza	Chittagong	2003-04

BEST MATCH BOWLING ANALYSIS

England	in Bangladesh	9- 79	S.J.Harmison	Dhaka	2003-04
Bangladesh	in Bangladesh	5-141	Mohammad Rafique	Dhaka	2003-04

HIGHEST AGGREGATE OF WICKETS IN A SERIES

England	in Bangladesh	9		S.J.Harmison, M.J.Hoggard, R.L.Johnson	2003-04
Bangladesh	in Bangladesh	10	(av 31.00)	Mohammad Rafique	2003-04

	Tests	Series E B D		Dhaka E B D		Chittagong E B D	
2003-04	2	2	–	–	1	–	–	1	–	–

TOURING TEAM REGISTER 2005

Bangladesh had not selected their 2005 touring team at the time of going to press. The following players represented Bangladesh in Test matches in 2004 and 2004-05:

BANGLADESH

Full Names	Birthdate	Birthplace	Team/Division	Type	F-C Debut
AFTAB AHMED	10.11.85	Chittagong	Chittagong	RHB/RM	2001-02
ALOK KAPALI	01.01.84	Sylhet	Sylhet	RHB/LB	2000-01
ENAMUL HAQUE II	05.12.86	Sylhet	Sylhet	LHB/SLA	2001-02
FAISAL HOSSAIN	26.10.78	Chittagong	Chittagong	RHB/RMF	2001-02
HABIBUL BASHAR	17.08.72	Nagakanda, Kushtia	Biman Bangladesh	RHB/OB	1997-98
HANNAN SARKAR	01.12.82	Dhaka	Barisal	RHB/RM	2000-01
JAVED OMAR	25.11.76	Dhaka	Dhaka	RHB/LB	1997-98
KHALED MASUD	08.02.76	Rajshahi	Rajshahi	RHB/WK	1997-98
MANJURAL RANA	04.05.84	Khulna	Khulna	LHB/SLA	2000-01
MASHRAFE MORTAZA	05.10.83	Norail, Khulna	Khulna	RHB/RM	2001-02
MOHAMMED ASHRAFUL	09.09.84	Dhaka	Dhaka	RHB/LB	2000-01
MOHAMMAD RAFIQUE	05.09.70	Dhaka	Dhaka	LHB/SLA	2000-01
MUSHFIQUR RAHMAN	01.01.80	Rajshahi	Rajshahi	RHB/RFM	1999-00
NAFIS IQBAL	31.01.85	Chittagong	Chittagong	RHB/RM	2000-01
NAZMUL HOSSAIN	06.10.87	Hobigonj	Bangladesh U-19	RHB/RMF	2004-05
RAJIN SALEH	20.11.83	Sylhet	Sylhet	RHB/OB	2000-01
TALHA JUBAIR	10.12.85	Faridpur, Dhaka	Dhaka	RHB/RM	2001-02
TAPASH BAISYA	25.12.82	Sylhet	Sylhet	RHB/RFM	2000-01
TAREQ AZIZ	04.09.83	Chittagong	Chittagong	RHB/RMF	2001-02

ENGLAND v AUSTRALIA

SERIES RECORDS

1876-77 to 2002-03

HIGHEST INNINGS TOTALS

England	in England	903-7d	The Oval	1938
	in Australia	636	Sydney	1928-29
Australia	in England	729-6d	Lord's	1930
	in Australia	659-8d	Sydney	1946-47

LOWEST INNINGS TOTALS

England	in England	52	The Oval	1948
	in Australia	45	Sydney	1886-87
Australia	in England	36	Birmingham	1902
	in Australia	42	Sydney	1887-88
HIGHEST MATCH AGGREGATE		1753 for 40 wickets	Adelaide	1920-21
LOWEST MATCH AGGREGATE		291 for 40 wickets	Lord's	1888

HIGHEST INDIVIDUAL INNINGS

England	in England	364	L.Hutton	The Oval	1938
	in Australia	287	R.E.Foster	Sydney	1903-04
Australia	in England	334	D.G.Bradman	Leeds	1930
	in Australia	307	R.M.Cowper	Melbourne	1965-66

HIGHEST AGGREGATE OF RUNS IN A SERIES

England	in England	732	(av 81.33)	D.I.Gower (6 Tests)	1985
	in Australia	905	(av 113.12)	W.R.Hammond	1928-29
Australia	in England	974	(av 139.14)	D.G.Bradman	1930
	in Australia	810	(av 90.00)	D.G.Bradman	1936-37

RECORD WICKET PARTNERSHIPS – ENGLAND

1st	323	J.B.Hobbs (178)/W.Rhodes (179)	Melbourne	1911-12
2nd	382	L.Hutton (364)/M.Leyland (187)	The Oval	1938
3rd	262	W.R.Hammond (177)/ D.R.Jardine (98)	Adelaide	1928-29
4th	288	N.Hussain (207)/G.P.Thorpe (138)	Birmingham	1997
5th	206	E.Paynter (216*)/D.C.S.Compton (102)	Nottingham	1938
6th	215	L.Hutton (364)/J.Hardstaff jr (169*)	The Oval	1938
	215	G.Boycott (107)/A.P.E.Knott (135)	Nottingham	1977
7th	143	F.E.Woolley (133*)/J.Vine (36)	Sydney	1911-12
8th	124	E.H.Hendren (169)/H.Larwood (70)	Brisbane	1928-29
9th	151	W.H.Scotton (90)/W.W.Read (117)	The Oval	1884
10th	130	R.E.Foster (287)/W.Rhodes (40*)	Sydney	1903-04

RECORD WICKET PARTNERSHIPS – AUSTRALIA

1st	329	G.R.Marsh (138)/M.A.Taylor (219)	Nottingham	1989
2nd	451	W.H.Ponsford (266)/D.G.Bradman (244)	The Oval	1934
3rd	276	D.G.Bradman (187)/A.L.Hassett (128)	Brisbane	1946-47
4th	388	W.H.Ponsford (181)/D.G.Bradman (304)	Leeds	1934
5th	405	S.G.Barnes (234)/D.G.Bradman (234)	Sydney	1946-47
6th	346	J.H.W.Fingleton (136)/D.G.Bradman (270)	Melbourne	1936-37
7th	165	C.Hill (188)/H.Trumble (46)	Melbourne	1897-98
8th	243	R.J.Hartigan (116)/C.Hill (160)	Adelaide	1907-08
9th	154	S.E.Gregory (201)/J.M.Blackham (74)	Sydney	1894-95
10th	127	J.M.Taylor (108)/A.A.Mailey (46*)	Sydney	1924-25

BEST INNINGS BOWLING ANALYSIS

England	in England	10- 53	J.C.Laker	Manchester	1956
	in Australia	8- 35	G.A.Lohmann	Sydney	1886-87
Australia	in England	8- 31	F.Laver	Manchester	1909
	in Australia	9-121	A.A.Mailey	Melbourne	1920-21

BEST MATCH BOWLING ANALYSIS

England	in England	19- 90	J.C.Laker	Manchester	1956
	in Australia	15-124	W.Rhodes	Melbourne	1903-04
Australia	in England	16-137	R.A.L.Massie	Lord's	1972
	in Australia	13- 77	M.A.Noble	Melbourne	1901-02

HIGHEST AGGREGATE OF WICKETS IN A SERIES

England	in England	46	(av 9.60)	J.C.Laker	1956
	in Australia	38	(av 23.18)	M.W.Tate	1924-25
Australia	in England	42	(av 21.26)	T.M.Alderman (6 Tests)	1981
	in Australia	41	(av 12.85)	R.M.Hogg (6 Tests)	1978-79

	Tests	Series			The Oval			Manchester			Lord's			Nottingham			Leeds			Birmingham			Sheffield		
		E	A	D	E	A	D	E	A	D	E	A	D	E	A	D	E	A	D	E	A	D	E	A	D
1880	1	1	-	-	1	-	-																			
1882	1	-	1	-	-	1	-																			
1884	3	1	-	2	-	-	1	-	-	1	1	-	-													
1886	3	3	-	-	1	-	-	1	-	-	1	-	-													
1888	3	2	1	-	1	-	-	1	-	-	-	1	-													
1890	2	2	-	-	1	-	-				1	-	-													
1893	3	1	-	2	1	-	-	-	-	1	-	-	1													
1896	3	2	1	-	1	-	-	-	1	-	1	-	-													
1899	5	-	1	4	-	-	1	-	-	1	-	1	-	-	-	1	-	-	1							
1902	5	1	2	2	1	-	-	-	1	-	-	-	1							-	-	1	-	1	-
1905	5	2	-	3	-	-	1	1	-	-	-	-	1	1	-	-	-	-	1							
1909	5	1	2	2	-	-	1	-	-	1	-	1	-				-	1	-	1	-	-				
1912	3	1	-	2	1	-	-	-	-	1	-	-	1													
1921	5	-	3	2	-	-	1	-	-	1	-	1	-	-	1	-	-	1	-							
1926	5	1	-	4	1	-	-	-	-	1	-	-	1	-	-	1	-	-	1							
1930	5	1	2	2	-	1	-	-	-	1	-	1	-	1	-	-	-	-	1							
1934	5	1	2	2	-	1	-	-	-	1	1	-	-	-	1	-	-	-	1							
1938	4	1	1	2	1	-	-				-	-	1	-	-	1	-	1	-							
1948	5	-	4	1	-	1	-	-	-	1	-	1	-	-	1	-	-	1	-							
1953	5	1	-	4	1	-	-	-	-	1	-	-	1	-	-	1	-	-	1							
1956	5	2	1	2	-	-	1	1	-	-	-	1	-	-	-	1	1	-	-							
1961	5	1	2	2	-	-	1	-	1	-	-	1	-				1	-	-	-	-	1				
1964	5	-	1	4	-	-	1	-	-	1	-	-	1	-	-	1	-	1	-							
1968	5	1	1	3	1	-	-	-	1	-	-	-	1				-	-	1	-	-	1				
1972	5	2	2	1	-	1	-	1	-	-	-	1	-	-	-	1	1	-	-							
1975	4	-	1	3	-	-	1				-	-	1				-	-	1	-	1	-				
1977	5	3	-	2	-	-	1	1	-	-	-	-	1	1	-	-	1	-	-							
1980	1	-	-	1							-	-	1													
1981	6	3	1	2	-	-	1	1	-	-	-	-	1	-	1	-	1	-	-	1	-	-				
1985	6	3	1	2	1	-	-	-	-	1	-	1	-	-	-	1	1	-	-	1	-	-				
1989	6	-	4	2	-	-	1	-	1	-	-	1	-	-	1	-	-	1	-	-	-	1				
1993	6	1	4	1	1	-	-	-	1	-	-	1	-	-	-	1	-	1	-	-	1	-				
1997	6	2	3	1	1	-	-	-	1	-	-	-	1	-	1	-	-	1	-	1	-	-				
2001	5	1	4	-	-	1	-				-	1	-	-	1	-	1	-	-	-	1	-				
	146	41	45	60	15	6	12	7	7	13	5	13	14	3	7	9	7	8	8	4	3	4	-	1	-

ENGLAND v AUSTRALIA – IN AUSTRALIA

	Tests	Series			Melbourne			Sydney			Adelaide			Brisbane			Perth		
		E	A	D	E	A	D	E	A	D	E	A	D	E	A	D	E	A	D
1876-77	2	1	1	-	1	1	-												
1878-79	1	-	1	-	-	1	-												
1881-82	4	-	2	2	-	-	2	-	2	-									
1882-83	4	2	2	-	1	1	-	1	1	-									
1884-85	5	3	2	-	2	-	-	-	2	-	1	-	-						
1886-87	2	2	-	-				2	-	-									
1887-88	1	1	-	-				1	-	-									
1891-92	3	1	2	-	-	1	-	-	1	-	1	-	-						
1894-95	5	3	2	-	2	-	-	1	1	-	-	1	-						
1897-98	5	1	4	-	-	2	-	1	1	-	-	1	-						
1901-02	5	1	4	-	-	2	-	1	1	-	-	1	-						
1903-04	5	3	2	-	1	1	-	2	-	-	-	1	-						
1907-08	5	1	4	-	1	1	-	-	2	-	-	1	-						
1911-12	5	4	1	-	2	-	-	1	1	-	1	-	-						
1920-21	5	-	5	-	-	2	-	-	2	-	-	1	-						
1924-25	5	1	4	-	1	1	-	-	2	-	-	1	-						
1928-29	5	4	1	-	1	1	-	1	-	-	1	-	-	1	-	-			

	Tests	Series			Melbourne			Sydney			Adelaide			Brisbane			Perth		
		E	A	D	E	A	D	E	A	D	E	A	D	E	A	D	E	A	D
1932-33	5	4	1	–	–	1	–	2	–	–	1	–	–	1	–	–	–	–	–
1936-37	5	2	3	–	–	2	–	1	–	–	–	1	–	1	–	–	–	–	–
1946-47	5	–	3	2	–	–	1	–	2	–	–	–	1	–	1	–	–	–	–
1950-51	5	1	4	–	1	1	–	–	1	–	–	1	–	–	1	–	–	–	–
1954-55	5	3	1	1	1	–	–	1	–	1	1	–	–	–	1	–	–	–	–
1958-59	5	–	4	1	–	2	–	–	–	1	–	1	–	–	1	–	–	–	–
1962-63	5	1	1	3	1	–	–	–	1	1	–	–	1	–	–	1	–	–	–
1965-66	5	1	1	3	–	–	2	1	–	–	–	1	–	–	–	1	–	–	–
1970-71	6	2	–	4	–	–	1	2	–	–	–	–	1	–	–	1	–	–	1
1974-75	6	1	4	1	1	–	1	–	1	–	–	1	–	–	1	–	–	1	–
1976-77	1	–	1	–	–	1	–	–	–	–	–	–	–	–	–	–	–	–	–
1978-79	6	5	1	–	–	1	–	2	–	–	1	–	–	1	–	–	1	–	–
1979-80	3	–	3	–	–	1	–	–	1	–	–	–	–	–	–	–	–	1	–
1982-83	5	1	2	2	1	–	–	–	–	1	–	1	–	–	1	–	–	–	1
1986-87	5	2	1	2	1	–	–	–	1	–	–	–	1	1	–	–	–	–	1
1987-88	1	–	–	1	–	–	–	–	–	1	–	–	–	–	–	–	–	–	–
1990-91	5	–	3	2	–	1	–	–	–	1	–	–	1	–	1	–	–	1	–
1994-95	5	1	3	1	–	1	–	–	–	1	1	–	–	–	1	–	–	1	–
1998-99	5	1	3	1	1	–	–	–	1	–	–	1	–	–	–	1	–	1	–
2002-03	5	1	4	–	–	1	–	1	–	–	–	1	–	–	1	–	–	1	–
	160	54	80	26	19	26	7	21	24	7	8	15	5	5	9	4	1	6	3
Totals	306	95	125	86															

Matches abandoned without a ball bowled (Manchester 1890 and 1938, Melbourne 1970-71) are excluded from these tables.

2000 RUNS

	Tests	I	NO	HS	Runs	Avge	100	50
D.G.Bradman (A)	37	63	7	334	5028	89.78	19	12
J.B.Hobbs (E)	41	71	4	187	3636	54.26	12	15
A.R.Border (A)	47	82	19	200*	3548	56.31	8	21
D.I.Gower (E)	42	77	4	215	3269	44.78	9	12
S.R.Waugh (A)	46	73	18	177*	3200	58.18	10	14
G.Boycott (E)	38	71	9	191	2945	47.50	7	14
W.R.Hammond (E)	33	58	3	251	2852	51.85	9	7
H.Sutcliffe (E)	27	46	5	194	2741	66.85	8	16
C.Hill (A)	41	76	1	188	2660	35.46	4	16
J.H.Edrich (E)	32	57	3	175	2644	48.96	7	13
G.A.Gooch (E)	42	79	0	196	2632	33.31	4	16
G.S.Chappell (A)	35	65	8	144	2619	45.94	9	12
M.A.Taylor (A)	33	61	2	219	2496	42.30	6	15
M.C.Cowdrey (E)	43	75	4	113	2433	34.26	5	11
L.Hutton (E)	27	49	6	364	2428	56.46	5	14
R.N.Harvey (A)	37	68	5	167	2416	38.34	6	12
V.T.Trumper (A)	40	74	5	185*	2263	32.79	6	9
D.C.Boon (A)	31	57	8	184*	2237	45.65	7	8
W.M.Lawry (A)	29	51	5	166	2233	48.54	7	13
M.E.Waugh (A)	29	51	7	140	2204	50.09	6	11
S.E.Gregory (A)	52	92	7	201	2193	25.80	4	8
W.W.Armstrong (A)	42	71	9	158	2172	35.03	4	6
I.M.Chappell (A)	30	56	4	192	2138	41.11	4	16
K.F.Barrington (E)	23	39	6	256	2111	63.96	5	13
A.R.Morris (A)	24	43	2	206	2080	50.73	8	8

D.G.Bradman holds the unique record of scoring 2000 runs in both countries in this series (2674 runs in England and 2354 in Australia); J.B.Hobbs is the only other batsman to score 2000 runs in either country (2493 runs in Australia).

100 WICKETS

	Tests	Balls	Runs	Wkts	Avge	Best	5wI	10wM
D.K.Lillee (A)	29	8516	3507	167	21.00	7- 89	11	4
I.T.Botham (E)	36	8479	4093	148	27.65	6- 78	9	2
H.Trumble (A)	31	7895	2945	141	20.88	8- 65	9	3
S.K.Warne (A)	26	7792	3040	132	23.03	8- 71	7	2
R.G.D.Willis (E)	35	7294	3346	128	26.14	8- 43	7	–
G.D.McGrath (A)	22	5221	2344	117	20.03	8- 38	7	–
M.A.Noble (A)	39	6845	2860	115	24.86	7- 17	9	2
R.R.Lindwall (A)	29	6728	2559	114	22.44	7- 63	6	–
W.Rhodes (E)	41	5791	2616	109	24.00	8- 68	6	1
S.F.Barnes (E)	20	5749	2288	106	21.58	7- 60	12	1
C.V.Grimmett (A)	22	9224	3439	106	32.44	6- 37	11	2
D.L.Underwood (E)	29	8000	2770	105	26.38	7- 50	4	2
A.V.Bedser (E)	21	7065	2859	104	27.49	7- 44	7	2
G.Giffen (A)	31	6457	2791	103	27.09	7-117	7	1
W.J.O'Reilly (A)	19	7864	2587	102	25.36	7- 54	8	3
R.Peel (E)	20	5216	1715	101	16.98	7- 31	5	1
C.T.B.Turner (A)	17	5195	1670	101	16.53	7- 43	11	2
T.M.Alderman (A)	17	4717	2117	100	21.17	6- 47	11	1
J.R.Thomson (A)	21	4951	2418	100	24.18	6- 46	5	–

100 WICKET-KEEPING DISMISSALS

	Tests	Ct	St	Total
R.W.Marsh (A)	42	141	7	148
I.A.Healy (A)	33	123	12	135
A.P.E.Knott (E)	34	97	8	105

R.W.Marsh (141 catches) and W.A.S.Oldfield (31 stumpings) hold the respective individual records in Anglo-Australian Tests.

TOURING TEAM REGISTER 2005

Australia had not selected their 2005 touring team at the time of going to press. The following players represented Australia in Test matches in 2004 and 2004-05:

AUSTRALIA

Full Names	Birthdate	Birthplace	Team	Type	F-C Debut
CLARKE, Michael John	02.04.81	Liverpool, NSW	NSW	RHB/SLA	1999-00
ELLIOTT, Matthew Thomas Gray	28.09.71	Chelsea, Vic	Vic	LHB/LM/SLC	1992-93
GILCHRIST, Adam Craig	14.11.71	Bellingen, NSW	WA	LHB/WK	1992-93
GILLESPIE, Jason Neil	19.04.75	Darlinghurst, NSW	SA	RHB/RFM	1994-95
HAURITZ, Nathan Michael	18.10.81	Wondai, Q	Q	RHB/OB	2001-02
HAYDEN, Matthew Lawrence	29.10.71	Kingaroy, Q	Q	LHB/RM	1991-92
KASPROWICZ, Michael Scott	10.02.72	S Brisbane, Q	Q	RHB/RFM	1989-90
KATICH, Simon Mathew	21.08.75	Middle Swan, WA	NSW	LHB/SLC	1996-97
LANGER, Justin Lee	21.11.70	Perth, WA	WA	LHB/WK	1991-92
#LEE, Brett	08.11.76	Wollongong, NSW	NSW	RHB/RF	1994-95
LEHMANN, Darren Scott	05.02.70	Gawler, SA	SA	LHB/SLA	1987-88
MacGILL, Stuart Charles Glyndwr	25.02.71	Mount Lawley, WA	NSW	RHB/LBG	1993-94
McGRATH, Glenn Donald	09.02.70	Dubbo, NSW	NSW	RHB/RFM	1992-93
MARTYN, Damien Richard	21.10.71	Darwin, NT	WA	RHB/RM	1990-91
PONTING, Ricky Thomas	19.12.74	Launceston, Tas	Tas	RHB/OB	1992-93
WARNE, Shane Keith	13.09.69	Ferntree Gully, Vic	Vic	RHB/LBG	1990-91
WATSON, Shane Robert	17.06.81	Ipswich, Q	Tas	RHB/RFM	2000-01

Selected mainly as 12th man for Australia's 11 Tests in 2004 or 2004-05 but he is likely to tour England.

THE FIRST-CLASS COUNTIES REGISTER, RECORDS AND 2004 AVERAGES

First-class career statistics are to the end of the 2004 season.

ABBREVIATIONS – General

*	not out/unbroken partnership	l-o	limited-overs
b	born	LOI	Limited-Overs Internationals
BB	Best innings bowling analysis	Tests	Official Test Matches
Cap	Awarded 1st XI County Cap	Tours	Overseas tours involving first-class
f-c	first-class		appearances
HS	Highest Score		

Awards

BHC	Benson and Hedges Cup 'Gold' Award
CGT	Gillette Cup, NatWest/Cheltenham & Gloucester Trophy Match Award
Wisden 2003	One of *Wisden Cricketers' Almanack's* Five Cricketers of 2003
YC 2004	Cricket Writers' Club Young Cricketer of 2004

ECB Competitions

BHC	Benson & Hedges Cup (1972-2002)
CC	(Frizzell) County Championship
CGT	Cheltenham & Gloucester Trophy
NL	(Totesport) National League
NWT	NatWest Trophy (1981-2000)
SL	Sunday League (1969-98)

Education

BHS	Boys' High School
C	College
CFE	College of Further Education
CHE	College of Higher Education
CS	Comprehensive School
GS	Grammar School
HS	High School
I	Institute
IHE	Institute of Higher Education
RGS	Royal Grammar School
S	School
SFC	Sixth Form College
SM	Secondary Modern School
SS	Secondary School
TC	Technical College
T(H)S	Technical (High) School
U	University
UMIST	University of Manchester Institute of Science and Technology
UWIC	University of Wales Institute, Cardiff

Playing Categories

LBG	Bowls right-arm leg-breaks and googlies
LF	Bowls left-arm fast
LFM	Bowls left-arm fast-medium
LHB	Bats left-handed
LM	Bowls left-arm medium pace
LMF	Bowls left-arm medium fast
OB	Bowls right-arm off-breaks
RF	Bowls right-arm fast
RFM	Bowls right-arm fast-medium
RHB	Bats right-handed
RM	Bowls right-arm medium pace
RMF	Bowls right-arm medium-fast
RSM	Bowls right-arm slow-medium
SLA	Bowls left-arm leg-breaks
SLC	Bowls left-arm 'Chinamen'
WK	Wicket-keeper

Teams (see also p 121)

ACT	Australian Capital Territory
ADBP	Agricultural Development Bank of P
B	Bangladesh
CD	Central Districts
EP	Eastern Province
GW	Griqualand West
HK	Hong Kong
K	Kenya
KRL	Khan Research Laboratories
NBP	National Bank of Pakistan
ND	Northern Districts
NSW	New South Wales
NT	Northern Transvaal
(O)FS	(Orange) Free State
PIA	Pakistan International Airlines
Q	Queensland
REDCO	Really Efficient Development Co
SAU	South African Universities
Tas	Tasmania
Vic	Victoria
WA	Western Australia
WAPDA	Water & Power Development Auth.
WP	Western Province

DERBYSHIRE

Formation of Present Club: 4 November 1870
Inaugural First-Class Match: 1871
Colours: Chocolate, Amber and Pale Blue
Badge: Rose and Crown
County Champions: (1) 1936
Gillette/NatWest/C & G Trophy Winners: (1) 1981
Benson and Hedges Cup Winners: (1) 1993
National League (Div 1) Winners: (0); best – 4th (Div 2) 2002
Sunday League Winners: (1) 1990
Twenty20 Cup Winners: (0) best – 3rd in Group 2003, 2004
Match Awards: CGT 49; BHC 71

Chief Executive: T.Sears, County Cricket Ground, Nottingham Road, Derby DE21 6DA • Tel: 01332 383211 • Fax: 01332 290251 • Email: post@dccc.org.uk • Web: www.dccc.org.uk

Director of Cricket/1st XI Coach: D.L.Houghton. **Academy Director/2nd XI Coach**: K.M.Krikken. **Captain**: L.D.Sutton. **Vice-Captain**: G.Welch. **Overseas Players**: M.J.Di Venuto and J.Moss. **2005 Beneficiary**: None. **Head Groundsman**: N.Godrich. **Scorer**: J.M.Brown. ‡ New registration. NO Not qualified for England.

NOADNAN, Muhammad Hassan SYED (M.A.O. College, Lahore), b Lahore, Pakistan 15 May 1974. 5'10". RHB, OB. Islamabad 1994-95, 2001-02. WAPDA 1997-98 to date (as an overseas player 2002-03 to date). Gujranwala 1997-98 to 1998-99. 49 f-c matches in Pakistan before his Derbyshire debut in 2003. Cap 2004. 1000 runs (1): 1380 (2004). HS 140 v Notts (Derby) 2004. BB 1-4 (CC). LO HS 113* v NZ (Derby) 2004. LO BB 2-13 v Leics (Derby) 2004 (NL).

NOBASSANO, Christopher Warwick Godfrey (Grey S, Port Elizabeth; Launceston Church GS; Tasmania U, Hobart), b East London, South Africa 11 Sep 1975. 6'2". British passport (English mother); son of the late B.S.Bassano (cricket writer, historian and broadcaster). RHB, LB. Debut 2001; cap 2002. First to score 100 in each innings on Championship debut – 186* and 106 v Glos (Derby) 2001. Tasmania 2002-03. 1000 runs (1): 1063 (2002). HS 186* (*see above*). Awards: CGT 2. LO HS 126* v Sussex (Arundel) 2003 (NL).

NOBOTHA, Anthony Greyvensteyn (Maritzburg C; Maritzburg Technikon), b Pretoria, South Africa 17 Nov 1976. 6'0". LHB, SLA. Natal/KwaZulu Natal 1995-96 to 1998-99. EP/Easterns 1999-00 to date. Derbyshire debut/cap 2004. HS 103 v and De BB 5-55 v DU (Derby) 2004. CC HS 52 v Essex (Derby) 2004. BB 8-53 Natal B v Northerns B (Pretoria) 1997-98. CC BB 4-66 v Durham (Derby) 2004. LO HS 60* Easterns v EP (Benoni) 2001-02. LO BB 3-16 SA Academy v NZ Academy (Pretoria) 1997.

NOBRYANT, James Douglas Campbell (Maritzburg C; Port Elizabeth U), b Durban, South Africa 4 Feb 1976. 6'0". RHB. E Province 1996-97 to date. Somerset 2003. F-c Tour (SA A): WI 2000-01. HS 234* EP v North West (Potchefstroom) 2002-03. UK HS 109* Sm v LU (Taunton) 2003 – on Sm/UK debut. CC HS 73 Sm v Hants (Taunton) 2003. BB (EP) 1-22. UK BB – . LO HS 105* EP v WP (Cape Town) 2000-01.

CHAPMAN, James Robert (St John Houghton SS; SE Derbyshire C), b Nottingham 19 May 1986. 6'2". LHB, RM. Debut 2004. Awaiting CC debut. HS 7 v DU (Derby) 2004.

DEAN, Kevin James (Leek HS; Leek CFE), b Derby 16 Oct 1975. 6'5". LHB, LMF. Debut 1996. Cap 1998. HS 54* v Worcs (Derby) 2002. 50 wkts (2): most – 83 (2002). BB 8-52 v Kent (Canterbury) 2000. 2 hat-tricks (1998, 2000). Award: CGT 1. LO HS 16* v Glam (Cardiff) 1998 (SL) and 16* v Middx (Derby) 2002 (NL). LO BB 5-32 v Glos (Derby) 1996 (SL).

NQDi VENUTO, Michael James (St Virgil's C; Hobart), b Hobart, Australia 12 Dec 1973. 6'0". LHB, RM/LB. Tasmania 1991-92 to date. Sussex 1999; cap 1999. Derbyshire debut/cap 2000; Appointed captain for 2004 but missed entire season – back surgery. **LOI** (A): 9 (1996-97 to 1997-98); HS 89 v SA (Johannesburg) 1996-97. F-c Tours: Z 1995-96 (Tas); Sc/Ire 1998 (Aus A). 1000 runs (4): most – 1538 (2002). HS 230 v Northants (Derby) 2002. BB (Tas) 1-0. UK BB (Sx) 1-3. De BB 1-16. Awards: CGT 1; BHC 1. LO HS 173* v Derbys CB (Derby) 2000 (NWT). LO BB (Tas) 1-10.

FRANCE, Benjaman John (Bromsgrove S; Oxford CFE), b Brunei 14 May 1982. 5'11". LHB, RM. Debut 2004. Suffolk 2003-04. HS 56 v Leics (Derby) 2004. LO HS 13 v Scot (Edinburgh) 2004.

‡NQFRIEND, Travis John (St George's C, Harare), b Kwekwe, Zimbabwe 7 Jan 1981. Son of I.S.Friend (Rhodesia B 1978-79). 6'2". RHB, RMF. Kolpak registration. Debut 1999-00 (Zimbabwe Academy). Midlands 2000-01 to date. **Tests** (Z): 13 (2001 to 2003-04); HS 81 and BB 5-31 v B (Dhaka) 2001-02. **LOI** (Z): 51 (2000-01 to 2003-04); HS 91 v K (Kwekwe) 2002-03; BB 4-55 v I (Sharjah) 2000-01. F-c Tours (Z): E 2003; I 2000-01, 2001-02; SL 2001-02; B 2001-02). HS 183 Midlands v Manicaland (Kwekwe) 2003-04. BB 5-16 Midlands v Matabeleland (Kwekwe) 2003-04. LO HS 91 (see LOI). LO BB 4-37 Midlands v Mashonaland (Harare) 2002-03.

GODDARD, Lee James (Batley GS; Huddersfield TC; Loughborough U), b Dewsbury, Yorks 22 Oct 1982. 5'10". RHB, WK. Loughborough U 2003. Derbyshire debut 2004. HS 23* LU v Somerset (Taunton) 2003 – on debut. De HS 8.

HAVELL, Paul Matthew Roger (Mentone GS, Melbourne; Warden Park S; Haywards Heath C), b Melbourne, Australia 4 Jul 1980. 6'3". LHB, RFM. Sussex 2001 (1 non-CC match). Derbyshire debut 2003. HS 13* v Yorks (Derby) 2004. BB 4-75 v Durham (Chester-le-St) 2004. LO HS 4 and LO BB 3-28 v Scot (Derby) 2004.

HEWSON, Dominic Robert (Cheltenham C; West of England U), b Cheltenham, Glos 3 Oct 1974. 5'8". RHB, occ RM. Gloucestershire 1996-2001. Derbyshire debut 2002. HS 168 Glos v Derbys (Bristol) 2001. De HS 102* v Glam (Cardiff) 2002 – on debut. BB 3-39 v Somerset (Taunton) 2004. LO HS 69 v Kent CB (Canterbury) 2003 (CGT). LO BB 4-25 v Scot (Edinburgh) 2003 (NL).

HUNTER, Ian David (Fyndoune Community C, Sacriston; Durham New C), b Durham City 11 Sep 1979. 6'2". RHB, RMF. Durham 2000-03. Derbyshire debut 2004. HS 65 Du v Northants (Northampton) 2002. De HS 6. BB 4-55 Du v Warwks (Birmingham) 2001. De BB 3-32 v Essex (Chelmsford) 2004 – on debut. LO HS 39 Du v Leics (Leicester) 2002 (BHC). LO BB 4-29 Du v Essex (Ilford) 2000 (NL).

LUNGLEY, Tom (St John Houghton SS; SE Derbyshire C), b Derby 25 Jul 1979. 6'1". LHB, RM. Debut 2000. No f-c appearances 2004. HS 47 v Warwks (Derby) 2001. BB 4-101 v Glam (Swansea) 2003. LO HS 45 v Essex (Chelmsford) 2001 (NL). LO BB 4-28 v Essex (Derby) 2001 (NL).

NQMOSS, Jonathan (Sydney C of E GS; Australian C of PE), b Manly, Sydney, Australia 4 May 1975. 6'1". RHB, RM. Victoria 2000-01 to date. Derbyshire debut/cap 2004. Berkshire 2001. HS 172* Vic v WA (Perth) 2003-04. De HS 147* and De BB 3-30 v Durham (Chester-le-St) 2004. BB 4-50 Vic v WA (Perth) 2002-03. LO HS 104 v Worcs (Derby) 2004 (NL). LO BB 5-47 Vic v Q (Melbourne) 2000 (NL).

PAGET, Christopher David (Repton S), b Stafford 2 Nov 1987. 6'0". RHB, OB. Debut 2004. HS 7 v Yorks (Derby) 2004. BB 3-63 v WI (Derby) 2004.

SHEIKH, Mohammad Avez (Broadway S), b Birmingham 2 Jul 1973. 6'0". LHB, RM. Warwickshire 1997-2003. Derbyshire debut 2004. HS 58* Wa v Northants (Northampton) 2000. De HS 42 v Yorks (Derby) 2004. BB 4-9 v Durham (Chester-le-St) 2004. LO HS 50* v Scot (Derby) 2004 (NL). LO BB 4-17 Wa v Yorks (Birmingham) 2001 (NL).

SPENDLOVE, Benjamin Lee (Trent C), b Belper 4 Nov 1978. 6'1". RHB, OB. Derbyshire 1997-2000, 2004 (l-o matches only). HS 63 v Warwks (Birmingham) 1999. LO HS 58 v Leics (Leicester) 1998 (NWT).

STUBBINGS, Stephen David (Frankston HS, Aus; Swinburne U, Aus), b Huddersfield, Yorks 31 Mar 1978. 6'3". LHB, OB. Debut 1997. Cap 2001. 1000 runs (1): 1047 (2001). HS 135* v Kent (Canterbury) 2000. LO HS 98* v Lancs (Derby) 2002 (NL).

SUTTON, Luke David (Millfield S; Durham U), b Keynsham, Somerset 4 Oct 1976. 5'11". RHB, WK. Somerset 1997-98. Derbyshire debut 2000; cap 2002; captain 2004. HS 140* (carried bat) v Sussex (Derby) 2001. LO HS 83 v Lancs (Derby) 2003 (NL).

WALKER, Nicholas Guy Eades (Haileybury Imperial Service C), b Enfield, Middlesex 7 Aug 1984. 6'2". RHB, RFM. Debut 2004. Hertfordshire 2002-04. HS 80 off 57 balls (4 sixes, 11 fours), the record score by a Derbyshire No. 11, adding 103 for 10th wicket with M.A.Sheikh, and BB 5-68, v Somerset (Derby) 2004. LO HS 43 v Scot (Derby) 2004 (NL). LO BB 3-49 Herts v Ireland (Bishop's Stortford) 2003 (CGT).

WELCH, Graeme (Hetton CS), b Durham City 21 Mar 1972. 5'11½". RHB, RM. Warwickshire 1994-2000; cap 1997. Derbyshire debut/cap 2001. F-c Tour: SA 1994-95 (Wa). HS 115* v Leics (Oakham) 2004. 50 wkts (3); most 65 (1997). BB 6-30 v Durham (Chester-le-St) 2001. Award: BHC 1. LO HS 82 v Sussex (Hove) 2004 (NL). LO BB 6-31 v Middx (Derby) 2002 (NL).

RELEASED/RETIRED

(Having made a first-class County appearance in 2004)

[NQ]**ALI, Syed Mohammad** Bukhari (Punjab C of Commerce), b Bahawalpur, Pakistan 8 Nov 1973. 6'0". Nephew of Taslim Arif (Pakistan 1979-80 to 1980-81). British passport. RHB, LFM. Lahore 1993-94. Railways 1993-94. Islamabad 1994-95. United Bank 1994-95. Rawalpindi 1995-96 to 1998-99. ADBP 1995-96 to 1998-99. Bahawalpur 1998-99. 55 f-c matches in Pakistan before his UK debut in 2002. Derbyshire 2002-04. HS 92 Bahawalpur v Lahore (Rahim Yar Khan) 1998-99. De HS 53 v Durham (Derby) 2002 – on debut. 50 wkts (0+1): 56 (1993-94). BB 6-37 Railways v National Bank (Faisalabad) 1993-94. De BB 4-75 v Glam (Cardiff) 2004. LO HS 19 v Lancs (Manchester) 2002 (CGT). LO BB 4-34 Railways v United Bank (Karachi) 1993-94.

DUMELOW, Nathan Robert Charles (Foremark Hall S; Denstone C), b Derby 30 Apr 1981. 5'9". RHB, OB. Derbyshire 2001-04. HS 75 v Hants (Southampton) 2003. BB 5-51 v WI (Derby) 2004. CC BB 5-78 (10-160 match) v Northants (Northampton) 2003. LO HS 52 v Surrey (Derby) 2002 (NL). LO BB 3-24 v Sussex (Hove) 2002 (NL).

[NQ]**GAIT, Andrew** Ian (Kearsney C; UNISA), b Bulawayo, Rhodesia 19 Dec 1978. British passport. 6'1". RHB. Free State 1998-99 to 2000-01. Derbyshire 2002-04. HS 175 v Northants (Northampton) 2002. LO HS 138* FS v GW (Bloemfontein) 2000-01 – Free State l-o record.

GUNTER, Neil Edward Lloyd (The Clere S; Newbury C), Basingstoke, Hants 12 May 1981. 6'0". LHB, RFM. Berkshire 2000-01. Derbyshire 2002-04. MCCYC. HS 20* v Hants (Southampton) 2003. BB 4-14 v WI A (Derby) 2002. CC BB 2-48 v Durham (Derby) 2003. LO HS 5 (Berks CGT) and 5 (NL). LO BB 2-34 v Worcs (Worcester) 2004 (NL).

[NQ]**POWELL, Daren** Brentlyle, b Malvenn, Jamaica 15 Apr 1978. RHB, RFM. Jamaica 2000-01 to date. Gauteng 2003-04. Derbyshire 2004. **Tests** (WI): 4 (2002 to 2002-03); HS 16 v B (Dhaka) 2002-03; BB 3-36 v B (Chittagong) 2002-03. **LOI** (WI): 2 (2002-03 to 2003); HS – ; BB 1-34. HS 56 Jamaica v Barbados (Lucas St, Barbados) 2004-05. De HS 17 v Glam (Derby) 2004. BB 6-49 v DU (Derby) 2004. CC BB 2-85 v Glam (Derby) 2004.

[NQ]**ROGERS, Christopher** John Llewellyn (Wesley C, Perth; Curtin U, Perth), b St George, Sydney, Australia 31 Aug 1977. Son of W.J.Rogers (NSW 1968-69 to 1969-70). 5'10". LHB, LBG. W Australia 1998-99 to date. Derbyshire 2004. Shropshire 2003. HS 194 WA v NSW (Perth) 2002-03. De HS 156 v Durham (Derby) 2004. LO HS 93 v Somerset (Derby) 2004 (CGT).

SELWOOD, Steven Andrew (Mill Hill S; Albany C, Loughborough U), b Barnet, Herts 24 Nov 1979. Son of T.Selwood (Middlesex and C Districts 1966-73). 6'0". LHB, SLA. Derbyshire 2001-04. HS 99 v Worcs (Derby) 2002. BB 1-8 (CC). LO HS 93 v Glos (Bristol) 2002 (NL). LO BB 1-7 (CGT).

R.M.Khan and D.K.Taylor left the staff having made no f-c appearances in 2004.

DERBYSHIRE 2004

RESULTS SUMMARY

	Place	Won	Lost	Tied	Drew	No Result
County Championship (2nd Division)	8th	1	6		9	
All First-Class Matches		2	7		9	
C & G Trophy	2nd Round					
National League (2nd Division)	9th	5	12			1
Twenty20 Cup	3rd in North Division					

COUNTY CHAMPIONSHIP AVERAGES

BATTING AND FIELDING

Cap		M	I	NO	HS	Runs	Avge	100	50	Ct/St
–	C.J.L.Rogers	6	11	2	156	498	55.33	1	3	6
2004	M.H.Adnan	16	28	4	140	1247	51.95	3	7	7
–	N.G.E.Walker	7	7	3	80	201	50.25	–	2	2
2002	C.W.G.Bassano	14	22	3	123*	814	42.84	2	6	4
2004	J.Moss	11	19	2	147*	608	35.76	1	4	2
2002	L.D.Sutton	15	25	3	131	684	31.09	1	2	30/3
2001	G.Welch	16	25	4	115*	609	29.00	1	1	12
2001	S.D.Stubbings	14	25	1	96	643	26.79	–	5	8
–	S.M.B.Ali	4	6	1	50	110	22.00	–	1	1
–	M.A.Sheikh	13	18	6	42	259	21.58	–	–	1
–	A.I.Gait	12	22	1	81	425	20.23	–	1	9
2004	A.G.Botha	10	17	2	52	302	20.13	–	1	5
1998	K.J.Dean	7	10	4	35	117	19.50	–	–	3
–	B.J.France	4	7	–	56	126	18.00	–	1	2
–	P.M.R.Havell	6	8	6	13*	30	15.00	–	–	2
–	J.D.C.Bryant	7	13	1	30	149	12.41	–	–	3
–	S.A.Selwood	3	6	–	38	63.	10.50	–	–	1
–	N.R.C.Dumelow	3	4	–	18	36	9.00	–	–	–

Also batted: L.J.Goddard (1 match) 8 (5 ct); D.R.Hewson (2) 0, 9; I.D.Hunter (1) 0, 6; C.D.Paget (3) 7, 0; D.B.Powell (1) 17, 13 (1 ct).

BOWLING

	O	M	R	W	Avge	Best	5wI	10wM
K.J.Dean	144	18	597	20	29.85	5-86	1	–
N.G.E.Walker	137.2	16	574	17	33.76	5-68	1	–
G.Welch	471.5	103	1525	45	33.88	5-57	3	–
M.A.Sheikh	298.3	69	945	26	36.34	4- 9	–	–
P.M.R.Havell	122.1	7	640	16	40.00	4-75	–	–
A.G.Botha	252	43	874	21	41.61	4-66	–	–
S.M.B.Ali	116.4	18	486	10	48.60	4-75	–	–
J.Moss	206.5	39	643	13	49.46	3-30	–	–

Also bowled: M.H.Adnan 37.3-2-154-1; N.R.C.Dumelow 86-12-306-2; B.J.France 4-0-20-0; D.R.Hewson 46-18-112-4; I.D.Hunter 14.3-1-52-3; C.D.Paget 36-4-137-0; D.B.Powell 29.1-2-132-2.

The First-Class Averages (pp 121–136) give the records of Derbyshire players in all first-class county matches (Derbyshire's other opponents being the West Indians and Durham UCCE).

DERBYSHIRE RECORDS

FIRST-CLASS CRICKET

Highest Total	For 645		v	Hampshire	Derby	1898
	V 662		by	Yorkshire	Chesterfield	1898
Lowest Total	For 16		v	Notts	Nottingham	1879
	V 23		by	Hampshire	Burton upon T	1958
Highest Innings	For 274	G.A.Davidson	v	Lancashire	Manchester	1896
	V 343*	P.A.Perrin	for	Essex	Chesterfield	1904

Highest Partnership for each Wicket

1st	322	H.Storer/J.Bowden	v	Essex	Derby	1929
2nd	417	K.J.Barnett/T.A.Tweats	v	Yorkshire	Derby	1997
3rd	316*	A.S.Rollins/K.J.Barnett	v	Leics	Leicester	1997
4th	328	P.Vaulkhard/D.Smith	v	Notts	Nottingham	1946
5th	302*†	J.E.Morris/D.G.Cork	v	Glos	Cheltenham	1993
6th	212	G.M.Lee/T.S.Worthington	v	Essex	Chesterfield	1932
7th	258	M.P.Dowman/D.G.Cork	v	Durham	Derby	2000
8th	198	K.M.Krikken/D.G.Cork	v	Lancashire	Manchester	1996
9th	283	A.Warren/J.Chapman	v	Warwicks	Blackwell	1910
10th	132	A.Hill/M.Jean-Jacques	v	Yorkshire	Sheffield	1986

† 346 runs were added for this wicket in two separate partnerships

Best Bowling	For 10- 40	W.Bestwick	v	Glamorgan	Cardiff	1921
(Innings)	V 10- 45	R.L.Johnson	for	Middlesex	Derby	1994
Best Bowling	For 17-103	W.Mycroft	v	Hampshire	Southampton	1876
(Match)	V 16-101	G.Giffen	for	Australians	Derby	1886

Most Runs – Season	2165	D.B.Carr	(av 48.11)	1959
Most Runs – Career	23854	K.J.Barnett	(av 41.12)	1979-98
Most 100s – Season	8	P.N.Kirsten		1982
Most 100s – Career	53	K.J.Barnett		1979-98
Most Wkts – Season	168	T.B.Mitchell	(av 19.55)	1935
Most Wkts – Career	1670	H.L.Jackson	(av 17.11)	1947-63
Most Career W-K Dismissals	1304	R.W.Taylor	(1157 ct; 147 st)	1961-84
Most Career Catches in the Field	563	D.C.Morgan		1950-69

LIST 'A' LIMITED-OVERS CRICKET

Highest Total	CGT	365-3		v	Cornwall	Derby	1986
	BHC	366-4		v	Combined U	Oxford	1991
	NL	292-9		v	Worcs	Knypersley	1985
Lowest Total	CGT	79		v	Surrey	The Oval	1967
	BHC	98		v	Worcs	Derby	1994
	NL	61		v	Hampshire	Portsmouth	1990
Highest Innings	CGT	173*	M.J.Di Venuto	v	Derbys CB	Derby	2000
	BHC	142	D.M.Jones	v	Minor C	Derby	1996
	NL	141*	C.J.Adams	v	Kent	Chesterfield	1992
Best Bowling	CGT	8-21	M.A.Holding	v	Sussex	Hove	1988
	BHC	6-33	E.J.Barlow	v	Glos	Bristol	1978
	NL	6- 7	M.Hendrick	v	Notts	Nottingham	1972

DURHAM

Formation of Present Club: 23 May 1882
Inaugural First-Class Match: 1992
Colours: Navy Blue, Yellow and Maroon
Badge: Coat of Arms of the County of Durham
County Champions: (0) 8th 1999, 8th (Div 1) 2000
Gillette/NatWest/C & G Trophy Winners: (0); best –
quarter-finalist 1992, 2001
Benson and Hedges Cup Winners: (0); best – quarter-finalist
1998, 2000, 2001
National League (Div 1) Winners: (0); best – 8th (Div 1)
2002
Sunday League Winners: (0); best – 7th 1993
Twenty20 Cup Winners: (0); best – 4th in Group 2004
Match Awards: CGT 24; BHC 20

Chief Executive: D.Harker, County Ground, Riverside, Chester-le-Street, Co Durham
DH3 3QR • Tel: 0191 387 1717 • Fax: 0191 387 1616 • Email:
reception.durham@ecb.co.uk • Web: www.durhamccc.co.uk

First XI Coach: M.D.Moxon. **Captain:** M.E.K.Hussey. **Vice-Captain:** No appointment.
Overseas Players: M.E.K.Hussey and A.A.Noffke. **2005 Beneficiary:** None. **Head
Groundsman:** D.Measor. **Scorer:** B.Hunt. ‡ New registration. NQ Not qualified for
England.
*Durham initially awarded caps immediately their players joined the staff but revised this
policy in 1998 and now cap players on merit, past 'awards' having been nullified.*

‡NOBENKENSTEIN, Dale Martin (Michaelhouse S), b Salisbury, Rhodesia 9 Jun 1974.
Son of M.M.Benkenstein (Rhodesia, Natal B 1970 to 1980); brother of B.R. (Natal B
1993-94) and B.N. (Natal B, GW 1994-96). RHB, RM/OB. Natal/KZ-Natal 1993-94 to
2003-04. Dolphins 2004-05. MCC 2004. **LOI** (SA): 23 (1998-99 to 2002-03); HS 69 v WI
(Cape Town) 1998-99; BB 3-5 v K (Colombo) 2002-03. Tours (SA A): WI 2000; NZ
1998-99 (SA); SL 1998-99. HS 259 KZ-Natal v Northerns (Durban) 2001-02. BB 3-27
Dolphins v Lions (Durban) 2004-05. UK HS 39 MCC v WI (Arundel) 2004. LO HS 107*
Natal v North West (Fochville) 1997-98. LO BB 4-23 Natal v Border (E London) 1996-97.

NOBREESE, Gareth Rohan (Kingston U of Technology, Jamaica), b Montego Bay, Jamaica
9 Jan 1976. 5'7". RHB, OB. Jamaica 1995-96 to date; captain/overseas player 2003-04 to
date. British passport. **Tests** (WI): 1 (2002-03); HS 5 and BB 2-108 v I (Madras) 2002-03.
F-c Tours (WI): I 2002-03. HS 165* v Somerset (Taunton) 2004. BB 7-60 Jamaica v
Barbados (Bridgetown) 2000-01. Du BB 5-41 (10-151 match) v Yorks (Scarborough) 2004 –
scored 35 and 68 to complete match double. LO HS 52* v Middx (Chester-le-St) 2004. LO
BB 3-24 Jamaica v Leeward Is (Spanish Town) 2001-02.

BRIDGE, Graeme David (Southmoor S, Sunderland), b Sunderland 4 Sep 1980. 5'8".
RHB, SLA. Debut 1999. HS 52 v Leics (Chester-le-St) 2004. BB 6-84 v Hants (Chester-le-
St) 2001. Awards: CGT 1; BHC 1. LO HS 50* v Leics (Leicester) 2002 (BHC). LO BB 4-20
v Hants (Chester-le-St) 2003 (NL).

COETZER, Kyle James (Aberdeen GS), b Aberdeen, Scotland 14 Apr 1984. RHB, RM.
Debut 2004. Scotland 2004. Registered but not contracted. HS 133* Scot v Kenya (Abu
Dhabi) 2004. Du HS 67 v Glam (Cardiff) 2004. LO HS 30 Durham CB v Glam (Darlington)
2003 (CGT).

16

COLLINGWOOD, Paul David (Blackfyne CS; Derwentside C), b Shotley Bridge 26 May 1976. 5'11". RHB, RMF. Debut 1996 v Northants (Chester-le-St) taking wicket of D.J.Capel with his first ball before scoring 91 and 16; cap 1998. **ECB contract 2004. Tests**: 2 (2003-04); HS 36 v SL (Galle) 2003-04. **LOI**: 70 (2001 to 2004-05); HS 100 v SL (Perth) 2002-03; BB 4-38 v NZ (Napier) 2001-02. F-c Tour: WI 2003-04; SL 2003-04. 1000 runs (1): 1108 (2001). HS 190 v SL (Chester-le-St) 2002. CC HS 153 v Warwks (Birmingham) 2001. BB 4-1 v Derbys (Derby) 2002. Awards: BHC 4. LO HS 118* v Notts (Chester-le-St) 2002 (NL). LO BB 4-31 v Yorks (Chester-le-St) 2000 (BHC).

DAVIES, Anthony **Mark** (Northfield CS, Billingham), b Stockton-on-Tees 4 Oct 1980. 6'3". RHB. RM. Debut 2002. HS 33 v Derbys (Darlington) 2002. 50 wkts (1): 50 (2004). BB 6-44 v Derbys (Chester-le-St) 2004. LO HS 31* v Warwks (Chester-le-St) 2002 (NL). LO BB 4-13 v Sussex (Chester-le-St) 2001 (NL).

HAMILTON, Gavin Mark (Hurstmere SS, Kent), b Broxburn, Scotland 16 Sep 1974. 6'1". LHB, RFM. Scotland 1993-94. Yorkshire debut 1994; cap 1998. Durham debut 2004. **Tests**: 1 (1999-00); HS 0 v SA (Johannesburg) 1999-00. **LOI** (Scot): 5 (1999); HS 76 and BB 2-36 v P (Chester-le-St) 1999. F-c Tours: SA 1999-00; 2 (WI+S) 1999. HS 125 Y v Hants (Leeds) 2000. Du HS 58 v Yorks (Scarborough) 2004. 50 wkts (1): 59 (1998). BB 7-50 (11-72 match) Y v Surrey (Leeds) 1998. Du BB 3-30 v DU (Chester-le-St) 2004 – on Du debut. Match double (79, 70; 5-69, 5-43) Y v Glam (Cardiff) 1998 – first instance for Yorks since 1964 (R.Illingworth). Award: BHC 1. LO HS 76 (*see LOI*) and 76 v Y (Scarborough) 2004 (NL). LO BB 5-16 Y v Hants (Leeds) 1998 (SL).

HARMISON, Stephen James (Ashington HS), b Ashington, Northumb 23 Oct 1978. 6'4". RHB, RF. Debut 1996; cap 1999. Northumberland 1996. **ECB contracts 2004-05. Tests**: 28 (2002 to 2004-05); HS 42 v SA (Cape Town) 2004-05 – first No 11 to top-score for England; BB 7-12 (9-73 match) v WI (Kingston) 2003-04; hat-trick v I (Nottingham) 2004. **LOI**: 25 (2002-03 to 2004-05); HS 13* v NZ (Chester-le-St) 2003; BB 4-22 v I (Lord's) 2004. F-c Tours: A 2002-03; SA 1998-99 (Eng A), 2004-05; WI 2003-04; I 1998-99 (Eng A); B 2003-04. HS 42 (*see Tests*). Du HS 36 v Kent (Canterbury) 1998. 50 wkts (2); most – 64 (1999). BB 7-12 (*see Tests*). Du BB 6-111 v Sussex Chester-le-St) 2001. LO HS 13* (*see LOI*). LO BB 4-22 (*see LOI*).

‡ᴺᵠ**HUSSEY, Michael** Edward Killeen (Prindiville Catholic C; Curtin U), b Morley, Perth, Australia 27 May 1975. Elder brother of D.J.Hussey (*see NOTTINGHAMSHIRE*). 5'11". LHB, RM. W Australia 1994-95 to date. Northamptonshire 2001-03; cap 2001; captain 2002-03. Gloucestershire 2004; cap 2004. Appointed Durham captain 2005. **LOI**: 1 (2003-04); HS 17* v I (Perth) 2003-04. F-c Tour (Aus A): Sc/Ire 1998. 1000 runs (3); most – 2055 (2001). HS 331* (Northants record) in 651 minutes v Somerset (Taunton) 2003. Also scored 329* Nh v Essex (Northampton) 2001 and 310 Nh v Glos (Bristol) 2002. BB 2-21 WA v Q (Perth) 1998-99. CC BB 1-5. Awards: BHC 3. LO HS 123 v Scot (Northampton) 2003 (NL). LO BB 3-52 WA v Vic (Melbourne) 1999-00 (MM).

KILLEEN, Neil (Greencroft CS; Derwentside C; Teesside U), b Shotley Bridge 17 Oct 1975. 6'2". RHB, RFM. Debut 1995; cap 1999. HS 48 v Somerset (Chester-le-St) 1995. 50 wkts (1): 58 (1999). BB 7-70 v Hants (Chester-le-St) 2003. Award: BHC 1. LO HS 32 v Middx (Lord's) 1996 (SL). LO BB 6-31 v Derbys (Derby) 2000 (NL).

LEWIS, Jonathan James Benjamin (King Edward VI S, Chelmsford; Roehampton IHE), b Isleworth, Middx 21 May 1970. 5'9½". RHB, RSM. Essex 1990-96; cap 1994; scored 116* on debut v Surrey (Oval). Durham debut 1997; cap 1998; captain 2000 (*part*) to 2004; benefit 2004. 1000 runs (4); most – 1252 (1997). HS 210* v OU (Oxford) 1997 – on Du debut. CC HS 160* v Derbys (Chester-le-St) 1997. BB 1-73. Award: BHC 1. LO HS 102 v Glos (Cheltenham) 1997 (NL).

LOWE, James Adam (Northallerton C, Yorks), b Bury St Edmunds, Suffolk 4 Nov 1982. 6'2". RHB, WK, occ OB. Debut 2003. Registered but not contracted. HS 80 v Hants (Southampton) 2003 – on debut.

MUCHALL, Gordon James (Durham S), b Newcastle upon Tyne, Northumb 2 Nov 1982. 6'1". RHB, RM. Northumberland 1999-2001. Debut 2002. F-c Tours (ECB Acad): SL 2002-03. HS 142* v Yorks (Scarborough) 2004. 127 v Middx (Lord's) 2002. BB 3-26 v Yorks (Leeds) 2003. LO HS 87 v Scot (Edinburgh) 2003 (NL). LO BB 1-15 (NL).

MUSTARD, Philip (Usworth CS), b Sunderland 8 Oct 1982. 5'11". LHB, WK. Debut 2002. HS 75 v SL (Chester-le-St) 2002 – on debut. CC HS 70* v Derbys (Derby) 2003. LO HS 41 v Somerset (Chester-le-St) 2003 (NL).

‡NOFFKE, Ashley** Allan b Nambour, Queensland, Australia 30 Apr 1977. RHB, RFM. Debut 1998-99 for Australian Academy. Queensland 1999-00 to date. Middlesex 2002-03; cap 2003. F-c Tours (A): E 2001 (part); WI 2003; Z 1998-99 (A Academy). HS 114* Q v S Aus (Brisbane) 2003-04. BB 8-24 (12-108 match) M v Derbys (Derby) 2002. LO HS 58 M v Sussex (Lord's) 2002 (BHC). LO BB 4-32 Q v Tasmania (Hobart) 2001-02 .

ONIONS, Graham (St Thomas More RCS, Blaydon), b Gateshead 9 Sep 1982. 6'2". RHB, RMF. Debut 2004. HS 20* v Leics (Chester-le-St) 2004. BB 3-110 v Leics (Leicester) 2004. LO HS 5 (Durham CB – CGT). LO BB 2-24 v Yorks (Scarborough) 2004 (NL).

PENG GILLENDER, Nicky (Newcastle upon Tyne RGS), b Newcastle upon Tyne, Northumb 18 Sep 1982. 6'2". RHB, OB. Debut 2000. Cap 2001. HS 158 v Durham UCCE (Chester-le-St) 2003. CC HS 133 v Glam (Cardiff) 2003. Scored 98 v Surrey (Chester-le-St) on debut. BB – Award: CGT 1. LO HS 121 v Worcs (Worcester) 2001 (NL).

PLUNKETT, Liam Edward (Nunthorpe SS; Teesside Tertiary C), b Middlesbrough, Yorks 6 Apr 1985. 6'3". RHB, RFM. Debut 2003. HS 54 v Notts (Chester-le-St) 2004. BB 6-74 v Hants (Chester-le-St) 2004. LO HS 21 and LO BB 3-35 v Yorks (Scarborough) 2004 (NL).

PRATT, Andrew (Willington Parkside CS; Durham New C), b Helmington Row, Crook 4 Mar 1975. Elder brother of G.J.Pratt. 6'0". LHB, WK. Debut 1997. Cap 2001. MCC YC. HS 93 v Glos (Chester-le-St) 2002. LO HS 86 v Derbys (Chester-le-St) 2001 (NL).

PRATT, Gary Joseph (Willington Parkside CS), b Bishop Auckland 22 Dec 1981. Younger brother of A.Pratt. 6'0". LHB, OB. Debut 2000. 1000 runs (1): 1055 (2003). HS 150 v Northants (Chester-le-St) 2003. LO HS 101* v Somerset (Taunton) 2003 (NL).

‡NOTHORP, Callum** David, b Mount Lawley, Perth, Australia 11 Feb 1975. English parents. RHB, RMF. W Australia 2002-03 to date. HS 26 WA v NSW (Newcastle) 2002-03. BB 3-59 WA v Tas (Perth) 2003-04. LO HS 12 and LO BB 4-46 WA v Tas (Hobart) 2002-03.

RELEASED/RETIRED

(Having made a first-class County appearance in 2004)

NOBLIGNAUT, Arnoldous Mauritius ('Andy') (Falcon C, Bulawayo; Eaglesvale S, Harare), b Salisbury, Rhodesia 1 Aug 1978. 6'1". LHB, RFM. Mashonaland 1997-98 to date. Durham 2004. Tasmania 2004-05. Tests (Z): 15 (2000-02 to 2003-04); HS 92 v WI (Harare) 2001; BB 5-73 v B (Bulawayo) 2000-01 – on debut. LOI (Z): 47 (1999-00 to 2003-04); HS 63* v K (Bulawayo) 2002-03; BB 4-43 v WI (Harare) 2003-04. HS 194 Mashonaland v Manicaland (Mutare) 2003-04. Du HS 56 v Leics (Leicester) 2004. BB 5-73 (see Tests). Du BB 2-109 v Leics (Leicester) 2004. LO HS 63* (see LOI). LO BB 4-43 (see LOI).

NOKING, Reon Dane (St Joseph's HS), b Good Fortune, Demerara, Guyana 6 Oct 1975. 6'3". RHB, RFM. Guyana 1995-96 to 2002-03. Northerns 2003-04. Durham 2004. Tests (WI): 14 (1998-99 to 2001); HS 12* v E (Lord's)2000; BB 5-51 v Z (Kingston) 1999-00. LOI (WI): 50 (1998-99 to 2004-05); HS 12* v A (St George's) 1998-99; BB 4-25 v P (Port-of-Spain) 1998-99. Tours (WI): E 2000, 2002 (WI A); SA 1997-98 (WI A), 1998-99; NZ 1999-00; I 1998-99(WI A); SL 2001-02; Z 2001; B 1999-00. HS 30 Guyana v Leeward Is (Charlestown) 1996-97. Du HS 3. BB 7-82 Guyana v I (Georgetown) 1996-97. Du BB 3-120 v Notts (Chester-le-St) 2004. LO HS 13* Guyana v Trinidad (Gros Islet) 2002-03. LO BB 4-25 (see LOI).

RELEASED/RETIRED continued on p 24

DURHAM 2004
RESULTS SUMMARY

	Place	Won	Lost	Tied	Drew	No Result
County Championship (2nd Division)	9th	2	8		6	
All First-Class Matches		2	8		7	
C & G Trophy	2nd Round					
National League (2nd Division)	6th	9	7			2
Twenty20 Cup	4th in North Division					

COUNTY CHAMPIONSHIP AVERAGES
BATTING AND FIELDING

Cap		M	I	NO	HS	Runs	Avge	100	50	Ct/St
–	G.J.Muchall	15	28	1	142*	970	35.92	1	5	13
–	M.J.North	16	29	1	219	879	31.39	2	3	8
–	Shoaib Akhtar	2	4	1	46	94	31.33	–	–	2
–	P.Mustard	3	5	–	60	148	29.60	–	1	9
1998	P.D.Collingwood	6	11	–	68	322	29.27	–	3	5
–	G.R.Breese	14	25	1	165*	685	28.54	1	3	12
1998	J.J.B.Lewis	16	29	1	127	729	26.03	1	4	7
2001	N.Peng	9	16	–	88	387	24.18	–	3	6
2001	A.Pratt	13	23	3	59	483	24.15	–	2	30/2
–	I.Pattison	3‡	4	–	33	92	23.00	–	–	3
–	J.A.Lowe	2	4	–	41	91	22.75	–	–	2
–	G.M.Hamilton	7	13	1	58	270	22.50	–	2	2
–	A.M.Blignaut	2	4	–	56	90	22.50	–	1	–
–	G.D.Bridge	10	16	3	52	291	22.38	–	2	1
–	L.E.Plunkett	9	14	3	54	242	22.00	–	1	2
–	K.J.Coetzer	6	10	–	67	212	21.20	–	1	–
–	G.J.Pratt	8	15	–	71	273	18.20	–	2	7
1999	N.Killeen	12	20	4	35*	218	13.62	–	–	1
–	A.M.Davies	10	17	8	29	110	12.22	–	–	2
–	P.Kumar	2	4	1	21	36	12.00	–	–	–
–	G.Onions	7	10	4	20*	60	10.00	–	–	2
–	R.D.King	2	4	–	3	4	1.00	–	–	1

Also batted: Tahir Mughal (1 match) 0, 17*; S.W.Tait (2) 0, 4.

BOWLING

	O	M	R	W	Avge	Best	5wI	10wM
A.M.Davies	304.2	75	938	50	18.76	6- 44	4	–
L.E.Plunkett	225.5	35	902	27	33.40	6- 74	1	–
P.D.Collingwood	137	37	455	12	37.91	3- 49	–	–
G.R.Breese	307.4	44	1163	28	41.53	5- 41	2	1
G.D.Bridge	204	43	648	15	43.20	4- 64	–	–
N.Killeen	323.4	81	1012	19	53.26	2- 39	–	–
Also bowled:								
G.J.Muchall	34	5	136	5	27.20	1- 1	–	–
Shoaib Akhtar	57.2	12	218	8	27.25	4- 64	–	–
P.Kumar	42	5	219	6	36.50	3- 78	–	–
R.D.King	38.5	6	206	5	41.20	3-120	–	–
G.M.Hamilton	64	9	249	5	49.80	2- 28	–	–
G.Onions	128.4	25	560	8	70.00	3-110	–	–

A.M.Blignaut 42-3-200-4; K.J.Coetzer 1-0-2-0; M.J.North 22.1-2-93-3; I.Pattison 39-7-129-2; Tahir Mughal 19-4-54-2; S.W.Tait 18-0-176-0.

The First-Class Averages (pp 121–136) give the records of Durham players in all first-class county matches (Durham's other opponents being Durham UCCE), with the exception of S.J.Harmison whose only first-class appearances were for England.

‡ Substituted by P.D.Collingwood v Glamorgan at Chester-le-Street.

DURHAM RECORDS

FIRST-CLASS CRICKET

Highest Total	For 645-6d		v	Middlesex	Lord's	2002
	V 810-4d		by	Warwicks	Birmingham	1994
Lowest Total	For 67		v	Middlesex	Lord's	1996
	V 56		by	Somerset	Chester-le-St^2	2003
Highest Innings	For 273	M.L.Love	v	Hampshire	Chester-le-St^2	2003
	V 501*	B.C.Lara	for	Warwicks	Birmingham	1994

Highest Partnership for each Wicket

1st	334*	S.Hutton/M.A.Roseberry	v	Oxford U	Oxford	1996
2nd	258	J.J.B.Lewis/M.L.Love	v	Notts	Chester-le-St^2	2001
3rd	205	G.Fowler/S.Hutton	v	Yorkshire	Leeds	1993
4th	224	G.J.Pratt/N.Peng	v	Durham UCCE	Chester-le-St^2	2003
5th	197	N.Peng/V.J.Wells	v	Derbys	Derby	2003
6th	193	D.C.Boon/P.D.Collingwood	v	Warwicks	Birmingham	1998
7th	127	D.R.Law/J.E.Brinkley	v	Hampshire	Chester-le-St^2	2001
8th	134	A.C.Cummins/D.A.Graveney	v	Warwicks	Birmingham	1994
9th	127	D.G.C.Ligertwood/S.J.E.Brown	v	Surrey	Stockton	1996
10th	103	M.M.Betts/D.M.Cox	v	Sussex	Hove	1996

Best Bowling	For	9- 64	M.M.Betts	v	Northants	Northampton	1997
(Innings)	V	9- 36	M.S.Kasprowicz	for	Glamorgan	Cardiff	2003
Best Bowling	For	14-177	A.Walker	v	Essex	Chelmsford	1995
(Match)	V	13-110	M.S.Kasprowicz	for	Glamorgan	Chester-le-St^2	2003

Most Runs – Season	1536	W.Larkins	(av 37.46)		1992
Most Runs – Career	7004	J.J.B.Lewis	(av 32.12)		1997-2004
Most 100s – Season	4	D.M.Jones			1992
	4	W.Larkins			1992
	4	J.E.Morris			1994
Most 100s – Career	14	J.E.Morris			1994-99
Most Wkts – Season	77	S.J.E.Brown	(av 25.87)		1996
Most Wkts – Career	518	S.J.E.Brown	(av 28.30)		1992-2002
Most Career W-K Dismissals	194	M.P.Speight	(189 ct; 5 st)		1997-2001
Most Career Catches in the Field	101	P.D.Collingwood			1996-2004

LIST 'A' LIMITED-OVERS CRICKET

Highest Total	CGT	326-4		v	Herefords	Chester-le-St^2	1995
	BHC	287-5		v	Leics	Leicester	1996
	NL	319-3		v	Worcs	Worcester	2004
Lowest Total	CGT	82		v	Worcs	Chester-le-St^1	1968
	BHC	133		v	Glos	Bristol	2001
	NL	72		v	Warwicks	Birmingham	2002
Highest Innings	CGT	132	M.A.Gough	v	Wales MC	Cardiff	2002
	BHC	145	J.E.Morris	v	Leics	Leicester	1996
	NL	131*	W.Larkins	v	Hampshire	Portsmouth	1994
Best Bowling	CGT	7-32	S.P.Davis	v	Lancashire	Chester-le-St^1	1983
	BHC	6-30	S.J.E.Brown	v	Northants	Chester-le-St^1	1997
	NL	6-31	N.Killeen	v	Derbyshire	Derby	2000

^{1} Chester-le-Street CC (Ropery Lane) ^{2} Riverside Ground

ESSEX

Formation of Present Club: 14 January 1876
Inaugural First-Class Match: 1894
Colours: Blue, Gold and Red
Badge: Three Seaxes above Scroll bearing 'Essex'
County Champions: (6) 1979, 1983, 1984, 1986, 1991, 1992
Gillette/NatWest/C & G Trophy Winners: (2) 1985, 1997
Benson and Hedges Cup Winners: (2) 1979, 1998
National League (Div 1) Winners: (0); best – 3rd 2003
Sunday League Winners: (3) 1981, 1984, 1985
Twenty20 Cup Winners: (0); best – Quarter-Finalist 2004
Match Awards: CGT 53; BHC 91

Chief Executive: D.E.East, County Ground, New Writtle Street, Chelmsford CM2 0PG •
Tel: 01245 252420 • Fax: 01245 254030 • Email: administration.essex@ecb.co.uk • Web:
www.essexcricket.org.uk

First XI Coach: G.A.Gooch. **Captain**: R.C.Irani. **Vice-Captain**: D.Gough. **Overseas Players**: A.R.Adams and Danish Kaneria. **2005 Beneficiary**: A.P.Grayson. **Head Groundsman**: S.G.Kerrison. **Scorer**: A.E.Choat. ‡ New registration. ^NQ Not qualified for England.

^NQ**ADAMS, Andre** Ryan (Westlake BHS, Auckland), b Mangere, Auckland, New Zealand 17 Jul 1975. 5'9". RHB, RMF. Auckland 1997-98 to date. Essex debut 2004, scoring 124; cap 2004. Herefordshire 2001. Tests (NZ): 1 (2001-02); HS 11 and BB 3-44 v E (Auckland) 2001-02 – on debut. LOI (NZ): 31 (2000-01 to 2004-05); HS 45 v P (Rawalpindi) 2001-02; BB 5-22 v I (Queenstown) 2002-03. HS 124 v Leics (Leics) 2004 (91 balls, 7 sixes, 13 fours; 100 off 80 balls) on UK debut. BB 5-40 Auckland v ND (Hamilton) 2003-04. Ex BB 5-93 v Notts (Southend) 2004. LO HS 90* N Island Selection XI v SL (New Plymouth) 2000-01. LO BB 5-7 Auckland v ND (Auckland) 1999-00.

BISHOP, Justin Edward (Bury St Edmunds County Upper S; John Snow C, Durham U), b Bury St Edmunds, Suffolk 4 Jan 1982. 6'0". LHB, LMF. Debut 1999. Durham UCCE 2002-04. British U 2003. HS 66 DU v Northants (Northampton) 2004. Ex HS 23* v Worcs (Southend) 2002. BB 5-148 v Leics (Chelmsford) 2001. LO HS 16* v Hants (Colchester) 2000 (NL). LO BB 3-33 v Worcs (Worcester) 2001 (NL).

BOPARA, Ravinder Singh (Brampton Manor S; Barking Abbey Sports C), b Newham, London 4 May 1985. 5'8". RHB, RMF. Debut 2002. HS 48 v Durham (Colchester) 2002 and 48 v Middx (Lord's) 2003. BB 1-23. LO HS 55 v Glos (Chelmsford) 2004. LO BB 2-10 v Hants (Chelmsford) 2004.

CLARKE, Andrew John (St Martin's S, Hutton; Brentwood CHE), b Brentwood 9 Nov 1975. 6'2". LHB, RM. MCC YC. Debut 2002. HS 41 v Warwks (Chelmsford) 2003. BB 5-54 v Glam (Swansea) 2002 – on debut. LO HS 18 v Warwks (Birmingham) 2004 (NL). LO BB 4-28 v Yorks (Chelmsford) 2003 (NL).

COOK, Alastair Nathan (Bedford S), b Gloucester 25 Dec 1984. 6'3". LHB, OB. Debut 2003. Essex 2nd XI debut 2000 when aged 15y 235d. England U-19 capt 2003-04. HS 126 v Leics (Chelmsford) 2004. LO HS 27 Essex CB v Essex (Chelmsford) 2003 (CGT).

COWAN, Ashley Preston (Framlingham C), b Hitchin, Herts 7 May 1975. 6'4". RHB, RFM. Debut 1995; cap 1997. No appearances 2003 (knee surgery). Cambridgeshire 1993. F-c Tour: WI 1997-98. HS 94 v Leics (Leicester) 1998. 50 wkts (1): 52 (1997). BB 6-47 v Glam (Cardiff) 1999. Hat-trick 1996. Award: BHC 1. LO HS 45 v Middx (Chelmsford) 2001 (BHC). LO BB 5-14 v Middx (Southgate) 2001 (NL).

21

NQDANISH PARABHA SHANKER **KANERIA** (St Patrick's HS; Government Islamia C), b Karachi, Pakistan 16 Dec 1980. 6'1". Cousin of Anil Dalpat (Pakistan) and second Hindu to represent Pakistan. RHB, LB. Karachi 1998-99 to 2001-02. PNSC 1998-99. Habib Bank 1999-00 to date. Essex debut/cap 2004. **Tests** (P): 23 (2000-01 to 2004-05); HS 15 v A (Sharjah) 2002-03; BB 7-77 v B (Dhaka) 2001-02. Test debut was his fourth f-c match. **LOI** (P): 10 (2001-02 to 2004); HS 3*; BB 3-31 v NZ (Dambulla) 2003. F-c Tours (P): A 2004-05; NZ 2003-04; SL 2001 (Pak A); K 2000 (Pak A). 50 wkts (1+1); most 63 (2004). HS 42 Habib Bank v Allied Bank (Sheikhupura) 2001-02. Ex HS 13* v Glam (Cardiff) 2004. BB 7-39 Karachi Whites v Gujranwala (Karachi) 2000-01. Ex BB 7-65 (13-186 match) v Yorks (Chelmsford) 2004. LO HS 15 PCB Whites v PCB Reds (Lahore) 2002-03. LO BB 5-24 Habib Bank v Lahore Blues (Lahore) 2001-02.

FLOWER, Andrew (Wainona HS, Harare), b Cape Town, South Africa 28 Apr 1968. 5'10". Elder brother of G.W.Flower (Zimbabwe). LHB, WK, occ RM. Mashonaland 1986-87 to 2002-03. MCC 1996-99. *Wisden* 2001. Essex debut/cap 2002. S Australia 2003-04. British passport after 2003 season. Qualified for England 2005. **Tests** (Z): 63 (1992-93 to 2002-03, 20 as captain); HS 232* v I (Nagpur) 2000-01. **LOI** (Z): 213 (1991-92 to 2002-03, 52 as captain); HS 145 v I (Colombo) 2002-03; scored 115* v SL (New Plymouth) on debut. F-c Tours (Z) (C=captain): E 2000C; SA 1999-00; WI 1999-00C; NZ 1995-96C, 1997-98, 2000-01; I 1992-93, 2000-01, 2001-02; P 1993-94C, 1996-97, 1998-99; SL 1996-97, 1997-98, 2001-02; B 2001-02. 1000 runs (3): 1244 (2003). HS 232* (*see Tests*). Ex HS 201* v Surrey (Oval) 2003. BB (Mashonaland) 1-1. Awards: BHC 2. LO HS 145 (*see LOI*). LO BB 1-21 (Mashonaland).

‡NQFLOWER, Grant William (St George's C), b Salisbury, Rhodesia 20 Dec 1970. 5'10". Younger brother of A Flower (*see Essex*). RHB, SLA. Mashonaland 1989-90. Leicestershire 2002 (one match); cap 2002. Kolpak registration. **Tests** (Z): 67 (1992-93 to 2003-04); HS 201* v P (Harare) 1994-95 sharing with G.W.Flower in fourth-wicket partnership of 269, the highest stand between brothers in Test cricket; BB 4-41 (8-104 match) v B (Chittagong) 2001-02. **LOI** (Z): 219 (1992-93 to 2003-04); HS 142* v B (Bulawayo) 2000-01; BB 4-32 v K (Dhaka) 1998-99. Tours (Z): E 2000; SA 1999-00; WI 1999-00; NZ 1995-96, 1997-98; I 1992-93, 2000-01, 2001-02; P 1993-94, 1996-97, 1998-99; SL 1996-97, 1997-98, 2001-02; B 2001-02. HS 243* Mashonaland v Matabeleland (Harare) 1996-97. CC HS 75 and CC BB 4-66 Le v Warwks (Birmingham) 2002. BB 7-31 Z v Lahore (Lahore) 1998-99. LO HS 148* Mashonaland v Midlands (Kwekwe) 2002-03. LO BB 4-32 (*see LOI*).

FOSTER, James Savin (Forest S, Snaresbrook; Collingwood C, Durham U), b Whipps Cross 15 Apr 1980. 6'0". RHB, WK. British U 2000. Essex debut 2000; cap 2001. Durham UCCE 2001. British U 2001. **ECB Contract 2002. Tests**: 7 (2001-02 to 2002-03); HS 48 v I (Bangalore) 2001-02. **LOI**: 11 (2001-02); HS 13 v I (Bombay) 2001-02. F-c Tours: A 2002-03; WI 2000-01 (Eng A); NZ 2001-02; I 2001-02. 1000 runs (1): 1037 (2004). HS 212 v Leics (Chelmsford) 2004. LO HS 56* v Sussex (Hove) 2001 (NL).

GOUGH, Darren (Priory CS, Lundwood), b Barnsley, Yorks 18 Sep 1970. 5'11". RHB, RF. Yorkshire 1989-2003; cap 1993; benefit 2001. Essex debut/cap 2004. *Wisden* 1998. **ECB contracts 2000-01-02. Tests**: 58 (1994 to 2003); HS 65 v NZ (Manchester) 1994 – on debut; BB 6-42 v SA (Leeds) 1998; hat-trick v A (Sydney) 1998-99 – first for E v A since 1899. **LOI**: 147 (1994 to 2004-5); HS 45 v A (Melbourne) 1994-95; BB 5-44 v Z (Sydney) 1994-95 and 5-44 v A (Lord's) 1997. Took wickets with his sixth balls in both Tests and LOI. F-c Tours: A 1994-95, 1998-99; SA 1991-92 (Y), 1992-93 (Y), 1993-94 (Eng A), 1995-96, 1999-00; NZ 1996-97; P 2000-01; SL 2000-01; Z 1996-97. HS 121 Y v Warwks (Leeds) 1996. Ex HS 50 v Leics (Chelmsford) 2004. 50 wkts (5); most – 67 (1996). BB 7-28 (10-80 match) Y v Lancs (Leeds) 1995 (not CC). CC BB 7-42 (10-96 match) Y v Somerset (Taunton) 1993. Ex BB 5-57 v Hants (Chelmsford) 2004. 2 hat-tricks (1995, 1998-99); took 4 wkts in 5 balls Y v Kent (Leeds) 1995. Awards: CGT 2; BHC 1. LO HS 72* Y v Leics (Leicester) 1991 (SL). LO BB 7-27 Y v Ire (Leeds) 1997 (NWT).

GRAYSON, Adrian Paul (Bedale CS), b Ripon, Yorks 31 Mar 1971. 6'1". RHB, SLA. Yorkshire 1990-95. Essex debut/cap 1996; benefit 2005. **LOI**: 2 (2000-01 to 2001-02); HS 6 and BB 3-40 v Z (Bulawayo) 2001-02. F-c Tour: SA Y 1991-92 (Y). 1000 runs (4); most – 1275 (2001). HS 189 v Glam (Chelmsford) 2001. BB 5-20 v Yorks (Scarborough) 2001. Award: BHC 1. LO HS 82* v Worcs (Chelmsford) 1997 (NWT). LO BB 4-25 Y v Glam (Cardiff) 1994 (SL).

IRANI, Ronald Charles (Smithills CS, Bolton), b Leigh, Lancs 26 Oct 1971. 6'3". RHB, RMF. Lancashire 1990-93. Essex debut/cap 1994; captain 2000 to date; benefit 2003. **Tests**: 3 (1996 to 1999); HS 41 v I (Lord's) 1996; BB 1-22. Took wicket of M.Azharuddin with his fifth ball in Test cricket. **LOI**: 31 (1996 to 2002-03); HS 53 and BB 5-26 v I (Oval) 2002. F-c Tours: NZ 1996-97, 1999-00 (Eng A); P 1995-96 (Eng A); Z 1996-97; B 1999-00 (Eng A). 1000 runs (5); most – 1196 (2000). HS 207* v Northants (Ilford) 2002. 50 wkts (1): 51 (1999). BB 6-71 v Notts (Nottingham) 2002. Awards: CGT 5; BHC 5. LO HS 158* v Glam (Chelmsford) 2004 (NL). LO BB 5-26 (see LOI).

JEFFERSON, William Ingleby (Beeston Hall S, Norfolk; Oundle S; St Hild & St Bede C, Durham U), b Derby 25 Oct 1979. Son of R.I.Jefferson (Cambridge U and Surrey 1961-66); grandson of J.Jefferson (Army 1919, Comb Services 1922). 6'10½". RHB, RMF. British U 2000-01. Essex debut 2000; cap 2002. Durham UCCE 2001-02. Scored 50 and 65 in first two LO innings. 1000 runs (1): 1555 (2004). HS 222 v Hants (Southampton) 2004. Awards: CGT 2. LO HS 132 v Essex CB (Chelmsford) 2003 (CGT).

MIDDLEBROOK, James Daniel (Pudsey Crawshaw S), b Leeds, Yorks 13 May 1977. 6'1". RHB, OB. Yorkshire 1998-2001. Essex debut 2002; cap 2003. HS 115 v Somerset (Taunton) 2004. 50 wkts (1): 56 (2002). BB 6-82 (10-170 match) Y v Hants (Southampton) 2000 – including 4 wickets in 5 balls. Ex BB 6-123 v Kent (Chelmsford) 2003. Hat-trick 2003. LO HS 47 v Worcs (Worcester) 2004 (CGT). LO BB 4-33 v Hants (Southend) 2002 (NL).

NAPIER, Graham Richard (The Gilberd S, Colchester), b Colchester 6 Jan 1980. 5'9½". RHB, RM. Debut 1997; cap 2003. F-c Tour (Eng A): I 2003-04. HS 106* v Notts (Nottingham) 2004. BB 5-56 v Derbys (Derby) 2004. Award: CGT 1. LO HS 79 Essex CB v Lancs CB (Chelmsford) 2000 (NWT). LO BB 6-29 v Worcs (Chelmsford) 2001 (NL).

PALLADINO, Antonio Paul (Cardinal Pole SS; Anglia Polytechnic U), b London Hospital 29 Jun 1983. 6'0". RHB, RMF. Cambridge UCCE 2003. Essex debut 2003. HS 41 v Notts (Nottingham) 2004. BB 6-41 v Kent (Canterbury) 2003. LO HS 16 Essex CB v Essex (Chelmsford) 2003. LO BB 3-32 v Glam (Chelmsford) 2003 (NL).

PETTINI, Mark Lewis (Comberton Village C; Hills Road SFC, Cambridge; Cardiff U), b Brighton, Sussex 7 Aug 1983. RHB, RM. 5'10". Debut 2001. British U (captain) 2004. HS 78 v Warwks (Chelmsford) 2003. LO 92* v Warwks (Birmingham) 2003 (CGT).

PHILLIPS, Timothy James (Felsted S; St Hild & St Bede C, Durham U), b Cambridge 13 Mar 1981. 6'1". LHB, SLA. Essex debut 1999. No appearances 2003-04. Durham UCCE 2001-02. HS 75 DU v Durham (Chester-le-St) 2002. Ex HS 42 and CC BB 4-102 v Middx (Southgate) 2002. BB 4-42 v SL A (Chelmsford) 1999 – on debut. LO HS 6 (NL). LO BB 2-36 v Middx (Chelmsford) 2002 (NL).

NQTen DOESCHATE, Ryan Neil (Fairbairn C; Cape Town U), b Port Elizabeth, South Africa 30 Jun 1980. 5'10½". RHB, RMF. Debut 2003. EU passport – Dutch ancestry. HS 31 v Sussex (Arundel) 2003. BB 3-29 v CU (Cambridge) 2004. CC BB 2-52 v Durham (Chester-le-St) 2004. LO HS – and BB 1-39 v Worcs (Worcester) 2003 (NL).

‡TUDOR, Alex Jeremy (St Mark's S, Hammersmith; City of Westminster C), b West Brompton, London 23 Oct 1977. 6'5". RHB, RF. Surrey 1995-2004; cap 1999. YC 1999. **Tests**: 10 (1998-99 to 2002-03); HS 99* v NZ (Birmingham) 1999 – record score by an England 'night-watchman'; BB 5-44 v A (Nottingham) 2001. **LOI**: 3 (2002); HS 6; BB 2-30 v I (Oval) 2002. F-c Tours: A 1998-99, 2002-03; SA 1999-00; WI 2000-01 (Eng A). HS 116 Sy v Essex (Oval) 2001. BB 7-48 Sy v Lancs (Oval) 2000. LO HS 56 Sy v Lancs (Croydon) 2004 (NL). LO BB 4-26 Sy v Hants (Oval) 2000 (NL).

RELEASED/RETIRED

(Having made a first-class County appearance in 2004)

NQBRANT, Scott Andrew (St Georges C, Harare; St Johns C, Harare; St Joseph's Nudgee C, Brisbane), b Harare, Zimbabwe 26 Jan 1983. 5'11½". RHB, LFM. Queensland 2001-02 to date. Essex 2003-04; cap 2003. HS 23 v Lancs (Manchester) 2003. BB 6-45 v Notts (Nottingham) 2003. LO HS 14* v Surrey (Chelmsford) 2003 (NL). LO BB 4-25 v Yorks (Leeds) 2003 (NL).

HABIB, A. – *see LEICESTERSHIRE.*

HUSSAIN, Nasser (Forest S, Snaresbrook; Durham U), b Madras, India 28 Mar 1968. Son of J.Hussain (Madras 1966-67); brother of M.Hussain (Worcs 1985). 5'11". RHB, LB. Essex 1987-2004; cap 1989; captain 1999; club captain 2000-04; benefit 1999. YC 1989. OBE 2002. *Wisden* 2002. **ECB contracts 2000-01-02-03-04. Tests:** 96 (1989-90 to 2004, 45 as captain); HS 207 v A (Birmingham) 1997. Scored 103* and made winning hit in his final f-c innings (v NZ, Lord's, 2004). **LOI:** 88 (1989-90 to 2002-03, 56 as captain – E record); HS 115 v I (Lord's) 2002. F-c Tours (C=captain): A 1998-99, 2002-03C; SA 1999-00C; WI 1989-90, 1991-92 (Eng A), 1993-94, 1997-98; NZ 1996-97, 2001-02C; I 2001-02C; P 1990-91 (Eng A), 1995-96C (Eng A), 2000-01C; SL 1990-91 (Eng A), 2000-01C, 2003-04; Z 1996-97; B 2003-04. 1000 runs (5); most – 1854 (1995). HS 207 (*see Tests*). Ex HS 206 v Kent (Chelmsford) 2003. BB 1-38. Awards: CGT 4; BHC 4. LO HS 161* v Glam (Chelmsford) 2003 (NL).

NQMcCOUBREY, Adrian George Agustus Mathew (Cambridge House BHS; Queens U, Belfast), b Ballymena, Co Antrim, N Ireland 3 Apr 1980. 5'10½". RHB, RFM. Ireland 1999-2000. Essex 2003-04. HS 2* (CC). BB 4-16 v CU (Cambridge) 2004. CC BB 3-40 v Durham (Chester-le-St) 2004. LO HS 11 Ire v Berks (Finchampstead) 2002. LO BB 2-20 Ire v Wilts (Salisbury) 2001.

STEPHENSON, John Patrick (Felsted S; Durham U), b Stebbing 14 Mar 1965. 6'1". RHB, RM. Essex 1985-94 and 2002-04 (2nd XI captain 2002-04); cap 1989. Hampshire 1995-2001; cap 1995; captain 1996-97; benefit 2001. Boland 1988-89. **Tests:** 1 (1989); HS 25 v A (Oval) 1989. F-c Tours: WI 1991-92 (Eng A); Z 1989-90 (Eng A). 1000 runs (5); most – 1887 (1990). HS 202* v Somerset (Bath) 1990. BB 7-44 (10-104 match) v Worcs (Worcester) 2002. Awards: CGT 1; BHC 5. LO HS 142 v Warwks (Birmingham) 1991 (BHC). LO BB 6-33 H v Worcs (Southampton) 1997 (SL). Appointed MCC Head of Cricket 2004.

Z.K.Sharif left the staff having made no f-c appearances in 2004.

DURHAM RELEASED/RETIRED (continued from p 18)

KUMAR, Pallav (Trinity S, Carlisle; Sunderland U), b Patna, India 13 Jul 1981. 6'1½" RHB, RM. Durham 2004. Cumberland 2003. HS 21 v Notts (Nottingham) 2004. BB 3-78 v Glam (Chester-le-St) 2004. LO HS 0 and LO BB 2-33 Cumb v Scot (Edinburgh) 2003 (CGT).

NQNORTH, Marcus James (Kent Street Sr HS), b Pakenham, Melbourne, Australia 28 Jul 1979. 6'1". LHB, OB. W Australia 1998-99 to date. Durham 2004. Tour (A Academy): Z 1998-99. 1000 runs (1): 1074 (2003-04). HS 219 v Glam (Cardiff) 2004. BB 4-16 v DU (Chester-le-St) 2004 – on DU debut. CC BB 2-45 v Yorks (Chester-le-St) 2004. LO HS 121* v Notts (Cleethorpes) 2004 (NL). LO BB 4-26 Durham CB v Bucks (Beaconsfield) 2001 (CGT).

PATTISON, Ian (Seaham CS), b Ryhope, Sunderland 5 May 1982. 5'10". RHB, RM. Durham 2002-04. HS 62 v Yorks (Leeds) 2003. BB 3-41 v Essex (Chester-le-St) 2002. LO HS 48* Durham CB v Leics CB (Gateshead) 2000 (NWT). LO BB 3-45 v Sussex (Chester-le-St) 2004 (CGT).

NQSHOAIB AKHTAR – *see WORCESTERSHIRE.*

NQTAHIR Mahmood MUGHAL (M.A.O. College, Lahore), b Daska, Pakistan 25 Apr 1977. 5'10". RHB, RFM. Gujranwala 1997-98 to 1998-99. ADBP 1998-99 to 2001-02. Sialkot 2001-02 to date. PCB 2002-03 to date. Durham 2004. HS 68* Sialkot v Lahore Blues (Lahore) 2001-02. Du HS 17* and Du BB 2-54 v Essex (Chester-le-St) 2004 – only f-c match. 50 wkts (0+2); most 83 (2001-02). BB 7-63 (11-141 match) Sialkot v Rest of NWFP (Sialkot) 2001-02. LO HS 118* Sialkot v NBP (Sialkot) 2002-03. LO BB 3-29 PCB Whites v PCB Blues (Lahore) 2002-03.

NQTAIT, Shaun William (Oakbank Area S, S Aus), b Bedford Park, Adelaide 22 Feb 1983. 6'4". RHB, RFM. S Australia 2002-03 to date. Durham 2004. HS 12 S Aus v Q (Brisbane) 2002-03. Du HS 4. BB 5-68 S Aus v Tas (Adelaide) 2002-03. LO HS 22* Aus A v Z (Perth) 2003-04. LO BB 8-43 S Aus v Tas (Adelaide) 2003-04.

ESSEX 2004

RESULTS SUMMARY

	Place	Won	Lost	Tied	Drew	No Result
County Championship (2nd Division)	5th	3	6		7	
All First-Class Matches		4	6		7	
C & G Trophy	Quarter-Finalist					
National League (1st Division)	6th	6	6	1		3
Twenty20 Cup	Quarter-Finalist					

COUNTY CHAMPIONSHIP AVERAGES

BATTING AND FIELDING

Cap		M	I	NO	HS	Runs	Avge	100	50	Ct/St
1994	R.C.Irani	9	15	4	164	694	63.09	3	2	1
2002	W.I.Jefferson	16	28	1	222	1411	52.25	5	5	13
2001	J.S.Foster	16	24	4	212	927	46.35	3	1	39/5
2002	A.Flower	16	28	3	172	1045	41.80	2	5	18
1996	A.P.Grayson	6	10	–	119	365	36.50	1	2	–
2003	G.R.Napier	14	22	4	106*	633	35.16	1	5	6
2002	A.Habib	13	21	–	157	722	34.38	1	4	3
1989	J.P.Stephenson	3	4	1	40	90	30.00	–	–	–
	A.N.Cook	12	21	2	126	568	29.89	1	4	18
2003	J.D.Middlebrook	15	22	1	115	583	27.76	1	3	4
2004	A.R.Adams	7	8	–	124	196	24.50	1	–	4
	R.S.Bopara	4	6	–	34	103	17.16	–	–	5
2004	D.Gough	7	10	1	50	144	16.00	–	1	–
1997	A.P.Cowan	5	7	2	25	63	12.60	–	–	3
	A.J.Clarke	4	6	–	28	50	8.33	–	–	1
2004	Danish Kaneria	11	13	7	13*	47	7.83	–	–	7
2003	S.A.Brant	6	8	1	19	39	5.57	–	–	–
	A.G.A.M.McCoubrey	5	7	4	2*	4	1.33	–	–	–

Also batted: N.Hussain (2 matches – cap 1989) 70, 0, 102 (2 ct); A.P.Palladino (2) 0, 41; M.L.Pettini (2) 67, 0, 10 (1 ct); R.N.ten Doeschate (1) 7.

BOWLING

	O	M	R	W	Avge	Best	5wI	10wM
D.Gough	226.4	52	672	30	22.40	5-57	1	–
A.R.Adams	157.4	23	561	23	24.39	5-93	1	–
Danish Kaneria	563	123	1609	63	25.53	7-65	4	1
A.P.Cowan	148	39	463	13	35.61	3-44	–	–
G.R.Napier	366.2	61	1444	39	37.02	5-56	1	–
J.D.Middlebrook	383.3	56	1423	32	44.46	5-26	1	–
Also bowled:								
J.P.Stephenson	55	7	223	8	27.87	3-28	–	–
A.J.Clarke	113	24	357	9	39.66	3-61	–	–
A.G.A.M.McCoubrey	103.4	17	491	8	61.37	3-40	–	–
S.A.Brant	167.2	36	597	9	66.33	2-86	–	–

R.S.Bopara 24-1-108-0; A.P.Grayson 40.1-2-167-0; A.Habib 7-1-18-0; A.P.Palladino 34-5-158-3; R.N.ten Doeschate 18-2-68-2.

The First-Class Averages (pp 121–136) give the records of Essex players in all first-class county matches (Essex's other opponents being Cambridge UCCE), with the exception of J.E.Bishop whose only first-class appearances were for Durham UCCE, A.N.Cook, A.Flower, J.S.Foster, N.Hussain, G.R.Napier and A.P.Palladino whose full county figures are as above, and:

J.P.Stephenson 4-5-2-71*-161-53.66-0-1-0ct. 64-9-247-8-30.87-3/28.

ESSEX RECORDS

FIRST-CLASS CRICKET

Highest Total	For	761-6d		v	Leics	Chelmsford	1990
	V	803-4d		by	Kent	Brentwood	1934
Lowest Total	For	30		v	Yorkshire	Leyton	1901
	V	14		by	Surrey	Chelmsford	1983
Highest Innings	For	343*	P.A.Perrin	v	Derbyshire	Chesterfield	1904
	V	332	W.H.Ashdown	for	Kent	Brentwood	1934

Highest Partnership for each Wicket

1st	316	G.A.Gooch/P.J.Prichard	v	Kent	Chelmsford	1994
2nd	403	G.A.Gooch/P.J.Prichard	v	Leics	Chelmsford	1990
3rd	347*	M.E.Waugh/N.Hussain	v	Lancashire	Ilford	1992
4th	314	Salim Malik/N.Hussain	v	Surrey	The Oval	1991
5th	316	N.Hussain/M.A.Garnham	v	Leics	Leicester	1991
6th	206	J.W.H.T.Douglas/J.O'Connor	v	Glos	Cheltenham	1923
	206	B.R.Knight/R.A.G.Luckin	v	Middlesex	Brentwood	1962
7th	261	J.W.H.T.Douglas/J.Freeman	v	Lancashire	Leyton	1914
8th	263	D.R.Wilcox/R.M.Taylor	v	Warwicks	Southend	1946
9th	251	J.W.H.T.Douglas/S.N.Hare	v	Derbyshire	Leyton	1921
10th	218	F.H.Vigar/T.P.B.Smith	v	Derbyshire	Chesterfield	1947

Best Bowling	For	10- 32	H.Pickett	v	Leics	Leyton	1895
(Innings)	V	10- 40	E.G.Dennett	for	Glos	Bristol	1906
Best Bowling	For	17-119	W.Mead	v	Hampshire	Southampton	1895
(Match)	V	17- 56	C.W.L.Parker	for	Glos	Gloucester	1925

Most Runs – Season	2559	G.A.Gooch	(av 67.34)		1984
Most Runs – Career	30701	G.A.Gooch	(av 51.77)		1973-97
Most 100s – Season	9	J.O'Connor			1929, 1934
	9	D.J.Insole			1955
Most 100s – Career	94	G.A.Gooch			1973-97
Most Wkts – Season	172	T.P.B.Smith	(av 27.13)		1947
Most Wkts – Career	1610	T.P.B.Smith	(av 26.68)		1929-51
Most Career W-K Dismissals	1231	B.Taylor	(1040 ct; 191 st)		1949-73
Most Career Catches in the Field	519	K.W.R.Fletcher			1962-88

LIST 'A' LIMITED-OVERS CRICKET

Highest Total	CGT	386-5		v	Wiltshire	Chelmsford	1988
	BHC	388-7		v	Scotland	Chelmsford	1992
	NL	316-4		v	Glamorgan	Chelmsford	2004
Lowest Total	CGT	57		v	Lancashire	Lord's	1996
	BHC	61		v	Lancashire	Chelmsford	1992
	NL	69		v	Derbyshire	Chesterfield	1974
Highest Innings	CGT	144	G.A.Gooch	v	Hampshire	Chelmsford	1990
	BHC	198*	G.A.Gooch	v	Sussex	Hove	1982
	NL	176	G.A.Gooch	v	Glamorgan	Southend	1983
Best Bowling	CGT	5- 8	J.K.Lever	v	Middlesex	Westcliff	1972
		5- 8	G.A.Gooch	v	Cheshire	Chester	1995
	BHC	5-13	J.K.Lever	v	Middlesex	Lord's	1985
	NL	8-26	K.D.Boyce	v	Lancashire	Manchester	1971

26

GLAMORGAN

Formation of Present Club: 6 July 1888
Inaugural First-Class Match: 1921
Colours: Blue and Gold
Badge: Gold Daffodil
County Champions: (3) 1948, 1969, 1997
Gillette/NatWest/C & G Trophy Winners: (0); best – finalist 1977
Benson and Hedges Cup Winners: (0); best – finalist 2000
National League (Div 1) Winners: (2) 2002, 2004
Sunday League Winners: (1) 1993
Twenty20 Cup Winners: (0); best – Semi-Finalist 2004
Match Awards: CGT 45; BHC 56

Chief Executive: M.J.Fatkin, Sophia Gardens, Cardiff, CF1 9XR • Tel: 029 2040 9380 • Fax: 029 2040 9390 • email: info@glamorgancricket.co.uk • Web: www.glamorgancricket.co.uk

First XI Coach: J.Derrick. **Captain**: R.D.B.Croft. **Vice-Captain**: No appointment.
Overseas Player: M.T.G.Elliott and M.S.Kasprowicz. **2005 Beneficiary**: M.P.Maynard (testimonial). **Head Groundsman**: L.A.Smith. **Scorer**: Dr Andrew K.Hignell. ‡ New registration. NQ Not qualified for England.

CHERRY, Daniel David (Tonbridge S; U of Wales, Swansea), b Newport, Gwent 7 Feb 1980. 5'9". LHB, RM. Debut 1998. No f-c appearances 2000-01. HS 47 v Glos (Cheltenham) 2002. LO HS 24 v Essex (Chelmsford) 2004.

COSKER, Dean Andrew (Millfield S), b Weymouth, Dorset 7 Jan 1978. 5'11". RHB, SLA. Debut 1996; cap 2000. F-c Tours (Eng A): SA 1998-99, SL 1997-98; Z 1998-99, K 1997-98. HS 49 v Sussex (Cardiff) 1999. BB 6-140 v Lancs (Colwyn Bay) 1998. LO HS 27* v Somerset (Taunton) 1999 (NL). LO BB 5-54 v Essex (Chelmsford) 2003 (NL).

CROFT, Robert Damien Bale (St John Lloyd Catholic CS, Llanelli; Neath Tertiary C; W Glam IHE), b Morriston 25 May 1970. 5'10½". RHB, OB. Debut 1989; cap 1992; benefit 2000; captain 2003 (*part*) to date. **Tests**: 21 (1996 to 2001); HS 37* v SA (Manchester) 1998; BB 5-95 v NZ (Christchurch) 1996-97. **LOI**: 50 (1996 to 2001); HS 32 v SL (Perth) 1998-99; BB 3-51 v SA (Oval) 1998. F-c Tours: A 1998-99; SA 1993-94 (Eng A), 1995-96 (Gm); WI 1991-92 (Eng A), 1997-98; NZ 1996-97; SL 2000-01, 2002-03; Z 1990-91 (Gm), 1994-95 (Gm), 1996-97. HS 143 v Somerset (Taunton) 1995. 50 wkts (7); most – 76 (1996). BB 8-66 (14-169 match) v Warwks (Swansea) 1992. Awards: CGT 2; BHC 2. LO HS 143 v Lincs (Lincoln) 2004 (CGT). LO BB 6-20 v Worcs (Cardiff) 1994 (SL).

DAVIES, Andrew Philip (Dwr-y-Felin CS; Christ C, Brecon), b Neath 7 Nov 1976. 5'11". LHB, RMF. Debut 1995. Wales (MC). HS 40 v Essex (Cardiff) 2001. BB 5-79 v Worcs (Cardiff) 2002. LO HS 24 v Sussex (Hove) 2001 (NL). LO BB 5-19 v Lincs (Sleaford) 2002 (CGT).

NQELLIOTT, Matthew Thomas Gray (Kyabram Secondary C; La Trobe U), b Chelsea, Victoria, Australia 28 Sep 1971. 6'3". LHB, LM/SLC. Victoria 1992-93 to date. Glamorgan 2000, 2004; cap 2000. Yorkshire 2002. *Wisden* 1997. **Tests** (A): 21 (1996-97 to 2004); HS 199 v E (Leeds) 1997. **LOI** (A): 1 (1997); HS 1 v E (Lord's) 1997. Tours (A): E 1995 (Young A), 1997; SA 1996-97; WI 1998-99. 1000 runs (3+5); most – 1429 (2003-04). HS 203 v Tasmania (Melbourne) 1995-96. UK HS 199 (*see Tests*). Gm HS 177 v Sussex (Colwyn Bay) 2000. BB (Vic) 1-3. Awards: CGT 2. LO HS 156 v Dorset (Bournemouth) 2000 (NWT).

‡GRANT, Richard Neil (Neath TC), b Neath 5 Jun 1984. RHB, RM. Joined staff 2005 – awaiting f-c debut. LO HS 21 v Essex (Chelmsford) 2004 (NL). LO BB 1-26 (NL).

‡**HARRISON, Adam** James (W Monmouth CS), b Newport, Gwent 30 Oct 1985. RHB, RMF. Younger brother of D.S.Harrison; son of S.C.Harrison (Glamorgan 1971-77). MCC 2004. Awaiting Glamorgan debut. HS 34* and BB 2-65 MCC v Sussex (Lord's) 2004.

HARRISON, David Stuart (W Monmouth CS; Usk C, Pontypool), b Newport, Gwent 30 Jul 1981. Elder brother of A.J.Harrison; son of S.C.Harrison (Glamorgan 1971-77). 6'4". RHB, RM. Glamorgan debut 1999. HS 88 v Essex (Chelmsford) 2004. 50 wkts (1): 57 (2004). BB 5-48 v Somerset (Swansea) 2004. LO HS 37* and LO BB 5-26 v Yorks (Leeds) 2002 (NL).

HEMP, David Lloyd (Olchfa CS; Millfield S; W Glamorgan C; Birmingham U), b Hamilton, Bermuda 8 Nov 1970. UK resident since 1976. 6'0". LHB, RM. Glamorgan 1991-96; cap 1994. Warwickshire 1997-2001; cap 1997. Wales (MC) 1992-94. F-c Tours: SA 1995-96 (Gm); I 1994-95 (Eng A); Z 1994-95 (Gm). 1000 runs (4); most – 1452 (1994). HS 186* Wa v Worcs (Birmingham) 2001. Gm 157 Gm v Glos (Abergavenny) 1995. BB 3-23 v SA A (Cardiff) 1996. CC BB 2-29 Wa v Glos (Birmingham) 2000. Awards: CGT 4; BHC 2. LO HS 121 v Comb U (Cardiff) 1995 (BHC). LO BB 4-32 Wa v Minor C (Lakenham) 1998 (BHC).

HUGHES, Jonathan (Coed-y-Land CS, Pontypridd), b Pontypridd 30 Jun 1981. 5'10". RHB, RM. Debut 2001. MCC YC. HS 110 v Leics (Cardiff) 2004. LO HS 51 v Derbys (Cardiff) 2003 (CGT).

JONES, Simon Philip (Coedcae CS; Millfield S), b Swansea 25 Dec 1978. Son of I.J.Jones (Glamorgan and England 1960-68). 6'3½". LHB, RF. Debut 1998; cap 2002. Unavailable 2003 (knee reconstruction). **ECB contracts 2004-05. Tests:** 12 (2002 to 2004-05); HS 44 v I (Lord's) 2002 – on debut; BB 5-57 v WI (Pt-of-Spain) 2003-04. LOI: 2 (2004-05); HS – ; BB 2-43 v Z (Bulawayo) 2004-05 – on debut. F-c Tours: A 2002-03 (part); SA 2004-05; WI 2003-04; I 2003-04 (Eng A – part). HS 46 v Yorks (Scarborough) 2001. BB 6-45 v Derbys (Cardiff) 2002. LO HS 12* v Notts (Nottingham) 1999 (NL). LO BB 2-42 (see LOI).

NQ**KASPROWICZ, Michael** Scott (Brisbane State HS), b South Brisbane, Australia 10 Feb 1972. 6'4". RHB, RFM. Queensland 1989-90 to date. Essex 1994; cap 1994. Leicestershire 1999; cap 1999. Glamorgan debut/cap 2002. **Tests** (A): 30 (1996-97 to 2004-05); HS 25 v I (Calcutta) 1997-98; BB 7-36 v E (Oval) 1997. **LOI** (A): 34 (1995-96 to 2004-05); HS 28* v E (Lord's) 1997; BB 5-45 v SL (Colombo) 2003-04. F-c Tours (A): E 1995 (Young A), 1997; I 1997-98, 2000-01; 2004-05; P 1998-99; SL 2003-04. HS 92 Australians v India A (Nagpur) 2000-01. Gm HS 78 v Glos (Cardiff) 2003. 50 wkts (4+3); most: 77 (2003). BB 9-36 (11-77 match) v Durham (Cardiff) 2003. Also 9-45 (13-110 match) v Durham (Chester-le-St) 2003. Hat-trick (Queensland 1998-99). LO HS 40 Le v Warwks (Leicester) 1999 (BHC). LO BB 5-45 (see LOI).

MAYNARD, Matthew Peter (David Hughes S, Anglesey), b Oldham, Lancs 21 Mar 1966. 5'10½". RHB, RM. Debut 1985 v Yorks (Swansea), scoring 102 out of 117 in 87 min, reaching 100 with 3 sixes off successive balls; cap 1987; captain 1996-2000; benefit 1996; testimonial 2005. Wisden 1997. N Districts 1990-91 to 1991-92. Otago 1996-97 to 1997-98. YC 1988. **Tests:** 4 (1988 to 1993-94); HS 35 v WI (Kingston) 1993-94. **LOI:** 14 (1993-94 to 2000); HS 41 v P (Manchester) 1996. F-c Tours: SA 1989-90 (Eng XI), 1995-96 (Gm – captain); WI 1993-94; Z 1994-95 (Gm). 1000 runs (13); most – 1803 (1991). HS 243 v Hants (Southampton) 1991. BB 3-21 v OU (Oxford) 1987. CC BB 1-3. Awards: CGT 5; BHC 9. LO HS 151* v Durham (Darlington) 1991 (NWT) and 151* v Middx (Lord's) 1996 (BHC). LO BB 1-13 (NL).

‡**O'SHEA, Michael** Peter, b Cardiff 24 Oct 1986. RHB, OB. England U-15, U-16, U-19. Joined staff 2005 – awaiting f-c debut.

POWELL, Michael John (Crickhowell SS; Pontypool CFE), b Abergavenny, Gwent 3 Feb 1977. 6'1". RHB, RSM. Debut 1997 scoring 200* v OU (Oxford); cap 2000. 1000 runs (3); most – 1234 (2003). HS 200* (see above). CC HS 198 v Durham (Chester-le-St) 2003. BB 2-39 v OU (Oxford) 1999. LO HS 91* v Leics (Cardiff) 2003 (NL). LO BB 1-26 (CGT).

‡**REES, Gareth** Peter (Coedcae CS; Bath U), b Swansea 8 Apr 1985. LHB, LM. Wales MC. Development Contract 2005. LO HS 15 Wales MC v Denmark (Abergavenny) 2003 (CGT).

SHAW, Adrian David (Llangatwg CS; Neath Tertiary C), b Neath 17 Feb 1972. 5'11". RHB, WK. Wales MC 1990-92. Debut 1994; cap 1999. One f-c appearance since 2001 – 2nd XI captain. HS 140 v OU (Oxford) 1999. CC HS 88* v Glos (Cardiff) 2000. LO HS 48 v Glos (Swansea) 1997 (SL).

THOMAS, Ian James (Bedwas CS; Bassaleg CS; UWIC), b Newport, Gwent 9 May 1979. 5'11". LHB, OB. Debut 1998. Wales MC. HS 82 v Essex (Southend) 2000 – on CC debut. BB 1-26 (CC). LO HS 93 v Durham CB (Darlington) 2003 (CGT). LO BB 1-27 (NL).

THOMAS, Stuart Darren (Graig CS, Llanelli; Neath Tertiary C), b Morriston 25 Jan 1975. 6'0". LHB, RFM. Debut v Derbys (Chesterfield) 1992, taking 5-80 when aged 17yr 217d; cap 1997. F-c Tours (Eng A): SA 1995-96 (Gm), 1998-99; NZ 1999-00; Z 1994-95 (Gm), 1998-99. HS 138 v Essex (Chelmsford) 2001. 50 wkts (5); most – 71 (1998). BB 8-50 Eng A v Zim A (Harare) 1998-99 – record Eng A analysis. CC BB 7-33 (10-83 match) v Durham (Cardiff) 2002. Award: BHC 1. LO HS 71* v Surrey (Oval) 2002 (CGT). LO BB 7-16 v Surrey (Swansea) 1998 (SL).

WALLACE, Mark Alexander (Crickhowell HS), b Abergavenny, Gwent 19 Nov 1981. 5'9". LHB, WK. Debut 1999; cap 2003. F-c Tour (ECB Acad): SL 2002-03. HS 121 v Durham (Chester-le-St) 2003. LO HS 39 v Warwks (Cardiff) 2002 (BHC).

WATKINS, Ryan Edward (Pontllanfraith CS; Cross Keys TC), b Abergavenny, Gwent 9 Jun 1983. 6'0". LHB, RM. Wales MC. Joined Glamorgan part-time staff 2002 – awaiting f-c debut. LO HS 0 (NL).

WHARF, Alexander George (Buttershaw Upper S; Thomas Danby C), b Bradford, Yorks 4 Jun 1975. 6'5". RHB, RMF. Yorkshire 1994-97. Nottinghamshire 1998-99. Glamorgan debut 2000, scoring 100* v OU (Oxford); cap 2000. **LOI**: 13 (2004 to 2004-05): HS 9; BB 4-24 v Z (Harare 2004-05. HS 101* v Northants (Northampton) 2000. 50 wkts (1): 52 (2003). BB 5-63 v Yorks (Swansea) 2001. LO HS 72 v Lancs (Manchester) 2004 (NL). LO BB 6-5 v Kent (Cardiff) 2004 (NL).

‡**WRIGHT, Ben** James, b Preston, Lancs 5 Dec 1987. RHB, RM. Joined staff 2005 – awaiting f-c debut.

RELEASED/RETIRED

(Having made a first-class County appearance in 2004)

DALE, Adrian (Chepstow CS; Swansea U), b Germiston, SA 24 Oct 1968 (to UK at 6 mths). 5'11½". RHB, RMF. Glamorgan1989-2004; cap 1992; benefit 2002. F-c Tours (Gm): SA 1993-94 (Eng A), 1995-96; Z 1990-91, 1994-95. 1000 runs (4); most – 1472 (1993). HS 214* v Middx (Cardiff) 1993. BB 6-18 v Warwks (Cardiff) 1993. Awards: CGT 2; BHC 3. LO HS 110 v Lincs (Swansea) 1994 (NWT). LO BB 6-22 v Durham (Colwyn Bay) 1993 (SL).

NQ**LEWIS, Michael** Llewellyn, b Greensborough, Victoria, Australia 29 Jun 1974. RHB, RFM. Victoria 1999-00 to date. Glamorgan 2004. HS 54* Vic v NSW (Sydney) 2001-02. Gm HS 0. BB 6-59 Vic v Q (Melbourne) 2003-04. Gm BB 4-39 v Essex (Chelmsford) 2004. LO HS 19 Vic v Tas (Melbourne) 2003-04. LO BB 4-41 Vic v WA (Perth) 2001-02.

GLAMORGAN 2004

RESULTS SUMMARY

	Place	Won	Lost	Tied	Drew	No Result
County Championship (2nd Division)	3rd	5	2		9	
All First-Class Matches		5	3		9	
C & G Trophy	3rd Round					
National League (1st Division)	1st	11	5			
Twenty20 Cup	Semi-Finalist					

COUNTY CHAMPIONSHIP AVERAGES

BATTING AND FIELDING

Cap		M	I	NO	HS	Runs	Avge	100	50	Ct/St
2000	M.T.G.Elliott	14	24	1	157	1245	54.13	4	5	15
1994	D.L.Hemp	16	27	4	102*	1037	45.08	1	9	12
1987	M.P.Maynard	15	24	3	163	906	43.14	3	4	14
1997	S.D.Thomas	13‡	17	5	105*	470	39.16	1	3	8
2000	M.J.Powell	15	25	2	124	895	38.91	1	7	13
1992	R.D.B.Croft	16	23	4	138	671	35.31	2	1	1
2000	D.A.Cosker	6	7	5	21*	54	27.00	–	–	7
–	D.D.Cherry	3	5	1	29	107	26.75	–	–	–
2003	M.A.Wallace	16	26	–	105	674	25.92	1	2	39/3
1992	A.Dale	7	13	3	44	241	24.10	–	–	3
2000	A.G.Wharf	10	15	1	78	307	21.92	–	3	4
–	D.S.Harrison	16	20	3	88	370	21.76	–	1	7
–	J.Hughes	10	13	–	110	267	20.53	1	–	5
2002	M.S.Kasprowicz	7	11	2	42	126	14.00	–	–	2
2002	S.P.Jones	8	7	4	20	33	11.00	–	–	2

Also batted: A.P.Davies (1 match) 6; M.L.Lewis (3) 0 (1 ct); I.J.Thomas (1) 29 (1 ct).

BOWLING

	O	M	R	W	Avge	Best	5wI	10wM
D.A.Cosker	138.1	37	372	15	24.80	3-40	–	–
D.S.Harrison	448.3	118	1465	53	27.64	5-48	3	–
S.P.Jones	215.1	31	808	26	31.07	5-77	2	–
R.D.B.Croft	629	140	1866	54	34.55	4-52	–	–
A.G.Wharf	249.5	38	1011	27	37.44	5-93	1	–
S.D.Thomas	290	30	1127	29	38.86	4-47	–	–
M.S.Kasprowicz	272.1	54	893	21	42.52	5-54	1	–
Also bowled:								
M.L.Lewis	53.1	5	253	6	42.16	4-39	–	–

A.Dale 13-2-42-0; A.P.Davies 31.4-4-130-2; M.T.G.Elliott 1-0-16-0; M.P.Maynard 7-0-27-0.

The First-Class Averages (pp 121–136) give the records of Glamorgan players in all first-class county matches (Glamorgan's other opponents being Sri Lanka A), with the exception of A.J.Harrison whose only first-class appearance was for the MCC, S.P.Jones whose full county figures are as above, and:

M.J.Powell 16-27-2-124-900-36.00-1-7-14ct. Did not bowl.

‡ Substituted by S.P.Jones v Hampshire at Southampton.

GLAMORGAN RECORDS

FIRST-CLASS CRICKET

Highest Total	For 718-3d		v	Sussex	Colwyn Bay	2000
	V 712		by	Northants	Northampton	1998
Lowest Total	For 22		v	Lancashire	Liverpool	1924
	V 33		by	Leics	Ebbw Vale	1965
Highest Innings	For 309*	S.P.James	v	Sussex	Colwyn Bay	2000
	V 322*	M.B.Loye	for	Northants	Northampton	1998

Highest Partnership for each Wicket

1st	374	M.T.G.Elliott/S.P.James	v	Sussex	Colwyn Bay	2000
2nd	252	M.P.Maynard/D.L.Hemp	v	Northants	Cardiff	2002
3rd	313	D.E.Davies/W.E.Jones	v	Essex	Brentwood	1948
4th	425*	A.Dale/I.V.A.Richards	v	Middlesex	Cardiff	1993
5th	264	M.Robinson/S.W.Montgomery	v	Hampshire	Bournemouth	1949
6th	230	W.E.Jones/B.L.Muncer	v	Worcs	Worcester	1953
7th	211	P.A.Cottey/O.D.Gibson	v	Leics	Swansea	1996
8th	202	D.Davies/J.J.Hills	v	Sussex	Eastbourne	1928
9th	203*	J.J.Hills/J.C.Clay	v	Worcs	Swansea	1929
10th	143	T.Davies/S.A.B.Daniels	v	Glos	Swansea	1982

Best Bowling	For 10-51	J.Mercer	v	Worcs	Worcester	1936
(Innings)	V 10-18	G.Geary	for	Leics	Pontypridd	1929
Best Bowling	For 17-212	J.C.Clay	v	Worcs	Swansea	1937
(Match)	V 16-96	G.Geary	for	Leics	Pontypridd	1929

Most Runs – Season	2276	H.Morris	(av 55.51)		1990
Most Runs – Career	34056	A.Jones	(av 33.03)		1957-83
Most 100s – Season	10	H.Morris			1990
Most 100s – Career	52	A.Jones			1957-83
	52	H.Morris			1981-97
Most Wkts – Season	176	J.C.Clay	(av 17.34)		1937
Most Wkts – Career	2174	D.J.Shepherd	(av 20.95)		1950-72
Most Career W-K Dismissals	933	E.W.Jones	(840 ct; 93 st)		1961-83
Most Career Catches in the Field	656	P.M.Walker			1956-72

LIST 'A' LIMITED-OVERS CRICKET

Highest Total	CGT	429		v	Surrey	The Oval	2002
	BHC	318-3		v	Combined U	Cardiff	1995
	NL	305-6		v	Worcs	Cardiff	2001
Lowest Total	CGT	76		v	Northants	Northampton	1968
	BHC	68		v	Lancashire	Manchester	1973
	NL	42		v	Derbyshire	Swansea	1979
Highest Innings	CGT	162*	I.V.A.Richards	v	Oxfordshire	Swansea	1993
	BHC	151*	M.P.Maynard	v	Middlesex	Lord's	1996
	NL	155*	J.H.Kallis	v	Surrey	Pontypridd	1999
Best Bowling	CGT	5-13	R.J.Shastri	v	Scotland	Edinburgh	1988
	BHC	6-20	S.D.Thomas	v	Combined U	Cardiff	1995
	NL	7-16	S.D.Thomas	v	Surrey	Swansea	1998

GLOUCESTERSHIRE

Formation of Present Club: 1871
Inaugural First-Class Match: 1870
Colours: Blue, Gold, Brown, Silver, Green and Red
Badge: Coat of Arms of the City and County of Bristol
County Champions (since 1890): (0); best – 2nd 1930, 1931, 1947, 1959, 1969, 1986
Gillette/NatWest/C & G Trophy Winners: (5) 1973, 1999, 2000, 2003, 2004
Benson and Hedges Cup Winners: (3) 1977, 1999, 2000
National League (Div 1) Winners: (1) 2000
Sunday League Winners: (0); best – 2nd 1988
Twenty20 Cup Winners: (0); best – Semi-Finalist 2003
Match Awards: CGT 65; BHC 72

Chief Executive: T.E.M.Richardson, County Ground, Nevil Road, Bristol BS7 9EJ • Tel: 0117 910 8000 • Fax: 0117 924 1193 • Email: info.glos@ecb.co.uk • Web: www.gloucestershire.cricinfo.com

First XI Coach: M.W.Alleyne. **Club/Limited-Overs Captain**: M.W.Alleyne. **Captain**: C.G.Taylor. **Vice-Captain**: No appointment. **Overseas Player**: U.D.U.Chandana. **2005 Beneficiary**: T.H.C.Hancock. **Head Groundsman**: S.P.Williams. **Scorer**: K.T.Gerrish.
‡ New registration. NQ Not qualified for England.
Gloucestershire revised their capping policy in 2004 and now award players with their County Caps when they make their first-class debut.

ADSHEAD, Stephen John (Bridley Moor HS, Redditch), b Worcester 29 Jan 1980. 5'9". RHB, WK. Herefordshire 1999. Leicestershire 2000 (one non-CC match). Worcestershire 2003 (2 matches). Gloucestershire debut/cap 2004. HS 63 v Glam (Cardiff) 2003 – on Worcs/CC debut. Gs HS 61 v Worcs (Worcester) 2004. LO HS 77* Shropshire v Northumb (Oswestry) 2003 (CGT).

‡ALI, Kadeer (Handsworth GS), b Moseley, Birmingham 7 Mar 1983. 6'1". Brother of M.M.Ali (*see* WARWICKSHIRE), cousin of Kabir Ali (*see* WORCESTERSHIRE). RHB, LB. Worcestershire 2000-04. F-c Tour (Eng A): I 2003-04. HS 99 Wo v Yorks (Worcester) 2003. BB (Wo) 1-15 . LO HS 66 Worcs CB v Sussex CB (Kidderminster) 2002 (CGT). LO BB 1-4 (Wo – CGT).

ALLEYNE, Mark Wayne (Harrison C, Barbados; Cardinal Pole S, London E9; Haringey Cricket C), b Tottenham, London 23 May 1968. 5'10". RHB, RM. Debut 1986; cap 1990; captain 1997-2003; club/limited-overs captain/1st XI coach 2004; benefit 1999. *Wisden* 2000. MBE 2004. **LOI**: 10 (1998-99 to 2000-01); HS 53 v SA (E London) 1999-00; BB 3-27 v SL (Sydney) 1998-99. F-c Tours (Eng A) (C=captain): WI 2000-01C; NZ 1999-00C; SL 1986-87 (Gs), 1992-93 (Gs); B 1999-00C. 1000 runs (6); most – 1189 (1998). HS 256 v Northants (Northampton) 1990. 50 wkts (1): 54 (1996). BB 6-49 v Middx (Lord's) 2000. Awards: CGT 3; BHC 3. LO HS 134* v Leics (Bristol) 1992 (SL). LO BB 5-27 v Comb U (Bristol) 1988 (BHC).

AVERIS, James Maxwell Michael (Cathedral S, Bristol; Portsmouth U; St Cross C, Oxford), b Bristol 28 May 1974. 5'11". RHB, RMF. Oxford U 1997; blue 1997; rugby blue 1996-97. Gloucestershire debut 1997; cap 2001. HS 48* v Surrey (Oval) 2004. BB 6-32 v Northants (Bristol) 2004. Award: BHC 1. LO HS 23* v Lancs (Manchester) 2000 (NL). LO BB 6-23 v Bucks (Ascott Park) 2003 (CGT).

BALL, Martyn Charles John (King Edmund SS; Bath CFE), b Bristol 26 Apr 1970. 5'8". RHB, OB. Debut 1988; cap 1996; benefit 2002. F-c 2001-02; SL 1992-93 (Gs). HS 75 v Somerset (Taunton) 2003. BB 8-46 (14-169 match) v Somerset (Taunton) 1993. Award: CGT 1. LO HS 51 v SL A (Cheltenham) 1999. LO BB 5-33 v Yorks (Leeds) 2003 (NL).

‡NOCHANDANA, Umagilıya Durage **Upul**, b Galle, Sri Lanka 5 Jul 1972. 5'8". RHB, LB. Tamil Union 1991-92 to date. **Tests** (SL): 14 (1998-99 to 2004); HS 92 v Z (Galle) 2001-02; BB 6-179 v P (Dhaka) 1998-99 – on debut. **LOI** (SL): 133 (1993-94 to 2004-05); HS 89 v WI (Bridgetown) 2003; BB 5-61 v SA (Colombo) 2004. F-c Tours (SL): E 1998, 2002; A 2004; SA 1997-98; 2000-01; I 2001-02 (Colombo Dist); P 1999-00; B 1998-99. HS 194 SL A v K (Matara) 2001-02. BB 7-80 Tamil U v Bloomfield (Colombo) 1998-99. LO HS 108 SL A v K (Moratuwa) 2001-02. LO BB 5-22 Tamil U v Chilaw Marians (Colombo) 2001-02.

FISHER, Ian Douglas (Beckfoot GS, Bingley; Thomas Danby C, Leeds), b Bradford, Yorks 31 Mar 1976. 5'10½". LHB, SLA. Yorkshire 1995-96 (Y in Zim) to 2001. Gloucestershire debut 2002; cap 2004. F-c Tour: Z 1995-96 (Y). HS 103* v Essex (Gloucester) 2002. BB 5-30 (10-123 match) v Durham (Bristol) 2003. LO HS 23 and BB 3-18 v Northants (Northampton) 2004 (NL).

GIDMAN, Alex Peter Richard (Wycliffe C), b High Wycombe, Bucks 22 Jun 1981. 6'3". RHB, RM. Debut 2002. Cap 2004. MCCYC. Appointed captain of Eng A tour to India 2003-04 but withdrew because of hand injury. HS 117 v Northants (Bristol) 2002. BB 3-33 v Middx (Cheltenham) 2002. LO HS 73 v Warwks (Birmingham) 2003 (NL). LO BB 3-26 v Warwks (Gloucester) 2003 (NL).

‡**GREENIDGE, Carl** Gary (Lodge S and St Michael S, Barbados; Heathcote S, Chingford; W Hatch HS; City of Westminster C), b Basingstoke, Hants 20 Apr 1978. Son of C.Gordon Greenidge (Hampshire, Barbados and West Indies 1970-92). 5'10". RHB, RMF. MCC YC. Surrey 1999-2000. Northamptonshire 2002-04. HS 46 Nh v Derbys (Derby) 2002. 50 wkts (1): 53 (2002). BB 6-40 Nh v Durham (Chester-le-St) 2002. LO HS 20 Nh v Sussex (Northampton) 2002 (NL). LO BB 3-22 Nh v Derbys (Northampton) 2002 (NL).

HANCOCK, Timothy Harold Coulter (St Edward's S, Oxford; Henley C), b Reading, Berks 20 Apr 1972. 5'10". RHB, RM. Debut 1991; cap 1998; benefit 2005. Oxfordshire 1990. F-c Tour: SL 1992-93 (Gs). 1000 runs (1): 1227 (1998). HS 220* v Notts (Nottingham) 1998. BB 3-5 v Essex (Colchester) 1998. Awards: CGT 4. LO HS 135 v Bucks (Ascott Park) 2003 (CGT). LO BB 6-58 v Scot (Bristol) 1997 (NWT).

HARDINGES, Mark Andrew (Malvern C; Bath U), b Gloucester 5 Feb 1978. 6'1". RHB, RMF. Debut 1999. Cap 2004. British U 2000..HS 172 v OU (Oxford) 2002. CC HS 68 v Warwks (Bristol) 2004. BB 2-16 v Essex (Bristol) 2000. Award: CGT 1. LO HS 65 v Notts (Nottingham) 2001 (NL). LO BB 4-19 v Salop (Shrewsbury) 2002 (CGT).

‡**KIRBY, Steven** Paul (Elton HS; Bury C), b Ainsworth, nr Bolton, Lancs 4 Oct 1977. 6'3½". RHB, RF. Leicestershire staff 1998 – no f-c appearances. Yorkshire 2001-04, debut as sub for M.J.Hoggard (England duty) taking 7-50; cap 2003. F-c Tour (Eng A): I 2003-04 (part). HS 57 Y v Hants (Leeds) 2002. 50 wkts (1): 67 (2003). BB 8-80 (13-154 match) v Somerset (Taunton) 2003. LO HS 15 Y v Leics (Leicester) 2003 (NL). LO BB 3-27 Y v Worcs (Scarborough) 2003 (NL).

LEWIS, Jonathan (Churchfields S, Swindon; Swindon C), b Aylesbury, Bucks 26 Aug 1975. 6'2". RHB, RMF. Debut 1995; cap 1998. Wiltshire 1993. Northamptonshire staff 1994. F-c Tour: WI 2000-01 (Eng A). HS 62 v Worcs (Cheltenham) 1999. 50 wkts (5); most – 74 (2003). BB 8-95 v Z (Gloucester) 2000. CC BB 7-56 (10-92 match) v Notts (Bristol) 1999. Hat-trick 2000. Awards: CGT 1; BHC 2. LO HS 33* v Somerset (Bristol) 1998 (BHC). LO BB 5-23 v Lancs (Cheltenham) 2004 (NL).

PEARSON, James Alexander, b Bristol 11 Sep 1983. LHB. Gloucestershire debut 2002. No appearances 2003-04. HS 51 v Northants (Bristol) 2002 – on debut. LO HS 7 and BB 1-29 Glos CB v Herefords (Brockhampton) 2001.

‡**RUDGE, William** Douglas (Clifton C), b Bristol 15 Jul 1983. RHB, RM. Joined staff 2005 – awaiting f-c debut. LO HS (Gs CB) 3 (CGT).

SILLENCE, Roger John (Highbury SS; Salisbury Art C), b Salisbury, Wilts 29 Jun 1977. 6'3". RHB, RMF. Debut 2001 taking 5-97 v Sussex (Hove). Cap 2004. Wiltshire 1996-2001. HS 101 v Derbys (Bristol) 2002. BB 5-63 v Durham (Bristol) 2002. LO HS (Wilts) 82 v Northants CB (Northampton) 1999 (NWT). LO BB 4-35 v WI A (Cheltenham) 2002.

‡**SNELL, Stephen** David, b Winchester, Hampshire 27 Feb 1983. RHB, WK. Joined staff 2005 – awaiting f-c debut. LO HS (H CB) 3 (CGT).

SPEARMAN, Craig Murray, b Auckland, New Zealand 4 Jul 1972. RHB. Auckland 1993-94 to 1995-96. Central Districts 1996-97 to date. Gloucestershire debut/cap 2002. **Tests** (NZ): 19 (1995-96 to 2000-01); HS 112 v Z (Auckland) 1995-96. **LOI** (NZ): 51 (1995-96 to 2000-01); HS 86 v Z (Harare) 2000-01. F-c Tours (NZ): SA 2000-01; WI 1995-96; I 1999-00; P 1996-97; SL 1997-98; Z 1997-98, 2000-01. 1000 runs (2): 1462 (2004). HS 341 v Middx (Gloucester) 2004 – record Gloucestershire score. BB 1-37 CD v Wellington (New Plymouth) 1999-00. Awards: CGT 3; BHC 1. LO HS 153 v Warwks (Gloucester) 2003 (NL).

TAYLOR, Christopher Glyn (Colston's Collegiate S), b Southmead, Bristol 27 Sep 1976. 5'7''. RHB, OB. Debut 2000, scoring 104 v Middx – first to score a hundred at Lord's in a Championship match on his first-class debut. Cap 2001. Captain 2004 to date. 1000 runs (1): 1077) 2004. HS 196 v Notts (Nottingham) 2001. BB 3-126 v Northants (Cheltenham) 2000. Award: BHC 1. LO HS 93 v Warwks (Bristol) 2002 (BHC). LO BB 2-5 v Northants (Northampton) 2004 (NL).

WESTON, William Philip Christopher (Durham S), b Durham City 16 Jun 1973. Son of M.P.Weston (Durham; England RFU); brother of R.M.S.Weston (*see MIDDLESEX*). 6'3''. LHB, LM. Worcestershire 1991-2002; cap 1995. Gloucestershire debut 2003; cap 2004. F-c Tours (Wo): Z 1993-94, 1996-97. 1000 runs (4); most – 1389 (1996). HS 205 Wo v Northants (Northampton) 1997. Gs HS 179 v Somerset (Taunton) 2003. BB 2-39 Wo v P (Worcester) 1992. Gs BB 1-8 (CC). Award: CGT 1. LO HS 134 Wo v Derbys (Derby) 2001 (NL). LO BB (Wo) 1-2 (SL).

WINDOWS, Matthew Guy Newman (Clifton C; Durham U), b Bristol 5 Apr 1973. Son of A.R.Windows (Glos and CU 1960-68). 5'7''. RHB, LM. Debut 1992; cap 1998. Combined U 1995. F-c Tours (Eng A): SA 1998-99; Z 1998-99. 1000 runs (3); most – 1173 (1998). HS 184 v Warwks (Cheltenham) 1996. BB (Comb U) 1-6. Gs BB – . Awards: CGT 1; BHC 2. LO HS 117 v Northants (Cheltenham) 2001 (NL). BB –

RELEASED/RETIRED

(Having made a first-class County appearance in 2004)

BRACKEN, Nathan Wade (Springwood HS, NSW), b Penrith, NSW, Australia 12 Sep 1977. 6'5''. RHB, LFM. NSW 1998-99 to date. Gloucestershire debut/cap 2004. **Tests** (A): 3 (2003-04); HS 6* and BB 2-12 v I (Brisbane) 2003-04 – on debut. **LOI** (A): 17 (2000-01 to 2003-04); HS 7*; BB 4-29 v I (Bombay) 2003-04. HS 38* NSW v Tas (Hobart) 2002-03. Gs HS 13* and BB 2-12 v Lancs (Manchester) 2004. BB 7-4 NSW v S Aus (29 all out) (Sydney) 2004-05. LO HS 16* NSW v Tas (Sydney) 2002-03. LO BB 5-38 NSW v Vic (Melbourne) 2001-02.

BRESSINGTON, Alastair Nigel (Marling GS, Stroud; UWIC), b Downend, Bristol 28 Nov 1979. 6'1''. LHB, RMF. Gloucestershire 2000, 2004; cap 2004. **Tests** HS 58* v Kent (Bristol) 2004. BB 4-36 v Glam (Bristol) 2000 – on debut. LO HS 54 Glos CB v Yorks CB (Cheltenham) 1999 (NWT). LO BB 3-21 Glos CB v Notts CB (Cheltenham) 2000 (NWT).

NQ**FRANKLIN, James** Edward Charles, b Wellington, New Zealand 7 Nov 1980. LHB, LFM. Wellington 1998-99 to date. Gloucestershire 2004; cap 2004. **Tests** (NZ): 6 (2000-01 to 2004-05); HS 23 and BB 5-28 (inc hat-trick) v B (Dhaka) 2004-05. **LOI** (NZ): 30 (2000-01 to 2004-05); HS 25* v Z (Taupo) 2000-01 – on debut; BB 5-42 v E (Chester-le-St) 2004. HS 108* Wellington v Otago (Dunedin) 2003-04. Gs HS 44 v Middx (Lord's) 2004. BB 7-60 v Lancs (Cheltenham) 2004 – on debut. LO HS 76 Wellington v Otago (Wellington) 2004-05. LO BB 5-42 (see LOI).

NQ**HUSSEY, M.E.K.** – *see DURHAM*.

34

RUSSELL, Robert Charles (*'Jack'*) (Archway CS; Bristol Poly – *"briefly"*), b Stroud 15 Aug 1963. 5'8½". LHB, WK, occ OB. Gloucestershire 1981-2004; youngest Glos wicket-keeper (17yr 307d), setting record for most match dismissals on f-c debut – 8 v SL (Bristol); cap 1985; benefit 1994; captain 1995; testimonial 2004. Kept throughout world record total without byes – 746-9d by Northants (Bristol) 2002. *Wisden* 1989. MBE 1996. **Tests:** 54 (1988 to 1997-98); HS 128* v A (Manchester) 1989; 11 ct v SA (Johannesburg) 1995-96 (Test record); 27 dis 1995-96 series v SA (Eng record). **LOI:** 40 (1987-88 to 1998-99); HS 50 v I (Nottingham) 1990. F-c Tours: A 1990-91, 1992-93 (Eng A); SA 1995-96; WI 1989-90, 1993-94, 1997-98; NZ 1991-92, 1996-97; P 1987-88; SL 1986-87 (Gs). 1000 runs (1): 1049 (1997). HS 129* Eng XI v Boland (Paarl) 1995-96. Gs HS 124 v Notts (Nottingham) 1996. BB 1-4. Awards: CGT 1; BHC 3. LO HS 119* v Brit U (Bristol) 1998 (BHC).

NQSHABBIR AHMED KHAN, b Khanewal, Pakistan 21 Apr 1976. 6'7". RHB, RFM. Multan 1997-98. WAPDA 1997-98 to 1999-00. Bahawalpur 1998-99. REDCO 1999-00. National Bank 2000-01 to date. Gloucestershire 2004; cap 2004. **Tests** (P): 7 (2003 to 2003-04); HS 24* v SA (Faisalabad) 2003-04; BB 5-48 v B (Karachi) 2003 on debut. **LOI** (P): 29 (1999-00 to 2004); HS 2 (*thrice*); BB 3-32 v B (Colombo) 2004. F-c Tours (P): WI 1999-00; NZ 2003-04; SL 2001 (Pak A). HS 50 National Bank v Allied Bank (Sheikhupura) 2000-01. Gs HS 34* v Sussex (Arundel) 2004. 50 wkts (0+1): 61 (2001-02). BB 7-70 National Bank v Lahore Blues (Okara) 2002-03. Gs BB 4-96 v Middx (Gloucester) 2004. LO HS 42 v Glam (Swansea) 2004 (NL). LO BB 5-24 WAPDA v Customs (Karachi) 1999-00.

NQSHOAIB MALIK (Government Arabic SS, Sialkot), b Sialkot, Pakistan 1 Feb 1982. 5'6". RHB, OB. Debut (Pakistan A) 1997. Gujranwala 1997-98 to 1998-99. PIA 1998-99 to 2000-01 date. Sialkot 2001-02. Gloucestershire 2003-04, cap 2004. **Tests** (P): 8 (2001 to 2004-05); HS 59 v SL (Faisalabad) 2004-05; BB 4-42 v SA (Lahore) 2003-04. **LOI** (P): 93 (1999-00 to 2004-05); HS 143 v I (Colombo) 2004; BB 4-19 v HK (Colombo) 2004. F-c Tours (P): E 1997 (Pak A); A 2004-05. HS 130* and BB 7-81 PIA v WAPDA (Faisalabad) 2000-01. Gs HS 63 v Northants (Bristol) 2004. Gs BB 3-76 v Worcs (Cheltenham) 2003. Award: CGT 1. LO HS 143 (*see LOI*). LO BB 5-35 PIA v Lahore Blues (Karachi) 2002-03.

SMITH, Andrew Michael (Queen Elizabeth GS, Wakefield; Exeter U; West of England U), b Dewsbury, Yorks 1 Oct 1967. 5'9". RHB, LMF. Gloucestershire 1991-2004; cap 1995; benefit 2001. **Tests:** 1 (1997); HS 4* v A (Leeds) 1997. F-c Tour: P 1995-96 (Eng A – *part*). HS 61 v Yorks (Gloucester) 1998. 50 wkts (5); most – 83 (1997). BB 8-73 (10-118 match) v Middx (Lord's) 1996. Awards: CGT 1; BHC 1. LO HS 26* v Kent (Moreton-in-M) 1996 (SL). LO BB 6-39 v Hants (Southampton) 1995 (BHC).

SCORING OF EXTRAS 2005

The variable penalties involved in scoring no-balls and wides in our international and county cricket remain unchanged from last season:

COMPETITION	NO-BALL PENALTY	WIDE PENALTY
Test Matches Limited-Overs Internationals }	1 + other runs scored	1 + other runs scored
County Championship Second XI Championship }	2 + other runs scored	1 + other runs scored
Tourist Matches (First-Class) Tourist Matches (Limited-Overs) }	1 + other runs scored	1 + other runs scored
C & G Trophy Totesport National League Twenty 20 Cup }	2 + other runs scored + for foot fault free hit next ball	1 + other runs scored

GLOUCESTERSHIRE 2004

RESULTS SUMMARY

	Place	Won	Lost	Tied	Drew	No Result
County Championship (1st Division)	**6th**	3	3		10	
All First-Class Matches		3	3		11	
C & G Trophy	Winners					
National League (1st Division)	5th	7	7	1		1
Twenty20 Cup	5th in Mid/West/Wales Division					

COUNTY CHAMPIONSHIP AVERAGES
BATTING AND FIELDING

Cap		M	I	NO	HS	Runs	Avge	100	50	Ct/St
2002	C.M.Spearman	16	27	2	341	1424	56.96	4	4	15
2001	C.G.Taylor	16	25	1	177	1077	44.87	4	4	6
1998	T.H.C.Hancock	8	12	1	77*	441	40.09	–	4	4
2004	S.J.Adshead	15	23	7	61	609	38.06	–	4	39/2
1990	M.W.Alleyne	4	5	1	77*	149	37.25	–	2	5
2004	M.E.K.Hussey	7	13	1	78	442	36.83	–	2	10
2004	W.P.C.Weston	16	27	1	135	922	35.46	2	4	18
2004	J.E.C.Franklin	3	6	2	44	134	33.50	–	–	1
2004	A.P.R.Gidman	15	23	–	82	745	32.39	–	8	12
1996	M.C.J.Ball	7	10	4	38	155	25.83	–	–	4
2004	Shabbir Ahmed	6	6	4	34*	51	25.50	–	–	1
1998	M.G.N.Windows	8	12	2	58	240	24.00	–	1	4
2001	J.M.M.Averis	12	11	4	48*	150	21.42	–	–	2
2004	I.D.Fisher	11	17	–	45	320	18.82	–	–	4
1998	J.Lewis	16	15	4	34*	193	17.54	–	–	1
2004	Shoaib Malik	6	9	1	63	134	16.75	–	1	2

Also batted: N.W.Bracken (2 matches – cap 2004) 8, 13*; A.N.Bressington (2 – cap 2004) 58*, 19*; M.A.Hardinges (1 – cap 2004) 68* (3 ct); R.C.Russell (1 – cap 1985) 2; R.J.Sillence (2 – cap 2004) 92, 4; A.M.Smith (2 – cap 1995) 3*, 9 (1 ct).

BOWLING

	O	M	R	W	Avge	Best	5wI	10wM
A.M.Smith	42.4	12	120	6	20.00	3- 34	–	–
J.E.C.Franklin	83.1	27	252	12	21.00	7- 60	1	–
J.Lewis	472.4	122	1440	57	25.26	7- 72	4	–
Shabbir Ahmed	169	38	605	18	33.61	4- 96	–	–
J.M.M.Averis	271.2	47	1075	26	41.34	6- 32	2	–
I.D.Fisher	320.4	61	1073	23	46.65	5-114	1	–
Shoaib Malik	176	30	530	10	53.00	3-109	–	–
M.C.J.Ball	169	23	564	10	56.40	3- 96	–	–
A.P.R.Gidman	173	22	695	12	57.91	2- 12	–	–

Also bowled:

N.W.Bracken | 39 | 12 | 106 | 5 | 21.20 | 2- 12 | – | –
M.W.Alleyne | 56.3 | 16 | 206 | 9 | 22.88 | 5- 71 | 1 | –
R.J.Sillence | 52 | 19 | 135 | 5 | 27.00 | 2- 50 | – | –

A.N.Bressington 12-0-93-1; T.H.C.Hancock 31-6-98-0; M.A.Hardinges 30-4-120-1; M.E.K.Hussey 8-2-22-0; C.G.Taylor 1-0-2-0; W.P.C.Weston 4-2-8-1.

The First-Class Averages (pp 121–136) give the records of Gloucestershire players in all first-class county matches (Gloucestershire's other opponents being Loughborough UCCE), with the exception of:

A.P.R.Gidman 16-24-0-82-778-32.41-0-8-13ct. 181-33-723-13-55.61-2/12.

In 2004 Gloucestershire awarded 1st XI caps to all their county's first-class debutants and previously uncapped f-c players.

GLOUCESTERSHIRE RECORDS

FIRST-CLASS CRICKET

Highest Total	For	695-9d		v	Middlesex	Gloucester	2004
	V	774-7d		by	Australians	Bristol	1948
Lowest Total	For	17		v	Australians	Cheltenham	1896
	V	12		by	Northants	Gloucester	1907
Highest Innings	For	341	C.M.Spearman	v	Middlesex	Gloucester	2004
	V	310*	M.E.K.Hussey	for	Northants	Bristol	2002

Highest Partnership for each Wicket

1st	395	D.M.Young/R.B.Nicholls	v	Oxford U	Oxford	1962
2nd	256	C.T.M.Pugh/T.W.Graveney	v	Derbyshire	Chesterfield	1960
3rd	336	W.R.Hammond/B.H.Lyon	v	Leics	Leicester	1933
4th	321	W.R.Hammond/W.L.Neale	v	Leics	Gloucester	1937
5th	261	W.G.Grace/W.O.Moberley	v	Yorkshire	Cheltenham	1876
6th	320	G.L.Jessop/J.H.Board	v	Sussex	Hove	1903
7th	248	W.G.Grace/E.L.Thomas	v	Sussex	Hove	1896
8th	239	W.R.Hammond/A.E.Wilson	v	Lancashire	Bristol	1938
9th	193	W.G.Grace/S.A.P.Kitcat	v	Sussex	Bristol	1896
10th	131	W.R.Gouldsworthy/J.G.Bessant	v	Somerset	Bristol	1923

Best Bowling	For	10-40	E.G.Dennett	v	Essex	Bristol	1906
(Innings)	V	10-66	A.A.Mailey	for	Australians	Cheltenham	1921
		10-66	K.Smales	for	Notts	Stroud	1956
Best Bowling	For	17-56	C.W.L.Parker	v	Essex	Gloucester	1925
(Match)	V	15-87	A.J.Conway	for	Worcs	Moreton-in-M	1914

Most Runs – Season	2860	W.R.Hammond	(av 69.75)	1933
Most Runs – Career	33664	W.R.Hammond	(av 57.05)	1920-51
Most 100s – Season	13	W.R.Hammond		1938
Most 100s – Career	113	W.R.Hammond		1920-51
Most Wkts – Season	222	T.W.J.Goddard	(av 16.80)	1937
	222	T.W.J.Goddard	(av 16.37)	1947
Most Wkts – Career	3170	C.W.L.Parker	(av 19.43)	1903-35
Most Career W-K Dismissals	1016	J.H.Board	(698 ct; 318 st)	1891-1914
	1016	R.C.Russell	(916 ct; 100 st)	1981-2002
Most Career Catches in the Field	718	C.A.Milton		1948-74

LIST 'A' LIMITED-OVERS CRICKET

Highest Total	CGT	401-7		v	Bucks	Wing	2003
	BHC	308-3		v	Ireland	Dublin	1996
	NL	344-6		v	Northants	Cheltenham	2001
Lowest Total	CGT	82		v	Notts	Bristol	1987
	BHC	62		v	Hampshire	Bristol	1975
	NL	49		v	Middlesex	Bristol	1978
Highest Innings	CGT	177	A.J.Wright	v	Scotland	Bristol	1997
	BHC	154*	M.J.Procter	v	Somerset	Taunton	1972
	NL	153	C.M.Spearman	v	Warwicks	Gloucester	2003
Best Bowling	CGT	6-21	C.A.Walsh	v	Kent	Bristol	1990
		6-21	C.A.Walsh	v	Cheshire	Bristol	1992
	BHC	6-13	M.J.Procter	v	Hampshire	Southampton	1977
	NL	6-52	J.N.Shepherd	v	Kent	Bristol	1983

HAMPSHIRE

Formation of Present Club: 12 August 1863
Inaugural First-Class Match: 1864
Colours: Blue, Gold and White
Badge: Tudor Rose and Crown
County Champions: (2) 1961, 1973
Gillette/NatWest/C & G Trophy Winners: (1) 1991
Benson and Hedges Cup Winners: (2) 1988, 1992
National League (Div 1) Winners: (0); best – 3rd 2004
Sunday League Winners: (3) 1975, 1978, 1986
Twenty20 Cup Winners: (0) – best Quarter-Finalist 2004
Match Awards: CGT 62; BHC 67

Chief Executive: N.S.Pike, The Rose Bowl, Botley Road, West End, Southampton SO30 3XH • Tel: 023 8047 2002 • Fax: 023 8047 2122 • Email: enquiries@rosebowlplc.com • Webs: www.hampshire.cricinfo.com • www.rosebowlplc.com

First XI Manager/Coach: V.P.Terry. **2nd XI Coach/Academy Director**: T.C.Middleton. **Captain**: S.K.Warne. **Vice-Captain**: *tba*. **Overseas Players**: S.M.Katich and S.K.Warne. **2005 Beneficiary**: A.D.Mullally. **Head Groundsman**: N.Gray. **Scorer**: V.H Isaacs. ‡ New registration. NQ Not qualified for England.

ADAMS, James Henry Kenneth (Sherborne S; University C, London; Loughborough U), b Winchester 23 Sep 1980. 6'2". LHB, LM. British U 2002-03. Hampshire debut 2002. Loughborough UCCE 2003-4 – scoring 107 v Somerset (Taunton) on debut. Dorset 1998. HS 107 (*above*). H HS 75 v Glam (Cardiff) 2004. BB 2-16 v Durham (Chester-le-St) 2004. LO HS 40 v Glam (Southampton) 2004 (NL).

BENHAM, Christopher Charles (Yately CS; Loughborough U), b Frimley, Surrey 24 Mar 1983. 6'1". RHB, RM/OB. Loughborough UCCE 2004. Hampshire debut 2004. HS 74 v Derbys (Derby) 2004 – on county debut. LO HS 0 (Hants CB) (CGT).

BROWN, Michael James (Queen Elizabeth GS, Blackburn; Collingwood C, Durham U), b Burnley, Lancs 9 Feb 1980. 6'0". RHB, OB. Middlesex 1999-2003. Durham UCCE 2001-02. British U 2001-02. Hampshire debut 2004. HS 109* v Glam (Southampton) 2004. LO HS 35 v Lancs (Southampton) 2004 (NL).

BRUCE, James Thomas Anthony (Eton C: St Hild & St Bede C, Durham U), b Hammersmith, London 17 Dec 1979. 6'1". RHB, RMF. Durham UCCE 2001-02. Hampshire debut 2003. HS 21* and BB 3-42 v Glam (Southampton) 2003. LO HS 6* (NL). LO BB 3-45 v Sussex (Hove) 2003 (NL).

BURROWS, Thomas George (Reading GS), b Wokingham, Berkshire 5 May 1985. 5'8". RHB, WK. Berkshire 2001 to 2003. Staff 2004 – awaiting first-class debut. LO HS Berks 1 (CGT).

CRAWLEY, John Paul (Manchester GS; Trinity C, Cambridge), b Maldon, Essex 21 Sep 1971. Brother of M.A.Crawley (Oxford U, Lancs and Notts 1987-94) and P.M. (Cambridge U 1992). 6'1". RHB, RM, occ WK. Lancashire 1990-2001; cap 1994; captain 1999-2001. Cambridge U 1991-93; blue 1991-92-93; captain 1992-93. Hampshire debut/cap 2002. YC 1994. **Tests**: 37 (1994 to 2002-03); HS 156* v SL (Oval) 1998. **LOI**: 13 (1994-95 to 1998-99); HS 73 v Z (Harare) 1996-97. F-c Tours: A 1994-95, 1998-99, 2002-03; SA 1993-94 (Eng A), 1995-96; WI 1995-96 (La), 1997-98, 2000-01 (Eng A); NZ 1996-97; Z 1996-97. 1000 runs (8); most – 1851 (1998). HS 301* v Notts (Nottingham) 2004. BB 1-90. Awards: BHC 2. LO HS 114 La v Notts (Manchester) 1995 (BHC).

‡^{NO}**ERVINE, Sean** Michael (Lomagundi C, Chinhoyi), b Harare, Zimbabwe 6 Dec 1982. Son of R.M.Ervine and nephew of B.B.Ervine (both Rhodesia 1977-78). Irish passport. 6'2". LHB, RM. Zimbabwe Academy 2000-01. Midlands 2001-02 to date. **Tests** (Z): 5 (2003 to 2003-04); HS 86 v B (Harare) 2002-04; BB 4-146 v A (Perth) 2003-04. **LOI** (Z): 42 (2001-02 to 2003-04): HS 100 v I (Adelaide) 2003-04; BB 3-29 v P (Sharjah) 2002-02. F-c Tours: E 2003; A 2003-04. HS 126 Midlands v Manicaland (Mutare) 2002-03. BB 6-82 Midlands v Mashonaland (Kwekwe) 2002-03. LO HS 100 (*see LOI*). LO BB 5-56 Z v WA (Perth) 2003-04.

‡**GRIFFITHS, David** Andrew, b Newport, IOW 10 Sep 1985. LHB, RFM. Joined staff 2005 – awaiting f-c debut.

^{NO}**KATICH, Simon** Mathew (Trinity C, WA; U of WA), b Middle Swan, Midland, W Australia 21 Aug 1975. 6'0". LHB. SLC. W Australia 1996-97 to 2001-02. NSW 2002-03. Durham 2000; cap 2000. Yorkshire 2002 (one match). Hampshire debut/cap 2003. **Tests** (A): 13 (2001 to 2004-05); HS 125 v I (Sydney) 2003-04; BB 6-65 v Z (Sydney) 2003-04. **LOI** (A): 11 (2000-01 to 2004-05); 76 v WI (Adelaide) 2003-04. F-c Tours (A): E 2001; I 2004-05; SL 1999-00, 2003-04. 1000 runs (2+3): most – 1632 (1998-99). HS 228* WA v S Aus (Perth) 2000-01. UK HS 168* A v MCC (Arundel) 2001. CC HS 143* v Yorks (Scarborough) 2003. BB 7-130 NSW v Vic (Melbourne) 2002-03. UK BB 4-21 H v Northants (Southampton) 2003. LO HS 136* NSW v Vic (Bowral) 2003-04. LO BB 3-21 Aus A v SA (Adelaide) 2001-02.

KENWAY, Derek Anthony (St George's S, Southampton; Barton Peveril C, Eastleigh), b Fareham 12 Jun 1978. 5'11". RHB, RM, occ WK. Debut 1997; cap 2001. 1000 runs (1): 1055 (1999). HS 166 v Notts (Southampton) 2001. BB 1-5. Award: CGT 1. LO HS 120* v Z (Southampton) 2003. LO BB 1-16 (CGT).

^{NO}**LAMB, Gregory** Arthur (Lomagundi C, Chinhoyi; Guildford C, Surrey), b Harare, Zimbabwe 4 Mar 1980. 5'11". RHB, RM/OB. CFX Academy 1998-99 to 1999-00. Mashonaland 2000-01.Hampshire debut 2004. F-c Tour (Zim A): SL 1999-00. HS 100* CFX Academy v Manicaland (Mutare) 1999-00. H HS 94 v Derbys (Derby) 2004 – on UK debut. BB 7-73 CFX Academy v Midlands (Kwekwe) 1999-00. LO HS 72* Zim A v Holland (Harare) 1999-00. LO BB (Zim) A 1-27.

LATOUF, Kevin John (Millfield S; Barton Peveril C), b Pretoria, South Africa 7 Sep 1985. 5'10". RHB, RM. Staff 2004 – awaiting first-class debut.

‡**LOGAN, Richard** James (Wolverhampton GS), b Stone, Staffs 28 Jan 1980. 6'1". RHB, RMF. Northamptonshire 1999-2000. Nottinghamshire 2001-04. HS 37* Nt v Hants (Nottingham) 2001. BB 6-93 Nt v Derbys (Nottingham) 2001. Award: CGT 1. LO HS 24 Nt v Northants (Northampton) 2001 (NL). LO BB 5-24 Nt v Suffolk (Mildenhall) 2001 (CGT).

‡^{NO}**MCLEAN, Jonathan** ('**Jono**') James (St Stithian's S), b Johannesburg, South Africa 11 Jul 1980. RHB, RM. W Province 2001-02 to 2003-04. Hampshire staff 2005. British passport. HS 57 WP v FS (Bloemfontein) 2002-03. LO HS (WP) 0.

MASCARENHAS, Adrian Dimitri (Trinity C, Perth, Australia), b Hammersmith, London 30 Oct 1977. 6'2". Resident in Australia 1979-96. RHB, RMF. Debut 1996, taking 6-88 v Glamorgan (Southampton); took 16 wickets in first two CC matches; cap 1998. Dorset 1996. HS 104 v Worcs (Southampton) 2001 and 104 v Durham (Chester-le-St) 2004. 50 wkts (1): 56 (2004). BB 6-25 v Derbys (Southampton) 2004. Awards: CGT 3. LO HS 79 v Worcs (Southampton) 1999 (NL) and 79 v Kent (Canterbury) 2004 (NL). LO BB 5-27 v Glos (Southampton) 2002 (NL).

MULLALLY, Alan David (Cannington HS, Perth, Australia; Wembley & Carlisle TC), b Southend-on-Sea, Essex 12 Jul 1969. 6'5". RHB, LFM. W Australia 1987-88 to 1989-90. Victoria 1990-91. Hampshire 1988 (1 match), 2000 to date; cap 2000; benefit 2005. Leicestershire 1990-99; cap 1993. **Tests**: 19 (1996 to 2001); HS 24 v P (Oval) 1996; BB 5-105 v A (Brisbane) 1998-99. **LOI**: 50 (1996 to 2001); HS 20 v Z (Harare) 1999; BB 4-18 v A (Brisbane) 1998-99. F-c Tours: A 1998-99; SA 1999-00; NZ 1996-97; Z 1996-97. HS 75 Le v Middx (Leicester) 1996. H HS 36 v Derbys (Derby) 2001. 50 wkts (5); most – 70 (1996). BB 9-93 (14-188 match) v Derbys (Derby) 2000. Award: CGT 1. UK HS 38 Le v Kent (Leicester) 1994 (SL). LO BB 6-38 Le v NZ (Leicester) 1990.

‡**PIETERSEN, Kevin** Peter (Maritzburg C; Natal U), b Pietermaritzburg, South Africa 27 Jun 1980. British passport (English mother) – qualified for England Oct 2004. 6'4". RHB, OB. Natal/KwaZulu-Natal 1997-98 to 1999-00. Nottinghamshire 2001-04; cap 2002. **LOI**: 11 (2004-05); HS 116 v SA (Pretoria) 2004-05; scored 454 runs (av 151.33) in 7-match series, including fastest England 100 off 69 balls (E London), v SA 2004-05. F-c Tour (Eng A): I 2003-04. 1000 runs (3): most – 1546 (2003). HS 254* Nt v Middx (Nottingham) 2002. BB 4-31 Nt v DU (Nottingham) 2003. CC BB 3-72 Nt v Hants (Nottingham) 2004. LO HS 147 Nt v Somerset (Taunton) 2002 (NL). LO BB 3-14 Nt v Middx (Lord's 2004 (NL).

NQ**POTHAS, Nic** (King Edward VII S; Rand Afrikaans U), b Johannesburg 18 Nov 1973. ECB qualified – EU (Greek) passport. 6'3". RHB, WK. Transvaal 1993-94 to 2000-01. Hampshire debut 2002; cap 2003. **LOI** (SA): 3 (2000-01); HS 24 v P (Singapore) 2000 – on debut. F-c Tours (SA): E 1996 (SA A); WI 2000-01 (SA A); SL 1998-99. HS 165 Gauteng v KZ-Natal (Johannesburg) 1998-99. H HS 146* v Worcs (Worcester) 2003. LO HS 101 Transvaal v EP (Johannesburg) 1995-96.

PRITTIPAUL, Lawrence Roland (St John's C, Southsea; Portsmouth C), b Portsmouth 19 Oct 1979. Cousin of S.Chanderpaul (Guyana and West Indies 1991-92 to date). 6'1". RHB, RM. Debut 2000. HS 152 v Derbys (Southampton) 2000. BB 3-17 v Worcs (Southampton) 2003. LO HS 61 v Notts (Southampton) 2000 (NL). LO BB 3-11 v Cheshire (Alderley Edge) 2004 (CGT).

TAYLOR, Billy Victor (Bitterne Park S, Southampton), b Southampton, Hants 11 Jan 1977. Brother of J.L.Taylor (Wiltshire 1998 to date). 6'3". LHB, RMF. Sussex 1999-2003. Hampshire debut 2004. Wiltshire 1996-98. HS 40 v Essex (Southampton) 2004. BB 5-73 v Essex (Chelmsford) 2004. Awards: CGT 1; BHC 1. LO HS 21* Sx v Notts (Cleethorpes) 1999 (NL). LO BB 5-28 Sx v Middx (Lord's) 2002 (BHC).

TOMLINSON, James Andrew (Harrow Way S, Andover; Cardiff U), b Winchester 12 Jun 1982. 6'1". LHB, LFM. Wiltshire 2001. British U 2002-03. Hampshire debut 2002. HS 23 v I (Southampton) 2002. CC HS 12* v Derbys (Derby) 2004. BB 6-63 v Derbys (Derby) 2003. LO HS 6 (NL). LO BB 2-15 v Sussex (Southampton) 2002 (NL).

TREMLETT, Christopher Timothy (Thornden S, Chandler's Ford; Taunton's C, Southampton), b Southampton 2 Sep 1981. Son of T.M.Tremlett (Hampshire 1976-91); grandson of M.F.Tremlett (Somerset, CD and England 1947-60). 6'7". RHB, RMF. Debut 2000. Cap 2004. F-c Tours (ECB Acad): SL 2002-03. HS 57 v Somerset (Southampton) 2004. BB 6-51 v Glam (Southampton) 2003. LO HS 38* v Cheshire (Alderley Edge) 2004 (CGT). LO BB 4-25 v Essex (Southend) 2002 (NL).

UDAL, Shaun David (Cove CS), b Cove, Farnborough 18 Mar 1969. Grandson of G.F.U.Udal (Middx 1932 and Leics 1946); great-great-grandson of J.S.Udal (MCC 1871-75). 6'2". RHB, OB. Debut 1989; cap 1992; benefit 2002. **LOI**: 10 (1994 to 1995); HS 11* v Z (Brisbane) 1994-95; BB 2-37 v A (Sydney) 1994-95. F-c Tours: A 1994-95; P 1995-96 (Eng A). HS 117* v Warwks (Southampton) 1997. 50 wkts (7); most – 74 (1993). BB 8-50 v Sussex (Southampton) 1992. Awards: CGT 1; BHC 2. LO HS 78 v Surrey (Guildford) 1997 (SL). LO BB 5-43 v Surrey (Oval) 1998 (SL).

NQ**WARNE, Shane** Keith (Hampton HS; Mentone GS), b Upper Ferntree Gully, Melbourne, Australia 13 Sep 1969. 6'0". RHB, LBG. Victoria 1990-91 to date; captain 1997-98 to 1998-99. Hampshire 2000, 2004; cap 2000; captain 2004 to date. *Wisden* 1993 (also one of *Five Cricketers of the Century*). **Tests** (A): 120 (1991-92 to 2004-05); HS 99 v NZ (Perth) 2001-02; BB 8-71 v E (Brisbane) 1994-95; hat-trick v E (Melbourne) 1994-95. **LOI** (A): 193 (1992-93 to 2002-03, 11 as captain); HS 55 v SA (Pt Elizabeth) 1993-94; BB 5-33 v WI (Sydney) 1996-97. F-c Tours (A): E 1993, 1997, 2001; SA 1993-94, 1996-97, 2001-02; WI 1994-95, 1998-99; NZ 1992-93, 1999-00; I 1997-98, 2000-01, 2004-05; P 1994-95, 2002-03 (in SL/Sharjah); SL 1992-93, 1999-00, 2003-04; Z 1991-92 (Aus B), 1999-00. HS 99 (*see Tests*). H HS 69 v Kent (Portsmouth) 2000. 50 wkts (4+1); most – 75 (1993). BB 8-71 (*see Tests*). H BB 6-34 v Kent (Canterbury) 2000. Award: BHC 1. LO HS 55 (*see LOI*). LO BB 5-33 (*see LOI*).

RELEASED/RETIRED continued on p 46

HAMPSHIRE 2004

RESULTS SUMMARY

	Place	Won	Lost	Tied	Drew	No Result
County Championship (2nd Division)	2nd	9	2		5	
All First-Class Matches		9	2		5	
C & G Trophy	3rd Round					
National League (1st Division)	3rd	7	6			3
Twenty20 Cup	Quarter-Finalist					

COUNTY CHAMPIONSHIP AVERAGES

BATTING AND FIELDING

Cap		M	I	NO	HS	Runs	Avge	100	50	Ct/St
2002	J.P.Crawley	13	21	3	301*	938	52.11	1	5	4
2003	N.Pothas	16	24	3	131*	834	39.71	3	4	45/5
2003	S.M.Katich	4	5	–	66	183	36.60	–	1	3
–	M.J.Clarke	12	20	–	140	709	35.45	3	2	20
–	J.H.K.Adams	8	15	3	75	425	35.41	–	2	1
1992	S.D.Udal	13	17	3	74	488	34.85	–	3	8
–	M.J.Brown	16	28	2	109*	838	32.23	2	6	12
2000	S.K.Warne	12	16	2	57	381	27.21	–	1	9
–	L.R.Prittipaul	5	9	–	49	231	25.66	–	–	3
2001	D.A.Kenway	14	23	1	101	552	25.09	1	1	9
1998	A.D.Mascarenhas	16	24	2	104	477	21.68	–	1	8
–	C.T.Tremlett	10	15	4	57	213	19.36	–	1	2
1999	W.S.Kendall	8	14	1	50	238	18.30	–	1	7
–	B.V.Taylor	11	16	6	40	177	17.70	–	–	3
2000	A.D.Mullally	10	10	5	22*	67	13.40	–	–	1
–	J.T.A.Bruce	4	5	1	9	10	2.50	–	–	1

Also batted (1 match each): C.C.Benham 74; G.A.Lamb 94, 7; J.A.Tomlinson 12* (1 ct); S.R.Watson 24, 112*.*

BOWLING

	O	M	R	W	Avge	Best	5wI	10wM
A.D.Mascarenhas	404.2	132	1046	56	18.67	6-25	4	–
C.T.Tremlett	268.2	56	867	39	22.23	4-29	–	–
S.D.Udal	247.4	40	869	39	22.28	6-79	1	–
S.K.Warne	411.5	88	1231	51	24.13	6-65	3	–
B.V.Taylor	298.1	59	1039	33	31.48	5-73	1	–
A.D.Mullally	245.4	69	711	18	39.50	6-68	1	–

Also bowled:
J.T.A.Bruce   88.0   11   375   9   41.66   3-74

J.H.K.Adams 19-6-61-2; M.J.Clarke 42.1-8-160-1; J.P.Crawley 4-1-24-0; S.M.Katich 18-1-61-0; W.S.Kendall 12-2-44-2; D.A.Kenway 2-2-0-0; G.A.Lamb 5-2-15-0; J.A.Tomlinson 20-7-43-1; L.R.Prittipaul 21-4-71-1; S.R.Watson 8.4-2-28-0.

Hampshire played no fixtures outside the County Championship in 2004. The First-Class Averages (pp 121–136) give the records of Hampshire players in all first-class county matches, with the exception of J.H.K.Adams and C.C.Benham whose full county figures are as above.

HAMPSHIRE RECORDS

FIRST-CLASS CRICKET

Highest Total	For 672-7d		v	Somerset	Taunton	1899
	V 742		by	Surrey	The Oval	1909
Lowest Total	For 15		v	Warwicks	Birmingham	1922
	V 23		by	Yorkshire	Middlesbrough	1965
Highest Innings	For 316	R.H.Moore	v	Warwicks	Bournemouth	1937
	V 303*	G.A.Hick	for	Worcs	Southampton	1997

Highest Partnership for each Wicket

1st	347	V.P.Terry/C.L.Smith	v	Warwicks	Birmingham	1987
2nd	321	G.Brown/E.I.M.Barrett	v	Glos	Southampton	1920
3rd	344	C.P.Mead/G.Brown	v	Yorkshire	Portsmouth	1927
4th	263	R.E.Marshall/D.A.Livingstone	v	Middlesex	Lord's	1970
5th	235	G.Hill/D.F.Walker	v	Sussex	Portsmouth	1937
6th	411	R.M.Poore/E.G.Wynyard	v	Somerset	Taunton	1899
7th	325	G.Brown/C.H.Abercrombie	v	Essex	Leyton	1913
8th	227	K.D.James/T.M.Tremlett	v	Somerset	Taunton	1985
9th	230	D.A.Livingstone/A.T.Castell	v	Surrey	Southampton	1962
10th	192	H.A.W.Bowell/W.H.Livsey	v	Worcs	Bournemouth	1921

Best Bowling	For 9- 25	R.M.H.Cottam	v	Lancashire	Manchester	1965
(Innings)	V 10- 46	W.Hickton	for	Lancashire	Manchester	1870
Best Bowling	For 16- 88	J.A.Newman	v	Somerset	Weston-s-Mare	1927
(Match)	V 17-119	W.Mead	for	Essex	Southampton	1895

Most Runs – Season	2854	C.P.Mead	(av 79.27)	1928
Most Runs – Career	48892	C.P.Mead	(av 48.84)	1905-36
Most 100s – Season	12	C.P.Mead		1928
Most 100s – Career	138	C.P.Mead		1905-36
Most Wkts – Season	190	A.S.Kennedy	(av 15.61)	1922
Most Wkts – Career	2669	D.Shackleton	(av 18.23)	1948-69
Most Career W-K Dismissals	700	R.J.Parks	(630 ct/70 st)	1980-92
Most Career Catches in the Field	629	C.P.Mead		1905-36

LIST 'A' LIMITED-OVERS CRICKET

Highest Total	CGT	371-4		v	Glamorgan	Southampton	1975
	BHC	321-1		v	Minor C (S)	Amersham	1973
	NL	335-6		v	Somerset	Taunton	2003
Lowest Total	CGT	98		v	Lancashire	Manchester	1975
	BHC	50		v	Yorkshire	Leeds	1991
	NL	43		v	Essex	Basingstoke	1972
Highest Innings	CGT	177	C.G.Greenidge	v	Glamorgan	Southampton	1975
	BHC	173*	C.G.Greenidge	v	Minor C (S)	Amersham	1973
	NL	172	C.G.Greenidge	v	Surrey	Southampton	1987
Best Bowling	CGT	7-30	P.J.Sainsbury	v	Norfolk	Southampton	1965
	BHC	6-25	S.J.Renshaw	v	Surrey	Southampton	1997
	NL	6-20	T.E.Jesty	v	Glamorgan	Cardiff	1975

KENT

Formation of Present Club: 1 March 1859
Substantial Reorganisation: 6 December 1870
Inaugural First-Class Match: 1864
Colours: Maroon and White
Badge: White Horse on a Red Ground
County Champions: (6) 1906, 1909, 1910, 1913, 1970, 1978
Joint Champions: (1) 1977
Gillette/NatWest/C & G Trophy Winners: (2) 1967, 1974
Benson and Hedges Cup Winners: (3) 1973, 1976, 1978
National League (Div 1) Winners: (1) 2001
Sunday League Winners: (4) 1972, 1973, 1976, 1995
Twenty20 Cup Winners: (0); best – 3rd in Group 2003
Match Awards: CGT 56; BHC 96

Chief Executive: P.E.Millman, St Lawrence Ground, Canterbury, CT1 3NZ • Tel: 01227 456886 • Fax: 01227 762168 • Email: kent@ecb.co.uk • Web: www.kentccc.com

First XI Coach: G.Ford. **Captain**: D.P.Fulton. **Vice-Captain**: M.J.Walker. **Overseas Player**: A.J.Hall. **2005 Beneficiary**: Youth and Benevolent Fund. **Head Groundsman**: M.G.Grantham. **Scorer**: J.C.Foley. ‡ New registration. ^{NQ} Not qualified for England.

CARBERRY, Michael Alexander (St John Rigby Catholic C), b Croydon, Surrey 29 Sep 1980. 6'0". LHB, OB. Surrey 2001-02. Kent debut 2003. HS 153* Sy v CU (Cambridge) 2002. K HS 137 v CU (Cambridge) 2003 – on Kent debut inc 109* before lunch 1st day. CC HS 112 v Worcs (Canterbury) 2004. BB 1-45. LO HS 79 v Worcs (Canterbury) 2003 (NL). LO BB 1-21 (NL).

‡COOK, Simon James (Matthew Arnold S), b Oxford 15 Jan 1977. 6'4". RHB, RM. Middlesex 1999-2004; cap 2003. HS 93* M v Notts (Lord's) 2001. BB 8-63 M v Northants (Northampton) 2002. LO HS 67* M v Durham (Lord's) 2003 (NL). LO BB 6-37 M v Leics (Leicester) 2004 (NL).

CUSDEN, Simon Mark James (Simon Langton GS, Canterbury), b Canterbury 21 Feb 1985. 6'5". RHB, RFM. Debut 2004. HS 12* v Sussex (Canterbury) 2004. BB 4-68 v Northants (Canterbury) 2004. LO HS 3 (NL). LO BB 1-29 (NL).

DENLY, Joseph Liam (Chaucer TC), b Canterbury 16 Mar 1986. 6'0". RHB, LB. Debut 2004. Awaiting CC debut. HS 0. LO HS 11 v SL A (Canterbury) 2004.

DENNINGTON, Matthew John (Northwood BS; UNISA), b Durban, South Africa16 Oct 1982. 6'1". RHB, RFM. Debut 2004. HS 50* v Surrey (Canterbury) 2004. BB 3-48 v Sussex (Canterbury) 2004. LO HS 26* v Glos (Cheltenham) 2004 (NL). LO BB 3-53 v Glam (Canterbury) 2004 (NL).

FERLEY, Robert Steven (King Edward VII HS; Sutton Valence S; Grey C, Durham U), b Norwich, Norfolk 4 Feb 1982. 5'8". RHB, SLA. Durham UCCE 2001-03. British U 2001-03. Kent debut 2003. Norfolk 2001. HS 78* DU v Durham (Chester-le-St) 2003. K HS 29 v Surrey (Canterbury) 2004. BB 4-76 v Surrey (Oval) 2003. LO HS 42 v Lancs (Manchester) 2004 (NL). LO BB 3-59 v Glam (Maidstone) 2003 (NL).

FULTON, David Paul (The Judd S; Kent U), b Lewisham 15 Nov 1971. 6'2". RHB, SLA, occ WK. Debut 1992; cap 1998; captain 2002 to date. PCA 2001. 1000 runs (3): most – 1892 (2001). HS 208* v Somerset (Canterbury) 2001. Scored 9 hundreds in 2001, including 208*, 104* and 197 in successive innings. BB 1-37 (not CC). LO HS 82 v Yorks (Leeds) 2001 (NL).

‡**NQHALL, Andrew** James (Alberton HS), b Alberton, Johannesburg, South Africa 31 Jul 1975. 6'0". RHB, RFM. Transvaal/Gauteng 1995-96 to 2001-02. Easterns 2001-02 to date. Durham CB 1999. Suffolk 2002. Worcestershire 2003-04. **Tests** (SA): 14 (2001-02 to 2004-05); HS 163 v I (Kanpur) 2004-05; BB 3-1 v SL (Johannesburg) 2002-03. **LOI** (SA): 46 (1998-99 to 2004-05); HS 81 v SL (Galle) 2000-01; BB 3-32 v B (Dhaka) 2002-03. F-c Tours (SA): E 2003; I 2004-05. HS 163 (*see Tests*). UK HS 104 Wo v Somerset (Bath) 2003. BB 6-77 (11-99 match) Easterns v WP (Port Elizabeth) 2002-03. CC BB 3-10 Wo v Durham (Stockton) 2003 and 3-10 Wo v Surrey (Worcester) 2004. Award: CGT 1. LO HS 129* Gauteng v Border (E London) 1999-00. LO BB 4-26 Wo v Leics (Oakham) 2004 (NL).

JONES, Geraint Owen (Harristown State HS, Toowoomba and MacGregor State HS, Brisbane, Australia), b Kundiawa, Papua New Guinea 14 Jul 1976. Welsh parents. 5'10". RHB, WK. Debut 2001; cap 2003. **ECB Contracts 2004-05**. **Tests**: 13 (2003-04 to 2004-05); HS 100 v NZ (Leeds) 2004. **LOI**: 23 (2003 to 2004-05); HS 80 v Z (Bulawayo) 2004-05. F-c Tours: SA 2004-05; WI 2003-04; SL 2003-04. HS 108* v Essex (Chelmsford) 2003. LO HS 74* v Glos (Beckenham) 2003 (NL).

JOSEPH, Robert ('Robbie') Hartman (Sutton Vallence S; St Mary's C, Twickenham), b Antigua 20 Jan 1982. Resided in England since 1997. RHB, RF. First-Class Counties XI 2000. Kent debut 2004. HS 26 and BB 3-47 v Middx (Canterbury) 2004. LO HS 3* (NL). LO BB 2-30 v Glos (Cheltenham) 2004 (NL).

KEY, Robert William Trevor (Colfe's S), b East Dulwich, London 12 May 1979. 6'1". RHB, RM/OB. Debut 1998; cap 2001. **Tests**: 15 (2002 to 2004-05); HS 221 v WI (Lord's) 2004. **LOI**: 5 (2003); HS 19 v WI (Lord's) 2004. F-c Tours: A 2002-03; SA 1998-99 (Eng A), 2004-05; SL 2002-03 (ECB Acad); Z 1998-99 (Eng A). 1000 runs (3): most – 1896 (2004). HS 221 (*see Tests*). K HS 199 v Surrey (Oval) 2004. LO HS 114 v Notts (Nottingham) 2002 (NL).

NQKHAN, Amjad (Skolenpa Duevej, Denmark), b Copenhagen, Denmark 14 Oct 1980. 6'0". RHB, RFM. Debut 2001. Denmark 1998-2000. HS 78 v Middx (Lord's) 2003. 50 wkts (1): 63 (2002). BB 6-52 v Yorks (Canterbury) 2002. LO HS 65* Denmark v Ire (Harare) 1999-00. LO BB 4-26 v Leics (Leicester) 2003 (NL).

NQO'BRIEN, Niall John (Marian C, Dublin), b Dublin, Ireland 8 Nov 1981. 5'6". LHB, WK. Irish passport. Debut 2004. HS 69 v Warwks (Birmingham) 2004. LO HS 27* v SL A (Canterbury) 2004.

PATEL, Minal Mahesh (Dartford GS; Erith TC), b Bombay, India 7 Jul 1970. 5'9". RHB, SLA. Debut 1989; cap 1994; benefit 2004. No appearances 2003 (back injury). **Tests**: 2 (1996); HS 27 and BB 1-101 v I (Nottingham) 1996. F-c Tour: I 1994-95 (Eng A). HS 82 v Leics (Canterbury) 2002. 50 wkts (3): most – 90 (1994). BB 8-96 v Lancs (Canterbury) 1994. LO HS 27* v Somerset (Canterbury) 2001 (CGT). LO BB 3-22 v Essex (Canterbury) 1999 (NL).

SAGGERS, Martin John (Springwood HS, King's Lynn; Huddersfield U), b King's Lynn, Norfolk 23 May 1972. 6'2". RHB, RMF. Durham 1996-98. Norfolk 1995-96. Kent debut 1999; cap 2001. **Tests**: 3 (2003-04 to 2004); HS 1 and BB 2-29 v B (Chittagong) 2003-04 on debut. F-c Tours: SL 2003-04; B 2003-04. HS 64 v Worcs (Canterbury) 2004. 50 wkts (4): most – 83 (2002). BB 7-79 v Durham (Chester-le-St) 2000. Awards: CGT 1; BHC 1. LO HS 34* Minor C v Leics (Jesmond) 1996 (BHC). LO BB 5-22 v Glos (Canterbury) 2001 (NL).

SHERIYAR, Alamgir (George Dixon S; Joseph Chamberlain SFC; Oxford Poly), b Birmingham 15 Nov 1973. 6'1". RHB, LFM. Leicestershire 1994-95. Worcestershire 1996-2002; cap 1997. Kent debut 2003. F-c Tours (Eng A): NZ 1999-00; B 1999-00. HS 21 Wo v Notts (Nottingham) 1997 and 21 Wo v Pak A (Worcester) 1997. K HS 18* v Essex (Chelmsford) 2003. 50 wkts (4): most – 92 (1999). BB 7-130 (10-172 match) Wo v Hants (Southampton) 1999. K BB 5-65 v Sussex (Hove) 2003. Hat-tricks (2): 1994 (Le), 1999 (Wo). LO HS 19 Wo v Derbys (Chesterfield) 1996 (SL). LO BB 4-18 Wo v Yorks (Leeds) 1997 (SL).

‡**STEVENS, Darren** Ian (Hinckley C), b Leicester 30 Apr 1976. 5'11". RHB, RM. Leicestershire 1997-2004; cap 2002. F-c Tours (ECB Acad): SL 2002-03. HS 149 Le v Essex (Southend) 2003. BB 2-50 Le v Somerset (Leicester) 2004. Award: CGT 1. LO HS 133 Le v Northumb (Jesmond) 2000 (NWT). LO BB 2-15 ECB Acad v SL A (Colombo) 2002-03.

STIFF, David Alexander (Batley GS; Wakefield C), b Dewsbury, Yorks 20 Oct 1984. RHB, RFM. England U-19 to Australia 2002-03. Debut 2004. HS 18 and CC BB 2-58 v Lancs (Tunbridge W) 2004. BB 3-88 v NZ (Canterbury) 2004. LO HS – and BB 1-27 Yorks CB v Glos CB (Bristol) 2001 (CGT).

TREDWELL, James Cullum (Southlands Community CS, New Romney), b Ashford 27 Feb 1982. 6'0". LHB, OB. Debut 2001. F-c Tour (Eng A): I 2003-04 (capt). HS 61 v Yorks (Leeds) 2002. BB 5-101 Eng A v E Zone (Amritsar) 2003-04. CC BB 4-49 v Sussex (Hove) 2003. LO HS 71 Kent CB v Bucks (Maidstone) 2001 (CGT). LO BB 3-7 v Norfolk (Horsford) 2002 (CGT).

‡[NQ]**VAN JAARSVELD, Martin** (Warmbaths S; Pretoria U), b Klerksdorp, South Africa 18 Jun 1974. 6'2". RHB, OB. N Transvaal/Northerns 1994-95 to 2003-04. Lions 2004-05. Northamptonshire 2004. **Tests** (SA): 9 (2002-03 to 2004-05); HS 73 v WI (Johannesburg) 2003-04. **LOI** (SA): 11(2002-03 to 2004); HS 45 v E (Birmingham) 2003; BB 1-0. Took wickets with his first and third balls in LOI. F-c Tours (SA): NZ 2003-04; I 2004-05; SL 1998-99 (SA A), 2004; Z 1998-99 (SA Acad). 1000 runs (0+1): 1268 (2001-02). HS 238* Northerns v GW (Kimberley) 1999-00. CC HS 114 Nh v Kent (Northampton) 2004. BB 2-30 SA A v SL A (Potchefstroom) 2003-04. Award: CGT 1. LO HS 123 NT v EP (Pretoria) 1996-97. LO BB 1-0 (see LOI).

WALKER, Matthew Jonathan (King's S, Rochester), b Gravesend 2 Jan 1974. Grandson of Jack Walker (Kent 1949). 5'8". LHB, RM. Debut 1992-93 (Z tour); UK Debut 1994; cap 2000. F-c Tour: Z 1992-93 (K). 1000 runs (2); most 1266 (2004). HS 275* v Somerset (Canterbury) 1996. BB 2-21 v Middx (Canterbury) 2004. Awards: BHC 3. LO HS 117 v Warwks (Canterbury) 1997 (BHC). LO BB 4-24 v Yorks (Leeds) 2001 (NL).

RELEASED/RETIRED

(Having made a first-class County appearance in 2004)

[NQ]**BEVAN, Michael** Gwyl (Western Creek HS, Canberra), b Belconnen, ACT, Australia 8 May 1970. 5'11½". LHB, SLC. S Australia 1989-90. NSW 1990-91 to date. Yorkshire 1995-96; cap 1995. Sussex 1998, 2000; cap 1998. Leicestershire 2002; cap 2002. **Tests** (A): 18 (1994-95 to 1997-98); HS 91 v P (Lahore) 1994-95; BB 6-82 (10-113 match) v WI (Adelaide) 1996-97. **LOI** (A): 232 (1993-94 to 2003-04); HS 108* v E (Oval) 1997; BB 3-36 v P (Melbourne) 1996-97. Tours (A): E 1997, 2001; SA 1996-97; I 1996-97; P 1994-95; Z 1991-92 (Aus B). 1000 runs (3+1); most – 1598 (1995). HS 216 NSW v Tas (Sydney) 2003-04. UK HS 174 Sx v Notts (Hove) 2000. K HS 66 v Middx (Southgate) 2004 – on K debut. BB 6-82 (see Tests). UK BB 3-25 v Warwks (Leicester) 2002. Awards: CGT 2; BHC 7. LO HS 157* Sx v Essex (Chelmsford) 2000 (BHC). LO BB 5-29 Y v Sussex (Eastbourne) 1996 (SL).

[NQ]**BUTLER, Ian** Gareth (home educated), b Otahuhu, Auckland, New Zealand 24 Nov 1981. 6'3". RHB, RFM. N Districts 2001-02 to date. Gloucestershire 2003. **Tests** (NZ): 8 (2001-02 to 2004-05); HS 26 v WI (Bridgetown) 2001-02; BB 6-46 v P (Wellington) 2003-04. **LOI** (NZ): 15 (2001-02 to 2004); HS 3; BB 3-41 v NZ (Cardiff) 2004. Dismissed M.E.Trescothick with his fifth ball in LOI. F-c Tours (NZ): WI 2001-02; I 2003-04; B 2004-05. HS 68 v Surrey (Canterbury) 2004. BB 6-46 (see Tests). CC BB 4-74 Gs v Worcs (Worcester) 2003. K BB 4-114 v Warwks (Birmingham) 2004. LO HS 18* v Glam (Cardiff) 2004 (NL). LO BB 3-41 (see LOI).

LOUDON, A.G. – see WARWICKSHIRE..

^{NQ}**MOHAMMAD SAMI**, b Karachi, Pakistan 24 Feb 1981. RGB, RF. Customs 1999-00. Karachi 2000-01. National Bank 2000-01 to 2001-02. Kent 2003-04. **Tests** (P): 18 (2000-01 to 2004-05); HS 49 v I (Rawalpindi) 2003-04; BB 5-36 v NZ (Auckland) 2000-01 on debut. **LOI** (P): 66 (2000-01 to 2004-05); HS 23 v I (Lahore) 2003-04; BB 5-10 v NZ (Lahore) 2003-04. F-c Tours (P): E 2001; A 2004-05; SA 2002-03; NZ 2000-01, 2003-04; SL 2002-03 (v A); Z 2002-03. HS 49 (*see Tests*). K HS 29 v Surrey (Oval) 2004. BB 8-64 (15-114 match) v Notts (Maidstone) 2003. LO HS 22 (*see LOI*). LO BB 6-20 v Glos (Canterbury) 2004 (NL).

SMITH, E.T. – *see MIDDLESEX.*

^{NQ}**SYMONDS, Andrew** (All Saints Anglican School, Mudgeeraba, Queensland), b Birmingham 9 Jun 1975. 6'1½". RHB, RMF/OB. Emigrated to Australia when 18 months old. Queensland 1994-95 to date. Gloucestershire 1995-96; cap 1996. Kent 1999, 2001, 2004; cap 1996-97. YC 1995. Surrendered England qualification by appearing for Australia A v WI 1996-97. **Tests** (A): 2 (2003-04); HS 24 and BB 1-68 v SL (Galle) 2003-04 – on debut. **LOI** (A): 111 (1998-99 to 2004-05); HS 143* v P (Johannesburg) 2002-03; BB 4-11 v I (Sydney) 1999-00. F-c Tours (A): Sc 1998 (Aus A); NZ 1994-95 (Aus Academy); SL 2003-04. 1000 runs (2); most – 1438 (1995). HS 254* Gs v Glam (Abergavenny) 1995 (including record 16 sixes); hit record 20 sixes in match. K HS 177 v Leics (Canterbury) 1999. BB 6-105 v Sussex (Tunbridge Wells) 2002. Awards: CGT 2; BHC 2. LO HS 146 v Lancs (Tunbridge W) 2004 (NL). LO BB 6-14 Aus A v Ind A (Los Angeles) 1999.

TROTT, Benjamin James (Court Fields Community S, Wellington; Richard Huish C, Taunton; Plymouth U), b Wellington, Somerset 14 Mar 1975. 6'5". RHB, RMF. Somerset 1997-98. Kent 2000-04. Devon 2000. HS 26 v Sussex (Tunbridge Wells) 2002. BB 6-13 (11-78 match) v Essex (Tunbridge Wells) 2001. Award: CGT 1. LO HS 3 (CGT). LO BB 5-18 v Cumb (Barrow) 2001 (CGT). Shahid Afridi appeared in l-o games without making a f-c appearance in 2004.

HAMPSHIRE RELEASED/RETIRED (continued from p 40)

(Having made a first-class County appearance in 2004)

^{NQ}**CLARKE, Michael** John (Westfield Sports HS, Sydney), b Liverpool, NSW, Australia 2 Apr 1981. 5'11". RHB, SLA. New South Wales 1999-00 to date. Hampshire debut/cap 2004.Captained Aus U-19 in 2000 world cup in Sri Lanka. Tests (A): 9 (2004-05); HS 151 v I (Bangalore) 2004-05 – on debut; scored 141 v NZ (Brisbane) 2004-05 – on home debut; BB 6-9 V I (Bombay) 2004-05. **LOI** (A): 44 (2002-03 to 2004-05); HS 105* v Z (Harare) 2004; BB 5-35 v SL (Dambulla) 2003-04. F-c Tours (A): WI 2002-03; I 2004-05. HS 140 v Notts (Nottingham) 2004 – scored 140, 103 and 109 in successive innings. BB 2-25 NSW v Tasmania (Hobart) 2001-02. H BB 1-52. LO HS 101* NSW v WA (Sydney) 2001-02 (ING). LO BB 4-42 (*see LOI*).

KENDALL, William Salwey (Bradfield C; Keble C, Oxford), b Wimbledon, Surrey 18 Dec 1973. 5'10". RHB, RM. Oxford U 1994-96; blue 1995-96. Hampshire debut 1996; cap 1999. 1000 runs (3); most – 1186 (1999). HS 201 v Sussex (Southampton) 1999. BB 3-37 OU v Derbys (Oxford) 1995. H BB 2-46 v Notts (Southampton) 1996. LO HS 110* v Middx (Southampton) 2002 (NL). LO BB 2-48 v Middx (Southampton) 2002 (BHC).

^{NQ}**WATSON, Shane** Robert (Ipswich GS), b Ipswich, Queensland, Australia 17 Jun 1981. 6'0". RHB, RFM. Tasmania 2000-01 to date. Hampshire 2004. Tests (A): 1 (2004-05); HS 31 and BB 1-32 v P (Sydney) 2004-05 – on debut. LOI (A): 32 (2001-02 to 2004-05); HS 77* v K (Nairobi) 2002; BB 3-27 v SL (Perth) 2002-03. F-c Tour (Aus): SA 2001-02 scoring 100* in only innings. HS 157 Tas v NSW (Sydney) 2003-04. H HS 112* v Somerset (Southampton) 2004 – on UK debut. BB 6-32 Tas v Q (Hobart) 2001-02. H BB – . LO HS 96 Tas v NSW (Devonport) 2001-02. LO BB 3-27 (*see LOI*).

D.A.Clapp, M.G.Dighton, J.R.C.Hamblin and J.Hibberd left the staff having made no f-c appearances in 2004.

KENT 2004
RESULTS SUMMARY

	Place	Won	Lost	Tied	Drew	No Result
County Championship (1st Division)	2nd	7	3		6	
All First-Class Matches		8	3		7	
C & G Trophy	3rd Round					
National League (1st Division)	8th	5	9			2
Twenty20 Cup	4th in South Division					

COUNTY CHAMPIONSHIP AVERAGES
BATTING AND FIELDING

Cap		M	I	NO	HS	Runs	Avge	100	50	Ct/St
2001	R.W.T.Key	10	17	1	199	1274	79.62	6	2	4
1999	A.Symonds	5	8	1	156*	506	72.28	3	1	6
2000	M.J.Walker	16	26	4	157	1234	56.09	4	8	16
2001	E.T.Smith	16	27	2	189	1269	50.76	4	5	5
1998	D.P.Fulton	15	26	1	122	1030	41.20	5	2	20
–	M.A.Carberry	10	17	3	112	555	39.64	2	3	3
–	A.G.R.Loudon	10	17	–	92	597	35.11	–	6	6
–	J.C.Tredwell	6	7	1	51*	197	32.83	–	1	7
–	I.G.Butler	5	8	2	68	185	30.83	–	1	2
–	N.J.O'Brien	14	19	4	69	439	29.26	–	3	33/5
–	M.J.Dennington	6	9	2	50*	108	15.42	–	1	2
–	A.Khan	7	8	2	29	91	15.16	–	–	–
–	M.G.Bevan	4	7	–	66	90	12.85	–	1	4
–	R.H.Joseph	7	9	3	26	77	12.83	–	–	3
1994	M.M.Patel	11	16	1	28	186	12.40	–	–	1
–	S.M.J.Cusden	4	6	4	12*	22	11.00	–	–	2
–	A.Sheriyar	6	7	4	12	32	10.66	–	–	–
2001	M.J.Saggers	6	7	–	64	74	10.57	–	1	4
–	Mohammad Sami	5	6	–	29	52	8.66	–	–	1
–	R.S.Ferley	2	4	–	29	33	8.25	–	–	1
–	B.J.Trott	5	7	1	12	28	4.66	–	–	1

Also batted: G.O.Jones (2 matches – cap 2003) 0, 20*, 1 (3 ct); D.A.Stiff (4) 4, 18, 5 (1 ct).

BOWLING

	O	M	R	W	Avge	Best	5wI	10wM
M.J.Saggers	152.5	43	410	15	27.33	4- 43	–	–
M.M.Patel	421.3	85	1206	41	29.41	5-138	1	–
A.Symonds	139.3	39	419	14	29.92	5-140	1	–
S.M.J.Cusden	100.3	17	404	13	31.07	4- 68	–	–
A.G.R.Loudon	192.2	32	653	21	31.09	6- 47	2	–
R.H.Joseph	165.2	31	648	19	34.10	3- 47	–	–
Mohammad Sami	140	32	526	14	37.57	6- 99	1	1
A.Sheriyar	156.3	23	633	16	39.56	5- 94	1	–
I.G.Butler	101.3	11	446	11	40.54	4-114	–	–
A.Khan	131.3	15	600	14	42.85	4- 47	–	–
B.J.Trott	153	23	538	10	53.80	4-109	–	–

Also bowled:

M.J.Walker 66 10 228 6 38.00 2- 21
M.J.Dennington 93 13 368 9 40.88 3- 48

M.G.Bevan 6-0-25-0; M.A.Carberry 27-0-157-2; R.S.Ferley 28-2-121-3; D.A.Stiff 62-10-299-3; J.C.Tredwell 124.1-16-495-3.

The First-Class Averages (pp 121–136) give the records of Kent players in all first-class county matches (Kent's other opponents being the New Zealanders and Oxford UCCE), with the exception of M.J.Saggers whose full county figures are as above, and:
   G.O.Jones 4-4-1-101-122-40.66-1-0-7ct/1st. Did not bowl.
   R.W.T.Key 11-19-2-199-1505-88.52-8-2-4ct. Did not bowl.
   M.M.Patel 12-17-1-44-230-14.37-0-0-1ct. 457-89-1317-47-28.02-5/56-2-0.
   J.C.Tredwell 7-7-1-51*-197-32.83-0-1-7ct. 124.1-16-495-3-165.00-1/51.

47

KENT RECORDS

FIRST-CLASS CRICKET

Highest Total	For 803-4d		v	Essex	Brentwood	1934
	V 676		by	Australians	Canterbury	1921
Lowest Total	For 18		v	Sussex	Gravesend	1867
	V 16		by	Warwicks	Tonbridge	1913
Highest Innings	For 332	W.H.Ashdown	v	Essex	Brentwood	1934
	V 344	W.G.Grace	for	MCC	Canterbury	1876

Highest Partnership for each Wicket

1st	300	N.R.Taylor/M.R.Benson	v	Derbyshire	Canterbury	1991
2nd	366	S.G.Hinks/N.R.Taylor	v	Middlesex	Canterbury	1990
3rd	321*	A.Hearne/J.R.Mason	v	Notts	Nottingham	1899
4th	368	P.A.de Silva/G.R.Cowdrey	v	Derbyshire	Maidstone	1995
5th	277	F.E.Woolley/L.E.G.Ames	v	New Zealand	Canterbury	1931
6th	315	P.A.de Silva/M.A.Ealham	v	Notts	Nottingham	1995
7th	248	A.P.Day/E.Humphreys	v	Somerset	Taunton	1908
8th	157	A.L.Hilder/A.C.Wright	v	Essex	Gravesend	1924
9th	171	M.A.Ealham/P.A.Strang	v	Notts	Nottingham	1997
10th	235	F.E.Woolley/A.Fielder	v	Worcs	Stourbridge	1909

Best Bowling	For 10- 30	C.Blythe	v	Northants	Northampton	1907
(Innings)	V 10- 48	C.H.G.Bland	for	Sussex	Tonbridge	1899
Best Bowling	For 17- 48	C.Blythe	v	Northants	Northampton	1907
(Match)	V 17-106	T.W.J.Goddard	for	Glos	Bristol	1939

Most Runs – Season	2894	F.E.Woolley	(av 59.06)		1928
Most Runs – Career	47868	F.E.Woolley	(av 41.77)		1906-38
Most 100s – Season	10	F.E.Woolley			1928
	10	F.E.Woolley			1934
Most 100s – Career	122	F.E.Woolley			1906-38
Most Wkts – Season	262	A.P.Freeman	(av 14.74)		1933
Most Wkts – Career	3340	A.P.Freeman	(av 17.64)		1914-36
Most Career W-K Dismissals	1253	F.H.Huish	(901 ct/352 st)		1895-1914
Most Career Catches in the Field	773	F.E.Woolley			1906-38

LIST 'A' LIMITED-OVERS CRICKET

Highest Total	CGT	384-6		v	Berkshire	Finchampstead	1994
	BHC	338-6		v	Somerset	Maidstone	1996
	NL	327-6		v	Leics	Canterbury	1993
Lowest Total	CGT	60		v	Somerset	Taunton	1979
	BHC	73		v	Middlesex	Canterbury	1979
	NL	83		v	Middlesex	Lord's	1984
Highest Innings	CGT	136*	C.L.Hooper	v	Berkshire	Finchampstead	1994
	BHC	143	C.J.Tavaré	v	Somerset	Taunton	1985
	NL	146	A.Symonds	v	Lancs	Tunbridge Wells	2004
Best Bowling	CGT	8-31	D.L.Underwood	v	Scotland	Edinburgh	1987
	BHC	6-41	T.N.Wren	v	Somerset	Canterbury	1995
	NL	6- 9	R.A.Woolmer	v	Derbyshire	Chesterfield	1979

LANCASHIRE

Formation of Present Club: 12 January 1864
Inaugural First-Class Match: 1865
Colours: Red, Green and Blue
Badge: Red Rose
County Champions (since 1890): (7) 1897, 1904, 1926,
1927, 1928, 1930, 1934
Joint Champions: (1) 1950
Gillette/NatWest/C & G Trophy Winners: (7) 1970, 1971,
1972, 1975, 1990, 1996, 1998
Benson and Hedges Cup Winners: (4) 1984, 1990, 1995, 1996
National League (Div 1) Winners: (1) 1999.
Sunday League Winners: (4) 1969, 1970, 1989, 1998
Twenty20 Cup Winners: (0); best – Semi-Finalist
Match Awards: CGT 78; BHC 86

Chief Executive: J.Cumbes, Old Trafford, Manchester M16 0PX • Tel: 0161 282 4000 •
Fax: 0161 282 4100 • Email: enquiries@lccc.co.uk • Web: www.lccc.co.uk
Cricket Manager/First XI Coach: M.Watkinson. **Captain:** M.J.Chilton. **Vice-Captain:**
S.G.Law. **Overseas Players:** B.J.Hodge and M.Muralitharan. **2005 Beneficiary:** G.Yates.
Head Groundsman: P.Marron. **Scorer:** A.West. ‡ New registration. NQ Not qualified for
England.

ANDERSON, James Michael (St Theodore RC HS and SFC, Burnley), b Burnley 30 Jul
1982. 6'2". LHB, RFM. England U-19. Debut 2002. YC 2003. **ECB contracts 2004-05.**
Tests: 12 (2003 to 2004-05); HS 21* v SA (Lord's) 2003; BB 5-73 v Z (Lord's) 2003 on
debut. **LOI:** 39 (2002-03 to 2004-05); HS 11 v NZ (Chester-le-St) 2004; BB 4-25 v Holland
(E London) 2003. Hat-trick v P (Oval) 2003 – 1st for Eng in 373 LOI. F-c Tours: SA
2004-05; WI 2003-04; SL 2003-04. HS 21* (*see Tests*). La HS 16 v Warwks (Manchester)
2002. 50 wkts (1): 50 (2002). BB 6-23 v Hants (Southampton) 2002. Hat-trick (Lancs)
2003. LO HS 11 (*see LOI*). LO BB 4-25 (*see LOI*).

CHAPPLE, Glen (West Craven HS; Nelson & Colne C), b Skipton, Yorks 23 Jan 1974.
6'1". RHB, RFM. Debut 1992; cap 1994; benefit 2004. F-c Tours (Eng A): A 1996-97; WI
1995-96 (La); I 1994-95. HS 155 v Somerset (Manchester) 2001. Scored 100 off 27 balls in
contrived circumstances v Glam (Manchester) 1993. 50 wkts (4); most – 55 (1994). BB 6-30
v Somerset (Blackpool) 2002. Awards: CGT 1; BHC 2. LO HS 81* v Derbys (Manchester)
2002 (CGT). LO BB 6-18 v Essex (Lord's) 1996 (NWT).

CHILTON, Mark James (Manchester GS; Durham U), b Sheffield, Yorks 2 Oct 1976. 6'3".
RHB, RM. Debut 1997. Cap 2002. Captain 2005. British U 1998. 1000 runs (1): 1154 (2003).
HS 125 v Middx (Manchester) 2003. BB 1-1. CC BB 1-10. Awards: CGT 2; BHC 4. LO HS 115
v Surrey (Croydon) 2004 (NL). LO BB 5-26 Brit U v Sussex (Cambridge) 1997 (BHC).

CORK, Dominic Gerald (St Joseph's C, Stoke-on-Trent; Newcastle CFE), b Newcastle-
under-Lyme, Staffs 7 Aug 1971. 6'2". RHB, RFM. Derbyshire 1990-2003; cap 1993; captain
1998-2003; benefit 2001. Lancashire debut/cap 2004. *Wisden* 1995. PCA 1995. Staffordshire 1989-90. **ECB contract 2001.** **Tests:** 37 (1995 to 2002); HS 59 v NZ (Auckland)
1996-97; BB 7-43 v WI (Lord's) 1995 – on debut (record England analysis by Test match
debutant); hat-trick v WI (Manchester) 1995 – the first in Test history to occur in the
opening over of a day's play. **LOI:** 32 (1992 to 2002-03); HS 31* v NZ (Napier) 1999-97;
BB 3-27 v WI (Lord's) 1995. F-c Tours: A 1992-93 (Eng A), 1998-99; SA 1993-94 (Eng A),
1995-96; WI 1991-92 (Eng A); NZ 1996-97; I 1994-95 (Eng A); P 2000-01 (*part*). HS 200*
De v Durham (Derby) 2000. La HS 109 v Surrey (Croydon) 2004. 50 wkts (7); most – 90
(1995). BB 9-43 (13-93 match) De v Northants (Derby) 1995. Took 8-53 before lunch on his
20th birthday De v Essex (Derby) 1991. 2 hat-tricks: 1994 and 1995 (*see Tests*). La BB
7-120 v Middx (Lord's) 2004. Awards: CGT 4; BHC 4. LO HS 93 De v Derbys CB (Derby)
2000 (NWT). LO BB 6-21 De v Glam (Chesterfield) 1997 (SL).

‡**CROFT, Steven** John (Highfield HS, Blackpool; Myerscough C), b Blackpool 11 Oct 1984. 5'10". RHB, RMF. Staff 2005 – awaiting first-class debut. LO HS 7 and BB 1-27 La CB v Oxon (Bodicote) 2002 (CGT).

NQ**CROOK, Andrew** Richard, b Modbury, S Australia 14 Oct 1980. 6'1". Elder brother of S.P.Crook. RHB, OB. British passport. S Australia 1998-99(one match). Lancashire debut 2004. HS 27 and BB 1-8 v Worcs (Worcester) 2004 – on debut.

NQ**CROOK, Steven** Paul (Rostrevor C; Magill U), b Modbury, S Australia 28 May 1983. Younger brother of A.R.Crook. 5'11". RHB, RFM. British passport. S Australia U-17, U-19. Lancashire 2003. HS 68 v Kent (Tunbridge W) 2004. BB 2-33 v Northants (Liverpool) 2004. LO HS 21 and BB 2-62 v Warwks (Birmingham) 2004 (NL).

‡**CROSS, Gareth** David (Moorside S; Eccles C), b Bury 20 Jun 1984. 5'9". RHB, WK. Staff 2005 – awaiting first-class debut. LO HS 21 La CB v Scot (Aberdeen) 2002 (CGT).

FLINTOFF, Andrew (Ribbleton Hall HS), b Preston 6 Dec 1977. 6'4". RHB, RFM. Debut 1995; cap 1998. YC 1998. *Wisden* 2003. PCA 2004. **ECB contracts 2000-02-03-04-05.** **Tests:** 45 (1998 to 2004-05); HS 167 vi WI (Birmingham) 2004; BB 5-58 v WI (Bridgetown) 2003-04. **LOI:** 80 (1998-99 to 2004); HS 123 v WI (Lord's) 2004; BB 4-14 v B (Chittagong) 2003-04. F-c Tours (Eng): A 2002-03 (*part*); SA 1998-99 (Eng A), 1999-00, 2004-05; WI 2003-04; NZ 2001-02; I 2001-02; SL 1997-98 (Eng A), 2003-04; Z 1998-99 (Eng A); K 1997-98 (Eng A). HS 167 (*see Tests*). BB 5-24 v Hants (Southampton) 1999. Awards: CGT 3; BHC 1. LO HS 143 (off 66 balls) v Essex (Chelmsford) 1999 (NL). LO BB 4-11 v Yorks (Leeds) 2002 (BHC).

HEGG, Warren Kevin (Unsworth HS, Bury; Stand C, Whitefield), b Whitefield 23 Feb 1968. 5'8". RHB, WK. Debut 1986; cap 1989; benefit 1999; captain 2002-04. **Tests:** 2 (1998-99); HS 15 v A (Sydney) 1998-99. F-c Tours: A 1996-97 (Eng A), 1998-99; WI 1986-87 (La), 1995-96 (La); NZ 2001-02; SL 1990-91 (Eng A); Z 1988-89 (La). HS 134 v Leics (Manchester) 1996. Held 11 catches (equalling world f-c match record) v Derbys (Chesterfield) 1989. Award: BHC 1. LO HS 81 v Yorks (Manchester) 1996 (BHC).

‡NQ**HODGE, Bradley** John (St Bede's C, Mentone; Deakin U), b Sandringham, Victoria, Australia 29 Dec 1974. 5'8". RHB, OB. Victoria 1993-94 to date. Australia A debut 1999-2000. Durham 2002. Leicestershire 2003-04; cap 2003; captain 2004 (*part*). F-c Tours (A): I 2004-05; Z 1998-99 (A Academy). 1000 runs (2+2); most 1548 (2004). HS 302* (Leics record) v Notts (Nottingham) 2003. BB 4-17 Aus A v WI (Hobart) 2000-01. Le BB 3-35 Le v LU (Leicester) 2003. CC BB (Le) 2-18 v Yorks (Leicester) 2004. LO HS 164 Aus A v SA A (Perth) 2002-03. LO BB 5-28 Aus A v SA A (Canberra) 2002-03.

HOGG, Kyle William (Saddleworth HS), b Birmingham 2 Jul 1983. Son of W.Hogg (Lancashire and Warwickshire 1976-83; grandson of S.Ramadhin (Trinidad, Lancashire and West Indies 1949-50 to 1965). 6'4". LHB, RFM. Debut 2001. F-c Tour (ECB Acad): SL 2002-03. HS 53 v Notts (Nottingham) 2003. BB 5-48 v Leics (Manchester) 2002 – on CC debut. LO HS 37* v Kent (Manchester) 2004 (NL). LO BB 4-20 v Hants (Southampton) 2002 (NL).

NQ**HORTON, Paul** James (St Margaret's HS), b Sydney, Australia 20 Sep 1982. 5'10". RHB, RM. Debut 2003. HS 22 v Warwks (Stratford) 2004. LO HS 42 v Warwks (Birmingham) 2004 (NL).

KEEDY, Gary (Garforth CS), b Wakefield, Yorks 27 Nov 1974. 6'0". LHB, SLA. Yorkshire 1994 (one match). Lancashire debut 1995; cap 2000. F-c Tour: WI 1995-96 (La). HS 57 v Yorks (Leeds) 2002. 50 wkts (2): most – 72 (2004). BB 7-95 (14-227 match) v Glos (Manchester) 2004. LO HS 10* v Essex (Manchester) 2002 (NL). LO BB 5-30 v Sussex (Manchester) 2000 (NL).

LAW, Stuart Grant (Craiglea State HS), b Herston, Brisbane, Australia 18 Oct 1968. 6'1". RHB, RM/LB. Queensland 1988-89 to 2003-04; captain 1994-95 to 1996-97, 1999-00 to 2001-02. Essex 1996-2001; cap 1996. Lancashire debut/cap 2002. *Wisden* 1997. PCA 1999. British Citizenship after 2004 season. **Tests** (A): 1 (1995-96); HS 54* v SL (Perth) 1995-96. **LOI** (A): 54 (1994-95 to 1998-99); HS 110 v Z (Hobart) 1994-95; BB 2-22 v P (Sydney) 1996-97. F-c Tours. E 1995 (Young A); Z 1991-92 (Aus B). 1000 runs (7+2); most – 1833 (1999). HS 263 Ex v Somerset (Chelmsford) 1999. La HS 236* v Warwks (Manchester) 2003. BB 5-39 Q v Tasmania (Brisbane) 1995-96. CC BB 3-27 Ex v Worcs (Chelmsford) 1997. La BB 1-24. Awards: CGT 5; BHC 1. LO HS 163 Young A v Surrey (Oval) 1995. LO BB 5-26 Q v SL (Cairns) 1995-96.

LOYE, Malachy Bernhard (Moulton S), b Northampton 27 Sep 1972. 6'2". RHB, OB. Northamptonshire 1991-2002; cap 1994. PCA 1998. Lancashire debut 2003 – scoring 126 v Surrey (Oval) and 113 v Notts (Manchester) in his first two innings; cap 2003. F-c Tours (Eng A): SA 1993-94, 1998-99; Z 1994-95 (Nh), 1998-99. 1000 runs (4); most – 1198 (1998). HS 322* Nh v Glam (Northampton) 1998 – record Northants score until 2001. La HS 184 v Warwks (Stratford) 2004. BB 1-8. Awards: CGT 2; BHC 1. LO HS 124* Nh v Northants CB (Northampton) 2001 (CGT).

MAHMOOD, Sajid Iqbal (North C, Bolton), b Bolton 21 Dec 1981. 6'4". RHB, RF. Debut 2002. **LOI**: 1 (2004); HS 1 and BB – v NZ (Bristol) 2004. F-c Tour (Eng A): I 2003-04. HS 94 v Sussex (Manchester) 2004. BB 5-37 v DU (Durham) 2003. CC BB 4-59 v Surrey (Manchester) 2004. LO HS 29 v Staffs (Stone) 2004 (CGT). LO BB 4-39 v Glam (Manchester) 2004 (NL).

‡**MARSHALL, Simon** James (Birkenhead S; Pembroke C, Cambridge), b Arrowe Park, Wirral, Cheshire 20 Sep 1982. 6'2½". RHB, LB. Cambridge U 2002-04; blue 2002-03-04. British U 2004. Hockey blue. Lancashire staff 2005 – awaiting county debut. Cheshire 2001-03. HS 126* CU v OU (Cambridge) 2003. BB 6-128 CU v Essex (Cambridge) 2002.

NQ**MURALITHARAN, Muthiah** (St Anthony's C, Kandy), b Kandy, Sri Lanka 17 Apr 1972. 5'5". RHB, OB. C Province 1989-90 to date. Tamil Union 1991-92 to date. Lancashire 1999 (taking 7-44 and 7-73 v Warwks at Southport on debut), 2001; cap 1999. Kent 2003; cap 2003. *Wisden* 1998. **Tests** (SL): 91 (1992-93 to 2004); HS 67 v I (Kandy) 2001-02; BB 9-51 (13-115 match) v Z (Kandy) 2001-02. **LOI** (SL): 237 (1993-94 to 2004); HS 19 v P (Dambulla) 2004; BB 7-30 v I (Sharjah) 2000-01. F-c Tours (SL): E 1991, 1998, 2002; A 1995-96; SA 1992-93 (SL U-24), 1994-95, 1997-98, 2000-01, 2002-03; WI 1996-97, 2003; NZ 1994-95, 1996-97; I 1993-94, 1997-98; P 1995-96, 1999-00, 2001-02; Z 1994-95, 1999-00, 2003-04. HS 67 (*see Tests*). 50 wkts (2+3); most – 97 (2001-02). Took 66 wkts in 7 CC matches 1999). BB 9-51 (13-115 match) (*see Tests*). La HS 21 v Kent (Canterbury) 2002. La BB 7-39 (11-61 match) v Derbys (Derby) 1999. Award: BHC 1. LO HS 19 (*see LOI*). LO BB 7-30 (*see LOI*).

NEWBY, Oliver James (Ribblesdale HS; Muerscough C), b Blackburn 26 Aug 1984. 5'5". RHB, RMF. Debut 2003. HS 0* and BB 2-32 v Northants (Liverpool) 2004 on CC debut. LO HS (Lancs CB) 3* (CGT). LO BB 2-37 v Glos (Manchester) 2004 (NL).

REES, Timothy Martyn (Canon Slade S and SFC, Bolton), b Loughborough, Leics 4 Sep 1984. 6'1". RHB, OB. Debut 2002. No appearances 2003-04. HS 16 v Somerset (Taunton) 2002 – on debut. LO HS 7* (NL).

SUTCLIFFE, Iain John (Leeds GS; Queen's C, Oxford), b Leeds, Yorks 20 Dec 1974. 6'2". LHB, occ OB. Oxford U 1994-96; blue 1995-96; boxing blue 1993-94. Leicestershire 1995-2002; cap 1997. Lancashire debut/cap 2003. F-c Tour (Le): SA 1996-97. 1000 runs (2): most – 1088 (2002). HS 203 Le v Glam (Cardiff) 2001. La HS 109 v Essex (Manchester) 2003. BB 2-21 OU v CU (Lord's) 1996. CC BB (Le) 1-7. La BB 1-11. Awards: CGT 1; BHC 1. LO HS 105* Le v Notts (Nottingham) 1998 (BHC).

YATES, Gary (Manchester GS), b Ashton-under-Lyne 20 Sep 1967. 6'0". RHB. OB. Lancashire 1990-2002; cap 1994; benefit 2005. Lancashire 2nd XI captain 2002-04. Appointed Assistant Coach 2005. HS 134* v Northants (Manchester) 1993. BB 6-64 v Kent (Manchester) 1999. LO HS 38 v Essex (Chelmsford) 1996 (SL). LO BB 4-34 v Warwks (Birmingham) 1994 (SL). Now Assistant Coach, he has made no f-c appearances since 2002.

RELEASED/RETIRED

(Having made a first-class County appearance in 2004)

CURRIE, Mark Robert (Poynton County HS; City of Westminster C), b Manchester 22 Sep 1979. 6'1". RHB, OB. Lancashire 2002-04. Cheshire 1999-2002. MCCYC. HS 97 v DU (Durham) 2003. CC HS 56 v Surrey (Manchester) 2003. LO HS 94 Cheshire v Lincs (Neston) 2002 (CGT).

HAYNES, Jamie Jonathan (St Edmunds C, Canberra; Canberra U), b Bristol 5 Jul 1974. 5'11". RHB, WK. Lancashire1996-2004. Represented Australian Capital Territory at cricket and Australian Rules football. HS 80 v SL A (Manchester) 1999. CC HS 57 v Surrey (Oval) 2001. LO HS 59* v Warwks CB (Blackpool) 2001 (CGT).

NQ**HOOPER, Carl** Llewellyn (Christchurch SS, Georgetown), b Georgetown, Guyana 15 Dec 1966. 6'1". RHB, OB. Demerara 1983-84. Guyana 1984-85 to 2002-03, scoring 130* in his final innings (captain 1996-97 to 2002-03). Kent 1992-94, 1996, 1998; cap 1992. Lancashire 2003-04; cap 2003. **Tests** (WI): 102 (1987-88 to 2002-03, 23 as captain); HS 233 v I (Georgetown) 2001-02; BB 5-26 v SL (Kingstown) 1996-97. **LOI** (WI): 227 (1986-87 to 2002-03, 49 as captain); HS 113* v I (Gwalior) 1987-88; BB 4-34 v P (Karachi) 1991-92. F-c Tours (WI) (C=captain): E 1988, 1991, 1995; A 1988-89, 1991-92, 1992-93, 1995-96, 1996-97; SA 1998-99; NZ 1986-87; I 1987-88, 1994-95, 2002-03C; P 1990-91, 1997-98, 2001-02C (Sharjah); SL 1993-94, 2001-02C; Z 1986-87 (Young WI), 1989-90 (Young WI, 2001C). 1000 runs (8+2); most – 1579 (1994). HS 236* K v Glam (Canterbury) 1993. La HS 201 v Middx (Manchester) 2003 – scored 201, 114 and 177 in successive f-c innings. BB 7-93 K v Surrey (Oval) 1998. La BB 6-51 v Essex (Chelmsford) 2003. Awards: NWT 1; BHC 1. LO HS 145 K v Leics (Leicester) 1996 (SL). LO BB 5-41 K v Essex (Maidstone) 1993 (SL).

MARTIN, Peter James (Danum S, Doncaster), b Accrington 15 Nov 1968. 6'4". RHB, RFM. Debut 1989; cap 1994; benefit 2002. **Tests**: 8 (1995 to 1997); HS 29 v WI (Lord's) 1995; BB 4-60 v SA (Durban) 1995-96. **LOI**: 20 (1995 to 1998-99); HS 6; BB 4-44 v WI (Oval) 1995 – on debut. F-c Tour: SA 1995-96. HS 133 v Durham (Gateshead) 1992. 50 wkts (4); most – 58 (1997). BB 8-32 (13-79 match) v Middx (Uxbridge) 1997. Awards: CGT 2. LO HS 35* v Worcs (Manchester) 1996 (SL). LO BB 5-16 v Warwks CB (Blackpool) 2001 (CGT).

NQ**MONGIA, D.** – see LEICESTERSHIRE.

SCHOFIELD, Christopher Paul (Wardle HS), b Birch Hill, Rochdale 6 Oct 1978. 6'2". LHB, LB. Lancashire1998-2004; cap 2002. **ECB contract 2000. Tests**: 2 (2000); HS 57 v Z (Nottingham) 2000. F-c Tours (Eng A): WI 2000-01; NZ 1999-00; B 1999-00. HS 99 v Warwks (Manchester) 2004. BB 6-120 Eng A v Bangladesh (Chittagong) 1999-00. La BB 5-48 v CU (Cambridge) 2000. CC BB 5-66 v Durham (Manchester) 1999. LO HS 69* v Ind A (Blackpool) 2003 and 69* v Surrey (Manchester) 2004 (NL). LO BB 5-31 v Derbys (Manchester) 2001 (NL).

SWANN, Alec James (Risade S; Sponne S, Towcester), b Northampton 26 Oct 1976. Son of R.Swann (Northumberland 1969-72; Bedfordshire 1988-95); elder brother of G.P.Swann (*see NOTTINGHAMSHIRE*). 6'1". RHB, RM/OB. Northamptonshire 1996-2001. Lancashire 2002-04; cap 2002. Bedfordshire 1994. 1000 runs (1): 1073 (2002). HS 154 Nh v Notts (Northampton) 1999. La HS 137 v DU (Durham) 2003. BB 2-30 Nh v Glos (Northampton) 2000. La BB 1-14. LO HS 83* Nh v Glos (Bristol) 2001 (BHC). BB –.

RELEASED/RETIRED continued on p 57

52

LANCASHIRE 2004

RESULTS SUMMARY

	Place	Won	Lost	Tied	Drew	No Result
County Championship (1st Division)	8th	2	4		10	
All First-Class Matches		2	4		10	
C & G Trophy	Quarter-Finalist					
National League (1st Division)	2nd	9	6			1
Twenty20 Cup	Semi-Finalist					

COUNTY CHAMPIONSHIP AVERAGES
BATTING AND FIELDING

Cap		M	I	NO	HS	Runs	Avge	100	50	Ct/St
–	D.Mongia	6	9	2	111	470	67.14	2	2	2
2002	S.G.Law	12	18	1	171*	867	51.00	3	1	17
2003	M.B.Loye	14	22	3	184	934	49.15	2	6	8
2002	C.P.Schofield	3	6	–	99	279	46.50	–	3	–
2003	C.L.Hooper	13	21	3	115	693	38.50	2	4	19
1994	G.Chapple	14	22	1	112	726	34.57	2	4	3
2003	I.J.Sutcliffe	14	24	1	104	788	34.26	1	6	5
2002	M.J.Chilton	16	27	2	124*	809	32.36	2	2	9
–	S.P.Crook	4‡	5	–	68	157	31.40	–	1	1
1989	W.K.Hegg	12	17	3	54	412	29.42	–	1	23/5
2004	D.G.Cork	14	20	2	109	437	24.27	1	2	17
–	S.I.Mahmood	11	14	3	94	233	21.18	–	1	2
–	A.R.Crook	2	4	–	27	68	17.00	–	–	1
2002	A.J.Swann	5	7	–	34	112	16.00	–	2	2
1994	P.J.Martin	6‡	7	2	33*	59	11.80	–	–	1
–	K.W.Hogg	4	7	–	23	72	10.28	–	–	–
–	J.J.Haynes	4	5	–	24	48	9.60	–	–	12/2
2000	G.Keedy	16	20	8	17	90	7.50	–	–	7
2003	J.M.Anderson	4	4	1	3	6	2.00	–	–	2

Also batted: P.J.Horton (1 match) 22; O.J.Newby (1) 0*; J.Wood (2 – cap 2003) 13*, 35 (1 ct).

BOWLING

	O	M	R	W	Avge	Best	5wI	10wM
J.M.Anderson	126	27	374	19	19.68	6- 49	1	1
G.Keedy	645.3	122	1849	72	25.68	7- 95	6	1
D.G.Cork	332.5	59	1144	38	30.10	7-120	3	–
P.J.Martin	115.5	34	319	10	31.90	4- 81	–	–
G.Chapple	374.4	80	1128	29	38.89	5-136	1	–
C.L.Hooper	234	51	595	15	39.66	4- 56	–	–
S.I.Mahmood	230	47	1010	23	43.91	4- 59	–	–
Also bowled:								
D.Mongia	50.2	9	157	5	31.40	1- 1	–	–
S.P.Crook	68.1	5	309	6	51.50	2- 33	–	–
K.W.Hogg	71	10	259	5	51.80	2- 16	–	–

M.J.Chilton 24-3-84-1; A.R.Crook 50-6-212-2; S.G.Law 5-1-16-0; M.B.Loye 1-0-1-0; O.J.Newby 35-6-107-2; C.P.Schofield 26.3-3-85-1; A.J.Swann 6-2-18-1; J.Wood 51-5-243-1.

Lancashire played no fixtures outside the County Championship in 2004. The First-Class Averages (pp 121–136) give the records of Lancashire players in all first-class county matches, with the exception of A.Flintoff whose only first-class appearances were for England, and J.M.Anderson whose full county figures are as above.

‡ Substituted by J.M.Anderson: S.P.Crook v Sussex (Manchester); P.J.Martin v Gloucestershire at Cheltenham.

LANCASHIRE RECORDS

FIRST-CLASS CRICKET

Highest Total	For 863		v	Surrey	The Oval	1990
	V 707-9d		by	Surrey	The Oval	1990
Lowest Total	For 25		v	Derbyshire	Manchester	1871
	V 22		by	Glamorgan	Liverpool	1924
Highest Innings	For 424	A.C.MacLaren	v	Somerset	Taunton	1895
	V 315*	T.W.Hayward	for	Surrey	The Oval	1898

Highest Partnership for each Wicket

1st	368	A.C.MacLaren/R.H.Spooner	v	Glos	Liverpool	1903
2nd	371	F.B.Watson/G.E.Tyldesley	v	Surrey	Manchester	1928
3rd	364	M.A.Atherton/N.H.Fairbrother	v	Surrey	The Oval	1990
4th	358	S.P.Titchard/G.D.Lloyd	v	Essex	Chelmsford	1996
5th	360	S.G.Law/C.L.Hooper	v	Warwicks	Birmingham	2003
6th	278	J.Iddon/H.R.W.Butterworth	v	Sussex	Manchester	1932
7th	248	G.D.Lloyd/I.D.Austin	v	Yorkshire	Leeds	1997
8th	158	J.Lyon/R.M.Ratcliffe	v	Warwicks	Manchester	1979
9th	142	L.O.S.Poidevin/A.Kermode	v	Sussex	Eastbourne	1907
10th	173	J.Briggs/R.Pilling	v	Surrey	Liverpool	1885

Best Bowling	For	10-46	W.Hickton	v	Hampshire	Manchester	1870
(Innings)	V	10-40	G.O.B.Allen	for	Middlesex	Lord's	1929
Best Bowling	For	17-91	H.Dean	v	Yorkshire	Liverpool	1913
(Match)	V	16-65	G.Giffen	for	Australians	Manchester	1886

Most Runs – Season	2633	J.T.Tyldesley	(av 56.02)	1901
Most Runs – Career	34222	G.E.Tyldesley	(av 45.20)	1909-36
Most 100s – Season	11	C.Hallows		1928
Most 100s – Career	90	G.E.Tyldesley		1909-36
Most Wkts – Season	198	E.A.McDonald	(av 18.55)	1925
Most Wkts – Career	1816	J.B.Statham	(av 15.12)	1950-68
Most Career W-K Dismissals	922†	G.Duckworth	(634 ct/288 st)	1923-38
Most Career Catches in the Field	556	K.J.Grieves		1949-64

† *W.K.Hegg (1987-2004) has retired with the second-highest aggregate of 874 dismissals (785 ct; 89 st)*

LIST 'A' LIMITED-OVERS CRICKET

Highest Total	CGT	381-3		v	Herts	Radlett	1999
	BHC	353-7		v	Notts	Manchester	1995
	NL	310-7		v	Somerset	Taunton	2003
Lowest Total	CGT	59		v	Worcs	Worcester	1963
	BHC	82		v	Yorkshire	Bradford	1972
	NL	68		v	Yorkshire	Leeds	2000
		68		v	Surrey	The Oval	2002
Highest Innings	CGT	135*	A.Flintoff	v	Surrey	The Oval	2000
	BHC	136	G.Fowler	v	Sussex	Manchester	1991
	NL	143	A.Flintoff	v	Essex	Chelmsford	1999
Best Bowling	CGT	6-18	G.Chapple	v	Essex	Lord's	1996
	BHC	6-10	C.E.H.Croft	v	Scotland	Manchester	1982
	NL	6-25	G.Chapple	v	Yorkshire	Leeds	1998

LEICESTERSHIRE

Formation of Present Club: 25 March 1879
Inaugural First-Class Match: 1894
Colours: Dark Green and Scarlet
Badge: Gold Running Fox on Green Ground
County Champions: (3) 1975, 1996, 1998
Gillette/NatWest/C & G Trophy Winners: (0); best – finalist 1992, 2001
Benson and Hedges Cup Winners: (3) 1972, 1975, 1985
National League (Div 1) Winners: (0); best – 2nd 2001
Sunday League Champions: (2) 1974, 1977
Twenty20 Cup Winners: (1) 2004
Match Awards: CGT 49; BHC 79

Operations Manager: A.J.Mackay, County Ground, Grace Road, Leicester LE2 8AD •
Tel: 0871 282 1879 • Fax: 0871 282 1873 • Email: enquiries@leicestershireccc.co.uk •
Web: www.leicestershireccc.co.uk

Director of Cricket: J.J.Whittaker. **Head Coach/Academy Director**: P.Whitticase.
Captain: H.D.Ackerman. **Vice-Captain**: D.L.Maddy. **Overseas Players**: M.F.Cleary and
D.Mongia. **2005 Beneficiary**: Leicestershire CCC 125 Years. **HeadGroundsman**:
A.Whiteman. **Scorer**: G.A.York. ‡ New registration. NQ Not qualified for England.

‡NQ**ACKERMAN**, Hylton Deon (**'HD'**) (Rondebosch BHS), b Cape Town, South Africa
14 Feb 1973. 5'11". Son of H.M.Ackerman (Border, NE Transvaal, Natal, Northants, W
Province 1963-81). RHB, RM. W Province 1993-94 to 2002-03. Gauteng 2003-04 to
2002-05. Lions 2004-05. Leicestershire debut/captain/cap 2005. Kolpak registration. **Tests**
(SA): 4 (1997-98): HS 57 v P (Durban) 1997-98 – on debut. F-c tours (SA): E 1996 (SA A); A
1995-96 (WP); SL 1995-96 (SA U-24), 1998-99; Z 2001-02, 1000 runs (1): 1373 (1997-98).
HS 202* WP v Northerns (Pretoria) 1997-98. LO HS 92 WP v Northerns (Pretoria) 2000-01.
BRIGNULL, David Stephen (Lancaster BSS; Wyggeston & Queen Elizabeth I SFC), b
Forest Gate, London 27 Nov 1981. 6'4". RHB, RMF. Debut 2003. HS 46 v Middx
(Leicester) 2003. BB 2-30 v Kent (Canterbury) 2003 – on debut. LO HS (Leics CB) 9*
(NWT). LO BB 3-40 v Worcs (Oakham) 2003 (NL).
‡**BROAD, Stuart** Christopher John, b Nottingham 24 Jun 1986. LHB, RM. Son of
B.C.Broad (Glos, Notts, OFS and England 1979-94). Joined staff 2005 – awaiting f-c debut.
NQ**CLEARY, Mark** Francis, b Moorabbin, Melbourne, Australia 19 Jul 1980. LHB, RFM.
South Australia 2002-03 to date. Australia A 2002-03. Leicestershire debut 2004. HS 58 S
Aus v Tas (Hobart) 2003-04. Le HS 38 v Durham (Leicester) 2004. BB 7-80 v Derbys
(Oakham) 2004. LO HS 70 S Aus v NSW (Adelaide) 2003-04. LO BB 4-55 S Aus v Tas
(Hobart) 2002-03.
DAGNALL, Charles Edward (Bridgewater HS, Worsley; UMIST), b Bury, Lancs 10 Jul
1976. 6'3". RHB, RMF. Warwickshire 1999-2001. Cumberland 1997-98. Leicestershire
debut 2002. HS 23* v Surrey (Oval) 2003. Le BB 6-50 Wa v Derbys (Derby) 2001. Le BB 5-66
v Essex (Leicester) 2003. Award: BHC 1. LO HS 28 v Worcs (Worcester) 2002 (NL). LO
BB 4-34 Wa v Derbys (Birmingham) 2000 (NL).
DeFREITAS, Phillip Anthony Jason (Willesden HS, London), b Scotts Head, Dominica
18 Feb 1966. 6'0". RHB, RFM. UK resident since 1976. Leicestershire 1985-88; cap 1986;
captain 2003-04 (*part*); benefit 2004. Lancashire 1989-93; cap 1989. Boland 1993-94 and
1995-96. Derbyshire 1994-99; cap 1994; captain 1997 (*part*). *Wisden* 1991. MCC YC. **Tests**:
44 (1986-87 to 1995-96); HS 88 v A (Adelaide) 1994-95; BB 7-70 v SL (Lord's) 1991.
LOI: 103 (1986-87 to 1997); HS 67 v SL (Faisalabad) 1995-96; BB 4-35 v A (Adelaide)
1986-87. F-c Tours: A 1986-87, 1990-91, 1994-95; WI 1989-90; NZ 1987-88, 1991-92; P
1987-88; I 1992-93; Z 1988-89 (La). HS 123* v Lancs (Leicester) 2000. 50 wkts (14); most
– 94 (1986). Took his 1000th f-c wicket 1999. BB 7-21 La v Middx (Lord's) 1989. Le BB
7-44 (13-86 match) v Essex (Southend) 1986. Hat-trick 1994. Awards: CGT 6; BHC 4. LO
HS 90 v Glos (Bristol) 2003 (NL). LO BB 5-13 La v Cumb (Kendal) 1989 (NWT).

FERRABY, Nicholas John (Oakham S; Loughborough U), b Market Harborough 31 May 1983. 6'0". RHB, RM. Staff 2004 – awaiting first-class debut. LO HS 1 (Leics CB) (CGT).

GIBSON, Ottis Delroy (Ellerslie SS), b Sion Hill, Bridgetown, Barbados 16 Mar 1969. 6'2". RHB, RFM. Barbados 1990-91 to 1997-98. 01. Border 1992-93 to 1994-95. Glamorgan 1994-96; cap 1994. Griqualand West 1998-99 to 1999-00. Gauteng 2000-01. Leicestershire debut 2004. Staffordshire 2001. **Tests** (WI): 2 (1995 to 1998-99); HS 37 v SA (Cape Town)1998-99; BB 2-81 v E (Lord's) 1995. **LOI** (WI): 15 (1995 to 1996-97); HS 52 v A (Brisbane) 1995-96; BB 5-40 v SL (Perth) 1995-96. Tours (WI): E 1995; A 1995-96; SA 1997-98 (WI A), 1998-99; SL 1996-97 (WI A). HS 101* WI v Somerset (Taunton) 1995. CC HS 97 Gm v Leics (Swansea) 1996. Le HS 60* v Yorks (Leicester 2004). 50 wkts (2): most – 60 (1994, 2004). BB 7-55 Border v Natal (Durban) 1994-95. Le BB 6-43 (11-141 match) v Notts (Leicester) 2004.Award: NWT 1. LO HS 102* Staffs v Northumb (Jesmond) 2001 (CGT). LO BB 5-19 Border v GW (Kimberley) 1992-93.

HABIB, Aftab (Millfield S; Taunton S), b Reading, Berks 7 Feb 1972. Cousin of Zahid Sadiq (Surrey and Derbys 1988-90). 5'11". RHB, RM. Middlesex 1992 (one match). Leicestershire 1995-2001; cap 1998. Essex 2002-04; cap 2002. **Tests**: 2 (1999); HS 19 v NZ (Lord's) 1999. F-c Tours (Eng A): WI 2000-01 (part); NZ 1999-00; B 1999-00. 1000 runs (2); most – 1055 (1999). HS 215 v Worcs (Leicester) 1996. BB 1-10. Award: BHC 1. LO HS 111 v Durham (Chester-le-St) 1997 (BHC). LO BB 2-5 v Ire (Dublin) 1999.

[NQ]**HENDERSON, Claude** William (Worcester HS), b Worcester, South Africa 14 Jun 1972. Elder brother of J.M.Henderson (Boland, North West and Transvaal 1994-95 to date). 6'1½". RHB, SLA. Boland 1990-91 to 1997-98. W Province 1998-99 to 2002-03. Leicestershire debut 2004 (first 'Kolpak' registration). **Tests** (SA): 7 (2001-02 to 2002-03); HS 30 and BB 4-116 v A (Adelaide) 2001-02. **LOI** (SA): 4 (2001-02); HS – ; BB 4-17 v Z (HarareaRAhhhhh) 2001-02. Tours (SA): A 2001-02; SL 1998-99 (SA A); Z 2001-02. HS 71 WP v KZ-Natal (Cape Town) 2003-04. Le HS 63 v Glam (Leicester 2004) – on UK debut. BB 7-57 Boland v EP (Paarl) 1994-95. Le BB 7-74 v Durham (Leicester) 2004. LO HS 32 Worcs CB v Kent CB (Kidderminster) 2000. LO BB 6-29 Boland v Easterns (Paarl) 1997-98.

LIDDLE, Christopher John (Nunthorpe CS), b Middlesbrough, Yorks 1 Feb 1984. 6'5". RHB, LFM. Staff 2004 – awaiting first-class debut.

MADDY, Darren Lee (Wreake Valley C), b Leicester 23 May 1974. 5'9". RHB, RM/OB. Debut 1994; cap 1996; benefit 2006. **Tests**: 3 (1999 to 1999-00); HS 24 v SA (Durban) 1999-00. **LOI**: 8 (1998 to 1999-00); HS 53 v Z (Harare) 1999-00. F-c Tours (Eng A): SA 1996-97 (Le), 1998-99, 1999-00 (Eng); SL 1997-98; Z 1998-99; K 1997-98. 1000 runs (4); most – 1187 (2002). HS 229* v LU (Leicester) 2003. CC HS 162 v Durham (Darlington) 1998. BB 5-37 v Hants (Southampton) 2002. Awards: CGT 1; BHC 8 (inc 5 in 1998). LO HS 151 v Minor C (Leicester) 1998 (BHC). LO BB 4-16 v Somerset (Taunton) 2000 (NL).

MASTERS, David Daniel (Fort Luton HS; Mid Kent CHE), b Chatham, Kent 22 Apr 1978. Son of K.D.Masters (Kent 1981-85, Surrey 1986). 6'4". RHB, RMF. Kent 2000-02. Leicestershire debut 2003. HS 119 v Sussex (Hove) 2003. BB 6-27 K v Durham (Tunbridge Wells) 2000. Le BB 5-53 v Warwks (Leicester) 2003. LO HS 27 v Kent (Canterbury) 2003 (NL). LO BB 5-20 K v Durham (Maidstone) 2002 (NL).

MAUNDERS, John Kenneth (Ashford HS; Spelthorne C), b Ashford, Middx 4 Apr 1981. 5'10". LHB, RM. Middlesex 1999 (one non-CC match); 2nd XI debut aged 16y 19d. Leicestershire debut 2003. HS 171 v Surrey (Leicester) 2003. BB 1-11. LO HS 49 M v Glam (Cardiff) 2001 (NL).

‡[NQ]**MONGIA, Dinesh**, b Chandigarh, India 17 Apr 1977. LHB, SLA. Punjab 1995-96 to date. Lancashire 2004. **LOI** (I): 49 (2000-01 to 2004-05); HS 159* v Z (Gauhati) 2001-02; BB 3-31 v Z (Mohali) 2001-02. F-c Tours (I): E 2002; WI 2001-02; SL 2001. 1000 runs (0+1): 1041 (2000-01). HS 308* Punjab v Jammu & Kashmir (Jullundur) 2000-01. CC HS 111 La v Glos (Cheltenham) 2004. BB 4-34 Punjab v Kerala (Palghat) 2003-04. CC BB 1-1. LO HS 159* (see LOI). LO BB 4-31 India B v India A (Bangalore) 2003-04.

56

NEW, Thomas James (Quarrydale S), b Sutton in Ashfield, Notts 18 Jan 1985. 5'10". LHB, WK. Debut 2004 HS 51* v Durham (Chester-le-St) 2004. LO HS (Leics CB) 6 (CGT).

NIXON, Paul Andrew (Ullswater HS, Penrith), b Carlisle, Cumberland 21 Oct 1970. 6'0". LHB, WK. Leicestershire 1989-99, 2003; cap 1994. Kent 2000-02; cap 2000. Cumberland 1987. MCC YC. F-c Tours: SA 1996-97 (Le); I 1994-95 (Eng A); P 2000-01. 1000 runs (1): 1046 (1994). HS 134* K v Hants (Canterbury) 2000. Le HS 131 v Hants (Leicester) 1994. Awards: CGT 1; BHC 3. LO HS 101 v SL A (Galle) 1998-99.

ROBINSON, Darren David John (Tabor HS, Braintree; Chelmsford CFE), b Braintree, Essex 2 Mar 1973. 5'10½". RHB, RMF. Essex 1993-2003; cap 1997. Leicestershire debut 2004. 1000 runs (2): most – 1474 (2002). HS 200 Ex v NZ (Chelmsford) 1999. CC HS 175 Ex v Glos (Gloucester) 2002. Le HS 154 v Notts (Leicester 2004). BB 1-7 (Ex). Awards: BHC 2. LO HS 137* Ex v Sussex (Hove) 1998 (BHC). LO BB (Ex)1-7 (SL).

SADLER, John Leonard (St Thomas A'Beckett S, Sandal), b Dewsbury, Yorks 19 Nov 1981. 5'11". LHB, LB. Yorkshire 2nd XI 2000-02. Leicestershire debut 2003. HS 145 v Surrey (Leicester) 2003 and 145 v Sussex (Hove) 2003. BB 1-22 (not CC). LO HS 88 v Yorks (Leeds) 2004 (NL).

SNAPE, Jeremy Nicholas (Denstone C; Durham U), b Stoke-on-Trent, Staffs 27 Apr 1973. 5'8½". RHB, OB. Northamptonshire 1992-97. Combined U 1994. Gloucestershire 1999-2002; cap 1999. Leicestershire debut 2003. **LOI**: 10 (2001-02 to 2002-03); HS 38 v I (Madras) 2001-02; BB 3-43 v Z (Bulawayo) 2001-02. F-c Tour: Z 1994-95 (Nh). HS 131 Gs v Sussex (Cheltenham) 2001. Le HS 66 v Notts (Leicester) 2004. BB 5-65 Nh v Durham (Northampton) 1995. Le BB 3-108 v Surrey (Leicester) 2003. Awards: BHC 3. LO HS 104* Gs v Notts (Nottingham) 2001 (NL). LO BB 5-32 Nh v Leics (Northampton) 1997 (BHC).

RELEASED/RETIRED

(Registered players who made a first-class appearance in 2004)

BRANDY, Damien Gareth (St John's, Epping; Harlow C), b Highgate, London 14 Sep 1981. 6'1". RHB, RMF. Leicestershire 2002-04. HS 52 v Kent (Canterbury) 2003. BB 2-11 v LU (Leicester) 2003. CC BB 2-86 v Surrey (Oval) 2004. LO HS 35 v Somerset (Leicester) 2002 (NL).

DAKIN, Jonathan Michael (King Edward VII S, Johannesburg) b Hitchin, Herts 28 Feb 1973. 6'4". LHB, RM. Leicestershire 1993-2001, 2004; cap 2000. Essex 2002-03; cap 2003. F-c Tour (Le): SA 1996-97. HS 190 v Northants (Northampton) 1997. BB 5-86 Ex v Middx (Lord's) 2003. Le BB 4-27 v Worcs (Worcester) 1999. Awards: CGT 1; BHC 1. LO HS 179 v Wales MC (Swansea) 2001 (CGT). LO BB 5-30 v Kent (Leicester) 1999 (NL).

^{NQ}**HODGE, B.J.** – see LANCASHIRE.

STEVENS, D.I. – see KENT.

G.W.Walker left the staff having made no f-c County appearances in 2004.

LANCASHIRE RELEASED/RETIRED (continued from p 52)

WOOD, John (Crofton HS; Wakefield District C; Leeds Poly), b Crofton, Yorks 22 Jul 1970. 6'3". RHB, RFM. GW (LO only) 1990-91. Durham 1992-2000; cap 1998. Lancashire 2001-04; cap 2003. HS 64 v Yorks (Leeds) 2002. 50 wkts (1): 62 (1998). BB 7-58 Du v Yorks (Leeds) 1999. La BB 4-17 v Hants (Southampton) 2002. LO HS 28* Du v Leics (Leicester) 2000 (BHC) and 28* Du v Notts (Nottingham) 2000 (NL). LO BB 5-49 v Glos (Manchester) 2002 (NL).

LEICESTERSHIRE 2004

RESULTS SUMMARY

	Place	Won	Lost	Tied	Drew	No Result
County Championship (2nd Division)	6th	4	5		7	
All First-Class Matches		4	6		7	
C & G Trophy	2nd Round					
National League (2nd Division)	7th	7	8			3
Twenty20 Cup	Winners					

COUNTY CHAMPIONSHIP AVERAGES
BATTING AND FIELDING

Cap		M	I	NO	HS	Runs	Avge	100	50	Ct/St
2003	B.J.Hodge	15	25	–	262	1548	61.92	5	4	6
2000	J.M.Dakin	4	7	3	71*	200	50.00	–	1	1
–	D.D.J.Robinson	15	26	–	154	1072	41.23	1	9	15
2002	D.I.Stevens	12	20	3	105	666	39.17	1	5	13
–	T.J.New	4	5	3	51*	74	37.00	–	1	8/1
1996	D.L.Maddy	16	28	2	145	790	30.38	1	6	23
–	O.D.Gibson	15	19	3	60*	480	30.00	–	4	5
–	M.F.Cleary	11	14	8	38	179	29.83	–	–	3
–	J.N.Snape	4	6	1	66	135	27.00	–	1	1
–	J.L.Sadler	13	23	2	95	533	25.38	–	3	7
1986	P.A.J.DeFreitas	13	20	3	78	394	23.17	–	1	1
1994	P.A.Nixon	12	21	3	63*	361	20.05	–	1	34/6
–	C.W.Henderson	16	21	3	63	295	16.38	–	2	6
–	J.K.Maunders	10	20	–	116	322	16.10	1	–	5
–	D.D.Masters	5	7	1	31	56	9.33	–	–	1
–	C.E.Dagnall	10	10	2	16	56	7.00	–	–	4

Also batted: D.G.Brandy (1 match) 7, 4.

BOWLING

	O	M	R	W	Avge	Best	5wI	10wM
O.D.Gibson	424.5	97	1445	60	24.08	6-43	5	2
C.E.Dagnall	209.4	42	741	24	30.87	4-37	–	–
P.A.J.DeFreitas	343.4	81	1064	31	34.32	4-49	–	–
M.F.Cleary	230	29	946	27	35.03	7-80	2	–
C.W.Henderson	469	132	1373	39	35.20	7-74	2	–
D.D.Masters	114	23	398	11	36.18	4-74	–	–
B.J.Hodge	95.5	14	365	10	36.50	2-18	–	–
D.L.Maddy	149.2	22	589	13	45.30	2-41	–	–
Also bowled:								
J.M.Dakin	102	22	372	7	53.14	2-66	–	–

J.K.Maunders 22-6-84-2; D.D.J.Robinson 4-0-38-0; J.L.Sadler 5-0-36-0; J.N.Snape 30.2-4-110-1; D.I.Stevens 13.2-1-50-2.

The First-Class Averages (pp 121–136) give the records of Leicestershire players in all first-class county matches (their other opponents being the New Zealanders), with the exception of G.W.Walker whose only first-class appearance was for Loughborough UCCE.

LEICESTERSHIRE RECORDS

FIRST-CLASS CRICKET

Highest Total	For 701-4d		v	Worcs	Worcester	1906
	V 761-6d		by	Essex	Chelmsford	1990
Lowest Total	For 25		v	Kent	Leicester	1912
	V 24		by	Glamorgan	Leicester	1971
	24		by	Oxford U	Oxford	1985
Highest Innings	For 302*	B.J.Hodge	v	Notts	Nottingham	2003
	V 341	G.H.Hirst	for	Yorkshire	Leicester	1905

Highest Partnership for each Wicket

1st	390	B.Dudleston/J.F.Steele	v	Derbyshire	Leicester	1979
2nd	289*	J.C.Balderstone/D.I.Gower	v	Essex	Leicester	1981
3rd	436*	D.L.Maddy/B.J.Hodge	v	L'boro UCCE	Leicester	2003
4th	290*	P.Willey/T.J.Boon	v	Warwicks	Leicester	1984
5th	322	B.F.Smith/P.V.Simmons	v	Notts	Worksop	1998
6th	284	P.V.Simmons/P.A.Nixon	v	Durham	Chester-le-St	1996
7th	219*	J.D.R.Benson/P.Whitticase	v	Hampshire	Bournemouth	1991
8th	172	P.A.Nixon/D.J.Millns	v	Lancashire	Manchester	1996
9th	160	W.W.Odell/R.T.Crawford	v	Worcs	Leicester	1902
10th	228	R.Illingworth/K.Higgs	v	Northants	Leicester	1977

Best Bowling	For 10- 18	G.Geary	v	Glamorgan	Pontypridd	1929
(Innings)	V 10- 32	H.Pickett	for	Essex	Leyton	1895
Best Bowling	For 16- 96	G.Geary	v	Glamorgan	Pontypridd	1929
(Match)	V 16-102	C.Blythe	for	Kent	Leicester	1909

Most Runs – Season		2446	L.G.Berry	(av 52.04)	1937
Most Runs – Career		30143	L.G.Berry	(av 30.32)	1924-51
Most 100s – Season		7	L.G.Berry		1937
		7	W.Watson		1959
		7	B.F.Davison		1982
Most 100s – Career		45	L.G.Berry		1924-51
Most Wkts – Season		170	J.E.Walsh	(av 18.96)	1948
Most Wkts – Career		2130	W.E.Astill	(av 23.19)	1906-39
Most Career W-K Dismissals		903	R.W.Tolchard	(794 ct/109 st)	1965-83
Most Career Catches in the Field		427	M.R.Hallam		1950-70

LIST 'A' LIMITED-OVERS CRICKET

Highest Total	CGT	406-5		v	Berkshire	Leicester	1996
	BHC	382-6		v	Minor C	Leicester	1998
	NL	344-4		v	Durham	Chester-le-St	1996
Lowest Total	CGT	56		v	Northants	Leicester	1964
	BHC	56		v	Minor C	Wellington	1982
	NL	36		v	Sussex	Leicester	1973
Highest Innings	CGT	201	V.J.Wells	v	Berkshire	Leicester	1996
	BHC	158*	B.F.Davison	v	Warwicks	Coventry	1972
	NL	154*	B.J.Hodge	v	Sussex	Horsham	2004
Best Bowling	CGT	6-20	K.Higgs	v	Staffs	Longton	1975
	BHC	6-25	V.J.Wells	v	Minor C	Leicester	1998
	NL	6-17	K.Higgs	v	Glamorgan	Leicester	1973

MIDDLESEX

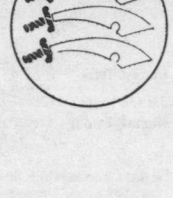

Formation of Present Club: 2 February 1864
Inaugural First-Class Match: 1864
Colours: Blue
Badge: Three Seaxes
County Champions (since 1890): (10) 1903, 1920, 1921, 1947,
1976, 1980, 1982, 1985, 1990, 1993
Joint Champions: (2) 1949, 1977
Gillette/NatWest/C & G Trophy Winners: (4) 1977, 1980, 1984, 1988
Benson and Hedges Cup Winners: (2) 1983, 1986
National League (Div 1) Winners: (0); best – 1st (Div 2) 2004
Sunday League Winners: (1) 1992
Twenty20 Cup Winners: (0); best – 4th in Group 2003
Match Awards: CGT 62; BHC 62

Secretary: V.J.Codrington, Lord's Cricket Ground, London NW8 8QN • Tel: 020 7289 1300 • Fax: 020 7289 5831 • Email: enquiries@middlesexccc.com • Web: www.middlesexccc.com

Head Coach: J.E.Emburey. **Assistant Coach**: J.C.Pooley. **Captain**: B.L.Hutton.
Vice-Captain: no appointment. **Overseas Players**: N.Hayward and S.B.Styris. **2005 Beneficiary**: None. **Head Groundsman**: M.Hunt. **Scorer**: D.K.Shelley. ‡ New registration. NQ Not qualified for England.

BETTS, Melvyn Morris (Fyndoune CS, Sacriston), b Sacriston, Co Durham 26 Mar 1975. 5'10". RHB, RFM. Durham 1993-2000; cap 1998. Warwickshire 2001-03; cap 2001. Middlesex debut 2004. F-c Tour (Eng A): Z 1998-99. HS 73 Wa v Lancs (Birmingham) 2003. M HS 31* v Warwks (Birmingham) 2004 – on Middx debut. BB 9-64 (Durham record; 13-143 match) v Northants (Northampton) 1997. M BB 5-89 v Worcs (Worcester) 2004. Award: BHC 1. LO HS 21 Du v Hants (Chester-le-St) 1997 (SL). LO BB 4-15 v Wales MC (Lamphey) 2004 (CGT).

COMPTON, Nicholas Richard Denis (Harrow S), b Durban, South Africa 26 Jun 1983. 6'1". Grandson of D.C.S.Compton (Middlesex, England, Holkar, Europeans, Commonwealth and Cavaliers 1936-64); great-nephew of L.H.Compton (Middlesex 1938-56). RHB, OB. Middlesex staff 2002. Debut 2004. HS 40 v Worcs (Worcester) 2004 – on CC debut. LO HS 86* v Lancs (Shenley) 2002 (NL).

DALRYMPLE, James William Murray (Radley C; St Peter's C, Oxford), b Nairobi, Kenya 21 Jan 1981. 5'11". RHB, OB. Oxford UCCE 2001-02; captain 2002; blue 2001-02. British U 2001-02. Middlesex debut 2001; cap 2004. HS 244 v Surrey (Oval) 2004. BB 5-49 OU v CU (Cambridge) 2003. M BB 4-66 v Kent (Canterbury) 2004. Awards: CGT 2. LO HS 107 v Glam (Lord's) 2004 (CGT). LO BB 4-14 v Essex (Southgate) 2001 (NL).

‡GODLEMAN, Billy Ashley (Islington Green S), b Camden, London 11 Feb 1989. LHB, LB. Joined staff 2005 – awaiting f-c debut.

NQHAYWARD, Mornantau ('Nantie') (Daniel Pienaar THS), b Uitenhage, South Africa 6 Mar 1977. RHB, RF. E Province 1995-96 to date. Worcestershire 2003. Middlesex debut 2004. **Tests** (SA): 16 (1999-00 to 2004); HS 14 v A (Melbourne) 2001-02; BB 5-56 v P (Durban) 2002-03. **LOI** (SA): 21 (1998 to 2001-02); HS 4; BB 4-31 v I (Sharjah) 1999-00. F-c Tours (SA): A 2001-02; I 1999-00; SL 2000-01, 2004. HS 55* EP v Boland (Pt Elizabeth) 1997-98. CC HS 28 Wo v Durham (Stockton) 2003. M HS 9. 50 wkts (1): 67 (2003). BB 6-31 (12-94 match) EP v Easterns (Pt Elizabeth) 1999-00. CC BB 5-46 Wo v Somerset (Worcester) 2003. M BB 4-41 v Surrey (Lord's) 2004. LO HS 19* EP v WP (Cape Town) 1996-97. LO BB 5-37 EP v KZ-Natal (Durban) 1998-99.

HUTCHISON, Paul Michael (Crawshaw HS, Pudsey), b Leeds, Yorks 9 Jun 1977. 6'3". LHB, LFM. Yorkshire 1995-96 (Y in Zim) to 2001; cap 1998. Sussex 2002-03. Middlesex debut 2004. F-c Tours (Eng A): SL 1997-98; Z 1995-96 (Y); K 1997-98. HS 30 Y v Essex (Scarborough) 1998. M HS 8. 50 wkts (1): 59 (1998). BB 7-31 Y v Sussex (Hove) 1998. M BB 3-50 v Surrey (Oval) 2004. Award: CGT 1. LO HS 20 Sx v Northants (Northampton) 2003 (NL). LO BB 4-29 Sx v Scot (Edinburgh) 2003 (NL).

HUTTON, Benjamin Leonard (Radley C; Durham U), b Johannesburg, South Africa 29 Jan 1977. Elder son of R.A.Hutton (Yorkshire, Transvaal & England 1962 to 1975-76); grandson of Sir Leonard (Yorkshire and England 1934-60); elder brother of O.R.Hutton (OU 2004). 6'2". LHB, RMF. British U 1998-99. Middlesex debut 1999; cap 2003; captain 2005. 1000 runs (1): 1129 (2004). HS 139 v Derbys (Southgate) 2001. BB 4-37 v SL (Shenley) 2002. CC BB 3-14 v Northants (Lord's) 2004. LO HS 77 v Durham (Chester-le-St) 2001 (NL). LO BB 5-45 v Derbys (Southgate) 2001 (NL).

^NQ**JOYCE, Edmund** Christopher (Presentation C; Bray, Co Wicklow; Trinity C, Dublin), b Dublin, Ireland 22 Sep 1978. 5'11". LHB, RM. Ireland 1997 to date. Middlesex debut 1999; cap 2002. Qualifies for England during 2005. 1000 runs (3); most 1267 (2004). HS 134 and BB 2-34 v CU (Cambridge) 2004. CC HS 129 v Glam (Cardiff) 2002 and 129 v Derbys (Lord's) 2002. CC BB 1-23. Award: CGT 1. LO HS 100* v Glam (Lord's) 2004 (CGT). LO BB 2-10 v Notts (Nottingham) 2003 (NL).

KEEGAN, Chad Blake (Durban HS), b Sandton, near Johannesburg, South Africa 30 Jul 1979. 6'1". RHB, RF. Debut 2001; cap 2003. MCC YC. Qualified for England March 2005. HS 44 v Surrey (Oval) 2004. 50 wkts (1): 63 (2003). BB 6-114 v Leics (Southgate) 2003. LO HS 50 v Notts (Lord's) 2003 (NL). LO BB 5-17 v Hants (Southgate) 2001 (NL).

^NQ**MORGAN, Eoin** Joseph Gerard, b Dublin, Ireland 10 Sep 1986. LHB, RM. British passport. Ireland 2004. Middlesex summer contract 2004. Ireland U-19 in 2003-04 youth world cup. Awaiting County debut. HS 7 Ire v Scot (Dublin) 2004. LO HS (Ire) 13* v Northants (Clontarf) 2004 (CGT).

‡**NAMBIAR**, Aneil Padman ('**Johnny**'), b Trivandrum, India 2 Mar 1984. RHB, RM. Awaiting f-c debut. LO HS (Oxon) 0 (CGT).

NASH, David Charles (Sunbury Manor S; Malvern C), b Chertsey, Surrey 19 Jan 1978. 5'8". RHB, occ LB, WK. Debut 1997; cap 2000. F-c Tour: SL 1997-98 (Eng A). HS 114 v Somerset (Lord's) 1998. BB 1-8. LO HS 67 v Sussex (Lord's) 2002 (BHC).

PEPLOE, Christopher Thomas (Twyford C of E HS; Surrey U, Roehampton), b Hammersmith, London 26 Apr 1981. 6'4". LHB, SLA. MCC YC. Debut 2003. HS 28* v Glos (Gloucester) 2004. BB 4-65 v Sussex (Hove) 2004. LO BB 1-32 (Middx CB) (CGT).

RANKIN, William Boyd, b Londonderry, Co Derry, N Ireland 5 Jul 1984. RHB, RMF. Brother of R.J.Rankin (Ireland U-19). Summer contract 2004. Ireland U-19 in 2003-04 youth world cup. Awaiting f-c debut.

‡**RICHARDSON, Alan** (Alleyne's HS; Stafford CFE; Durham U), b Newcastle-under-Lyme, Staffs 6 May 1975. 6'2". RHB, RMF. Derbyshire 1995 (one match). Warwickshire 1999-2004, cap 2002. Staffordshire 1996-98. HS 91 Wa v Hants (Birmingham) 2002 – adding 214 for 10th wicket with N.V.Knight. BB 8-46 Wa v Sussex (Birmingham) 2002. LO HS 18 Wa v Surrey (Oval) (NL). LO BB 5-35 Wa v Staffs (Stone) 2002 (CGT).

SCOTT, Ben James Matthew (Whitton S, Richmond; Richmond C), b Isleworth, Middx 4 Aug 1981. 5'8". RHB, WK. Surrey 2003. HS 101* v Northants (Lord's) 2004. LO HS 42 v Worcs (Lord's) 2004 (NL).

SHAH, Owais Alam (Isleworth & Syon S), b Karachi, Pakistan 22 Oct 1978. 6'0". RHB, OB. Debut 1996; cap 2000; captain 2004 (part). **LOI:** 15 (2001 to 2002-03); HS 62 v P (Lord's) 2001. F-c Tours (Eng A): A 1996-97; SL 1997-98. 1000 runs (4); most 1336 (2004). HS 203 v Derbys (Southgate) 2001. BB 3-33 v Glos (Bristol) 1999. Award: BHC 1. LO HS 134 v Sussex (Arundel) 1999 (NL). LO BB 2-2 v Glam (Cardiff) 1998 (BHC).

‡**SMITH, Edward** Thomas (Tonbridge S; Peterhouse, Cambridge), b Pembury, Kent 19 Jul 1977. 6'2". RHB, RM. Cambridge U 1996-98, scoring 101 v Glam (Cambridge) on debut; blue 1996-97 *(injured 1998)*. Kent 1996-2004; cap 2001. British U 1998. **Tests**: 3 (2003); HS 64 v SA (Nottingham) 2003 on debut. F-c Tour (Eng A): I 2003-04. 1000 runs (5): most – 1534 (2003). Scored 135, 0, 149, 113, 203 and 108 in successive f-c innings 2003. HS 213 K v Warwks (Canterbury) 2003. LO HS 122 K v Glam (Maidstone) 2003 (NL).

STRAUSS, Andrew John (Radley C; Durham U), b Johannesburg, South Africa 2 Mar 1977. 5'11". LHB, LM. Debut 1998; cap 2001; captain 2002 *(part)* to 2004 *(part)*. Oxfordshire 1996. **ECB contracts 2004-05**. **Tests**: 12 (2004 to 2004-05); HS 147 v SA (Johannesburg) 2004-05. Scored 112 & 83 (run out) v NZ (Lord's) on debut and 126 & 94* v SA (Pt Elizabeth) 2004-05 on his debut overseas. **LOI**: 29 (2003-04 to 2004-05); HS 100 v WI (Lord's) 2004. F-c Tour: SA 2004-05. 1000 runs (3); most – 1529 (2003). HS 176 v Durham (Lord's) 2001. BB 1-27. Award: CGT 1. LO HS 127 v Lancs (Manchester) 2003 (NL).

‡**STYRIS, Scott** Bernard (Hamilton BHS), b Brisbane, Australia 10 Jul 1975. 5'10". RHB, RM. N Districts 1994-95 to date. **Tests** (NZ): 19 (2002 to 2004-05); HS 170 v SA (Auckland) 2003-04; BB 3-28 v I (Wellington) 2002-03. **LOI** (NZ): 94 (1999-00 to 2004-05); HS 141 v SL (Bloemfontein) 2002-03; BB 6-25 v WI (Pt-of-Spain) 2002. F-c Tours (NZ): E 2004; A 2004-05; WI 2001-02; I 2003-04; SL 2002-03; B 2004-05. HS 212* ND v Otago (Hamilton) 2001-02. UK HS 108 NZ v E (Nottingham) 2004. BB 6-32 ND v Otago (Gisborne) 1999-00. UK BB 3-88 v E (Leeds) 2004. LO HS 141 *(see LOI)*. LO BB 6-25 *(see LOI)*.

WEEKES, Paul Nicholas (Homerton House SS, Hackney), b Hackney, London 8 Jul 1969. 5'10". LHB, OB. Debut 1990; cap 1993; benefit 2002. F-c Tour: I 1994-95 (Eng A). MCC YC. 1000 runs (2); most – 1218 (1996). HS 171* v Somerset (Uxbridge) 1996. BB 8-39 v Glam (Lord's) 1996. Awards: CGT 2; BHC 4. LO HS 143* v Cornwall (St Austell) 1995 (NWT). LO BB 4-17 v Kent (Lord's) 2001 (BHC).

WHELAN, Christopher David, b Liverpool, Lancs 8 May 1986. RHB, RMF. Summer contract 2004. Awaiting f-c debut. LO HS 6 (NL).

‡**WRIGHT, Christopher** Julian Clement (Eggars S, Alton; Anglia Polytechnic U), b Chipping Norton, Oxon 14 Jul 1985. 6'3". RHB, RFM. CU 2004. Middlesex debut 2004. HS 57 CU v Essex (Cambridge) 2004. M HS 0. BB 2-70 CU v Middx (Cambridge) 2004. LO HS 0 (NL). LO BB 1-34 (NL).

RELEASED/RETIRED

(Having made a first-class County appearance in 2004)

NQ**AGARKAR, Ajit** Bhalchandra, b Bombay 4 Dec 1977. 5'9". RHB, RFM. Bombay 1996-97 to date. Middlesex 2004. **Tests** (I): 22 (1998-99 to 2004-05); HS 109* v E (Lord's) 2002; BB 6-41 v A (Adelaide) 2003-04. **LOI** (I): 134 (1997-98 to 2004-05); HS 95 v WI (Jamshedpur) 2002-03; BB 6-42 v A (Melbourne) 2003-04. F-c Tours (I): E 2002; A 1999-00, 2003-04; SA 2001-02; NZ 2002-03; P 2003-04; Z 1998-99, 2001; B 2000-01. HS 109* *(see Tests)*. M HS 22 v Worcs (Worcester) 2004 – on debut. BB 6-41 *(see Tests)*. M BB 5-81 v Glos (Lord's) 2004. LO HS 95 *(see LOI)*. LO BB 6-18 Bombay v Gujarat (Ahmedabad) 2004-05.

BLOOMFIELD, Timothy Francis (Halliford S, Shepperton), b Ashford 31 May 1973. 6'2". RHB, RMF. Middlesex 1997-2004; cap 2001. Berkshire 1996. HS 31* v Northants (Northampton) 2002. 50 wkts (1): 50 (2001). BB 5-36 v Glam (Cardiff) 1999. Award: CGT 1. LO HS 15 v Warwks (Lord's) 1998 (SL) and 15 v Somerset (Taunton) 2003 (NL). LO BB 4-17 v Somerset (Southgate) 2000 (NWT).

NQ**CLARK, Stuart** Rupert, b Sutherland, Sydney, Australia 28 Sep 1975. RHB, RFM. NSW 1997-98 to date. Middlesex 2004. HS 35 NSW v WA (Newcastle) 2002-03. M HS 34 v Northants (Northampton) 2004 – on UK debut. BB 6-84 NSW v Tas (Hobart) 2002-03. M BB 3-28 v Sussex (Hove) 2004. LO HS 26* v Sussex (Hove) 2004 (NL). LO BB 4-26 NSW v Tas (Sydney) 1997-98.

RELEASED/RETIRED continued on p 68

MIDDLESEX 2004

RESULTS SUMMARY

	Place	Won	Lost	Tied	Drew	No Result
County Championship (1st Division)	**4th**	4	4		8	
All First-Class Matches		4	4		9	
C & G Trophy	Quarter-Finalist					
National League (2nd Division)	1st	12	6			
Twenty20 Cup	5th in South Division					

COUNTY CHAMPIONSHIP AVERAGES

BATTING AND FIELDING

Cap		M	I	NO	HS	Runs	Avge	100	50	Ct/St
2000	O.A.Shah	16	29	5	140*	1280	53.33	4	8	18
1993	P.N.Weekes	16	26	3	118	1001	43.52	2	9	14
2002	E.C.Joyce	13	23	2	123	906	43.14	1	7	12
2003	B.L.Hutton	16	29	1	126	1129	40.32	5	3	23
2004	J.W.M.Dalrymple	15	24	4	244	767	38.35	1	3	9
2002	S.G.Koenig	16	29	2	171	971	35.96	2	4	4
2000	D.C.Nash	11	16	4	81*	416	34.66	–	3	26/2
–	L.Klusener	6	8	1	68*	170	24.28	–	2	2
–	B.J.M.Scott	6	11	3	101*	190	23.75	1	–	6/3
2003	C.B.Keegan	5	4	–	44	75	18.75	–	2	2
2003	S.J.Cook	11	14	–	40	243	17.35	–	–	5
–	N.R.D.Compton	3	5	–	40	80	16.00	–	–	3
–	C.T.Peploe	7	11	2	28*	135	15.00	–	–	3
–	M.M.Betts	6	7	2	31*	75	15.00	–	–	3
–	A.B.Agarkar	3	4	2	22	27	13.50	–	–	2
–	M.Hayward	11	13	5	9	40	5.00	–	–	4
–	P.M.Hutchison	7	9	2	8	25	3.57	–	–	3

Also batted: T.F.Bloomfield (1 match – cap 2001) 8; S.R.Clark (3) 34, 11, 24; G.D.McGrath (2) 24, 4, 0; A.J.Strauss (1 – cap 2001) 95, 19*; C.J.C.Wright (1) 0.

BOWLING

	O	M	R	W	Avge	Best	5wI	10wM
S.R.Clark	89	23	217	10	21.70	3-28	–	–
C.B.Keegan	161	29	550	20	27.50	5-36	2	–
M.Hayward	289	54	918	31	29.61	4-41	–	–
S.J.Cook	346	77	1008	34	29.64	6-89	2	–
A.B.Agarkar	93.3	20	323	10	32.30	5-81	1	–
J.W.M.Dalrymple	277.5	37	1001	26	38.50	4-66	–	–
M.M.Betts	135.4	27	507	13	39.00	5-89	1	–
C.T.Peploe	212.2	51	672	17	39.52	4-65	–	–
P.N.Weekes	325.3	34	1166	26	44.84	5-76	1	–
L.Klusener	170.3	18	673	13	51.76	4-89	–	–
Also bowled:								
G.D.McGrath	100.4	41	215	9	23.88	4-59		
B.L.Hutton	113	23	353	8	44.12	3-14		
P.M.Hutchison	160	25	551	9	61.22	3-50		

T.F.Bloomfield 20-3-55-1; E.C.Joyce 32-2-135-1; S.G.Koenig 3-1-7-0; D.C.Nash 2-0-8-0; O.A.Shah 18-4-54-1; C.J.C.Wright 20-3-50-0.

The First-Class Averages (pp 121–136) give the records of Middlesex players in all first-class county matches (their other opponents being Cambridge UCCE), with the exception of M.A.Richards and T.E.Savill whose only first-class appearances were for Oxford UCCE and Cambridge UCCE respectively, A.J.Strauss and C.J.C.Wright whose full county figures are as above, and:
  S.G.Koenig 17-31-2-171-1038-35.79-2-5-5ct. 3-1-7-0.

MIDDLESEX RECORDS

FIRST-CLASS CRICKET

Highest Total	For	642-3d		v	Hampshire	Southampton	1923
	V	734-5d		by	Lancashire	Manchester	2003
Lowest Total	For	20		v	MCC	Lord's	1864
	V	31		by	Glos	Bristol	1924
Highest Innings	For	331*	J.D.B.Robertson	v	Worcs	Worcester	1949
	V	341	C.M.Spearman	for	Glos	Gloucester	2004

Highest Partnership for each Wicket

1st	372	M.W.Gatting/J.L.Langer	v	Essex	Southgate	1998
2nd	380	F.A.Tarrant/J.W.Hearne	v	Lancashire	Lord's	1914
3rd	424*	W.J.Edrich/D.C.S.Compton	v	Somerset	Lord's	1948
4th	325	J.W.Hearne/E.H.Hendren	v	Hampshire	Lord's	1919
5th	338	R.S.Lucas/T.C.O'Brien	v	Sussex	Hove	1895
6th	270	J.D.Carr/P.N.Weekes	v	Glos	Lord's	1994
7th	271*	E.H.Hendren/F.T.Mann	v	Notts	Nottingham	1925
8th	182*	M.H.C.Doll/H.R.Murrell	v	Notts	Lord's	1913
9th	160*	E.H.Hendren/T.J.Durston	v	Essex	Leyton	1927
10th	230	R.W.Nicholls/W.Roche	v	Kent	Lord's	1899

Best Bowling	For	10- 40	G.O.B.Allen	v	Lancashire	Lord's	1929
(Innings)	V	9- 38	R.C.R.Glasgow†	for	Somerset	Lord's	1924
Best Bowling	For	16-114	G.Burton	v	Yorkshire	Sheffield	1888
(Match)		16-114	J.T.Hearne	v	Lancashire	Manchester	1898
	V	16-109	C.W.L.Parker	for	Glos	Cheltenham	1930

Most Runs – Season	2669	E.H.Hendren	(av 83.41)	1923
Most Runs – Career	40302	E.H.Hendren	(av 48.81)	1907-37
Most 100s – Season	13	D.C.S.Compton		1947
Most 100s – Career	119	E.H.Hendren		1907-37
Most Wkts – Season	158	F.J.Titmus	(av 14.63)	1955
Most Wkts – Career	2361	F.J.Titmus	(av 21.27)	1949-82
Most Career W-K Dismissals	1223	J.T.Murray	(1024 ct/199 st)	1952-75
Most Career Catches in the Field	561	E.H.Hendren		1907-37

LIST 'A' LIMITED-OVERS CRICKET

Highest Total	CGT	304-7		v	Surrey	The Oval	1995
		304-8		v	Cornwall	St Austell	1995
	BHC	325-5		v	Leics	Leicester	1992
	NL	337-5		v	Somerset	Southgate	2003
Lowest Total	CGT	41		v	Essex	Westcliff	1972
	BHC	73		v	Essex	Lord's	1985
	NL	23		v	Yorkshire	Leeds	1974
Highest Innings	CGT	158	G.D.Barlow	v	Lancashire	Lord's	1984
	BHC	143*	M.W.Gatting	v	Sussex	Hove	1985
	NL	147*	M.R.Ramprakash	v	Worcs	Lord's	1990
Best Bowling	CGT	6-15	W.W.Daniel	v	Sussex	Hove	1980
	BHC	7-12	W.W.Daniel	v	Minor C (E)	Ipswich	1978
	NL	6- 6	R.W.Hooker	v	Surrey	Lord's	1969

† R.C.Robertson-Glasgow

NORTHAMPTONSHIRE

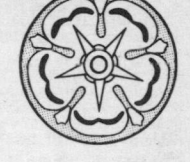

Formation of Present Club: 31 July 1878
Inaugural First-Class Match: 1905
Colours: Maroon
Badge: Tudor Rose
County Champions: (0); best – 2nd 1912, 1957, 1965, 1976
Gillette/NatWest/C & G Trophy Winners: (2) 1976, 1992
Benson and Hedges Cup Winners: (1) 1980
National League (Div 1) Winners: (0); best – 3rd 2000
Sunday League Winners: (0); best – 3rd 1991
Twenty20 Cup Winners: (0); best – 4th in Group 2003
Match Awards: CGT 57; BHC 62

Chief Executive: M.J.Tagg County Ground, Wantage Road, Northampton, NN1 4TJ • Tel: 01604 514455 • Fax: 01604 514488 • Email: post@nccc.co.uk • Web: www.nccc.co.uk

Director of Cricket/First XI Coach: K.P.Wessels. **Captain**: D.J.G.Sales. **Vice-Captain**: no appointment. **Overseas Players**: M.L.Love and D.G.Wright. **2005 Beneficiary**: Club Centenary Appeal. **Head Groundsman**: P.Marshall. **Scorer**: A.C.Kingston. ‡ New registration. NQ Not qualified for England.

AFZAAL, Usman (Manvers Pierrepont CS; S Notts C), b Rawalpindi, Pakistan 9 Jun 1977. 6'0". LHB, SLA. Debut 1995; cap 2000. Northamptonshire debut 2004. **Tests**: 3 (2001); HS 54 v A (Oval) 2001; BB 1-49. F-c Tours: SA 1996-97 (Nt); WI 2000-01 (Eng A); NZ 2001-02. 1000 runs (4): most – 1365 (2004). HS 167* v Sussex (Northampton) 2004. BB 4-101 v Glos (Nottingham) 1998. Nh BB 3-65 v Kent (Northampton) 2004. Award: CGT 1. LO HS 105 Nt v Somerset (Taunton) 2003 (NL). LO BB 3-4 v Cambs (Northampton) 2004 (CGT).

NQBROPHY, Gerard Louis (Christian Brothers C, Boksburg; Witwatersrand TC), b Welkom, South Africa 26 Nov 1975. 5'11". British/EU passport. RHB, WK. Transvaal 1996-97 to 1998-99. Free State 1999-00 to 2000-01. Northamptonshire debut 2002. HS 185 SA Academy v Zim President's XI (Harare) 1998-99. Nh HS 181 v Sussex (Hove) 2004. LO HS 57* v NZ (Northampton) 2004.

BROWN, Jason Fred (St Margaret Ward HS & SFC), b Newcastle-under-Lyme, Staffs 10 Oct 1974. 6'0". RHB, OB. Debut 1996; cap 2000. Staffordshire 1994-95. F-c Tours: WI 2000-01 (*part*) (Eng A); SL 2000-01 (*no f-c*). HS 38 v Hants (Northampton) 2003. 50 wkts (2): most – 66 (2003). BB 7-69 v Durham (Chester-le-St) 2003. Award: CGT 1. LO HS 16 v Lancs (Manchester) 2002 (NL). LO BB 5-19 v Cambs (Northampton) 2004 (CGT).

COVERDALE, Paul Stephen (Wellingborough S; Loughborough U), b Harrogate, Yorks 24 Jul 1983. Son of S.P.Coverdale (Yorkshire, Cambridge U and Northamptonshire 1973-80, 1987; Northants Secretary-Manager/Chief Executive 1985-2004). 5'10". RHB, RM. Emerging player contract – awaiting f-c debut. LO HS 19 Northants CB v Leics CB (Barwell) 2001. LO BB 1-21 (CGT).

GOODE, Christopher Martin (Huxlow CS, Irthlingborough; Tresham C), b Kettering 12 Oct 1984. 6'2". RHB, RMF. Emerging player contract. Debut 2004. HS 0. BB 1-70.

HUGGINS, Thomas Benjamin (Kimbolton S; De Montfort U), b Peterborough 8 Mar 1983. 6'3". RHB, OB. Debut 2003. Emerging player contract. Cambridgeshire 2001. HS 82* v Middx (Oxford) 2004. LO HS 16 v Kent (Canterbury) 2004 (NL).

JONES, Philip Steffan (Stradey CS, Llanelli; Neath TC; Loughborough U; Homerton C, Cambridge), b Llanelli, Carms, Wales 9 Feb 1974. 6'2". RHB, RMF. Cambridge U 1997; blue 1997. Somerset debut 1997; cap 2001. Northamptonshire debut 2004. Wales MC 1992-96. HS 105 Sm v NZ (Taunton) 1999. CC HS 63 Sm v Northants (Taunton) 2003. Nh HS 37 v Kent (Canterbury) 2004. 50 wkts (1): 59 (2001). BB 6-67 CU v OU (Lord's) 1997. Nh BB 6-110 (match 10-156) Sm v Warwks (Birmingham) 2002. Nh BB 3-75 v Sussex (Hove) 2004. LO HS 27 Sm v Northants (Northampton) 2000 (NL). LO BB 6-56 v Ire (Clontarf) 2004 (CGT).

KING, Richard Eric (Bedford Modern S; Loughborough U), b Hitchin, Herts 3 Jan 1984. 6'0". RHB, LMF. Loughborough UCCE 2003. Northants emerging player contract awaiting County debut. HS 17 LU v Somerset (Taunton) 2003 – on debut. BB 1-108 (LU). LO HS 2 (Northants CB). LO BB 2-39 Northants CB v Yorks CB (Northampton) 2002 (CGT).

NQLOUW, Johann (Fraserburg HS; Port Elizabeth U), b Cape Town, South Africa 12 Apr 1979. 6'2". RHB, RFM. Griqualand West 2000-01 to 2002-03. E Province 2003-04. Dolphins 2004-05. Northamptonshire debut 2004. Kolpak registration. HS 124 EP v Boland (Pt Elizabeth) 2003-04. Nh HS 63 and BB 5-44 v Middx (Northampton) 2004. 50 wkts (1): 60 (2004). BB 6-108 GW v Border (East London) 2002-03. LO HS 72 GW v Northerns (Kimberley) 2000-01. LO BB 5-27 v Warwks (Northampton) 2004 (NL).

‡NQLOVE, Martin Lloyd (Toowoomba GS; Queensland U), b Mundubbera, Queensland, Australia 30 Mar 1974. 6'1". RHB, OB. Queensland 1992-93 to date. Durham 2001-03; cap 2001. Northamptonshire debut 2004; captain 2005. **Tests** (A): 5 (2002-03 to 2003); HS 100* v B (Cairns) 2003. F-c Tours (A): E 1995 (Young A); WI 2003. 1000 (1+3): most – 1364 (2001). HS 300* Q v Vic (Melbourne) 2003-04. CC HS 273 (Durham record) v Hants (Chester-le-St) 2003 . Nh HS 161* v Worcs (Worcester) 2004 – scored 133* in first innings. Averages 394 for Northants. BB (Q) 1-5. LO HS 127* Q v NSW (Brisbane) 2001-02.

PANESAR, Mudhsuden Singh *'Monty'* (Stopsley HS; Bedford Modern S; Loughborough U), b Luton, Beds 25 Apr 1982. 6'0". LHB, SLA. Bedfordshire 1998-99. Debut 2001. Loughborough U 2004. F-c Tours (ECB Acad): SL 2002-03. HS 28 v CU (Cambridge) 2003. BB 5-77 ECB Acad v SL Acad XI (Colombo) 2002-03. CC HS 10 and Nh BB 4-11 (8-131 match) v Leics (Northampton) 2001 – on debut. LO HS 16* v Essex (Colchester) 2002 (NL). LO BB 5-20 ECB Acad v SL Acad XI (Colombo) 2002-03.

PHILLIPS, Ben James (Langley Park S and SFC, Beckenham), b Lewisham, London 30 Sep 1974. 6'6". RHB, RFM. Kent 1996-99. Northamptonshire debut 2002 (one non-CC match). HS 100* K v Lancs (Manchester) 1997. Nh HS 90 v Warwks (Birmingham) 2004. BB 5-47 K v Sussex (Horsham) 1997. Nh BB 5-106 v Glos (Bristol) 2004. Award: CGT 1. LO HS 44* v Kent (Canterbury) 2004 (NL). LO BB 4-25 K v Northants (Canterbury) 2000 (NL).

‡NQPIETERSEN, Charl, b Kimberley, South Africa 6 Jan 1983. LHB, LMF. Griqualand West 2001-02 to 2003-04. Kolpak registration. HS 45 GW v N West (Kimberley) 2003-04. BB 6-43 GW v Boland (Kimberley) 2002-03. LO HS 14* GW v KZ-Natal (Kimberley) 2003-04. LO BB 4-32 GW v KZ-Natal (Pietermaritzburg) 2003-04.

‡PYTHIAN, Mark John, b Peterborough 26 Apr 1985. RHB, WK. Emerging player contract – awaiting f-c debut.

ROBERTS, Timothy William (Bishop's Stopford S, Kettering; Durham U), b Kettering 4 Mar 1978. Younger brother of A.R.Roberts (Northants 1987-98). 5'7". RHB, OB. British U 1999. Bedfordshire 2000. Lancashire debut 2001. Northamptonshire debut 2003. HS 89 v Lancs (Northampton) 2004. BB 1-10 (not CC). LO HS 131 v Notts (Nottingham) 2003 (NL).

SALES, David John Grimwood (Caterham S; Cumnor House S), b Carshalton, Surrey 3 Dec 1977. 6'0". RHB, RM. Debut 1996 v Worcs (Kidderminster) scoring 0 and 210* – record Championship score on f-c debut; youngest (18yr 237d) to score 200 in a Championship match; cap 1999; captain 2004. Wellington 2001-02. F-c Tours (Eng A): NZ 1999-00; SL 1997-98; K 1997-98; B 1999-00. Sustained severe knee injury prior to start of England A tour of WI 2000-01 – no f-c appearances 2001. 1000 runs (2); most – 1291 (1999). HS 303* v Essex (Northampton) 1999 – youngest Englishman (21y 240d) to score a f-c 300. BB 4-25 v SL A (Northampton) 1999. CC BB 2-7 v Yorks (Scarborough) 1999. Award: BHC 1. LO HS 133* v Notts (Northampton) 2003 (NL). LO BB 4-...

‡SHAFAYAT, Bilal Mustapha (Greenwood Dale; Nottingham Bluecoat SFC), b Nottingham 10 Jul 1984. 5'7". RHB, RMF. Nottinghamshire 2001-2004. Captained Eng U-19 tour of Australia 2002-03. F-c Tour (Eng A): I 2003-04. HS 105 and BB 1-22 Nt v DU (Nottingham) 2003. CC HS 104 Nt v Worcs (Nottingham) 2004. LO HS 66 Nt v Somerset (Taunton) 2002 (NL). LO BB 4-35 Nt v Somerset (Nottingham) 2002 (NL).

‡**WAKE, Cameron** John (Oundle S), b Kettering 28 Jun 1985. Son of J.R.Wake (Bedfordshire). RHB, LB. Emerging player contract – awaiting f-c debut.

NQ**WESSELS, Matthewus** Hendrik (**'Riki'**) (Woodridge C, Pt Elizabeth; Northants U), b Nambour, Queensland, Australia 12 Nov 1985. Left Australia when 2 months old. Son of K.C.Wessels (OFS, Sussex, WP, NT, Q, FP, Australia and South Africa 1973-74 to 1999-00). 5'11". RHB, WK. MCC 2004. Kolpak registration. Awaiting Northamptonshire debut. HS 34 MCC v WI (Arundel) 2004 – on debut.

WHITE, Andrew Rowland (Regent House GS; Ulster U), b Newtownards, Co Down, N Ireland 3 Jul 1980. 6'0". RHB, OB. Ireland 2004, scoring 152* on debut (*see HS*). Northamptonshire debut 2004. HS 152* Ire v Holland (Deventer) 2004 – on f-c debut. Nh HS 22 v Middx (Lord's) 2004 – on Northants debut. BB 2-19 v Warwks (Northampton) 2004. Award: CGT 1. LO HS 44 Ire v Northants (Dublin) 2004. LO BB 3-43 Ire v Surrey (Dublin) 2004.

WHITE, Robert Allan (Stowe S; Durham U; Loughborough U), b Chelmsford, Essex 15 Oct 1979. 5'11". RHB, LB. Debut 2000. Loughborough UCCE 2003. British U 2003. HS 277 and BB 2-30 v Glos (Northampton) 2002 – highest maiden f-c hundred in UK; included 107 before lunch on first day. LO HS 101 v Glam (Northampton) 2004 (NL). LO BB 2-18 v Sussex (Northampton) 2002 (NL).

NQ**WRIGHT, Damien** Geoffrey (Terrigal HS, NSW), b Casino, NSW, Australia 25 Jul 1975. 6'1". RHB, RFM. Tasmania 1997-98 to date. Scotland 2001 (CGT). Northamptonshire 2003. Withdrew from 2004 overseas player contract with Derbyshire because of a knee injury. F-c Tours (Aus A): SA 2002-03. HS 111 Tas v Vic (Hobart) 2004-05. Nh HS 46 and BB 3-38 v Hants (Northampton) 2003 – on CC debut. BB 6-25 Tas v S Aus (Hobart) 2004-05. LO HS 55 Scot v Middx CB (Southgate) 2001 (CGT). LO BB 4-23 Tas v Vic (Melbourne) 2001-02.

RELEASED/RETIRED

(Having made a first-class County appearance in 2004)

ANDERSON, Ricaldo Sherman Glenroy (Alperton HS; Barnet C; North West London C; London Cricket C), b Hammersmith, London 22 Sep 1976. 5'10". RHB, RMF. Essex 1999-2001. Northamptonshire 2002-04. HS 67* Ex v Sussex (Chelmsford) 2000. Nh HS 51 v Essex (Northampton) 2002. 50 wkts (1): 50 (1999). BB 6-34 (11-111 match) Ex v Northants (Ilford) 2000. NH BB 4-97 v Derbys (Derby) 2002 on Nh debut. LO HS 22 Ex v Sussex (Hove) 2001 (NL) and 22 v Derbys (Derby) 2002 (NL). LO BB 3-28 v Glos (Northampton) 2002 (BHC).

BAILEY, Tobin Michael Barnaby (Bedford S; Loughborough U), b Kettering 28 Aug 1976. 5'10". RHB, WK. Northamptonshire 1996-2004; cap 2003. British U 1998. Bedfordshire 1994-96. HS 101* v Somerset (Taunton) 2003. LO HS 52 Brit U v Glos (Bristol) 1997 (CGT).

CAWDRON, Michael John (Cheltenham C), b Luton, Beds 7 Oct 1974. 6'2". LHB, RM. Gloucestershire staff 1994-2001; debut 1999 – taking 15 wickets in first four innings. Northamptonshire 2003-04. HS 42 Gs v Hants (Bristol) 1999 – on debut. Nh HS 24 v Hants (Northampton) 2003 – on Northants debut. BB 6-25 (10-74 match) FCC Select XI v NZ A (Milton Keynes) 2004. Nh BB 6-87 v Durham (Chester-le-St) 2003. LO HS 50 Gs v Essex (Cheltenham) 1995 (SL). LO BB 4-17 Gs v Warwks (Cheltenham) 1999 (NL).

COOK, Jeffrey William (James Cook HS, Kogarah, NSW), b Sydney, Australia 2 Feb 1972. 6'4". LHB, RM. UK resident since 1993 – England qualified 2000. Northamptonshire 2000-04; cap 2003. NSW U-19. HS 137 v Glos (Cheltenham) 2000. BB 5-31 v Durham (Northampton) 2003. Awards: CGT 1; BHC 1. LO HS 130 Northants CB v Wilts (Northampton) 1999 (NWT). LO BB 4-35 v Glos (Bristol) 2002 (NL).

GREENIDGE, C.G. – *see GLOUCESTERSHIRE.*

JENNINGS, Craig James Robert (Hagley Park HS), b Rugeley, Staffs 13 Nov 1984. 6'0". RHB, RMF. Northamptonshire 2004. HS 6. BB 1-64. LO HS 3 (L). LO BB (Nh CB)1-29 (CGT).

POWELL, Mark John (Campion S, Bugbrooke; Loughborough U), b Northampton 4 Nov 1980. 5'11". RHB, OB. Northamptonshire 2000-04. HS 108* v Glam (Cardiff) 2002. LO HS 70 v Derbys (Derby) 2003 (NL).

NQ**ROFE, Paul** Cameron (Prince Alfred C; Flinders U), b Adelaide, Australia 16 Jan 1981. 6'6". RHB, RFM. S Australia 2000-01 to date. Northamptonshire 2004. HS 18 S Aus v Q (Adelaide) 2000-01. Nh HS 15* v Kent (Canterbury) 2004. BB 7-52 S Aus v NSW (Adelaide) 2001-02. Nh BB 4-109 v Middx (Lord's) 2004. LO HS (S Aus) 6*. LO BB 3-23 v Surrey (Northampton) 2004 (NL).

SHANTRY, A.J. – *see WARWICKSHIRE.*

SWANN, G.P. – *see NOTTINGHAMSHIRE.*

NQ**VAN JAARSVELD, M.** – **see** *KENT.*

MIDDLESEX RELEASED/RETIRED (continued from p 62)

COOK, S.J. – *see KENT.*

NQ**KLUSENER, Lance** (Durban HS), b Durban, South Africa 4 Sep 1971. 5'10". LHB, RM/OB. Natal/KwaZulu-Natal 1993-94 to 2003-04. Dolphins 2004-05. Nottinghamshire 2002. *Wisden* 1999. **Tests** (SA): 49 (1996-97 to 2004); HS 174 v E (Pt Elizabeth) 1999-00; BB 8-64 v I (Calcutta) 1996-97 – on debut. **LOI** (SA): 171 (1995-96 to 2004); HS 103* v NZ (Auckland) 1998-99; BB 6-49 v SL (Lahore) 1997-98. F-c Tours (SA): E 1998; A 1997-98, 2001-02; WI 2000-01; NZ 1998-99; I 1996-97, 1999-00; P 1997-98; SL 1998-99, 2000-01, 2004; Z 1999-00, 2001-02. HS 174 (*see Tests*). M HS 68* v Glos (Gloucester) 2004. BB 8-34 Natal v WP (Durban) 1995-96. M BB 4-89 v Lancs (Lord's) 2004 – on Middx debut. Award: BHC 1. LO HS 142* SA v Northants (Northampton) 1998. LO BB 6-49 (*see LOI*).

NQ**KOENIG, Sven** Gaetan (Hilton C; Cape Town U), b Durban, South Africa 9 Dec 1973. ECB qualified – EU (Italian) passport. 5'10". LHB, OB. Western Province 1993-94 to 1996-97. Transvaal/Gauteng 1997-98 to 2000-01. Middlesex 2002-04; cap 2002. F-c Tour (SA A): E 1996. 1000 runs (3): most 1251 (2002). HS 171 v Lancs (Manchester) 2004. BB (Gauteng) 1-0. M BB 1-19. LO HS 116 v Essex (Chelmsford) 2002 (CGT).

NQ**McGRATH, Glenn** Donald (Narromine HS), b Dubbo, NSW, Australia 9 Feb 1970. 6'6". RHB, RF. New South Wales 1992-93 to date. Worcestershire 2000; cap 2000. Middlesex 2004. *Wisden* 1997. **Tests** (A): 106 (1993-94 to 2004-05); HS 61 v NZ (Brisbane) 2004-05; BB 8-24 v P (Perth) 2004-05. **LOI** (A): 200 (1993-94 to 2004-05); HS 11 v NZ (Auckland) 1999-00; BB 7-15 v Namibia (Potchefstroom) 2002-03. Tours (A): E 1997, 2001; SA 1993-94, 1996-97, 2002-02; WI 1994-95, 1998-99, 2002-03; NZ 1999-00; I 1996-97, 2000-01, 2004-05; P 1994-95, 1998-99, 2002-03 (in SL and Sharjah); SL 1999-00; Z 1999-00. HS 61 (*see Tests*). UK HS 55 Wo v Notts (Worcester) 2000. M HS 24 and BB 4-59 v Kent (Southgate) 2004 – on Middx debut. 50 wkts (1+1); most – 80 (2000). BB 8-24 (*see Tests*). CC BB 8-41 (12-116 match) Wo v Northants (Worcester) 2000. LO HS 11 (*see LOI*). LO BB 7-15 (*see LOI*).

B.J.Duncan, M.A.Richards and D.L.S.van Bunge left the staff having made no Middlesex f-c appearances in 2004.

NORTHAMPTONSHIRE 2004

RESULTS SUMMARY

	Place	Won	Lost	Tied	Drew	No Result
County Championship (1st Division)	9th	1	4		11	
All First-Class Matches		1	4		12	
C & G Trophy	Quarter-Finalist					
National League (1st Division)	4th	8	8			
Twenty20 Cup	6th in Mid/West/Wales Division					

COUNTY CHAMPIONSHIP AVERAGES

BATTING AND FIELDING

Cap		M	I	NO	HS	Runs	Avge	100	50	Ct/St
–	M.L.Love	2	4	3	161*	394	394.00	2	1	3
1999	D.J.G.Sales	16	25	5	171	1230	61.50	1	12	18
–	U.Afzaal	16	28	5	167*	1365	59.34	4	7	9
–	M.van Jaarsveld	7	13	–	114	484	37.23	1	1	7
–	G.L.Brophy	15	24	2	181	744	33.81	1	4	27/2
–	T.B.Huggins	8	13	2	82*	342	31.09	–	2	3
–	T.W.Roberts	16	29	2	89	748	27.70	–	6	10
2003	J.W.Cook	5	8	–	114	204	25.50	1	1	4
1999	G.P.Swann	13	21	–	54	435	20.71	–	1	12
–	B.J.Phillips	15	21	3	90	327	18.16	–	3	2
–	J.Louw	16	22	3	63	342	18.00	–	1	8
–	P.S.Jones	8	9	1	37	139	17.37	–	–	1
–	R.A.White	4	8	–	52	139	17.37	–	1	3
–	M.J.Powell	6	11	–	48	190	17.27	–	–	1
2003	T.M.B.Bailey	2	4	1	20	37	12.33	–	–	1/4
–	P.C.Rofe	5	6	4	15*	20	10.00	–	–	1
2000	J.F.Brown	13	15	6	34	82	9.11	–	–	4
–	C.G.Greenidge	3	4	1	8*	13	4.33	–	–	–

Also batted: C.M.Goode (1 match) 0; C.J.R.Jennings (1) 6; A.J.Shantry (2) 2*, 0*, 5 (1 ct); A.R.White (2) 22,0.

BOWLING

	O	M	R	W	Avge	Best	5wI	10wM
J.Louw	463.3	89	1591	60	26.51	5- 44	3	–
B.J.Phillips	408.3	107	1175	31	37.90	5-106	1	–
G.P.Swann	403.2	71	1168	30	38.93	4- 94	–	–
P.C.Rofe	167.5	42	505	12	42.08	4-109	–	–
J.F.Brown	584.3	133	1523	36	42.30	5-113	1	–
P.S.Jones	220	33	792	10	79.20	3- 75	–	–
Also bowled:								
C.G.Greenidge	56.2	6	277	9	30.77	3- 71	–	–
J.W.Cook	84	14	285	5	57.00	3- 42	–	–

U.Afzaal 51.3-7-196-4; G.L.Brophy 1-0-1-0; C.M.Goode 16-3-70-1; C.J.R.Jennings 14-3-64-1; T.W.Roberts 1-1-0-0; D.J.G.Sales 2-1-2-0; A.J.Shantry 35-10-110-3; M.van Jaarsveld 4-2-8-0; A.R.White 26-3-62-2; R.A.White 12-1-52-1.

The First-Class Averages (pp 121-136) give the records of Northamptonshire players in all first-class county matches (Northamptonshire's other opponents being Durham UCCE), with the exception of M.S.Panesar whose only first-class appearances were for Loughborough UCCE.

NORTHAMPTONSHIRE RECORDS

FIRST-CLASS CRICKET

Highest Total	For 781-7d		v	Notts	Northampton 1995
	V 673-8d		by	Yorkshire	Leeds 2003
Lowest Total	For 12		v	Glos	Gloucester 1907
	V 33		by	Lancashire	Northampton 1977
Highest Innings	For 331*	M.E.K.Hussey	v	Somerset	Taunton 2003
	V 333	K.S.Duleepsinhji	for	Sussex	Hove 1930

Highest Partnership for each Wicket

1st	375	R.A.White/M.J.Powell	v	Glos	Northampton 2002
2nd	344	G.Cook/R.J.Boyd-Moss	v	Lancashire	Northampton 1986
3rd	393	A.Fordham/A.J.Lamb	v	Yorkshire	Leeds 1990
4th	370	R.T.Virgin/P.Willey	v	Somerset	Northampton 1976
5th	401	M.B.Loye/D.Ripley	v	Glamorgan	Northampton 1998
6th	376	R.Subba Row/A.Lightfoot	v	Surrey	The Oval 1958
7th	293	D.J.G.Sales/D.Ripley	v	Essex	Northampton 1999
8th	164	D.Ripley/N.G.B.Cook	v	Lancashire	Manchester 1987
9th	156	R.Subba Row/S.Starkie	v	Lancashire	Northampton 1955
10th	148	B.W.Bellamy/J.V.Murdin	v	Glamorgan	Northampton 1925

Best Bowling	For 10-127	V.W.C.Jupp	v	Kent	Tunbridge W 1932
(Innings)	V 10- 30	C.Blythe	for	Kent	Northampton 1907
Best Bowling	For 15- 31	G.E.Tribe	v	Yorkshire	Northampton 1958
(Match)	V 17- 48	C.Blythe	for	Kent	Northampton 1907

Most Runs – Season	2198	D.Brookes	(av 51.11)	1952
Most Runs – Career	28980	D.Brookes	(av 36.13)	1934-59
Most 100s – Season	8	R.A.Haywood		1921
Most 100s – Career	67	D.Brookes		1934-59
Most Wkts – Season	175	G.E.Tribe	(av 18.70)	1955
Most Wkts – Career	1097	E.W.Clark	(av 21.31)	1922-47
Most Career W-K Dismissals	810	K.V.Andrew	(653 ct/157 st)	1953-66
Most Career Catches in the Field	469	D.S.Steele		1963-84

LIST 'A' LIMITED-OVERS CRICKET

Highest Total	CGT	360-2		v	Staffs	Northampton 1990
	BHC	304-6		v	Scotland	Northampton 1995
	NL	319-7		v	Scotland	Northampton 2003
Lowest Total	CGT	62		v	Leics	Leicester 1974
	BHC	85		v	Sussex	Northampton 1978
	NL	41		v	Middlesex	Northampton 1972
Highest Innings	CGT	145	R.J.Bailey	v	Staffs	Stone 1991
	BHC	134	R.J.Bailey	v	Glos	Northampton 1987
	NL	172*	W.Larkins	v	Warwicks	Luton 1983
Best Bowling	CGT	7-37	N.A.Mallender	v	Worcs	Northampton 1984
	BHC	5-14	F.A.Rose	v	Minor C	Luton 1998
	NL	7-39	A.Hodgson	v	Somerset	Northampton 1976

NOTTINGHAMSHIRE

Formation of Present Club: March/April 1841
Substantial Reorganisation: 11 December 1866
Inaugural First-Class Match: 1864
Colours: Green and Gold
Badge: Badge of City of Nottingham
County Champions (since 1890): (4) 1907, 1929, 1981, 1987
Gillette/NatWest/C & G Trophy Winners: (1) 1987
Benson and Hedges Cup Winners: (1) 1989
National League (Div 1) Winners: (0); best – 5th 2001
Sunday League Winners: (1) 1991
Twenty20 Cup Winners: (0); best – 6th in Group 2003, 2004
Match Awards: CGT 46; BHC 76

Chief Executive: D.G.Collier, Trent Bridge, Nottingham NG2 6AG • Tel: 0115 982 3000 • Fax: 0115 945 5730 • Email: administration.notts@ecb.co.uk • Webs: www.nottsccc.co.uk and www.trentbridge.co.uk

First XI Coach: M.Newell. **Captain**: S.P.Fleming. **Vice-Captain**: P.J.Franks. **Overseas Players**: S.P.Fleming and D.J.Hussey. **2005 Beneficiary**: J.E.R.Gallian. **Head Groundsman**: S.Birks. **Scorer**: G.Stringfellow. ‡ New registration. NQ Not qualified for England.

ALLEYNE, David (Enfield GS; Hertford Regional C; City & Islington C), b York 17 Apr 1976. 5'11". RHB, WK. Middlesex 2001-02. Nottinghamshire debut 2004. HS 49* M v Derbys (Derby) 2002. Nt HS 43* v OU (Oxford) 2004 on Nt debut. LO HS 58 M v Notts (Nottingham) 2000 (NL).

BICKNELL, Darren John (Robert Haining County SS; Guildford TC), b Guildford, Surrey 24 Jun 1967. Elder brother of M.P.Bicknell (*see SURREY*). 6'4". LHB, SLA. Surrey 1987-99; cap 1990; benefit 1999. Nottinghamshire debut/cap 2000. F-c Tours (Eng A): WI 1991-92; P 1990-91; SL 1990-91; Z 1989-90. 1000 runs (8); most – 1888 (1991). HS 235* Sy v Notts (Nottingham) 1994. Nt HS 180* v Warwks (Birmingham) 2000 – sharing unbroken 1st wkt stand of 406 with G.E.Welton. BB 3-7 Sy v Sussex (Guildford) 1996. Nt BB 3-33 v Essex (Nottingham) 2004. Awards: CGT 1; BHC 6. LO HS 135* Sy v Yorks (Oval) 1989 (NWT). LO BB (Sy) 1-11 (SL).

CLOUGH, Gareth David (Pudsey Grangefield S), b Leeds, Yorks 23 May 1978. 6'0". RHB, RM. Yorkshire 1998. Nottinghamshire debut 2001. No f-c appearances 2004. HS 55 v Ind A (Nottingham) 2003. CC HS 33 Y v Glam (Cardiff) 1998 – on debut. BB 3-69 v Glos (Nottingham) 2001. LO HS 42* v Durham (Nottingham) 2003 (NL). LO BB 4-32 v Sussex (Horsham) 2003 (NL).

EALHAM, Mark Alan (Stour Valley SS, Chartham), b Willesborough, Ashford, Kent 27 Aug 1969. Son of A.G.E.Ealham (Kent 1966-82). 5'9". RHB, RMF. Kent 1989-2003; cap 1992; benefit 2003. Nottinghamshire debut/cap 2004. No f-c appearances 2004. **Tests**: 8 (1996 to 1998); HS 53* v A (Birmingham) 1997; BB 4-21 v I (Nottingham) 1996. **LOI**: 64 (1996 to 2001); HS 45 v WI (Bridgetown) 1997-98; BB 5-15 v Z (Kimberley) 1999-00 – Eng record. F-c Tours: A 1996-97 (Eng A); SA 1999-00 (*part*); SL 1997-98; Z 1992-93 (K); K 1997-98. 1000 runs (1): 1055 (1997). HS 153* K v Northants (Canterbury) 2001. Nt HS 139 v Leics (Leicester) 2004. BB 8-36 (10-74 match) K v Warwks (Birmingham) 1996. Nt BB 4-43 v Leics (Nottingham) 2004. Awards: CGT 2; BHC 6. LO HS 112 K v Derbys (Maidstone) 1995 (off 44 balls – SL record). LO BB 6-53 K v Hants (Basingstoke) 1993 (SL).

‡**NQFLEMING, Stephen** Paul (Cashmere HS, Canterbury; Christchurch C of Ed), b Christchurch, New Zealand 1 Apr 1973. 6'3". LHB, RSM. Canterbury 1991-92 to 1999-00. Wellington 2000-01 to date. Middlesex 2001; cap 2001. Yorkshire 2003. Nottinghamshire captain 2005. **Tests** (NZ): 89 (1993-94 to 2004-05, 65 as captain); HS 274* v SL (Colombo) 2002-03. **LOI** (NZ): 228 (1993-94 to 2004-05, 170 as captain); HS 134* v SA (Johannesburg) 2002-03; BB 1-8. F-c Tours (NZ) (C=captain): E 1994, 1999C, 2004C; A 1997-98C, 2001-02C, 2004-05C; SA 1993-94 (Cant), 1994-95, 2000-01C; WI 1995-96; I 1995-96, 1999-00C, 2003-04C; P 1996-97; SL 1997-98C, 2002-03C; Z 1997-98C, 2000-01C. 1000 (1): 1091 (2001). HS 274* (*see Tests*). CC HS 151 M v Notts (Nottingham) 2001. LO HS 139* Y v Warwks (Leeds) 2003. LO BB (NZ) 1-3.

FRANKS, Paul John (Southwell Minster CS), b Mansfield 3 Feb 1979. 6'2". LHB, RMF. Debut 1996; cap 1999. Canterbury 2002-03. YC 2000. **LOI**: 1 (2000); HS 4 v WI (Nottingham) 2000. F-c Tours (Eng A): SA 1998-99; WI 2000-01; NZ 1999-00; B 1999-00. HS 123* v Leics (Leicester) 2003. 50 wkts (2); most – 63 (1999). BB 7-56 v Middx (Lord's) 2000. Hat-trick 1997. Awards: CGT 2. LO HS 84* v Lincs (Lincoln) 2003 (CGT). LO BB 6-27 v Durham (Chester-le-St) 2000 (NL).

GALLIAN, Jason Edward Riche (Pittwater House S, Sydney; Keble C, Oxford), b Manly, Sydney, Australia 25 Jun 1971. Qualified for England 1994. 6'0". RHB, RM. Lancashire 1990-97, taking wicket of D.A.Hagan (OU) with his first ball; cap 1994. Debut 1998; captain 1998 (part) to 2004; benefit 2005. Captained Australia YC v England YC 1989-90, scoring 158* in 1st 'Test'. **Tests**: 3 (1995 to 1995-96); HS 28 v SA (Pt Elizabeth) 1995-96. F-c Tours: A 1996-97 (Eng A); I 1995-96 (La); SA 1995-96 (part); I 1994-95 (Eng A); P 1995-96 (Eng A). 1000 runs (5); most – 1156 (1996). HS 312 La v Derbys (Manchester) 1996 (record score at Old Trafford). Nt HS 190 v Derbys (Nottingham) 2004. BB 6-115 La v Surrey (Southport) 1996. Nt BB 2-28 v Warwks (Nottingham) 1999. Awards: CGT 2; BHC 2. LO HS 134 La v Notts (Manchester) 1995 (BHC). LO BB 5-15 La v Minor C (Leek) 1995 (BHC).

HARRIS, Andrew James (Hadfield CS; Glossopdale Community C), b Ashton-under-Lyne, Lancs 26 Jun 1973. 6'1". RHB, RM. Derbyshire 1994-99; cap 1996. Nottinghamshire debut/cap 2000. F-c Tour: A 1996-97 (Eng A). HS 41* v Northants (Northampton) 2002. Dismissed 'Timed Out' v DU (Nottingham) 2003 – third instance in f-c cricket. 50 wkts (2); most – 72 (1996). BB 7-54 (11-122 match) v Northants (Nottingham) 2002. Award: CGT 1. LO HS 16* v Kent (Tunbridge Wells) 2002 (NL). LO BB 5-35 v Hants (Nottingham) 2000 (NL).

HODGKINSON, Richard (West Notts C), b Mansfield 9 Dec 1983. RHB, RFM. Nottinghamshire staff 2003 – awaiting first-class debut. LO HS – and LO BB 2-36 Notts CB v Oxon (Oxford) 2001.

NQHUSSEY, David John, b Morley, Perth, Australia 15 Jul 1977. Younger brother of M.E.K.Hussey (*see DURHAM*). RHB, OB. Victoria 2002-03 to date. Nottinghamshire debut (and cap) 2004 scoring 107* v Oxford UCCE (Oxford) – UK debut. 1000 runs (1): 1315 (2004). HS 212* Vic v NSW (Newcastle) 2003-04. Nt HS 170 v Hants (Nottingham) 2004 (scored 170, 116 and 140 in successive innings). BB 1-6 Vic and Nt (not CC). LO HS 118* Sussex CB v Essex CB (Chelmsford) 2001 (CGT). LO BB 3-48 Sussex CB v Glos (Horsham) 2001 (CGT).

McMAHON, Paul Joseph (Trinity RC CS, Nottingham; Wadham C, Oxford), b Wigan, Lancs 12 Mar 1983. 6'2". RHB, OB. Debut 2002. Oxford UCCE 2003-04; captain 2004; blue 2003-04. British U 2004. HS 99 OU v CU (Oxford) 2004. Nt HS 30 v Middlesex (Lord's) 2003. BB 4-59 v Essex (Chelmsford) 2003. LO HS 0 and LO BB – (NL).

NOON, Wayne Michael (Caistor S), b Grimsby, Lincs 5 Feb 1971. 5'9". RHB, WK. Northamptonshire 1989-93. Nottinghamshire debut 1994; cap 1995; benefit 2003. Canterbury 1994-95. Worcs 2nd XI debut when aged 15yr 199d. F-c Tours: SA 1991-92 (Nh), 1996-97 (Nt). No f-c appearances 2004. HS 83 v Northants (Northampton) 1997. LO HS 46 v Warwks (Birmingham) 1998 (BHC).

PATEL, Samit Rohit (Worksop C), b Leicester 30 Nov 1984. 5'8". RHB, SLA. Debut 2002. Notts 2nd XI debut 1999 when aged 14yr 274d. No f-c appearances 2004. HS 55 v Lancs (Nottingham) 2003 – on CC debut. LO HS 44 v Somerset (Nottingham) 2003 (NL). LO BB 2-14 v Yorks (Leeds) 2002 (NL).

READ, Christopher Mark Wells (Torquay GS, Bath U), b Paignton, Devon 10 Aug 1978. 5'8". RHB, WK. Gloucestershire (L-O) 1997. Nottinghamshire debut 1998; cap 1999. Devon 1995-97. **Tests:** 11 (1999 to 2003-04); HS 38* v B (Chittagong) 2003-04. **LOI:** 28 (1999-00 to 2003-04); HS 30* v SA (Manchester) 2003. F-c Tours: SA 1998-99 (Eng A), 1999-00; WI 2000-01 (Eng A); SL 1997-98 (Eng A), 2002-03 (ECB Acad), 2003-04; Z 1998-99 (Eng A); B 2003-04; K 1997-98 (Eng A). HS 160 v Warwks (Nottingham) 1999. Award: CGT 1. LO HS 119* v Northants (Northampton) 2003 (NL).

SHRECK, Charles Edward (Truro S), b Truro, Cornwall 6 Jan 1978. 6'7". RHB, RFM. Cornwall 1997-2002. Nottinghamshire debut 2003. Award: CGT 1. HS 19 v Essex (Chelmsford) 2003. BB 6-46 v Durham (Chester-le-St) 2004. LO HS 9 Cornwall v Cumb (Netherfield) 1999 (CGT). LO BB 5-19 Cornwall v Worcs (Truro) 2002 (CGT). Took 5-35 v Worcs (Nottingham) 2002 (NL) – on 1st XI debut.

SIDEBOTTOM, Ryan Jay (King James's GS, Almondbury), b Huddersfield, Yorks 15 Jan 1978. Son of A.Sidebottom (Yorks, OFS and England 1973-91). 6'3". LHB, LFM. Yorkshire 1997-2003; cap 2000. Nottinghamshire debut/cap 2004. **Tests:** 1 (2001); HS 4 v P (Lord's) 2001; **LOI:** 2 (2001-02); HS 2*; BB 1-42 (twice). F-c Tour (Eng A): WI 2000-01. HS 54 Y v Glam (Cardiff) 1998. Nt HS 15* and BB 5-86 v Glam (Nottingham) 2004. BB 7-97 Y v Derbys (Leeds) 2003. LO HS 30* Y v Glam (Leeds) 2002 (NL). LO BB 6-40 Y v Glam (Cardiff) 1998 (SL).

SINGH, Anurag (King Edward's, Birmingham; Gonville & Caius C, Cambridge), b Kanpur, India 9 Sep 1975. 5'11½". RHB, OB. Warwickshire 1995-2000. Cambridge U 1996-98; blue 1996-97-98; captain 1997-98. British U 1998 (captain). Worcestershire 2001-03. Nottinghamshire debut 2004. 1000 runs (2); most – 1167 (2002). HS 187 Wo v Glos (Bristol) 2002. Nt HS 112 v Glam (Cardiff) 2004. Awards: CGT 1; BHC 1. LO HS 123 Brit U v Somerset (Taunton) 1996 (BHC).

NQSMITH, Gregory James (Pretoria BHS; Pretoria Technikon), b Pretoria, South Africa 30 Oct 1971. ECB qualified – British passport. 6'4". RHB, LFM. N Transvaal/Northerns 1993-94 to date. Nottinghamshire debut/cap 2001. F-c Tour (SA A): E 1996. HS 68 NT v WP (Pretoria) 1995-96. Nt HS 44* v Sussex (Nottingham) 2001. 50 wkts (2): most – 51 (2003). BB 8-53 (11-74 match) v Essex (Nottingham) 2002. Awards: BHC 2. LO HS 17* v Durham (Chester-le-St) 2004 (NL). LO BB 5-11 NT v GW (Kimberley) 1995-96.

SMITH, Will Rew (Bedford S; Collingwood C, Durham), b Luton, Beds 28 Sep 1982. 5'9". RHB, OB. Debut 2002 – awaiting CC debut. Durham UCCE 2003 –04; captain 2004. British U 2004. Notts 2nd XI debut 1999 when aged 16y 309d. HS 48 DU v Durham (Chester-le-ST) 2004. Nt HS 38* v WI A (Nottingham) 2002 – on debut. BB 2-83 DU v Derbys (Derby) 2004. LO HS 16 v Durham (Nottingham) 2002 (NL).

‡SWANN, Graeme Peter (Sponne SS, Towcester), b Northampton 24 Mar 1979. Son of R.Swann (Northumberland 1969-72; Bedfordshire 1988-95); younger brother of A.J.Swann (see LANCASHIRE). 6'0". RHB, OB. Northamptonshire 1998-04; cap 1999. Bedfordshire 1996. **LOI:** 1 (1999-00); dnb v SA (Bloemfontein) 1999-00. F-c Tours (Eng A): SA 1998-99, 1999-00 (Eng); WI 2000-01 (part); Z 1998-99. HS 183 Nh v Glos (Bristol) 2002 – including 114 before lunch on third day. 50 wkts (1): 57 (1999). BB 7-33 Nh v Derbys (Northampton) 2003. LO HS 83 Nh v Leics (Northampton) 2001 (NL). LO BB 5-35 Nh v Durham (Chester-le-St) 1999 (NL).

WARREN, Russell John (Kingsthorpe Upper S), b Northampton 10 Sep 1971. 6'1". RHB, OB. Northamptonshire 1992-2002; cap 1995. Nottinghamshire debut 2003. Cap 2004. 1000 runs (1): 1303 (2001). HS 201* Nh v Glam (Northampton) 1996. Award: CGT 1. Nt HS 134 v Leics (Nottingham) 2004. LO HS 100* Nh v Ire (Northampton) 1994 (NWT).

RELEASED/RETIRED continued on p 79

73

NOTTINGHAMSHIRE 2004

RESULTS SUMMARY

	Place	Won	Lost	Tied	Drew	No Result
County Championship (2nd Division)	1st	9	2		5	
All First-Class Matches		9	2		6	
C & G Trophy	3rd Round					
National League (2nd Division)	3rd	9	4	1		4
Twenty20 Cup	6th in North Division					

COUNTY CHAMPIONSHIP AVERAGES

BATTING AND FIELDING

Cap		M	I	NO	HS	Runs	Avge	100	50	Ct/St
2004	D.J.Hussey	16	22	3	170	1208	63.57	6	2	24
2002	K.P.Pietersen	14	19	1	167	965	53.61	4	3	17
1999	C.M.W.Read	13	18	2	130	807	50.43	2	6	35/3
1998	J.E.R.Gallian	16	24	2	190	1032	46.90	3	7	16
2000	D.J.Bicknell	16	24	1	175	1066	46.34	5	1	4
2004	M.A.Ealham	15	19	1	139	819	45.50	3	3	13
2004	R.J.Warren	12	17	1	134	697	43.56	2	3	4
1999	P.J.Franks	16	21	5	57*	610	38.12	–	5	2
–	A.Singh	5	8	1	112*	332	47.42	1	2	3
–	R.J.Logan	3	4	2	25*	45	22.50	–	–	3
2001	G.J.Smith	12	12	3	35	201	22.33	–	–	1
2002	S.C.G.MacGill	14	12	2	28	126	12.60	–	–	2
–	C.E.Shreck	7	6	4	13*	16	8.00	–	–	1
2004	R.J.Sidebottom	10	10	2	15*	49	6.12	–	–	3

Also batted: D.Alleyne (3 matches) 27, 14*, 28 (8 ct); A.J.Harris (2 – cap 2000) 1*, 13, 10; P.J.McMahon (1) 0*, 0 (1 ct); B.M.Shafayat (1) 13, 3.

BOWLING

	O	M	R	W	Avge	Best	5wI	10wM
C.E.Shreck	216	42	793	29	27.34	6- 46	2	–
R.J.Sidebottom	258	59	859	30	28.63	5- 86	1	–
P.J.Franks	341.1	67	1251	42	29.78	7- 72	2	–
G.J.Smith	315.1	63	1109	34	32.61	5- 35	2	–
M.A.Ealham	304	85	910	26	35.00	4- 43	–	–
R.J.Logan	75.1	9	353	10	35.30	4- 34	–	–
S.C.G.MacGill	400	74	1395	39	35.76	7-109	2	1
Also bowled:								
A.J.Harris	67	15	196	9	21.77	4- 22	–	–
D.J.Bicknell	39.4	2	135	6	22.50	3- 33	–	–
K.P.Pietersen	81.5	7	365	7	52.14	3- 72	–	–

D.J.Hussey 64.2-5-284-1; P.J.McMahon 43-4-169-3; B.M.Shafayat 2-0-16-0.

The First-Class Averages (pp 121–136) give the records of Nottinghamshire players in all first-class county matches (Nottinghamshire's other opponents being Oxford UCCE), with the exception of W.R.Smith whose only first-class appearances were for Durham UCCE and BUSA, P.J.McMahon whose full county figures are as above, and:

K.P.Pietersen 15-20-1-167-1027-54.05-4-4-17ct. 81.5-7-365-7-52.14-3/72.

NOTTINGHAMSHIRE RECORDS

FIRST-CLASS CRICKET

Highest Total	For 739-7d		v	Leics	Nottingham	1903
	V 781-7d		by	Northants	Northampton	1995
Lowest Total	For 13		v	Yorkshire	Nottingham	1901
	V 16		by	Derbyshire	Nottingham	1879
	16		by	Surrey	The Oval	1880
Highest Innings	For 312*	W.W.Keeton	v	Middlesex	The Oval	1939
	V 345	C.G.Macartney	for	Australians	Nottingham	1921

Highest Partnership for each Wicket

1st	406*	D.J.Bicknell/G.E.Welton	v	Warwicks	Birmingham	2000
2nd	398	A.Shrewsbury/W.Gunn	v	Sussex	Nottingham	1890
3rd	369	W.Gunn/J.R.Gunn	v	Leics	Nottingham	1903
4th	361	A.O.Jones/J.R.Gunn	v	Essex	Leyton	1905
5th	266	A.Shrewsbury/W.Gunn	v	Sussex	Hove	1884
6th	372*	K.P.Pietersen/J.E.Morris	v	Derbyshire	Derby	2001
7th	301	C.C.Lewis/B.N.French	v	Durham	Chester-le-St	2000
8th	220	G.F.H.Heane/R.Winrow	v	Somerset	Nottingham	1935
9th	170	J.C.Adams/K.P.Evans	v	Somerset	Taunton	1994
10th	152	E.B.Alletson/W.Riley	v	Sussex	Hove	1911
	152	U.Afzaal/A.J.Harris	v	Worcs	Nottingham	2000

Best Bowling	For 10-66	K.Smales	v	Glos	Stroud	1956
(Innings)	V 10-10	H.Verity	for	Yorkshire	Leeds	1932
Best Bowling	For 17-89	F.C.Matthews	v	Northants	Nottingham	1923
(Match)	V 17-89	W.G.Grace	for	Glos	Cheltenham	1877

Most Runs – Season		2620	W.W.Whysall	(av 53.46)	1929
Most Runs – Career		31592	W.W.Whysall	(av 35.69)	1902-32
Most 100s – Season		9	W.W.Whysall		1928
		9	M.J.Harris		1971
		9	B.C.Broad		1990
Most 100s – Career		65	J.Hardstaff jr		1930-55
Most Wkts – Season		181	B.Dooland	(av 14.96)	1954
Most Wkts – Career		1653	T.G.Wass	(av 20.34)	1896-1920
Most Career W-K Dismissals		957	T.W.Oates	(733 ct/224 st)	1897-1925
Most Career Catches in the Field		466	A.O.Jones		1892-1914

LIST 'A' LIMITED-OVERS CRICKET

Highest Total	CGT	344-6		v	Northumb	Jesmond	1994
	BHC	296-6		v	Kent	Nottingham	1989
	NL	329-6		v	Derbyshire	Nottingham	1993
Lowest Total	CGT	123		v	Yorkshire	Scarborough	1969
	BHC	74		v	Leics	Leicester	1987
	NL	66		v	Yorkshire	Bradford	1969
Highest Innings	CGT	149*	D.W.Randall	v	Devon	Torquay	1988
	BHC	130*	C.E.B.Rice	v	Scotland	Glasgow	1982
	NL	167*	P.Johnson	v	Kent	Nottingham	1993
Best Bowling	CGT	6-10	K.P.Evans	v	Northumb	Jesmond	1994
	BHC	6-22	M.K.Bore	v	Leics	Leicester	1980
		6-22	C.E.B.Rice	v	Northants	Northampton	1981
	NL	6-12	R.J.Hadlee	v	Lancashire	Nottingham	1980

SOMERSET

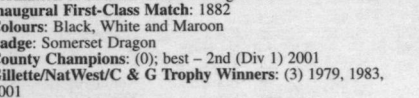

Formation of Present Club: 18 August 1875
Inaugural First-Class Match: 1882
Colours: Black, White and Maroon
Badge: Somerset Dragon
County Champions: (0); best – 2nd (Div 1) 2001
Gillette/NatWest/C & G Trophy Winners: (3) 1979, 1983, 2001
Benson and Hedges Cup Winners: (2) 1981, 1982
National League (Div 1) Winners: (0); best – 4th 2001
Sunday League Winners: (1) 1979
Twenty20 Cup Winners: (0); best – 4th in Group 2004
Match Awards: CGT 63; BHC 70

Chief Executive: P.W.Anderson, County Ground, Taunton TA1 1JT • Tel: 01823 272946 • Fax: 01823 332395 • Email: enquiries@somersetcountycc.co.uk • Web: www.somersetcountycc.co.uk

First XI Coach: M.Garaway. **Director of Academy:** K.J.Shine. **Captain:** G.C.Smith. **Vice-Captain:** *tba*. **Overseas Players:** N.A.M.McLean and G.C.Smith (reserve – S.T.Jayasuriya). **2005 Beneficiary:** none. **Head Groundsman:** P.W.Frost. **Scorer:** G.A.Stickley. ‡ New registration. ^NQ Not qualified for England.

ANDREW, Gareth Mark (Ansford Community S; Richard Huish C), b Yeovil 27 Dec 1983. 6'0". LHB, RMF. Debut 2003. Somerset 2nd XI debut 1999 when aged 15y 247d. HS 44 and BB 4-63 v SLA (Taunton) 2004. CC HS 15 v Durham (Chester-le-St) 2004. CC BB 3-14 v Derbys (Taunton) 2003. LO HS 23 v Hants (Southampton) 2003 (NL). LO BB 4-48 v Scot (Taunton) 2004 (NL).

BLACKWELL, Ian David (Brookfield Community S), b Chesterfield, Derbys 10 Jun 1978. 6'2". LHB, SLA. Derbyshire 1997-99. Somerset debut 2000; cap 2001. **LOI:** 18 (2002-03 to 2003-04); HS 82 v I (Colombo) 2002-03; BB 3-26 v A (Adelaide) 2002-03. 1000 runs (1): 1160 (2003). HS 247* v Derbys (Taunton) 2003 – off 156 balls and including 204 off 98 balls in reduced post-lunch session. BB 7-90 v Glam (Taunton) 2004 and 7-90 v Notts (Nottingham) 2004. Awards: CGT 1; BHC 1. LO HS 111 v Sussex (Hove) 2003 (NL). LO BB 4-24 v Kent (Taunton) 2002 (NL)

BURNS, Michael (Walney CS), b Barrow-in-Furness, Lancs 6 Feb 1969. 6'0". RHB, RM, WK. Cumberland 1988-90. Warwickshire 1992-96. Somerset debut 1997; cap 1999; captain 2003-04. Scored earliest hundred in UK f-c matches (160 v OU (Taunton) on 7 Apr 2000). 1000 runs (2): most – 1133 (2003). HS 221 v Yorks (Bath) 2001. BB 6-54 v Leics (Taunton) 2001. Awards: CGT 1; BHC 1. LO HS 115* v Middx (Taunton) 1997 (SL). LO BB 4-39 v Glos (Taunton) 1997 (SL).

CADDICK, Andrew Richard (Papanui HS), b Christchurch, NZ 21 Nov 1968. Son of English emigrants – qualified for England 1992. 6'5". RHB, RFM. Debut 1991; cap 1992; benefit 1999. Represented NZ in 1987-88 Youth World Cup. *Wisden* 2000. **ECB contracts 2000-01-02-03. Tests:** 62 (1993 to 2002-03); HS 49* v A (Birmingham) 2001; BB 7-46 v SA (Durban) 1999-00. **LOI:** 54 (1993 to 2002-03); HS 36 v A (Oval) 2001; BB 4-19 v SA (Johannesburg) 1999-00. F-c Tours: A 1992-93 (Eng A), 2002-03; SA 1999-00; WI 1993-94, 1997-98; NZ 1996-97, 2001-02; P 2000-01; SL 2000-01; Z 1996-97. HS 92 v Worcs (Worcester) 1995. 50 wkts (9) inc 100 (1): 105 (1998). BB 9-32 (12-120 match) v Lancs (Taunton) 1993. Awards: CGT 2. LO HS 39 v Hants (Taunton) 1996 (SL). LO BB 6-30 v Glos (Taunton) 1992 (NWT).

DURSTON, Wesley John (Millfield S; University C, Worcester), b Taunton 6 Oct 1980. 5'10". RHB, OB. Debut 2002. HS 55 v WI A (Taunton) 2002 – on debut. CC HS 47 v Notts (Nottingham) 2004. BB 3-23 v SL A (Taunton) 2004. CC BB 1-16. LO HS 51* v Middx (Southgate) 2003 (NL). LO BB 1-32 Somerset CB v Staffs (Walsall) 2000 (CGT).

EDWARDS, Neil James (Cape Cornwall CS; Richard Huish C), b Treliske, Cornwall 14 Oct 1983. 6'3". LHB, RM. Debut 2002. HS 160 v Hants (Taunton) 2003. BB 1-16.

FRANCIS, John Daniel (King Edward VI S, Southampton; Durham U; Loughborough U), b Bromley, Kent 13 Nov 1980. Younger brother of S.R.G.Francis. 5'11". LHB, SLA. Hampshire 2001-03. British U 2002-03. Loughborough UCCE 2003. Somerset debut 2004. HS 110 v Hants (Taunton) 2004. BB (H) 1-1. Sm BB 1-4. LO HS 103* H v Northants (Southampton) 2002 (NL).

FRANCIS, Simon Richard George (Yardley Court, Tonbridge; King Edward VI S, Southampton; Durham U), b Bromley, Kent 15 Aug 1978. Elder brother of J.D.Francis. 6'2". RHB, RMF. Hampshire 1997-2000. British U 1998-99. Somerset debut 2002. F-c Tour (Eng A): I 2003-04. HS 44 v Yorks (Taunton) 2003. BB 5-42 v Glam (Taunton) 2004. Hat-trick 2003. LO HS 33* v Derbys (Taunton) 2003 (NL). LO BB 8-66 v Derbys (Derby) 2004 (CGT) – record l-o Sm analysis.

GAZZARD, Carl Matthew (Mounts Bay CS, Penzance; Richard Huish C), b Penzance, Cornwall 15 Apr 1982. 6'0". RHB, WK. Debut 2002. Cornwall 1998 to date. HS 44* v SL A (Taunton) 2004. CC HS 41 v Northants (Taunton) 2003. LO HS 157 v Derbys (Derby) 2004 (NL).

HILDRETH James Charles (Millfield S), b Milton Keynes, Bucks 9 Sep 1984. 5'10", RHB, RMF. Debut 2003. HS 108 v Notts (Nottingham) 2004. BB 2-39 v Hants (Taunton) 2004. LO HS 85 v Notts (Nottingham) 2004 (NL). LO BB (Somerset CB) 1-44 (CGT).

JOHNSON, Richard Leonard (Sunbury Manor S; S Pelthorne C), b Chertsey, Surrey 29 Dec 1974. 6'2". RHB, RFM. Middlesex 1992-2000; cap 1995. Somerset debut/cap 2001. **Tests**: 3 (2003 to 2003-04); HS 26 v SL (Galle) 2003-04; BB 6-33 v Z (Chester-le-St) 2003 on debut, including wickets with his third and fourth balls. Hit first ball in Test cricket for four. **LOI**: 10 (2003 to 2003-04); HS 10 v SA (Manchester) 2003; BB 3-22 v B (Dhaka) 2003-04. Took wicket with his second ball in LOI. F-c Tours: I 1994-95 (Eng A – *part*), 2001-02; SL 2003-04, B 2003-04. HS 118 v Glos (Bristol) 2003 (100 off 75 balls). Won Walter Lawrence Trophy 2004 for 63-ball hundred v Durham (Chester-le-St). 50 wkts (4); most – 62 (2001). BB 10-45 M v Derbys (Derby) 1994 (second youngest to take all ten wickets in any f-c match). Sm BB 7-43 (10-75 match) v Hants (Bath) 2002. Award: CGT 1. LO HS 53 v Derbys (Derby) 2003 (NL). LO BB 5-50 M v Kent (Lord's) 1997 (NWT).

LARAMAN, Aaron William (Enfield GS), b Enfield, Middx 10 Jan 1979. 6'5". RHB, RFM. Middlesex 1998-2002. Somerset debut 2003. HS 148* v Glos (Taunton) 2004. BB 5-58 v Derbys (Taunton) 2004. LO HS 50* v Derbys (Derby) 2004 (CGT). LO BB 6-42 M v Glam (Cardiff) 2000 (NL).

NQ**McLEAN, Nixon** Alexei McNamara (Crapan SS, St Vincent), b Stubbs, St Vincent 20 Jul 1973. 6'4". LHB, RFM. Windward Is 1991-92 to 2000-01. Hampshire 1998-99; cap 1998. KwaZulu-Natal 2001-02 to date. Somerset debut/cap 2003. **Tests** (WI): 19 (1997-98 to 2000-01); HS 46 v P (Georgetown) 1999-00; BB 3-53 v SA (Cape Town) 1998-99. **LOI** (WI): 45 (1996-97 to 2002-03); HS 50* v Z (Canterbury) 2000; BB 3-21 v Z (Perth) 2000-01. F-c Tours (WI): **E** 2000; A 1996-97, 2000-01; SA 1997-98 (WI A), 1998-99. HS 76 v Glos (Taunton) 2003. 50 wkts (2): most – 65 (2003). BB 7-28 WI v FS (Bloemfontein) 1998-99. UK BB 6-79 (11-124 match) Sm v Yorks (Scarborough) 2004. LO HS 50* (*see LOI*). LO BB 5-26 WI Select XI v P (St John's) 1999-00.

MUNDAY, Michael Kenneth (Truro S, Cornwall; Corpus Christi C, Oxford), b Nottingham 22 Oct 1984. 5'7½". RHB, LB. Oxford U 2003-04; blue 2003-4. Awaiting Somerset debut. Cornwall 2001-03. HS 14 OU v Surrey (Oxford) 2004. BB 5-83 OU v CU (Cambridge) 2003. LO HS – and BB 1-39 Cornwall v Sussex (Truro) 2001 (CGT).

PARSONS, Keith Alan (The Castle S, Taunton; Richard Huish C), b Taunton 2 May 1973. Identical twin brother of K.J.Parsons (Somerset staff 1992-94). 6'1". RHB, RM. Debut 1992; cap 1999; benefit 2004. HS 193* v WI (Taunton) 2000. CC·HS 139 v Northants (Taunton) 2001. BB 5-13 v Lancs (Taunton) 2000. Awards: CGT 2. LO HS 121 v Worcs (Taunton) 2002 (CGT). LO BB 5-39 v Derbys (Derby) 2004 (NL).

PARSONS, Michael (Ladymead Community S, Taunton; Richard Huish C), b Taunton 26 Nov 1984. 5'11". RHB, RMF. Somerset l-o debut 2002 – awaiting f-c debut. LO HS 1* (NL). LO BB 3-70 Somerset CB v Cornwall (Camborne) 2002.

‡NOSMITH, Graeme Craig (King Edward VII S, Johannesburg), b Johannesburg. South Africa 1 Feb 1981. 6'3". LHB, OB. UCB Invitation XI 1999-00, scoring 187 on debut v GW (Kimberley). W Province 2000-01 to 2003-04. WP/Boland 2004-05. Gauteng (l-o) 1999-00. Somerset captain 2005. *Wisden* 2003. **Tests** (SA): 33 (2001-02 to 2004-05, 25 as captain); HS 277 v E (Birmingham) 2003; BB 1-9. **LOI** (SA): 63 (2001-02 to 2004-05, 41 as captain); HS 115* v E (E London) 2004-05; BB 1-24. F-c Tours (SA) (C=captain): E 2003C; WI 2003-04C; NZ 2003-04C; I 2004-05C; P 2003-04C; SL 2004C; B 2002-03C. HS 277 (*see Tests*). BB 1-9 (*see Tests*). LO HS 117* WP v N West (Cape Town) 2001-02. LO BB 3-35 WP v FS (Bloemfontein) 2001-02.

NOSUPPIAH, Arul Vivasvan (Exeter U), b Kuala Lumpur, Malaysia 30 Aug 1983. Son of R.Suppiah (Kuala Lumpur). Brother of R.V.Suppiah (Malaysia – vice-captain). 6'0". RHB, SLA. Somerset debut 2002. Malaysia 1999-2001. HS 33 v SL A (Taunton) 2004. CC HS 21 v Lancs (Taunton) 2002 – on debut. BB 3-46 v WI A (Taunton) 2002. CC BB 2-36 v Leics (Leicester) 2004. LO HS 70 Somerset CB v Cornwall (Camborne) 2002 (CGT). LO BB 2-36 v Leics (Leicester) 2002 (NL).

TRESCOTHICK, Marcus Edward (Sir Bernard Lovell S), b Keynsham 25 Dec 1975. 6'2". LHB, RM. Debut 1993; cap 1999; joint captain 2002. PCA 2000. **ECB contracts 2001-02-03-04-05. Tests:** 59 (2000 to 2004-05, 1 as captain); HS 219 v SA (Oval) 2003; BB 1-34. **LOI:** 99 (2000 to 2004-05, 3 as captain); HS 137 v P (Lord's) 2001; BB 2-7 v Z (Manchester) 2000. F-c Tours: A 2002-03; SA 1004-05; WI 2003-04; NZ 1999-00 (Eng A), 2001-02; I 2001-02; P 2000-01; SL 2000-01, 2003-04; B 1999-00 (Eng A), 2003-04. HS 219 (*see Tests*). Sm HS 190 v Middx (Taunton) 1999. BB 4-36 (inc hat-trick) v Young A (Taunton) 1995. CC BB 4-82 v Yorks (Leeds) 1998. Hat-trick 1995. Awards: CGT 4; BHC 3. LO HS 137 (*see LOI*). LO BB 4-50 v Northants (Northampton) 2000 (NL).

TURNER, Robert Julian (Millfield S; Magdalene C, Cambridge), b Malvern, Worcs 25 Nov 1967. 6'1½". RHB, WK. Brother of S.J.Turner (Somerset 1984-85). Cambridge U 1988-91; blue 1988-89-90-91; captain 1991. Somerset debut 1991; cap 1994; benefit 2002. Cambridgeshire 1990. F-c Tours (Eng A):· NZ 1999-00; B 1999-00. Held 7 catches in an innings v Northants (Taunton) 2001. 1000 runs (2); most – 1217 (1999). HS 144 v Kent (Taunton) 1997. Award: BHC 1. LO HS 70 v Glam (Cardiff) 1996 (BHC).

WOOD, Matthew James (Exmouth Community C; Exeter U), b Exeter, Devon 30 Sep 1980. 5'11". RHB, OB. Debut 2001. 2nd XI debut 1997 when aged 16y 345d. Devon 1998-2000. HS 196 v Kent (Taunton) 2002. LO HS 88* v Durham (Taunton) 2002 (NL).

RELEASED/RETIRED

(Registered players who made a first-class County appearance in 2004)

BOWLER, Peter Duncan (Scots C, Sydney, Aus; Daramalan C, Canberra, Aus; Nottingham Trent U), b Plymouth, Devon 30 Jul 1963. 6'1". RHB, OB, occ WK. Leicestershire 1986 – first to score hundred on f-c debut for Leics (100* and 62 v Hants). Tasmania 1986-87. Derbyshire 1988-94; cap 1989; scored 155* v CU (Cambridge) on debut – first instance of hundreds on debut for two counties. Somerset 1995-2004; cap 1995; captain 1997-98; benefit 2000. 1000 runs (10), inc 2000 (1): 2044 (1992). HS 241* De v Hants (Portsmouth) 1992. Sm HS 207 v Surrey (Taunton) 1996. BB 3-25 v Northants (Taunton) 1998. Awards: BHC 4. LO HS 138* De v Somerset (Derby) 1993 (SL). LO BB 3-31 De v Glos (Cheltenham) 1991 (SL).

COX, Jamie (Wynyard HS; Deakin U), b Burnie, Tasmania, Australia 15 Oct 1969. 6'0". RHB, OB. Tasmania 1987-88 to date; captain 2000-01 to date. Somerset 1999-2004; cap 1999; captain 1999-2002. F-c Tours: Z 1991-92 (Aus B), 1995-96 (Tas). 1000 runs (4+2); most – 1617 (1999). HS 250 v Notts (Nottingham) 2004. BB 3-46 v Middx (Taunton) 1999. Awards: CGT 2. LO HS 131 v Derbys (Derby) 2004 (CGT). LO BB 3-28 v Durham (Taunton) 1999 (NL).

DUTCH, Keith Philip (Nower Hill HS; Weald C), b Harrow, Middlesex 21 Mar 1973. 5'10". RHB, OB. Middlesex 1993-2000. Somerset 2001-04; cap 2001. MCC YC. HS 118 v Essex (Taunton) 2001. BB 6-62 M v Essex (Chelmsford) 2000. Sm BB 5-26 v Yorks (Scarborough) 2004. Award: CGT 1. LO HS 93 v Z (Taunton) 2003 (NL). LO BB 6-40 v Northants (Northampton) 2001 (NL).

HUNT, Thomas Aaron *'Thos'* (Acton HS: St Clement Danes S), b Melbourne, Australia 19 Jan 1982. 6'2". Resident in UK since 1985 (English parents). LHB, RMF. Middlesex 2002-03. Somerset 2004. No CC appearance. HS (M) 3. Sm HS 1*. BB 3-43 M v CU (Cambridge) 2002 – on debut. Sm BB 2-85 v LU (Taunton) 2004. LO HS (M) 0 (NL). LO BB (M) 1-24 (NL).

NQPONTING, Ricky Thomas (Brooks HS), b Launceston, Australia 19 Dec 1974. 5'10". RHB, OB. Tasmania 1992-93 to date. Awarded Somerset cap with contract 2004. **Tests** (A): 85 (1995-96 to 2004-05, 10 as captain); HS 257 v I (Melbourne) 2003 04; BB 1-0. **LOI** (A) : 217 (1994-95 to 2004-05, 86 as captain); HS 145 v Z (Delhi) 1997-98; BB 1-12. F-c Tours (A) (C=captain): E 1995 (Young Aus), 1997, 2001; SA 2001-02; WI 1994-95, 1998-99, 2002-03; NZ ; I 1996-97, 1997-98, 2000-01, 2004-05C (*part*); P 1998-99, 2002-03 (in SL/Sharjah); SL 1999-00, 2003-04; Z 1995-96 (Tas), 1999-00. HS 257 (*see Tests*). Sm HS 117 v Glam (Taunton) 2004. Scored 112 v Yorks (Scarborough) on Sm debut. BB 2-10 A v Bombay (Bombay) 2000-01. LO HS 145 (*see LOI*). LO BB 3-34 Tasmania v WA (Hobart) 1996-97 (MM).

T.Webley left the staff having made no Somerset appearances in 2004. N.D.Hancock (Devon) appeared in one NL game.

NOTTINGHAMSHIRE RELEASED/RETIRED (continued from p 73)

(Having made a first-class County appearance in 2004)

LOGAN, R.L. – *see HAMPSHIRE.*

NQMacGILL, Stuart Charles Glyndwr (Christ Church GS, Perth), b Mount Lawley, W Australia 25 Feb 1971. Grandson of C.W.T. (WA 1938-39), son of T.M.D. (WA 1968-69). 6'0". RHB, LBG. W Australia 1993-94. NSW 1996-97 to date. Somerset 1997 (unregistered). Devon 1997 to 1998 (NWT only). Nottinghamshire 2002-04; cap 2002. **Tests** (A): 33 (1997-98 to 2004-05); HS 43 v E (Melbourne) 1998-99; BB 7-50 (12-107 match) v E (Sydney) 1998-99. **LOI** (A): 3 (1999-00); HS 1 and BB 4-19 v P (Sydney) 1999-00 – on debut. F-c Tours (A): SA 2001-02; WI 1998-99, 2002-03; P 1998-99, 2002-03. HS 53 NSW v S Aus (Sydney) 2001-02. Nt HS 28 v Hants (Nottingham) 2004. 50 wkts (0+2): 60 (2002-03). BB 8-111 (14-165 match) v Middx (Nottingham) 2002. LO HS 26 v Durham (Chester-le-St) 2004 (NL). LO BB 5-40 NSW v ACT (Canberra) 1998-99.

PIETERSEN, K.P. – *see HAMPSHIRE.*

SHAFAYAT, B.M. – *see NORTHAMPTONSHIRE.*

D.S.Lucas (*see YORKSHIRE*) left the staff having made no f-c appearances in 2004.

SOMERSET 2004

RESULTS SUMMARY

	Place	Won	Lost	Tied	Drew	No Result
County Championship (2nd Division)	4th	4	5		7	
All First-Class Matches		5	5		8	
C & G Trophy	3rd Round					
National League (2nd Division)	8th	6	11			1
Twenty20 Cup	4th in Mid/West/Wales Division					

COUNTY CHAMPIONSHIP AVERAGES

BATTING AND FIELDING

Cap		M	I	NO	HS	Runs	Avge	100	50	Ct/St
–	R.T.Ponting	3	4	1	117	297	99.00	2	1	7
2001	I.D.Blackwell	10	14	2	131	745	62.08	2	5	3
1995	P.D.Bowler	14	24	6	187*	957	53.16	3	3	9
1999	J.Cox	12	19	1	250	841	46.72	2	4	6
–	J.C.Hildreth	13	20	2	108	760	42.22	2	5	12
–	J.D.Francis	8	13	1	110	500	41.66	2	3	6
–	M.J.Wood	9	13	3	113	402	40.20	1	2	4
1999	M.Burns	15	21	2	124*	732	38.52	1	4	17
1999	K.A.Parsons	3	4	1	55	114	38.00	–	1	2
2001	K.P.Dutch	6	8	1	72	248	35.42	–	2	2
2001	R.L.Johnson	13	11	1	101*	246	24.60	1	1	3
–	A.W.Laraman	9	8	2	66*	144	24.00	–	1	3
–	N.J.Edwards	8	16	–	87	380	23.75	–	1	8
1994	R.J.Turner	15	17	3	46	319	22.78	–	–	61/4
1992	A.R.Caddick	13	13	4	54	192	21.33	–	1	5
–	S.R.G.Francis	11	10	6	15	46	11.50	–	–	6
2003	N.A.M.McLean	10	11	3	22*	61	7.62	–	–	1

Also batted (1 match each): G.M.Andrew 15 (1 ct); W.J.Durston 47 (4 ct); C.M.Gazzard 18;
A.V.Suppiah 0.

BOWLING

	O	M	R	W	Avge	Best	5wI	10wM
K.P.Dutch	124	21	448	19	23.57	5-26	2	–
N.A.M.McLean	322.1	62	1127	43	26.20	6-79	3	1
A.W.Laraman	134	26	486	15	32.40	5-58	1	–
I.D.Blackwell	342.1	85	956	27	35.40	7-90	2	–
A.R.Caddick	534.3	98	1922	54	35.59	6-80	4	–
S.R.G.Francis	295.5	51	1201	33	36.39	5-42	2	–
R.L.Johnson	389.5	90	1323	36	36.75	7-69	2	–

Also bowled: G.M.Andrew 16-3-63-3; P.D.Bowler 2-1-2-0; M.Burns 40.4-6-149-3;
W.J.Durston 24-6-73-1; N.J.Edwards 15-1-68-1; J.D.Francis 15.3-3-55-1; J.C.Hildreth
17-1-76-2; K.A.Parsons 37-7-183-0; R.T.Ponting 5-2-6-0; A.V.Suppiah 7-0-36-2; M.J.Wood
2-0-6-0.

The First-Class Averages (pp 121–136) give the records of Somerset players in all first-class
county matches (Somerset's other opponents being Sri Lanka A and Loughborough UCCE),
with the exception of M.K.Munday, M.E.Trescothick and T.Webley whose only first-class
appearances were for Oxford UCCE, England and Cambridge UCCE respectively.

SOMERSET RECORDS

FIRST-CLASS CRICKET

Highest Total	For	705-9d		v	Hampshire	Taunton	2003
	V	811		by	Surrey	The Oval	1899
Lowest Total	For	25		v	Glos	Bristol	1947
	V	22		by	Glos	Bristol	1920
Highest Innings	For	322	I.V.A.Richards	v	Warwicks	Taunton	1985
	V	424	A.C.MacLaren	for	Lancashire	Taunton	1895

Highest Partnership for each Wicket

1st	346	H.T.Hewett/L.C.H.Palairet	v	Yorkshire	Taunton	1892
2nd	290	J.C.W.MacBryan/M.D.Lyon	v	Derbyshire	Burton upon T	1924
3rd	319	P.M.Roebuck/M.D.Crowe	v	Leics	Taunton	1984
4th	310	P.W.Denning/I.T.Botham	v	Glos	Taunton	1980
5th	235	J.C.White/C.C.C.Case	v	Glos	Taunton	1927
6th	265	W.E.Alley/K.E.Palmer	v	Northants	Northampton	1961
7th	279	R.J.Harden/G.D.Rose	v	Sussex	Taunton	1997
8th	172	I.V.A.Richards/I.T.Botham	v	Leics	Leicester	1983
	172	A.R.K.Pierson/P.S.Jones	v	N Zealanders	Taunton	1999
9th	183	C.H.M.Greetham/H.W.Stephenson	v	Leics	Weston-s-Mare	1963
	183	C.J.Tavaré/N.A.Mallender	v	Sussex	Hove	1990
10th	163	I.D.Blackwell/N.A.M.McLean	v	Derbyshire	Taunton	2003

Best Bowling	For	10- 49	E.J.Tyler	v	Surrey	Taunton	1895
(Innings)	V	10- 35	A.Drake	for	Yorkshire	Weston-s-Mare	1914
Best Bowling	For	16- 83	J.C.White	v	Worcs	Bath	1919
(Match)	V	17-137	W.Brearley	for	Lancashire	Manchester	1905

Most Runs – Season	2761	W.E.Alley	(av 58.74)	1961
Most Runs – Career	21142	H.Gimblett	(av 36.96)	1935-54
Most 100s – Season	11	S.J.Cook		1991
Most 100s – Career	49	H.Gimblett		1935-54
Most Wkts – Season	169	A.W.Wellard	(av 19.24)	1938
Most Wkts – Career	2166	J.C.White	(av 18.02)	1909-37
Most Career W-K Dismissals	1007	H.W.Stephenson	(698 ct/309 st)	1948-64
Most Career Catches in the Field	381	J.C.White		1909-37

LIST 'A' LIMITED-OVERS CRICKET

Highest Total	CGT	413-4		v	Devon	Torquay	1990
	BHC	349-7		v	Ireland	Taunton	1997
	NL	377-9		v	Sussex	Hove	2003
Lowest Total	CGT	58		v	Middlesex	Southgate	2000
	BHC	98		v	Middlesex	Lord's	1982
	NL	58		v	Essex	Chelmsford	1977
Highest Innings	CGT	162*	C.J.Tavaré	v	Devon	Torquay	1990
	BHC	177	S.J.Cook	v	Sussex	Hove	1990
	NL	175*	I.T.Botham	v	Northants	Wellingborough	1986
Best Bowling	CGT	8-66	S.R.G.Francis	v	Derbyshire	Derby	2004
	BHC	7-24	Mushtaq Ahmed	v	Ireland	Taunton	1997
	NL	6-24	I.V.A.Richards	v	Lancashire	Manchester	1983

SURREY

Formation of Present Club: 22 August 1845
Inaugural First-Class Match: 1864
Colours: Chocolate
Badge: Prince of Wales' Feathers
County Champions (since 1890): (18) 1890, 1891, 1892, 1894, 1895, 1899, 1914, 1952, 1953, 1954, 1955, 1956, 1957, 1958, 1971, 1999, 2000, 2002
Joint Champions: (1) 1950
Gillette/NatWest/C & G Trophy Winners: (1) 1982
Benson and Hedges Cup Winners: (3) 1974, 1997, 2001
National League (Div 1) Winners: (1) 2003
Sunday League Winners: (1) 1996
Twenty20 Cup Winners: (1) 2003
Match Awards: CGT 57; BHC 76

Chief Executive: P.C.J.Sheldon, Kennington Oval, London, SE11 5SS • Tel: 020 7582 6660 • Fax: 020 7735 7769 • E-mail: enquiries@surreycricket.com • Web: www.surreycricket.com

First XI Coach: S.J.Rixon. **Captain**: M.A.Butcher. **Vice-Captain**: M.R.Ramprakash. **Overseas Players**: Azhar Mahmood and Harbhajan Singh. **2005 Beneficiary**: M.A.Butcher. **Head Groundsman**: W.H.Gordon. **Scorer**: K.R.Booth. ‡ New registration. NQ Not qualified for England.

NQ**AZHAR MAHMOOD** SAGAR (F.G. No. 1 HS, Islamabad, b Multan, Pakistan 28 Feb 1975. 5'11". RHB, RFM. Islamabad 1993-94 to 1997-98, 2001-02. United Bank 1996-97. Rawalpindi 1998-99. PIA 1999-00 to 2001-02. Surrey debut 2002; cap 2004. **Tests** (P): 21 (1997-98 to 2001); HS 136 v SA (Johannesburg) 1997-98; BB 4-50 v E (Lord's) 2001. Scored 128* and 50* v SA (Rawalpindi) 1997-98 on debut. **LOI** (P): 139 (1996-97 to 2004-05); HS 67 v I (Adelaide) 1999-00; BB 6-18 v WI (Sharjah) 1999-00. F-c Tours (P): E 2001; A 1999-00; SA 1997-98; I 1998-99; SL 2000-01; Z 1997-98. HS 136 (*see Tests*). Sy HS 98 v Notts (Nottingham) 2003. 50 wkts (0+1): 59 (1996-97). BB 8-61 v Lancs (Oval) 2002. LO HS 100* P v Aus A (Perth) 1999-00. LO BB 6-18 (*see LOI*).

BATTY, Jonathan Neil (Wheatley Park S, Oxon; Repton S; Durham U; Keble C, Oxford), b Chesterfield, Derbys 18 Apr 1974. 5'10". RHB, WK. Minor C 1994. Comb U 1995. Oxford U 1996; blue 1996. Surrey debut 1997; cap 2001; captain 2004. Oxfordshire 1993-96. HS 168* v Essex (Chelmsford) 2003. BB 1-21. LO HS 66 v Essex and 66 v Northants – (Oval) 2004 (NL).

BENNING, James Graham Edward (Beacon S; Chesham S; Caterham S), b Mill Hill, N London 4 May 1983. 6'0". RHB, RM. Debut 2003. Buckinghamshire 2000-01. HS 128 and BB 1-28 v OU (Oxford) 2004. CC HS 47 v Essex (Oval) 2003. CC BB 1-39. LO HS 71 v Warwks (Guildford) 2004. BB 4-43 v Leics (Oval) 2003 (NL).

BICKNELL, Martin Paul (Robert Haining County SS), b Guildford 14 Jan 1969. Younger brother of D.J.Bicknell (*see NOTTINGHAMSHIRE*). 6'3". RHB, RFM. Debut 1986; cap 1989; benefit 1997. *Wisden* 2000. **Tests**: 4 (1993 to 2003); HS 15 v SA (Leeds) 2003; BB 4-84 v SA (Oval) 2003. **LOI**: 7 (1990-91); HS 31* v A (Perth) 1990-91; BB 3-55 v NZ (Christchurch) 1990-91. F-c Tours: A 1990-91; SA 1993-94 (Eng A); Z 1989-90 (Eng A). HS 141 v Essex (Chelmsford) 2003. 50 wkts (11); most – 72 (2001). BB 9-45 v CU (Oval) 1988. CC BB 9-47 (16-119 match) v Leics (Guildford) 2000. Took his 1000th f-c wicket 2004. Awards: BHC 3. LO HS 66* v Northants (Oval) 1991 (NWT). LO BB 7-30 v Glam (Oval) 1999 (NL).

BROWN, Alistair Duncan (Caterham S), b Beckenham, Kent 11 Feb 1970. 5'10". RHB, occ LB. Debut 1992; cap 1994; benefit 2002. **LOI:** 16 (1996 to 2001); HS 118 v I (Manchester) 1996. 1000 runs (7); most – 1382 (1993). HS 295* v Leics (Oakham) 2000 – record score (all levels) in Rutland. BB 1-11. Awards: CGT 1; BHC 4. LO HS 268 v Glam (Oval) 2002 (CGT) – world record 1-o score (160 balls, 12 sixes, 30 fours). LO BB 3-39 v Notts (Nottingham) 2000 (NL).

BUTCHER, Mark Alan (Trinity S; Archbishop Tenison's S, Croydon), b Croydon 23 Aug 1972. Son of A.R.Butcher (Surrey, Glamorgan and England 1972-92); brother of G.P.Butcher (Glamorgan 1994-98; Surrey 1999-2001). 5'11". LHB, RM/OB. Debut 1992; cap 1996; captain 2005; benefit 2005. **ECB contracts 2002-03-04-05. Tests:** 71 (1997 to 2004-05, 1 as captain); HS 173* v A (Leeds) 2001; BB 4-42 v A (Birmingham) 2001. F-c Tours: A 1996-97 (Eng A), 1998-99, 2002-03; SA 1999-00; WI 1997-98; NZ 2001-02; I 2001-02; SL 2003-04; B 2003-04. 1000 runs (7); most – 1604 (1996). HS 259 v Leics (Leicester) 1999. BB 5-86 v Lancs (Manchester) 2000. Awards: CGT 2; BHC 3. LO HS 104 v Yorks (Oval) 2003 (NL). LO BB 3-23 v Sussex (Oval) 1992 (SL).

CLARKE, Rikki (Broadwater SS; Godalming C), b Orsett, Essex 29 Sep 1981. 6'4". RHB, RFM. Debut 2002 – scoring 107* v CU (Cambridge). YC 2002. **Tests:** 2 (2003-04); HS 55 and BB 2-7 v B (Chittagong) 2003-04. **LOI:** 17 (2003 to 2004); HS 37 v SA (Birmingham) 2003; BB 2-28 v B (Dhaka) 2003-04. F-c Tours: WI 2003-04; SL 2003-04 (ECB Acad); B 2003-04. HS 153* v Somerset (Taunton) 2002. BB 4-21 v Leics (Leicester) 2003. LO HS 98* v Derbys (Derby) 2002 (NL). LO BB 4-50 v Glos (Oval) 2004 (NL).

CLINTON, Richard Selvey (Colfes S), b Sidcup, Kent 1 Sep 1981. Son of G.S.Clinton (Kent and Surrey 1974-90). 6'3". LHB, RM. Kent staff 1999-2000 – no f-c appearances. Essex 2001-02. Loughborough U. 2004. Surrey debut 2004. HS 107 Ex v CU (Cambridge) 2002. CC HS 73 v Worcs (Oval) 2004 – on Sy debut. BB 2-30 Ex v A (Chelmsford) 2001. CC BB – . LO HS 56 Ex v Durham (Ilford) 2001 (NL).

NQ**DERNBACH, Jade** Winston (St John the Baptist S), b Johannesburg, South Africa 3 Mar 1986. 6'1½". RHB, RMF. Italian passport. UK resident since 1998. Debut 2003 when aged 17 – awaiting CC debut. 'Sir Jack Hobbs Fair Play Award' 2003. HS 3 and BB 1-74 v Ind A (Oval) 2003.

DOSHI, Nayan Dilip, b Nottingham 6 Oct 1978. Son of D.R.Doshi (Bengal, Notts, Warwks, Saurashtra, Herts and India 1968-69 to 1986). Saurashtra 2001-02 to 2003-04. Surrey debut 2004. Buckinghamshire 2001. HS 29* v Lancs (Croydon) 2004. BB 7-110 (10-183 match) v Sussex (Hove) 2004. LO HS 38* Saurashtra v Baroda (Bombay) 2001-02. LO BB (Bucks) 1-12 (CGT).

†NQ**HARBHAJAN SINGH** PLAHA, b Jullundur City, India 3 Jul 1980. 6'0". RHB, OB. Punjab 1997-98 to date. **Tests** (I): 43 (1997-98 to 2004-05); HS 66 v Z (Bulawayo) 2001; BB 8-84 (15-217 match) v A (Madras) 2000-01. Took 28 wickets, including a hat-trick, in 2 Tests v Australia 2000-01. **LOI** (I): 93 (1997-98 to 2003-04); HS 46 v A (Vishakapatnam) 2000-01; BB 5-43 v E (Bombay) 2001-02. Tours (I): E 2002; A 2003-04; SA 2001-02; WI 2001-02; NZ 1998-99, 2002-03; SL 1998-99, 2001; Z 1998-99, 2001; B 2004-05. HS 84 Punjab v Haryana (Amritsar) 2000-01. UK HS 54 I v E (Nottingham) 2002. 50 wkts (0+1): 70 (2000-01). BB 8-84 (15-217 match) (see Tests). Hat-trick (India 2000-01). UK HS 84 I v Essex (Chelmsford) 2002. LO HS 46 (see LOI). LO BB 5-43 (see LOI).

HODD, Andrew John (Bexhill C), b Chichester, Sussex 12 Jan 1984. RHB, WK. Sussex 2003 (1 match). Surrey staff 2004. Awaiting Surrey and CC debuts. HS – Sx v Z (Hove) 2003. LO HS 3 Sx v WI (Hove) 2002.

‡**MILLER, Daniel** James (Ewell Castle S; Kingston-upon-Thames C; Loughborough U), b Hammersmith, London 12 Jun 1983. LHB, RFM. Summer contract 2005. Awaiting f-c debut. LO HS 1 v Northants (Croydon) 2002 (NL).

‡NQMOHAMMAD AKRAM AWAN, b Islamabad, Pakistan 10 Sep 1972. 6'2". RHB, RFM. Rawalpindi 1992-93 to 1998-99, 2001-02 to date. Allied Bank 1996-97 to 2000-01. Northamptonshire 1997. Essex 2003. Sussex 2004; cap 2004. **Tests** (P): 9 (1995-96 to 2001-02); HS 10* and BB 5-138 v A (Perth) 1999-00. **LOI** (P): 23 (1995-96 to 2000-01; HS 7*; BB 2-28 v I (Toronto) 1997. F-c Tours (P): E 1996; A 1995-96. HS 35* Sx v Warwks (Birmingham) 2004. BB 8-49 (10-142 match) Ex v Surrey (Oval) 2003. LO HS 33 Allied Bank v Faisalabad (Faisalabad) 1998-99. LO BB 4-19 Nh v Surrey (Northampton) 1997 (SL)

MURTAGH, Timothy James (John Fisher S; St Mary's C), b Lambeth 2 Aug 1981. Nephew of A.J.Murtagh (Hampshire and E Province 1973-7). 6'0". LHB, RFM. British U 2000-03. Surrey debut 2001. HS 74* v Middx (Oval) 2004. BB 6-86 Brit U v P (Nottingham) 2001. Sy BB 5-39 v Leics (Oval) 2002. LO HS 28 v Warwks (Birmingham) 2004 (NL). LO BB 4-31 v Warwks (Croydon) 2001 (NL).

NEWMAN, Scott Alexander (Trinity S, Croydon; Coulsdon C; Brighton U), b Epsom 3 Nov 1979. 6'2". LHB, RM. Debut 2002 – scoring 99 v Hants (Oval) 2002. F-c Tour (Eng A): I 2003-04. 1000 runs (1): 1277 (2004). HS 183 v Leics (Oval) 2002. LO HS 106 v Essex (Oval) 2004 (NL).

ORMOND, James (St Thomas More S, Nuneaton), b Walsgrave, Coventry, Warwks 20 Aug 1977. 6'3". RHB, RFM. Leicestershire 1995-2001; cap 1999. Surrey debut 2002; cap 2003. **Tests**: 2 (2001 to 2001-02); HS 18 v A (Oval) 2001; BB 1-70. F-c Tours: NZ 2001-02; I 2001-02; SL 1997-98 (Eng A); K 1997-98 (Eng A). HS 57 v Glos (Bristol) 2004. Sy HS 47 v Middx (Guildford) 2003. 50 wkts (4); most – 52 (1999, 2004). BB 6-33 (9-62 match) Le v Somerset (Leicester) 1998. Sy BB 6-34 v LU (Oval) 2003. Sy CC BB 6-62 v Worcs (Oval) 2004. Hat-trick (4 wkts in 6 balls) 2003. Awards: BHC 2. LO HS 18* Le v Somerset (Lord's) 2001 (CGT). LO BB 4-12 Le v Middx (Leicester) 1998 (SL).

RAMPRAKASH, Mark Ravin (Gayton HS; Harrow Weald SFC), b Bushey, Herts 5 Sep 1969. 5'9". RHB, RM. Middlesex 1987-2000; cap 1990; captain 1997-99. Surrey debut 2001 – scoring 146 v Kent (Oval); cap 2002. YC 1991. **ECB contract 2000. Tests**: 52 (1991 to 2001-02); HS 154 v WI (Bridgetown) 1997-98; BB 1-2. **LOI**: 18 (1991 to 2001-02); HS 51 v WI (Pt-of-Spain) 1997-98; BB 3-28 v Z (Harare) 2001-02. F-c Tours: A 1994-95 (part), 1998-99; SA 1995-96; WI 1991-92 (Eng A), 1993-94, 1997-98; NZ 1991-92, 2001-02; I 1994-95 (Eng A), 2001-02; P 1990-91 (Eng A); SL 1990-91 (Eng A). 1000 runs (14) inc 2000 (1): 2258 (1995). HS 279* v Notts (Croydon) 2003. BB 3-32 M v Glam (Lord's) 1998. Sy BB 2-35 v Northants (Northampton) 2004. Awards: CGT 3; BHC 4. LO HS 147* M v Worcs (Lord's) 1990 (SL). LO BB 5-38 M v Leics (Lord's) 1993 (SL).

SAKER, Neil Clifford (Raynes Park HS; Nescot C), b Tooting, London 20 Sep 1984. 6'4". RHB, RFM. Debut 2003. No f-c appearance 2004. HS 5. BB 1-71.

SALISBURY, Ian David Kenneth (Moulton CS), b Northampton 21 Jan 1970. 5'11". RHB, LBG. Sussex 1989-96; cap 1991. Surrey debut 1997; cap 1998. MCC YC. YC 1992. *Wisden* 1992. **Tests**: 15 (1992 to 2000-01); HS 50 v P (Manchester) 1992; BB 4-163 v WI (Georgetown) 1993-94. **LOI**: 4 (1992-93 to 1993-94); HS 5; BB 3-41 v WI (Pt-of-Spain) 1993-94. F-c Tours: WI 1991-92 (Eng A), 1993-94; I 1992-93; 1994-95 (Eng A); P 1990-91 (Eng A), 1995-96 (Eng A), 2000-01; SL 1990-91 (Eng A). HS 101* v Leics (Oval) 2003. 50 wkts (6); most – 87 (1992). BB 8-60 (12-91 match) v Somerset (Oval) 2000. Awards: CGT 1; BHC 2. LO HS 59* v Glam (Oval) 2004 (NL). LO BB 5-30 Sx v Leics (Leicester) 1992 (SL).

SAMPSON, Philip James (Pretoria BHS, SA), b Manchester 6 Sep 1980. 6'1". RHB, RFM. Debut 2002. Buckinghamshire 1999. HS 42 v CU (Cambridge) 2002 – on debut. CC HS 32* v Essex (Oval) 2003. BB 5-121 v Warwks (Guildford) 2004. LO HS 16 v Middx (Croydon) 2002 (NL). LO BB 3-42 v Kent (Oval) 2002 (BHC).

THORPE, Graham Paul (Weydon CS; Farnham SFC), b Farnham 1 Aug 1969. 5'10". LHB, RM. Debut 1988; cap 1991; benefit 2000. *Wisden* 1997. **ECB contracts 2001-02-04-05. Tests:** 98 (1993 to 2004-05); HS 200* v NZ (Christchurch) 2001-02; scored 114* v A (Nottingham) 1993 on debut. **LOI:** 82 (1993 to 2002, 3 as captain); HS 89 v Z (Brisbane) 1994-95 and 89 v H (Peshawar) 1995-96; BB 2-15 v I (Manchester) 1996. F-c Tours: A 1992-93 (Eng A), 1994-95, 1998-99 (*part*); SA 1995-96, 2004-05; WI 1991-92 (Eng A), 1993-94, 1997-98, 2003-04; NZ 1996-97, 2001-02; I 2001-02 (*part*); P 1990-91 (Eng A), 2000-01; SL 1990-91 (Eng A), 2000-01, 2003-04; Z 1989-90 (Eng A), 1996-97; B 2003-04. 1000 runs (9); most – 1895 (1992). HS 223* Eng XI v S Aus (Adelaide) 1998-99. Sy HS 222 v Glam (Oval) 1997. BB 4-40 v A (Oval) 1993. CC BB 2-14 v Derbys (Oval) 1996. Awards: CGT 4; BHC 1. LO HS 145* v Lancs (Oval) 1994 (NWT). LO BB 3-21 v Somerset (Oval) 1991 (SL).

RELEASED/RETIRED

(Having made a first-class County appearance in 2004)

HOLLIOAKE, Adam John (St Joseph's C, Sydney; St Patrick's C, Ballarat; St George's C, Weybridge; Surrey Tutorial C), b Melbourne, Australia 5 Sep 1971. Elder brother of the late B.C.Hollioake (Surrey and England 1996-2001). 5'11". RHB, RMF. Surrey 1993-2004, scoring 13 and 123 v Derbys (Ilkeston) on debut; cap 1995; captain 1997-2003; benefit 2004. Qualified for England 1992. *Wisden* 2002. Retires after 2004 season. **Tests:** 4 (1997 to 1997-98); HS 45 and BB 2-31 v A (Nottingham) 1997 – on debut. **LOI:** 35 (1996 to 1999, 14 as captain); HS 83* v SA (Dhaka) 1998-99; BB 4-23 v P (Birmingham) 1996 – on debut. F-c Tours: A 1996-97 (Eng A – captain); WI 1997-98. 1000 runs (2); most – 1522 (1996). HS 208 v Leics (Oval) 2002. BB 5-62 v Glam (Swansea) 1998. Awards: CGT 2; BHC 1. LO HS 117* v Sussex (Hove) 2002 (CGT). LO BB 6-17 v Kent (Canterbury) 2003 (NL).

NQKHAN, Zaheer (KTS HS; RBNB C), b Shrirampur, Maharashtra, India 7 Oct 1978. 6'2". RHB, LFM. Baroda 1999-00 to date. Surrey 2004. **Tests** (I): 37 (2000-01 to 2004-05); HS 75 v B (Dhaka) 2004-05 – record score by No. 11 in Tests; BB 5-29 v NZ (Hamilton) 2002-03. **LOI** (I): 89 (2000-01 to 2002-03); HS 34* v NZ (Wellington) 2002-03; BB 4-19 v B (Dhaka) 2002-03. F-c Tours (I): E 2002; A 2003-04; SA 2001-02; WI 2001-02; NZ 2002-03; P 2003-04 (*part*); SL 2001; Z 2001; B 2000-01, 2004-05. HS 75 (*see Tests*). UK HS 14* (*twice*)I v E (Nottingham) 2002. Sy HS 2*. BB 6-25 Baroda v Punjab (Baroda) 2001-02. UK BB 3-90 I v E (Lord's) 2002. Sy BB 1-48. LO HS 34* (*see LOI*). LO BB 4-19 (*see LOI*).

NQSAQLAIN MUSHTAQ (Govt Muslim League HS, M.A.O. College, Lahore), b Lahore, Pakistan 29 Dec 1976. Brother of Sibtain Mushtaq (Lahore 1988-89). 5'11". RHB, OB. Islamabad 1994-95. PIA 1994-95 to 2001-02. Surrey 1997-2004; cap 1998. *Wisden* 1999. **Tests** (P): 49 (1995-96 to 2003-04); HS 101* v NZ (Christchurch) 2000-01; BB 8-164 v E (Lahore) 2000-01 (all eight wickets to fall). **LOI** (P): 169 (1995-96 to 2003-04); HS 37* v A (Brisbane) 1999-00; BB 5-20 v E (Rawalpindi) 2000-01, 2 hat-tricks. F-c Tours (P): E 1996, 2001; A 1995-96, 1996-97, 1999-00; SA 1997-98, 2002-03; WI 1999-00; NZ 2000-01; I 1998-99, SL 1996-97; Z 1997-98, 2002-03; B 1999-00, 1999, 2001-02. HS 101* (*see Tests*). Sy HS 69 v Middx (Lord's) 2003. 50 wkts (5+1); most – 66 (2000). BB 8-65 (11-107 match) v Derbys (Oval) 1988. Took 7-11 (including 7-5 in 34 balls) v Derbys (Oval) 2000. Three hat-tricks, all for Surrey 1997 and 1999 (2). Awards: CGT 2. LO HS 38* v Yorks (Leeds) 2001 (NL). LO BB 5-20 (*see LOI*).

SHAHID, Nadeem (Ipswich S), b Karachi, Pakistan 23 Apr 1969. 6'0". RHB, LB. Essex 1989-94. Surrey 1995-2004; cap 1998. Suffolk 1988. 1000 runs (1): 1003 (1990). HS 150 v Sussex (Oval) 2002. BB 3-91 Ex v Surrey (Oval) 1990. Sy BB 3-93 v SA A (Oval) 1996. LO HS 109* v Notts (Nottingham) 2000 (NL). LO BB 3-30 v Bucks (Oval) 1998 (NWT).

TUDOR, A.J. – *see ESSEX.*

G.S.Blewett appeared in l-o games without making a f-c appearance in 2004.

SURREY 2004

RESULTS SUMMARY

	Place	Won	Lost	Tied	Drew	No Result
County Championship (1st Division)	3rd	5	5		6	
All First-Class Matches		5	5		7	
C & G Trophy	2nd Round					
National League (1st Division)	9th	4	9			3
Twenty20 Cup	Finalist					

COUNTY CHAMPIONSHIP AVERAGES

BATTING AND FIELDING

Cap		M	I	NO	HS	Runs	Avge	100	50	Ct/St
2002	M.R.Ramprakash	16	28	4	161	1451	60.45	6	6	5
1991	G.P.Thorpe	3	5	1	89	211	52.75	–	1	–
1994	A.D.Brown	14	23	1	170	1094	49.72	4	5	15
–	S.A.Newman	16	28	1	131	1162	43.03	2	9	9
–	T.J.Murtagh	11	17	8	74*	374	41.55	–	4	8
1996	M.A.Butcher	4	8	–	184	298	37.25	1	–	1
2001	J.N.Batty	16	27	2	145	899	35.96	3	3	47/5
–	R.Clarke	10	17	–	112	530	31.17	1	2	15
2004	Azhar Mahmood	12	20	1	84	577	30.36	–	4	8
1989	M.J.Bicknell	12	18	3	47*	415	27.66	–	–	3
–	R.S.Clinton	5	8	–	73	205	25.62	–	2	8
1998	I.D.K.Salisbury	8	13	1	77	285	23.75	–	1	1
1995	A.J.Hollioake	10	17	1	106	377	23.56	1	2	6
2003	J.Ormond	16	24	5	57	330	17.36	–	1	4
–	J.G.E.Benning	5	9	1	35*	137	17.12	–	–	2
1998	N.Shahid	2	4	–	53	54	13.50	–	1	1
–	N.D.Doshi	9	13	3	29*	134	13.40	–	–	2
–	P.J.Sampson	2	4	2	11*	13	6.50	–	–	–
1998	Saqlain Mushtaq	3	4	–	14	17	4.25	–	–	1

Also batted (1 match each): A.J.Tudor (cap 1999) 0 (3 ct); Z.Khan 2*.

BOWLING

	O	M	R	W	Avge	Best	5wI	10wM
Saqlain Mushtaq	86.4	9	304	12	25.33	4-107	–	–
N.D.Doshi	265.2	45	875	33	26.51	7-110	3	2
Azhar Mahmood	336.3	77	1138	38	29.94	5- 54	1	–
M.J.Bicknell	363	88	1198	40	29.95	5-128	1	–
J.Ormond	580.2	138	1800	48	37.50	6- 62	1	–
T.J.Murtagh	243.3	50	873	20	43.65	5- 74	1	–
Also bowled:								
P.J.Sampson	34.3	4	154	6	25.66	5-121	1	–
A.J.Hollioake	60.3	7	237	6	39.50	3- 69	–	–
R.Clarke	109.3	16	518	9	57.55	3- 47	–	–
I.D.K.Salisbury	182.1	26	587	7	83.85	2- 32	–	–

J.G.E.Benning 6.3-0-37-0; A.D.Brown 13.3-3-43-0; R.S.Clinton 1-0-9-0; Z.Khan 26.4-2-101-1; M.R.Ramprakash 22-4-52-2; A.J.Tudor 22-4-118-4.

The First-Class Averages (pp 121–136) give the records of Surrey players in all first-class county matches (Surrey's other opponents being Oxford UCCE), with the exception of M.A.Butcher, R.S.Clinton and G.P.Thorpe whose full county figures are as above.

SURREY RECORDS

FIRST-CLASS CRICKET

Highest Total	For 811		v	Somerset	The Oval	1899
	V 863		by	Lancashire	The Oval	1990
Lowest Total	For 14		v	Essex	Chelmsford	1983
	V 16		by	MCC	Lord's	1872
Highest Innings	For 357*	R.Abel	v	Somerset	The Oval	1899
	V 366	N.H.Fairbrother	for	Lancashire	The Oval	1990

Highest Partnership for each Wicket

1st	428	J.B.Hobbs/A.Sandham	v	Oxford U	The Oval	1926
2nd	371	J.B.Hobbs/E.G.Hayes	v	Hampshire	The Oval	1909
3rd	413	D.J.Bicknell/D.M.Ward	v	Kent	Canterbury	1990
4th	448	R.Abel/T.W.Hayward	v	Yorkshire	The Oval	1899
5th	308	J.N.Crawford/F.C.Holland	v	Somerset	The Oval	1908
6th	298	A.Sandham/H.S.Harrison	v	Sussex	The Oval	1913
7th	262	C.J.Richards/K.T.Medlycott	v	Kent	The Oval	1987
8th	205	I.A.Greig/M.P.Bicknell	v	Lancashire	The Oval	1990
9th	168	E.R.T.Holmes/E.W.J.Brooks	v	Hampshire	The Oval	1936
10th	173	A.Ducat/A.Sandham	v	Essex	Leyton	1921

Best Bowling	For	10-43	T.Rushby	v	Somerset	Taunton	1921
(Innings)	V	10-28	W.P.Howell	for	Australians	The Oval	1899
Best Bowling	For	16-83	G.A.R.Lock	v	Kent	Blackheath	1956
(Match)	V	15-57	W.P.Howell	for	Australians	The Oval	1899

Most Runs – Season	3246	T.W.Hayward	(av 72.13)	1906
Most Runs – Career	43554	J.B.Hobbs	(av 49.72)	1905-34
Most 100s – Season	13	T.W.Hayward		1906
	13	J.B.Hobbs		1925
Most 100s – Career	144	J.B.Hobbs		1905-34
Most Wkts – Season	252	T.Richardson	(av 13.94)	1895
Most Wkts – Career	1775	T.Richardson	(av 17.87)	1892-1904
Most Career W-K Dismissals	1221	H.Strudwick	(1035 ct/186 st)	1902-27
Most Career Catches in the Field	605	M.J.Stewart		1954-72

LIST 'A' LIMITED-OVERS CRICKET

Highest Total	CGT	438-5		v	Glamorgan	The Oval	2002
	BHC	361-8		v	Notts	The Oval	2001
	NL	375-4		v	Yorkshire	Scarborough	1994
Lowest Total	CGT	74		v	Kent	The Oval	1967
	BHC	89		v	Notts	Nottingham	1984
	NL	64		v	Worcs	Worcester	1978
Highest Innings	CGT	268	A.D.Brown	v	Glamorgan	The Oval	2002
	BHC	167*	A.J.Stewart	v	Somerset	The Oval	1994
	NL	203	A.D.Brown	v	Hampshire	Guildford	1997
Best Bowling	CGT	7-33	R.D.Jackman	v	Yorkshire	Harrogate	1970
	BHC	5-15	S.G.Kenlock	v	Ireland	The Oval	1995
	NL	7-30	M.P.Bicknell	v	Glamorgan	The Oval	1999

SUSSEX

Formation of Present Club: 1 March 1839
Substantial Reorganisation: August 1857
Inaugural First-Class Match: 1864
Colours: Dark Blue, Light Blue and Gold
Badge: County Arms of Six Martlets
County Champions: (1) 2003
Gillette/NatWest/C & G Trophy Winners: (4) 1963, 1964, 1978, 1986
Benson and Hedges Cup Winners: (0); best – semi-finalist 1982, 1999
National League (Div 1) Winners: (0); best – 9th 2000
Sunday League Winners: (1) 1982
Twenty20 Cup Winners: (0); best – 2nd in Group 2003
Match Awards: CGT 61; BHC 64

Chief Executive: H.H.Griffiths, County Ground, Eaton Road, Hove BN3 3AN • Tel: 01273 827100 • Fax: 01273 771549 • Email: info@sussexcricket.co.uk • Web: www.sussexcricket.co.uk

First XI Coach: P.Moores. **Captain**: C.J.Adams. **Vice-Captain**: R.J.Kirtley. **Overseas Players**: Mushtaq Ahmed, Naved-ul-Hasan and M.J.Nicholson. **2005 Beneficiary**: M.A.Robinson (testimonial). **Head Groundsman**: D.J.Traill. **Scorers**: M.J.Charman and J.F.Hartridge. ‡ New registration. NQ Not qualified for England.

ADAMS, Christopher John (Repton S), b Whitwell, Derbyshire 6 May 1970. 6'0". RHB, RM/OB. Derbyshire 1988-97; cap 1992. Sussex debut/cap 1998; captain 1998 to date; benefit 2003. *Wisden* 2003. **Tests**: 5 (1999-00); HS 31 v SA (Cape Town) 1999-00; BB 1-42. **LOI**: 5 (1998 to 1999-00); HS 42 v SA (Cape Town) 1999-00. F-c Tour: SA 1999-00. 1000 runs (6); most – 1742 (1996). HS 239 De v Hants (Southampton) 1996. Sx HS 217 v Lancs (Manchester) 2002. BB 4-28 v Durham (Chester-le-St) 2001. Awards: CGT 5; BHC 6. LO HS 163 v Middx (Arundel) 1999 (NL). LO BB 5-16 v Middx (Hove) 1998 (SL).

AMBROSE, Timothy Raymond (Merewether HS, NSW; TAFE C), b Newcastle, NSW, Australia 1 Dec 1982. ECB qualified – British/EU passport. 5'7". RHB, WK. Debut 2001; cap 2003. HS 149 v Yorks (Leeds) 2002. Award: CGT 1. LO HS 95 v Bucks (Beaconsfield) 2002 (CGT).

NQ**DAVIS**, Mark Jeffrey Gronow (Grey HS; Pretoria U), b Port Elizabeth, South Africa 10 Oct 1971. ECB qualified – British/EU passport. 6'2". RHB, OB. N Transvaal/Northerns 1990-91 to date. MCC 1999 and 2000. Sussex debut 2001; cap 2002. HS 168 v Middx (Hove) 2003. BB 8-37 (12-84 match) NT B v W Transvaal (Potchefstroom) 1994-95. Sx BB 6-97 v Surrey (Hove) 2002. Award: BHC 1. LO HS 37 v Hants (Hove) 2003 (NL). LO BB 4-14 v Lancs (Manchester) 2003 (NL).

NQ**GOODWIN**, Murray William (Newton Moore HS, Bunbury, WA), b Salisbury, Rhodesia 11 Dec 1972. Younger brother of D.G.Goodwin (Zimbabwe 1986-97 to 1998-99). 5'9". Emigrated to Australia in Nov 1986. Gained Australian citizenship in Sep 1997. Kolpak registration 2005. RHB, LB. W Australia 1994-95 to 1996-97, 2000-01 to date. Mashonaland 1997-98 to 1998-99. Sussex debut/cap 2001. Holland 1997. **Tests** (Z): 19 (1997-98 to 2000); HS 166* v P (Bulawayo) 1997-98. **LOI** (Z): 71 (1997-98 to 2000); HS 112* v WI (Chester-le-St) 2000; BB 1-12. F-c Tours (Z): E 2000, SA 1999-00; WI 1999-00; NZ 1997-98; P 1998-99; SL 1997-98. 1000 runs (3+1); most – 1654 (2001). HS 335* (Sussex record) v Leics (Hove) 2003. BB 2-23 Z v Lahore City (Lahore) 1998-99. Sx BB –. Awards: BHC 2. LO HS 167 WA v NSW (Perth) 2000-01 (MC) – Australian l-o record. LO BB 1-9 Mashonaland v Eng A (Harare) 1998-99.

HOPKINSON, Carl Daniel (Brighton C), b Brighton 14 Sep 1981. 5'11". RHB, RM. Debut 2002. HS 33 and CC BB 1-35 v Warwks (Hove) 2002 – on debut. BB 1-20. LO HS 67* and BB 3-19 v Scot (Edinburgh) 2003 (NL).

KIRTLEY, Robert James (Clifton C), b Eastbourne 10 Jan 1975. 6'0". RHB, RFM. Debut 1995; cap 1998. Mashonaland 1996-97. **Tests**: 4 (2003 to 2003 04); HS 12 v SL (Colombo) 2003-04; BB 6-34 v SA (Nottingham) 2003 on debut. **LOI**: 11 (2001-02 to 2004-05); HS 1 (*twice*); BB 2-33 v Z (Harare) 2001-02 on debut, and 2-33 v B (Dhaka) 2003-04. F-c Tours: NZ 1999-00 (Eng A); SL 2003-04; B 1999-00 (Eng A). HS 59 v Durham (Eastbourne) 1998. 50 wkts (6); most – 75 (2001). BB 7-21 v Hants (Southampton) 1999. Took 5-53 (7-88 match) for Mashonaland v Eng XI (Harare) 1996-97. Award: CGT 1. LO HS 30* v Middx (Lord's) 2003 (CGT). LO BB 5-33 v Essex (Chelmsford) 2002 (BHC).

LEWRY, Jason David (Durrington HS, Worthing), b Worthing 2 Apr 1971. 6'2". LHB, LFM. Debut 1994; cap 1996; benefit 2002. F-c Tour: Z 1998-99 (Eng A). HS 72 v Surrey (Oval) 2004. 50 wkts (4); most – 62 (1998). BB 8-106 v Leics (Hove) 2003. 2 hat-tricks (1998, 2001). LO HS 16* v Yorks (Arundel) 2004 (NL). LO BB 4-29 v Somerset (Bath) 1995 (SL).

MARTIN-JENKINS, Robin Simon Christopher (Radley C; Durham U), b Guildford, Surrey 28 Oct 1975. Son of C.D.A.Martin-Jenkins (*Times* Chief Cricket Correspondent/ BBC Commentator). 6'5". RHB, RFM. Debut 1995; cap 2000. British U 1996. 1000 runs (1): 1008 (2002). HS 205* v Somerset (Taunton) 2002. BB 7-51 v Leics (Horsham) 2002. Award: BHC 1. LO HS 68* v Northants (Hove) 2003 (NL). LO BB 4-22 v Kent (Canterbury) 2002 (BHC).

MONTGOMERIE, Richard Robert (Rugby S; Worcester C, Oxford), b Rugby, Warwks 3 Jul 1971. 5'10½". RHB, OB. Oxford U 1991-94; blue 1991-92-93-94; captain 1994; half blues for rackets and real tennis. Northamptonshire 1991-98; cap 1995. Sussex debut/cap 1999. F-c Tour: Z 1994-95 (Nh). 1000 runs (5); most – 1704 (2001). HS 196 v Hants (Hove) 2002. BB 1-0. Award: CGT 1. LO HS 129* v Z (Hastings) 2000.

[NQ]MUSHTAQ AHMED (Mahmoodia HS, Sahiwal), b Sahiwal, Pakistan 28 Jun 1970. 5'5". RHB, LBG. Multan 1986-87, 1988-89, 1990 91. United Bank 1987-88 to 1996-97. Islamabad 1994-95. Lahore 1996-97, 2000-01. Peshawar 1998-99. National Bank 1999-00 to date. REDCO 1999-00. Somerset 1993-95, 1997-98; cap 1993. Surrey 2002 (2 matches). Sussex debut/cap 2003. *Wisden* 1996. PCA 2003. **Tests** (P): 52 (1989-90 to 2003-04); HS 59 v SA (Rawalpindi) 1997-98; BB 7-56 (10-171 match) v NZ (Christchurch) 1995-96. **LOI** (P): 144 (1988-89 to 2003-014); HS 34* v SA (Colombo) 2000-01; BB 5-36 v I (Toronto) 1996-97. F-c Tours (P): E 1992, 1996; A 1989-90, 1991-92, 1992-93, 1995-96, 1996-97, 1999-00; SA 1997-98; WI 1992-93, 1999-00; NZ 1992-93, 1993-94, 1995-96, 2000-01; I 1998-99; SL 1994-95, 1996-97, 2000-01; Z 1997-98. HS 90 Sm v Sussex (Taunton) 1993. Sx HS 62 v Warwks (Horsham) 2004. 50 wkts (6+2) inc 100 (1): 103 (2003). Took 1000th f-c wicket 2004. BB 9-93 Multan v Peshawar (Sahiwal) 1990-91. Sx BB 7-73 (13-140 match) v Worcs (Hove) 2004. Awards: NWT 2; BHC 2. LO HS 41 Sm v Durham (Taunton) 1998 (SL). LO BB 7-24 Sm v Ire (Taunton) 1997 (BHC).

NASH, Christopher David (Collyers SFC; Loughborough U), b Cuckfield 19 May 1983. 5'11". RHB, OB. Sussex debut 2002 – no appearances 2003-04. Loughborough UCCE 2003-04. British U 2004. HS 63 LU v Somerset (Taunton) 2004. BB (LU) 1-5. Sx HS 0* and BB 1-81 v Warwks (Birmingham) 2002 – on debut.

NAVED-UL-HASAN, Rana, b Sheikhupura, Pakistan 28 Feb 1978. RHB, RMF. Debut Pakistan A 1995-96. Lahore 1999-00. Customs 2000-01. Sheikhupura 2000-01 to 2001-02. Allied Bank 2001-02. PCB Blues 2002-03. WAPDA 2002-03 to 2003-04. Sialkot 2002-03 to date. Herefordshire 2002. **Tests** (P): 2 (2004-05); HS 11 and BB 3-83 v SL (Karachi) 2004-05 – on debut. **LOI** (P): 22 (2002-03 to 2004-05); HS 29 v A (Melbourne) 2004-05; BB 4-25 v I (Birmingham) 2004. Tour (P): A 2004-05. HS 117 Sheikhupura v Lahore Whites (Sheikhupura) 2001-02. 50 wkts (3); most –91 (2000-01). BB 7-49 Sheikhupura v Sialkot (Muridke) 2001-02. LO HS 70* Lahore v Habib Bank (Sheikhupura) 1999-00. LO BB 4-25 (*see LOI*).

NICHOLSON, Matthew James (Knox GS; Edith Cowan U, Perth), b St Leonards, Sydney, Australia 2 Oct 1974. 6'6". RHB, RFM. W Australia.1996-97 to 2002-03. NSW 2003-04 to date. Missed entire 1997-98 season (salmonella poisoning, glandular fever, Ross River fever, chronic fatigue syndrome). **Tests** (A): 1 (1998-99); HS 9 and BB 3-56 v E (Melbourne) 1998-99. Tour (A): Z 1999-00. HS 101* WA v S Africans (Perth) 2001-02. BB 7-77 WA v Eng XI (Perth) 1998-99. LO HS 25 NSW v Q (Sydney 2003-04. LO BB 3-34 NSW v S Aus (Sydney) 2003-04.

PRIOR, Matthew James (Brighton C), b Johannesburg, South Africa 24 Feb 82. 6'2". RHB, WK. Debut 2001; cap 2003. **LOI**: 1 (2004-05); HS 35 v Z (Bulawayo) 2004-05. F-c Tour (Eng A): I 2003-04. 1000 runs (2); most – 1158 (2004). HS 201* v LU (Hove) 2004. CC HS 153* v Essex (Colchester) 2003. LO HS 119 v Durham (Hove) 2004 (NL).

TURK, Neil Richard Keith (Sackville S, E Grinstead; Exeter U), b Cuckfield 28 Apr 1983. 6'0". LHB, RM. Awaiting f-c debut. LO HS 36 v Essex (Chelmsford) 2002 (NL).

WARD, Ian James (Millfield S), b Plymouth, Devon 30 Sep 1972. 5'8½". LHB, RM. Surrey 1992, 1996-2003; cap 2000. Sussex debut/cap 2004. **Tests**: 5 (2001); HS 39 v P (Lord's) 2001 – on debut. F-c Tours (Eng A): WI 2000-01; NZ 1999-00; B 1999-00. 1000 runs (5); most 1759 (2002) – including 114, 112, 156 and 118 in successive innings. HS 168* Sy v Kent (Canterbury) 2002. Sx HS 160 v Warwks (Horsham) 2004. BB 1-1 (Sy – *twice*). Award: CGT 1. LO HS 136 v Leics (Horsham) 2004 (NL). LO BB 2-27 Sy v Sussex (Hove) 2002 (BHC).

WRIGHT, Luke James (Belvoir HS; Ratcliffe C; Loughborough U), b Grantham, Lincs 7 Mar 1985. 5'11". Younger brother of A.S.Wright (Leicestershire 2001-02). RHB, RM. Leicestershire 2003 (one f-c match). Sussex debut 2004. HS 100 v LU (Hove) 2004 – on Sx debut. CC HS 18 and BB 1-74 v Kent (Canterbury) 2004. LO HS 25* v Scot (Edinburgh) 2004 (NL). LO BB 4-12 v Middx (Hove) 2004 (NL).

YARDY, Michael Howard (William Parker S, Hastings), b Pembury, Kent 27 Nov 1980. 6'0". LHB, LM. Debut 2000. HS 115 v Surrey (Hove) 2004. BB 1-13. LO HS 88* v Derbys (Hove) 2004 (NL). LO BB 3-30 v Warwks (Hove) 2002 (BHC).

RELEASED/RETIRED

(Having made a first-class County appearance in 2004)

COTTEY, Phillip Anthony (Bishopston CS, Swansea), b Swansea, Glamorgan 2 Jun 1966. 5'4". RHB, OB. Glamorgan 1986-98; cap 1992. Sussex 1999-2004; cap 1999. E Transvaal 1991-92. F-c Tours (Gm): SA 1995-96; Z 1990-91, 1994-95. 1000 runs (8); most – 1543 (1996). HS 203 and BB 4-49 Gm v Leics (Swansea) 1996. Sx HS 188 v Warwks (Hove) 2003. LO HS 96 Gm v Sussex (Hove) 1998 (BHC). LO BB 5-49 v Somerset (Taunton) 2004 (NL).

INNES, Kevin John (Weston Favell Upper S), b Wellingborough, Northants 24 Sep 1975. 5'10". RHB, RM. Northamptonshire 2nd XI debut 1990 (aged 14yr 8m – Nh record). Northamptonshire 1994-2001. Sussex 2002-04. HS 103* v Notts (Horsham) 2003 – when a nominated substitute for R.J.Kirtley. BB 4-41 v Surrey (Hove) 2002. LO HS 55 Nh v Worcs (Worcester) 2000 (NL). LO BB 5-41 v Middx (Lord's) 2003 (NL).

[NQ]**MOHAMMAD AKRAM** – *see SURREY.*

[NQ]**VOROS, Jason** Alexander, b Canberra, Australia 31 Dec 1976. LHB, LFM. Hungarian passport – EU qualified 1 May 2004. Sussex 2004. No CC appearances. HS 3* and BB 4-40 v LU (Hove) 2004 – on debut. LO HS 11* ACT v Q (Brisbane) 1998-99 (MM). LO BB 3-28 ACT v Tasmania (Canberra) 1998-99 (MM).

J.A.G.Green, a non-contracted player, made no Sussex appearances in 2004.

SUSSEX 2004

RESULTS SUMMARY

	Place	Won	Lost	Tied	Drew	No Result
County Championship (1st Division)	5th	4	5		7	
All First-Class Matches		4	5		9	
C & G Trophy	3rd Round					
National League (2nd Division)	5th	9	7	1		1
Twenty20 Cup	6th in South Division					

COUNTY CHAMPIONSHIP AVERAGES

BATTING AND FIELDING

Cap		M	I	NO	HS	Runs	Avge	100	50	Ct/St
1998	C.J.Adams	16	25	4	200	1003	47.76	4	2	14
2004	I.J.Ward	15	23	1	160	985	44.77	4	3	5
–	M.H.Yardy	2	4	–	115	154	38.50	1	–	–
2003	M.J.Prior	16	23	–	123	852	37.04	2	5	21/2
1999	P.A.Cottey	9	13	–	185	466	35.84	1	–	7
1999	R.R.Montgomerie	16	25	1	82	809	33.70	–	7	11
2001	M.W.Goodwin	16	25	2	119	756	32.86	2	4	9
2003	Mushtaq Ahmed	16	22	4	62	416	23.11	–	2	6
2000	R.S.C.Martin-Jenkins	15	21	1	64*	412	20.60	–	2	5
2004	Mohammad Akram	13	17	7	35*	198	19.80	–	–	2
1996	J.D.Lewry	10	13	4	72	150	16.66	–	1	2
1998	R.J.Kirtley	12	17	4	53*	209	16.07	–	1	3
2002	M.J.G.Davis	9	12	2	43	156	15.60	–	–	5
2003	T.R.Ambrose	8	11	–	56	148	13.45	–	1	20/1

Also batted: K.J.Innes (2 matches) 22, 5, 3; L.J.Wright (1) 0, 18 (1 ct).

BOWLING

	O	M	R	W	Avge	Best	5wI	10wM
Mushtaq Ahmed	751.2	153	2226	82	27.14	7-73	6	2
J.D.Lewry	231.2	62	732	25	29.28	5-66	1	–
M.J.G.Davis	219.3	37	637	19	33.52	4-57	–	–
Mohammad Akram	401.1	69	1451	43	33.74	4-85	–	–
R.S.C.Martin-Jenkins	358.4	91	1082	29	37.31	5-96	1	–
R.J.Kirtley	424.5	89	1336	33	40.48	4-32	–	–

Also bowled: C.J.Adams 10-2-35-0; K.J.Innes 32-5-109-3; R.R.Montgomerie 4-0-9-0; L.J.Wright 27.5-2-96-1; M.H.Yardy 13-2-46-0.

The First-Class Averages (pp 121–136) give the records of Sussex players in all first-class county matches (Sussex's other opponents being the MCC and Loughborough UCCE), with the exception of C.D.Nash whose only first-class appearances were for Loughborough UCCE and BUSA.

91

SUSSEX RECORDS

FIRST-CLASS CRICKET

Highest Total	For 705-8d		v	Surrey	Hastings	1902
	V 726		by	Notts	Nottingham	1895
Lowest Total	For 19		v	Surrey	Godalming	1830
	19		v	Notts	Hove	1873
	V 18		by	Kent	Gravesend	1867
Highest Innings	For 335*	M.W.Goodwin	v	Leics	Hove	2003
	V 322	E.Paynter	for	Lancashire	Hove	1937

Highest Partnership for each Wicket

1st	490	E.H.Bowley/J.G.Langridge	v	Middlesex	Hove	1933
2nd	385	E.H.Bowley/M.W.Tate	v	Northants	Hove	1921
3rd	298	K.S.Ranjitsinhji/E.H.Killick	v	Lancashire	Hove	1901
4th	326*	J.Langridge/G.Cox	v	Yorkshire	Leeds	1949
5th	297	J.H.Parks/H.W.Parks	v	Hampshire	Portsmouth	1937
6th	255	K.S.Duleepsinhji/M.W.Tate	v	Northants	Hove	1930
7th	344	K.S.Ranjitsinhji/W.Newham	v	Essex	Leyton	1902
8th	291	R.S.C.Martin-Jenkins/M.J.G.Davis	v	Somerset	Taunton	2002
9th	178	H.W.Parks/A.F.Wensley	v	Derbyshire	Horsham	1930
10th	156	G.R.Cox/H.R.Butt	v	Cambridge U	Cambridge	1908

Best Bowling	For 10- 48	C.H.G.Bland	v	Kent	Tonbridge	1899
(Innings)	V 9- 11	A.P.Freeman	for	Kent	Hove	1922
Best Bowling	For 17-106	G.R.Cox	v	Warwicks	Horsham	1926
(Match)	V 17- 67	A.P.Freeman	for	Kent	Hove	1922

Most Runs – Season	2850	J.G.Langridge	(av 64.77)	1949
Most Runs – Career	34152	J.G.Langridge	(av 37.69)	1928-55
Most 100s – Season	12	J.G.Langridge		1949
Most 100s – Career	76	J.G.Langridge		1928-55
Most Wkts – Season	198	M.W.Tate	(av 13.47)	1925
Most Wkts – Career	2211	M.W.Tate	(av 17.41)	1912-37
Most Career W-K Dismissals	1176	H.R.Butt	(911 ct/265 st)	1890-1912
Most Career Catches in the Field	779	J.G.Langridge		1928-55

LIST 'A' LIMITED-OVERS CRICKET

Highest Total	CGT	384-9		v	Ireland	Belfast	1996
	BHC	316-3		v	Essex	Chelmsford	2000
	NL	323-5		v	Leics	Horsham	2004
Lowest Total	CGT	49		v	Derbyshire	Chesterfield	1969
	BHC	61		v	Middlesex	Hove	1978
	NL	59		v	Glamorgan	Hove	1996
Highest Innings	CGT	158	R.K.Rao	v	Derbyshire	Derby	1997
	BHC	157*	M.G.Bevan	v	Essex	Chelmsford	2000
	NL	163	C.J.Adams	v	Middlesex	Arundel	1999
Best Bowling	CGT	6- 9	A.I.C.Dodemaide	v	Ireland	Downpatrick	1990
	BHC	5- 8	Imran Khan	v	Northants	Northampton	1978
	NL	7-41	A.N.Jones	v	Notts	Nottingham	1986

WARWICKSHIRE

Formation of Present Club: 8 April 1882
Substantial Reorganisation: 19 January 1884
Inaugural First-Class Match: 1894
Colours: Dark Blue, Gold and Silver
Badge: Bear and Ragged Staff
County Champions: (6) 1911, 1951, 1972, 1994, 1995, 2004
Gillette/NatWest/C & G Trophy Winners: (5) 1966, 1968, 1989, 1993, 1995
Benson and Hedges Cup Winners: (2) 1994, 2002
National League (Div 1) Winners: (0); best – 3rd 2001, 2002
Sunday League Winners: (3) 1980, 1994, 1997
Twenty20 Cup Winners: (0); best – Finalist 2003
Match Awards: CGT 76; BHC 69

Chief Executive: D.L.Amiss MBE, County Ground, Edgbaston, Birmingham, B5 7QU • Tel: 0121 446 4422 • Fax: 0121 446 4544 • Email addresses: info@thebears.co.uk • info@edgbaston.com • Web: www.thebears.co.uk

Director of Coaching/First XI Coach: R.J.Inverarity. **Captain**: N.V.Knight.
Vice-Captain: D.R.Brown. **Overseas Player**: H.H.Streak. **2005 Beneficiary**: D.R.Brown.
Head Groundsman: S.J.Rouse. **Scorer**: D.E.Wainwright. ‡ New registration. ^{NQ} Not qualified for England.

ALI, Moeen Munir, b Birmingham 18 Jun 1987. Brother of Kadeer Ali and cousin of Kabir Ali of Worcestershire. 6'0". LHB, OB. Joined Warwickshire staff 2003 when aged 15. Awaiting 1st XI debut.

‡ANYON, James Edward (Garstang HS; Preston C; Loughborough U), b Lancaster, Lancs 5 May 1983. 6'1". LHB, RFM. Loughborough U 2003-04. Warwickshire staff 2005 – awaiting County debut. Cumberland 2003. HS 21 LU v Leics (Leicester) 2003. BB 3-57 LU v Glos (Bristol) 2004. LO HS 0 and BB 1-46 Cumberland v Scotland (Edinburgh) 2003 (CGT).

BELL, Ian Ronald (Princethorpe C), b Walsgrave-on-Sowe 11 Apr 1982. 5'9". RHB, RM. Debut 1999; cap 2001. YC 2004. **Tests**: 1 (2004); HS 70 v WI (Oval) 2004 – on debut. **LOI**: 8 (2004-05); HS 75 v Z (Harare) 2004-05 – on debut; BB 3-9 v Z (Bulawayo) 2004-05 – taking a wicket with his third ball in LOI. F-c Tour (Eng A): WI 2000-01 (*part*;) SL 2002-03 (ECB Acad). 1000 runs (1): 1714 (2004). HS 262* v Sussex (Horsham) 2004. BB 4-4 v Middx (Lord's) 2004. Awards: CGT 1; BHC 2. LO HS 125 and BB 5-41 v Essex (Chelmsford) 2003 (NL).

BROWN, Douglas Robert (Alloa Academy; W London IHE), b Stirling, Scotland 29 Oct 1969. 6'2". RHB, RFM. Scotland 1989. Warwickshire debut 1991-92 (cap 1995; benefit 2005. Wellington 1995-96. **LOI**: 9 (1997-98); HS 21 v WI (Bridgetown) 1997-98; BB 2-28 v WI (Sharjah) 1997-98. F-c Tours (Wa): SA 1991-92, 1994-95; SL 1997-98 (Eng A). 1000 runs (1): 1028 (2003). HS 203 v Sussex (Hove) 2000. 50 wkts (3); most – 81 (1997). BB 8-89 (11-154 match) F-C Counties XI v Pak A (Chelmsford) 1997. Wa BB 7-66 v Durham (Chester-le-St) 1999. Awards: CGT 1; BHC 1. LO HS 108 v Essex (Birmingham) 2003 (CGT). LO BB 5-31 v Worcs (Worcester) 1997 (BHC).

^{NQ}CARTER, Neil Miller (Hottentots Holland HS; Cape Technicon), b Cape Town, South Africa 29 Jan 1975. ECB qualified – British passport. 6'2". LHB, LFM. Boland 1999-00 to 2000-01. Warwickshire debut 2001. HS 103 v Sussex (Hove) 2002 – completed maiden hundred off 67 balls. BB 6-63 Boland v GW (Kimberley) 2000-01. Wa BB 5-75 v Surrey (Birmingham) 2003. Award: CGT 1. LO HS 75 v Leics (Birmingham) 2003 (NL). LO BB 5-31 v Durham (Birmingham) 2002 (NL).

FROST, Tony (James Brinkley HS; Stoke-on-Trent C), b Stoke-on-Trent, Staffs 17 Nov 1975. 5'11". RHB, WK. Debut 1997; cap 1999. HS 135* v Sussex (Horsham) 2004. CC HS 103 v Yorks (Birmingham) 2002. LO HS 47 v Beds (Luton) (CGT).

GILES, Ashley Fraser (George Abbot S, Guildford), b Chertsey, Surrey 19 Mar 1973. 6'3". RHB, SLA. Debut 1993; cap 1996. **ECB contracts 2001-02-03-04-05. Tests**: 45 (1998 to 2004-05): HS 52 v Z (Lord's) 2003 and 52 v WI (Oval) 2004; BB 5-57 v WI (Birmingham) 2004. **LOI**: 54 (1997 to 2004-05); HS 41 v SA (Pretoria) 2004-05; BB 5-57 v I (Delhi) 2001-02. F-c Tours: A 1996-97 (Eng A), 2002-03 (part); NZ 2001-02; I 2001-02; P 2000-01; SL 1997-98 (Eng A), 2000-01, 2003-04; B 2003-04; K 1997-98 (Eng A). HS 128* v Sussex (Hove) 2000. 50 wkts (2); most – 64 (1996). BB 8-90 (12-135 match) v Northants (Northampton) 2000. Awards: CGT 2; BHC 1. LO HS 107 v Derbys (Birmingham) 2000 (NWT). LO BB 5-21 v Norfolk (Birmingham) 1997 (NWT).

KNIGHT, Nicholas Verity (Felsted S; Loughborough U), b Watford, Herts 28 Nov 1969. 6'0". LHB, occ RM. Essex 1991-94; cap 1994. Warwickshire debut 1994-95 (SA tour); cap 1995; captain 2004 to date; benefit 2004. **Tests**: 17 (1995 to 2001); HS 113 v P (Leeds) 1996. **LOI**: 100 (1996 to 2002-03); HS 125* v P (Nottingham) 1996. F-c Tours: SA 1994-95 (Wa), 1999-00 (part); NZ 1996-97; I 1994-95 (Eng A); SL 1997-98 (Eng A – captain); P 1995-96 (Eng A); Z 1996-97; K 1997-98 (Eng A – captain). 1000 runs (5); most – 1520 (2002). HS 303* v Middx (Lord's) 2004. BB 1-61. Awards: CGT 4; BHC 4. LO HS 151 v Somerset (Birmingham) 1995 (NWT). LO BB 1-14 (SL).

‡**LOUDON, Alexander** Guy Rushworth (Wellesley House; Eton C; Collingwood C, Durham U), b Westminster, London 6 Sep 1980. Younger brother of H.J.H.Loudon (Durham UCCE 2001). 6'3". RHB, OB. Durham UCCE 2001-03; captain 2003. Kent 2003-04. HS 172 DU (record) v Durham (Chester-le-St) 2003. CC HS 92 K v Warwks (Birmingham) 2004. BB 6-47 K v Middx (Canterbury) 2004. LO HS 53 Kent CB v Leics CB (Hinckley) 2001 (CGT). LO BB 4-48 K v Essex (Colchester) 2004 (NL).

PENNEY, Trevor Lionel (Prince Edward S, Salisbury), b Salisbury, Rhodesia 12 Jun 1968. 6'0". RHB, RM. Qualified for England 1992. Boland 1991-92. Warwickshire debut 1991-92 (SA tour); UK debut v CU (Cambridge) 1992, scoring 102*; cap 1994; benefit 2003. No f-c appearances 2002, 2004. Mashonaland 1993-94; 1997-98 to date. F-c Tours (Wa): SA 1991-92, 1992-93, 1994-95; Z 1993-94. 1000 runs (2); most – 1295 (1996). HS 151 v Middx (Lord's) 1992. BB 3-18 Mashonaland v Mashonaland U-24 (Harare) 1993-94. Wa BB 1-40 (Z tour). Awards: CGT 3. LO HS 90 v Cornwall (St Austell) 1996 (NWT). LO BB 1-8 (NWT).

PIPER, Keith John (Haringey Cricket C), b Leicester 18 Dec 1969. 5'6". RHB, WK. Warwickshire debut 1989; cap 1992; benefit 2001 No f-c appearances 2004. F-c Tours (Wa): SA 1991-92, 1992-93, 1994-95; I 1994-95 (Eng A); P 1995-96 (Eng A); Z 1993 94. HS 116* v Durham (Birmingham) 1994. BB 1-57. LO HS 38* v Leics (Birmingham) 1999 (NL).

POWELL, Michael James (Lawrence Sheriff S, Rugby), b Bolton, Lancs 5 Apr 1975. 5'11". RHB, RM. Debut 1996; cap 1999; captain 2001-03. Oxford UCCE 2001-02. F-c Tour (Eng A): WI 2000-01. 1000 runs (1): 1046 (2000). HS 236 v OU (Oxford) 2001. CC HS 145 v Northants (Northampton) 2000. BB 2-16 v OU (Oxford) 1998. CC BB 2-29 v Somerset (Taunton) 2002. Award: BHC 1. LO HS 101* v Northants (Birmingham) 2002 (BHC). LO BB 5-40 v Kent (Canterbury) 2002 (CGT).

NQ**PRETORIUS, Dewald** (Dr Viljoen HS), b Pretoria, South Africa 6 Dec 1977. 6'3". RHB, RF. Free State 1997-98 to date. Durham 2003. Warwickshire debut 2004. Kolpak registration 2005. **Tests** (SA): 4 (2001-02 to 2003); HS 9; BB 4-115 v E (Birmingham) 2003. F-c Tours (SA): E 2003; Sc/Ire 1999 (SA A). HS 43 FS v WP (Bloemfontein) 1998-99. UK HS 16 Du v Glos (Chester-le-St) 2003. Wa HS 14 v Sussex (Birmingham) 2004. BB 6-49 SA A v Ind A (Bloemfontein) 2001-02. UK BB 4-15 Du v Yorks (Leeds) 2003. Wa HS 4-119 v Sussex (Horsham) 2004. LO HS 7* (twice – FS and Du). LO BB 4-31 Du v Somerset (Taunton) 2003 (NL).

‡**SHANTRY, Adam** John (Priory S; Shrewsbury SFC), b Bristol 13 Nov 1982. 6'2½". Son of B.K.Shantry (Gloucestershire 1978-79). LHB, LFM. Northamptonshire 2003-04. Shropshire 2001. HS 38* and BB 3-8 (3 wkts in 5 balls) Nh v Somerset (Northampton) 2003 – on CC debut. LO HS 15 Nh CB v Yorks CB (Northampton) 2002 (CGT). LO BB 5-37 Nh v NZ (Northampton) 2004.

NQ**STREAK, Heath** Hilton (Falcon C), b Bulawayo, Rhodesia 16 Mar 1974. 6'1". Son of D.H.Streak (Rhodesia 1976-77 to 1978-79). RHB, RFM. Debut for Zimbabwe B v Kent (Harare) 1992-93. Matabeleland 1993-94 to 2003-04. Hampshire 1995. Warwickshire debut 2004. **Tests** (Z): 59 (1993-94 to 2003-04, 21 as captain); HS 127* v WI (Harare) 2003-04; BB 6-87 v E (Lord's) 2003. **LOI** (Z): 183 (1993-94 to 2003-04, 68 as captain); HS 79* v NZ (Auckland) 2000-01; BB 5-32 v I (Bulawayo) 1996-97. F-c Tours (Z) (C=captain): E 1993, 2000, 2003C; A 1994-95, 2003-04C; WI 1999-00; NZ 1995-96, 1997-98, 2000-01C; I 2000-01C, 2001-02; P 1993-94, 1998-99; SL 1996-97, 1997-98, 2001-02; B 2001-02. HS 131 Matabeleland – v Mashonaland CD (Bulawayo) 1995-96 and 131 v Midlands (Bulawayo) 2003-04. Wa HS 61 and BB 7-80 (13-158 match) v Northants (Birmingham) 2004 – on Wa debut. 50 wkts (1): 53 (1995). BB 7-55 Matabeleland – v Mashonaland (Bulawayo) 2003-04. LO HS 90* Matabeleland v Manicaland (Bulawayo) 2003-04. LO BB 5-32 (*see LOI*).

TAHIR, Naqaash (Moseley S; Spring Hill C), b Birmingham 14 Nov 1983. 5'10". RHB, RFM. Debut 2004. HS 49 v Worcs (Worcester) 2004. BB 4-43 v Worcs (Birmingham) 2004 – on CC debut.

NQ**TROTT, Ian Jonathan** Leonard (Rondebosch BHC; Stellenbosch U), b Cape Town, South Africa 22 Apr 1981. 6'0". Stepbrother of K.C.Jackson (WP and Boland 1988-89 to 2001-02). RHB, RM. Boland 2002-01. W Province 2001-02. EU/British passport. Warwickshire debut 2003 scoring 134. 1000 runs (1): 1170 (2004). HS 134 v Sussex (Birmingham) 2003 – on UK debut. BB 7-39 v Kent (Canterbury) 2003. LO HS 108* Boland v North West (Paarl) 2000-01. LO BB 2-32 Boland v EP (Paarl) 1999-00.

TROUGHTON, Jamie Oliver (*'Jim'*) (Trinity S; Leamington Spa; Birmingham U), b Camden, London 2 Mar 1979. Great-grandson of H.T.Crichton (Warwicks 1908). 5'11". LHB, SLA. Debut 2001, cap 2002. **LOI**: 6 (2003); HS 20 v P (Lord's) 2003. F-c Tour (ECB Acad): SL 2002-03. 1000 runs (1): 1067 (2002). HS 131* v Hants (Southampton) 2002. BB 3-1 v CU (Cambridge) 2004. CC BB 2-106 v Glos (Bristol) 2004. Awards: CGT 2. LO HS 115* and BB 4-23 Warwks CB v Cumb (Millom) 2001 (CGT).

WAGH, Mark Anant (King Edward's S, Birmingham; Keble C, Oxford), b Birmingham 20 Oct 1976. 6'2". RHB, OB. Oxford U 1996-98; blue 1996-97-98; captain 1997. Warwickshire debut 1997; cap 2000. British U 1998. Mashonaland A 1998-99. F-c Tour (Eng A): I 2003-04. 1000 runs (4): most – 1277 (2001). HS 315 v Middx (Lord's) 2001. BB 7-222 v Lancs (Birmingham) 2003. Award: CGT 1. LO HS 102* v Kent (Birmingham) 2004 (NL). LO BB 4-35 v Glam (Birmingham) 2004 (NL).

WARREN, Nick Alexander (Wheelers Lane S; Solihull SFC), b Moseley, Birmingham 26 Jun 1982. 5'11". RHB, RMF. No appearances 2003. 2nd XI debut 1998 when aged 16y 76d. HS 11 v WI A (Birmingham) 2002. BB 3-60 and CC HS 0 v Northants (Northampton) 2004. LO HS 2 and LO BB 3-34 v Kent (Canterbury) 2002 (NL).

WESTWOOD, Ian James (Wheelers Lane S; Solihull SFC), b Birmingham 13 Jul 1982. 5'7½". LHB, OB. Debut 2003 – awaiting CC debut. HS 38 v Northants (Northampton) 2004. LO HS 55 and BB 1-28 Warwks CB v Cambs (March) 2001 (CGT).

RELEASED/RETIRED

(Having made a first-class County appearance in 2004)

^{NO}**HOGG,** George **Bradley,** b Narrogin, W Australia 6 Feb 1971. LHB, SLC. W Australia 1993-94 to date. Warwickshire 2004. **Tests** (A): 4 (1996-97 to 2003-04); HS 17* v WI (Port-of-Spain) 2002-03; BB 2-40 v WI (Georgetown) 2002-03. **LOI** (A): 57 (1996-97 to 2004-05); HS 71* v E (Melbourne) 2002-03; BB 5-32 v WI (Melbourne) 2004-05. F-c Tours (A): WI 2002-03; I 1996-97. HS 158 v Surrey (Birmingham) 2004. BB 5-53 WA v NSW (Sydney) 1999-00. Wa BB 4-90 v Kent (Beckenham) 2004. Award: CGT 1. LO HS 94* v Northants (Birmingham) 2004 (CGT). LO BB 5-23 v Essex (Birmingham) 2004 (NL).

RICHARDSON, A. – *see MIDDLESEX.*

WAGG, Graham Grant (Ashlawn S, Rugby), b Rugby, 28 Apr 1983. 6'0". RHB, LM. Warwickshire 2002-04; contract terminated after ECB imposed a 15-month ban, expiring 1 Jan 2006, for taking cocaine. F-c Tour (Eng A): I 2003-04. HS 74 v Ind A (Birmingham) 2003. BB 4-43 and CC HS 51 v Somerset (Birmingham) 2002 – on debut. LO HS 45 v Eng A v Karnataka (Bangalore) 2003-04. LO BB 4-50 v Kent (Birmingham) 2002 (NL).

J.I.Clifford, H.R.Jones, T.Mees, D.P.Ostler, J.A.Spires and S.A.Taylor left the staff having made no f-c appearances in 2004.

COUNTY CAPS AWARDED IN 2004

Derbyshire	M.H.Adnan, A.G.Botha, J.Moss
Durham	–
Essex	A.R.Adams, Danish Kaneria, D.Gough
Glamorgan	–
Gloucestershire	S.J.Adshead, N.W.Bracken, A.N.Bressington, I.D.Fisher, J.E.C.Franklin, A.P.R.Gidman, M.A.Hardinges, M.E.K.Hussey, Shabbir Ahmed, Shoaib Malik, R.J.Sillence, W.P.C.Weston.
Hampshire	M.J.Clarke, C.T.Tremlett
Kent	–
Lancashire	D.G.Cork
Leicestershire	–
Middlesex	J.W.M.Dalrymple
Northamptonshire	–
Nottinghamshire	M.A.Ealham, D.J.Hussey, R.J.Sidebottom, R.J.Warren
Somerset	–
Surrey	Azhar Mahmood
Sussex	Mohammad Akram, I.J.Ward
Warwickshire	–
Worcestershire	N.M.Malik, R.W.Price
Yorkshire	R.K.J.Dawson

Gloucestershire award caps on first-class debut. Worcestershire award club colours on Championship debut.

WARWICKSHIRE 2004

RESULTS SUMMARY

	Place	Won	Lost	Tied	Drew	No Result
County Championship (1st Division)	1st	5	0		11	
All First-Class Matches		6	0		11	
C & G Trophy	Semi-Finalist					
National League (1st Division)	7th	7	8			1
Twenty20 Cup	Quarter-Finalist					

COUNTY CHAMPIONSHIP AVERAGES

BATTING AND FIELDING

Cap		M	I	NO	HS	Runs	Avge	100	50	Ct/St
2001	I.R.Bell	15	25	4	262*	1498	71.33	6	4	6
–	G.B.Hogg	11	12	2	158	662	66.20	1	7	4
1995	N.V.Knight	15	28	6	303*	1256	57.09	2	8	9
–	I.J.L.Trott	16	27	6	115	1126	53.61	1	10	11
1995	D.R.Brown	16	21	3	162	911	50.61	3	2	7
1999	M.J.Powell	9	15	2	134	630	48.46	2	2	4
1999	T.Frost	16	18	5	135*	488	37.53	1	1	44/4
2000	M.A.Wagh	16	29	2	167	928	34.37	1	5	14
2002	J.O.Troughton	13	16	–	120	528	33.00	1	4	2
–	H.H.Streak	6	9	2	61	180	25.71	–	1	–
–	N.M.Carter	13	15	4	95	245	22.27	–	1	3
–	N.Tahir	11	12	5	49	150	21.42	–	–	1
2002	A.Richardson	7	4	2	17	26	13.00	–	–	2
–	D.Pretorius	9	6	3	14	31	10.33	–	–	1

Also batted (1 match each): A.F.Giles (cap 1996) 70; N.A.Warren 0; I.J.Westwood 3, 38.

BOWLING

	O	M	R	W	Avge	Best	5wI	10wM
H.H.Streak	159	29	522	24	21.75	7- 80	2	1
I.R.Bell	137.4	32	400	14	28.57	4- 4	–	–
N.Tahir	194.4	26	766	26	29.46	4- 43	–	–
D.R.Brown	412.4	91	1273	38	33.50	5- 53	2	–
D.Pretorius	245	43	936	24	39.00	4-119	–	–
N.M.Carter	349.4	71	1189	27	44.03	4- 50	–	–
M.A.Wagh	281.4	44	977	18	54.27	3- 85	–	–
G.B.Hogg	256.2	39	881	14	62.92	4- 90	–	–

Also bowled:

A.Richardson | 144 | 28 | 532 | 6 | 88.66 | 2- 62 | – | –

A.F.Giles 62-17-128-4; M.J.Powell 8-0-51-0; I.J.L.Trott 23-5-86-3; J.O.Troughton 123-27-344-3; N.A.Warren 17-3-60-3.

The First-Class Averages (pp 121–136) give the records of Warwickshire's players in all first-class county matches (Warwickshire's other opponents being Cambridge UCCE), with the exception of A.F.Giles whose full county figures are as above, and:
I.R.Bell 16-27-4-262*-1556-67.65-6-5-7ct. 146.4-34-422-16-26.37-4/4.

WARWICKSHIRE RECORDS

FIRST-CLASS CRICKET

Highest Total	For	810-4d		v	Durham	Birmingham	1994
	V	887		by	Yorkshire	Birmingham	1896
Lowest Total	For	16		v	Kent	Tonbridge	1913
	V	15		by	Hampshire	Birmingham	1922
Highest Innings	For	501*	B.C.Lara	v	Durham	Birmingham	1994
	V	322	I.V.A.Richards	for	Somerset	Taunton	1985

Highest Partnership for each Wicket

1st	377*	N.F.Horner/K.Ibadulla	v	Surrey	The Oval	1960
2nd	465*	J.A.Jameson/R.B.Kanhai	v	Glos	Birmingham	1974
3rd	327	S.P.Kinneir/W.G.Quaife	v	Lancashire	Birmingham	1901
4th	470	A.I.Kallicharran/G.W.Humpage	v	Lancashire	Southport	1982
5th	322*	B.C.Lara/K.J.Piper	v	Durham	Birmingham	1994
6th	220	H.E.Dollery/J.Buckingham	v	Derbyshire	Derby	1938
7th	289*	I.R.Bell/T.Frost	v	Sussex	Horsham	2004
8th	228	A.J.W.Croom/R.E.S.Wyatt	v	Worcs	Dudley	1925
9th	154	G.W.Stephens/A.J.W.Croom	v	Derbyshire	Birmingham	1925
10th	214	N.V.Knight/A.Richardson	v	Hampshire	Birmingham	2002

Best Bowling	For	10-41	J.D.Bannister	v	Comb Servs	Birmingham	1959
(Innings)	V	10-36	H.Verity	for	Yorkshire	Leeds	1931
Best Bowling	For	15-76	S.Hargreave	v	Surrey	The Oval	1903
(Match)	V	17-92	A.P.Freeman	for	Kent	Folkestone	1932

Most Runs – Season	2417	M.J.K.Smith	(av 60.42)	1959
Most Runs – Career	35146	D.L.Amiss	(av 41.64)	1960-87
Most 100s – Season	9	A.I.Kallicharran		1984
	9	B.C.Lara		1994
Most 100s – Career	78	D.L.Amiss		1960-87
Most Wkts – Season	180	W.E.Hollies	(av 15.13)	1946
Most Wkts – Career	2201	W.E.Hollies	(av 20.45)	1932-57
Most Career W-K Dismissals	800	E.J.Smith	(662 ct/138 st)	1904-30
Most Career Catches in the Field	422	M.J.K.Smith		1956-75

LIST 'A' LIMITED-OVERS CRICKET

Highest Total	CGT	392-5		v	Oxfordshire	Birmingham	1984
	BHC	369-8		v	Minor C	Jesmond	1996
	NL	310-5		v	Lancs	Birmingham	2004
Lowest Total	CGT	98		v	Leics	Leicester	1998
	BHC	91		v	Glos	Bristol	2002
	NL	59		v	Yorks	Leeds	2001
Highest Innings	CGT	206	A.I.Kallicharran	v	Oxfordshire	Birmingham	1984
	BHC	137*	T.A.Lloyd	v	Lancashire	Birmingham	1985
	NL	134*	D.P.Ostler	v	Glos	Birmingham	2001
Best Bowling	CGT	6-32	K.Ibadulla	v	Hampshire	Birmingham	1965
		6-32	A.I.Kallicharran	v	Oxfordshire	Birmingham	1984
	BHC	7-32	R.G.D.Willis	v	Yorkshire	Birmingham	1981
	NL	6-15	A.A.Donald	v	Yorkshire	Birmingham	1995

WORCESTERSHIRE

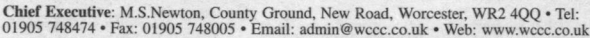

Formation of Present Club: 11 March 1865
Inaugural First-Class Match: 1899
Colours: Dark Green and Black
Badge: Shield Argent a Fess between three Pears Sable
County Championships: (5) 1964, 1965, 1974, 1988, 1989
Gillette/NatWest/C & G Trophy Winners: (1) 1994
Benson and Hedges Cup Winners: (1) 1991
National League (Div 1) Winners: (0); best – 2nd 1999, 2002
Sunday League Winners: (3) 1971, 1987, 1988
Twenty20 Cup Winners: (0); best – Quarter-Finalist 2004
Match Awards: CGT 55; BHC 72

Chief Executive: M.S.Newton, County Ground, New Road, Worcester, WR2 4QQ • Tel: 01905 748474 • Fax: 01905 748005 • Email: admin@wccc.co.uk • Web: www.wccc.co.uk

Director of Cricket/First XI Coach: T.M.Moody. **Captain**: V.S.Solanki. **Vice-Captain**: G.J.Batty. **Overseas Players**: Shoaib Akhtar and Vaas. **2005 Beneficiary**: none. **Head Groundsman**: T.Packwood. **Scorer**: N.D.Smith. ‡ New registration. NQ Not qualified for England.
Worcestershire revised their capping policy in 2002 and now award players with their County Colours when they make their Championship debut.

ALI, Kabir (Moseley CS and SFC), b Moseley, Birmingham 24 Nov 1980. 6'0". Cousin of Kadeer Ali (*see Gloucestershire*). RHB, RMF. Debut 1999. F-c Tour: SL 2002-03 (ECB Acad). **Tests**: 1 (2003); HS 9 and BB 3-80 v SA (Leeds) 2003 on debut. **LOI**: 8 (2003 to 2004-05); HS 25 v SA (Pretoria) 2004-05; BB 3-44 v SA (Durban) 2004-05. HS 84* v Durham (Stockton) 2003. 50 wkts (2); most – 71 (2002). BB 8-53 (*before lunch first day*) v Yorks (Scarborough) 2003. Award: BHC 1. LO HS 92 v Essex (Worcester) 2003 (NL). LO BB 5-36 v Yorks (Leeds) 2002 (NL).

BATTY, Gareth Jon (Bingley GS), b Bradford, Yorks 13 Oct 1977. Younger brother of J.D.Batty (Yorkshire and Somerset 1989-96). 5'11". RHB, OB. Yorkshire 1997. Surrey 1999-2001. Worcestershire debut 2002. **Tests**: 5 (2003-04); HS 38 v SL (Kandy) 2003-04; BB 3-55 v SL (Galle) 2003-04. Took wicket with his third ball in Test cricket. **LOI**: 6 (2002-03 to 2004-05); HS 3; BB 2-40 v WI (Gros Islet) 2003-04. F-c Tours: WI 2003-04; SL 2002-03 (ECB Acad); SL 2003-04; B 2003-04. HS 133 v Surrey (Oval) 2004. 50 wkts (2); most – 60 (2003). BB 7-52 (10-113 match) v Northants (Northampton) 2004. LO HS 83* Sy v Yorks (Oval) 2001 (NL). LO BB 4-36 Sy v Kent (Canterbury) 2001 (NL) and 4-36 v Notts (Nottingham) 2002 (NL).

DAVIES, Steven Michael (King Charles I S, Kidderminster), b Bromsgrove 17 Jun 1986. LHB, WK. Staff 2004 – awaiting first-class debut. Worcs 2nd XI debut 2001 when 15yr 8d. LO HS 13 Worcs CB v Worcs (Worcester) 2003 (CGT).

De BRUYN, Zander (Helpmekaar HS; Randburg HS; Rand Afrikaans U, Jo'burg), b Johannesburg, South Africa 5 Jul 1975. 6'0". RHB, RMF. Transvaal B 1995-96 to 1996-97. Gauteng 1996-97 to 2001-02. Easterns 2002-03 to 2003-04. Titans 2004-05. MCC 2000. Kolpak registration. **Tests** (SA): 3 (2004-05); HS 83 v I (Kanpur) 2004-05 – on debut; BB 2-32 v I (Calcutta) 2004-05. F-c Tour (SA): I 2004-05. HS 266* Easterns v GW (Kimberley) 2003-04. BB 6-120 Transvaal B v WP B (Cape Town) 1996-97. LO HS 113* Surrey CB v Hunts (Cheam) 2001. LO BB 5-44 Easterns v WP (Cape Town) 2003-04.

HICK, Graeme Ashley (Prince Edward HS, Salisbury), b Salisbury, Rhodesia 23 May 1966. 6'3". RHB, OB. Zimbabwe 1983-84 to 1985-86. Worcestershire debut 1984; cap 1986; benefit 1999; captain 2000-02. N Districts 1987-88 to 1988-89. Queensland 1990-91. *Wisden* 1986. PCA 1988. **ECB contract 2000. Tests:** 65 (1991 to 2000-01); HS 178 v I (Bombay) 1992-93; BB 4-126 v NZ (Wellington) 1991-92. Took wicket with third ball in Test cricket. **LOI:** 120 (1991 to 2000-01); HS 126* v SL (Adelaide) 1998-99; BB 5-33 v Z (Harare) 1999-00. F-c Tours: E 1985 (Z); A 1994-95, 1998-99 *(part)*; SA 1995-96, 1999-00 *(part)*; WI 1993-94; NZ 1991-92; I 1992-93; SL 1993-84 (Z), 1992-93, 2000-01; Z 1990-91 (Wo), 1996-97 (Wo). 1000 runs (18+1) inc 2000 (3); most – 2713 (1988); youngest to score 2000 (1986). Scored 1019 runs before June 1988, including a record 410 runs in April. Fewest innings for 10,000 runs in county cricket (179). Youngest (24) to score 50 f-c hundreds. Second youngest (32) to score 100 f-c hundreds. Scored 645 runs without being dismissed (UK record) in 1990. HS 405* (Worcs record and then second highest in UK f-c matches) v Somerset (Taunton) 1988. BB 5-18 v Leics (Worcester) 1995. Awards: CGT 5; BHC 11. LO HS 172* v Devon (Worcester) 1987 (NWT). LO BB 5-19 E v Pak A (Lahore) 1998-99.

KHALID, Shaftab Ahmad (Dormers Wells HS; W Thames C; Middlesex U), b Lahore, Pakistan 6 Oct 1982. 5'11". RHB, OB. Debut 2003. F-c Tour (Eng A): I 2003-04. HS 15 Eng A v Tamil Nadu (Madras) 2003-04. CC HS 13 v Glam (Worcester) 2003 – on CC debut. BB 4-131 v Northants (Northampton) 2003. LO HS 9* (CGT). LO BB 2-40 v Essex (Worcester) 2003 (NL).

LEATHERDALE, David Anthony (Pudsey Grangefield S), b Bradford, Yorks 26 Nov 1967. 5'10½". RHB, RM. Debut 1988; cap 1994; benefit 2003. No f-c appearances 2004. F-c Tours (Wo): Z 1993-94, 1996-97. 1000 runs (1): 1001 (1998). HS 157 v Somerset (Worcester) 1991. BB 5-20 v Glos (Worcester) 1998. Awards: CGT 1; BHC 1. LO HS 80 v Yorks (Worcester) 2003 (CGT). LO BB 5-9 v Durham (Chester-le-St) 2002 (NL).

MALIK Muhammad Nadeem, (Wilford Meadows CS; Bilborough C), b Nottingham 6 Oct 1982. 6'5". RHB, RFM. Nottinghamshire 2001-03. Worcestershire debut 2004. Notts 2nd XI debut 1999 when aged 16y 337d. HS 39* v NZ (Worcester) 2004. CC HS 30* Nt v Essex (Nottingham) 2003. BB 5-57 Nt v Derbys (Nottingham) 2001. Wo BB 5-88 v Kent (Canterbury) 2004 – on Wo debut. LO HS 11 Nt v Worcs (Nottingham) 2002 (NL). LO BB 4-42 v Sussex (Worcester) 2004 (NL).

[NQ]**MASON, Matthew** Sean (Mazenod C, Lesmurdie, WA), b Claremont, Perth, Australia 20 Mar 1974. ECB qualified – British passport. 6'5". RHB, RFM. W Australia 1996-97 to 1997-98. Worcestershire debut 2002. HS 63 v Warwks (Worcester) 2004. 50 wkts (2); most – 53 (2003). BB 6 68 v Durham (Worcester) 2003. LO HS 25 v Durham (Worcester) 2004 (NL). LO BB 4-34 v Surrey (Guildford) 2003 (NL).

MITCHELL, Daryl Keith Henry (Prince Henry's HS; University C, Worcester), b Badsey, near Evesham 25 Nov 1983. 5'10". RHB, RM. Worcestershire staff 2003 – awaiting 1st XI debut.

MOORE, Stephen Colin (St Stithian's C, Johannesburg; Exeter U), b Johannesburg, South Africa 4 Nov 1980. 6'1". RHB, RM. Debut 2003. 1000 runs (1): 1004 (2004). HS 146 v Surrey (Worcester) 2004. BB 1-13. LO HS 93* v Durham (Chester-le-St) 2004 (NL). LO BB 1-1 (NL).

PETERS, Stephen David (Coopers Coborn & Co S), b Harold Wood, Essex 10 Dec 1978. 5'11". RHB, occ LB. Essex 1996-2001, scoring 110 and 12* v CU (Cambridge) on debut. Worcestershire debut 2002. 1000 runs (1): 1177 (2003). HS 165 v Somerset (Bath) 2003. BB (Ex) 1-19 (not CC). Award: CGT 1. LO HS 82 v Leics (Oakham) 2003 (NL).

PIPE, David James (Queensbury S, Bradford), b Bradford, Yorks 16 Dec 1977. 5'11". RHB, WK. Debut 1998. HS 104* v Hants (Southampton) 2003. LO HS 56 Worcs CB v Kent CB (Kidderminster) 2000 (NWT). Held 8 catches v Herts (Hertford) 2001 (CGT) to equal l-o record.

PRICE, Raymond William (Watershed C), b Salisbury, Rhodesia 12 Jun 1976. 6'2". RHB, SLA. Mashonaland CD 1995-96. Zimbabwe Academy 1998-99 to 2000-01. Midlands 1999-00 to date. Worcestershire debut 2004. Kolpak registration 2005. **Tests** (Z): 18 (1999-00 to 2003-04); HS 36 v A (Perth) 2003-04; BB 6-73 (10-161 match) v WI (Harare) 2003-04. **LOI** (Z): 26 (2002-03 to 2003-04); HS 20* v B (Harare) 2003-04;BB 2-16 v WI (Bulawayo) 2003-04. F-c Tours (Z): E 2003; A 2003-04; I 2001-02, SL 1999-00 (Zim A); K 2001-02 (Zim A). HS 117* Midlands v Manicaland (Mutare) 2003-04. Wo HS 76 * v Lancs (Worcester) 2004. BB 8-35 Midlands v CFX Academy)Kwekwe) 2001-02. Wo BB 4-83 v Warwks (Worcester) 2004. LO HS 35 Zim A v Eng A (Harare) 1998-99. LO BB 4-29 Midlands v Mashonaland (Harare) 2002-03.

‡**NQSHOAIB AKHTAR** (Elliott HS; Government C, Rawalpindi), b Rawalpindi, Pakistan 13 Aug 1975. 5'11½". RHB, RF. PIA 1994-95 to 1995-96. Rawalpindi 1994-95 to 1998-99. ADBP 1996-97 to 1997-98. KRL 2001-02. Somerset (one match) 2001. Durham 2003-04. **Tests** (P): 36 (1997-98 to 2004-05); HS 37 and BB 6-11 v NZ (Lahore) 2001-02. **LOI** (P): 120 (1997-98 to 2004-05); HS 43 v E (Cape Town) 2002-03; BB 6-16 v NZ (Karachi) 2002-03. F-c Tours (P): E (Pak A) 1997; A 1999-00, 2004-05; SA 1997-98; NZ 2003-04; WI 1998-99; SL 2002-03; Z 1997-98, 2002-03; B 1998-99, 2001-02. HS 59* KRL v PIA (Lahore) 2001-02. CC HS 46 Du v Somerset (Taunton) 2004. 50 wkts (0+1): 69 (1996-97). BB 6-11 (see Tests). CC BB 4-9 Du v Somerset (Chester-le-St) 2003. LO HS 56 KRL v Habib Bank (Lahore) 2002-03. LO BB 6-16 (see LOI).

SMITH, Benjamin Francis (Kibworth HS), b Corby, Northants 3 Apr 1972. 5'9". RHB, RM. Leicestershire 1990-2001; cap 1995. Central Districts 2001-02. Worcestershire debut 2002; captain 2003 to 2004 (part). F-c Tour (Le): SA 1996-97. 1000 runs (6); most – 1289 (2003). HS 204 Le v Surrey (Oval) 1998. Wo HS 187 v Glos (Worcester) 2004. BB (Le) 1-5. Wo BB 1-45. Awards: CGT 3. LO HS 115 Le v Somerset (Weston-s-M) 1995 (SL). LO BB 1-2 (CGT).

SOLANKI, Vikram Singh (Regis S, Wolverhampton), b Udaipur, India 1 Apr 1976. 6'0". RHB, OB. Debut 1995; cap 1998. Kolpak captain 2005. F-c Tours (Eng A): SA 1999-00 (Eng – part); WI 2000-01; NZ 1999-00; Z 1996-97 (Wo), 1998-99; B 1999-00. **LOI**: 35 (1999-00 to 2004-05); HS 106 v SA (Oval) 2003. 1000 runs (2); most – 1339 (1999). HS 185 Eng A v Bangladesh (Chittagong) 1999-00. Wo HS 171 v Glos (Cheltenham) 1999. BB 5-40 v Middx (Lord's) 2004. Awards: CGT 4; BHC 1. LO HS 164* v Worcs CB (Worcester) 2003 (CGT). LO BB 2-5 v Middx (Lord's) 2004 (NL).

‡**NQVAAS**, Warnakulasooriya Patabendige Ushantha **Chaminda** Joseph, b Mattumagala 27 Jan 1974. LHB, LFM. Colts 1990-91 to date. Hampshire 2003. **Tests**: 82 (1994-95 to 2004-05); HS 74* v Z (Colombo) 2001-02; BB 7-71 (14-191 match) v WI (Colombo) 2001-02. **LOI**: 249 (1993-94 to 2004-05); HS 50* v P (Sharjah) 2000-01; BB 8-19 v Z (Colombo) 2001-02, including the first of two LOI hat tricks. F-c Tours (SL): E 2002; A 1995-96, 2004; SA 1997-98, 2000-01, 2002-03; WI 2003; NZ 1994-95, 1996-97; I 1997-98; P 1995-96, 1998-99, 1999-00, 2001-02, 2004-05; Z 1994-95, 1999-00, 2003-04. HS 104 Uva Province v N Central Province (Dambulla) 2003-04. CC HS 35 H v Worcs (Southampton) 2003. 50 wkts (0+2); most 62 (2001-02). BB 7-71 (see Tests). CC BB 4-82 H v Derbys (Southampton) 2003 – on CC debut. LO HS 62* Colts v Sinhalese (Colombo) 1999-00. LO BB 8-19 (see LOI).

WIGLEY, David Harry (St Mary's RCS, Menstom, Ilkley; Loughborough U), b Bradford, Yorks 26 Oct 1981. 6'4". RHB, RFM. Yorkshire 2002 (one match). Loughborough UCCE 2003-04. British U 2004. Worcestershire debut 2003 – no f-c appearances then. HS 23* LU and BB 4-133 v Somerset (Taunton) 2004. CC HS 15 Y v Surrey (Guildford) 2002 – on debut – and 15 plus CC BB 2-56 v Yorks (Worcester) 2003 – on Worcs debut. LO HS 2 (NL). LO BB 4-37 v Leics (Worcester) 2004 (NL).

RELEASED/RETIRED continued on p 107

WORCESTERSHIRE 2004

RESULTS SUMMARY

	Place	Won	Lost	Tied	Drew	No Result
County Championship (1st Division)	7th	3	6		7	
All First-Class Matches		3	6		8	
C & G Trophy	Finalist					
National League (2nd Division)	2nd	11	5			2
Twenty20 Cup	Quarter-Finalist					

COUNTY CHAMPIONSHIP AVERAGES

BATTING AND FIELDING

Cap		M	I	NO	HS	Runs	Avge	100	50	Ct/St
1986	G.A.Hick	16	27	3	262	1349	56.20	3	6	25
2004c	R.W.Price	3	5	2	76*	146	48.66	–	1	1
2002c	B.F.Smith	15	23	3	187	930	46.50	2	6	17
2001	A.J.Bichel	14	18	1	142	717	42.17	3	2	3
1998	V.S.Solanki	13	18	–	107	757	42.05	1	6	10
2003c	S.C.Moore	16	27	3	146	957	39.87	3	4	7
1986	S.J.Rhodes	16	19	8	59*	412	37.45	–	2	42/4
2003c	A.J.Hall	11	17	2	81	519	34.60	–	5	15
2002c	S.D.Peters	16	27	–	123	898	33.25	3	3	13
2002c	G.J.Batty	12	18	3	133	470	31.33	1	2	7
2002c	Kadeer Ali	5	8	–	66	181	22.62	–	1	4
2002c	M.S.Mason	16	19	6	63	193	14.84	–	1	4
2002c	Kabir Ali	8	9	1	31	93	11.62	–	–	2
2004c	M.N.Malik	7	8	1	7	9	1.28	–	–	1

Also batted: M.A.Harrity (3 matches – 2003c) 0, 0; S.A.Khalid (3 – 2003c) 0, 1*, 6* (1 ct); D.J.Pipe (2 – 2002c) 12.

BOWLING

	O	M	R	W	Avge	Best	5wI	10wM
M.S.Mason	574.1	174	1517	51	29.74	5-62	1	–
G.J.Batty	492.1	129	1381	45	30.68	7-52	2	1
M.N.Malik	179	31	714	23	31.04	5-88	1	–
Kabir Ali	248	45	899	28	32.10	5-60	1	–
A.J.Hall	330.3	70	1055	29	36.37	3-10	–	–
R.W.Price	169.1	50	420	10	42.00	4-83	–	–
A.J.Bichel	398.5	75	1549	33	46.93	5-87	2	–

Also bowled:
V.S.Solanki 74.3 7 240 6 40.00 5-40 1 –
Kadeer Ali 14-1-51-1; M.A.Harrity 65-15-240-4; G.A.Hick 5-1-16-1; S.A.Khalid 86.3-17-277-4; S.C.Moore 23-3-99-2; S.D.Peters 2-0-12-0.

The First-Class Averages (pp 121–136) give the records of Worcestershire's players in all first-class county matches (Worcestershire's other opponents being the New Zealanders), with the exception of D.H.Wigley whose only first-class appearances were for Loughborough UCCE and BUSA.

2004c Denotes awarded Worcestershire 1st XI colours, a system which replaced capping in 2002.

WORCESTERSHIRE RECORDS

FIRST-CLASS CRICKET

Highest Total	For 670-7d		v	Somerset	Worcester	1995
	V 701-4d		by	Leics	Worcester	1906
Lowest Total	For 24		v	Yorkshire	Huddersfield	1903
	V 30		by	Hampshire	Worcester	1903
Highest Innings	For 405*	G.A.Hick	v	Somerset	Taunton	1988
	V 331*	J.D.B.Robertson	for	Middlesex	Worcester	1949

Highest Partnership for each Wicket

1st	309	F.L.Bowley/H.K.Foster	v	Derbyshire	Derby	1901
2nd	300	W.P.C.Weston/G.A.Hick	v	Indians	Worcester	1996
3rd	438*	G.A.Hick/T.M.Moody	v	Hampshire	Southampton	1997
4th	281	J.A.Ormrod/Younis Ahmed	v	Notts	Nottingham	1979
5th	393	E.G.Arnold/W.B.Burns	v	Warwicks	Birmingham	1909
6th	265	G.A.Hick/S.J.Rhodes	v	Somerset	Taunton	1988
7th	256	D.A.Leatherdale/S.J.Rhodes	v	Notts	Nottingham	2002
8th	184	S.J.Rhodes/S.R.Lampitt	v	Derbyshire	Kidderminster	1991
9th	181	J.A.Cuffe/R.D.Burrows	v	Glos	Worcester	1907
10th	119	W.B.Burns/G.A.Wilson	v	Somerset	Worcester	1906

Best Bowling	For	9- 23	C.F.Root	v	Lancashire	Worcester	1931
(Innings)	V	10- 51	J.Mercer	for	Glamorgan	Worcester	1936
Best Bowling	For	15- 87	A.J.Conway	v	Glos	Moreton-in-M	1914
(Match)	V	17-212	J.C.Clay	for	Glamorgan	Swansea	1937

Most Runs – Season	2654	H.H.I.Gibbons	(av 52.03)		1934
Most Runs – Career	34490	D.Kenyon	(av 34.18)		1946-67
Most 100s – Season	10	G.M.Turner			1970
	10	G.A.Hick			1988
Most 100s – Career	96	G.A.Hick			1984-2004
Most Wkts – Season	207	C.F.Root	(av 17.52)		1925
Most Wkts – Career	2143	R.T.D.Perks	(av 23.73)		1930-55
Most Career W-K Dismissals	1095	S.J.Rhodes	(991 ct/104 st)		1985-2004
Most Career Catches in the Field	416	G.A.Hick			1984-2004

LIST 'A' LIMITED-OVERS CRICKET

Highest Total	CGT	404-3		v	Devon	Worcester	1987
	BHC	314-5		v	Lancashire	Manchester	1980
	NL	307-4		v	Derbyshire	Worcester	1975
Lowest Total	CGT	98		v	Durham	Chester-le-St	1968
	BHC	70		v	Glos	Worcester	2002
	NL	86		v	Yorkshire	Leeds	1969
Highest Innings	CGT	180*	T.M.Moody	v	Surrey	The Oval	1994
	BHC	143*	G.M.Turner	v	Warwicks	Birmingham	1976
	NL	160	T.M.Moody	v	Kent	Worcester	1991
Best Bowling	CGT	7-19	N.V.Radford	v	Beds	Bedford	1991
	BHC	6- 8	N.Gifford	v	Minor C (S)	High Wycombe	1979
	NL	6-26	A.P.Pridgeon	v	Surrey	Worcester	1978

YORKSHIRE

Formation of Present Club: 8 January 1863
Substantial Reorganisation: 10 December 1891
Inaugural First-Class Match: 1864
Colours: Dark Blue, Light Blue and Gold
Badge: White Rose
County Championships (since 1890): (30) 1893, 1896, 1898, 1900, 1901, 1902, 1905, 1908, 1912, 1919, 1922, 1923, 1924, 1925, 1931, 1932, 1933, 1935, 1937, 1938, 1939, 1946, 1959, 1960, 1962, 1963, 1966, 1967, 1968, 2001
Joint Champions: (1) 1949
Gillette/NatWest/C & G Trophy Winners: (3) 1965, 1969, 2002
Benson and Hedges Cup Winners: (1) 1987
National League (Div 1) Winners: (0); best – 2nd 2000
Sunday League Winners: (1) 1983
Twenty20 Cup Winners: (0); best – 2nd in Group 2003
Match Awards: CGT 49; BHC 80

Chief Executive: C.J.Graves, Headingley Cricket Ground, Leeds, LS6 3BU • Tel: 0113 278 7394 • Fax: 0113 278 4099 • Email: cricket@yorkshireccc.org.uk • Web: www.yorkshireccc.org.uk

Director of Cricket: D.Byas. **Batting Coach**: K.Sharp. **Bowling Coach**: S.Oldham. **Captain**: C.White. **Vice-Captain**: none. **Overseas Players**: I.J.Harvey and P.A.Jaques. **2005 Beneficiary**: M.P.Vaughan. **Head Groundsman**: A.W.Fogarty. **Scorer**: J.T.Potter. ‡ New registration. NQ Not qualified for England.

BLAIN, John Angus Rae (Penicuik HS; Jewel & Esk Valley C), b Edinburgh, Scotland 4 Jan 1979. 6'1". RHB, RMF. Scotland 1996-99. Northamptonshire 1997-2003. Yorkshire debut 2004. **LOI** (Scot): 5 (1999); HS 9 and BB 4-37 v B (Edinburgh) 1999. HS 34 Nh v Surrey (Northampton) 2001. Y HS 28* v Notts (Nottingham) 2004 and 28* v Derbys (Leeds) 2004. BB 6-42 Nh v Kent (Canterbury) 2001. Y BB 4-38 v Derbys (Leeds) 2004. Award: BHC 1. LO HS 29 Scot v UAE (Dubai) 2003-04. LO BB 5-24 Nh v Derbys (Derby) 1997 (SL).

BLAKEY, Richard John (Rastrick GS), b Huddersfield 15 Jan 1967. 5'9". RHB, WK. Debut 1985; cap 1987; benefit 1998. YC 1987. No f-c appearances 2004. **Tests**: 2 (1992-93); HS 6. **LOI**: 3 (1992 to 1992-93); HS 25 v P (Lord's) 1992 – on debut. F-c **Tours**: SA 1991-92 (Y); WI 1986-87 (Y); I 1992-93; P 1990-91 (Eng A); SL 1990-91 (Eng A); Z 1989-90 (Eng A), 1995-96 (Y). 1000 runs (6); most – 1361 (1987). HS 223* v Northants (Leeds) 2003. BB 1-68. Awards: BHC 2. LO HS 130* v Kent (Scarborough) 1991 (SL).

BRESNAN, Timothy Thomas (Castleford HS and TC; Pontefract New C), b Pontefract 28 Feb 1985. 6'0". RHB, RMF. Debut 2003. HS 52 v Ind A (Leeds) 2003. CC HS 35 v Leics (Leicester) 2004. BB 3-32 v Durham (Scarborough) 2004. LO HS 61 v Leics (Leeds) 2003 (NL). BB 3-29 v Essex (Leeds) 2003 (NL).

DAWOOD, Ismail (Batley GS), b Dewsbury, Yorks 23 Jul 1976. 5'8". RHB, WK. Northamptonshire 1994. Worcestershire 1996-97. Glamorgan 1998-99. British U 2004. Yorkshire debut 2004. Hertfordshire 2002 (CGT). HS 102 Gm v Glos (Cardiff) 1999. Y HS 75 v Durham (Scarborough) 2004. LO HS 60 Herts v Warwks GIs (Coventry) 2002.

DAWSON, Richard Kevin James (Batley GS; Exeter U), b Doncaster 4 Aug 1980. 6'3". RHB, OB. British U 2000. Yorkshire debut 2001. Cap 2004. Devon 1999-2000. **Tests**: 7 (2000-02 to 2002-03); HS 19* v A (Perth) 2002-03; BB 4-134 v I (Chandigarh) 2001-02 – on debut. F-c **Tours**: A 2002-03; NZ 2001-02; I 2001-02; SL 2002-03 (ECB Acad). HS 87 v Kent (Canterbury) 2002. BB 6-82 v Glam Scarborough) 2001. LO HS 41 v Leics (Scarborough) 2002 (NL). LO BB 4-13 v Derbys (Derby) 2002 (BHC).

GALE, Andrew William (Whitcliffe Mount S; Heckmondwike GS), b Dewsbury 28 Nov 1983. 6'2". LHB, LB. England U-19 to Australia 2002-03. Debut 2004. HS 29 v Derbys (Leeds) 2004. LO HS 70* v Somerset (Scarborough) 2004 (NL).

GUY, Simon Mark (Wickersley CS), b Rotherham 17 Nov 1978. 5'7". RHB, WK. Debut 2000. No 1st appearances 2002. HS 42 v Somerset (Taunton) 2000. LO HS 29 v Leics (Leeds) 2001 (NL).

^{NO}**HARVEY, Ian** Joseph (Wonthaggi TC), b Wonthaggi, Victoria, Australia 10 Apr 1972. 5'10". RHB, RMF. Victoria 1993-94 to date. Gloucestershire 1999-2003/cap 1999. Yorkshire debut 2004. *Wisden* 2003. **LOI** (A): 73 (1997-98 to 2004); HS 48* v WI (Kingston) 2003; BB 4-16 v B (Darwin) 2003. F-c Tour: NZ 1994-95 (Aus Academy). HS 136 Vic v S Aus (Melbourne) 1995-96. UK HS 130* Gs v Middx (Lord's) 2001. Y HS 95 v Essex (Leeds) – on Y debut. BB 8-101 Aus A v SA A (Adelaide) 2002-03. UK BB 6-19 (10-32 match) Gs v Sussex (Hove) 2000. Y BB 3-38 v Derbys (Leeds) 2004. Hat-trick (Victoria 2001-02). Awards: CGT 3; BHC 4. LO HS 96 Gs v Essex (Chelmsford) 2003 (NL). LO BB 5-19 Gs v Northants (Bristol) 2000 (NL).

HOGGARD, Matthew James (Grangefield S, Pudsey), b Leeds 31 Dec 1976. 6'2". RHB, RFM. Debut 1996; cap 2000. Free State 1998-99 to 1999 00. **ECB contracts 2001-02-03-04-05.** **Tests:** 38 (2000 to 2004-05); HS 38 v WI (Oval) 2004; BB 7-61 (12-205 match) v SA (Johannesburg) 2004-05; hat-trick v WI (Bridgetown) 2003-04. **LOI:** 24 (2001-02 to 2004-05); HS 5; BB 5-49 v Z (Harare) 2001-02. F-c Tours: A 2002-03; SA 2004-05; WI 2003-04; NZ 2001-02; I 2001-02; P 2000-01; SL 2000-01, 2003-04; B 2003-04. HS 89* v Glam (Leeds) 2004. 50 wkts (1): 50 (2000). BB 7-49 v Somerset (Leeds) 2003. Hat-trick 2003-04. LO HS 7* (*twice*). LO BB 5-28 v Leics (Leicester) 2000 (NL).

^{NO}**JAQUES, Philip** Anthony Anthony (Fig Tree HS, Wollongong; Australian C of PE, Homebush), b Wollongong, NSW, Australia 3 May 1979. 6'1". LHB, SLC. British passport (English parents). NSW 2000-01 to 2001-02, 2003-04. Northamptonshire 2003; cap 2003. Yorkshire debut 2004. 1000 runs (2); most – 1409 (2003). HS 243 v Hants (Southampton) 2004. First to score 200s for and against Yorks (222 for Northants 2003). LO HS 117 Nh v Hants (Northampton) 2003 (NL).

‡^{NO}**KRUIS, Gideon** Jacobus (St Albans C), b Pretoria 9 May 1974. N Transvaal B 1993-94 to 1995-96. N Transvaal 1995-96 to 1996-97. Griqualand West 1997-98 to 2003-04. Eagles 2004-05. MCC 2000, 2001. HS 59 GW v B (Kimberley) 2000-01. BB 7-58 GW v Northerns (Pretoria) 1997-98. LO HS 28* GW v WP (Kimberley) 2000-01. LO BB 4-26 GW v Boland (Kimberley) 1999-00.

LAWSON, Mark Anthony Kenneth (Castle Hall Language C, Mirfield), b Leeds 24 Oct 1985. 5'8". RHB, LB. Debut 2004. HS 14 and BB 5-62 v Durham (Scarborough) 2004.

‡**LUCAS, David** Scott (Djanogly CTC, Nottingham), b Nottingham 19 Aug 1978. 6'2". RHB, LMF. Nottinghamshire 1999-2002. HS 49 Nt v DU (Nottingham) 2002. CC HS 46* Nt v Middx (Nottingham) 2000. LO HS 5-104 Nt v Essex (Nottingham) 1999. LO HS 19* Nt v Sussex (Hove) 1999 (NL). LO BB 4-27 Nt v Derbys (Derby) 2000 (NL).

LUMB, Michael John (St Stithians C, Johannesburg), b Johannesburg, South Africa 12 Feb 1980. Son of R.G.Lumb (Yorkshire 1970-84); nephew of A.J.S.Smith (SAU and Natal 1971-72 to 1983-84). 6'0". LHB, RM. Debut 2000; ECB qualified and CC debut 2001; cap 2003. F-c Tour (Eng A): I 2003-04. 1000 runs (1): 1038 (2003). HS 124 v Surrey (Guildford) 2002. BB 2-10 v Kent (Canterbury) 2001. LO HS 92 v Glam (Colwyn Bay) 2003 (NL).

McGRATH, Anthony (Yorkshire Martyrs CS), b Bradford 6 Oct 1975. 6'2". RHB, RM. Debut 1995; cap 1999; captain 2003. **Tests:** 4 (2003); HS 81 v Z (Chester-le-St) 2003; BB 3-16 v Z (Lord's) 2003 on debut. **LOI:** 14 (2003 to 2004); HS 52 v SA (Manchester) 2003; BB 1-13. F-c Tours (Eng A): A 1996-97; P 1995-96; Z 1995-96 (Y). HS 174 and BB 5-39 v Derbys (Derby) 2004. Awards: CGT 2; BHC 1. LO HS 109* v Minor C (Leeds) 1997 (BHC). LO BB 4-41 v Surrey (Leeds) 2003 (NL).

PYRAH, Richard Michael (Ossett S; Wakefield C), b Dewsbury 1 Nov 1982. 6'0". RHB, RM. Yorkshire 2004. HS 39 v Somerset (Taunton) 2004. LO HS 42 v Durham (Scarborough) 2004 (NL). LO BB 5-50 Yorks CB v Somerset (Scarborough) 2002 (CGT).

SAYERS, Joseph John (St Mary's RC CS, Menston; Worcester C, Oxford) b Leeds 5 Nov 1983. 6'0". LHB, OB. Oxford U 2002-04; blue 2002-03-04. Yorkshire debut 2004. HS 147 OU v CU (Oxford) 2004. Y HS 62 v Somerset (Taunton) 2004. LO HS 62 v Glos (Leeds) 2003 (NL).

SHAHZAD, Ajmal, Huddersfield 27 Jul 1985. RHB, RMF. First British-born Asian to play for Yorkshire. Yorkshire Academy player awaiting f-c debut. LO HS 5 v Worcs (Leeds) 2004 (NL).

SILVERWOOD, Christopher Eric Wilfred (Garforth CS), b Pontefract 5 Mar 1975. 6'1". RHB, RFM. Debut 1993; cap 1996; benefit 2004. YC 1996. **Tests**: 6 (1996-97 to 2002-03); HS 10 v A (Perth) 2002-03; BB 5-91 v SA (Cape Town) 1999-00. **LOI**: 7 (1996-97 to 2001-02); HS 12 v NZ (Auckland) 1996-97; BB 3-43 v Z (Bulawayo) 2001-02. F-c Tours: A 2002-03 (*part*); SA 1999-00 (*part*); WI 1997-98, 2000-01 (Eng A); NZ 1996-97; Z 1995-96 (Y), 1996-97. HS 70 v Essex (Chelmsford) 2001. 50 wkts (2): most – 59 (1999). BB 7-93 (12-148 match) v Kent (Leeds) 1997. Awards: CGT 2; BHC 2. LO HS 61 v Northants (Northampton) 2002 (CGT). LO BB 5-28 v Scot (Leeds) 1996 (BHC).

TAYLOR, Christopher Robert (Benton Park HS, Rawdon), b Leeds 21 Feb 1981. 6'4". RHB, RMF. Debut 2001. HS 52* v Surrey (Leeds) 2002. LO HS 28 v Glos (Leeds) 2003 (NL).

THORNICROFT, Nicholas David (Easingwold S), b York 23 Jan 1985. 5'11". LHB, RMF. Debut 2002. HS 30 v Notts (Leeds) 2004. BB 2-27 v Durham (Chester-le-St) 2004. LO HS 8* (NL). LO BB 5-42 v Glos (Leeds) 2003 (NL).

VAUGHAN, Michael Paul (Silverdale CS, Sheffield), b Manchester, Lancs 29 Oct 1974. 6'2". RHB, OB. Debut 1993; cap 1995; benefit 2005. *Wisden* 2002. PCA 2002. ECB **contracts 2000-01-02-03-04-05. Tests**: 55 (1999-00 to 2004-05, 24 as captain); HS 197 and BB 2-71 v I (Nottingham) 2002. Scored Eng record 1,481 runs (avge 61.70) with six hundreds in 2002. **LOI**: 66 (2000-01 to 2004-05, 40 as captain); HS 90* v Z (Bulawayo) 2004-05; BB 4-22 v SL (Manchester) 2002. F-c Tours (C=captain): A 1996-97 (Eng A), 2002-03; SA 1998-99C (Eng A), 1999-00, 2004-05C; WI 2003-04C; NZ 2001-02; I 1994-95 (Eng A), 2001-02; P 2000-01; SL 2000-01, 2003-04C; Z 1995-96 (Y), 1998-99C (Eng A); B 2003-04C. 1000 runs (4); most – 1244 (1995). HS 197 (*see Tests*). Y HS 183 v Glam (Cardiff) 1996. BB 4-39 v OU (Oxford) 1994. CC BB 4-47 v Somerset (Leeds) 2001. Awards: CGT 3; BHC 2. LO HS 125* v Somerset (Taunton) 2001 (BHC). LO BB 4-22 (*see LOI*).

WAINWRIGHT, David John (Hemsworth HS and SFC); b Pontefract 21 Mar 1985. LHB, SLA. Debut 2004. HS 5 v Somerset (Taunton) 2004 – on debut.

WHITE, Craig (Flora Hill HS, Bendigo, Australia; Bendigo HS), b Morley 16 Dec 1969. 6'0". RHB, RFM. Debut 1990; cap 1993; benefit 2002; captain 2004. Victoria 1990-91 (2 matches). **ECB contracts 2000-01. Tests**: 30 (1994 to 2002-03); HS 121 v I (Ahmedabad) 2001-02; BB 5-32 v WI (Oval) 2000. **LOI**: 51 (1994-95 to 2002 03); HS 57* v A (Melbourne) 2002-03; BB 5-21 v Z (Bulawayo) 1999-00. F-c Tours: A 1994-95, 1996-97 (Eng A), 2002-03; SA 1991-92 (Y), 1992-93 (Y); NZ 1996-97, 2001-02; I 2001-02; P 1995-96 (Eng A), 2000-01; SL 2000-01; Z 1996-97 (*part*). HS 186 v Lancs (Manchester) 2001. BB 8-55 v Glos (Gloucester) 1998 – inc hat-trick. Hat-trick 1998. Awards: CGT 4; BHC 4. LO HS 148 v Leics (Leicester) 1997 (SL). LO BB 5-19 v Somerset (Scarborough) 2002 (NL).

WOOD, Matthew James (Shelley HS & SFC), b Huddersfield 6 Apr 1977. 5'9". RHB, OB. Debut 1997; cap 2001. 1000 runs (3): most – 1432 (2003). HS 207 v Somerset (Taunton) 2003. BB 1-4. Awards: CGT 2; BHC 1. LO HS 160 v Devon (Exmouth) 2004 (CGT). LO BB 3-45 v Cambs (March) 2003 (CGT).

RELEASED/RETIRED

(Having made a first-class County appearance in 2004)

CRAVEN, Victor John (Harrogate GS), b Harrogate 31 Jul 1980. 6'0". LHB, RM. Yorkshire 2000-04. HS 81* and BB 2-18 v Derbys (Derby) 2004. LO HS 59 v Durham (Leeds) 2002 (NL). BB 4-22 v Kent (Scarborough) 2003 (NL).

GRAY, Andrew Kenneth Donovan, b Armadale, W Australia 19 May 1974. RHB, OB. British passport. Yorkshire 2001-04. HS 104 v Somerset (Taunton) 2003. BB 4-128 v Surrey (Oval) 2001. LO HS 30* v Leics (Leicester) 2003 (NL). LO BB 4-34 v Kent (Leeds) 2002 (NL).

KIRBY, S. P. – *see GLOUCESTERSHIRE.*

SABBATICAL

NQLEHMANN, Darren Scott (Gawler HS), b Gawler, S Australia 5 Feb 1970. 5'10. LHB, SLA. S Australia 1987-88 to 1989-90, 1993-94 to date; captain 1998-99 to date. Victoria 1990-91 to 1992-93. Yorkshire 1997-98, 2000, 2002, 2004; cap 1997; captain 2002; currently contracted and expected to return in 2006. *Wisden* 2000. **Tests** (A): 27 (1997-98 to 2004-05); HS 177 v D (Cairns) 2003; BB 3-42 v SL (Colombo) 2003-04. **LOI** (A): 117 (1996-97 to 2004-05); HS 119 v SL (Perth) 2002-03; BB 4-7 v Z (Harare) 2004. F-c Tours (A): E 1991 (Vic); SA 2001-02; WI 2002-03; I 1997-98, 2004-05; P 1998-99; SL 2003-04. 1000 runs (4+5); most – 1575 (1997). HS 255 S Aus v Queensland (Adelaide) 1996-97. Y HS 252 v Lancs (Leeds) 2001. BB 4-35 v Essex (Chelmsford) 2004. Awards: CGT 1; BHC 5. LO HS 191 v Notts (Scarborough) 2001 (NL). LO BB 4-26 v Devon (Exmouth) 2002 (CGT).

WORCESTERSHIRE RELEASED/RETIRED (continued from p 101)

(Having made a first-class County appearance in 2004)

ALI, Kadeer – *See GLOUCESTERSHIRE.*

NQBICHEL, Andrew John (Laidley HS; Ipswich C, Queensland), b Laidley, Queensland, Australia 27 Aug 1970. RHB, RFM. 5'11". Queensland 1992-93 to date. Worcestershire 2001-02, 2004; cap 2001. **Tests** (A): 19 (1996-97 to 2003-04); HS 71 v WI (Bridgetown) 2002-03; BB 5-60 v WI (Melbourne) 2000-01. **LOI** (A): 67 (1996-97 to 2003-04); HS 64 v NZ (Pt Elizabeth) 2002-03; BB 7-20 v E (Pt Elizabeth) 2002-03. F-c Tours (A): E 1997; SA 1996-97, 2001-02; WI 1998-99, 2002-03; P 2002-03 (in Sharjah); Scot 1998 (Aus A). HS 142 v Northants (Worcester) 2004. 50 wkts (1+1): most – 66 (2001). BB 9-93 (10-131 match) v Glos (Worcester) 2002. Awards: GGT 1; BHC 3. LO HS 100 v Glam (Cardiff) 2001 (BHC). LO BB 7-20 (*see LOI*).

NQHALL, A.J. – *see KENT.*

NQHARRITY, Mark Andrew (Taperoo HS), b Semaphore, S Australia 9 Mar 1974. British passport (English father). 6'4". RHB, LFM. S Australia 1993-94 to date. Worcestershire debut 2003. HS 19 S Aus v Vic (Melbourne) 2001-02. Wo HS 16 v Z (Worcester) 2003. CC HS 5*. BB 5-65 S Aus v Tasmania (Hobart) 2002-02. Wo BB 4-39 v Durham (Worcester) 2003. LO HS 15 v Glos (Worcester) 2003 (NL). LO BB 5-42 S Aus v Vic (Adelaide) 1997-98.

RHODES, Steven John (Lapage Middle S; Carlton-Bolling S, Bradford), b Bradford, Yorks 17 Jun 1964. Son of W.E. (Notts 1961-64). 5'7". RHB, WK. Yorkshire 1981-84. Worcestershire debut 1985; cap 1986; benefit 1996; captain 2004 (part). *Wisden* 1994. **Tests**: 11 (1994 to 1994-95); HS 65* v SA (Leeds) 1994. **LOI**: 9 (1989 to 1994-95); HS 56 v SA (Manchester) 1994. F-c Tours: A 1994-95; SA 1993-94 (Eng A); WI 1991-92 (Eng A); SL 1985-86 (Eng B), 1990-91 (Eng A); Z 1989-90 (Eng A), 1990-91 (Wo), 1993-94 (Wo), 1996-97 (Wo – captain). 1000 runs (2); most – 1018 (1995). HS 124 v Notts (Nottingham) 2002. Awards: CGT 1; BHC 2. LO HS 105 v Lancs (Manchester) 1991 (RAC).

J.C.Farrow and J.D.Whitney left the staff having made no f-c appearances in 2004.

YORKSHIRE 2004
RESULTS SUMMARY

	Place	Won	Lost	Tied	Drew	No Result
County Championship (2nd Division)	7th	3	4		9	
All First-Class Matches		3	4		9	
C & G Trophy	Semi-Finalist					
National League (2nd Division)	4th	10	6			2
Twenty20 Cup	5th in North Division					

COUNTY CHAMPIONSHIP AVERAGES
BATTING AND FIELDING

Cap		M	I	NO	HS	Runs	Avge	100	50	Ct/St
1997	D.S.Lehmann	7	11	1	120	592	59.20	1	5	2
–	P.A.Jaques	11	19	–	243	1118	58.84	3	5	11
1999	A.McGrath	9	16	–	174	728	45.50	3	1	6
2001	M.J.Wood	16	27	2	123	955	38.20	1	7	.24
–	J.J.Sayers	5	9	–	62	311	34.55	–	3	–
–	I.Dawood	8	14	5	75	310	34.44	–	1	12/2
–	V.J.Craven	6	8	1	81*	202	28.85	–	1	2
–	R.M.Pyrah	4	7	1	39	158	26.33	–	–	–
–	C.R.Taylor	4	5	1	43*	105	26.25	–	1	1
–	I.J.Harvey	7	11	–	95	273	24.81	–	1	4
2003	M.J.Lumb	13	23	1	83	546	24.81	–	4	8
–	R.K.J.Dawson	15	23	–	81	564	24.52	–	3	11
1993	C.White	7	12	1	60	265	24.09	–	1	4
2000	M.J.Hoggard	5	8	3	89*	107	21.40	–	1	2
1996	C.E.W.Silverwood	7	10	2	37	150	18.75	–	–	3
–	J.A.R.Blain	9	13	6	28*	94	13.42	–	–	1
–	T.T.Bresnan	10	15	3	45	143	11.91	–	–	3
–	A.W.Gale	4	7	–	29	78	11.14	–	–	2
–	S.M.Guy	8	12	–	26	124	10.33	–	–	21/2
–	M.A.K.Lawson	3	5	1	14	33	8.25	–	–	1
2003	S.P.Kirby	13	16	5	14*	39	3.54	–	–	2

Also batted: A.K.D.Gray (2 matches) 10, 27, 0 (2 ct); N.D.Thornicroft (2) 30, 4, 6 (1 ct); D.J.Wainwright (1) 5.

BOWLING

	O	M	R	W	Avge	Best	5wI	10wM
D.S.Lehmann	105.4	19	261	15	17.40	4-35	–	–
C.White	88.2	18	282	11	25.63	3-50	–	–
C.E.W.Silverwood	174.3	33	570	22	25.90	3-18	–	–
J.A.R.Blain	188	26	804	30	26.80	4-38	–	–
T.T.Bresnan	160.3	31	557	17	32.76	3-32	–	–
R.K.J.Dawson	379.4	71	1255	36	34.86	5-40	1	–
S.P.Kirby	327.1	53	1132	31	36.51	3-64	–	–
Also bowled:								
N.D.Thornicroft	44.2	10	168	6	28.00	2-27	–	–
V.J.Craven	51.4	8	191	6	31.83	2-18	–	–
M.A.K.Lawson	75.3	6	308	9	34.22	5-62	1	–
A.McGrath	102	21	280	8	35.00	5-39	1	–
M.J.Hoggard	121.5	22	393	9	43.66	3-50	–	–
I.J.Harvey	154	41	430	7	61.42	3-38	–	–

A.K.D.Gray 31-3-89-2; P.A.Jaques 2-0-18-0; M.J.Lumb 1-0-2-0; R.M.Pyrah 6-4-2-0; D.J.Wainwright 3-1-5-0; M.J.Wood 1-0-1-0.

Yorkshire played no fixtures outside the County Championship in 2004. The First-Class Averages (pp 121–136) give the records of Yorkshire players in all first-class county matches, with the exception of M.P.Vaughan whose only first-class appearances were for England, and I.Dawood, M.J.Hoggard and J.J.Sayers whose full county figures are as above.

YORKSHIRE RECORDS

FIRST-CLASS CRICKET

Highest Total	For 887		v	Warwicks	Birmingham	1896
	V 681-7d		by	Leics	Bradford	1996
Lowest Total	For 23		v	Hampshire	Middlesbrough	1965
	V 13		by	Notts	Nottingham	1901
Highest Innings	For 341	G.H.Hirst	v	Leics	Leicester	1905
	V 318*	W.G.Grace	for	Glos	Cheltenham	1876

Highest Partnership for each Wicket

1st	555	P.Holmes/H.Sutcliffe	v	Essex	Leyton	1932
2nd	346	W.Barber/M.Leyland	v	Middlesex	Sheffield	1932
3rd	323*	H.Sutcliffe/M.Leyland	v	Glamorgan	Huddersfield	1928
4th	330	M.J.Wood/D.R.Martyn	v	Glos	Leeds	2003
5th	340	E.Wainwright/G.H.Hirst	v	Surrey	The Oval	1899
6th	276	M.Leyland/E.Robinson	v	Glamorgan	Swansea	1926
7th	254	W.Rhodes/D.C.F.Burton	v	Hampshire	Dewsbury	1919
8th	292	R.Peel/Lord Hawke	v	Warwicks	Birmingham	1896
9th	192	G.H.Hirst/S.Haigh	v	Surrey	Bradford	1898
10th	149	G.Boycott/G.B.Stevenson	v	Warwicks	Birmingham	1982

Best Bowling	For	10-10	H.Verity	v	Notts	Leeds	1932
(Innings)	V	10-37	C.V.Grimmett	for	Australians	Sheffield	1930
Best Bowling	For	17-91	H.Verity	v	Essex	Leyton	1933
(Match)	V	17-91	H.Dean	for	Lancashire	Liverpool	1913

Most Runs – Season	2883	H.Sutcliffe	(av 80.08)	1932
Most Runs – Career	38561	H.Sutcliffe	(av 50.20)	1919-45
Most 100s – Season	12	H.Sutcliffe		1932
Most 100s – Career	112	H.Sutcliffe		1919-45
Most Wkts – Season	240	W.Rhodes	(av 12.72)	1900
Most Wkts – Career	3608	W.Rhodes	(av 16.00)	1898-1930
Most Career W-K Dismissals	1186	D.Hunter	(863 ct/323 st)	1888-1909
Most Career Catches in the Field	665	J.Tunnicliffe		1891-1907

LIST 'A' LIMITED-OVERS CRICKET

Highest Total	CGT	411-6		v	Devon	Exmouth	2004
	BHC	317-5		v	Scotland	Leeds	1986
	NL	352-6		v	Notts	Scarborough	2001
Lowest Total	CGT	76		v	Surrey	Harrogate	1970
	BHC	81		v	Lancs	Leeds	2002
	NL	54		v	Essex	Leeds	2003
Highest Innings	CGT	160	M.J.Wood	v	Devon	Exmouth	2004
	BHC	142	G.Boycott	v	Worcs	Worcester	1980
	NL	191	D.S.Lehmann	v	Notts	Scarborough	2001
Best Bowling	CGT	7-27	D.Gough	v	Ireland	Leeds	1997
	BHC	6-27	A.G.Nicholson	v	Minor C (N)	Middlesbrough	1972
	NL	7-15	R.A.Hutton	v	Worcs	Leeds	1969

FIRST-CLASS UMPIRES 2005

† New appointment
See page 10 for key to abbreviations.

BENSON, Mark Richard (Sutton Valence S), b Shoreham, Sussex 6 Jul 1958. LHB, OB. Kent 1980-95; cap 1981; captain 1991-96 (did not play in 1996); benefit 1991. **Tests:** 1 (1986); HS 30 v I (Birmingham) 1986. **LOI:** 1 (1986; HS 24). 1000 runs (11); most – 1725 (1987). HS 257 K v Hants (Southampton) 1991. BB 2-55 K v Surrey (Dartford) 1986. F-c career: 292 matches; 18387 runs @ 40.23, 48 hundreds; 5 wickets @ 98.60; 140 ct. Appointed 2000. Umpired 3 Tests (2004-05) and 10 LOI (2004 to 2004-05).

BURGESS, Graham Iefvion (Millfield S), b Glastonbury, Somerset 5 May 1943. RHB, RM. Somerset 1966-79; cap 1968; testimonial 1977. HS 129 Sm v Glos (Taunton) 1973. BB 7-43 (13-75 match) Sm v OU (Oxford) 1975. F-c career: 252 matches; 7129 runs @ 18.90, 2 hundreds; 474 wickets @ 28.57. Appointed 1991.

CONSTANT, David John, b Bradford-on-Avon, Wilts 9 Nov 1941. LHB, SLA. Kent 1961-63. Leicestershire 1965-68. HS 80 Le v Glos (Bristol) 1966. BB 1-28. F-c career: 61 matches; 1517 runs @ 19.20; 1 wicket @ 36.00. Appointed 1969. Umpired 36 Tests (1971 to 1988) and 33 LOI (1972 to 2001). Represented Gloucestershire at bowls 1984-86.

COWLEY, Nigel Geoffrey (Dutchy Manor SS, Mere), b Shaftesbury, Dorset 1 Mar 1953. RHB, OB. Dorset 1972. Hampshire 1974-89; cap 1978; benefit 1988. Glamorgan 1990. 1000 runs (1): 1042 (1984). HS 109* H v Somerset (Taunton) 1977. BB 6-48 H v Leics (Southampton) 1982. F-c career: 271 matches; 7309 runs @ 23.35, 2 hundreds; 437 wickets @ 34.04. Appointed 2000.

DUDLESTON, Barry (Stockport S), b Bebington, Cheshire 16 Jul 1945. RHB, SLA. Leicestershire 1966-80; cap 1969; benefit 1980. Gloucestershire 1981-83. Rhodesia 1976-77 to 1979-80. 1000 runs (8); most – 1374 (1970). HS 202 Le v Derbys (Leicester) 1979. BB 4-6 Le v Surrey (Leicester) 1972. F-c career: 295 matches; 14747 runs @ 32.48, 32 hundreds; 47 wickets @ 29.04. Appointed 1984. Umpired 2 Tests (1991 to 1992) and 4 LOI (1992 to 2001).

EVANS, Jeffery Howard, b Llanelli, Carms 7 Aug 1954. No f-c appearances. Appointed 2001.

GOULD, Ian James (Westgate SS, Slough), b Taplow, Bucks 19 Aug 1957. LHB, WK. Middlesex 1975 to 1980-81, 1996; cap 1977. Auckland 1979-80. Sussex 1981-90; cap 1981; captain 1987; benefit 1990. MCC YC. **LOI:** 18 (1982-83 to 1983; HS 42). Tours: A 1982-83; P 1980-81 (Int); Z 1980-81 (M). HS 128 M v Worcs (Worcester) 1978. BB 3-10 Sx v Surrey (Oval) 1989. Middlesex coach 1991-2000. Reappeared in one match (v OU) 1996. F-c career: 298 matches; 8756 runs @ 26.05, 4 hundreds; 7 wickets @ 52.14; 603 dismissals (536 ct, 67 st). Appointed 2002.

HAMPSHIRE, John Harry (Oakwood THS, Rotherham), b Thurnscoe, Yorks 10 Feb 1941. RHB, LB. Son of J. (Yorks 1937); brother of A.W. (Yorks 1975). Yorkshire 1961-81; cap 1963; benefit 1976; captain 1979-80. Leicestershire 1980-81 (tour). Derbyshire 1982-84; cap 1982. Tasmania 1967-68 to 1978-79. **Tests:** 8 (1969 to 1975); 403 runs @ 26.86, HS 107 v WI (Lord's) 1969 on debut (only England player to score hundred at Lord's on Test debut). Tours: A 1970-71; SA 1972-73 (DHR), 1974-75 (DHR); WI 1964-65 (Cav); NZ 1970-71; P 1967-68 (Cwlth XI); SL 1969-70; Z 1980-81 (Le XI). 1000 runs (15); most – 1596 (1978). HS 183* Y v Sussex (Hove) 1971. BB 7-52 Y v Glam (Cardiff) 1963. F-c career: 577 matches; 28059 runs @ 34.55, 43 hundreds; 30 wickets @ 54.56; 445 ct. Appointed 1985. Umpired 21 Tests (1989 to 2001-02) and 20 LOI (1989 to 2001). International Panel 1999 to *2001-02*.

HARRIS, Michael John ('*Pasty*') (Gerrans S, nr Truro), b St Just-in-Roseland, Cornwall 25 May 1944. RHB, LB, WK. Middlesex 1964-68; cap 1967. Nottinghamshire 1969-82; cap 1970; benefit 1977. E Province 1971-72. Wellington 1975-76. 1000 runs (11); most – 2238 (1971). Equalled Notts record with 9 hundreds in 1971. HS 201* Nt v Glam (Nottingham)

1973. BB 4-16 Nt v Warwks (Nottingham) 1969. F-c career: 344 matches; 19196 runs @ 36.70, 41 hundreds; 79 wickets @ 43.78; 302 dismissals (288 ct, 14 st). Appointed 1998.

HARTLEY, Peter John (Greenhead GS; Bradford C), b Keighley, Yorks 18 Apr 1960. RHB, RMF. Warwickshire 1982. Yorkshire 1985-97; cap 1987; benefit 1996. Hampshire 1998-2000; cap 1998. Tours (Y): SA 1991-92; WI 1986-87; Z 1995-96. HS 127* Y v Lancs (Manchester) 1988. 50 wkts (7); most – 81 (1995). BB 9-41 (inc hat-trick, 4 wkts in 5 balls and 5 in 9; 11-68 match) Y v Derbys (Chesterfield) 1995. Hat-trick 1995. F-c career: 232 matches; 4321 runs @ 19.91, 2 hundreds; 683 wickets @ 30.21. Appointed 2003.

HOLDER, John Wakefield (Combermere S), b St George, Barbados 19 Mar 1945. RHB, RFM. Hampshire 1968-72. HS 33 H v Sussex (Hove) 1971. BB 7-79 H v Glos (Gloucester) 1972. Hat-trick 1972. F-c career: 47 matches; 374 runs @ 10.68; 139 wickets @ 24.56. Appointed 1983. Umpired 11 Tests (1988 to 2001) and 19 LOI (1988 to 2001).

HOLDER, Vanburn Alonza (Richmond SM), b Deans Village, St Michael, Barbados 8 Oct 1945. RHB, RFM. Barbados 1966-67 to 1977-78. Worcestershire 1968-80; cap 1970; benefit 1979. Shropshire 1981. **Tests** (WI): 40 (1969 to 1978-79); 682 runs @ 14.20, HS 42 v NZ (P-o-S) 1971-72; 109 wkts @ 33.27, BB 6-28 v A (P-o-S) 1977-78. **LOI** (WI): 12. Tours (WI): E 1969, 1973, 1976; A 1975 76; I 1974-75, 1978-79; P 1973-74 (RW), 1974-75; SL 1974-75, 1978-79. HS 122 Barbados v Trinidad (Bridgetown) 1973-74. BB 7-40 Wo v Glam (Cardiff) 1974. F-c career: 311 matches; 3559 runs @ 13.03, 1 hundred; 947 wickets @ 24.48. Appointed 1992.

JESTY, Trevor Edward (Privet County SS, Gosport), b Gosport, Hants 2 Jun 1948. RHB, RM. Hampshire 1966-84; cap 1971; benefit 1982. Surrey 1985-87; cap 1985; captain 1985. Lancashire 1987-88 to 1991; cap 1989. Border 1973-74. GW 1974-75 to 1980-81. Canterbury 1979-80. *Wisden* 1982. **LOI:** 10. Tours: WI 1987-88 (La), 1982-83 (Int); Z 1988-89 (La). 1000 runs (10); most – 1645 (1982). HS 248 H v CU (Cambridge) 1984. Scored 122* La v OU (Oxford) 1991 in his final f-c innings. 50 wkts (2); most – 52 (1981). BB 7-75 H v Worcs (Southampton) 1976. F-c career: 490 matches; 21916 runs @ 32.71, 35 hundreds; 585 wickets @ 27.47. Appointed 1994.

JONES, Allan Arthur (St John's C, Horsham), b Horley, Surrey 9 Dec 1947. RHB, RFM. Sussex 1966-69. Somerset 1970-75; cap 1972. Middlesex 1976-79; cap 1976. Glamorgan 1980-81. Northern Transvaal 1972-73. Orange Free State 1976-77. HS 33 M v Kent (Canterbury) 1978. BB 9-51 Sm v Sussex (Hove) 1972. F-c career: 214 matches; 799 runs @ 5.39; 549 wickets @ 28.07. Appointed 1985. Umpired 1 LOI (1996).

KITCHEN, Mervyn John (Backwell SM, Nailsea), b Nailsea, Somerset 1 Aug 1940. LHB, RM. Somerset 1960-79; cap 1966; testimonial 1973. Tour: Rhodesia 1972-73 (Int W). 1000 runs (7); most – 1730 (1968). HS 189 Sm v Pakistanis (Taunton) 1967. BB 1-4. F-c career: 354 matches; 15230 runs @ 26.25, 17 hundreds; 2 wickets @ 54.50. Appointed 1982. Umpired 20 Tests (1990 to 2000) and 28 LOI (1983 to 2001). International Panel 1995 to 1999.

LEADBEATER, Barrie (Harehills SS), b Harehills, Leeds, Yorks 14 Aug 1943. RHB, RM. Yorkshire 1966-79; cap 1969; joint benefit with G.A.Cope 1980. Tour: WI 1969-70 (DN). HS 140* Y v Hants (Portsmouth) 1976. BB 1-1. F-c career: 147 matches; 5373 runs @ 25.34, 1 hundred; 1 wicket @ 5.00. Appointed 1981. Umpired 5 LOI (1983 to 2000).

LLONG, Nigel James (Ashford North S), b Ashford, Kent 11 Feb 1969. LHB, OB. Kent 1990-98; cap 1993. Tour: Z 1992-93 (K). HS 130 K v Hants (Canterbury) 1996. BB 5-21 K v Middx (Canterbury) 1996. F-c career: 68 matches; 3024 runs @ 31.17, 6 hundreds; 35 wickets @ 35.97. Appointed 2002.

LLOYDS, Jeremy William (Blundell's S), b Penang, Malaya 17 Nov 1954. LHB, OB. Somerset 1979-84; cap 1982. Gloucestershire 1985-91; cap 1985. Orange Free State 1983-84 to 1987-88. Tour (Glos): SL 1986-87. 1000 runs (3); most – 1295 (1986). HS 132* Sm v Northants (Northampton) 1982. BB 7-88 Sm v Essex (Chelmsford) 1982. F-c career: 267 matches; 10679 runs @ 31.04, 10 hundreds; 333 wickets @ 38.86; 229 ct. Appointed 1998. Umpired 4 Tests (2003-04 to 2004-05) and 10 LOI (2000 to 2004).

MALLENDER, Neil Alan (Beverley GS), b Kirk Sandall, Yorks 13 Aug 1961. RHB, RFM. Northamptonshire 1980-86 and 1995-96; cap 1984. Somerset 1987-94; cap 1987; benefit 1994. Otago 1983-84 to 1992-93; captain 1990-91 to 1992-93. **Tests:** 2 (1992); 8 runs @ 2.66, HS 4; 10 wkts @ 21.50, BB 5-50 v P (Leeds) 1992 – on debut. Tour: Z 1994-95 (Nh). HS 100* Otago v CD (Palmerston N) 1991-92. UK HS 87* Sm v Sussex (Hove) 1990. 50 wkts (6); most – 56 (1983). BB 7-27 Otago v Auckland (Auckland) 1984-85. UK BB 7-41 Nh v Derbys (Northampton) 1982. F-c career: 345 matches; 4709 runs @ 17.18, 1 hundred; 937 wickets @ 26.31; 111 ct. Appointed 1999. Umpired 3 Tests (2003-04) and 22 LOI (2001 to 2003-04), including 2002-03 World Cup. **Elite Panel 2004**.

PALMER, Roy (Southbroom SM, Devizes), b Devizes, Wilts 12 Jul 1942. RHB, RFM. Younger brother of K.E.Palmer, MBE (Somerset and England 1955-69). Somerset 1965-70. HS 84 Sm v Leics (Taunton) 1967. BB 6-45 Sm v Middx (Lord's) 1967. F-c career: 74 matches; 1037 runs @ 13.29; 172 wickets @ 31.62. Appointed 1980. Umpired 2 Tests (1992 to 1993) and 8 LOI (1983 to 1995).

SHARP, George (Elwick Road SS, Hartlepool), b West Hartlepool, Co Durham 12 Mar 1950. RHB, WK, occ LM. Northamptonshire 1968-85; cap 1973; benefit 1982. HS 98 Nh v Yorks (Northampton) 1983. BB 1-47. F-c career: 306 matches; 6254 runs @ 19.85; 1 wicket @ 70.00; 655 dismissals (565 ct, 90 st). Appointed 1992. Umpired 15 Tests (1996 to 2001-02) and 31 LOI (1995-96 to 2001-02). International Panel 1996 to 2001-02.

SHEPHERD, David Robert (Barnstaple GS; St Luke's C, Exeter), b Bideford, Devon 27 Dec 1940. RHB, RM. Gloucestershire 1965-79; cap 1969; joint benefit with J.Davey 1978. Scored 108 on debut (v OU). Devon 1959-64. 1000 runs (2); most – 1079 (1970). HS 153 Gs v Middx (Bristol) 1968. BB 1-1. F-c career: 282 matches; 10672 runs @ 24.47, 12 hundreds; 2 wickets @ 53.00. Appointed 1981. Umpired 86 Tests (1985 to 2004-05) and a record 164 LOI (1983 to 2004), including 1987-88, 1991-92, 1995-96, 1999 and 2002-03 World Cups (3 finals). International Panel 1994 to 2001-02. **Elite Panel 2001-02 to date**.

STEELE, John Frederick (Endon SS), b Brown Edge, Staffs 23 Jul 1946. RHB, SLA. Brother of D.S. (Northants, Derbys and England 1963-84). Leicestershire 1970-83; cap 1971; benefit 1983. Glamorgan 1984-86; cap 1984. Natal 1973-74 to 1977-78. Staffordshire 1965-69. Tour: SA 1974-75 (DHR). 1000 runs (6); most – 1347 (1972). HS 195 Le v Derbys (Leicester) 1971. BB 7-29 Natal B v GW (Umzinto) 1973-74 and 7-29 Le v Glos (Leicester) 1980. F-c career: 379 matches; 15054 runs @ 28.95, 21 hundreds; 584 wickets @ 27.04; 413 ct. Appointed 1997.

WHITEHEAD, Alan Geoffrey Thomas, b Butleigh, Somerset 28 Oct 1940. LHB, SLA. Somerset 1957-61. HS 15 Sm v Hants (Southampton) 1959 and 15 Sm v Leics (Leicester) 1960. BB 6-74 Sm v Sussex (Eastbourne) 1959. F-c career: 38 matches; 137 runs @ 5.70; 67 wickets @ 34.41. Appointed 1970. Umpired 5 Tests (1982 to 1987) and 14 LOI (1979 to 2001).

WILLEY, Peter (Seaham SS), b Sedgefield, Co Durham 6 Dec 1949. RHB, OB. Northamptonshire 1966-83; cap 1971; benefit 1981. Leicestershire 1984-91; cap 1984; captain 1987. E Province 1982-83 to 1984-85. Northumberland 1992. **Tests:** 26 (1976 to 1986); 1184 runs @ 26.90, HS 102* v WI (St John's) 1980-81; 7 wkts @ 65.14, BB 2-73 v WI (Lord's) 1980. **LOI:** 26. Tours: A 1979-80; SA 1972-73 (DHR), 1981-82 (SAB); WI 1980-81, 1985-86; I 1979-80; SL 1977-78 (DHR). 1000 runs (10); most – 1783 (1982). HS 227 Nh v Somerset (Northampton) 1976. 50 wkts (3); most – 52 (1979). BB 7-37 Nh v OU (Oxford) 1975. F-c career: 559 matches; 24361 runs @ 30.56, 44 hundreds; 756 wickets @ 30.95. Appointed 1993. Umpired 25 Tests (1995-96 to 2003-04) and 34 LOI (1996 to 2003), including 1999 and 2002-03 World Cups. International Panel 1996 to 2001-02 and 2003-04.

RESERVE FIRST-CLASS LIST: Rob J.Bailey, Neil L.Bainton, Stephen A.Garratt, †Darrell B.Hair (58 Tests and 108 LOI), Richard K.Illingworth, Richard A.Kettleborough, R.Tim Robinson.

Test Match and LOI statistics to 3 March and 13 February 2005 inclusive respectively.

INTERNATIONAL UMPIRES AND REFEREES 2005

ELITE PANEL OF UMPIRES 2005

The Elite Panel of ICC Umpires and Referees was introduced in April 2002 to raise standards and guarantee impartial adjudication. Two umpires from this panel stand in Test matches while one officiates with a home umpire from the Supplementary International Panel in limited-overs internationals.

Full Names	Birthdate	Birthplace	Tests	Debut	LOI	Debut
ALIM Sarwar DAR	06.06.68	Jhang, Pakistan	17	2003-04	44	1999-00
BOWDEN, Brent Fraser	11.04.63	Auckland, N Zealand	23	1999-00	69	1994-95
BUCKNOR, Stephen Anthony	31.05.46	Montego Bay, Jamaica	99	1988-89	131	1988-89
HAIR, Darrell Bruce	30.09.52	Mudgee, Australia	58	1991-92	108	1991-92
HARPER, Daryl John	23.10.61	Adelaide, Australia	48	1998-99	94	1993-94
KOERTZEN, Rudolf Eric ('Rudi')	26.03.49	Knysna, S Africa	59	1992-93	132	1992-93
SHEPHERD, David Robert	27.12.40	Bideford, England	86	1985	164	1983
TAUFEL, Simon James Arthur	21.01.71	Sydney, Australia	21	2000-01	75	1998-99

ELITE PANEL OF REFEREES 2005

Full Names	Birthdate	Birthplace	Tests	Debut	LOI	Debut
BROAD, Brian Christopher	29.09.57	Bristol, England	9	2003-04	30	2003-04
CROWE, Jeffrey John	14.09.58	Auckland, N Zealand	5	2004-05	11	2003-04
HURST, Alan George	15.07.50	Melbourne, Australia	2	2004-05	3	2004-05
LLOYD, Clive Hubert	31.08.44	Georgetown, Guyana	43	1992-93	101	1992-93
MADUGALLE, Ranjan Senerath	22.04.59	Kandy, Sri Lanka	72	1993-94	167	1993-94
MAHANAMA, Roshan Siriwardena	31.05.66	Colombo, England	4	2004	16	2004
PROCTER, Michael John	15.09.46	Durban, S Africa	28	2001-02	77	2001-02
VISWANATH, Gundappa Ranganath	12.02.49	Bhadravati, India	15	1999-00	78	1998-99

INTERNATIONAL PANEL OF UMPIRES 2005

Nominated by their respective cricket boards, members from this panel officiate in home LOIs and supplement the Elite panel for Test matches. Specialist third umpires have been selected to undertake adjudication involving television replays.

			Third Umpire
Australia	S.J.Davis	P.D.Parker	R.L.Parry
Bangladesh	A.F.M.Akhtaruddin	Mahbubur Rahman	Nadir Shah
England	M.R.Benson	J.W.Lloyds	N.J.Llong
India	K.Hariharan	A.V.Jayaprakash	I.Sivaram
New Zealand	D.B.Cowie	A.L.Hill	E.A.Watkin
Pakistan	Asad Rauf	Nadeem Ghauri	Zamir Haider
South Africa	I.L.Howell	B.G.Jerling	K.H.Hurter
Sri Lanka	E.A.R.de Silva	T.H.Wijewardene	R.Martinez
West Indies	B.R.Doctrove	E.A.Nicholls	B.E.W.Morgan
Zimbabwe	K.C.Barbour	R.B.Tiffin	D.Frost

Test Match and LOI statistics to 3 March and 13 February 2005 inclusive respectively.

UNIVERSITY FIRST-CLASS REGISTER 2004

‡ Represented British Universities v New Zealanders

BRITISH UNIVERSITIES
(Excluding players listed above)

Full Names	Birthdate	Birthplace	University	Bat/Bowl	F-C Debut
‡DAWOOD, Ismail	23.07.76	Dewsbury	Bradford/Leeds	RHB/WK	1994
‡SHIRAZI, Damien Cyrus	23.03.83	Neath	Southampton	LHB/RM	2004

CAMBRIDGE († Blue 2004)

Full Names	Birthdate	Birthplace	College	Bat/Bowl	F-C Debut
AKRAM, Mohammed Adnan	17.11.83	Leytonstone	(Anglia PU)	RHB/RM	2003
AKRAM, Mohammed Arfan	17.11.83	Leytonstone	(Anglia PU)	RHB/LB	2003
†BANERJEE, Vikram	20.03.84	Bradford	Downing	LHB/SLA	2004
BUCKHAM, Craig Thomas	09.08.83	Ashford (Kent)	(Anglia PU)	RHB/LB	2004
†CLARKE, Adam Charles Spencer	10.11.81	Sherwood, N'ham	Downing	RHB/RMF	2001
EDWARDS, Philip Duncan	16.04.84	Minster, I of Sheppey	(Anglia PU)	RHB/RFM	2004
HARVEY, Thomas Frederick Charles	04.02.80	Chatham	(Anglia PU)	LHB/OB	2004
HEMBRY, Tobias Digby Charles	16.11.83	Ipswich	(Anglia PU)	LHB	2004
†HEYWOOD, James John Neville	24.09.82	Eastbourne	Homerton	RHB/WK	2003
†HILLYARD, Christopher Martin	14.05.83	Edinburgh	Jesus	LHB/LM	2004
JAMES, Gareth David	01.12.84	Walthamstow	(Anglia PU)	RHB/LB	2004
KAY, Matthew Adam	09.11.82	Enfield	(Anglia PU)	RHB/LB	2004
LEE, Nicholas Trevor	16.10.83	Dartford	(Anglia PU)	RHB/LB	2004
MANN, Richard James	26.09.82	Ipswich	St John's	LHB/OB	2003
†‡MARSHALL, Simon James	20.09.82	Birkenhead	Pembroke	RHB/OB	2002
†NEWMAN, Anush Raj Ignatius	03.02.84	Ealing	Jesus	RHB, OB	2004
†NOBLE, David Jonathan	08.11.82	Manchester	Emmanuel	RHB/RM	2002
PALLADINO, Antonio Paul	29.06.83	London	(Anglia PU)	RHB/RMF	2003
PARK, Garry Terence	19.04.83	Empangeni, SA	(Anglia PU)	RHB/RMF	2003
†SAVILL, Thomas Edward	16.05.83	Sheffield	Homerton	RHB/RFM	2002
†SHANKAR, Adrian	07.05.82	Ascot	Queens	RHB/OB	2002
†SINGH, Anirudh	28.12.83	Birmingham	Gonville & Caius	RHB/LB	2003
†WEBLEY, Thomas	02.03.83	Bristol	(Anglia PU)	LHB/SLA	2004
WRIGHT, Christopher Julian Clement	14.07.85	Chipping Norton	(Anglia PU)	RHB/RFM	2004

OXFORD († Blue 2004)

Full Names	Birthdate	Birthplace	College	Bat/Bowl	F-C Debut
AIREY, Stuart James	18.03.83	Cleethorpes	(Brookes U)	RHB/RMF	2003
‡ANWAR, Omar Sohail	01.07.83	Harrow	(Brookes U)	RHB	2003
†CLINTON, Paul James Selvey	30.08.83	Dartford	Keble	RHB/RM	2004
DALEY, Stephen Robert	15.04.77	Atherton, Australia	Magdalen	LHB/RMF	2003
†DALRYMPLE, Simon Hedley	06.06.83	Worcester	Christ Church	RHB/RM	2002
†DORAN, Graeme Paul	02.12.79	Liverpool	St Edmund Hall	RHB/WK	2004
†FOX, Daniel Richard	03.03.83	Birmingham	Greyfriars	RHB	2004
†HAWINKELS, Stephen John	12.03.82	Cape Town, SA	University	RHB/RM	2001
HOWARD, William Oliver Fitzalen	13.02.81	Guildford	(Brookes U)	RHB/WK	2004
HUTTON, Oliver Richard	27.05.79	Johannesburg, SA	OXILP#	LHB/RM	2004
KNAPPETT, Joshua Philip Thomas	15.04.85	Westminster	(Brookes U)	RHB/WK	2004
‡LINLEY, Timothy Edward	23.03.82	Leeds	(Brookes U)	RHB	2003
†‡McMAHON, Paul Joseph	12.03.83	Wigan	Wadham	RHB/OB	2002
†MUNDAY, Michael Kenneth	22.10.84	Nottingham	Corpus Christi	RHB/LB	2003
PARKER, Luke Charles	27.09.83	Coventry	(Brookes U)	RHB/RM	2004
RICHARDS, Mali Alexander	02.09.83	Taunton	(Brookes U)	LHB/RM	2004
†SAYERS, Joseph John	05.11.83	Leeds	Worcester	LHB/OB	2002
†SUMAN, Amit Kumar	10.12.80	Sahibganj, India	Pembroke	RHB/LM	1998-99
†UPADHYAY, Amit Madhusoodhan	29.09.78	Bombay, India	St Antony's	RHB/OB	2004
†WYATT, Alexander August	23.06.76	Melbourne, Aus	New	RHB/LB	2002

Oxford Institute of Legal Practice

DURHAM

Full Names	Birthdate	Birthplace	College	Bat/Bowl	F-C Debut
BISHOP, Justin Edward	04.01.82	Bury St Edmunds	John Snow	LHB/LMF	1999
BROWN, David Owen	08.12.82	Burnley	Collingwood	RHB/RM	2003
BURNELL, William Fleet	07.01.85	Havering	St Aidan's	RHB/RM	2004
CARPENTER, Edward James	10.09.82	Hammersmith	Grey	RHB/SLA	2004
CLARKE, Adam Peter Augustus	13.09.84	Greenwich	St Hild & St Bede	RHB/RMF	2004
‡DAGGETT, Lee Martin	01.10.82	Bury	John Snow	RHB/RMF	2003
DALE, Mark Adam Paul	16.03.82	Hucknall	George Stephenson	RHB/RM	2003
HOLLINGSWORTH, Simon Christopher	01.10.83	Chertsey	St Cuthbert's Society	RHB/RM	2004
HOWELLS, Peter William	09.10.81	Stockton-on-Tees	St Aidan's	RHB/WK	2004
LONGHURST, Neil James	21.11.84	Rotherham	John Snow	LHB/RMF	2004
MAIDEN, Alastair Jonathan	15.09.82	Stourbridge	Collingwood	RHB/RM	2002
READ, Glen George	04.09.81	Cuckfield	Collingwood	LHB/LM	2004
‡SMITH, Will Rew	28.09.82	Luton	Collingwood	RHB/OB	2002
SOMERVILLE-HENDRIE, John William	22.06.83	Hillingdon	George Stephenson	RHB/RFM	2003

LOUGHBOROUGH

Full Names	Birthdate	Birthplace		Bat/Bowl	F-C Debut
‡ADAMS, James Henry Kenneth	23.09.80	Winchester		LHB/LM	2002
ANYON, James Edward	05.05.83	Lancaster		LHB/RFM	2003
ATRI, Vikram	09.03.83	Hull		RHB/OB	2002
BENHAM, Christopher Charles	24.03.83	Frimley		RHB/RM-OB	2004
CLINTON, Richard Selvey	01.09.81	Sidcup		LHB/RM	2001
HARRISON, Paul William	22.05.84	Cuckfield		RHB/WK	2004
LEWIS, Philip David	04.10.81	Liss		RHB/RFM	2003
‡NASH, Christopher David	19.05.83	Cuckfield		RHB/OB	2002
PANESAR, Mudhsuden Singh	25.04.82	Luton		LHB/SLA	2001
ROSENBERG, Marc Christopher	10.02.82	Johannesburg, South Africa		RHB/RM	2004
WALKER, George William	12.05.84	Norwich		LHB/SLA	2002
‡WIGLEY, David Harry	26.10.81	Bradford		RHB/RFM	2002
WILKINSON, Richard Malcolm	24.11.82	Birkenhead		RHB/RM	2004

TOURING TEAMS FIRST-CLASS REGISTER 2004

NEW ZEALAND

Full Names	Birthdate	Birthplace	Team	Type	F-C Debut
ASTLE, Nathan John	15.09.71	Christchurch	Canterbury	RHB/RM	1991-92
BOND, Shane Edward	07.06.75	Christchurch	Canterbury	RHB/RF	1996-97
CAIRNS, Christopher Lance	13.06.70	Picton	Canterbury	RHB/RFM	1988
FLEMING, Stephen Paul	01.04.73	Christchurch	Wellington	LHB/RSM	1991-92
FRANKLIN, James Edward Charles	07.11.80	Wellington	Wellington	LHB/LFM	1998-99
HOPKINS, Gareth James	24.11.76	Lower Hutt	Otago	RHB/WK	1997-98
McCULLUM, Brendon Barrie	27.09.81	Dunedin	Canterbury	RHB/WK	1999-00
McMILLAN, Craig Douglas	13.09.76	Christchurch	Canterbury	RHB/RM	1994-95
MARTIN, Christopher Stewart	10.12.74	Christchurch	Canterbury	RHB/RFM	1997-98
MILLS, Kyle David	15.03.79	Auckland	Auckland	RHB/RFM	1998-99
ORAM, Jacob David Philip	28.07.78	Palmerston North	C Districts	LHB/RMF	1997-98
PAPPS, Michael Hugh William	02.07.79	Christchurch	Canterbury	RHB/WK	1998-99
RICHARDSON, Mark Hunter	11.06.71	Hastings	Auckland	LHB/LM	1989-90
STYRIS, Scott Bernard	10.07.75	Brisbane, Australia	N Districts	RHB/RMF	1994-95
TUFFEY, Daryl Raymond	11.06.78	Milton	N Districts	RHB/RFM	1996-97
VETTORI, Daniel Luca	27.01.79	Auckland	N Districts	RHB/SLA	1996-97

WEST INDIES

Full Names	Birthdate	Birthplace	Team	Type	F-C Debut
BANKS, Omari Ahmed Clemente	17.07.82	Anguilla	Leeward Is	RHB/OB	2000-01
BAUGH, Carlton Seymour	23.06.82	Kingston	Jamaica	RHB/LBG/WK	2000-01
BEST, Tino la Bertram	26.08.81	St Michael	Barbados	RHB/RFM	2001-02
BRAVO, Dwayne James John	07.10.83	Santa Cruz	Trinidad	RHB/RFM	2001-02
CHANDERPAUL, Shivnarine	18.08.74	Unity Village	Guyana	LHB/LB	1991-92
COLLINS, Pedro Tyrone	12.08.76	Boscobelle	Barbados	RHB/LFM	1996-97
COLLYMORE, Corey Dalanelo	21.12.77	Boscobelle	Barbados	RHB/RMF	1998-99
EDWARDS, Fidel Henderson	06.02.82	St Peter	Barbados	RHB/RF	2001-02
GAYLE, Christopher Henry	21.09.79	Kingston	Jamaica	LHB/OB	1998-99
JACOBS, Ridley Detamore	26.11.67	Swetes, Antigua	Leeward Is	LHB/WK	1991-92
JOSEPH, Sylvester Cleofoster	05.09.78	New Winthorpes, Antigua	Leeward Is	RHB/RM	1996-97
LARA, Brian Charles	02.05.69	Santa Cruz	Trinidad	LHB/LBG	1987-88
LAWSON, Jermaine Jay Charles	13.01.82	Spanish Town	Jamaica	RHB/RF	2000-01
MOHAMMED, Dave	08.10.79	Princes Town	Trinidad	LHB/SLC	2000-01
RAMPAUL, Ravindranath	15.10.84	Preysal	Trinidad	LHB/RFM	2001-02
SARWAN, Ramnaresh Ronnie	23.06.80	Wakenaam I	Guyana	RHB/LB	1995-96
SMITH, Dwayne Romel	12.04.83	St Michael	Barbados	RHB/RM	2001-02
SMITH, Devon Sheldon	21.10.81	Sauters, Grenada	Windward Is	LHB/OB	1998-99

SRI LANKA A

Full Names	Birthdate	Birthplace	Team	Type	F-C Debut
DANIEL, Gerald Ian	17.08.81	Colombo	Bloomfield	RHB	1999-00
DIAS, Wadugamudalige Joseph Maurice Ranga	14.08.79	Kandy	Tamil Union	RHB/RFM	1999-00
FERNANDO, Charith Sylvester	30.12.82	Badulla	Chilaw Marians	LHB/WK	2001
GAJANAKE, Malintha Krishantha	05.10.80	Colombo	Tamil Union	RHB/OB	2000-01
JAYAWARDENA, Hewasandatchige Asiri Prasanna Wishvanath	09.10.79	Colombo	Colombo	RHB/WK	1997-98
KALAVITIGODA, Shantha	23.12.77	Colombo	Colts	RHB/LB	1997-98
KULASEKARA, Mudiyanselage Dinesh Nuwan	22.07.82	Nittambuwa	Galle	RHB/RFM	2002-03
LOKUARACHCHI, Kaushal Samaraweera	20.05.82	Colombo	Bloomfield	RHB/LB	2000-01
MENDIS, Balapuwaduge Manukulasuriya Amith Jeewan	15.01.83	Colombo	Sinhalese	LHB/LB	2000-01
MIRANDO, Magina Thilan Thushara	01.03.81	Balapitiya	Nondescripts	LHB/LFM	1998-99
MUBARAK, Jehan	10.01.81	Washington	Colombo	LHB/OB	1999-00
PERERA, Wagawattage Maithree Bathiya	28.04.77	Colombo	Moors	RHB/LB	1996-97
PRASAD, Kariyawasam Tirana Gamage Dammika	30.05.83	Ragama	Sinhalese	RHB/RFM	2001-02
RAMYAKUMARA, Wijekoon Mudiyanselage Gayan	21.12.76	Gampaha	Tamil Union	LHB/LM	1996-97
SURAJ, Mohamed Marshuk	30.01.85	Matara	Matara	RHB/OB	2004

THE 2004 FIRST-CLASS SEASON
STATISTICAL HIGHLIGHTS

FIRST TO INDIVIDUAL TARGETS

1000 RUNS	R.W.T.Key	Kent	2 June
2000 RUNS	–	Most 1896 – R.W.T.Key (Kent)	
100 WICKETS	–	Most 84 – Mushtaq Ahmed (Sussex)	

TEAM HIGHLIGHTS

HIGHEST INNINGS TOTALS (†*County record*)

708-9d	Essex v Leicestershire	Chelmsford
695-9d†	Gloucestershire v Middlesex	Gloucester
654-8d	Somerset v Nottinghamshire	Nottingham
642	Essex v Glamorgan	Chelmsford
Highest first-class total by a losing team		
641-4d	Hampshire v Nottinghamshire	Nottingham
634-9d	Leicestershire v Durham	Leicester
619-6d	Worcestershire v Gloucestershire	Worcester
618	Sussex v Kent	Hove
615	Kent v Lancashire	Tunbridge Wells
612	Nottinghamshire v Hampshire	Nottingham
608-7d	Warwickshire v Middlesex	Lord's
600-6d	Warwickshire v Sussex	Horsham

HIGHEST FOURTH INNINGS TOTALS

453-9	Durham (set 451) v Somerset	Taunton
429-5	Kent (set 429) v Worcestershire	Canterbury
410	Kent (set 530) v Middlesex	Southgate

LOWEST INNINGS TOTALS

88	Derbyshire v West Indians	Derby
91	Durham v Derbyshire	Chester-le-St
93	Durham v Nottinghamshire	Chester-le-St
96	Derbyshire v Nottinghamshire	Derby

MATCH AGGREGATES OF 1500 RUNS

1617-36	Essex (642, 165) v Glamorgan (587, 223-6)	Chelmsford
1576-35	England (568, 325-5d) v West Indies (416, 267) (1st Test)	Lord's
1548-20	Hampshire (641-4d, 295-6d) v Nottinghamshire (612)	Nottingham
1532-39	Glamorgan (435, 335) v Essex (437, 325-9)	Cardiff
1522-35	Worcestershire (453, 405-6d) v Kent (420, 244-9)	Worcester

BATSMEN'S MATCH (Qualification: 1200 runs, average 70 per wicket)

77.40 (1548-20)	Hampshire (641-4d, 295-6d) v Nottinghamshire (612)	Nottingham

LARGE MARGINS OF VICTORY

409 runs	Glamorgan (333, 468-9d) beat Leicestershire (255, 137)	Cardiff

ALL ELEVEN SCORING DOUBLE FIGURES

Glamorgan (474) v Derbyshire	Derby
England (470) v West Indies (4th Test)	The Oval

SIXTY EXTRAS IN AN INNINGS

B	LB	W	NB			
88	9	16	11	52	Sussex (618) v Kent	Hove

```
70  –  11  15  44  Somerset (400-8d) v Durham            Chester-le-St
63   5  13   5  40  Worcestershire (401) v Kent           Canterbury
62  25  21   3  13  England (526) v New Zealand (2nd Test) Leeds
```
Under ECB regulations, Test matches excluded, two penalty extras were scored for each no-ball.

BATTING HIGHLIGHTS

TRIPLE HUNDREDS († *County record*)

J.P.Crawley	301*	Hampshire v Nottinghamshire	Nottingham
N.V.Knight	303*	Warwickshire v Middlesex	Lord's
C.M.Spearman	341†	Gloucestershire v Middlesex	Gloucester

DOUBLE HUNDREDS

C.J.Adams		200	Sussex v Northamptonshire	Hove
I.R.Bell		262*	Warwickshire v Sussex	Horsham
J.Cox		250	Somerset v Nottinghamshire	Nottingham
J.W.M.Dalrymple		244	Middlesex v Surrey	The Oval
J.S.Foster		212	Essex v Leicestershire	Chelmsford
G.A.Hick	(2)	204*	Worcestershire v New Zealanders	Worcester
		262	Worcestershire v Gloucestershire	Worcester
B.J.Hodge	(3)	240	Leicestershire v Essex	Chelmsford
		221	Leicestershire v Derbyshire	Oakham
		262	Leicestershire v Durham	Leicester
P.A.Jaques		243	Yorkshire v Hampshire	Southampton
W.I.Jefferson		222	Essex v Hampshire	Southampton
R.W.T.Key		221	England v West Indies (1st Test)	Lord's
M.J.North		219	Durham v Glamorgan	Cardiff
M.J.Prior		201*	Sussex v Loughborough UCCE	Hove
C.M.Spearman		237	Gloucestershire v Warwickshire	Bristol

HUNDREDS IN THREE CONSECUTIVE INNINGS

I.R.Bell (Warwickshire)	112 and 181	v Lancashire	Manchester
	121	v Kent	Birmingham
M.J.Clarke (Hampshire)	140 and 103	v Nottinghamshire	Nottingham
	109	v Glamorgan	Cardiff
D.J.Hussey (Nottinghamshire)	170	v Hampshire	Nottingham
	116	v Essex	Southend
	140	v Leicestershire	Nottingham
M.R.Ramprakash (Surrey)	130 and 100*	v Worcestershire	The Oval
	134	v Lancashire	Croydon

HUNDRED IN EACH INNINGS OF A MATCH

I.R.Bell	112	181	Warwickshire v Lancashire	Manchester
M.J.Clarke	140	103	Hampshire v Nottinghamshire	Nottingham
B.J.Hodge	105	158	Leicestershire v Glamorgan	Leicester
B.L.Hutton	100	107	Middlesex v Kent	Southgate
W.I.Jefferson	167	100*	Essex v Nottinghamshire	Nottingham
R.W.T.Key	114	117*	Kent v New Zealanders	Canterbury
M.L.Love	133*	161*	Northamptonshire v Worcestershire	Worcester
S.D.Peters	123	117	Worcestershire v Kent	Worcester
M.R.Ramprakash	130	100*	Surrey v Worcestershire	The Oval
M.E.Trescothick	105	107	England v West Indies (2nd Test)	Birmingham
M.P.Vaughan	103	101*	England v West Indies (1st Test)	Lord's
M.J.Walker	157	100*	Kent v Sussex	Canterbury

FASTEST HUNDRED (WALTER LAWRENCE TROPHY)

R.L.Johnson (101*) 63 balls	Somerset v Durham	Chester-le-St

HUNDRED BEFORE LUNCH

		Day		
D.S.Lehmann	15*-120	3	Yorkshire v Durham	Chester-le-St
M.A.Wagh	0*-105	1	Warwks v Cambridge UCCE	Cambridge

HUNDRED ON FIRST-CLASS DEBUT

D.R.Fox	104	Oxford U v Cambridge U	Oxford

HUNDRED ON FIRST-CLASS DEBUT IN BRITISH ISLES

A.R.Adams	124	Essex v Leicestershire	Leicester
D.J.Hussey	107*	Nottinghamshire v Oxford UCCE	Oxford
S.R.Watson	112*	Hampshire v Somerset	Southampton

CARRYING BAT THROUGH COMPLETED INNINGS

M.T.G.Elliott	77*	Glamorgan (169) v Hampshire	Cardiff
J.J.B.Lewis	35*	Durham (91) v Derbyshire	Chester-le-St
R.R.Montgomerie	60*	Sussex (195) v Lancashire	Hove
M.J.Wood	66*	Yorkshire (160) v Somerset	Scarborough

LONG INNINGS

Min	Balls			
644	488	N.V.Knight (303*)	Warwickshire v Middlesex	Lord's

NOTABLE PARTNERSHIPS († County record)

First Wicket

265	W.I.Jefferson/A.N.Cook	Essex v Leicestershire	Chelmsford

Second Wicket

291	A.J.Strauss/R.W.T.Key	England v West Indies (1st Test)	Lord's
255	R.W.T.Key/E.T.Smith	Kent v Middlesex	Canterbury
254	N.V.Knight/I.R.Bell	Warwickshire v Middlesex	Lord's

Third Wicket

417	G.A.Hick/B.F.Smith	Worcestershire v Gloucestershire	Worcester
299	D.J.Bicknell/K.P.Pietersen	Nottinghamshire v Derbyshire	Derby
283	C.M.Spearman/C.G.Taylor	Gloucestershire v Middlesex	Gloucester

Fifth Wicket

298	E.C.Joyce/J.W.M.Dalrymple	Middlesex v Surrey	The Oval
254	I.R.Bell/D.R.Brown	Warwickshire v Lancashire	Manchester
243	J.N.Batty/A.D.Brown	Surrey v Gloucestershire	The Oval
236	M.J.Walker/M.A.Carberry	Kent v Worcestershire	Canterbury

Sixth Wicket

218	J.Hughes/R.D.B.Croft	Glamorgan v Leicestershire	Cardiff

Seventh Wicket

289*†	I.R.Bell/T.Frost	Warwickshire v Sussex	Horsham
229	M.J.Prior/L.J.Wright	Sussex v Loughborough UCCE	Hove

Eighth Wicket

198	J.D.Middlebrook/A.R.Adams	Essex v Leicestershire	Leicester
163	M.P.Maynard/R.D.B.Croft	Glamorgan v Essex	Chelmsford
158	S.R.Watson/S.D.Udal	Hampshire v Somerset	Southampton
154	M.A.Hardinges/R.J.Sillence	Gloucestershire v Warwickshire	Bristol

Ninth Wicket

157*	A.W.Laraman/R.L.Johnson	Somerset v Durham	Chester-le-St

Tenth Wicket

120	D.J.Hussey/S.C.G.MacGill	Nottinghamshire v Durham	Nottingham
113	S.I.Mahmood/G.Keedy	Lancashire v Sussex	Manchester
106	T.J.Murtagh/J.Ormond	Surrey v Middlesex	The Oval
105	R.C.Irani/S.A.Brant	Essex v Nottinghamshire	Southend
104	M.R.Ramprakash/J.Ormond	Surrey v Gloucestershire	Bristol
103	M.A.Sheikh/N.G.E.Walker	Derbyshire v Somerset	Derby

BOWLING HIGHLIGHTS

EIGHT OR MORE WICKETS IN AN INNINGS

L.M.Daggett	8-94	Durham UCCE v Durham	Chester-le-St

TEN OR MORE WICKETS IN A MATCH

J.M.Anderson		10- 81	Lancashire v Worcestershire	Manchester
G.J.Batty		10-113	Worcestershire v Northamptonshire	Northampton
G.R.Breese		10-151	Durham v Yorkshire	Scarborough
Danish Kaneria		13-186	Essex v Yorkshire	Chelmsford
N.D.Doshi	(2)	11-182	Surrey v Lancashire	Manchester
		10-183	Surrey v Sussex	Hove
F.H.Edwards		10- 83	West Indians v Derbyshire	Derby
O.D.Gibson	(2)	11-141	Leicestershire v Nottinghamshire	Leicester
		10-147	Leicestershire v Essex	Leicester
G.Keedy		14-227	Lancashire v Gloucestershire	Manchester
S.C.G.MacGill		10-233	Nottinghamshire v Essex	Southend
N.A.M.McLean		11-124	Somerset v Yorkshire	Scarborough
Mohammad Sami		10-138	Kent v Northamptonshire	Northampton
Mushtaq Ahmed (2)		10-149	Sussex v Middlesex	Lord's
		13-140	Sussex v Worcestershire	Hove
H.H.Streak		13-158	Warwickshire v Northamptonshire	Birmingham

OUTSTANDING INNINGS ANALYSIS

I.R.Bell	4-1-4-4	Warwickshire v Middlesex	Lord's

HAT-TRICKS - None

200 RUNS CONCEDED IN AN INNINGS

R.D.B.Croft	58-9-203-3	Glamorgan v Essex	Chelmsford

MATCH DOUBLE (100 RUNS AND 10 WICKETS)

G.R.Breese	35, 68; 5-41, 5-110 Durham v Yorkshire	Scarborough

WICKET-KEEPER'S MATCH DOUBLE (100 RUNS AND 10 DISMISSALS)

J.N.Batty	129ct, 18*; 8 ct, 2 st Surrey v Kent	The Oval

SIX OR MORE WICKET-KEEPING DISMISSALS IN AN INNINGS

J.N.Batty	8 ct	Surrey v Kent	The Oval
J.N.Batty	4 ct, 2 st	Surrey v Lancashire	Manchester
N.J.O'Brien	6 ct	Kent v Middlesex	Canterbury
R.J.Turner	5 ct, 1 st	Somerset v Hampshire	Southampton

NINE OR MORE WICKET-KEEPING DISMISSALS IN A MATCH

J.N.Batty	7 ct, 4 st	Surrey v Lancashire	Manchester
J.N.Batty	10 ct	Surrey v Kent	The Oval
N.J.O'Brien	7ct, 2 st	Kent v Middlesex	Canterbury

NO BYES CONCEDED IN TOTAL OF 500 OR MORE

619-6d	S.J.Adshead	Gloucestershire v Worcestershire	Worcester
566-9d	R.D.Jacobs	West Indies v England (2nd Test)	Birmingham
534	L.Sutton	Derbyshire v Leicestershire	Oakham
504-9d	G.L.Brophy	Northamptonshire v Lancashire	Northampton

SIX CATCHES IN A MATCH IN THE FIELD

A.N.Cook	6 ct	Essex v Durham	Chester-le-St

2004 FIRST-CLASS AVERAGES

These averages involve the 498 cricketers who appeared in the 174 first-class matches played by 28 teams in England and Wales during the 2004 season.

'Cap' denotes the season in which the player was awarded a 1st XI cap by the county he represented in 2004. For Worcestershire players, '2004' denotes the award of county colours in 2004. Gloucestershire now cap players on their first-class debut.

Team abbreviations: BU – British Universities; CU – Cambridge University/Cambridge UCCE; De – Derbyshire; Du – Durham; DU – Durham UCCE; E – England; Ex – Essex; Gm – Glamorgan; Gs – Gloucestershire; H – Hampshire; K – Kent; La – Lancashire; Le – Leicestershire; LU – Loughborough UCCE; M – Middlesex; MCC – Marylebone Cricket Club; Nh – Northamptonshire; Nt – Nottinghamshire; NZ – New Zealand (ers); OU – Oxford University/Oxford UCCE; SL – Sri Lanka A; Sm – Somerset; Sy – Surrey; Sx – Sussex; Wa – Warwickshire; WI – West Indies (ians); Wo – Worcestershire; Y – Yorkshire.

† Left-handed batsman.

BATTING AND FIELDING

	Cap	M	I	NO	HS	Runs	Avge	100	50	Ct/St
Adams, A.R.(Ex)	2004	7	8	–	124	196	24.50	1	–	4
Adams, C.J.(Sx)	1998	16	25	4	200	1003	47.76	4	?	14
† Adams, J.H.K.(LU/BU/H)	–	12	20	3	75	511	30.05	–	2	2
Adnan, M.H.(De)	2004	18	31	4	140	1380	51.11	3	8	11
Adshead, S.J.(Gs)	2004	15	23	7	61	609	38.06	–	4	39/2
† Afzaal, U.(Nh)	–	16	28	5	167*	1365	59.34	4	7	9
Agarkar, A.B.(M)	–	3	4	2	22	27	13.50	–	–	2
Airey, S.J.(OU)	–	3	3	1	72	96	48.00	–	1	1
† Akram, Adnan M.(CU)	–	2	3	–	128	148	49.33	1	–	–
Akram, Arfan M.(CU)	–	2	4	1	21	24	8.00	–	–	–
Ali, Kabir (Wo)	2002ᶜ	8	9	1	31	93	11.62	–	–	2
Ali, Kadeer (Wo)	2002ᶜ	6	10	–	66	216	21.60	–	1	4
Ali, S.M.B.(De)	–	4	6	1	50	110	22.00	–	1	1
Alleyne, D. (Nt)	–	4	4	2	43*	112	56.00	–	–	11
Alleyne, M.W.(Gs)	1990	5	6	1	77*	171	34.20	–	2	5
Ambrose, T.R.(Sx)	2003	10	15	–	60	257	17.13	–	2	21/1
† Anderson, J.M.(La/E)	2003	7	8	3	12	29	5.80	–	–	4
Anderson, R.S.G.(Nh)	–	1	1	1	33*	33	–	–	–	–
† Andrew, G.M.(Sm)	–	2	3	–	44	59	19.66	–	–	2
Anwar, O.S.(OU/BU)	–	4	3	–	82	98	32.66	–	1	1
† Anyon, J.E.(LU)	–	2	1	1	2*	2	–	–	–	–
Astle, N.J.(NZ)	–	6	10	1	93	343	38.11	–	3	1
Atri, V.(LU)	–	3	5	1	30	84	21.00	–	–	–
Averis, J.M.M.(Gs)	2001	13	11	4	48*	150	21.42	–	–	2
Azhar Mahmood(Sy)	2004	12	20	1	84	577	30.36	–	4	8
Bailey, T.M.B.(Nh)	2003	5	5	2	52*	89	29.66	–	1	3/4
Ball, M.C.J.(Gs)	1996	8	10	4	38	155	25.83	–	–	5
† Banerjee, V.(CU)	–	1	2	–	19	32	16.00	–	–	–
Banks, O.A.C.(WI)	–	5	10	2	90	224	28.00	–	1	1
Bassano, C.W.G.(De)	2002	14	22	3	123*	814	42.84	2	6	4
Batty, G.J.(Wo)	2002ᶜ	12	18	3	133	470	31.33	1	2	7
Batty, J.N.(Sy)	2001	17	29	2	145	933	34.55	3	3	50/6
Baugh, C.S.(WI)	–	4	8	1	150*	304	43.42	1	1	10/2
Bell, I.R.(Wa)	2001	18	29	4	262*	1714	68.56	6	7	12
Benham, C.C.(LU/H)	–	4	6	1	74	202	40.40	–	1	–
Benkenstein, D.M.(MCC)	–	1	2	–	39	48	24.00	–	–	–
Benning, J.G.E.(Sy)	–	6	11	1	128	265	26.50	1	–	3
Best, T.L.(WI)	–	2	2	–	3	3	1.50	–	–	1

F-C	Cap	M	I	NO	HS	Runs	Avge	100	50	Ct/St
Betts, M.M.(M)	–	7	8	2	31*	87	14.50	–	–	3
† Bevan, M.G.(K)	–	4	7	–	66	90	12.85	–	1	2
Bichel, A.J.(Wo)	2001	14	18	1	142	717	42.17	3	2	3
† Bicknell, D.J.(Nt)	2000	17	26	1	175	1080	43.20	5	1	4
Bicknell, M.P.(Sy)	1989	13	19	3	47*	447	27.93	–	–	4
† Bishop, J.E.(DU)	–	3	5	1	66	148	37.00	–	2	2
† Blackwell, I.D.(Sm)	2001	11	16	2	131	864	61.71	2	6	5
Blain, J.A.R.(Y)	–	9	13	6	28*	94	13.42	–	–	1
† Blignaut, A.M.(Du)	–	2	4	–	56	90	22.50	–	1	–
Bloomfield, T.F.(M)	2001	1	1	–	8	8	8.00	–	–	–
Bond, S.E.(NZ)	–	3	2	–	7	7	3.50	–	–	4
Bopara, R.S.(Ex)	–	5	8	1	40*	156	22.28	–	–	5
† Botha, A.G.(De)	2004	11	18	2	103	405	25.31	1	1	5
Bowler, P.D.(Sm)	1995	16	27	6	187*	1034	49.23	3	3	11
Bracken, N.W.(Gs)	2004	2	2	1	13*	21	21.00	–	–	–
Brandy, D.G.(Le)	–	1	2	–	7	11	5.50	–	–	–
Brant, S.A.(Ex)	2003	7	8	1	19	39	5.57	–	–	–
Bravo, D.J.J.(WI)	–	7	14	–	118	358	25.57	1	2	4
Breese, G.R.(Du)	–	14	25	1	165*	685	28.54	1	3	12
Bresnan, T.T.(Y)	–	10	15	3	35	143	11.91	–	–	3
† Bressington, A.N.(Gs)	2004	3	3	3	58*	83	–	–	1	1
Bridge, G.D.(Du)	–	11	18	3	52	321	21.40	–	2	1
Brignull, D.S.(Le)	–	1	2	2	0*	0	–	–	–	–
Brophy, G.L.(Nh)	–	16	25	2	181	744	32.34	1	4	27/2
Brown, A.D.(Sy)	1994	15	24	2	170	1155	52.50	4	6	15
Brown, D.O.(DU)	–	3	5	–	65	85	17.00	–	1	1
Brown, D.R.(Wa)	1995	17	22	3	162	957	50.36	3	2	7
Brown, J.F.(Nh)	2000	13	15	6	34	82	9.11	–	–	4
Brown, M.J.(H)	–	16	28	2	109*	838	32.23	2	6	12
Bruce, J.T.A.(H)	–	4	5	1	9	10	2.50	–	–	1
Bryant, J.D.C.(De)	–	9	16	1	30	169	11.26	–	–	3
Buckham, C.T.(CU)	–	1	2	1	8	12	12.00	–	–	–
Burnell, W.F.(DU)	–	2	4	–	49	57	14.25	–	–	–
Burns, M.(Sm)	1999	16	22	2	124*	733	36.65	1	4	17
† Butcher, M.A.(Sy/E)	1996	7	14	1	184	403	31.00	1	1	3
Butler, I.G.(K)	–	5	8	2	68	185	30.83	–	1	2
Caddick, A.R.(Sm)	1992	14	14	4	54	204	20.40	–	1	5
Cairns, C.L.(NZ)	–	6	10	–	82	349	34.90	–	4	–
† Carberry, M.A.(K)	–	12	19	4	112	639	42.60	2	4	5
Carpenter, E.J.(DU)	–	3	4	1	0*	0	0.00	–	–	2
† Carter, N.M.(Wa)	–	14	15	4	95	245	22.27	–	1	3
† Cawdron, M.J.(Nh)	–	1	–	–	–	–	–	–	–	1
† Chanderpaul, S.(WI)	–	6	12	3	128*	583	64.77	2	2	4
† Chapman, J.R.(De)	–	1	1	–	7	7	7.00	–	–	–
Chapple, G.(La)	1994	14	22	1	112	726	34.57	2	4	3
† Cherry, D.D.(Gm)	–	3	5	1	29	107	26.75	–	–	–
Chilton, M.J.(La)	2002	16	27	2	124*	809	32.36	2	2	9
Clark, S.R.(M)	–	3	3	–	34	69	23.00	–	–	–
Clarke, A.C.S.(CU)	–	1	2	1	22	29	29.00	–	–	–
† Clarke, A.J.(Ex)	–	5	6	–	28	50	8.33	–	–	2
Clarke, A.P.A.(DU)	–	1	1	–	0	0	0.00	–	–	–
Clarke, M.J.(H)	2004	12	20	–	140	709	35.45	3	2	20
Clarke, R.(Sy)	–	10	17	–	112	530	31.17	1	2	15
† Cleary, M.F.(Le)	–	11	14	8	38	179	29.83	–	–	3
Clinton, P.J.S.(OU)	–	2	1	–	6	6	6.00	–	–	–
† Clinton, R.S.(LU/Sy)	–	7	12	1	73	265	24.09	–	2	10
Coetzer, K.J.(Du)	–	6	10	–	67	212	21.20	–	1	–
Collingwood, P.D.(Du)	1998	6	11	–	68	322	29.27	–	3	5

122

F-C	Cap	M	I	NO	HS	Runs	Avge	100	50	Ct/St
Collins, P.T.(WI)	–	4	8	2	19*	37	6.16	–	–	2
Collymore, C.D.(WI)	–	3	6	1	10	33	6.60	–	–	–
Compton, N.R.D.(M)	–	4	7	2	40	111	22.20	–	–	3
† Cook, A.N.(Ex/MCC)	–	14	24	2	126	718	32.63	1	5	21
Cook, J.W.(Nh)	2003	6	9	–	114	222	24.66	1	1	4
Cook, S.J.(M)	2003	12	15	–	40	251	16.73	–	–	6
Cork, D.G.(La)	2004	14	20	2	109	437	24.27	1	2	17
Cosker, D.A.(Gm)	2000	7	9	6	21*	68	22.66	–	–	8
Cottey, P.A.(Sx)	1999	11	17	–	185	510	30.00	1	–	7
Cowan, A.P.(Ex)	1997	5	7	2	25	63	12.60	–	–	3
Cox, J.(Sm)	1999	13	20	1	250	1013	53.31	3	4	7
† Craven, V.J.(Y)	–	6	8	1	81*	202	28.85	–	1	2
Crawley, J.P.(H)	2002	13	21	3	301*	938	52.11	1	5	4
Croft, R.D.B.(Gm)	1992	17	25	4	138	712	33.90	2	1	2
Crook, A.R.(La)	–	2	4	–	27	68	17.00	–	–	–
Crook, S.P.(La)	–	4	5	–	68	157	31.40	–	1	1
Cusden, S.M.J.(K)	–	4	6	4	12*	22	11.00	–	–	2
Daggett, L.M.(DU/BU)	–	3	3	1	7	11	5.50	–	–	–
Dagnall, C.E.(Le)	–	11	12	2	17	75	7.50	–	–	4
† Dakin, J.M.(Le)	2000	5	9	3	71*	210	35.00	–	1	1
Dale, A.(Gm)	1992	7	13	3	44	241	24.10	–	–	3
Dale, M.A.P.(DU)	–	3	6	1	48	166	33.20	–	–	–
Dalrymple, J.W.M.(M)	2004	16	25	4	244	848	40.38	1	4	9
Dalrymple, S.H.(OU)	–	1	1	–	13	13	13.00	–	–	1
Daniel, G.I.(SL)	–	3	5	–	72	177	35.40	–	2	2
Danish Kaneria (Ex)	2004	11	13	7	13*	47	7.83	–	–	7
Davies, A.M.(Du)	–	10	17	8	29	110	12.22	–	–	2
† Davies, A.P.(Gm)	–	2	3	–	6	10	3.33	–	–	–
Davis, M.J.G.(Sx)	2002	10	14	3	43	171	15.54	–	–	6
Dawood, I.(BU/Y)	–	9	14	5	75	310	34.44	–	1	13/2
Dawson, R.K.J.(Y)	2004	15	23	–	81	564	24.52	–	3	11
† Dean, K.J.(De)	1998	7	10	4	35	117	19.50	–	–	3
DeFreitas, P.A.J.(Le)	1986	13	20	3	78	394	23.17	–	1	1
Denly, J.L.(K)	–	1	1	–	0	0	0.00	–	–	–
Dennington, M.J.(K)	–	7	9	2	50*	108	15.42	–	1	2
Dias, W.J.M.R.(SL)	–	1	1	–	23	23	23.00	–	–	1
Doran, G.P.(OU)	–	1	1	1	9*	9	–	–	–	3/2
Doshi, N.D.(Sy)	–	9	13	3	29*	134	13.40	–	–	2
Dumelow, N.R.C.(De)	–	4	6	–	18	50	8.33	–	–	–
Durston, W.J.(Sm)	–	2	3	–	47	86	28.66	–	–	8
Dutch, K.P.(Sm)	2001	6	8	1	72	248	35.42	–	2	2
Ealham, M.A.(Nt)	2004	16	20	2	139	871	48.38	3	4	13
Edwards, F.H.(WI)	–	6	9	3	5*	20	3.33	–	–	2
† Edwards, N.J.(Sm)	–	10	19	–	93	537	28.26	–	2	11
Edwards, P.D.(CU)	–	3	5	3	43	65	32.50	–	–	–
† Elliott, M.T.G.(Gm)	2000	15	26	1	157	1346	53.84	4	6	15
Ferley, R.S.(K)	–	4	5	–	29	34	6.80	–	–	1
† Fernando, C.S.(SL)	–	1	2	–	44	52	26.00	–	–	2/1
Fisher, I.D.(Gs)	2004	11	17	–	45	320	18.82	–	–	4
† Fleming, S.P.(NZ)	–	5	9	–	117	482	53.55	1	3	6
Flintoff, A.(La/E)	1998	7	11	1	167	603	60.30	1	6	7
† Flower, A.(MCC/Ex)	2002	17	29	3	172	1121	43.11	2	6	18
Foster, J.S.(MCC/Ex)	2001	17	25	5	212	1037	51.85	4	1	45/6
Fox, D.R.(OU)	–	1	1	–	104	104	104.00	1	–	–
† France, B.J.(De)	–	4	7	–	56	126	18.00	–	1	2
† Francis, J.D.(Sm)	–	10	16	1	110	554	36.93	2	3	6
Francis, S.R.G.(Sm)	–	11	10	6	15	46	11.50	–	–	6
† Franklin, J.E.C.(NZ/Gs)	2004	4	8	3	44	155	31.00	–	–	2

123

F-C	Cap	M	I	NO	HS	Runs	Avge	100	50	Ct/St
† Franks, P.J.(Nt)	1999	17	22	5	57*	634	37.29	–	5	2
† Frost, T.(Wa)	1999	17	19	6	135*	568	43.69	1	2	47/6
Fulton, D.P.(K)	1998	16	28	1	122	1106	40.96	5	3	21
Gait, A.I.(De)	–	14	25	1	81	509	21.20	–	2	12
Gajanayake, M.K.(SL)	–	3	5	–	29	105	21.00	–	–	9/1
† Gale, A.W.(Y)	–	4	7	–	29	78	11.14	–	–	2
Gallian, J.E.R.(Nt)	1998	17	25	2	190	1121	48.73	3	8	16
† Gayle, C.H.(WI)	–	6	11	–	105	569	51.72	1	4	3
Gazzard, C.M.(Sm)	–	2	3	1	44*	97	48.50	–	–	3
Gibson, O.D.(Le)	–	15	19	3	60*	480	30.00	–	4	5
Gidman, A.P.R.(MCC/Gs)	2004	17	25	–	91	869	34.76	–	9	13
Giles, A.F.(Wa/E)	–	8	10	2	70	289	36.12	–	2	3
Goddard, L.J.(De)	–	2	1	–	8	8	8.00	–	–	7
Goode, C.M.(Nh)	–	1	1	–	0	0	0.00	–	–	–
Goodwin, M.W.(Sx)	2001	17	27	2	119	875	35.00	3	4	9
Gough, D.(Ex)	2004	7	10	1	50	144	16.00	–	1	–
Gray, A.K.D.(Y)	–	2	3	–	27	37	12.33	–	–	2
Grayson, A.P.(Ex)	1996	6	10	–	119	365	36.50	1	2	–
Greenidge, C.G.(Nh)	–	4	4	1	8*	13	4.33	–	–	–
† Gunter, N.E.L.(De)	–	2	3	1	15*	27	13.50	–	–	2
Guy, S.M.(Y)	–	8	12	–	26	124	10.33	–	–	21/2
Habib, A.(Ex)	2002	14	22	–	157	776	35.27	1	5	3
Hall, A.J.(Wo)	2003c	12	19	2	81	558	32.82	–	5	16
† Hamilton, G.M.(Du)	–	8	15	1	58	320	22.85	–	2	3
Hancock, T.H.C.(Gs)	1998	9	13	1	77*	481	40.08	–	4	4
Hardinges, M.A.(Gs)	2004	1	1	1	68*	68	–	–	1	3
Harmison, S.J.(E)	1999	7	8	4	36*	80	20.00	–	–	2
Harris, A.J.(Nt)	2000	2	3	1	13	24	12.00	–	–	–
Harrison, A.J.(MCC)	–	1	1	–	34*	34	–	–	–	–
Harrison, D.S.(Gm)	–	17	22	4	88	395	21.94	–	1	8
Harrison, P.W.(LU)	–	3	4	1	27	77	25.66	–	–	4
Harrity, M.A.(Wo)	2003c	4	3	1	3*	3	1.50	–	–	–
Harvey, I.J.(Y)	–	7	11	–	95	273	24.81	–	1	4
† Harvey, T.F.C.(CU)	–	1	1	–	21	21	21.00	–	–	–
† Havell, P.M.R.(De)	–	8	10	6	13*	32	8.00	–	–	2
Hawinkels, S.J.(OU)	–	3	4	–	27	79	19.75	–	–	–
Haynes, J.J.(La)	–	4	5	–	24	48	9.60	–	–	12/2
Hayward, M.(M)	–	11	13	5	9	40	5.00	–	–	4
Hegg, W.K.(La)	1989	12	17	3	54	412	29.42	–	1	23/5
† Hembry, T.D.C.(CU)	–	2	4	–	28	56	14.00	–	–	1
† Hemp, D.L.(Gm)	1994	17	29	4	102*	1120	44.80	1	10	15
Henderson, C.W.(Le)	–	16	21	3	63	295	16.38	–	2	6
Hewson, D.R.(De)	–	2	2	–	9	9	4.50	–	–	–
Heywood, J.J.N.(CU)	–	1	2	1	0*	0	0.00	–	–	1
Hick, G.A.(Wo)	1986	17	29	4	262	1589	63.56	4	6	25
Hildreth, J.C.(Sm)	–	13	20	2	108	760	42.22	2	5	12
† Hillyard, C.M.(CU)	–	1	2	–	20	31	15.50	–	–	–
Hodge, B.J.(Le)	2003	15	25	–	262	1548	61.92	5	4	6
† Hogg, G.B.(Wa)	–	12	13	3	158	706	70.60	1	7	6
† Hogg, K.W.(La)	–	4	7	–	23	72	10.28	–	–	–
Hoggard, M.J.(Y/E/MCC)	2000	13	18	5	89*	239	18.38	–	1	4
Hollingsworth, S.C.(DU)	–	3	5	–	30	65	13.00	–	–	2
Hollioake, A.J.(Sy)	1995	11	19	1	106	412	22.88	1	2	6
Hooper, C.L.(La)	2003	13	21	3	115	693	38.50	2	4	19
Hopkins, G.J.(NZ)	–	1	1	–	71	71	71.00	–	1	2
Hopkinson, C.D.(Sx)	–	1	2	–	13	13	6.50	–	–	–
Horton, P.J.(La)	–	1	1	–	22	22	22.00	–	–	–
Howard, W.O.F.(OU)	–	2	1	–	33	33	33.00	–	–	1

124

F-C	Cap	M	I	NO	HS	Runs	Avge	100	50	Ct/St
Howells, P.W.(DU)	–	3	5	2	25*	58	19.33	–	–	7
Huggins, T.B.(Nh)	–	9	14	2	82*	355	29.58	–	2	3
Hughes, J.(Gm)	–	11	15	–	110	361	24.06	1	1	5
† Hunt, T.A.(Sm)	–	1	1	1	1*	1	–	–	–	–
Hunter, I.D.(De)	–	1	2	–	6	6	3.00	–	–	–
Hussain, N.(Ex/E)	1989	3	5	1	103*	309	77.25	2	1	5
Hussey, D.J.(Nt)	2004	17	23	4	170	1315	69.21	7	2	24
† Hussey, M.E.K.(Gs)	2004	7	13	1	78	442	36.83	–	2	10
Hutchison, P.M.(M)	–	8	10	3	8	25	3.57	–	–	3
Hutton, B.L.(M)	2003	16	29	1	126	1129	40.32	5	3	23
† Hutton, O.R.(OU)	–	1	2	–	18	23	11.50	–	–	3
Innes, K.J.(Sx)	–	3	4	–	38	68	17.00	–	–	1
Irani, R.C.(Ex)	1994	10	16	4	164	695	57.91	3	2	1
† Jacobs, R.D.(WI)	–	4	7	2	117*	242	48.40	1	1	10/1
James, G.D.(CU)	–	2	4	1	33*	63	21.00	–	–	1
† Jaques, P.A.(Y)	–	11	19	–	243	1118	58.84	3	5	11
Jayawardena, H.A.P.W.(SL)	–	2	3	1	48*	76	38.00	–	–	1
Jefferson, W.I.(Ex)	2002	17	29	1	222	1555	55.53	6	5	15
Jennings, C.J.R.(Nh)	–	1	1	–	6	6	6.00	–	–	–
Johnson, R.L.(Sm)	2001	15	14	2	101*	297	24.75	1	1	3
Jones, G.O.(K/E)	2003	11	13	1	101	433	36.08	2	1	34/3
Jones, P.S.(Nh)	–	8	9	1	37	139	17.37	–	–	1
† Jones, S.P.(Gm/E/MCC)	2002	11	11	5	20	45	7.50	–	–	2
Joseph, R.H.(K)	–	7	9	3	26	77	12.83	–	–	3
Joseph, S.C.(WI)	–	4	8	–	114	367	45.87	1	2	2
† Joyce, E.C.(M)	2002	14	25	2	134	1055	45.86	2	7	12
Kalavitigoda, S.(SL)	–	2	3	–	39	66	22.00	–	–	1
Kasprowicz, M.S.(Gm)	2002	7	11	2	42	126	14.00	–	–	2
† Katich, S.M.(H)	2003	4	5	–	66	183	36.60	–	1	3
Kay, M.A.(CU)	–	1	1	–	21	21	21.00	–	–	1
† Keedy, G.(La)	2000	16	20	8	17	90	7.50	–	–	7
Keegan, C.B.(M)	2003	5	4	–	44	75	18.75	–	–	2
Kendall, W.S.(H)	1999	8	14	1	50	238	18.30	–	1	7
Kenway, D.A.(H)	2001	14	23	1	101	552	25.09	1	1	9
Key, R.W.T.(MCC/K/E)	2001	16	27	3	221	1896	79.00	9	3	8
Khalid, S.A.(Wo)	2003c	3	3	2	6*	7	7.00	–	–	1
Khan, A.(K)	–	9	9	2	29	107	15.28	–	–	–
Khan, Z.(Sy)	–	1	1	1	2*	2	–	–	–	–
Killeen, N.(Du)	1999	13	22	5	35*	269	15.82	–	–	1
King, R.D.(Du)	–	2	4	–	3	4	1.00	–	–	1
Kirby, S.P.(Y)	2003	13	16	5	14*	39	3.54	–	–	2
Kirtley, R.J.(Sx)	1998	13	18	5	53*	212	16.30	–	1	3
† Klusener, L.(M)	–	6	8	1	68*	170	24.28	–	2	2
Knappett, J.P.T.(OU)	–	2	2	–	45	45	22.50	–	–	2
† Knight, N.V.(Wa)	1995	16	30	6	303*	1324	55.16	2	8	9
† Koenig, S.G.(M/MCC)	2002	18	33	2	171	1125	36.29	2	6	6
Kulasekara, M.D.N.(SL)	–	3	4	–	38	77	19.25	–	–	2
Kumar, P.(Du)	–	2	4	1	21	36	12.00	–	–	–
Lamb, G.A.(H)	–	1	2	1	94	101	101.00	–	1	–
† Lara, B.C.(WI)	–	5	10	1	113*	420	46.66	1	2	10
Laraman, A.W.(Sm)	–	11	11	2	66*	186	20.66	–	1	5
Law, S.G.(La)	2002	12	18	1	171*	867	51.00	3	1	17
Lawson, J.J.C.(WI)	–	4	6	3	4*	11	3.66	–	–	2
Lawson, M.A.K.(Y)	–	3	5	1	14	33	8.25	–	–	1
Lee, N.T.(CU)	–	1	2	–	15	15	7.50	–	–	–
† Lehmann, D.S.(Y)	1997	7	11	1	120	592	59.20	1	5	2
Lewis, J.(Gs)	1998	16	15	4	34*	193	17.54	–	–	1
Lewis, J.J.B.(Du)	1998	17	31	1	127	757	25.23	1	4	7

125

F-C	Cap	M	I	NO	HS	Runs	Avge	100	50	Ct/St
Lewis, M.L.(Gm)	–	3	1	–	0	0	0.00	–	–	1
Lewis, P.D.(LU)	–	3	3	1	43*	101	50.50	–	–	1
† Lewry, J.D.(Sx)	1996	11	14	4	72	159	15.90	–	1	2
Linley, T.E.(OU/BU)	–	4	3	–	8	16	5.33	–	–	–
Logan, R.J.(Nt)	–	3	4	2	25*	45	22.50	–	–	3
Lokuarachchi, K.S.(SL)	–	2	3	–	91	106	35.33	–	1	–
† Longhurst, N.J.(DU)	–	2	3	–	29	61	20.33	–	–	–
Loudon, A.G.R.(K)	–	11	17	–	92	597	35.11	–	6	6
Louw, J.(Nh)	–	16	22	3	63	342	18.00	–	1	8
Love, M.L.(Nh)	–	2	4	3	161*	394	394.00	2	1	3
Lowe, J.A.(Du)	–	2	4	–	41	91	22.75	–	–	2
Loye, M.B.(La)	2003	14	22	3	184	934	49.15	2	6	8
† Lumb, M.J.(Y)	2003	13	23	1	83	546	24.81	–	4	8
McCoubrey, A.G.A.M.(Ex)	–	6	7	4	2*	4	1.33	–	–	3
McCullum, B.B.(NZ)	–	7	11	1	96	342	34.20	–	3	13/3
MacGill, S.C.G.(Nt)	2002	15	12	2	28	126	12.60	–	–	8
McGrath, A.(Y)	1999	9	16	–	174	728	45.50	3	1	6
McGrath, G.D.(M)	–	2	3	–	24	28	9.33	–	–	–
† McLean, N.A.M.(Sm)	2003	10	11	3	22*	61	7.62	–	–	1
McMahon, P.J.(OU/BU/Nt)	–	6	6	2	99	153	38.25	–	1	3
McMillan, C.D.(NZ)	–	6	9	1	86	245	30.62	–	2	–
Maddy, D.L.(Le)	1996	17	30	2	145	900	32.14	1	7	24
Mahmood, S.I.(La)	–	11	14	3	94	233	21.18	–	1	2
Maiden, A.J.(DU)	–	2	2	–	20	33	16.50	–	–	–
Malik, M.N.(Wo)	2004[c]	8	9	2	39*	48	6.85	–	–	2
† Mann, R.J.(CU)	–	1	2	–	24	26	13.00	–	–	3
Marshall, S.J.(CU/BU)	–	4	6	–	98	218	36.33	–	1	–
Martin, C.S.(NZ)	–	6	9	5	7	13	3.25	–	–	2
Martin, P.J.(La)	1994	6	7	2	33*	59	11.80	–	–	1
Martin-Jenkins, R.S.C.(Sx)	2000	16	23	1	64*	424	19.27	–	2	6
Mascarenhas, A.D.(H)	1998	16	24	2	104	477	21.68	1	–	8
Mason, M.S.(Wo)	2002[c]	17	20	6	63	205	14.64	–	1	5
Masters, D.D.(Le)	–	6	9	1	31	74	9.25	–	–	3
† Maunders, J.K.(Le)	–	11	22	–	116	461	20.95	1	2	4
Maynard, M.P.(Gm)	1987	15	24	3	163	906	43.14	3	4	14
Mendis, B.M.A.J. (SL)	–	2	4	–	34	64	16.00	–	–	3
Middlebrook, J.D.(Ex)	2003	16	24	2	115	723	32.86	2	3	4
Mills, K.D.(NZ)	–	2	4	2	42*	57	28.50	–	–	–
† Miranda, M.T.T.(SL)	–	2	3	–	20	25	8.33	–	–	–
Mohammad Akram (Sx)	2004	14	18	8	35*	199	19.90	–	–	2
Mohammad Sami (K)	–	5	6	–	29	52	8.66	–	–	1
† Mohammed, D.(WI)	–	2	3	–	23	36	12.00	–	–	1
† Mongia, D.(La)	–	6	9	2	111	470	67.14	2	2	2
Montgomerie, R.R.(Sx)	1999	18	29	1	85	1010	36.07	–	10	12
Moore, S.C.(Wo)	2003[c]	17	29	3	146	1004	38.61	3	4	7
Moss, J. (De)	2004	12	20	2	147*	608	33.77	1	4	5
† Mubarak, J. (SL)	–	3	5	–	83	235	47.00	–	3	4
Muchall, G.J.(Du)	–	16	30	1	142*	975	33.62	1	5	14
Mullally, A.D.(H)	2000	10	10	5	22*	67	13.40	–	–	1
Munday, M.K.(OU)	–	4	3	1	14	15	7.50	–	–	–
† Murtagh, T.J.(Sy)	–	11	17	8	74*	374	41.55	–	4	8
Mushtaq Ahmed (Sx)	2003	17	24	5	62	424	22.31	–	2	6
† Mustard, P.(Du)	–	3	5	–	60	148	29.60	–	1	9
Napier, G.R.(MCC/Ex)	2003	15	23	4	106*	637	33.52	1	5	7
Nash, C.D.(LU/BU)	–	4	5	1	63	134	33.50	–	2	2
Nash, D.C.(M)	2000	12	17	4	113	529	40.69	1	3	26/2
† New, T.J.(Le)	–	5	7	3	51*	94	23.50	–	1	11/1
Newby, O.J.(La)	–	1	1	1	0*	0	–	–	–	–

F-C	Cap	M	I	NO	HS	Runs	Avge	100	50	Ct/St
Newman, A.R.I.(CU)	–	1	2	–	17	17	8.50	–	–	
† Newman, S.A.(Sy)	–	17	30	1	131	1277	44.03	3	9	11
† Nixon, P.A.(Le)	1994	12	21	3	63*	361	20.05	–	1	34/6
Noble, D.J.(CU)	–	1	2	–	14	24	12.00	–	–	
† North, M.J.(Du)	–	17	31	1	219	969	32.30	2	4	8
† O'Brien, N.J.(K)	–	14	19	4	69	439	29.26	–	3	33/5
Onions, G.(Du)	–	8	12	5	20*	76	10.85	–	–	2
† Oram, J.D.P.(NZ)	–	5	7	2	103*	263	52.60	1	1	3
Ormond, J.(Sy)	2003	17	24	5	57	330	17.36	–	1	4
Paget, C.D.(De)	–	4	4	2	7	7	3.50	–	–	
Palladino, A.P.(CU/Ex)	–	3	2	–	41	41	20.50	–	–	
† Panesar, M.S.(LU)	–	3	3	1	12*	12	6.00	–	–	1
Papps, M.H.W.(NZ)	–	5	9	–	126	241	26.77	1	1	4
Park, G.T.(CU)	–	3	5	1	36	87	21.75	–	–	10
Parker, L.C.(OU)	–	3	3	–	27	32	10.66	–	–	1
Parsons, K.A.(Sm)	1999	3	4	1	55	114	38.00	–	1	2
Patel, M.M.(K/MCC)	1994	13	19	1	44	238	13.22	–	–	1
Pattison, I.(Du)	–	3	4	–	33	92	23.00	–	–	3
Peng, N.(Du)	2001	10	18	–	88	417	23.16	–	3	6
† Peploe, C.T.(M)	–	8	12	2	28*	140	14.00	–	–	3
Perera, W.M.B.(SL)	–	3	5	1	86*	209	52.25	–	2	3
Peters, S.D.(Wo)	2002c	17	29	–	123	907	31.27	3	3	13
Pettini, M.L.(Ex)	–	3	5	–	67	104	20.80	–	1	1
Phillips, B.J.(Nh)	–	15	21	3	90	327	18.16	–	3	2
Pietersen, K.P.(MCC/Nt)	2002	16	21	1	167	1044	52.20	4	4	19
Pipe, D.J.(Wo)	2002c	3	3	–	12	20	6.66	–	–	–
Plunkett, L.E.(Du)	–	10	16	4	54	302	25.16	–	1	2
Ponting, R.T.(Sm)	–	3	4	1	117	297	99.00	2	1	7
Pothas, N.(H)	2003	16	24	3	131*	834	39.71	3	4	45/5
Powell, D.B.(De)	–	2	3	–	17	33	11.00	–	–	1
Powell, M.J.(Gm)	2000	16	27	2	124	900	36.00	1	7	14
Powell, M.J.(Nh)	–	7	12	–	49	239	19.91	–	–	2
Powell, M.J.(Wa/MCC)	1999	10	17	2	134	657	43.80	2	2	5
Prasad, K.T.G.D.(SL)	–	1	1	–	10	10	10.00	–	–	–
† Pratt, A.(Du)	2001	14	25	3	68	618	28.09	–	4	33/2
Pratt, G.J.(Du)	–	9	17	–	71	324	19.05	–	2	7
Pretorius, D.(Wa)	–	9	6	3	14	31	10.33	–	–	1
Price, R.W.(Wo)	2004c	3	5	2	76*	146	48.66	–	1	1
Prior, M.J.(Sx)	2003	18	26	1	201*	1158	46.32	3	6	25/2
Prittipaul, L.R.(H)	–	5	9	–	49	231	25.66	–	–	3
Pyrah, R.M.(Y)	–	4	7	1	39	158	26.33	–	–	
Ramprakash, M.R.(Sy)	2002	17	29	5	161	1564	65.16	7	6	7
† Ramyakumara, W.M.G.(SL)	–	2	4	2	67*	150	75.00	–	2	1
Read, C.M.W.(Nt)	1999	13	18	2	130	807	50.43	2	6	35/3
† Read, G.G.(DU)	–	1	2	1	9	10	10.00	–	–	
Rhodes, S.J.(Wo)	1986	17	21	9	59*	433	36.08	–	2	44/4
† Richards, M.A.(OU)	–	2	1	–	5	5	5.00	–	–	1
Richardson, A.(Wa)	2002	7	4	2	17	26	13.00	–	–	2
† Richardson, M.H.(NZ)	–	6	11	1	101	583	58.30	1	3	4
Roberts, T.W.(Nh)	–	17	29	2	89	748	27.70	–	6	12
Robinson, D.D.J.(Le)	–	16	28	–	154	1087	38.82	1	9	18
Rofe, P.C.(Nh)	–	5	6	4	15*	20	10.00	–	–	1
† Rogers, C.J.L.(De)	–	6	11	2	156	498	55.33	1	3	6
Rosenberg, M.C.(LU)	–	2	2	–	3	6	3.00	–	–	
† Russell, R.C.(Gs)	1985	2	2	1	28*	30	30.00	–	–	1
Sadler, J.L.(Le)	–	14	25	2	95	566	24.60	–	3	7
Saggers, M.J.(MCC/K/E)	2001	9	9	–	64	74	8.22	–	1	4
Sales, D.J.G.(Nh)	1999	16	25	5	171	1230	61.50	1	12	18

127

F-C	Cap	M	I	NO	HS	Runs	Avge	100	50	Ct/St
Salisbury, I.D.K.(Sy)	1998	9	13	1	77	285	23.75	–	1	3
Sampson, P.J.(Sy)	–	2	4	2	11*	13	6.50	–	–	–
Saqlain Mushtaq (Sy)	1998	3	4	–	14	17	4.25	–	–	1
Sarwan, R.R.(WI)	–	6	12	–	139	319	26.58	1	1	7
Savill, T.E.(CU)	–	4	6	–	29	54	9.00	–	–	3
† Sayers, J.J.(OU/Y)	–	8	13	–	147	518	39.84	1	4	1
Schofield, C.P.(La)	2002	3	6	–	99	279	46.50	–	3	–
Scott, B.J.M.(M)	–	7	13	4	101*	236	26.22	1	–	8/3
† Selwood, S.A.(De)	–	4	8	–	38	68	8.50	–	–	1
Shabbir Ahmed (Gs)	2004	6	6	4	34*	51	25.50	–	–	1
Shafayat, B.M.(Nt)	–	1	2	–	13	16	8.00	–	–	–
Shah, O.A.(M)	2000	17	30	5	140*	1336	53.44	4	9	19
Shahid, N.(Sy)	1998	3	6	1	53	109	21.80	–	1	2
Shankar, A.(CU)	–	2	4	–	40	45	11.25	–	–	–
† Shantry, A.J.(Nh)	–	2	3	2	5	7	7.00	–	–	1
† Sheikh, M.A.(De)	–	13	18	6	42	259	21.58	–	–	1
Sheriyar, A.(K)	–	8	8	5	12	36	12.00	–	–	–
† Shirazi, D.C.(BU)	–	1	–	–	–	–	–	–	–	–
Shoaib Akhtar (Du)	–	2	4	1	46	94	31.33	–	–	2
Shoaib Malik (Gs)	2004	6	9	1	63	134	16.75	–	1	2
Shreck, C.E.(Nt)	–	8	6	4	13*	16	8.00	–	–	2
† Sidebottom, R.J.(Nt)	2004	10	10	2	15*	49	6.12	–	–	3
Sillence, R.J.(Gs)	2004	2	2	–	92	96	48.00	–	1	–
Silverwood, C.E.W.(Y)	1996	7	10	2	37	150	18.75	–	–	3
Singh, A.(Nt)	–	5	8	1	112*	332	47.42	1	2	3
Singh, A.(CU)	–	3	6	1	38*	76	15.20	–	–	1
Smith, A.M.(Gs)	1995	3	2	1	9	12	12.00	–	–	1
Smith, B.F.(Wo)	2002ᶜ	16	25	3	187	1036	47.09	2	7	17
Smith, D.R.(WI)	–	4	7	–	55	130	18.57	–	1	1
† Smith, D.S.(WI)	–	5	10	–	142	294	29.40	1	–	6
Smith, E.T.(K)	2001	18	30	4	189	1277	49.11	4	5	6
Smith, G.J.(Nt)	2001	13	12	3	35	201	22.33	–	–	2
Smith, W.R.(DU/BU)	–	4	6	1	48	91	18.20	–	–	4
Snape, J.N.(Le)	–	5	8	1	66	140	20.00	–	1	1
Solanki, V.S.(Wo)	1998	13	18	–	107	757	42.05	1	6	10
Somerville-Hendrie, J.W.(DU)	–	2	4	1	23	30	10.00	–	–	1
Spearman, C.M.(Gs)	2002	17	28	2	341	1462	56.23	4	4	15
Stephenson, J.P.(Ex/MCC)	1989	5	7	2	71*	226	45.20	–	2	1
Stevens, D.I.(Le)	2002	13	22	3	105	689	36.26	1	5	13
Stiff, D.A.(K)	–	6	4	1	18	30	10.00	–	–	1
† Strauss, A.J.(M/E)	2001	8	16	2	137	704	50.28	2	4	11
Streak, H.H.(Wa)	–	6	9	2	61	180	25.71	–	1	–
† Stubbings, S.D.(De)	2001	16	28	1	96	743	27.51	–	6	8
Styris, S.B. (NZ)	–	7	12	–	108	299	24.91	1	–	5
Suman, A.K.(OU)	–	4	4	2	24*	45	22.50	–	–	1
Suppiah, A.V.(Sm)	–	2	3	–	33	44	14.66	–	–	1
Suraj, M.M.(SL)	–	3	4	2	14*	29	14.50	–	–	–
† Sutcliffe, I.J.(La)	2003	14	24	1	104	788	34.26	1	6	5
Sutton, L.D.(De)	2002	16	27	3	131	747	31.12	1	2	34/3
Swann, A.J.(La)	2002	5	7	–	34	112	16.00	–	–	2
Swann, G.P.(Nh)	1999	14	22	–	54	485	22.04	–	2	13
Symonds, A.(K)	1999	5	8	1	156*	506	72.28	3	1	6
Tahir Mughal (Du)	–	1	2	1	17*	17	17.00	–	–	–
Tahir, N.(Wa)	–	12	12	5	49	150	21.42	–	–	1
Tait, S.W.(Du)	–	2	2	–	4	4	2.00	–	–	–
† Taylor, B.V.(H)	–	11	16	6	40	177	17.70	–	–	3
Taylor, C.G.(Gs)	2001	16	25	1	177	1077	44.87	4	4	6
Taylor, C.R.(Y)	–	4	5	1	43*	105	26.25	–	–	1

F-C	Cap	M	I	NO	HS	Runs	Avge	100	50	Ct/St
Ten Doeschate, R.N.(Ex)	–	2	1	–	7	7	7.00	–	–	1
† Thomas, I.J.(Gm)	–	2	3	–	68	106	35.33	–	1	2
† Thomas, S.D.(Gm)	1997	14	19	5	105*	499	35.64	1	3	8
Thornicroft, N.D.(Y)	–	2	3	–	30	40	13.33	–	–	1
† Thorpe, G.P.(Sy/E/MCC)	1991	10	17	3	114	770	55.00	2	4	7
† Tomlinson, J.A.(H)	–	1	1	1	12*	12	–	–	–	1
† Tredwell, J.C.(MCC/K)	–	8	8	1	51*	237	33.85	–	1	7
Tremlett, C.T.(H)	2004	10	15	4	57	213	19.36	–	1	2
† Trescothick, M.E.(E)	1999	7	14	2	132	641	53.41	3	2	6
Trott, B.J.(K)	–	5	7	1	12	28	4.66	–	–	1
Trott, I.J.L.(Wa)	–	17	28	6	115	1170	53.18	1	10	12
† Troughton, J.O.(Wa)	2002	14	18	1	120	587	34.52	1	5	4
Tudor, A.J.(Sy)	1999	2	2	1	18*	18	18.00	–	–	3
Tuffey, D.R.(NZ)	–	5	7	2	14*	57	11.40	–	–	5
Turner, R.J.(Sm)	1994	16	18	3	46	346	23.06	–	–	61/4
Udal, S.D.(H)	1992	13	17	3	74	488	34.85	–	3	8
Upadhyay, A.M.(OU)	–	1	1	–	34	34	34.00	–	–	2
Van Jaarsveld, M.(Nh)	–	7	13	–	114	484	37.23	1	1	7
Vaughan, M.P.(E)	1995	6	10	1	103	414	46.00	2	2	7
† Vettori, D.L.(NZ)	–	6	8	–	77	250	31.25	–	2	1
† Voros, J.A.(Sx)	–	1	1	1	3*	3	–	–	–	–
Wagg, G.G.(Wa)	–	1	–	–	–	–	–	–	–	–
Wagh, M.A.(Wa)	2000	17	30	2	167	1033	36.89	2	5	16
† Wainwright, D.J.(Y)	–	1	1	–	5	5	5.00	–	–	–
† Walker, G.W.(LU)	–	1	1	–	5	5	5.00	–	–	–
† Walker, M.J.(K)	2000	17	27	4	157	1266	55.04	4	8	17
Walker, N.G.E.(De)	–	8	9	3	80	221	36.83	–	2	3
† Wallace, M.A.(Gm)	2003	16	28	–	105	776	27.71	1	3	41/3
† Ward, I.J.(Sx)	2004	16	25	1	160	1032	43.00	4	3	5
Warne, S.K.(H)	2000	12	16	2	57	381	27.21	–	1	9
Warren, N.A.(Wa)	–	1	1	–	0	0	0.00	–	–	–
Warren, R.J.(Nt)	2004	13	19	2	134	784	46.11	2	4	4
Watson, S.R.(H)	–	1	2	1	112*	136	136.00	1	–	–
† Webley, T.(CU)	–	3	5	–	93	173	34.60	–	1	1
† Weekes, P.N.(M)	1993	16	26	3	118	1001	43.52	2	9	14
Welch, G.(De)	2001	16	25	4	115*	609	29.00	1	1	12
Wessels, M.H.(MCC)	–	1	2	–	34	35	17.50	–	–	4/1
† Weston, W.P.C.(Gs)	2004	17	28	1	135	961	35.59	2	4	18
† Westwood, I.J.(Wa)	–	1	2	–	38	41	20.50	–	–	–
Wharf, A.G.(Gm)	2000	10	15	1	78	307	21.92	–	3	4
White, A.R.(Nh)	–	2	2	–	22	22	11.00	–	–	–
White, C.(Y)	1993	7	12	1	60	265	24.09	–	1	4
White, R.A.(Nh)	–	5	9	–	52	158	17.55	–	1	3
Wigley, D.H.(LU/BU)	–	4	3	1	23*	34	17.00	–	–	2
Wilkinson, R.M.(LU)	–	2	2	–	49	69	34.50	–	–	–
† Willoughby, C.M. (MCC)	–	1	2	1	4*	4	4.00	–	–	–
Windows, M.G.N.(Gs)	1998	9	13	2	58	249	22.63	–	1	4
Wood, J.(La)	2003	2	1	–	35	48	48.00	–	–	1
Wood, M.J.(Sm)	–	11	16	4	128*	604	50.33	2	3	5
Wood, M.J.(Y)	2001	16	27	2	123	955	38.20	1	7	24
Wright, C.J.C.(CU/M)	–	4	5	–	57	96	19.20	–	1	3
Wright, L.J. (Sx)	–	2	3	–	100	118	39.33	1	–	1
Wyatt, A.A.(OU)	–	1	1	–	1	1	1.00	–	–	1
† Yardy, M.H.(Sx)	–	4	8	1	115	239	34.14	1	–	3

BOWLING

See BATTING and FIELDING section for details of matches, caps and teams

	Cat	O	M	R	W	Avge	Best	5wI	10wM
Adams, A.R.	RMF	157.4	23	561	23	24.39	5- 93	1	–
Adams, C.J.	RM/OB	10	2	35	0				
Adams, J.H.K.	LM	23	6	77	2	38.50	2- 16	–	–
Adnan, M.H.	OB	37.3	2	154	1	154.00	1- 4	–	–
Afzaal, U.	SLA	51.3	7	196	4	49.00	3- 65	–	–
Agarkar, A.B.	RFM	93.3	20	323	10	32.30	5- 81	1	–
Airey, S.J.	RMF	35	7	151	0				
Akram, Adnan M.	RM	3	1	3	0				
Akram, Arfan M.	LB	5.1	1	30	1	30.00	1- 30	–	–
Ali, Kabir	RMF	248	45	899	28	32.10	5- 60	1	–
Ali, Kadeer	LB	21	1	106	1	106.00	1- 15	–	–
Ali, S.M.B.	LFM	116.4	18	486	10	48.60	4- 75	–	–
Alleyne, M.W.	RM	66.3	19	227	11	20.63	5- 71	1	–
Anderson, J.M.	RFM	181.1	35	593	26	22.80	6- 49	1	1
Anderson, R.S.G.	RMF	21	3	54	2	27.00	1- 11	–	–
Andrew, G.M.	RMF	40	5	179	7	25.57	4- 63	–	–
Anyon, J.E.	RFM	30	8	119	4	29.75	3- 57	–	–
Averis, J.M.M.	RMF	285.2	51	1099	28	39.25	6- 32	2	–
Azhar Mahmood	RMF	336.3	77	1138	38	29.94	5- 54	1	–
Ball, M.C.J.	OB	183	25	609	11	55.36	3- 96	–	–
Banerjee, V.	SLA	34	6	107	0				
Banks, O.A.C.	OB	131	19	527	11	47.90	3- 50	–	–
Batty, G.J.	OB	492.1	129	1381	45	30.68	7- 52	2	1
Bell, I.R.	RM	149.4	34	438	16	27.37	4- 4	–	–
Benkenstein, D.M.	RM/OB	10	1	63	0				
Benning, J.G.E.	RM	24.3	5	92	1	92.00	1- 28	–	–
Best, T.L.	RFM	35	3	165	5	33.00	4- 47	–	–
Betts, M.M.	RFM	147.4	30	577	13	44.38	5- 89	1	–
Bevan, M.G.	SLC	6	0	25	0				
Bichel, A.J.	RFM	398.5	75	1549	33	46.93	5- 87	2	–
Bicknell, D.J.	SLA	39.4	2	135	6	22.50	3- 33	–	–
Bicknell, M.P.	RFM	387	95	1266	43	29.44	5-128	1	–
Bishop, J.E.	LMF	81	16	263	6	43.83	3- 81	–	–
Blackwell, I.D.	SLA	345.1	85	972	27	36.00	7- 90	1	–
Blain, J.A.R.	RMF	188	26	804	30	26.80	4- 38	–	–
Blignaut, A.M.	RFM	42	3	200	4	50.00	2-109	–	–
Bloomfield, T.F.	RMF	20	3	55	1	55.00	1- 55	–	–
Bond, S.E.	RF	44	7	200	4	50.00	2- 46	–	–
Bopara, R.S.	RMF	24	1	108	0				
Botha, A.G.	SLA	291	62	938	26	36.07	5- 55	1	–
Bowler, P.D.	OB	2	1	2	0				
Bracken, N.W.	LFM	39	12	106	5	21.20	2- 12	–	–
Brant, S.A.	LFM	188.2	42	666	12	55.50	2- 34	–	–
Bravo, D.J.J.	RFM	146.4	29	486	20	24.30	6- 55	1	–
Breese, G.R.	OB	307.4	44	1163	28	41.53	5- 41	2	1
Bresnan, T.T.	RMF	160.3	31	557	17	32.76	3- 32	–	–
Bressington, A.N.	RMF	21	2	138	1	138.00	1- 38	–	–
Bridge, G.D.	SLA	235	60	680	19	35.78	4- 64	–	–
Brignull, D.S.	RMF	29	3	121	2	60.50	2- 78	–	–
Brophy, G.L.	(WK)	1	0	1	0				
Brown, A.D.	LB	13.3	3	43	0				
Brown, D.O.	RM	39	5	202	5	40.40	2- 48	–	–
Brown, D.R.	RFM	425.4	97	1293	40	32.32	5- 53	2	–
Brown, J.F.	OB	584.3	133	1523	36	42.30	5-113	1	–

130

F-C	Cat	O	M	R	W	Avge	Best	5wI	10wM
Bruce, J.T.A.	RMF	88	11	375	9	41.66	3- 74	–	–
Buckham, C.T.	LB	15	1	79	0				
Burns, M.	RM	44.4	7	155	3	51.66	3- 46	–	–
Butler, I.G.	RFM	101.3	11	446	11	40.54	4-114	–	–
Caddick, A.R.	RFM	578.5	110	2026	56	36.17	6- 80	4	–
Cairns, C.L.	RFM	143.1	24	516	18	28.66	5- 79	1	–
Carberry, M.A.	OB	27	0	157	2	78.50	1- 56	–	–
Carpenter, E.J.	SLA	53.1	11	155	1	155.00	1- 47	–	–
Carter, N.M.	LFM	367.4	79	1209	27	44.77	4- 50	–	–
Cawdron, M.J.	RM	20	7	46	1	46.00	1- 46	–	–
Chapple, G.	RFM	374.4	80	1128	29	38.89	5-136	1	–
Chilton, M.J.	RM	24	3	84	1	84.00	1- 39	–	–
Clark, S.R.	RFM	89	23	217	10	21.70	3- 28	–	–
Clarke, A.C.S.	RMF	24	8	56	2	28.00	2- 56	–	–
Clarke, A.J.	RM	131	25	444	12	37.00	3- 32	–	–
Clarke, A.P.A.	RMF	5.4	1	19	0				
Clarke, M.J.	SLA	42.1	8	160	1	160.00	1- 52	–	–
Clarke, R.	RFM	109.3	16	518	9	57.55	3- 47	–	–
Cleary, M.F.	RFM	230	29	946	27	35.03	7- 80	2	–
Clinton, R.S.	RM	3	0	30	0				
Coetzer, K.J.	RM	1	0	2	0				
Collingwood, P.D.	RMF	137	37	455	12	37.91	3- 49	–	–
Collins, P.T.	LMF	109	9	453	13	34.84	4-113	–	–
Collymore, C.D.	RFM	104	29	316	6	52.66	2- 66	–	–
Cook, A.N.	OB	1	0	12	0				
Cook, J.W.	RM	99	19	307	7	43.85	3- 42	–	–
Cook, S.J.	RM	371	82	1072	35	30.62	6- 89	2	–
Cork, D.G.	RFM	332.5	59	1144	38	30.10	7-120	3	–
Cosker, D.A.	SLA	174.1	42	513	17	30.17	3- 40	–	–
Cowan, A.P.	RFM	148	39	463	13	35.61	3- 44	–	–
Cox, J.	OB	1	0	8	0				
Craven, V.J.	RM	51.4	8	191	6	31.83	2- 18	–	–
Crawley, J.P.	RM	4	1	24	0				
Croft, R.D.B.	OB	674	146	2006	57	35.19	4- 52	–	–
Crook, A.R.	OB	50	6	212	2	106.00	1- 8	–	–
Crook, S.P.	RFM	68.1	5	309	6	51.50	2- 33	–	–
Cusden, S.M.J.	RFM	100.3	17	404	13	31.07	4- 68	–	–
Daggett, L.M.	RMF	66.1	5	236	12	19.66	8- 94	1	–
Dagnall, C.E.	RM	256.4	46	923	29	31.82	4- 37	–	–
Dakin, J.M.	RM	137	28	490	8	61.25	2- 66	–	–
Dale, A.	RMF	13	2	42	0				
Dale, M.A.P.	RM	8	0	34	1	34.00	1- 34	–	–
Dalrymple, J.W.M.	OB	306.5	47	1083	28	38.67	4- 66	–	–
Daniel, G.I.	RM	8	0	30	0				
Danish Kaneria	LB	563	123	1609	63	25.53	7- 65	4	1
Davies, A.M.	RM	304.2	75	938	50	18.76	6- 44	4	–
Davies, A.P.	RMF	55.4	7	203	3	67.66	2- 95	–	–
Davis, M.J.G.	OB	235.3	40	662	21	31.52	4- 57	–	–
Dawson, R.K.J.	OB	379.4	71	1255	36	34.86	5- 40	1	–
Dean, K.J.	LMF	144	18	597	20	29.85	5- 86	1	–
DeFreitas, P.A.J.	RFM	343.4	81	1064	31	34.32	4- 49	–	–
Dennington, M.J.	RFM	93	13	368	9	40.88	3- 48	–	–
Dias, W.J.M.R.	RFM	22	6	93	1	93.00	1- 52	–	–
Doshi, N.D.	SLA	265.2	45	875	33	26.51	7-110	3	2
Dumelow, N.R.C.	OB	126	20	488	9	54.22	5- 51	1	–
Durston, W.J.	OB	35	6	115	4	28.75	3- 23	–	–
Dutch, K.P.	OB	124	21	448	19	23.57	5- 26	2	–
Ealham, M.A.	RMF	317	90	952	26	36.61	4- 43	–	–

F-C	Cat	O	M	R	W	Avge	Best	5wI	10wM
Edwards, F.H.	RF	139.2	14	610	14	43.57	5- 22	2	1
Edwards, N.J.	RM	25	1	110	2	55.00	1- 16	–	–
Edwards, P.D.	RFM	83	12	341	3	113.66	1- 31	–	–
Elliott, M.T.G.	LM/SLC	1.3	0	26	0				
Ferley, R.S.	SLA	51.4	6	192	5	38.40	3-107	–	–
Fisher, I.D.	SLA	320.4	61	1073	23	46.65	5-114	1	–
Flintoff, A.	RFM	193.2	41	588	24	24.50	3- 25	–	–
France, B.J.	RM	4	0	20	0				
Francis, J.D.	SLA	36.3	9	120	2	60.00	1- 4	–	–
Francis, S.R.G.	RMF	295.5	51	1201	33	36.39	5- 42	2	–
Franklin, J.E.C.	LFM	126.2	33	415	18	23.05	7- 60	1	–
Franks, P.J.	RMF	352	68	1287	43	29.93	7- 72	2	–
Gajanayake, M.K.	OB	2	0	24	0				
Gayle, C.H.	OB	66.1	13	189	10	18.90	5- 34	1	–
Gibson, O.D.	RFM	424.5	97	1445	60	24.08	6- 43	5	2
Gidman, A.P.R.	RM	210	39	827	16	51.68	2- 12	–	–
Giles, A.F.	SLA	362.1	79	939	35	26.82	5- 57	2	–
Goode, C.M.	RMF	16	3	70	1	70.00	1- 70	–	–
Gough, D.	RF	226.4	52	672	30	22.40	5- 57	1	–
Gray, A.K.D.	OB	31	3	89	2	44.50	1- 20	–	–
Grayson, A.P.	SLA	40.1	2	167	0				
Greenidge, C.G.	RMF	83.2	14	346	10	34.60	3- 71	–	–
Gunter, N.E.L.	RFM	45.1	5	215	5	43.00	3- 52	–	–
Habib, A.	RM	7	1	18	0				
Hall, A.J.	RFM	347	72	1124	30	37.46	3- 10	–	–
Hamilton, G.M.	RFM	79	11	288	8	36.00	3- 30	–	–
Hancock, T.H.C.	RM	37	8	105	2	52.50	2- 7	–	–
Hardinges, M.A.	RMF	30	4	120	1	120.00	1- 78	–	–
Harmison, S.J.	RF	301	64	966	38	25.42	6- 46	1	–
Harris, A.J.	RM	67	15	196	9	21.77	4- 22	–	–
Harrison, A.J.	RMF	25.4	3	108	3	36.00	2- 65	–	–
Harrison, D.S.	RM	480.3	123	1584	57	27.78	5- 48	3	–
Harrity, M.A.	LFM	94	19	382	8	47.75	3-111	–	–
Harvey, I.J.	RM	154	41	430	7	61.42	3- 38	–	–
Harvey, T.F.C.	OB	37	7	110	4	27.50	3- 43	–	–
Havell, P.M.R.	RFM	178.1	20	814	21	38.76	4- 75	–	–
Hawinkels, S.J.	RM	3	0	12	0				
Hayward, M.	RF	289	54	918	31	29.61	4- 41	–	–
Henderson, C.W.	SLA	469	132	1373	39	35.20	7- 74	2	–
Hewson, D.R.	RM	46	18	112	4	28.00	3- 39	–	–
Hick, G.A.	OB	9	1	40	1	40.00	1- 1	–	–
Hildreth, J.C.	RMF	17	1	76	2	38.00	2- 39	–	–
Hodge, B.J.	OB	95.5	14	365	10	36.50	2- 18	–	–
Hogg, G.B.	SLC	297.2	54	956	18	53.11	4- 90	–	–
Hogg, K.W.	RFM	71	10	259	5	51.80	2- 16	–	–
Hoggard, M.J.	RFM	385.5	80	1360	42	32.38	4- 32	–	–
Hollioake, A.J.	RM	78.3	7	290	7	41.42	3- 69	–	–
Hooper, C.L.	OB	234	51	595	15	39.66	4- 56	–	–
Hopkinson, C.D.	RM	10	2	34	1	34.00	1- 20	–	–
Hunt, T.A.	RMF	28	4	124	2	62.00	2- 85	–	–
Hunter, I.D.	RMF	14.3	1	52	3	17.33	3- 32	–	–
Hussey, D.J.	RM/OB	72.2	10	290	2	145.00	1- 6	–	–
Hussey, M.E.K.	RM	8	2	22	0				
Hutchison, P.M.	LFM	182.4	28	645	11	58.63	3- 50	–	–
Hutton, B.L.	RMF	113	23	353	8	44.12	3- 14	–	–
Hutton, O.R.	RM	6	1	36	0				
Innes, K.J.	RM	46.3	7	156	3	52.00	2- 50	–	–
Jaques, P.A.	SLC	2	0	18	0				

F-C	Cat	O	M	R	W	Avge	Best	5wI	10wM
Jennings, C.J.R.	RMF	14	3	64	1	64.00	1- 64	–	–
Johnson, R.L.	RFM	449.5	104	1512	44	34.36	7- 69	2	–
Jones, P.S.	RMF	220	33	792	10	79.20	3- 75	–	–
Jones, S.P.	RF	310.1	53	1155	34	33.97	5- 77	2	–
Joseph, R.H.	RF	165.2	31	648	19	34.10	4- 47	–	–
Joseph, S.C	OB	7	1	23	0				
Joyce, E.C.	RM	41	3	169	3	56.33	2- 34	–	–
Kasprowicz, M.S.	RFM	272.1	54	893	21	42.52	5- 54	1	–
Katich, S.M.	SLC	18	1	61	0				
Kay, M.A.	LB	4	0	13	0				
Keedy, G.	SLA	645.3	122	1849	72	25.68	7- 95	6	1
Keegan, C.B.	RFM	161	29	550	20	27.50	5- 36	2	–
Kendall, W.S.	RM	12	2	44	2	22.00	1- 12	–	–
Kenway, D.A.	RM	2	2	0	0				
Khalid, S.A.	OB	86.3	17	277	4	69.25	2- 20	–	–
Khan, A.	RFM	170.3	24	756	20	37.80	4- 47	–	–
Khan, Z.	LFM	26.4	2	101	1	101.00	1- 48	–	–
Killeen, N.	RFM	343.4	83	1056	19	55.57	2- 39	–	–
King, R.D.	RFM	38.5	6	206	5	41.20	3-120	–	–
Kirby, S.P.	RFM	327.1	53	1132	31	36.51	3- 64	–	–
Kirtley, R.J.	RFM	446.5	97	1381	37	37.32	4- 32	–	–
Klusener, L.	RMF	170.3	18	673	13	51.76	4- 89	–	–
Koenig, S.G.	OB	3	1	7	0				
Kulasekara, M.D.N.	RFM	102.1	15	407	12	33.91	6-109	1	–
Kumar, P.	RM	42	5	219	6	36.50	3- 78	–	–
Lamb, G.A.	OB	5	2	15	0				
Laraman, A.W.	RFM	180.3	43	638	22	29.00	5- 58	1	–
Law, S.G.	RM/LB	5	1	16	0				
Lawson, J.J.C.	RF	105.3	13	471	13	36.23	4- 94	–	–
Lawson, M.A.K.	LB	75.3	6	308	9	34.22	5- 62	1	–
Lehmann, D.S.	SLA	105.4	19	261	15	17.40	4- 35	–	–
Lewis, J.	RMF	472.4	121	1440	57	25.26	7- 72	4	–
Lewis, M.L.	RFM	53.1	5	253	6	42.16	4- 39	–	–
Lewis, P.D.	RFM	64	16	229	7	32.71	3- 58	–	–
Lewry, J.D.	LFM	259.2	64	849	27	31.44	5- 66	1	–
Linley, T.E.	RMF	72	14	287	9	31.88	3- 44	–	–
Logan, R.J.	RMF	75.1	9	353	10	35.30	4- 34	–	–
Lokuarachchi, K.S.	LB	63	10	223	5	44.60	2- 62	–	–
Loudon, A.G.R.	OB	192.2	32	653	21	31.09	6- 47	2	–
Louw, J.	RFM	463.3	89	1591	60	26.51	5- 44	3	–
Loye, M.B.	OB	1	0	1	0				
Lumb, M.J.	RM	1	0	2	0				
McCoubrey, A.G.A.M.	RFM	126.4	22	563	15	37.53	4- 16	–	–
MacGill, S.C.G.	LBG	410	80	1408	40	35.20	7-109	2	1
McGrath, A.	RM	102	21	280	8	35.00	5- 39	1	–
McGrath, G.D.	RFM	100.4	41	215	9	23.88	4- 59	–	–
McLean, N.A.M.	RFM	322.1	62	1127	43	26.20	6- 79	3	1
McMahon, P.J.	OB	172	36	551	12	45.91	4- 68	–	–
McMillan, C.D.	RM	9	3	30	0				
Maddy, D.L.	RM/OB	169.2	24	686	15	45.73	2- 41	–	–
Mahmood, S.I.	RMF	230	27	1010	23	43.91	4- 59	–	–
Malik, M.N.	RFM	204	35	781	24	32.54	5- 88	1	–
Marshall, S.J.	LB	96	18	324	6	54.00	3- 42	–	–
Martin, C.S.	RFM	161.5	34	624	14	44.57	4- 92	–	–
Martin, P.J.	RFM	115.5	34	319	10	31.90	4- 81	–	–
Martin-Jenkins, R.S.C.	RFM	388.4	101	1166	30	38.86	5- 96	1	–
Mascarenhas, A.D.	RMF	404.2	132	1046	56	18.67	6- 25	4	–
Mason, M.S.	RFM	597.1	181	1582	52	30.42	5- 62	1	–

133

F-C	Cat	O	M	R	W	Avge	Best	5wI	10wM
Masters, D.D.	RMF	149	29	533	14	38.07	4- 74	–	–
Maunders, J.K.	RM	22	6	84	2	42.00	1- 11	–	–
Maynard, M.P.	RM	7	0	27	0				
Middlebrook, J.D.	OB	394.3	57	1459	34	42.91	5- 26	1	–
Mills, K.D.	RMF	31	6	117	3	39.00	3- 51	–	–
Mirando, M.T.T.	LFM	64.5	8	280	7	40.00	3- 51	–	–
Mohammad Akram	RFM	432.1	76	1581	46	34.36	4- 85	–	–
Mohammad Sami	RF	140	32	526	14	37.57	6- 99	1	1
Mohammed, D.	SLC	60	10	171	5	34.20	3- 47	–	–
Mongia, D.	SLA	50.2	9	157	5	31.40	1- 1	–	–
Montgomerie, R.R.	OB	8	0	26	0				
Moore, S.C.	RM	27	3	127	3	42.33	1- 13	–	–
Moss, J.	RM	207.5	39	646	14	46.14	3- 30	–	–
Mubarak, J.	OB	17	3	65	2	32.50	1- 20	–	–
Muchall, G.J.	RM	43	7	161	6	26.83	1- 1	–	–
Mullally, A.D.	LFM	245.4	69	711	18	39.50	6- 68	1	–
Munday, M.K.	LB	60.3	13	257	10	25.70	4- 36	–	–
Murtagh, T.J.	RFM	243.3	50	873	20	43.65	5- 74	1	–
Mushtaq Ahmed	LBG	791.2	164	2318	84	27.59	7- 73	6	2
Napier, G.R.	RM	403.3	65	1595	42	37.97	5- 56	1	–
Nash, C.D.	OB	13	1	47	2	23.50	1- 5	–	–
Nash, D.C.	(WK)	2	0	8	0				
Newby, O.J.	RMF	35	6	107	2	53.50	2- 32	–	–
Newman, A.R.I.	OB	14	1	70	2	35.00	2- 70	–	–
Noble, D.J.	RMF	13	2	70	0				
North, M.J.	OB	34.1	6	109	7	15.57	4- 16	–	–
Onions, G.	RMF	146.4	32	593	9	65.88	3-110	–	–
Oram, J.D.P.	RMF	95.4	19	319	3	106.33	2- 76	–	–
Ormond, J.	RFM	609.2	143	1909	52	36.71	6- 62	1	–
Paget, C.D.	OB	56	6	206	3	68.66	3- 63	–	–
Palladino, A.P.	RMF	62	7	267	3	89.00	1- 28	–	–
Panesar, M.S.	SLA	86	23	197	5	39.40	3- 28	–	–
Parker, L.C.	RM	1	0	13	0				
Parsons, K.A.	RM	37	7	183	0				
Patel, M.M.	SLA	475	91	1416	49	28.89	5- 56	2	–
Pattison, I.	RM	39	7	129	2	64.50	1- 30	–	–
Peploe, C.T.	SLA	242.2	59	745	17	43.82	4- 65	–	–
Perera, W.M.B.	LB	69	5	244	5	48.80	2- 24	–	–
Peters, S.D.	LB	2	0	12	0				
Phillips, B.J.	RFM	408.3	107	1175	31	37.90	5-106	1	–
Pietersen, K.P.	OB	81.5	7	365	7	52.14	3- 72	–	–
Plunkett, L.E.	RFM	247.5	37	964	31	31.09	6- 74	1	–
Ponting, R.T.	RM/OB	5	2	6	0				
Powell, D.B.	RFM	70.3	14	253	10	25.30	6- 49	1	–
Powell, M.J.(Wa)	RM	8	0	51	0				
Prasad, K.T.G.D.	RFM	25	5	115	1	115.00	1- 94	–	–
Pratt, G.J.	OB	2	0	2	0				
Pretorius, D.	RFM	245	43	936	24	39.00	4-119	–	–
Price, R.W.	SLA	169.1	50	420	10	42.00	4- 83	–	–
Prittipaul, L.R.	RM/OB	21	4	71	1	71.00	1- 14	–	–
Pyrah, R.M.	RM	6	4	2	0				
Ramprakash, M.R.	RM	24	4	68	2	34.00	2- 35	–	–
Ramyakumara, W.M.G.	LM	41	4	172	2	86.00	1- 44	–	–
Read, G.G.	LM	14	5	45	1	45.00	1- 45	–	–
Richards, M.A.	RMF	15	3	62	0				
Richardson, A.	RMF	144	28	532	6	88.66	2- 62	–	–
Richardson, M.H.	SLA	6	0	28	1	28.00	1- 24	–	–
Roberts, T.W.	OB	13	7	10	1	10.00	1- 10	–	–

F-C	Cat	O	M	R	W	Avge	Best	5wI	10wM
Robinson, D.D.J.	RMF	7	0	64	0			–	–
Rofe, P.C.	RFM	167.5	42	505	12	42.08	4-109	–	–
Rosenberg, M.C.	RM	6.1	0	27	1	27.00	1- 27	–	–
Sadler, J.L.	LB	6.4	0	58	1	58.00	1- 22	–	–
Saggers, M.J.	RMF	259.5	72	717	23	31.17	4- 43	–	–
Sales, D.J.G.	RM	2	1	2	0			–	–
Salisbury, I.D.K.	LBG	222.1	39	660	13	50.76	3- 30	–	–
Sampson, P.J.	RFM	34.3	4	154	6	25.66	5-121	1	–
Saqlain Mushtaq	OB	86.4	9	304	12	25.33	4-107	–	–
Sarwan, R.R.	LB	39	1	145	0			–	–
Savill, T.E.	RFM	96	10	435	10	43.50	3- 93	–	–
Schofield, C.P.	LB	26.3	3	85	1	85.00	1- 13	–	–
Shabbir Ahmed	RFM	169	38	605	18	33.61	4- 96	–	–
Shafayat, B.M.	RMF	2	0	16	0			–	–
Shah, O.A.	OB	22	5	67	1	67.00	1- 9	–	–
Shahid, N.	LB	3	3	0	0				
Shantry, A.J.	LFM	35	10	110	3	36.66	2- 67	–	–
Sheikh, M.A.	RM	298.3	69	945	26	36.34	4- 9	–	–
Sheriyar, A.	LFM	199.3	33	772	18	42.88	5- 94	1	–
Shoaib Akhtar	RF	57.2	12	218	8	27.25	4- 64	–	–
Shoaib Malik	OB	176	30	530	10	53.00	3-109	–	–
Shreck, C.E.	RMF	235	51	823	31	26.54	6- 46	2	–
Sidebottom, R.J.	LFM	258	59	859	30	28.63	5- 86	1	–
Sillence, R.J.	RMF	52	19	135	5	27.00	2- 50	–	–
Silverwood, C.E.W.	RFM	174.3	33	570	22	25.90	3- 18	–	–
Smith, A.M.	LMF	54.3	22	127	8	15.87	3- 34	–	–
Smith, D.R.	RMF	54	12	163	5	32.60	3- 4	–	–
Smith, G.J.	LFM	336.1	69	1161	39	29.76	5- 35	3	–
Smith, W.R.	OB	35	4	127	2	63.50	2- 83	–	–
Snape, J.N.	OB	36.2	5	133	1	133.00	1- 78	–	–
Solanki, V.S.	OB	74.3	7	240	6	40.00	5- 40	1	–
Somerville-Hendrie, J.W.	RFM	42	7	145	4	36.25	3- 51	–	–
Stephenson, J.P.	RM	74	11	285	9	31.66	3- 28	–	–
Stevens, D.I.	RM	17.2	1	80	3	26.66	2- 50	–	–
Stiff, D.A.	RFM	88	13	419	7	59.85	3- 88	–	–
Streak, H.H.	RFM	159	29	522	24	21.75	7- 80	2	1
Styris, S.B.	RMF	96.3	18	325	7	46.42	3- 88	–	–
Suman, A.K.	LMF	90.3	24	278	7	39.71	3- 44	–	–
Suppiah, A.V.	SLA	25	1	105	4	26.25	2- 36	–	–
Suraj, M.M.	OB	134.4	21	498	11	45.27	5- 40	1	–
Swann, A.J.	RM/OB	6	2	18	1	18.00	1- 14	–	–
Swann, G.P.	OB	403.2	71	1168	30	38.93	4- 94	–	–
Symonds, A.	RMF/OB	139.3	39	419	14	29.92	5-140	1	–
Tahir Mughal	RFM	19	4	54	2	27.00	2- 54	–	–
Tahir, N.	RFM	207.4	33	791	28	28.25	4- 43	–	–
Tait, S.W.	RFM	18	0	176	0			–	–
Taylor, B.V.	RMF	298.1	59	1039	33	31.48	5- 73	1	–
Taylor, C.G.	OB	1	0	2	0			–	–
Ten Doeschate, R.N.	RFM	36.5	7	117	7	16.71	3- 29	–	–
Thomas, I.J.	OB	1	0	6	0			–	–
Thomas, S.D.	RFM	320.3	32	1252	34	36.82	4- 47	–	–
Thornicroft, N.D.	RMF	44.2	10	168	6	28.00	2- 27	–	–
Tomlinson, J.A.	LFM	20	7	43	1	43.00	1- 9	–	–
Tredwell, J.C.	OB	152.1	21	583	7	83.28	3- 20	–	–
Tremlett, C.T.	RMF	268.2	56	867	39	22.23	4- 29	–	–
Trescothick, M.E.	RM	4	0	10	0			–	–
Trott, B.J.	RFM	153	23	538	10	53.80	4-109	–	–
Trott, I.J.L.	RM	31	10	96	3	32.00	1- 1	–	–

135

F-C	Cat	O	M	R	W	Avge	Best	5wI	10wM
Troughton, J.O.	SLA	125.2	28	345	6	57.50	3- 1	–	–
Tudor, A.J.	RF	33	7	157	6	26.16	4- 61	–	–
Tuffey, D.R.	RFM	133.1	31	444	8	55.50	4- 57	–	–
Udal, S.D.	OB	247.4	40	869	39	22.28	6- 79	1	–
Van Jaarsveld, M.	OB	4	2	8	0				
Vaughan, M.P.	OB	7	0	25	0				
Vettori, D.L.	SLA	173.1	22	612	20	30.60	5- 92	1	–
Voros, J.A.	LFM	20.5	6	62	5	12.40	4- 40	–	–
Wagg, G.G.	LM	18	7	33	4	8.25	3- 21	–	–
Wagh, M.A.	OB	306.2	56	1020	20	51.00	3- 85	–	–
Wainwright, D.J.	SLA	3	1	5	0				
Walker, G.W.	SLA	7	0	29	0				
Walker, M.J.	RM	66	10	228	6	38.00	2- 21	–	–
Walker, N.G.E.	RFM	151.2	17	667	18	37.05	5- 68	1	–
Warne, S.K.	LBG	411.5	88	1231	51	24.13	6- 65	3	–
Warren, N.A.	RMF	17	3	60	3	20.00	3- 60	–	–
Watson, S.R.	RFM	8.4	2	28	0				
Webley, T.	SLA	3	0	13	0				
Weekes, P.N.	OB	325.3	34	1166	26	44.84	5- 76	1	–
Welch, G.	RM	471.5	103	1525	45	33.88	5- 57	3	–
Weston, W.P.C.	LB	4	2	8	1	8.00	1- 8	–	–
Wharf, A.G.	RMF	249.5	38	1011	27	37.44	5- 93	1	–
White, A.R.	OB	26	3	62	2	31.00	2- 19	–	–
White, C.	RFM	88.2	18	282	11	25.63	3- 50	–	–
White, R.A.	LB	32	6	98	3	32.66	2- 46	–	–
Wigley, D.H.	RFM	93	16	350	10	35.00	4-133	–	–
Wilkinson, R.M.	RM	37	6	133	1	133.00	1- 36	–	–
Willoughby, C.M.	LMF	38.5	11	114	5	22.80	5- 48	1	–
Wood, J.	RFM	51	5	243	4	60.75	2- 70	–	–
Wood, M.J.(Sm)	OB	2	0	6	0				
Wood, M.J.(Y)	OB	1	0	1	0				
Wright, C.J.C.	RFM	103	19	379	6	63.16	2- 70	–	–
Wright, L.J.	RMF	33.5	4	104	1	104.00	1- 74	–	–
Wyatt, A.A.	LB	20	9	40	2	20.00	2- 22	–	–
Yardy, M.H.	LM	33	4	135	1	135.00	1- 18	–	–

COUNTY BENEFITS AWARDED FOR 2005

Derbyshire	–
Durham	–
Essex	A.P.Grayson
Glamorgan	M.P.Maynard (Testimonial)
Gloucestershire	T.H.C.Hancock
Hampshire	A.D.Mullally
Kent	–
Lancashire	G.Yates
Leicestershire	–
Middlesex	–
Northamptonshire	Club Centenary Appeal
Nottinghamshire	J.E.R.Gallian
Somerset	Club Benefit
Surrey	M.A.Butcher
Sussex	M.A.Robinson (Testimonial)
Warwickshire	D.R.Brown
Worcestershire	–
Yorkshire	M.P.Vaughan

COUNTY CHAMPIONSHIP 2004
FRIZZELL FINAL TABLES

DIVISION 1

	P	W	L	T	D	Bat	Bowl	Deduct Points	Total Points
1 WARWICKSHIRE (5)	16	5	–	–	11	65	43		222.0
2 Kent (4)	16	7	3	–	6	43	41	–	206.0
3 Surrey (3)	16	5	5	–	6	60	42	0.5	195.5
4 Middlesex (6)	16	4	4	–	8	48	43	–	179.0
5 Sussex (1)	16	4	5	–	7	46	42	–	172.0
6 Gloucestershire (-)	16	3	3	–	10	49	41	–	172.0
7 Worcestershire (-)	16	3	6	–	7	51	40	–	161.0
8 Lancashire (2)	16	2	4	–	10	44	44	2.0	154.0
9 Northamptonshire (-)	16	1	4	–	11	35	41	–	134.0

DIVISION 2

	P	W	L	T	D	Bat	Bowl	Deduct Points	Total Points
1 NOTTINGHAMSHIRE (-)	16	9	2	–	5	66	40		252.0
2 Hampshire (8)	16	9	2	–	5	42	40	–	228.0
3 Glamorgan (5)	16	5	2	–	9	48	44	1.5	196.5
4 Somerset (7)	16	4	5	–	7	47	44	–	175.0
5 Essex (-)	16	3	6	–	7	50	45	–	165.0
6 Leicestershire (-)	16	4	5	–	7	39	42	1.5	163.5
7 Yorkshire (4)	16	3	4	–	9	44	40	–	162.0
8 Derbyshire (9)	16	1	6	–	9	36	40	–	126.0
9 Durham (6)	16	2	8	–	6	28	41	2.5	118.5

2003 final positions for that division are shown in brackets.

SCORING OF CHAMPIONSHIP POINTS 2004

(a) For a win, 14 points, plus any points scored in the first innings.

(b) In a tie, each side to score seven points, plus any points scored in the first innings.

(c) In a drawn match, each side to score four points, plus any points scored in the first innings (see also paragraph (f) below).

(d) If the scores are equal in a drawn match, the side batting in the fourth innings to score seven points plus any points scored in the first innings, and the opposing side to score four points plus any points scored in the first innings.

(e) First Innings Points (awarded only for performances **in the first 130 overs** of each first innings and retained whatever the result of the match).
   • A maximum of five batting points to be available as under:-
   200 to 249 runs – 1 point; 250 to 299 runs – 2 points; 300 to 349 runs – 3 points; 350 to 399 runs – 4 points; 400 runs or over – 5 points.
   • A maximum of three bowling points to be available as under:-
   3 to 5 wickets taken – 1 point; 6 to 8 wickets taken – 2 points; 9 to 10 wickets taken – 3 points.

(f) If play starts when fewer than eight hours' playing time remains (in which event a one innings match shall be played as provided for in First-Class Playing Condition 18), no first innings points shall be scored. The side winning on the one innings to score 14 points. In a tie, each side to score seven points. In a drawn match, each side to score four points. If the scores are equal in a drawn match, the side batting in the second innings to score seven points and the opposing side to score four points.

(g) If a match is abandoned without a ball being bowled, each side to score four points.

(h) The side which has the highest aggregate of points gained at the end of the season shall be the Champion County of their respective Division. Should any sides in the Championship table be equal on points, the following tie-breakers will be applied in the order stated: most wins, least losses, team achieving most points in contests between teams level on points, most wickets taken, most runs scored. At the end of the season, the top three teams from the Second Division will be promoted and the bottom three teams from the First Division will be relegated.

COUNTY CHAMPIONS

The English County Championship was not officially constituted until December 1889. Prior to that date there was no generally accepted method of awarding the title; although the 'least matches lost' method existed, it was not consistently applied. Rules governing playing qualifications were agreed in 1873 and the first unofficial points system 15 years later.

Research has produced a list of champions dating back to 1826, but at least seven different versions exist for the period from 1864 to 1889 (see *The Wisden Book of Cricket Records*). Only from 1890 can any authorised list of county champions commence.

That first official Championship was contested between eight counties: Gloucestershire, Kent, Lancashire, Middlesex, Nottinghamshire, Surrey, Sussex and Yorkshire. The remaining counties were admitted in the following seasons: 1891 – Somerset, 1895 – Derbyshire, Essex, Hampshire, Leicestershire and Warwickshire, 1899 – Worcestershire, 1905 – Northamptonshire, 1921 – Glamorgan, and 1992 – Durham.

The Championship pennant was introduced by the 1951 champions, Warwickshire, and the Lord's Taverners' Trophy was first presented in 1973. The first sponsors, Schweppes (1977 to 1983), were succeeded by Britannic Assurance (1984 to 1998), PPP Healthcare (1999-2000), CricInfo (2001) and Frizzell (2002 to date). Based on their previous season's positions, the 18 counties were separated into two divisions in 2001.

1890	Surrey	1930	Lancashire	1970	Kent
1891	Surrey	1931	Yorkshire	1971	Surrey
1892	Surrey	1932	Yorkshire	1972	Warwickshire
1893	Yorkshire	1933	Yorkshire	1973	Hampshire
1894	Surrey	1934	Lancashire	1974	Worcestershire
1895	Surrey	1935	Yorkshire	1975	Leicestershire
1896	Yorkshire	1936	Derbyshire	1976	Middlesex
1897	Lancashire	1937	Yorkshire	1977	{ Kent
1898	Yorkshire	1938	Yorkshire		{ Middlesex
1899	Surrey	1939	Yorkshire	1978	Kent
1900	Yorkshire	1946	Yorkshire	1979	Essex
1901	Yorkshire	1947	Middlesex	1980	Middlesex
1902	Yorkshire	1948	Glamorgan	1981	Nottinghamshire
1903	Middlesex	1949	{ Middlesex	1982	Middlesex
1904	Lancashire		{ Yorkshire	1983	Essex
1905	Yorkshire	1950	{ Lancashire	1984	Essex
1906	Kent		{ Surrey	1985	Middlesex
1907	Nottinghamshire	1951	Warwickshire	1986	Essex
1908	Yorkshire	1952	Surrey	1987	Nottinghamshire
1909	Kent	1953	Surrey	1988	Worcestershire
1910	Kent	1954	Surrey	1989	Worcestershire
1911	Warwickshire	1955	Surrey	1990	Middlesex
1912	Yorkshire	1956	Surrey	1991	Essex
1913	Kent	1957	Surrey	1992	Essex
1914	Surrey	1958	Surrey	1993	Middlesex
1919	Yorkshire	1959	Yorkshire	1994	Warwickshire
1920	Middlesex	1960	Yorkshire	1995	Warwickshire
1921	Middlesex	1961	Hampshire	1996	Leicestershire
1922	Yorkshire	1962	Yorkshire	1997	Glamorgan
1923	Yorkshire	1963	Yorkshire	1998	Leicestershire
1924	Yorkshire	1964	Worcestershire	1999	Surrey
1925	Yorkshire	1965	Worcestershire	2000	Surrey
1926	Lancashire	1966	Yorkshire	2001	Yorkshire
1927	Lancashire	1967	Yorkshire	2002	Surrey
1928	Lancashire	1968	Yorkshire	2003	Sussex
1929	Nottinghamshire	1969	Glamorgan	2004	Warwickshire

COUNTY CHAMPIONSHIP RESULTS 2004

DIVISION 1

	GLOS	KENT	LANCS	MIDDX	N'HANTS	SURREY	SUSSEX	WARWKS	WORCS
GLOS	–	Bristol K 7w	Chelt Drawn	Glos Gs 10w	Bristol Drawn	Bristol Gs 6w	Bristol Drawn	Bristol Drawn	Chelt Wo 5w
KENT	Cant Drawn	–	Tun W K 7w	Cant K I/49	Cant K 194	Cant Drawn	Cant K 236	Beck'm Drawn	Cant K 5w
LANCS	Man Drawn	Man Drawn	–	Man Drawn	L'pool Drawn	Man Sy 147	Man Sx 8w	Man Drawn	Man La 219
MIDDX	Lord's Drawn	S'gate M 119	Lord's Drawn	–	Lord's Drawn	Lord's M 6w	Lord's Sx 143	Lord's Wa I/8	Lord's Drawn
N'HANTS	No'ton Drawn	No'ton K 145	No'ton Drawn	No'ton Drawn	–	No'ton Nh 6w	No'ton Drawn	No'ton Drawn	No'ton Wo 9w
SURREY	Oval Drawn	Oval Sy 7w	Croydon Sy I/55	Oval Drawn	Oval Drawn	–	Oval Drawn	Guild Wa 7w	Oval Sy 68
SUSSEX	Arundel Gs 9w	Hove Sx I/45	Hove La 10w	Hove M 5w	Hove Drawn	Hove Sy 37	–	Horsham Drawn	Hove Sx 7w
WARWKS	B'ham Drawn	B'ham Drawn	Stratford Drawn	B'ham Drawn	B'ham Wa 8w	B'ham Wa 7w	B'ham Drawn	–	B'ham Wa 9w
WORCS	Worcs Wo I/86	Worcs Drawn	Worcs Drawn	Worcs M 6w	Worcs Drawn	Worcs Drawn	Worcs Drawn	Worcs Drawn	–

DIVISION 2

	DERBYS	DURHAM	ESSEX	GLAM	HANTS	LEICS	NOTTS	SOM'T	YORKS
DERBYS		Derby Drawn	Derby Drawn	Derby Gm 128	Derby H 91	Derby Drawn	Derby Nt I/56	Derby Drawn	Derby Drawn
DURHAM	C-le-St De 165	–	C-le-St Drawn	C-le-St Gm 201	C-le-St Drawn	C-le-St Le 6w	C-le-St Nt I/80	C-le-St Drawn	C-le-St Y 320
ESSEX	Chelms Ex 8w	Colchester Drawn	–	Chelms Gm 4w	Chelms H 114	Chelms Drawn	S'end Nt 8w	Chelms Drawn	Chelms Y 137
GLAM	Cardiff Drawn	Cardiff Drawn	Cardiff Drawn	–	Cardiff H 9w	Cardiff Gm 409	Cardiff Drawn	Swansea Gm 7w	Col Bay Drawn
HANTS	So'ton Drawn	So'ton H 3w	So'ton Ex 384	So'ton Drawn	–	So'ton H I/18	So'ton Nt I/44	So'ton H 275	So'ton Drawn
LEICS	Oakham Le 6w	Leics Le I/26	Leics Ex 48	Leics Drawn	Leics H 86	–	Leics Le 92	Leics Sm 75	Leics Drawn
NOTTS	N'ham Nt 10w	N'ham Nt 3w	N'ham Nt 3w	N'ham Drawn	N'ham Drawn	N'ham Drawn	–	N'ham Sm 10w	N'ham Drawn
SOM'T	Taunton Drawn	Taunton Du 1w	Taunton Drawn	Taunton Sm 8w	Taunton H 10r	Taunton Drawn	Bath Nt 7w	–	Taunton Drawn
YORKS	Leeds Drawn	Scar Du 210	Leeds Y 7w	Leeds Drawn	Leeds H 119	Leeds Drawn	Leeds Nt 244	Scar Sm 10w	–

COUNTY CHAMPIONSHIP RESULTS 2005

KEEP YOUR OWN RECORD (see page 139)

DIVISION 1

	GLAM	GLOS	HANTS	KENT	MIDDX	NOTTS	SURREY	SUSSEX	WARWKS
GLAM	–	Cardiff	Cardiff	Cardiff	Cardiff	Cardiff	Cardiff	Swansea	Col Bay
GLOS	Bristol	–	Chelt	Bristol	Bristol	Bristol	Bristol	Chelt	Glos
HANTS	So'ton	So'ton	–	So'ton	So'ton	So'ton	So'ton	So'ton	So'ton
KENT	Cant	Maidstone	Cant	–	Cant	Cant	Tun W	Cant	Cant
MIDDX	Southgate	Lord's	Southgate	Lord's	–	Lord's	Lord's	Lord's	Lord's
NOTTS	N'ham	N'ham	N'ham	N'ham	N'ham	–	N'ham	N'ham	N'ham
SURREY	Oval	Oval	Oval	Guildford	Oval	Oval	–	Oval	Croydon
SUSSEX	Hove	Hove	Hove	Hove	Hove	Arundel	Hove	–	Horsham
WARWKS	B'ham	B'ham	B'ham	B'ham	B'ham	B'ham	B'ham	B'ham	–

DIVISION 2

	DERBYS	DURHAM	ESSEX	LANCS	LEICS	N'HANTS	SOM'T	WORCS	YORKS
DERBYS	–	Derby	Derby	Derby	Derby	Derby	Derby	Derby	Derby
DURHAM	C-le-St	–	C-le-St	C-le-St	C-le-St	C-le-St	C-le-St	C-le-St	C-le-St
ESSEX	Chelms	Southend	–	Chelms	Chelms	Chelms	Colchester	Chelms	Chelms
LANCS	Man	Man	Man	–	Man	Man	Man	B'pool	Man
LEICS	Leics	Leics	Leics	Leics	–	Leics	Oakham	Leics	Leics
N'HANTS	No'ton	No'ton	No'ton	No'ton	No'ton	–	No'ton	No'ton	No'ton
SOM'T	Taunton	Taunton	Taunton	Taunton	Taunton	Taunton	–	Bath	Taunton
WORCS	Worcs	Worcs	Worcs	Worcs	Worcs	Worcs	Worcs	–	Worcs
YORKS	Leeds	Scar	Leeds	Leeds	Scar	Leeds	Leeds	Leeds	–

NATWEST TRIANGULAR SERIES 2004

Manchester 24 June (floodlit). England v **New Zealand**. Match abandoned without a ball being bowled.

Birmingham 26 June. Toss: New Zealand. **New Zealand v West Indies** – match reduced to 21 overs and abandoned (rain). West Indies122-4 (21 overs). New Zealand 97-2 (13.4 overs). No award.

Nottingham 27 June. Toss: West Indies. **WEST INDIES** beat **England** by seven wickets. England 147 (38.2; A.J.Strauss 43, D.J.J.Bravo 3-26). West Indies 148-3 (32.2; C.H.Gayle 60*). Award: D.J.J.Bravo.

Chester-le-Street 29 June (floodlit). Toss: New Zealand. **NEW ZEALAND** beat **England** by seven wickets. England 101 (32.5; J.E.C.Franklin 5-42). New Zealand 103-3 (17.2; S.J.Harmison 3-38). Award: J.E.C.Franklin.

Leeds 1 July (floodlit). Toss: England. **ENGLAND** beat **West Indies** by seven wickets. West Indies 159 (40.1; R.R.Sarwan 46, S.J.Harmison 3-31, J.M.Anderson 3-37). England 160-3 (22; M.E.Trescothick 55, A.J.Strauss 44*). Award: S.J.Harmison.

Cardiff 3 July. Toss: New Zealand. **NEW ZEALAND** beat **West Indies** by five wickets. West Indies 216 (46.2; B.C.Lara 55, R.R.Sarwan 54; C.L.Cairns 3-29, I.G.Butler 3-41). New Zealand 220-5 (46; S.P.Fleming 45, H.J.H.Marshall 75*, D.J.J.Bravo 3-36). Award: H.J.H.Marshall.

Bristol 4 July. Toss: New Zealand. **NEW ZEALAND** beat **England** by six wickets. England 237-7 (50; A.J.Strauss 61, A.Flintoff 106), I.G.Butler 3-57). New Zealand 241-4 (47.2; S.P.Fleming 99, N.J.Astle 53, H.J.H.Marshall 55). Award: S.P.Fleming.

Lord's 6 July. Toss: West Indies. **WEST INDIES** beat **England** by seven wickets. England 285-7 (50; A.J.Strauss 100, A.Flintoff 123, C.H.Gayle 3-57). West Indies 286-3 (49.1; C.H.Gayle 132*, R.R.Sarwan 89). Award: C.H.Gayle.

Southampton 8 July. Toss: West Indies. **New Zealand v West Indies**. Match abandoned without a ball being bowled.

	Played	Won	Lost	No Result	Points	NRR
New Zealand	6	3	–	3	25	1.40
West Indies	6	2	2	2	18	–0.37
England	6	1	4	1	11	–0.58

Final – Lord's 10 July

Toss: West Indies. **NEW ZEALAND** beat **West Indies** by 107 runs. New Zealand 266 (49.2; S.P.Fleming 67, N.J.Astle 57, H.J.H.Marshall 44, C.D.McMillan 52, R.R.Sarwan 3-31). West Indies 159 (41.2; D.S.Smith 44, D.L.Vettori 5-30). Award: D.L.Vettori. Series Award: S.P.Fleming.

NATWEST CHALLENGE 2004

Nottingham, 1 September. Toss: England. **ENGLAND** beat **India** by seven wickets. India 170 (43.5; M.Kaif 50, S.J.Harmison 3-41 including a hat-trick, A.G.Wharf 3-30). England 171-3 (32.2; V.S.Solanki 52, A.J.Strauss 41*). Award: A.G.Wharf.

The Oval, 3 September. Toss: India. **ENGLAND** beat **India** by 70 runs. England 307-5 (50; V.S.Solanki 48, A.Flintoff 99, P.D.Collingwood 79*). India 237 (46.3; M.Kaif 51, Harbhajan Singh 41*, D.Gough 4-50, A.F.Giles 3-26). Award: A.Flintoff.

Lord's, 5 September. Toss: India. **INDIA** beat **England** by 23 runs. India 204 (49.3; S.C.Ganguly 90, R.Dravid 52, S.J.Harmison 4-22). England 181 (48.2; M.P.Vaughan 74, A.Nehra 3-26, Harbhajan Singh 3-28). Award: S.C.Ganguly.

ICC CHAMPIONS TROPHY 2004

QUALIFYING ROUNDS TABLE

Pool A

	Played	Won	Lost	No Result	Tied	Points	NRR
AUSTRALIA	2	2	–	–	–	4	+3.237
New Zealand	2	1	1	–	–	2	+1.603
United States of America	2	–	2	–	–	0	–5.121

Pool B

	Played	Won	Lost	No Result	Tied	Points	NRR
WEST INDIES	2	2	–	–	–	4	+1.471
South Africa	2	1	1	–	–	2	+1.552
Bangladesh	2	–	2	–	–	0	–3.111

Pool C

	Played	Won	Lost	No Result	Tied	Points	NRR
PAKISTAN	2	2	–	–	–	4	+1.413
India	2	1	1	–	–	2	+0.944
Kenya	2	–	2	–	–	0	–2.747

Pool D

	Played	Won	Lost	No Result	Tied	Points	NRR
ENGLAND	2	2	–	–	–	4	+2.716
Sri Lanka	2	1	1	–	–	2	–0.252
Zimbabwe	2	–	2	–	–	0	–1.885

Semi-Finals

Birmingham 21 September. Toss: England. **ENGLAND** beat **Australia** by six wickets. Australia 259-9 (50 overs; D.R.Martyn 65, M.J.Clarke 42, D.Gough 3-48). England 262-4 (46.3; M.E.Trescothick 81, M.P.Vaughan 86, A.J.Strauss 52*). Award: M.P.Vaughan.

Southampton 22 September. Toss: Pakistan. **WEST INDIES** beat **Pakistan** by seven wickets. Pakistan 131 (38.2). West Indies 132-3 (28.1; R.R.Sarwan 56*). Award: R.R.Sarwan.

Final

The Oval 25 September. Toss: West Indies. **WEST INDIES** beat **England** by two wickets. England 217 (49.4; M.E.Trescothick 104, W.W.Hinds 3-24). West Indies 218-8 (48.5; S.Chanderpaul 47, C.O.Browne 35* and I.D.R.Bradshaw 34* added 71* off 92 balls for the ninth wicket). Award: I.D.R.Bradshaw.

CHELTENHAM & GLOUCESTER TROPHY 2004 RESULTS CHART

SECOND ROUND 5, 6, 17 May	THIRD ROUND 26, 29, 30 May	QUARTER-FINALS 15, 16 June	SEMI-FINALS 17 July	FINAL 28 August
Holland†				
GLOUCESTERSHIRE†	GLOUCESTERSHIRE†	GLOUCESTERSHIRE†	GLOUCESTERSHIRE†	GLOUCESTERSHIRE (£53,000)
Cheshire†				
HAMPSHIRE	Hampshire			
Wales MC†				
MIDDLESEX†	MIDDLESEX†	Middlesex (£11,500)		
Lincolnshire†				
GLAMORGAN	Glamorgan			
Leicestershire				
DEVON†	DEVON†	YORKSHIRE	Yorkshire (£16,500)	
Dorset†				
YORKSHIRE	YORKSHIRE			
Staffordshire†				
LANCASHIRE	LANCASHIRE	Lancashire† (£11,500)		
Durham†				
SUSSEX	Sussex†			
Cambridgeshire				
NORTHAMPTONSHIRE†	NORTHAMPTONSHIRE†	Northamptonshire (£11,500)	Warwickshire† (£16,500)	Worcestershire (£27,000)
Surrey				
IRELAND†	Ireland†			
Shropshire				
WARWICKSHIRE†	WARWICKSHIRE†	WARWICKSHIRE†		
Berkshire				
KENT†	Kent			
Wiltshire				
NOTTINGHAMSHIRE†	Nottinghamshire†	Essex (£11,500)	WORCESTERSHIRE	
Scotland†				
ESSEX	ESSEX			
Derbyshire†				
SOMERSET	Somerset	WORCESTERSHIRE†		
Herefordshire				
WORCESTERSHIRE†	WORCESTERSHIRE†			

† Home team. Winning teams are in capitals. Prize-money shown in brackets.

2004 C & G TROPHY FINAL

GLOUCESTERSHIRE v WORCESTERSHIRE

At Lord's, London on 28 August
Result: **GLOUCESTERSHIRE** won by eight wickets
Toss: Gloucestershire. Award: V.S.Solanki

WORCESTERSHIRE		Runs	Balls	4/6	Fall
V.S.Solanki	st Adshead b Ball	115	136	14	4-202
S.C.Moore	c Adshead b Lewis	0	12	–	1- 4
G.A.Hick	c Adshead b Lewis	0	4	–	2- 4
B.F.Smith	c Hussey b Lewis	1	9	–	3- 8
D.A.Leatherdale	c Hancock b Averis	66	118	3	5-218
A.J.Bichel	st Adshead b Ball	19	15	-/2	6-231
A.J.Hall	c Hussey b Averis	1	3	–	8-232
G.J.Batty	c Weston b Averis	1	2	–	7-232
*†S.J.Rhodes	not out	1	1	–	
M.S.Mason	b Averis	1	2	–	9-234
R.W.Price	not out	2	1	–	
Extras	(B 2, LB 4, W 17, NB 6)	29			
Total	(50 overs; 9 wickets; 213 minutes)	**236**			

GLOUCESTERSHIRE		Runs	Balls	4/6	Fall
W.P.C.Weston	not out	110	129	12/1	
C.M.Spearman	c Rhodes b Batty	70	77	9	1-141
M.E.K.Hussey	b Price	20	25	3	3-171
C.G.Taylor	not out	22	34	2	
T.H.C.Hancock					
* M.W.Alleyne					
A.P.R.Gidman					
† S.J.Adshead					
M.C.J.Ball					
J.Lewis					
J.M.M.Averis					
Extras	(B 3, LB 2, W 6, NB 4)	15			
Total	(43.5 overs; 2 wickets; 176 minutes)	**237**			

GLOS	O	M	R	W	WORCS	O	M	R	W
Lewis	10	2	32	3	Mason	10	0	40	0
Averis	10	3	23	4	Bichel	7	0	46	0
Alleyne	8	0	32	0	Hall	5	0	28	0
Gidman	7	1	40	0	Leatherdale	2.5	0	25	0
Ball	9	0	65	2	Price	9	0	51	1
Hussey	6	0	38	0	Batty	10	0	42	1

Scores after 15 overs: Worcestershire 34-3; Gloucestershire 83-0.

Umpires: N.A.Mallender and P.Willey.

CHELTENHAM & GLOUCESTER TROPHY

PRINCIPAL RECORDS 1963-2004
(Including Gillette Cup and NatWest Trophy Matches)

Highest Total	438-5	Surrey v Glamorgan	The Oval	2002
Highest Total in a Final	322-5	Warwicks v Sussex	Lord's	1993
Highest Total Batting Second	429	Glamorgan v Surrey	The Oval	2002
Highest Total to Win Batting Second	329-5	Sussex v Derbyshire	Derby	1997
Lowest Total	39	Ireland v Sussex	Hove	1985
Lowest Total in a Final	57	Essex v Lancashire	Lord's	1996
Lowest Total to Win Batting First	98	Worcs v Durham	Chester-le-St	1968

Highest Score	268	A.D.Brown	Surrey v Glamorgan	The Oval	2002
Fastest Hundred	36 balls	G.D.Rose	Somerset v Devon	Torquay	1990
Most Hundreds	8	R.A.Smith	Hampshire		1985-03
Most Runs	2547	(av 48.98)	G.A.Gooch	Essex	1973-96

Highest Partnership for each Wicket

1st	311	A.J.Wright/N.J.Trainor	Glos v Scotland	Bristol	1997
2nd	286	I.S.Anderson/A.Hill	Derbys v Cornwall	Derby	1986
3rd	309*	T.S.Curtis/T.M.Moody	Worcs v Surrey	The Oval	1994
4th	234*	D.Lloyd/C.H.Lloyd	Lancashire v Glos	Manchester	1978
5th	166	M.A.Lynch/G.R.J.Roope	Surrey v Durham	The Oval	1982
6th	226	N.J.Llong/M.V.Fleming	Kent v Cheshire	Bowdon	1999
7th	170	D.R.Brown/A.F.Giles	Warwicks v Essex	Birmingham	2003
8th	112	A.L.Penberthy/J.E.Emburey	Northants v Lancs	Manchester	1996
9th	87	M.A.Nash/A.E.Cordle	Glamorgan v Lincs	Swansea	1974
10th	81	S.Turner/R.E.East	Essex v Yorkshire	Leeds	1982

Best Bowling	8-21	M.A.Holding	Derbys v Sussex	Hove	1988
Most Wickets	88	(av 14.35)	A.A.Donald	Warwks/Worcs 1987-02

Most Wicket-Keeping Dismissals in an Innings

8 (8ct)	D.J.Pipe	Worcs v Herts	Hertford	2001

Most Match Wins: 88 – Lancashire.　　　　**Most Cup/Trophy Wins:** 7 – Lancashire

GILLETTE CUP WINNERS

1963	Sussex	1970	Lancashire	1977	Middlesex
1964	Sussex	1971	Lancashire	1978	Sussex
1965	Yorkshire	1972	Lancashire	1979	Somerset
1966	Warwickshire	1973	Gloucestershire	1980	Middlesex
1967	Kent	1974	Kent		
1968	Warwickshire	1975	Lancashire		
1969	Yorkshire	1976	Northamptonshire		

NATWEST TROPHY WINNERS

1981	Derbyshire	1988	Middlesex	1995	Warwickshire
1982	Surrey	1989	Warwickshire	1996	Lancashire
1983	Somerset	1990	Lancashire	1997	Essex
1984	Middlesex	1991	Hampshire	1998	Lancashire
1985	Essex	1992	Northamptonshire	1999	Gloucestershire
1986	Sussex	1993	Warwickshire	2000	Gloucestershire
1987	Nottinghamshire	1994	Worcestershire		

CHELTENHAM & GLOUCESTER TROPHY WINNERS

2001	Somerset	2003	Gloucestershire	2004	Gloucestershire
2002	Yorkshire				

TOTESPORT NATIONAL LEAGUE 2004

FIRST DIVISION

		P	W	L	T	NR	Pts	NRR
1	GLAMORGAN (5) (£54,000)	16	11	5	–	–	44	4.08
2	Lancashire (-) (£27,000)	16	9	6	–	–	38	–3.39
3	Hampshire (-)	16	7	6	–	3	34	0.81
4	Northamptonshire (-)	16	8	8	–	–	32	1.85
5	Gloucestershire (2)	16	7	7	1	1	32	3.34
6	Essex (3)	16	6	6	1	3	32	1.00
7	Warwickshire (4)	16	7	8	–	1	30	4.60
8	Kent (6)	16	5	9	–	2	24	–6.46
9	Surrey (1)	16	4	9	–	3	22	–7.26

SECOND DIVISION

		P	W	L	T	NR	Pts	NRR
1	MIDDLESEX (4) (£20,000)	18	12	6	–	–	48	–0.11
2	Worcestershire (-) (£11,000)	18	11	5	–	2	48	14.17
3	Nottinghamshire (5)	18	9	4	1	4	46	9.74
4	Yorkshire (-)	18	10	6	–	2	44	2.76
5	Sussex (8)	18	9	7	1	1	40	7.90
6	Durham (7)	18	9	7	–	2	40	2.49
7	Leicestershire (-)	18	7	8	–	3	34	–0.10
8	Somerset (9)	18	6	11	–	1	26	–1.66
9	Derbyshire (6)	18	5	12	–	1	22	–16.04
10	Scotland (10)	18	2	14	–	2	12	–17.56

Win = 4 points. Tie (T)/No Result (NR) = 2 points. Positions of counties finishing equal on points are decided by most wins or, if equal, by higher net run-rate (NRR – overall run-rate in all matches, i.e. total runs scored times 100 divided by balls received, minus the run-rate of its opponents in those same matches). Horizontal rules segregate the counties relegated and promoted for the 2005 competition. 2004 final positions for that division are shown in brackets.

HIGHEST BATTING AGGREGATE– Div 1	686	(av 98.00) M.T.G.Elliott		Glamorgan
– Div 2	807	(av 57.64) P.N.Weekes		Middlesex
HIGHEST BOWLING AGGREGATE – Div 1	34	(av 15.67) J.Louw		Northamptonshire
– Div 2	39	(av 15.35) S.J.Cook		Middlesex

SUNDAY LEAGUE CHAMPIONS

1969	Lancashire	1979	Somerset	1989	Lancashire
1970	Lancashire	1980	Warwickshire	1990	Derbyshire
1971	Worcestershire	1981	Essex	1991	Nottinghamshire
1972	Kent	1982	Sussex	1992	Middlesex
1973	Kent	1983	Yorkshire	1993	Glamorgan
1974	Leicestershire	1984	Essex	1994	Warwickshire
1975	Hampshire	1985	Essex	1995	Kent
1976	Kent	1986	Hampshire	1996	Surrey
1977	Leicestershire	1987	Worcestershire	1997	Warwickshire
1978	Hampshire	1988	Worcestershire	1998	Lancashire

NATIONAL LEAGUE CHAMPIONS

1999	Lancashire	2001	Kent	2003	Surrey
2000	Gloucestershire	2002	Glamorgan	2004	Glamorgan

SCOTLAND

TOTESPORT NATIONAL LEAGUE REGISTER 2004

Full Names	Birthdate	Birthplace	Bat/Bowl	F-C Debut
ASIM BUTT	24.10.67	Lahore, Pakistan	RHB/LMF	1983-84
BRINKLEY, James Edward	13.03.74	Helensburgh	RHB/RFM	1993-94
BRUCE, Stewart	02.04.69	Edinburgh	LHB/LFM	–
COETZER, Stuart Charles	31.01.82	Grahamstown, S Africa	RHB/WK	–
COLES, Cameron Alan Ross	23.05.74	Moura, Australia	RHB/OB	–
ENGLISH, Cedric Vaughan	13.09.73	Kimberley, S Africa	RHB/RFM	1990-91

Full Names	Birthdate	Birthplace	Bat/Bowl	F-C Debut
GOUDIE, Gordon	12.08.87	Aberdeen	RHB/RFM	–
HAQ, Rana Majid Khan	11.12.83	Paisley	LHB/OB	2004
HOFFMAN, Paul Jacob Christopher	14.01.70	Rockhampton, Australia	RHB/RMF	2004
KNOX, Steven Thomas	16.02.74	Barrow-in-Furness	RHB/RM	–
LOCKHART, Douglas Ross	19.01.76	Glasgow	RHB/WK	1996
MAIDEN, Gregor Ian	22.07.79	Glasgow	RHB/OB	1999
MORE, Robert Edwards	01.06.82	Edinburgh	LHB/OB	–
NEL, Johann Dewald	06.06.80	Klerksdorp, S Africa	RHB/RMF	2004
REIFER, Floyd Lamonte	23.07.72	Christ Church, Barbados	LHB/RM/WK	1991-92
SMITH, Colin John Ogilvie	27.09.72	Aberdeen	RHB/WK	1999
SMITH, Simon James Stevenson	08.12.79	Ashington	RHB/WK	2004
SRIRAM, Sridharan	21.02.76	Madras, India	LHB/SLA	1993-94
STANGER, Ian Michael	05.10.71	Glasgow	RHB/RMF	1997
WATSON, Ryan Robert	12.11.76	Salisbury, Rhodesia	RHB/RM	2004
WATTS, David Fraser	05.06.79	King's Lynn, Norfolk	RHB/RM	1999
WILLIAMSON, John Greig	20.12.68	Glasgow	RHB/RM	1994
WRIGHT, Craig McIntyre	28.04.74	Paisley	RHB/RMF	1997
YASIR ARAFAT Satti	12.03.82	Rawalpindi, Pakistan	RHB/RMF	1997-98

NATIONAL (SUNDAY) LEAGUE 1969-2004
PRINCIPAL RECORDS

Highest Total	377-9	Somerset v Sussex	Hove	2003
Highest Total Batting Second	323-5	Sussex v Leics	Horsham	2004
Lowest Total	23	Middlesex v Yorks	Leeds	1974
Largest Victory (Runs)	220	Somerset v Glamorgan	Neath	1990
Highest Scores	203 A.D.Brown	Surrey v Hampshire	Guildford	1997
	191 D.S.Lehmann	Yorks v Notts	Scarborough	2001
	176 G.A.Gooch	Essex v Glamorgan	Southend	1983
	175* I.T.Botham	Somerset v Northants	Wellingborough	1986
Fastest Hundred	44 balls M.A.Ealham	Kent v Derbyshire	Maidstone	1995
Most Sixes (Inns)	13 I.T.Botham	Somerset v Northants	Wellingborough	1986
Highest Partnership for each Wicket				
1st	239 G.A.Gooch/B.R.Hardie	Essex v Notts	Nottingham	1985
2nd	273 G.A.Gooch/K.S.McEwan	Essex v Notts	Nottingham	1983
3rd	228* M.W.Goodwin/C.J.Adams	Sussex v Middlesex	Hove	2003
4th	219 C.G.Greenidge/C.L.Smith	Hampshire v Surrey	Southampton	1987
5th	220* C.C.Lewis/P.A.Nixon	Leics v Kent	Canterbury	1999
6th	167 C.L.Cairns/C.M.W.Read	Notts v Sussex	Nottingham	2003
7th	164 J.N.Snape/M.A.Hardinges	Glos v Notts	Nottingham	2001
8th	116* N.D.Burns/P.A.J.DeFreitas	Leics v Northants	Leicester	2001
9th	105 D.G.Moir/R.W.Taylor	Derbyshire v Kent	Derby	1984
10th	82 G.Chapple/P.J.Martin	Lancashire v Worcs	Manchester	1996
Best Bowling	8-26 K.D.Boyce	Essex v Lancashire	Manchester	1971
	7-15 R.A.Hutton	Yorkshire v Worcs	Leeds	1969
	7-16 S.D.Thomas	Glamorgan v Surrey	Swansea	1998
	7-30 M.P.Bicknell	Surrey v Glamorgan	The Oval	1999
	7-39 A.Hodgson	Northants v Somerset	Northampton	1976
	7-41 A.N.Jones	Sussex v Notts	Nottingham	1986
Four Wkts in Four Balls	A.Ward	Derbyshire v Sussex	Derby	1970
	V.C.Drakes	Notts v Derbys	Nottingham	1999
Most Economical Analysis				
	8-8-0-0 B.A.Langford	Somerset v Essex	Yeovil	1969
Most Expensive Analysis				
	9-0-99-1 M.R.Strong	Northants v Glos	Cheltenham	2001
Most Wicket-Keeping Dismissals in an Innings				
	7 (6ct, 1st) R.W.Taylor	Derbyshire v Lancs	Manchester	1975
Most Catches in an Innings by a Fielder				
	5 J.M.Rice	Hampshire v Warwicks	Southampton	1978

TWENTY20 CUP 2004
GROUP TABLES

MIDLANDS/WALES/WEST	P	W	L	T	NR	Pts	NRR
1 GLAMORGAN	5	4	1	–	–	8	0.41
2 Worcestershire	5	3	2	–	–	6	–0.26
3 Warwickshire	5	3	2	–	–	6	0.61
4 Somerset	5	2	2	–	1	5	–0.38
5 Gloucestershire	5	1	3	–	1	3	–0.37
6 Northamptonshire	5	1	4	–	–	2	–0.46

NORTH	P	W	L	T	NR	Pts	NRR
1 LEICESTERSHIRE	5	3	1	–	1	7	0.21
2 LANCASHIRE	5	3	2	–	–	6	0.27
3 Derbyshire	5	2	2	–	1	5	–0.03
4 Nottinghamshire	5	2	3	–	–	4	–0.55
5 Durham	5	2	3	–	–	4	0.26
6 Yorkshire	5	2	3	–	–	4	–0.10

SOUTH	P	W	L	T	NR	Pts	NRR
1 SURREY	5	4	–	–	1	9	2.13
2 Hampshire	5	3	2	–	–	6	0.32
3 Essex	5	2	2	–	1	5	0.52
4 Kent	5	2	3	–	–	4	–0.20
5 Middlesex	5	1	3	–	1	3	–1.23
6 Sussex	5	1	3	–	1	3	–1.71

SEMI-FINALS
Played at Edgbaston, Birmingham, on 7 August

SURREY beat Lancashire by one run. Toss: Surrey. Surrey 133 (20 overs; A.D.Brown 32, G. Keedy 3-25). Lancashire 132-8 (20 overs). Award: Azhar Mahmood (13 and 2-22).

LEICESTERSHIRE beat Glamorgan by 21 runs. Toss: Leicestershire. Leicestershire 165-5 (20 overs; D.L.Maddy 72). Glamorgan 144 (18.5 overs; D.L.Hemp 44, M.F.Cleary 3-20, C.W.Henderson 3-26). Award: D.L.Maddy (72 and 1-22).

LEADING AVERAGES

BATTING (Qual: 4 Inns, Avge 45)		M	I	NO	HS	Runs	Avge	100	50	SR
A.J.Hollioake	Surrey	7	7	4	65*	183	61.00	–	1	156.41
A.J.Bichel	Worcestershire	6	6	3	58*	180	60.00	–	1	125.00
C.J.Adams	Sussex	4	4	2	38*	106	53.00	–	–	108.16
D.L.Maddy	Leicestershire	7	7	0	111	356	50.85	1	3	173.65
P.N.Weekes	Middlesex	4	4	1	55*	150	50.00	–	1	94.93
I.J.L.Trott	Warwickshire	5	5	3	39	93	46.50	–	–	104.49
J.J.B.Lewis	Durham	5	4	2	49*	91	45.50	–	–	88.34
M.J.Walker	Kent	5	5	2	48*	136	45.33	–	–	108.80
P.A.Jaques	Yorkshire	5	5	1	92	180	45.00	–	1	132.35

BOWLING (Qualification: 10 wkts)		O	M	R	W	Avge	BB	4w	R/Over
S.M.B.Ali	Derbyshire	15	–	95	10	9.50	3-24	–	6.33
A.D.Mascarenhas	Hampshire	20.5	2	121	12	10.08	5-14	1	5.80
A.J.Hollioake	Surrey	25	–	208	20	10.40	5-34	2	8.32
G.B.Hogg	Warwickshire	21.5	–	142	13	10.92	4- 9	2	6.50
J.M.M.Averis	Gloucestershire	14	–	111	10	11.10	3- 7	–	7.92
M.F.Cleary	Leicestershire	25	–	199	15	13.26	3-11	–	7.96
G.Keedy	Lancashire	23	–	138	10	13.80	3-25	–	6.00
M.N.Malik	Worcestershire	20	–	156	10	15.60	3-23	–	7.80
A.P.Davies	Glamorgan	23.1	1	159	10	15.90	3-17	–	6.86
A.G.Wharf	Glamorgan	25.1	–	202	11	18.36	3-23	–	8.02

TWENTY20 CUP FINAL

LEICESTERSHIRE v SURREY

At Edgbaston, Birmingham, on 7 August.
Result: **LEICESTERSHIRE** won by seven wickets
Toss: Surrey. Award: B.J.Hodge.

SURREY		Runs	Balls	4/6	Fall
A.D.Brown	c Sadler b Henderson	64	41	9/2	3-109
J.G.E.Benning	c Henderson b Gibson	5	4	1	1- 11
S.A.Newman	c Cleary b Dagnall	21	27	2	2- 91
M.R.Ramprakash	not out	23	24	2	
R.Clarke	c Cleary b Henderson	13	13	–/1	4-135
A.J.Hollioake	c Hodge b Cleary	4	5	–	5-141
Azhar Mahmood	b Cleary	13	6	1/1	6-160
*†J.N.Batty	not out	1	1	–	
J.Ormond					
P.J.Sampson					
N.D.Doshi					
Extras	(B 6, LB 6, W 10, NB 2)	24			
Total	(20 overs; 6 wickets)	**168**			

LEICESTERSHIRE		Runs	Balls	4/6	Fall
* B.J.Hodge	not out	77	53	10/1	
D.L.Maddy	b Sampson	22	17	3	1- 62
D.I.Stevens	c Azhar Mahmood b Hollioake	20	22	3	2-114
J.L.Sadler	c Clarke b Hollioake	6	7	1	3-122
J.N.Snape	not out	34	16	3/2	
† P.A.Nixon					
O.D.Gibson					
D.G.Brandy					
C.W.Henderson					
M.F.Cleary					
C.E.Dagnall					
Extras	(LB 3, W 7)	10			
Total	(19.1 overs; 3 wickets)	**169**			

LEICESTER	O	M	R	W	SURREY	O	M	R	W
Cleary	4	0	38	2	Azhar Mahmood	3.1	0	33	0
Gibson	3	0	21	1	Clarke	2	0	27	0
Dagnall	4	0	36	1	Sampson	2	0	14	1
Maddy	2	0	16	0	Ormond	4	0	30	0
Snape	4	0	30	0	Doshi	4	0	26	0
Henderson	3	0	15	2	Hollioake	4	0	36	2

Umpires: I.J.Gould and N.J.Llong

Prize Money: Winner £42,000; Runner-up £21,000; Losing Semi-finalist £10,500;
Losing Quarter-finalist £5,000.

MINOR COUNTIES CHAMPIONSHIP

FINAL TABLES 2004

	P	W	L	D	T	Bonus Points Bat	Bonus Points Bowl	Total Points
EASTERN DIVISION								
BEDFORDSHIRE	6	3	–	3		17	19	96
Staffordshire	6	2	1	2	1	17	20	85
Buckinghamshire	6	2	1	3	–	18	20	82
Suffolk	6	2	1	3	–	17	21	82
Northumberland	6	2	1	3	–	13	21	78
Hertfordshire	6	2	2	2	–	14	20	74
Cumberland	6	2	2	2	–	9	24	73
Norfolk	6	–	1	4	1	19	17	60
Cambridgeshire	6	–	3	3	–	14	18	44
Lincolnshire	6	–	3	3	–	15	16	43†
WESTERN DIVISION								
DEVON	6	5	1	–	–	18	17	115
Shropshire	6	3	1	2	–	15	19	90
Wales MC	6	3	2	1	–	20	15	87
Berkshire	6	2	1	3	–	17	21	82
Wiltshire	6	2	2	2	–	14	22	76
Cornwall	6	2	3	1	–	16	27	69
Cheshire	6	1	1	4	–	14	17	63
Oxfordshire	6	2	3	1	–	7	18	61
Dorset	6	1	3	2	–	11	22	57
Herefordshire	6	–	4	2	–	15	18	41

† Two points deducted for a slow over rate. Win = 16 points. Draw/Tie = 4 points.

CHAMPIONSHIP FINAL

At The Maer Ground, Exmouth on 12, 13, 14 September. Toss: Devon. **DEVON drew with BEDFORDSHIRE – TITLE SHARED.** Bedfordshire 214 (68.3 overs; J.E.P.Walford 52, N.D.Hancock 7-80) and 170-4 (53; A.J.Trott 83*, J.E.P.Walford 55*). Devon 288-9 (70; A.V.Suppiah 97, S.J.Watts 4-104, A.J.Trott 4-51).

MCCA KNOCK-OUT TROPHY FINAL

At Lord's, London, on 6 September. Toss: Berkshire. **BERKSHIRE beat NORTHUMBER-LAND by seven wickets.** Northumberland 237 (49.3; S.P.Naylor 4-49). Berkshire 240-3 (42.4; J.R.Perkins 73, B.H.D.Mordt 72*, J.R.Wood 51).

MINOR COUNTIES RECORDS

Highest Total	621		Surrey II v Devon	The Oval	1928
Lowest Total	14		Cheshire v Staffs	Stoke	1909
Highest Score	282	E.Garnett	Berkshire v Wiltshire	Reading	1908
Most Runs – Season	1212	A.F.Brazier	Surrey II		1949
Record Partnership:					
2nd wkt	388*	T.H.Clark/A.F.Brazier	Surrey II v Sussex II	The Oval	1949
Best Bowling – Innings	10- 11	S.Turner	Cambs v Cumberland	Penrith	1987
– Match	18-100	N.W.Harding	Kent II v Wiltshire	Swindon	1937
Most Wickets – Season	119	S.F.Barnes	Staffordshire		1906

MINOR COUNTIES CHAMPIONS

1895	Norfolk / Durham / Worcestershire	1932	Buckinghamshire	1974	Oxfordshire
		1933	*Undecided*	1975	Hertfordshire
		1934	Lancashire II	1976	Durham
1896	Worcestershire	1935	Middlesex II	1977	Suffolk
1897	Worcestershire	1936	Hertfordshire	1978	Devon
1898	Worcestershire	1937	Lancashire II	1979	Suffolk
1899	Northamptonshire / Buckinghamshire	1938	Buckinghamshire	1980	Durham
		1939	Surrey II	1981	Durham
1900	Glamorgan / Durham / Northamptonshire	1946	Suffolk	1982	Oxfordshire
		1947	Yorkshire II	1983	Hertfordshire
		1948	Lancashire II	1984	Durham
1901	Durham	1949	Lancashire II	1985	Cheshire
1902	Wiltshire	1950	Surrey II	1986	Cumberland
1903	Northamptonshire	1951	Kent II	1987	Buckinghamshire
1904	Northamptonshire	1952	Buckinghamshire	1988	Cheshire
1905	Norfolk	1953	Berkshire	1989	Oxfordshire
1906	Staffordshire	1954	Surrey II	1990	Hertfordshire
1907	Lancashire II	1955	Surrey II	1991	Staffordshire
1908	Staffordshire	1956	Kent II	1992	Staffordshire
1909	Wiltshire	1957	Yorkshire II	1993	Staffordshire
1910	Norfolk	1958	Yorkshire II	1994	Devon
1911	Staffordshire	1959	Warwickshire II	1995	Devon
1912	*In abeyance*	1960	Lancashire II	1996	Devon
1913	Norfolk	1961	Somerset II	1997	Devon
1920	Staffordshire	1962	Warwickshire II	1998	Staffordshire
1921	Staffordshire	1963	Cambridgeshire	1999	Cumberland
1922	Buckinghamshire	1964	Lancashire II	2000	Dorset
1923	Buckinghamshire	1965	Somerset II	2001	Cheshire / Lincolnshire
1924	Berkshire	1966	Lincolnshire		
1925	Buckinghamshire	1967	Cheshire	2002	Herefordshire / Norfolk
1926	Durham	1968	Yorkshire II		
1927	Staffordshire	1969	Buckinghamshire	2003	Lincolnshire
1928	Berkshire	1970	Bedfordshire	2004	Bedfordshire / Devon
1929	Oxfordshire	1971	Yorkshire II		
1930	Durham	1972	Bedfordshire		
1931	Leicestershire II	1973	Shropshire		

LEADING CHAMPIONSHIP BATTING AVERAGES
(Qualifications: 8 innings; average 35.00)

		M	I	NO	HS	Runs	Avge	100	50
R.C.Driver	Cornwall	5	8	2	183	545	90.83	2	2
B.J.France	Suffolk	5	9	2	179*	566	80.85	1	4
R.I.Dawson	Devon	7	11	2	143*	598	66.44	3	1
R.Cook	Lincolnshire	6	10	3	148	455	65.00	2	1
A.D.Mawson	Suffolk	5	8	1	146	427	61.00	3	–
A.R.Roberts	Bedfordshire	7	11	2	123	519	57.66	1	4
D.D.Cherry	Wales MC	6	10	–	170	565	56.50	3	2
K.T.Medlycott	Buckinghamshire	6	10	1	111	508	56.44	1	5
C.Amos	Norfolk	6	12	2	121	556	55.60	2	2
B.Parker	Northumberland	6	9	–	183	476	52.88	2	1
R.E.Watkins	Wales MC	5	9	2	89	364	52.00	–	4
N.D.Hancock	Devon	7	11	4	79	363	51.85	–	3
C.R.Borrett	Norfolk	6	11	2	111	462	51.33	1	3
D.M.Ward	Hertfordshire	6	9	–	111	443	49.22	2	1
K.J.Barnett	Staffordshire	6	11	2	150*	438	48.66	1	2
B.J.Frazer	Hertfordshire	6	9	3	85	291	48.50	–	2
Baqar Rizvi	Wiltshire	6	11	1	96	459	45.90	–	5

		M	I	NO	HS	Runs	Avge	100	50
C.J.Rogers	Norfolk	6	12	2	142*	456	45.60	2	1
A.V.Suppiah	Devon	5	8	–	108	360	45.00	1	1
C.W.Boroughs	Herefordshire	6	10	–	142	446	44.60	2	–
C.Jones	Cambridgeshire	6	10	–	103	435	43.50	1	3
P.D.Atkins	Buckinghamshire	6	9	4	61*	217	43.40	–	1
N.M.K.Smith	Shropshire	6	8	1	142	302	43.14	1	1
D.N.Leech	Cheshire	6	10	–	118	430	43.00	1	2
A.Worthy	Northumberland	5	9	1	85	342	42.75	–	3
M.W.Patterson	Bedfordshire	7	8	4	101*	170	42.50	1	–
D.E.Barnes	Cumberland	6	11	2	135	373	41.44	1	1
J.P.Whittaker	Cheshire	6	8	3	70*	207	41.40	–	1
R.P.Harvey	Staffordshire	5	10	–	160	411	41.10	1	1
S.P.White	Hertfordshire	6	8	4	76	160	40.00	–	1
M.C.Dobson	Lincolnshire	6	10	–	115	393	39.30	1	3
J.A.Knott	Bedfordshire	7	12	–	107	468	39.00	2	1
S.A.Trigg	Cheshire	6	10	–	86	379	37.90	–	3
G.R.Treagus	Dorset	6	10	1	96	340	37.77	–	3
A.J.Hall	Cheshire	5	8	–	160	300	37.50	1	1
M.S.Coles	Wiltshire	6	11	–	111	412	37.45	1	2
T.C.Z.Lamb	Dorset	5	8	1	91	257	36.71	–	2
S.A.Richardson	Cumberland	6	11	1	95	365	36.50	–	3
J.E.P.Walford	Bedfordshire	7	12	1	91	401	36.45	–	4
C.A.Hunkin	Cornwall	5	8	2	54	217	36.16	–	1
I.A.Hawtin	Oxfordshire	6	10	2	117*	289	36.12	1	1
A.T.Heather	Northumberland	6	10	–	120	357	35.70	1	–
G.D.Freear	Cambridgeshire	5	8	–	73	285	35.62	–	3
T.G.Sharp	Cornwall	6	10	–	113	354	35.40	2	–
D.J.R.Exall	Herefordshire	6	8	2	83	211	35.16	–	1

LEADING CHAMPIONSHIP BOWLING AVERAGES
(Qualification: 20 wickets)

		O	M	R	W	Avge	BB	5w	10w
Z.A.Sher	Buckinghamshire	120	25	385	20	19.25	6- 83	2	–
S.A.Roberts	Herefordshire	187.3	37	609	29	21.00	6- 90	3	1
N.A.Denning	Berkshire	137.3	34	487	23	21.17	5- 50	2	–
A.Jones	Devon	179.4	51	466	21	22.19	4- 41	–	–
A.J.Procter	Devon	241.4	74	640	27	23.70	4- 44	–	–
S.Rashid	Bedfordshire	174.5	39	571	24	23.79	8- 55	1	–
N.D.Hancock	Devon	223.4	40	801	33	24.27	7- 80	2	–
D.Follett	Staffordshire	158.1	32	557	22	25.31	6- 98	2	–
C.D.Crowe	Berkshire	183.3	41	585	23	25.43	6- 73	2	–
D.B.Pennett	Cheshire	142.1	29	513	20	25.65	6- 73	1	–
C.Brown	Norfolk	224	41	668	26	25.69	5-115	1	–
D.E.Malcolm	Suffolk	191.4	43	678	25	27.12	4- 50	–	–
I.D.Hunter	Cumberland	207.1	48	683	25	27.32	7-111	1	–
M.J.Symington	Northumberland	159	30	562	20	28.10	5- 36	1	–
T.J.Mason	Shropshire	149.3	19	601	21	28.61	6- 76	2	–
M.P.Eccles	Norfolk	159	29	613	21	29.19	7- 74	1	1
T.C.Hicks	Dorset	156.5	38	584	20	29.20	4- 87	–	–
S.J.Watts	Bedfordshire	219.3	47	715	22	32.50	5-119	1	–
M.J.Rawnsley	Herefordshire	238.2	69	719	21	34.23	3- 41	–	–

152

SECOND XI CHAMPIONSHIP 2004
FINAL TABLE

	P	W	L	D	Deduct	Bonus Points Bat	Bonus Points Bowl	Total Points	Avge
1 SOMERSET (7)	6	3	–	3	–	23	16	93	15.50
2 Sussex (14)	9	4	1	4	–	25	31	128	14.22
3 Lancashire (8)	13	6	1	6	–	37	36	181	13.92
4 Warwickshire (12)	12	4	2	6	0.5	37	38	154.5	12.88
5 Nottinghamshire (9)	12	4	2	6	–	33	39	152	12.67
6 Essex (13)	8	3	2	3	–	25	18	97	12.13
7 Leicestershire (11)	10	3	1	6	3.0	22	35	120	12.00
8 Yorkshire (1)	8	2	–	6	0.5	16	27	94.5	11.81
9 Gloucestershire (10)	9	2	3	4	–	25	25	97	10.78
10 Hampshire (3)	9	2	3	4	–	29	23	96	10.67
11 Derbyshire (18)	9	1	3	5	–	22	31	87	9.67
12 Middlesex (15)	7	1	2	4	0.5	17	16	62.5	8.93
13 Kent (2)	6	1	3	2	–	10	21	53	8.83
14 Northamptonshire (4)	11	1	3	7	–	27	27	96	8.73
15 Surrey (6)	12	2	5	5	0.5	28	29	104.5	8.71
16 Glamorgan (16)	6	–	1	5	–	14	8	42	7.00
17 Durham (5)	9	–	4	5	–	19	24	63	7.00
18 Worcestershire (17)	6	–	3	3	0.5	15	14	40.5	6.75

Win = 14 points, plus any first-innings points.
Draw = 4 points, plus any first-innings points.
2003 final positions are shown in brackets.

SECOND XI TROPHY 2004

Semi-Finals
ESSEX beat DURHAM by four wickets at Billericay.
WORCESTERSHIRE beat NORTHAMPTONSHIRE by nine wickets at Worcester.

Final
WORCESTERSHIRE beat ESSEX by eight wickets at Worcester.

SECOND XI CHAMPIONS

1959	Gloucestershire	1975	Surrey	1991	Yorkshire
1960	Northamptonshire	1976	Kent	1992	Surrey
1961	Kent	1977	Yorkshire	1993	Middlesex
1962	Worcestershire	1978	Sussex	1994	Somerset
1963	Worcestershire	1979	Warwickshire	1995	Hampshire
1964	Lancashire	1980	Glamorgan	1996	Warwickshire
1965	Glamorgan	1981	Hampshire	1997	Lancashire
1966	Surrey	1982	Worcestershire	1998	Northamptonshire
1967	Hampshire	1983	Leicestershire	1999	Middlesex
1968	Surrey	1984	Yorkshire	2000	Middlesex
1969	Kent	1985	Nottinghamshire	2001	Hampshire
1970	Kent	1986	Lancashire	2002	Kent
1971	Hampshire	1987	Kent/Yorkshire	2003	Yorkshire
1972	Nottinghamshire	1988	Surrey	2004	Somerset
1973	Essex	1989	Middlesex		
1974	Middlesex	1990	Sussex		

YOUNG CRICKETER OF THE YEAR

This annual award, made by The Cricket Writers' Club (founded 1946), is currently restricted to players qualified for England, Andrew Symonds meeting that requirement at the time of his award, and under the age of 23 on 1st May. In 1986 their ballot resulted in a dead heat. Up to 4 March 2005 their selections have gained a tally of 1,839 Test match caps (shown in brackets).

1950	R.Tattersall (16)	1978	D.I.Gower (117)
1951	P.B.H.May (66)	1979	P.W.G.Parker (1)
1952	F.S.Trueman (67)	1980	G.R.Dilley (41)
1953	M.C.Cowdrey (114)	1981	M.W.Gatting (79)
1954	P.J.Loader (13)	1982	N.G.Cowans (19)
1955	K.F.Barrington (82)	1983	N.A.Foster (29)
1956	B.Taylor	1984	R.J.Bailey (4)
1957	M.J.Stewart (8)	1985	D.V.Lawrence (5)
1958	A.C.D.Ingleby-Mackenzie	1986 {	A.A.Metcalfe
1959	G.Pullar (28)		J.J.Whitaker (1)
1960	D.A.Allen (39)	1987	R.J.Blakey (2)
1961	P.H.Parfitt (37)	1988	M.P.Maynard (4)
1962	P.J.Sharpe (12)	1989	N.Hussain (96)
1963	G.Boycott (108)	1990	M.A.Atherton (115)
1964	J.M.Brearley (39)	1991	M.R.Ramprakash (52)
1965	A.P.E.Knott (95)	1992	I.D.K.Salisbury (15)
1966	D.L.Underwood (86)	1993	M.N.Lathwell (2)
1967	A.W.Greig (58)	1994	J.P.Crawley (37)
1968	R.M.H.Cottam (4)	1995	A.Symonds (2-Australia)
1969	A.Ward (5)	1996	C.E.W.Silverwood (6)
1970	C.M.Old (46)	1997	B.C.Hollioake (2)
1971	J.Whitehouse	1998	A.Flintoff (45)
1972	D.R.Owen-Thomas	1999	A.J.Tudor (10)
1973	M.Hendrick (30)	2000	P.J.Franks
1974	P.H.Edmonds (51)	2001	O.A.Shah
1975	A.Kennedy	2002	R.Clarke (2)
1976	G.Miller (34)	2003	J.M.Anderson (12)
1977	I.T.Botham (102)	2004	I.R.Bell (1)

THE PROFESSIONAL CRICKETERS' ASSOCIATION

PLAYER OF THE YEAR

Founded in 1967, the Professional Cricketers' Association introduced this award, decided by their membership, in 1970. Since 1998 it has been presented at their Annual Awards Dinner at the Royal Albert Hall.

1970 {	M.J.Procter	1987	R.J.Hadlee
	J.D.Bond	1988	G.A.Hick
1971	L.R.Gibbs	1989	S.J.Cook
1972	A.M.E.Roberts	1990	G.A.Gooch
1973	P.G.Lee	1991	Waqar Younis
1974	B.Stead	1992	C.A.Walsh
1975	Zaheer Abbas	1993	S.L.Watkin
1976	P.G.Lee	1994	B.C.Lara
1977	M.J.Procter	1995	D.G.Cork
1978	J.K.Lever	1996	P.V.Simmons
1979	J.K.Lever	1997	S.P.James
1980	R.D.Jackman	1998	M.B.Loye
1981	R.J.Hadlee	1999	S.G.Law
1982	M.D.Marshall	2000	M.E.Trescothick
1983	K.S.McEwan	2001	D.P.Fulton
1984	R.J.Hadlee	2002	M.P.Vaughan
1985	N.V.Radford	2003	Mushtaq Ahmed
1986	C.A.Walsh	2004	A.Flintoff

FIRST-CLASS CAREER RECORDS

Compiled by **PHILIP BAILEY**

The following career records are for all players who appeared in first-class cricket during the 2004 season and are complete to the end of that season. Some players who did not appear in 2004 but who may do so in 2005 are included.

BATTING AND FIELDING

'1000' denotes instances of scoring 1000 runs in a season. Where these have been achieved outside the British Isles they are shown after a plus sign.

	M	I	NO	HS	Runs	Avge	100	50	1000	Ct/St
Ackerman, H.D.	110	179	19	202*	6776	42.35	18	38	0+1	89
Adams, A.R.	36	53	1	124	1073	20.63	1	6	–	17
Adams, C.J.	273	447	33	239	15753	38.05	41	72	6	313
Adams, J.H.K.	28	51	5	107	1260	27.39	1	5	–	11
Adnan, M.H.	77	125	19	140	4884	46.07	7	36	1	44
Adshead, S.J.	18	28	8	63	711	35.55	–	5	–	46/4
Afzaal, U.	147	254	25	167*	8057	35.18	17	44	4	72
Agarkar, A.B.	56	75	12	109*	1440	22.85	2	6	–	22
Airey, S.J.	6	7	2	72	196	39.20	–	1	–	2
Akram, Adnan M.	5	7	–	128	310	44.28	1	1	–	–
Akram, Arfan M.	5	9	2	110	215	30.71	1	–	–	3
Ali, Kabir	56	75	15	84*	1178	19.63	–	5	–	12
Ali, Kadeer	25	43	1	99	810	19.28	–	5	–	10
Ali, S.M.B.	84	112	26	92	1247	14.50	–	5	–	26
Alleyne, D.	9	11	3	49*	260	32.50	–	–	–	23
Alleyne, M.W.	327	535	52	256	14876	30.79	22	71	6	272/3
Ambrose, T.R.	40	66	4	149	2078	33.51	2	14	–	62/8
Anderson, J.M.	33	40	25	21*	145	9.66	–	–	–	11
Anderson, R.S.G.	40	52	6	67*	683	14.84	–	2	–	7
Andrew, G.M.	6	8	–	44	95	11.87	–	–	–	4
Anwar, O.S.	7	7	–	99	226	32.28	–	2	–	1
Anyon, J.E.	5	4	1	21	23	7.66	–	–	–	2
Astle, N.J.	134	213	21	223	7464	38.87	17	36	–	107
Atri, V.	9	16	3	98	422	32.46	–	3	–	5
Averis, J.M.M.	56	70	16	48*	662	12.25	–	–	–	12
Azhar Mahmood	108	169	20	136	4323	29.01	4	25	–	84
Bailey, T.M.B.	52	71	12	101*	1324	22.44	1	6	–	97/18
Ball, M.C.J.	180	274	53	75	4408	19.94	–	15	–	212
Banerjee, V.	1	2	–	19	32	16.00	–	–	–	–
Banks, O.A.C.	33	51	10	90	939	22.90	–	5	–	20
Bassano, C.W.G.	50	87	9	186*	2703	34.65	5	18	1	30
Batty, G.J.	61	96	14	133	1834	22.36	1	8	–	43
Batty, J.N.	111	164	24	168*	4284	30.60	9	16	–	284/38
Baugh, C.S.	30	52	8	158*	1792	40.72	5	8	–	57/7
Bell, I.R.	67	112	10	262*	4341	42.55	10	22	1	37
Benham, C.C.	4	6	1	74	202	40.40	–	1	–	–
Benkenstein, D.M.	104	152	15	259	5743	41.91	13	33	–	72
Benning, J.G.E.	8	14	1	128	352	27.07	1	–	–	3
Best, T.L.	34	40	12	42*	300	10.71	–	–	–	10
Betts, M.M.	106	154	35	73	1743	14.64	–	5	–	37
Bevan, M.G.	218	364	63	216	17038	56.60	59	75	3+1	117
Bichel, A.J.	132	170	14	142	3699	23.71	5	13	–	72
Bicknell, D.J.	289	504	40	235*	17858	38.48	44	77	8	102
Bicknell, M.P.	280	341	83	141	6237	24.17	3	22	–	97

155

F-C	M	I	NO	HS	Runs	Avge	100	50	1000	Ct/St
Bishop, J.E.	24	33	5	66	433	15.46	–	4	–	5
Blackwell, I.D.	94	144	9	247*	4976	36.85	13	20	1	39
Blain, J.A.R.	31	37	15	34	253	11.50	–	–	–	6
Blakey, R.J.	348	554	87	223*	14674	31.42	13	86	6	778/57
Blignaut, A.M.	42	64	4	194	1712	28.53	2	7	–	26
Bloomfield, T.F.	58	62	25	31*	306	8.27	–	–	–	8
Bond, S.E.	39	44	17	66*	441	16.33	–	2	–	20
Bopara, R.S.	13	22	5	48	484	28.47	–	–	–	14
Botha, A.G.	55	88	12	103	1611	21.19	1	6	–	41
Bowler, P.D.	318	542	59	241*	19567	40.51	45	101	10	232/1
Bracken, N.W.	38	51	21	38*	449	14.96	–	–	–	10
Brandy, D.G.	9	14	2	52	187	15.58	–	1	–	3
Brant, S.A.	23	26	9	23	111	6.52	–	–	–	7
Bravo, D.J.J.	38	73	5	197	2229	32.77	5	11	–	27
Breese, G.R.	63	101	15	165*	2438	28.34	2	16	–	47
Bresnan, T.T.	14	19	3	52	224	14.00	–	1	–	4
Bressington, A.N.	9	9	6	58*	125	41.66	–	1	–	4
Bridge, G.D.	37	61	10	52	881	17.27	–	3	–	18
Brignull, D.S.	4	6	2	46	58	14.50	–	–	–	–
Brophy, G.L.	50	83	13	185	2456	35.08	5	11	–	119/7
Brown, A.D.	199	312	30	295*	12206	43.28	36	51	7	207/1
Brown, D.O.	6	11	–	65	308	28.00	–	3	–	2
Brown, D.R.	179	270	36	203	7467	31.91	9	40	1	110
Brown, J.F.	75	88	39	38	376	7.67	–	–	–	17
Brown, M.J.	28	48	6	109*	1332	31.71	2	10	–	24
Bruce, J.T.A.	18	22	7	21*	105	7.00	–	–	–	5
Bryant, J.D.C.	79	142	16	234*	4156	32.98	8	19	–	53
Buckham, C.T.	1	2	1	8	12	12.00	–	–	–	–
Burnell, W.F.	2	4	–	49	57	14.25	–	–	–	–
Burns, M.	145	231	13	221	7164	32.86	8	49	2	138/7
Butcher, M.A.	230	396	30	259	14498	39.61	29	79	7	215
Butler, I.G.	34	41	13	68	460	16.42	–	2	–	8
Caddick, A.R.	217	287	55	92	3360	14.48	–	6	–	75
Cairns, C.L.	216	340	38	158	10680	35.36	13	71	1	78
Carberry, M.A.	34	57	6	153*	1997	39.15	4	11	–	15
Carpenter, E.J.	3	4	1	0*	0	0.00	–	–	–	2
Carter, N.M.	43	53	12	103	812	19.80	1	2	–	12
Cawdron, M.J.	25	32	4	42	396	14.14	–	–	–	5
Chandana, U.D.U.	129	174	13	194	5096	31.65	8	28	–	102
Chanderpaul, S.	170	278	45	303*	11735	50.36	34	55	1	103
Chapman, J.R.	1	1	–	7	7	7.00	–	–	–	–
Chapple, G.	176	242	52	155	4683	24.64	6	19	–	57
Cherry, D.D.	10	15	1	47	256	18.28	–	–	–	4
Chilton, M.J.	96	156	10	125	4688	32.10	12	17	1	80
Clark, S.R.	41	59	16	35	557	12.95	–	–	–	11
Clarke, A.C.S.	3	4	1	44	73	24.33	–	–	–	–
Clarke, A.J.	10	14	2	41	179	14.91	–	–	–	4
Clarke, A.P.A.	1	1	–	0	0	0.00	–	–	–	–
Clarke, M.J.	48	86	5	140	3065	37.83	11	11	–	50
Clarke, R.	36	58	5	153*	2006	37.84	5	9	–	40
Cleary, M.F.	24	34	8	58	480	18.46	–	1	–	11
Clinton, P.J.S.	2	1	–	6	6	6.00	–	–	–	–
Clinton, R.S.	20	35	3	107	790	24.68	1	4	–	14
Clough, G.D.	9	13	1	55	133	11.08	–	1	–	3
Coetzer, K.J.	8	13	3	133*	358	35.80	1	1	–	–
Collingwood, P.D.	105	182	11	190	5344	31.25	8	31	1	109
Collins, P.T.	83	103	27	25	507	6.67	–	–	–	21

156

F-C	M	I	NO	HS	Runs	Avge	100	50	1000	Ct/St
Collymore, C.D.	55	75	35	20	347	8.67	–	–	–	18
Compton, N.R.D.	4	7	2	40	111	22.20	–	–	–	3
Cook, A.N.	17	30	3	126	957	35.44	1	8	–	24
Cook, J.W.	55	88	7	137	2378	29.35	3	13	–	20
Cook, S.J.	66	87	11	93*	1347	17.72	–	3	–	23
Cork, D.G.	237	354	46	200*	7742	25.13	6	44	–	173
Cosker, D.A.	109	130	41	49	1015	11.40	–	–	–	78
Cottey, P.A.	277	448	51	203	14567	36.69	31	73	8	182
Cowan, A.P.	105	156	30	94	2241	17.78	–	9	–	51
Cox, J.	256	451	31	250	18252	43.45	51	78	4+2	118
Craven, V.J.	33	55	6	81*	1206	24.61	–	6	–	18
Crawley, J.P.	287	471	48	301*	19788	46.78	43	112	8	185
Croft, R.D.B.	301	441	83	143	9378	26.19	6	42	–	145
Crook, A.R.	3	5	–	27	69	13.80	–	–	–	–
Crook, S.P.	6	6	–	68	184	30.66	–	1	–	2
Currie, M.R.	3	5	1	97	216	54.00	–	2	–	3
Cusden, S.M.J.	4	6	4	12*	22	11.00	–	–	–	2
Daggett, L.M.	6	8	4	7	21	5.25	–	–	–	–
Dagnall, C.E.	31	32	10	23*	223	10.13	–	–	–	5
Dakin, J.M.	79	119	14	190	2937	27.97	5	14	–	22
Dale, A.	251	413	35	214*	12586	33.29	23	58	4	107
Dale, M.A.P.	4	8	1	48	179	25.57	–	–	–	–
Dalrymple, J.W.M.	36	60	8	244	1943	37.36	4	6	–	25
Dalrymple, S.H.	2	3	1	15*	40	20.00	–	–	–	3
Daniel, G.I.	66	114	9	156*	3263	31.07	7	15	–	43
Danish Kaneria	64	74	37	42	271	7.32	–	–	–	23
Davies, A.M.	29	49	18	33	358	11.54	–	–	–	5
Davies, A.P.	23	28	4	40	264	11.00	–	–	–	4
Davis, M.J.G.	121	181	30	168	2857	18.92	2	7	–	68
Dawood, I.	27	44	8	102	796	22.11	1	2	–	60/5
Dawson, R.K.J.	65	99	10	87	1938	21.77	–	7	–	35
Dean, K.J.	96	130	41	54*	1059	11.89	–	2	–	20
De Bruyn, Z.	48	87	11	266*	3018	39.71	5	17	0+1	20
DeFreitas, P.A.J.	368	526	50	123*	10929	22.96	10	54	–	127
Denly, J.L.	1	1	1	0	0	0.00	–	–	–	–
Dennington, M.J.	7	9	2	50*	108	15.42	–	1	–	2
Dernbach, J.W.	1	1	–	3	3	3.00	–	–	–	–
Dias, W.J.M.R.	42	72	9	75*	1010	16.03	–	4	–	23
Di Venuto, M.J.	189	331	16	13331	230	42.32	28	86	4	208
Doran, G.P.	1	1	1	9*	9	–	–	–	–	3/2
Doshi, N.D.	19	29	4	29*	206	8.24	–	–	–	3
Dumelow, N.R.C.	25	41	4	75	781	21.10	–	6	–	5
Durston, W.J.	5	9	1	55	215	26.87	–	1	–	13
Dutch, K.P.	72	102	10	118	1868	20.30	1	11	–	72
Ealham, M.A.	208	324	49	153*	9011	32.76	10	56	1	109
Edwards, F.H.	22	32	11	18	88	4.19	–	–	–	5
Edwards, N.J.	16	30	–	160	955	31.83	1	3	–	13
Edwards, P.D.	3	5	3	43	65	32.50	–	–	–	–
Elliott, M.T.G.	173	316	26	203	14810	51.06	47	66	3+5	195
Ervine, S.M.	30	48	6	126	1510	35.95	4	8	–	36
Ferley, R.S.	22	29	7	78*	433	19.68	–	2	–	8
Fernando, C.S.	39	61	10	109	1504	29.49	2	5	–	104/9
Fisher, I.D.	61	87	15	103*	1652	22.94	1	7	–	17
Fleming, S.P.	179	299	27	274*	11320	41.61	22	67	1	235
Flintoff, A.	124	191	13	167	6509	36.56	14	34	–	138
Flower, A.	190	320	57	232*	13494	51.30	36	68	3	332/21
Flower, G.W.	149	259	22	243*	9307	39.27	19	51	–	139

F-C	M	I	NO	HS	Runs	Avge	100	50	1000	Ct/St
Foster, J.S.	72	108	13	212	2995	31.52	5	11	1	176/19
Fox, D.R.	1	1	–	104	104	104.00	1	–	–	–
France, B.J.	4	7	–	56	126	18.00	–	1	–	2
Francis, J.D.	32	56	3	110	1445	27.26	2	9	–	19
Francis, S.R.G.	49	63	27	44	337	9.36	–	–	–	11
Franklin, J.E.C.	48	72	13	108*	1656	28.06	1	7	–	14
Franks, P.J.	115	169	34	123*	3577	26.49	2	17	–	43
Friend, T.J.	41	60	9	183	1671	32.76	3	6	–	31
Frost, T.	68	96	14	135*	2265	27.62	3	10	–	163/15
Fulton, D.P.	169	297	18	208*	10323	37.00	25	42	3	243
Gait, A.I.	63	118	2	175	3093	26.66	4	19	–	55
Gajanayake, M.K.	42	74	4	95	1529	21.84	–	8	–	32/1
Gale, A.W.	4	7	–	29	78	11.14	–	–	–	2
Gallian, J.E.R.	187	323	31	312	11334	38.81	29	55	5	160
Gayle, C.H.	107	192	15	259*	7848	44.33	19	39	0+1	97
Gazzard, C.M.	6	10	2	44*	237	29.62	–	–	–	11/1
Gibson, O.D.	134	198	26	101*	4051	23.55	1	21	–	55
Gidman, A.P.R.	35	58	3	117	1834	33.34	1	15	–	25
Giles, A.F.	158	213	40	128*	4647	26.86	3	20	–	66
Goddard, L.J.	5	6	2	23*	56	14.00	–	–	–	9
Goode, C.M.	1	1	–	0	0	0.00	–	–	–	–
Goodwin, M.W.	149	261	20	335*	11213	46.52	34	46	3+1	96
Gough, D.	209	283	52	121	3771	16.32	1	15	–	43
Gray, A.K.D.	18	26	3	104	649	28.21	1	2	–	16
Grayson, A.P.	181	298	25	189	8655	31.70	16	43	4	121
Greenidge, C.G.	32	34	5	46	234	8.06	–	–	–	12
Gunter, N.E.L.	7	8	3	20*	74	14.80	–	–	–	5
Guy, S.M.	21	31	3	42	345	12.32	–	–	–	58/6
Habib, A.	145	219	27	215	8164	42.52	20	43	2	71
Hall, A.J.	81	118	17	153	3456	34.21	3	26	–	65
Hamilton, G.M.	91	126	21	125	2779	26.46	2	17	–	32
Hancock, T.H.C.	180	313	20	220*	8344	28.47	7	51	1	113
Harbhajan Singh	86	113	25	84	1640	18.63	–	5	–	38
Hardinges, M.A.	11	12	2	172	327	32.70	1	1	–	6
Harmison, S.J.	99	137	36	36*	861	8.52	–	–	–	18
Harris, A.J.	92	129	33	41*	836	8.70	–	–	–	28
Harrison, A.J.	1	1	–	34*	34	–	–	–	–	–
Harrison, D.S.	37	52	9	88	722	16.79	–	2	–	11
Harrison, P.W.	3	4	1	27	77	25.66	–	–	–	4
Harrity, M.A.	84	103	53	19	254	5.08	–	–	–	26
Harvey, I.J.	127	211	18	136	6222	32.23	9	36	–	92
Harvey, T.F.C.	1	1	–	21	21	21.00	–	–	–	–
Havell, P.M.R.	13	16	11	13*	42	8.40	–	–	–	4
Hawinkels, S.J.	7	11	–	78	322	29.27	–	1	–	1
Haynes, J.J.	20	29	4	80	491	19.64	–	3	–	47/4
Hayward, M.	102	110	39	55*	814	11.46	–	1	–	31
Hegg, W.K.	333	483	93	134	10800	27.69	7	52	–	816/89
Hembry, T.D.C.	2	4	–	28	56	14.00	–	–	–	1
Hemp, D.L.	202	338	33	186*	10697	35.07	19	61	4	133
Henderson, C.W.	131	175	44	71	2073	15.82	–	5	–	50
Hewson, D.R.	73	132	8	168	2796	22.54	3	15	–	34
Heywood, J.J.N.	3	4	1	8	11	3.66	–	–	–	4
Hick, G.A.	470	777	76	405*	37505	53.50	126	142	18+1	596
Hildreth, J.C.	14	22	2	108	769	38.45	2	5	–	12
Hillyard, C.M.	1	2	–	20	31	15.50	–	–	–	–
Hodd, A.J.	1	–	–	–	–	–	–	–	–	2
Hodge, B.J.	145	259	23	302*	10977	46.51	33	40	2+2	79

158

F-C	M	I	NO	HS	Runs	Avge	100	50	1000	Ct/St
Hogg, G.B.	85	124	27	158	3328	34.30	3	23	–	49
Hogg, K.W.	19	25	1	53	430	17.91	–	3	–	7
Hoggard, M.J.	104	129	47	89*	745	9.08	–	1	–	26
Hollingsworth, S.C.	3	5	–	30	65	13.00	–	–	–	2
Hollioake, A.J.	173	263	21	208	9376	38.74	18	55	2	157
Hooper, C.L.	339	535	52	236*	23034	47.68	69	104	8+2	375
Hopkins, G.J.	61	98	16	175*	2370	28.90	4	7	–	138/10
Hopkinson, C.D.	3	5	1	33	62	15.50	–	–	–	2
Horton, P.J.	2	2	1	22	24	24.00	–	–	–	1
Howard, W.O.F.	5	6	–	72	131	21.83	–	1	–	2/2
Howells, P.W.	3	5	2	25*	58	19.33	–	–	–	7
Huggins, T.B.	10	16	2	82*	395	28.21	–	2	–	3
Hughes, J.	29	44	1	110	1045	24.30	1	4	–	17
Hunt, T.A.	4	2	1	3	4	4.00	–	–	–	–
Hunter, I.D.	22	34	4	65	583	19.43	–	2	–	6
Hussain, N.	334	545	53	207	20698	42.06	52	108	5	350
Hussey, D.J.	32	44	6	212*	2281	60.02	11	5	1	36
Hussey, M.E.K.	154	276	19	331*	13169	51.24	32	59	3	164
Hutchison, P.M.	60	63	30	30	277	8.39	–	–	–	12
Hutton, B.L.	78	131	12	139	3923	32.96	13	13	1	92
Hutton, O.R.	1	2	–	18	23	11.50	–	–	–	3
Innes, K.J.	45	70	17	103*	1256	23.69	1	3	–	15
Irani, R.C.	196	321	40	207*	10730	38.18	22	56	5	69
Jacobs, R.D.	146	234	53	149	6702	37.02	13	37	–	417/32
James, G.D.	2	4	1	33*	63	21.00	–	–	–	–
Jaques, P.A.	39	68	1	243	3249	48.49	9	15	2	28
Jayasuriya, S.T.	219	343	32	340	12625	40.59	27	60	0+1	145
Jayawardena, H.A.P.W.	91	138	15	131	2707	22.00	2	11	–	221/42
Jefferson, W.I.	51	93	9	222	3357	39.96	9	13	1	47
Jennings, C.J.R.	1	1	–	6	6	6.00	–	–	–	–
Johnson, R.L.	143	196	27	118	3068	18.15	2	7	–	55
Jones, G.O.	37	49	8	108*	1704	41.56	4	10	–	101/10
Jones, P.S.	77	93	24	105	1244	18.02	1	3	–	17
Jones, S.P.	60	69	19	46	527	10.54	–	–	–	12
Joseph, R.H.	8	10	4	26	77	12.83	–	–	–	3
Joseph, S.C.	55	98	5	211*	2796	30.06	5	12	–	49
Joyce, E.C.	62	101	11	134	3865	42.94	11	18	3	50
Kalavitigoda, S.	87	139	6	169	4077	30.65	8	18	–	85
Kasprowicz, M.S.	210	285	61	92	4024	17.96	–	11	–	84
Katich, S.M.	119	206	30	228*	9030	51.30	26	46	2+3	120
Kay, M.A.	1	1	–	21	21	21.00	–	–	–	1
Keedy, G.	123	141	71	57	769	10.98	–	1	–	36
Keegan, C.B.	38	44	5	44	448	11.48	–	–	–	11
Kendall, W.S.	140	230	25	201	6822	33.27	10	33	3	118
Kenway, D.A.	92	161	15	166	4362	29.87	7	20	1	82/1
Key, R.W.T.	126	216	11	221	7985	38.95	24	30	3	80
Khalid, S.A.	9	7	2	15	44	8.80	–	–	–	3
Khan, A.	34	38	7	78	556	17.93	–	2	–	6
Khan, Z.	56	70	12	48	765	13.18	–	–	–	21
Killeen, N.	84	126	26	48	1186	11.86	–	–	–	20
King, R.D.	76	96	32	30	391	6.10	–	–	–	10
King, R.E.	3	5	–	17	19	3.80	–	–	–	–
Kirby, S.P.	48	63	14	57	342	6.97	–	1	–	13
Kirtley, R.J.	133	185	55	59	1566	12.04	–	3	–	43
Klusener, L.	125	173	35	174	4731	34.28	6	27	–	70
Knappett, J.P.T.	2	2	–	45	45	22.50	–	–	–	2
Knight, N.V.	206	349	39	303*	13880	44.77	34	66	5	261

159

F-C	M	I	NO	HS	Runs	Avge	100	50	1000	Ct/St
Koenig, S.G.	135	234	13	171	8820	39.90	16	50	3	63
Kruis, G.J.	69	108	25	59	1190	14.33	–	2	–	30
Kulasekara, M.D.N.	29	41	12	95	642	22.13	–	1	–	10
Kumar, P.	2	4	1	21	36	12.00	–	–	–	–
Lamb, G.A.	17	25	4	100*	592	28.19	1	3	–	9
Lara, B.C.	236	396	11	501*	19835	51.51	55	84	3+1	297
Laraman, A.W.	38	43	10	148*	1142	34.60	1	5	–	15
Law, S.G.	307	507	56	263	23099	51.21	68	107	7+2	344
Lawson, J.J.C.	35	45	11	28*	251	7.38	–	–	–	11
Lawson, M.A.K.	3	5	1	14	33	8.25	–	–	–	1
Lee, N.T.	1	2	–	15	15	7.50	–	–	–	–
Lehmann, D.S.	239	406	28	255	21573	57.07	69	98	4+5	125
Lewis, J.	132	185	39	62	1920	13.15	–	3	–	29
Lewis, J.J.B.	186	332	25	210*	9971	32.47	16	61	4	104
Lewis, M.L.	41	52	15	54*	363	9.81	–	1	–	23
Lewis, P.D.	5	6	2	43*	115	28.75	–	–	–	1
Lewry, J.D.	124	170	39	72	1430	10.91	–	2	–	28
Linley, T.E.	5	4	–	8	23	5.75	–	–	–	–
Logan, R.J.	37	52	11	37*	425	10.36	–	–	–	14
Lokuarachchi, K.S.	44	63	5	91	1332	22.96	–	4	–	22
Longhurst, N.J.	2	3	–	29	61	20.33	–	–	–	–
Loudon, A.G.R.	22	35	1	172	1120	32.94	1	7	–	16
Louw, J.	39	60	8	124	1151	22.13	1	5	–	21
Love, M.L.	161	279	29	300*	12980	51.92	31	61	1+3	191
Lowe, J.A.	3	6	–	80	171	28.50	–	1	–	2
Loye, M.B.	180	287	26	322*	10345	39.63	28	43	4	87
Lucas, D.S.	22	28	8	49	436	21.80	–	–	–	3
Lumb, M.J.	54	95	6	124	2739	30.77	4	17	1	28
Lungley, T.	19	32	5	47	356	13.18	–	–	–	6
McCoubrey, A.G.A.M.	10	12	6	2*	6	1.00	–	–	–	3
McCullum, B.B.	31	55	3	142	1545	29.71	2	10	–	72/5
MacGill, S.C.G.	135	164	41	53	1182	9.60	–	1	–	62
McGrath, A.	139	238	16	174	7098	31.97	13	32	–	84
McGrath, G.D.	160	162	54	55	786	7.27	–	1	–	43
McLean, J.J.	6	8	–	57	162	20.25	–	1	–	7
McLean, N.A.M.	139	209	31	76	2399	13.47	–	3	–	40
McMahon, P.J.	14	18	2	99	261	16.31	–	1	–	6
McMillan, C.D.	114	185	22	168*	6600	40.49	12	39	–	48
Maddy, D.L.	188	306	20	229*	9475	33.12	18	48	4	195
Mahmood, S.I.	19	24	4	94	348	17.40	–	1	–	3
Maiden, A.J.	6	9	–	53	177	19.66	–	2	–	2
Malik, M.N.	22	25	9	39*	147	9.18	–	–	–	3
Mann, R.J.	4	7	–	63	207	29.57	–	2	–	5
Marshall, S.J.	12	20	3	126*	629	37.00	1	3	–	3
Martin, C.S.	70	84	35	25	185	3.77	–	–	–	16
Martin, P.J.	213	246	61	133	3594	19.42	2	7	–	56
Martin-Jenkins, R.S.C.	101	160	18	205*	4179	29.42	3	22	1	29
Mascarenhas, A.D.	119	178	17	104	3755	23.32	4	15	–	49
Mason, M.S.	42	53	13	63	572	14.30	–	3	–	9
Masters, D.D.	51	62	13	119	539	11.00	1	1	–	16
Maunders, J.K.	24	46	2	171	1251	28.43	3	5	–	10
Maynard, M.P.	394	641	60	243	24779	42.64	59	131	13	371/7
Mendis, B.M.A.J.	29	53	8	152*	969	21.53	1	3	–	33
Middlebrook, J.D.	73	108	10	115	2109	21.52	2	7	–	32
Mills, K.D.	34	49	16	117*	1294	39.21	1	9	–	11
Mirando, M.T.T.	57	91	11	103*	1220	15.25	1	2	–	20
Mohammad Akram	94	123	34	35*	784	8.80	–	–	–	26

F-C	M	I	NO	HS	Runs	Avge	100	50	1000	Ct/St
Mohammad Sami	47	63	28	49	407	11.62	–	–	–	13
Mohammed, D.	25	38	4	52	521	15.32	–	1	–	11
Mongia, D.	79	115	12	308*	5489	53.29	18	20	0+1	94
Montgomerie, R.R.	199	346	30	196	11452	36.24	24	63	5	189
Moore, S.C.	19	33	4	146	1101	37.96	3	4	1	9
Morgan, E.J.G.	1	2	–	7	7	3.50	–	–	–	–
Moss, J.	40	64	6	172*	2483	42.81	4	17	–	17
Mubarak, J.	49	86	7	169	2382	30.15	1	17	–	46
Muchall, G.J.	47	86	2	142*	2467	29.36	4	13	–	34
Mullally, A.D.	230	258	70	75	1615	8.59	–	2	–	44
Munday, M.K.	8	6	3	14	15	5.00	–	–	–	2
Muralitharan, M.	175	214	62	67	1737	11.42	–	1	–	97
Murtagh, T.J.	26	39	17	74*	555	25.22	–	4	–	11
Mushtaq Ahmed	248	312	42	90	4279	15.84	–	17	–	105
Mustard, P.	17	29	1	75	709	25.32	–	3	–	53/3
Napier, G.R.	57	88	17	106*	2145	30.21	2	12	–	27
Nash, C.D.	8	13	2	63	363	33.00	–	4	–	4
Nash, D.C.	115	162	33	114	4283	33.20	7	20	–	239/19
Naved-ul-Hasan	56	78	9	117	1728	25.04	1	7	–	33
New, T.J.	5	7	3	51*	94	23.50	–	1	–	11/1
Newby, O.J.	2	1	1	0*	0	–	–	–	–	–
Newman, A.R.I.	1	2	–	17	17	8.50	–	–	–	–
Newman, S.A.	25	45	2	183	1759	40.90	4	11	1	18
Nicholson, M.J.	52	78	15	101*	1363	21.63	1	3	–	25
Nixon, P.A.	265	387	84	134*	9519	31.41	14	40	1	703/58
Noble, D.J.	6	10	3	21	94	13.42	–	–	–	–
Noffke, A.A.	55	63	13	114*	1293	25.86	1	4	–	19
Noon, W.M.	92	145	23	83	2527	20.71	–	12	–	195/20
North, M.J.	58	101	7	219	3540	37.65	9	17	0+1	39
O'Brien, N.J.	14	19	4	69	439	29.26	–	3	–	33/5
Onions, G.	8	12	5	20*	76	10.85	–	–	–	2
Oram, J.D.P.	48	74	11	155	2349	37.28	4	13	–	27
Ormond, J.	110	133	32	57	1553	15.37	–	2	–	24
Paget, C.D.	4	4	2	7	7	3.50	–	–	–	–
Palladino, A.P.	9	7	3	41	65	16.25	–	–	–	2
Panesar, M.S.	19	22	10	28	81	6.75	–	–	–	7
Papps, M.H.W.	53	97	9	192	3087	35.07	7	14	–	51/1
Park, G.T.	6	9	1	68	219	27.37	–	1	–	10
Parker, L.C.	3	3	–	27	32	10.66	–	–	–	1
Parsons, K.A.	112	182	18	193*	4412	26.90	5	24	–	101
Patel, M.M.	173	233	45	82	3163	16.82	–	11	–	89
Patel, S.R.	2	3	–	55	99	33.00	–	1	–	1
Pattison, I.	7	11	–	62	215	19.54	–	1	–	5
Pearson, J.A.	3	6	1	51	114	22.80	–	1	–	2
Peng, N.	58	101	2	158	2450	24.74	4	11	–	35
Penney, T.L.	158	248	45	151	7975	39.28	15	36	2	94/2
Peploe, C.T.	10	14	3	28*	153	13.90	–	–	–	5
Perera, W.M.B.	86	131	21	220*	3909	35.53	4	25	–	97
Peters, S.D.	107	177	16	165	4996	31.03	9	25	1	80
Pettini, M.L.	10	18	1	78	475	27.94	–	5	–	7
Phillips, B.J.	50	69	9	100*	1047	17.45	1	5	–	11
Phillips, T.J.	17	25	3	75	388	17.63	–	1	–	7
Pietersen, C.	14	25	7	45	326	18.11	–	–	–	2
Pietersen, K.P.	72	113	11	254*	5512	54.03	19	24	3	76
Pipe, D.J.	19	28	3	104*	455	18.20	1	1	–	38/5
Piper, K.J.	199	275	44	116*	4618	19.99	2	14	–	502/34
Plunkett, L.E.	17	28	9	54	466	24.52	–	1	–	4

F-C	M	I	NO	HS	Runs	Avge	100	50	1000	Ct/St
Ponting, R.T.	171	285	39	257	14219	57.80	52	55	–	173
Pothas, N.	131	203	31	165	6129	35.63	12	30	–	350/33
Powell, D.B.	36	44	7	38	392	10.59	–	–	–	13
Powell, M.J. (Gm)	119	197	18	200*	6996	39.08	16	35	3	74
Powell, M.J. (Nh)	27	44	3	108*	1024	24.97	2	4	–	40
Powell, M.J. (Wa)	112	186	7	236	5903	32.97	11	33	1	81
Prasad, K.T.G.D.	15	19	3	77*	180	11.25	–	1	–	4
Pratt, A.	62	105	14	93	1974	21.69	–	10	–	150/12
Pratt, G.J.	47	84	1	150	2217	26.71	1	14	1	32
Pretorius, D.	61	65	17	43	452	9.41	–	–	–	13
Price, R.W.	61	101	19	117*	1401	17.08	1	6	–	19
Prior, M.J.	69	107	10	201*	3648	37.60	8	18	2	135/6
Prittipaul, L.R.	23	36	2	152	975	28.67	1	4	–	18
Pyrah, R.M.	4	7	1	39	158	26.33	–	–	–	–
Ramprakash, M.R.	357	589	75	279*	24787	48.22	73	116	14	201
Ramyakumara, W.M.G.	78	122	14	148	3817	35.34	6	22	–	39
Read, C.M.W.	139	212	32	160	5082	28.23	4	26	–	380/20
Read, G.G.	1	2	1	9	10	10.00	–	–	–	–
Rees, T.M.	1	1	–	16	16	16.00	–	–	–	1
Rhodes, S.J.	440	618	166	124	14839	32.82	12	72	2	1139/124
Richards, M.A.	2	1	–	5	5	5.00	–	–	–	1
Richardson, A.	64	62	25	91	392	10.59	–	1	–	18
Richardson, M.H.	150	254	31	306	9758	43.75	20	47	0+1	87
Roberts, T.W.	29	46	2	89	1121	25.47	–	8	–	21
Robinson, D.D.J.	152	268	13	200	8236	32.29	16	42	2	129
Rofe, P.C.	38	56	20	18	225	6.25	–	–	–	10
Rogers, C.J.L.	40	72	6	194	2908	44.06	9	14	–	36
Rosenberg, M.C.	2	2	–	3	6	3.00	–	–	–	–
Russell, R.C.	465	690	145	129*	16861	30.93	11	89	–	1192/128
Sadler, J.L.	21	36	3	145	1000	30.30	2	4	–	12
Saggers, M.J.	84	104	26	64	792	10.15	–	2	–	21
Saker, N.C.	2	3	–	5	6	2.00	–	–	–	–
Sales, D.J.G.	122	189	17	303*	6547	38.06	12	35	2	97
Salisbury, I.D.K.	284	367	73	101*	5941	20.20	2	20	–	180
Sampson, P.J.	5	9	4	42	91	18.20	–	–	–	–
Saqlain Mushtaq	171	237	53	101*	3056	16.60	1	12	–	61
Sarwan, R.R.	123	208	17	261*	7259	38.00	15	42	–	84
Savill, T.E.	12	16	3	29	134	10.30	–	–	–	7
Sayers, J.J.	16	27	1	147	913	35.11	2	6	–	3
Schofield, C.P.	68	95	14	99	2423	29.91	–	20	–	40
Scott, B.J.M.	9	16	5	101*	315	28.63	1	1	–	14/3
Selwood, S.A.	25	48	1	99	901	19.17	–	4	–	4
Shabbir Ahmed	66	89	22	50	778	11.61	–	1	–	15
Shafayat, B.M.	26	48	1	105	1332	28.34	2	7	–	10/1
Shah, O.A.	130	216	18	203	7617	38.46	19	39	4	91
Shahid, N.	148	235	27	150	6453	31.02	9	35	1	153
Shankar, A.	10	16	–	143	332	20.75	1	–	–	5
Shantry, A.J.	5	6	4	38*	62	31.00	–	–	–	2
Shaw, A.D.	77	103	16	140	1906	21.90	1	9	–	180/14
Sheikh, M.A.	33	45	13	58*	831	25.96	–	2	–	4
Sheriyar, A.	150	162	64	21	816	8.32	–	–	–	22
Shirazi, D.C.	1	–	–	–	–	–	–	–	–	–
Shoaib Akhtar	105	143	44	59*	1170	11.81	–	1	–	32
Shoaib Malik	53	76	10	130*	1544	23.39	4	6	–	25
Shreck, C.E.	19	21	10	19	67	6.09	–	–	–	3
Sidebottom, R.J.	70	89	26	54	673	10.68	–	1	–	26
Sillence, R.J.	12	16	–	101	367	22.93	1	1	–	3

162

F-C	M	I	NO	HS	Runs	Avge	100	50	1000	Ct/St
Silverwood, C.E.W.	142	190	38	70	2325	15.29	–	6	–	31
Singh, A. (Nt)	100	165	7	187	5136	32.50	10	23	2	40
Singh, A. (CU)	4	8	1	38*	98	14.00	–	–	–	–
Smith, A.M.	157	206	62	61	1756	12.19	–	4	–	31
Smith, B.F.	248	384	45	204	13774	40.63	32	69	6	130
Smith, D.R.	29	46	4	114	1175	27.97	4	1	–	24
Smith, D.S.	63	115	5	181	4183	38.02	9	21	0+1	57
Smith, E.T.	134	227	14	213	8690	40.79	22	37	5	49
Smith, G.C.	53	89	6	277	4369	52.63	13	14	–	68
Smith, G.J.	126	157	53	68	1461	14.04	–	2	–	25
Smith, W.R.	8	13	2	48	216	19.63	–	–	–	6
Snape, J.N.	111	165	30	131	3874	28.69	3	22	–	71
Solanki, V.S.	170	276	19	185	9167	35.66	15	52	2	210
Somerville-Hendrie, J.W.	4	5	2	23	31	10.33	–	–	–	–
Spearman, C.M.	149	267	15	341	9654	38.30	21	46	2	140
Spendlove, B.L.	20	36	2	63	656	19.29	–	2	–	10
Stephenson, J.P.	302	510	56	202*	14772	32.53	25	78	5	182
Stevens, D.I.	80	134	8	149	3542	28.11	4	23	–	64
Stiff, D.A.	6	4	1	18	30	10.00	–	–	–	1
Strauss, A.J.	89	155	11	176	6142	42.65	13	31	3	52
Streak, H.H.	134	202	37	131	4523	27.41	6	21	–	45
Stubbings, S.D.	72	130	6	135*	3697	29.81	6	19	1	27
Styris, S.B.	72	119	14	212*	3354	31.94	6	15	–	48
Suman, A.K.	12	12	6	24*	73	12.16	–	–	–	4
Suppiah, A.V.	5	8	–	33	87	10.87	–	–	–	2
Suraj, M.M.	3	4	2	14*	29	14.50	–	–	–	–
Sutcliffe, I.J.	147	233	19	203	7204	33.66	11	39	2	76
Sutton, L.D.	70	125	16	140*	3265	29.95	5	10	–	129/7
Swann, A.J.	77	123	4	154	3305	27.77	8	14	1	56
Swann, G.P.	108	161	8	183	3979	26.00	4	17	–	75
Symonds, A.	173	290	28	254*	11130	42.48	33	45	2	121
Tahir Mughal	58	90	11	68*	1524	19.29	–	6	–	29
Tahir, N.	12	12	5	49	150	21.42	–	–	–	1
Tait, S.W.	16	23	10	12	62	4.76	–	–	–	3
Taylor, B.V.	39	48	17	40	360	11.61	–	–	–	5
Taylor, C.G.	59	104	6	196	3334	34.02	9	10	1	38
Taylor, C.R.	15	25	2	52*	402	17.47	–	2	–	7
Ten Doeschate, R.N.	4	5	–	31	55	11.00	–	–	–	2
Thomas, I.J.	28	46	4	82	941	22.40	–	6	–	19
Thomas, S.D.	162	220	44	138	3703	21.03	2	17	–	56
Thornicroft, N.D.	6	10	4	30	50	8.33	–	–	–	1
Thorp, C.D.	6	8	–	26	66	8.25	–	–	–	2
Thorpe, G.P.	325	541	75	223*	21185	45.46	48	117	9	281
Tomlinson, J.A.	15	24	11	23	73	5.61	–	–	–	5
Tredwell, J.C.	29	40	6	61	772	22.70	–	3	–	33
Tremlett, C.T.	41	56	16	57	720	18.00	–	1	–	13
Trescothick, M.E.	175	302	18	219	10033	35.32	17	58	–	190
Trott, B.J.	34	37	11	26	150	5.76	–	–	–	8
Trott, I.J.L.	44	78	9	134	2733	39.60	3	22	1	29
Troughton, J.O.	43	68	7	131*	2594	42.52	8	13	1	19
Tudor, A.J.	92	120	27	116	2041	21.94	1	6	–	27
Tuffey, D.R.	65	77	18	89*	788	13.35	–	3	–	29
Turner, R.J.	241	367	67	144	9242	30.80	10	45	2	681/49
Udal, S.D.	229	327	61	117*	6269	23.56	1	28	–	105
Upadhyay, A.M.	1	1	–	34	34	34.00	–	–	–	2
Vaas, W.P.U.C.J.	134	174	37	104	2884	21.05	1	13	–	40
Van Jaarsveld, M.	99	167	16	238*	6831	45.23	19	31	0+1	114

F-C	M	I	NO	HS	Runs	Avge	100	50	1000	Ct/St
Vaughan, M.P.	209	368	22	197	13336	38.54	36	54	4	100
Vettori, D.L.	95	130	19	137*	2459	22.15	2	13	–	43
Voros, J.A.	1	1	1	3*	3	–	–	–	–	–
Wagg, G.G.	10	15	2	74	284	21.84	–	2	–	2
Wagh, M.A.	125	208	18	315	7335	38.60	18	32	4	69
Wainwright, D.J.	1	1	–	5	5	5.00	–	–	–	–
Walker, G.W.	4	5	3	37*	74	24.66	–	–	–	2
Walker, M.J.	133	219	25	275*	6529	33.65	14	26	2	98
Walker, N.G.E.	8	9	3	80	221	36.83	–	2	–	3
Wallace, M.A.	69	111	10	121	2796	27.68	4	12	–	201/9
Ward, I.J.	128	214	17	168*	7955	40.38	21	41	3	69
Warne, S.K.	219	296	36	99	4629	17.80	–	16	–	174
Warren, N.A.	2	3	1	11	13	6.50	–	–	–	–
Warren, R.J.	132	217	25	201*	7285	37.94	15	37	1	119/5
Watson, S.R.	28	49	6	157	2038	47.39	7	10	–	13
Webley, T.	12	21	2	104	601	31.63	1	3	–	4
Weekes, P.N.	212	331	44	171*	9870	34.39	18	50	2	203
Welch, G.	139	213	35	115*	3904	21.93	1	15	–	56
Wessels, M.H.	1	2	–	34	35	17.50	–	–	–	4/1
Weston, W.P.C.	202	354	33	205	10970	34.17	21	53	4	117
Westwood, I.J.	2	3	–	38	60	20.00	–	–	–	–
Wharf, A.G.	72	104	18	101*	1696	19.72	2	8	–	33
White, A.R.	4	5	1	152*	252	63.00	1	1	–	1
White, C.	234	371	48	186	10217	31.63	16	49	–	148
White, R.A.	18	34	1	277	1012	30.66	1	6	–	10
Wigley, D.H.	7	9	2	23*	91	13.00	–	–	–	2
Wilkinson, R.M.	2	2	–	49	69	34.50	–	–	–	1
Willoughby, C.M.	85	96	39	17*	234	4.10	–	–	–	23
Windows, M.G.N.	154	271	19	184	8497	33.71	16	45	3	88
Wood, J.	115	163	24	64	1762	12.67	–	3	–	28
Wood, M.J. (Sm)	45	79	5	196	2640	35.67	7	15	–	13
Wood, M.J. (Y)	105	183	18	207	5615	34.03	15	23	3	87
Wright, C.J.C.	4	5	–	57	96	19.20	–	1	–	3
Wright, D.G.	52	75	15	65	1272	21.20	–	6	–	23
Wright, L.J.	3	5	1	100	129	32.25	1	–	–	1
Wyatt, A.A.	3	4	1	10*	19	6.33	–	–	–	1
Yardy, M.H.	38	66	8	115	1725	29.74	1	8	–	27

BOWLING

'50wS' denotes instances of taking 50 or more wickets in a season. Where these have been achieved outside the British Isles they are shown after a plus sign.

	Runs	Wkts	Avge	Best	5wI	10wM	50wS
Ackerman, H.D.	57	0					
Adams, A.R.	3174	136	23.33	5- 40	5	–	–
Adams, C.J.	1890	41	46.09	4- 28	–	–	–
Adams, J.H.K.	223	6	37.16	2- 16	–	–	–
Adnan, M.H.	174	1	174.00	1- 4	–	–	–
Afzaal, U.	3543	70	50.61	4-101	–	–	–
Agarkar, A.B.	4892	174	28.11	6- 41	8	–	–
Airey, S.J.	369	4	92.25	2- 32	–	–	–
Akram, Adnan M.	163	3	54.33	2- 85	–	–	–
Akram, Arfan M.	113	5	22.60	3- 41	–	–	–
Ali, Kabir	5542	205	27.03	8- 53	10	2	2
Ali, Kadeer	163	1	163.00	1- 15	–	–	–
Ali, S.M.B.	8607	264	32.60	6- 37	11	2	0+1
Alleyne, M.W.	13572	414	32.78	6- 49	9	–	1

164

F-C	Runs	Wkts	Avge	Best	5wI	10wM	50wS
Ambrose, T.R.	1	0					
Anderson, J.M.	3110	122	25.49	6- 23	7	1	1
Anderson, R.S.G.	3452	122	28.29	6- 34	8	1	1
Andrew, G.M.	489	17	28.76	4- 63	–	–	–
Anyon, J.F.	494	7	70.57	3- 57	–	–	–
Astle, N.J.	3948	118	33.45	6- 22	2	–	–
Averis, J.M.M.	5408	126	42.92	6- 32	5	–	–
Azhar Mahmood	9421	375	25.12	8- 61	14	3	0+1
Bailey, T.M.B.	3	0					
Ball, M.C.J.	13352	356	37.50	8- 46	12	1	–
Banerjee, V.	107	0					
Banks, O.A.C.	3446	90	38.28	7- 70	3	1	–
Bassano, C.W.G.	11	0					
Batty, G.J.	5921	196	30.20	7- 52	7	1	2
Batty, J.N.	61	1	61.00	1- 21	–	–	–
Bell, I.R.	994	29	34.27	4- 4	–	–	–
Benkenstein, D.M.	1245	31	40.16	2- 4	–	–	–
Benning, J.G.E.	173	2	86.50	1- 28	–	–	–
Best, T.L.	2692	120	22.43	7- 33	6	1	–
Betts, M.M.	9797	321	30.52	9- 64	14	2	–
Bevan, M.G.	5207	115	45.27	6- 82	1	1	–
Bichel, A.J.	13747	524	26.23	9- 93	25	5	1+1
Bicknell, D.J.	928	29	32.00	3- 7	–	–	–
Bicknell, M.P.	25405	1025	24.78	9- 45	41	4	11
Bishop, J.E.	2197	55	39.94	5-148	1	–	–
Blackwell, I.D.	6390	156	40.96	7- 90	7	–	–
Blain, J.A.R.	3219	89	36.16	6- 42	2	–	–
Blakey, R.J.	68	1	68.00	1- 68	–	–	–
Blignaut, A.M.	3901	114	34.21	5- 73	3	–	–
Bloomfield, T.F.	5291	157	33.70	5- 36	6	–	1
Bond, S.E.	3471	128	27.11	5- 37	6	–	–
Bopara, R.S.	304	3	101.33	1- 23	–	–	–
Botha, A.G.	4454	143	31.14	8- 53	3	1	–
Bowler, P.D.	2051	34	60.32	3- 25	–	–	–
Bracken, N.W.	3350	112	29.91	5- 22	4	–	–
Brandy, D.G.	172	4	43.00	2- 11	–	–	–
Brant, S.A.	2008	60	33.46	6- 45	1	–	–
Bravo, D.J.J.	1500	68	22.05	6- 11	4	–	–
Breese, G.R.	4747	184	25.79	7- 60	9	3	–
Bresnan, T.T.	816	24	34.00	3- 32	–	–	–
Bressington, A.N.	584	17	34.35	4- 36	–	–	–
Bridge, G.D.	2960	84	35.23	6- 84	1	–	–
Brignull, D.S.	356	9	39.55	2- 30	–	–	–
Brophy, G.L.	1	0					
Brown, A.D.	504	2	252.00	1- 11	–	–	–
Brown, D.O.	292	6	48.66	2- 48	–	–	–
Brown, D.R.	13619	477	28.55	8- 89	19	4	3
Brown, J.F.	8659	284	30.48	7- 69	14	3	2
Bruce, J.T.A.	1593	33	48.27	3- 42	–	–	–
Bryant, J.D.C.	37	1	37.00	1- 22	–	–	–
Buckham, C.T.	79	0					
Burns, M.	2743	65	42.20	6- 54	1	–	–
Butcher, M.A.	4190	124	33.79	5- 86	1	–	–
Butler, I.G.	3261	109	29.91	6- 46	2	–	–
Caddick, A.R.	24322	953	25.52	9- 32	65	15	9
Cairns, C.L.	18278	643	28.42	8- 47	30	6	3
Carberry, M.A.	251	3	83.66	1- 45	–	–	–
Carpenter, E.J.	155	1	155.00	1- 47	–	–	–

165

F-C	Runs	Wkts	Avge	Best	5wI	10wM	50wS
Carter, N.M.	4094	104	39.36	6- 63	4	–	–
Cawdron, M.J.	1848	74	24.97	6- 25	6	1	–
Chandana, U.D.U.	8220	351	23.41	7- 80	15	1	–
Chanderpaul, S.	2213	54	40.98	4- 48	–	–	–
Chapple, G.	15191	516	29.43	6- 30	21	1	4
Cherry, D.D.	0	0					
Chilton, M.J.	590	7	84.28	1- 1	–	–	–
Clark, S.R.	4286	128	33.48	6- 84	5	–	–
Clarke, A.C.S.	158	8	19.75	3- 44	–	–	–
Clarke, A.J.	762	26	29.30	5- 54	1	–	–
Clarke, A.P.A.	19	0					
Clarke, M.J.	454	6	75.66	2- 25	–	–	–
Clarke, R.	2015	47	42.87	4- 21	–	–	–
Cleary, M.F.	2189	73	29.98	7- 80	3	–	–
Clinton, R.S.	60	2	30.00	2- 30	–	–	–
Clough, G.D.	544	9	60.44	3- 69	–	–	–
Coetzer, K.J.	3	0					
Collingwood, P.D.	3121	77	40.53	4- 31	–	–	–
Collins, P.T.	7362	268	27.47	6- 53	6	–	0+1
Collymore, C.D.	4403	162	27.17	7- 57	7	–	–
Cook, A.N.	23	0					
Cook, J.W.	1391	36	38.63	5- 31	1	–	–
Cook, S.J.	5410	168	32.20	8- 63	4	–	–
Cork, D.G.	20077	760	26.41	9- 43	31	5	7
Cosker, D.A.	9411	257	36.61	6-140	2	–	–
Cottey, P.A.	954	16	59.62	4- 49	–	–	–
Cowan, A.P.	9236	283	32.63	6- 47	8	–	1
Cox, J.	450	5	90.00	3- 46	–	–	–
Craven, V.J.	584	15	38.93	2- 18	–	–	–
Crawley, J.P.	225	1	225.00	1- 90	–	–	–
Croft, R.D.B.	30078	839	35.84	8- 66	36	6	7
Crook, A.R.	377	3	125.66	1- 8	–	–	–
Crook, S.P.	464	8	58.00	2- 33	–	–	–
Cusden, S.M.J.	404	13	31.07	4- 68	–	–	–
Daggett, L.M.	553	15	36.86	8- 94	1	–	–
Dagnall, C.E.	2746	87	31.56	6- 50	2	–	–
Dakin, J.M.	5572	162	34.39	5- 86	1	–	–
Dale, A.	8274	217	38.12	6- 18	4	–	–
Dale, M.A.P.	66	1	66.00	1- 34	–	–	–
Dalrymple, J.W.M.	2657	56	47.44	5- 49	1	–	–
Daniel, G.I.	157	3	52.33	2- 48	–	–	–
Danish Kaneria	7317	315	23.22	7- 39	24	3	1+1
Davies, A.M.	2389	97	24.62	6- 44	5	–	1
Davies, A.P.	1792	45	39.82	5- 79	1	–	–
Davis, M.J.G.	8191	229	35.76	8- 37	5	1	–
Dawson, R.K.J.	5797	141	41.11	6- 82	5	–	–
Dean, K.J.	8866	352	25.18	8- 52	15	4	2
De Bruyn, Z.	2229	69	32.30	6-120	1	–	–
DeFreitas, P.A.J.	34403	1236	27.83	7- 21	61	6	14
Dennington, M.J.	368	9	40.88	3- 48	–	–	–
Dernbach, J.W.	74	1	74.00	1- 74	–	–	–
Dias, W.J.M.R.	1796	73	24.60	6- 41	3	–	–
Di Venuto, M.J.	480	5	96.00	1- 0	–	–	–
Doshi, N.D.	1530	47	32.55	7-110	4	2	–
Dumelow, N.R.C.	2132	41	52.00	5- 51	3	1	–
Durston, W.J.	305	8	38.12	3- 23	–	–	–
Dutch, K.P.	4187	115	36.40	6- 62	3	–	–
Ealham, M.A.	13085	451	29.01	8- 36	19	1	–

F-C	Runs	Wkts	Avge	Best	5wI	10wM	50wS
Edwards, F.H.	2384	60	39.73	5- 22	4	1	–
Edwards, N.J.	181	2	90.50	1- 16	–	–	–
Edwards, P.D.	341	3	113.66	1- 31	–	–	–
Elliott, M.T.G.	666	10	66.60	1- 3	–	–	–
Ervine, S.M.	2191	55	39.83	6- 82	2	–	–
Ferley, R.S.	1864	44	42.36	4- 76	–	–	–
Fisher, I.D.	4949	126	39.27	5- 30	7	1	–
Fleming, S.P.	129	0					
Flintoff, A.	5895	169	34.88	5- 24	2	–	–
Flower, A.	250	6	41.66	1- 1	–	–	–
Flower, G.W.	4867	145	33.56	7- 31	3	–	–
Foster, J.S.	6	0					
France, B.J.	20	0					
Francis, J.D.	155	4	38.75	1- 1	–	–	–
Francis, S.R.G.	4764	126	37.80	5- 42	3	–	–
Franklin, J.E.C.	3732	157	23.77	7- 60	4	–	–
Franks, P.J.	9832	336	29.26	7- 56	11	–	2
Friend, T.J.	3154	79	39.92	5- 16	2	–	–
Frost, T.	15	0					
Fulton, D.P.	112	1	112.00	1- 37	–	–	–
Gajanayake, M.K.	584	25	23.36	3- 13	–	–	–
Gallian, J.E.R.	3919	95	41.25	6-115	1	–	–
Gayle, C.H.	2589	65	39.83	5- 34	1	–	–
Gibson, O.D.	13519	485	27.87	7- 55	22	5	2
Gidman, A.P.R.	1710	31	55.16	3- 33	–	–	–
Giles, A.F.	13877	483	28.73	8- 90	23	3	2
Goode, C.M.	70	1	70.00	1- 70	–	–	–
Goodwin, M.W.	355	7	50.71	2- 23	–	–	–
Gough, D.	20250	757	26.75	7- 28	28	3	5
Gray, A.K.D.	1359	30	45.30	4-128	–	–	–
Grayson, A.P.	6038	136	44.39	5- 20	1	–	–
Greenidge, C.G.	3403	97	35.08	6- 40	4	–	1
Gunter, N.E.L.	602	17	35.41	4- 14	–	–	–
Guy, S.M.	8	0					
Habib, A.	80	1	80.00	1- 10	–	–	–
Hall, A.J.	6345	247	25.68	6- 77	9	1	–
Hamilton, G.M.	6368	248	25.67	7- 50	9	2	1
Hancock, T.H.C.	1785	46	38.80	3- 5	–	–	–
Harbhajan Singh	9275	354	26.20	8- 84	21	3	0+1
Hardinges, M.A.	737	14	52.64	2- 16	–	–	–
Harmison, S.J.	9739	338	28.81	7- 12	9	–	2
Harris, A.J.	9511	300	31.70	7- 54	12	3	2
Harrison, A.J.	108	3	36.00	2- 65	–	–	–
Harrison, D.S.	3109	101	30.78	5- 48	4	–	1
Harrity, M.A.	8491	216	39.31	5- 65	2	–	–
Harvey, I.J.	9712	354	27.43	8-101	14	2	–
Harvey, T.F.C.	110	4	27.50	3- 43	–	–	–
Havell, P.M.R.	1328	35	37.94	4- 75	–	–	–
Hawinkels, S.J.	145	2	72.50	1- 44	–	–	–
Hayward, M.	9999	354	28.24	6- 31	9	2	1
Hegg, W.K.	7	0					
Hemp, D.L.	778	17	45.76	3- 23	–	–	–
Henderson, C.W.	14031	474	29.60	7- 57	15	–	–
Hewson, D.R.	203	5	40.60	3- 39	–	–	–
Hick, G.A.	10308	232	44.43	5- 18	5	1	–
Hildreth, J.C.	76	2	38.00	2- 39	–	–	–
Hodge, B.J.	2395	57	42.01	4- 17	–	–	–
Hogg, G.B.	5804	129	44.99	5- 53	4	–	–

F-C	Runs	Wkts	Avge	Best	5wI	10wM	50wS
Hogg, K.W.	1396	36	38.77	5- 48	1	–	–
Hoggard, M.J.	9726	363	26.79	7- 49	11	–	1
Hollioake, A.J.	4927	120	41.05	5- 62	1	–	–
Hooper, C.L.	19595	555	35.30	7- 93	18	–	–
Hopkins, G.J.	13	0					
Hopkinson, C.D.	77	2	38.50	1- 20	–	–	–
Hunt, T.A.	409	9	45.44	3- 43	–	–	–
Hunter, I.D.	1946	48	40.54	4- 55	–	–	–
Hussain, N.	323	2	161.50	1- 38	–	–	–
Hussey, D.J.	375	4	93.75	1- 6	–	–	–
Hussey, M.E.K.	467	9	51.88	2- 21	–	–	–
Hutchison, P.M.	5001	179	27.93	7- 31	7	1	1
Hutton, B.L.	1554	31	50.12	4- 37	–	–	–
Hutton, O.R.	36	0					
Innes, K.J.	2461	79	31.15	4- 41	–	–	–
Irani, R.C.	10007	339	29.51	6- 71	9	–	1
Jacobs, R.D.	0	0					
Jaques, P.A.	53	0					
Jayasuriya, S.T.	5348	169	31.64	5- 34	2	–	–
Jennings, C.J.R.	64	1	64.00	1- 64	–	–	–
Johnson, R.L.	12945	480	26.96	10- 45	19	3	4
Jones, G.O.	4	0					
Jones, P.S.	7705	198	38.91	6- 67	5	1	1
Jones, S.P.	5511	164	33.60	6- 45	9	1	–
Joseph, R.H.	704	20	35.20	3- 47	–	–	–
Joseph, S.C.	197	4	49.25	2- 13	–	–	–
Joyce, E.C.	564	6	94.00	2- 34	–	–	–
Kalavitigoda, S.	39	0					
Kasprowicz, M.S.	22302	847	26.33	9- 36	47	6	4+3
Katich, S.M.	2790	73	38.21	7-130	3	–	–
Kay, M.A.	13	0					
Keedy, G.	11887	363	32.74	7- 95	18	4	2
Keegan, C.B.	3918	120	32.65	6-114	5	–	1
Kendall, W.S.	736	15	49.06	3- 37	–	–	–
Kenway, D.A.	159	4	39.75	1- 5	–	–	–
Key, R.W.T.	44	0					
Khalid, S.A.	673	14	48.07	4-131	–	–	–
Khan, A.	3603	101	35.67	6- 52	4	–	1
Khan, Z.	5996	206	29.10	6- 25	14	3	–
Killeen, N.	7005	221	31.69	7- 70	7	–	1
King, R.D.	6496	250	25.98	7- 82	10	1	–
King, R.E.	313	1	313.00	1-108	–	–	–
Kirby, S.P.	5231	184	28.42	8- 80	9	3	1
Kirtley, R.J.	13444	513	26.20	7- 21	27	4	6
Klusener, L.	9874	363	27.20	8- 34	14	4	–
Knight, N.V.	230	1	230.00	1- 61	–	–	–
Koenig, S.G.	102	2	51.00	1- 0	–	–	–
Kruis, G.J.	6632	228	29.08	7- 58	10	1	–
Kulasekara, M.D.N.	2330	96	24.27	6-109	5	1	0+1
Kumar, P.	219	6	36.50	3- 78	–	–	–
Lamb, G.A.	574	26	22.07	7- 73	1	–	–
Lara, B.C.	416	4	104.00	1- 1	–	–	–
Laraman, A.W.	2612	79	33.06	5- 58	1	–	–
Law, S.G.	4165	82	50.79	5- 39	1	–	–
Lawson, J.J.C.	3178	111	28.63	7- 78	3	–	–
Lawson, M.A.K.	308	9	34.22	5- 62	1	–	–
Lehmann, D.S.	3214	94	34.19	4- 35	–	–	–
Lewis, J.	12527	469	26.71	8- 95	24	3	5

168

F-C	Runs	Wkts	Avge	Best	5wI	10wM	50wS
Lewis, J.J.B.	121	1	121.00	1- 73	–	–	–
Lewis, M.L.	4057	130	31.20	6- 59	4	–	–
Lewis, P.D.	402	10	40.20	3- 58	–	–	–
Lewry, J.D.	11683	432	27.04	8-106	25	4	4
Linley, T.F.	350	9	38.88	3- 44	–	–	–
Logan, R.J.	3723	107	34.79	6- 93	4	–	–
Lokuarachchi, K.S.	3159	121	26.10	5-103	1	–	0+1
Loudon, A.G.R.	1205	30	40.16	6- 47	2	–	–
Louw, J.	3640	121	30.08	6-108	4	–	1
Love, M.L.	11	1	11.00	1- 5	–	–	–
Loye, M.B.	61	1	61.00	1- 8	–	–	–
Lucas, D.S.	1909	52	36.71	5-104	1	–	–
Lumb, M.J.	114	4	28.50	2- 10	–	–	–
Lungley, T.	1334	42	31.76	4-101	–	–	–
McCoubrey, A.G.A.M.	842	23	36.60	4- 16	–	–	–
MacGill, S.C.G.	17228	570	30.22	8-111	34	6	0+2
McGrath, A.	1762	61	28.88	5- 39	1	–	–
McGrath, G.D.	14631	704	20.78	8- 38	37	7	1+1
McLean, N.A.M.	13142	484	27.15	7- 28	19	3	2
McMahon, P.J.	1249	32	39.03	4- 59	–	–	–
McMillan, C.D.	2633	75	35.10	6- 71	1	–	–
Maddy, D.L.	4602	149	30.88	5- 37	4	–	–
Mahmood, S.I.	1685	46	36.63	5- 37	2	–	–
Malik, M.N.	1984	59	33.62	5- 57	3	–	–
Marshall, S.J.	1463	17	86.05	6-128	1	–	–
Martin, C.S.	6585	205	32.12	6- 76	8	1	0+1
Martin, P.J.	16677	606	27.51	8- 32	17	1	4
Martin-Jenkins, R.S.C.	7731	229	33.75	7- 51	5	–	–
Mascarenhas, A.D.	7867	272	28.92	6- 25	10	–	1
Mason, M.S.	3588	131	27.38	6- 68	4	–	2
Masters, D.D.	4418	129	34.24	6- 27	4	–	–
Maunders, J.K.	122	2	61.00	1- 11	–	–	–
Maynard, M.P.	895	6	149.16	3- 21	–	–	–
Mendis, B.M.A.J.	290	7	41.42	3- 67	–	–	–
Middlebrook, J.D.	6632	177	37.46	6- 82	5	1	1
Mills, K.D.	2455	90	27.27	5- 50	1	–	–
Mirando, M.T.T.	4344	134	32.41	6- 83	5	–	–
Mohammad Akram	8891	325	27.35	8- 49	14	1	–
Mohammad Sami	5071	166	30.54	8- 64	11	2	–
Mohammed, D.	2099	78	26.91	5- 63	1	–	–
Mongia, D.	659	19	34.68	4- 34	–	–	–
Montgomerie, R.R.	134	2	67.00	1- 0	–	–	–
Moore, S.C.	127	3	42.33	1- 13	–	–	–
Moss, J.	1912	60	31.86	4- 50	–	–	–
Mubarak, J.	513	9	57.00	2- 0	–	–	–
Muchall, G.J.	571	15	38.06	3- 26	–	–	–
Mullally, A.D.	19953	708	28.18	9- 93	31	4	5
Munday, M.K.	562	24	23.41	5- 83	1	–	–
Muralitharan, M.	19388	1015	19.10	9- 51	87	25	2+3
Murtagh, T.J.	2032	57	35.64	6- 86	3	–	–
Mushtaq Ahmed	28205	1080	26.11	9- 93	76	23	6+2
Napier, G.R.	4562	117	38.99	5- 56	2	–	–
Nash, C.D.	457	5	91.40	1- 5	–	–	–
Nash, D.C.	52	1	52.00	1- 8	–	–	–
Naved-ul-Hasan	6062	265	22.87	7- 49	16	2	0+3
Newby, O.J.	189	3	63.00	2- 32	–	–	–
Newman, A.R.I.	70	2	35.00	2- 70	–	–	–
Newman, S.A.	5	0					

F-C	Runs	Wkts	Avge	Best	5wI	10wM	50wS
Nicholson, M.J.	5538	189	29.30	7- 77	7	–	–
Nixon, P.A.	22	0					
Noble, D.J.	599	9	66.55	3- 66	–	–	–
Noffke, A.A.	5770	191	30.20	8- 24	9	1	–
Noon, W.M.	34	0					
North, M.J.	1171	28	41.82	4- 16	–	–	–
Onions, G.	593	9	65.88	3-110	–	–	–
Oram, J.D.P.	2177	78	27.91	5- 30	1	–	–
Ormond, J.	11048	381	28.99	6- 33	19	1	4
Paget, C.D.	206	3	68.66	3- 63	–	–	–
Palladino, A.P.	861	14	61.50	6- 41	1	–	–
Panesar, M.S.	1875	56	33.48	5- 77	1	–	–
Papps, M.H.W.	4	0					
Park, G.T.	261	0					
Parker, L.C.	13	0					
Parsons, K.A.	3858	88	43.84	5- 13	2	–	–
Patel, M.M.	15900	519	30.63	8- 96	25	9	3
Patel, S.R.	10	0					
Pattison, I.	295	7	42.14	3- 41	–	–	–
Peng, N.	2	0					
Penney, T.L.	184	6	30.66	3- 18	–	–	–
Peploe, C.T.	984	19	51.78	4- 65	–	–	–
Perera, W.M.B.	2661	83	32.06	4- 21	–	–	–
Peters, S.D.	31	1	31.00	1- 19	–	–	–
Phillips, B.J.	3530	121	29.17	5- 47	3	–	–
Phillips, T.J.	1704	32	53.25	4- 42	–	–	–
Pietersen, C.	1400	36	38.88	6- 43	1	–	–
Pietersen, K.P.	2598	55	47.23	4- 31	–	–	–
Piper, K.J.	60	1	60.00	1- 57	–	–	–
Plunkett, L.E.	1636	50	32.72	6- 74	2	–	–
Ponting, R.T.	716	13	55.07	2- 10	–	–	–
Pothas, N.	5	0					
Powell, D.B.	2941	106	27.74	6- 49	5	–	–
Powell, M.J. (Gm)	132	2	66.00	2- 39	–	–	–
Powell, M.J. (Nh)	12	0					
Powell, M.J. (Wa)	627	10	62.70	2- 16	–	–	–
Prasad, K.T.G.D.	1114	50	22.28	6- 25	2	1	–
Pratt, G.J.	19	0					
Pretorius, D.	5866	219	26.78	6- 49	7	–	–
Price, R.W.	7206	225	32.02	8- 35	15	3	–
Prittipaul, L.R.	443	9	49.22	3- 17	–	–	–
Pyrah, R.M.	2	0					
Ramprakash, M.R.	2172	34	63.88	3- 32	–	–	–
Ramyakumara, W.M.G.	3213	114	28.18	7- 25	2	1	–
Read, C.M.W.	25	0					
Read, G.G.	45	1	45.00	1- 45	–	–	–
Rhodes, S.J.	30	0					
Richards, M.A.	62	0					
Richardson, A.	5419	166	32.64	8- 46	4	1	–
Richardson, M.H.	1911	44	43.43	5- 77	1	–	–
Roberts, T.W.	20	1	20.00	1- 10	–	–	–
Robinson, D.D.J.	279	1	279.00	1- 7	–	–	–
Rofe, P.C.	3635	120	30.29	7- 52	6	1	–
Rogers, C.J.L.	12	0					
Rosenberg, M.C.	27	1	27.00	1- 27	–	–	–
Russell, R.C.	68	1	68.00	1- 4	–	–	–
Sadler, J.L.	98	1	98.00	1- 22	–	–	–
Saggers, M.J.	7666	327	23.44	7- 79	15	–	4

F-C	Runs	Wkts	Avge	Best	5wI	10wM	50wS
Saker, N.C.	179	1	179.00	1- 71	–	–	–
Sales, D.J.G.	169	9	18.77	4- 25	–	–	–
Salisbury, I.D.K.	25164	773	32.55	8- 60	34	6	6
Sampson, P.J.	415	17	24.41	5-121	1	–	–
Saqlain Mushtaq	17433	759	22.96	8- 65	56	15	5+1
Sarwan, R.R.	1374	39	35.23	6- 62	1	–	–
Savill, T.E.	1317	26	50.65	3- 86	–	–	–
Sayers, J.J.	12	0					
Schofield, C.P.	5347	171	31.26	6-120	4	–	–
Selwood, S.A.	95	2	47.50	1- 8	–	–	–
Shabbir Ahmed	6587	279	23.60	7- 70	15	–	0+1
Shafayat, B.M.	192	1	192.00	1- 22	–	–	–
Shah, O.A.	749	18	41.61	3- 33	–	–	–
Shahid, N.	2146	45	47.68	3- 91	–	–	–
Shantry, A.J.	263	10	26.30	3- 8	–	–	–
Shaw, A.D.	7	0					
Sheikh, M.A.	2336	62	37.67	4- 9	–	–	–
Sheriyar, A.	14904	498	29.92	7-130	23	3	4
Shoaib Akhtar	9668	372	25.98	6- 11	22	2	0+1
Shoaib Malik	4157	154	26.99	7- 81	5	1	–
Shreck, C.E.	1701	54	31.50	6- 46	3	–	–
Sidebottom, R.J.	5288	209	25.30	7- 97	9	1	–
Sillence, R.J.	1092	32	34.12	5- 63	2	–	–
Silverwood, C.E.W.	12289	461	26.65	7- 93	20	1	2
Singh, A. (Nt)	111	0					
Singh, A. (CU)	19	0					
Smith, A.M.	13158	533	24.68	8- 73	22	5	5
Smith, B.F.	350	3	116.66	1- 5	–	–	–
Smith, D.R.	629	24	26.20	4- 46	–	–	–
Smith, D.S.	34	0					
Smith, E.T.	59	0					
Smith, G.C.	295	4	73.75	1- 9	–	–	–
Smith, G.J.	10919	394	27.71	8- 53	16	2	2
Smith, W.R.	127	2	63.50	2- 83	–	–	–
Snape, J.N.	5361	109	49.18	5- 65	1	–	–
Solanki, V.S.	3549	78	45.50	5- 40	4	1	–
Somerville-Hendrie, J.W.	358	8	44.75	3- 51	–	–	–
Spearman, C.M.	55	1	55.00	1- 37	–	–	–
Stephenson, J.P.	12782	392	32.60	7- 44	11	1	–
Stevens, D.I.	413	6	68.83	2- 50	–	–	–
Stiff, D.A.	419	7	59.85	3- 88	–	–	–
Strauss, A.J.	58	1	58.00	1- 27	–	–	–
Streak, H.H.	10974	405	27.09	7- 55	12	2	1
Stubbings, S.D.	77	0					
Styris, S.B.	4200	142	29.57	6- 32	6	–	–
Suman, A.K.	808	23	35.13	3- 44	–	–	–
Suppiah, A.V.	204	8	25.50	3- 46	–	–	–
Suraj, M.M.	498	11	45.27	5- 40	1	–	–
Sutcliffe, I.J.	329	9	36.55	2- 21	–	–	–
Swann, A.J.	326	6	54.33	2- 30	–	–	–
Swann, G.P.	8959	284	31.54	7- 33	12	2	1
Symonds, A.	6278	170	36.92	6-105	2	–	–
Tahir Mughal	5923	278	21.30	7- 63	23	5	0+2
Tahir, N.	791	28	28.25	4- 43	–	–	–
Tait, S.W.	1584	53	29.88	5- 68	2	–	–
Taylor, B.V.	3532	104	33.96	5- 73	2	–	–
Taylor, C.G.	222	3	74.00	3-126	–	–	–
Ten Doeschate, R.N.	239	7	34.14	3- 29	–	–	–

F-C	Runs	Wkts	Avge	Best	5wI	10wM	50wS
Thomas, I.J.	38	1	38.00	1- 26	–	–	–
Thomas, S.D.	15412	495	31.13	8- 50	18	1	5
Thornicroft, N.D.	473	10	47.30	2- 27	–	–	–
Thorp, C.D.	531	10	53.10	3- 59	–	–	–
Thorpe, G.P.	1378	26	53.00	4- 40	–	–	–
Tomlinson, J.A.	1585	30	52.83	6- 63	1	–	–
Tredwell, J.C.	2679	62	43.20	5-101	1	–	–
Tremlett, C.T.	3534	134	26.37	6- 51	3	–	–
Trescothick, M.E.	1530	36	42.50	4- 36	–	–	–
Trott, B.J.	2999	88	34.07	6- 13	4	1	–
Trott, I.J.L.	531	14	37.92	7- 39	1	–	–
Troughton, J.O.	544	6	90.66	3- 1	–	–	–
Tudor, A.J.	7908	280	28.24	7- 48	13	–	–
Tuffey, D.R.	5636	213	26.46	7- 12	9	1	–
Turner, R.J.	58	0					
Udal, S.D.	21324	643	33.16	8- 50	30	4	7
Vaas, W.P.U.C.J.	11878	479	24.79	7- 71	20	2	0+1
Van Jaarsveld, M.	427	8	53.37	2- 30	–	–	–
Vaughan, M.P.	5092	113	45.06	4- 39	–	–	–
Vettori, D.L.	9960	298	33.42	7- 87	17	1	–
Voros, J.A.	62	5	12.40	4- 40	–	–	–
Wagg, G.G.	726	23	31.56	4- 43	–	–	–
Wagh, M.A.	4553	98	46.45	7-222	2	–	–
Wainwright, D.J.	5	0					
Walker, G.W.	190	1	190.00	1- 92	–	–	–
Walker, M.J.	791	15	52.73	2- 21	–	–	–
Walker, N.G.E.	667	18	37.05	5- 68	1	–	–
Ward, I.J.	197	3	65.66	1- 1	–	–	–
Warne, S.K.	24452	946	25.84	8- 71	47	8	4+1
Warren, N.A.	150	5	30.00	3- 60	–	–	–
Warren, R.J.	0	0					
Watson, S.R.	1487	53	28.05	6- 32	2	1	–
Webley, T.	357	6	59.50	2- 57	–	–	–
Weekes, P.N.	11656	285	40.89	8- 39	5	–	–
Welch, R.J.	12277	381	32.22	6- 30	14	1	3
Weston, W.P.C.	658	5	131.60	2- 39	–	–	–
Westwood, I.J.	57	0					
Wharf, A.G.	6402	188	34.05	5- 63	3	–	1
White, A.R.	159	4	39.75	2- 19	–	–	–
White, C.	11103	390	28.46	8- 55	11	–	–
White, R.A.	319	9	35.44	2- 30	–	–	–
Wigley, D.H.	746	15	49.73	4-133	–	–	–
Wilkinson, R.M.	133	1	133.00	1- 36	–	–	–
Willoughby, C.M.	7468	319	23.41	7- 56	11	3	0+1
Windows, M.G.N.	131	2	65.50	1- 6	–	–	–
Wood, J.	10787	318	33.92	7- 58	11	–	1
Wood, M.J. (Sm)	68	0					
Wood, M.J. (Y)	39	2	19.50	1- 4	–	–	–
Wright, C.J.C.	379	6	63.16	2- 70	–	–	–
Wright, D.G.	5051	154	32.79	6- 39	2	–	–
Wright, L.J.	199	1	199.00	1- 74	–	–	–
Wyatt, A.A.	221	4	55.25	2- 22	–	–	–
Yardy, M.H.	610	4	152.50	1- 13	–	–	–

LIMITED-OVERS 'LIST A' CAREER RECORDS

Compiled by **PHILIP BAILEY**

The following career records, to the end of the 2004 season, include all players currently registered with first-class counties. These records are restricted to performances in limited-overs matches of 'List A' status as defined by the Association of Cricket Statisticians and Historians. The following matches qualify for List A status and are included in the figures that follow: Limited-Overs Internationals; other international matches (e.g. Commonwealth Games, 'A' team internationals); premier domestic limited-overs tournaments in Test status countries; official tourist matches against the main first-class teams.

The following matches do NOT qualify for inclusion: World Cup warm-up games; tourist matches against first-class teams outside the major domestic competitions (e.g. universities, Minor Counties, etc.); festival, pre-season friendly games and Twenty20 Cup matches).

Editor's note: I have deducted from Philip's match totals for A.R.Adams, S.P.Fleming and S.B.Styris the LOI scheduled between New Zealand and West Indies at Southampton on 8 July 2004. Although the ICC has ruled this should count as a match because the toss was made, Law 16 clearly states that the umpire's call of 'play' heralds the start of a match and not the toss.

	M	Runs	Avge	HS	100	50	Wkts	Avge	Best	Ct/St
Ackerman, H.D.	114	2926	32.51	92	–	20	0	–	–	41
Adams, A.R.	77	843	19.60	90*	–	1	108	26.59	5- 7	16
Adams, C.J.	312	9937	40.39	163	18	64	32	38.03	5-16	151
Adams, J.H.K.	6	102	17.00	40	–	–	0	–	–	4
Adnan, M.H.	48	1277	33.60	113*	2	10	5	25.80	2-13	17
Adshead, S.J.	28	312	17.33	77*	–	1	–	–	–	35/13
Afzaal, U.	114	3027	34.39	105	1	24	39	24.00	3- 4	31
Ali, Kabir	88	494	13.72	92	–	1	127	22.78	5-36	17
Ali, Kadeer	20	492	25.89	66	–	4	1	25.00	1- 4	–
Alleyne, D.	30	256	11.13	58	–	1	–	–	–	22/6
Alleyne, M.W.	422	8175	27.52	134*	5	33	407	29.38	5-27	171/1
Ambrose, T.R.	46	1054	25.70	95	–	6	–	–	–	49/5
Anderson, J.M.	53	64	7.11	11	–	–	86	23.51	4-25	8
Andrew, G.M.	21	93	8.45	23	–	–	22	28.81	4-48	7
Anyon, J.E.	1	0	0.00	0	–	–	1	46.00	1-46	1
Averis, J.M.M.	122	310	10.33	23*	–	–	188	23.59	6-23	17
Azhar Mahmood	221	2804	20.46	100*	1	11	231	32.51	6-18	67
Ball, M.C.J.	254	1642	14.03	51	–	1	248	32.02	5-33	123
Bassano, C.W.G.	62	1646	31.05	126*	5	6	–	–	–	12
Batty, G.J.	95	1133	18.27	83*	–	4	74	35.48	4-36	35
Batty, J.N.	113	1120	17.23	66	–	5	–	–	–	116/16
Bell, I.R.	66	2019	35.42	125	1	17	20	36.65	5-41	21
Benham, C.C.	1	0	0.00	0	–	–	–	–	–	–
Benkenstein, D.M.	159	3333	30.86	107*	1	14	44	24.15	4-23	52
Benning, J.G.E.	15	275	19.64	71	–	2	13	24.23	4-43	5
Betts, M.M.	85	344	9.82	21	–	–	104	28.50	4-15	15
Bicknell, D.J.	232	7430	37.71	135*	10	51	3	27.33	1-11	55
Bicknell, M.P.	329	1546	15.61	66*	–	2	421	25.29	7-30	76
Bishop, J.E.	23	58	5.80	16*	–	–	26	28.61	3-33	4
Blackwell, I.D.	160	3330	25.03	111	1	20	116	34.64	4-24	40
Blain, J.A.R.	38	108	13.50	29	–	–	56	25.26	5-24	9
Blakey, R.J.	385	7661	31.14	130*	3	37	–	–	–	375/61
Blignaut, A.M.	72	798	17.34	63*	–	5	61	43.21	4-43	16
Bopara, R.S.	22	347	21.68	55	–	1	12	24.08	2-10	4
Botha, A.G.	56	520	17.33	60*	–	1	49	29.12	3-16	22
Breese, G.R.	43	513	19.00	52*	–	1	38	32.47	3-24	12
Bresnan, T.T.	60	533	20.50	61	–	1	55	33.36	3-29	15
Bridge, G.D.	47	322	15.33	50*	–	1	54	26.94	4-20	8
Brignull, D.S.	13	31	7.75	9*	–	–	16	28.00	3-40	7

L-O	M	Runs	Avge	HS	100	50	Wkts	Avge	Best	Ct/St
Brophy, G.L.	52	803	24.33	57*	–	4	–	–	–	47/11
Brown, A.D.	319	9221	31.47	268	16	40	11	35.54	3-39	105
Brown, D.R.	263	4235	23.26	108	1	21	315	26.18	5-31	66
Brown, J.F.	96	84	5.60	16	–	–	93	35.22	5-19	24
Brown, M.J.	5	78	15.60	35	–	–	–	–	–	2
Bruce, J.T.A.	4	6	6.00	4*	–	–	4	25.00	3-45	–
Bryant, J.D.C.	81	1905	28.43	105*	1	13	–	–	–	14
Burns, M.	213	4632	25.87	115*	2	31	58	30.50	4-39	98/15
Burrows, T.G.	1	1	1.00	1	–	–	–	–	–	1
Butcher, M.A.	155	3079	27.24	104	1	17	49	45.10	3-23	48
Caddick, A.R.	232	740	10.42	39	–	–	301	26.41	6-30	34
Carberry, M.A.	35	596	18.62	79	–	4	1	41.00	1-21	13
Carter, N.M.	81	847	15.40	75	–	1	106	26.87	5-31	11
Chandana, U.D.U.	206	2677	20.12	108	1	9	239	26.45	5-22	118
Chapple, G.	218	1390	15.97	81*	–	6	244	29.22	6-18	52
Cherry, D.D.	2	28	14.00	24	–	–	0	–	–	1
Chilton, M.J.	111	2821	30.66	115	4	15	40	24.07	5-26	36
Clarke, A.J.	41	63	5.72	18	–	–	53	24.41	4-28	9
Clarke, R.	66	1047	20.52	98*	–	5	42	38.54	4-50	30
Cleary, M.F.	33	212	16.30	70	–	1	33	35.84	4-55	9
Clinton, R.S.	13	153	21.85	56	–	1	0	–	–	2
Clough, G.D.	58	418	20.90	42*	–	–	51	36.39	4-32	19
Coetzer, K.J.	6	70	14.00	30	–	–	–	–	–	3
Collingwood, P.D.	198	4929	31.59	118*	3	28	105	34.81	4-31	96
Compton, N.R.D.	15	214	23.77	86*	–	1	0	–	–	2
Cook, A.N.	10	97	12.12	27	–	–	–	–	–	5
Cook, S.J.	108	898	16.32	67*	–	2	130	28.30	6-37	14
Cork, D.G.	243	3499	21.20	93	–	19	302	27.61	6-21	95
Cosker, D.A.	119	283	8.08	27*	–	–	126	32.21	5-54	41
Coverdale, P.S.	3	33	11.00	19	–	–	1	48.00	1-21	2
Cowan, A.P.	146	1028	14.27	45	–	–	177	27.94	5-14	49
Crawley, J.P.	252	6959	31.48	114	6	45	0	–	–	72/4
Croft, R.D.B.	343	5528	24.13	143	4	27	360	31.77	6-20	83
Croft, S.J.	2	11	11.00	7	–	1	1	34.00	1-27	–
Crook, S.P.	9	58	9.66	21	–	–	5	61.60	2-62	3
Cross, G.D.	2	23	11.50	21	–	–	–	–	–	4/1
Cusden, S.M.J.	5	5	2.50	3	–	–	3	53.66	1-29	–
Dagnall, C.E.	52	185	10.88	28	–	–	69	23.37	4-34	6
Dalrymple, J.W.M.	53	901	26.50	107	2	2	42	30.69	4-14	21
Danish Kaneria	69	81	4.50	15	–	–	106	23.58	5-24	14
Davies, A.M.	60	163	7.76	31*	–	–	59	29.32	4-13	9
Davies, A.P.	68	130	11.81	24	–	–	103	23.86	5-19	8
Davies, S.M.	3	25	25.00	13	–	–	–	–	–	–
Davis, M.J.G.	150	895	16.88	37	–	–	135	37.35	4-14	34
Dawood, I.	36	531	21.24	60	–	3	–	–	–	33/9
Dawson, R.K.J.	67	262	7.93	41	–	–	72	25.93	4-13	24
Dean, K.J.	114	228	8.76	16*	–	–	127	30.22	5-32	20
De Bruyn, Z.	63	1523	33.84	113*	2	7	46	26.78	5-44	13
DeFreitas, P.A.J.	479	5181	18.56	90	–	13	539	27.92	5-13	101
Denly, J.L.	1	11	11.00	11	–	–	–	–	–	–
Dennington, M.J.	13	82	11.71	26*	–	–	6	77.33	3-53	3
Di Venuto, M.J.	198	5940	33.18	173*	8	32	5	36.20	1-10	74
Doshi, N.D.	20	83	13.83	38*	–	–	8	77.87	1-12	3
Durston, W.J.	13	230	25.55	51*	–	2	3	69.00	1-32	1
Ealham, M.A.	358	5759	25.03	112	1	25	401	27.38	6-53	93
Elliott, M.T.G.	115	4256	44.33	156	12	23	0	–	–	45
Ervine, S.M.	69	1313	27.93	100	1	7	75	33.28	5-56	9
Ferley, R.S.	14	163	20.37	42	–	–	18	26.66	3-59	4
Ferraby, N.J.	2	1	0.50	1	–	–	0	–	–	–

L-O	M	Runs	Avge	HS	100	50	Wkts	Avge	Best	Ct/St
Fisher, I.D.	40	105	7.00	23	–	–	46	23.54	3-18	12
Fleming, S.P.	343	10105	34.25	139*	14	59	2	15.50	1- 3	163
Flintoff, A.	207	5098	30.71	143	6	28	185	22.49	4-11	82
Flower, A.	351	11581	38.34	145	11	91	1	103.00	1-21	247/48
Flower, G.W.	291	8675	33.75	148*	11	53	152	36.50	4-32	116
Foster, J.S.	68	799	20.48	56*	–	2	–	–	–	90/16
France, B.J.	2	21	10.50	13	–	–	–	–	–	–
Francis, J.D.	41	1163	35.24	103*	1	8	–	–	–	8
Francis, S.R.G.	55	210	12.35	33*	–	–	58	35.51	8-66	12
Franks, P.J.	120	1344	21.67	84*	–	4	154	26.32	6-27	20
Friend, T.J.	79	962	16.30	91	–	3	75	36.21	4-37	25
Frost, T.	55	297	15.63	47	–	–	–	–	–	47/13
Fulton, D.P.	97	1750	20.58	82	–	6	0	–	–	45
Gale, A.W.	14	266	20.46	70*	–	1	–	–	–	6
Gallian, J.E.R.	199	5676	31.53	134	8	34	55	32.87	5-15	68
Gazzard, C.M.	27	677	27.08	157	1	3	–	–	–	24/1
Gibson, O.D.	164	2201	21.57	102*	1	4	234	24.71	5-19	44
Gidman, A.P.R.	50	941	25.43	73	–	3	14	52.85	3-26	20
Giles, A.F.	201	1945	21.14	107	1	5	250	24.38	5-21	64
Goodwin, M.W.	229	7004	35.02	167	10	44	7	43.71	1- 9	71
Gough, D.	346	1725	12.68	72*	–	1	488	24.46	7-27	59
Grant, R.N.	2	26	13.00	21	–	–	1	54.00	1-26	–
Gray, A.K.D.	31	130	10.83	30*	–	–	25	33.72	4-34	8
Grayson, A.P.	246	3426	20.39	82*	–	11	206	33.16	4-25	68
Greenidge, C.G.	49	86	6.14	20	–	–	53	36.66	3-22	14
Guy, S.M.	9	50	10.00	29	–	–	–	–	–	11/3
Habib, A.	155	2928	26.61	111	1	12	2	29.00	2- 5	52
Hall, A.J.	161	3313	31.55	129*	3	18	158	28.43	4-26	42
Hamblin, J.R.C.	48	656	16.82	61	–	2	28	32.39	4-29	14
Hamilton, G.M.	119	1680	25.84	76	–	8	128	25.11	5-16	21
Hancock, T.H.C.	209	4145	22.40	135	2	18	47	24.82	6-58	67
Harbhajan Singh	117	595	11.90	46	–	–	151	27.72	5-43	41
Hardinges, M.A.	31	281	12.21	65	–	1	23	39.39	4-19	11
Harmison, S.J.	75	83	5.18	13*	–	–	89	32.01	4-22	12
Harris, A.J.	114	150	6.25	16*	–	–	143	29.97	5-35	26
Harrison, D.S.	29	156	13.00	37*	–	–	26	37.80	5-26	3
Harvey, I.J.	256	4701	23.98	96	–	21	399	20.85	5-19	71
Havell, P.M.R.	5	8	2.66	4	–	–	3	38.66	3-28	–
Hayward, M.	118	169	9.94	19*	–	–	157	27.91	5-37	23
Hegg, W.K.	392	3207	20.42	81	–	5	–	–	–	447/57
Hemp, D.L.	211	4207	25.65	121	5	19	11	16.18	4-32	79
Henderson, C.W.	146	560	17.50	32	–	–	191	24.31	6-29	37
Hewson, D.R.	72	1186	20.80	69	–	5	22	28.27	4-25	19
Hick, G.A.	590	20437	41.79	172*	39	132	225	29.55	5-19	265
Hildreth, J.C.	24	508	24.19	85	–	2	1	50.00	1-44	10
Hodd, A.J.	2	4	2.00	3	–	–	–	–	–	3
Hodge, B.J.	136	4516	38.27	164	9	23	30	34.60	5-28	56
Hodgkinson, R.	1	–	–	–	–	–	2	18.00	2-36	–
Hogg, K.W.	50	247	14.52	37*	–	–	54	27.51	4-20	10
Hoggard, M.J.	107	54	3.37	7*	–	–	158	22.70	5-28	12
Hopkinson, C.D.	28	349	16.61	67*	–	1	12	39.75	3-19	17
Horton, P.J.	6	95	23.75	42	–	–	–	–	–	–
Huggins, T.B.	5	30	7.50	16	–	–	–	–	–	–
Hughes, J.	5	95	19.00	51	–	1	–	–	–	1
Hunter, I.D.	49	219	8.42	39	–	–	57	29.91	4-29	12
Hussey, D.J.	34	941	39.20	118*	2	2	9	38.88	3-48	13
Hussey, M.E.K.	159	5640	44.76	123	9	42	16	32.87	3-52	78
Hutchison, P.M.	52	97	8.81	20	–	–	69	21.84	4-29	8
Hutton, B.L.	91	1286	20.74	77	–	6	38	31.76	5-45	40

L-O	M	Runs	Avge	HS	100	50	Wkts	Avge	Best	Ct/St
Irani, R.C.	279	6510	30.00	158*	5	37	309	25.22	5-26	69
Jaques, P.A.	44	1706	42.65	117	3	13	–	–	–	9
Jayasuriya, S.T.	382	11043	31.46	189	19	61	313	34.48	6-29	117
Jefferson, W.I.	52	1831	38.14	132	4	10	–	–	–	25
Johnson, R.L.	165	1034	12.30	53	–	1	183	31.96	5-50	18
Jones, G.O.	50	713	20.37	74*	–	2	–	–	–	58/8
Jones, P.S.	129	382	11.93	27	–	–	184	27.86	6-56	25
Jones, S.P.	10	26	13.00	12*	–	–	4	105.75	1-34	1
Joseph, R.H.	6	6	–	3*	–	–	7	28.14	2-30	–
Joyce, E.C.	81	2146	34.06	100*	1	15	2	63.50	2-10	27
Kasprowicz, M.S.	193	931	14.54	40	–	–	257	25.99	5-45	40
Katich, S.M.	128	4111	39.15	136*	6	30	24	30.37	3-21	66
Keedy, G.	21	19	6.33	10*	–	–	22	32.00	5-30	1
Keegan, C.B.	68	492	16.40	50	–	1	98	25.56	5-17	15
Kendall, W.S.	130	2113	21.78	110*	1	7	5	47.40	2-48	59
Kenway, D.A.	102	2467	26.52	120*	2	14	1	16.00	1-16	56/7
Key, R.W.T.	111	2912	29.71	114	1	20	–	–	–	16
Khalid, S.A.	10	13	6.50	9*	–	–	4	71.00	2-40	1
Khan, A.	30	218	12.82	65*	–	1	31	33.29	4-26	9
Killeen, N.	165	567	9.61	32	–	–	232	23.39	6-31	29
King, R.E.	2	2	1.00	2	–	–	2	33.00	2-39	1
Kirby, S.P.	29	38	4.22	15	–	–	24	44.20	3-27	6
Kirtley, R.J.	161	334	10.12	30*	–	–	229	23.93	5-33	46
Knight, N.V.	377	12010	37.76	151	24	64	2	44.50	1-14	163
Kruis, G.J.	64	258	9.96	28*	–	–	81	29.96	4-26	17
Lamb, G.A.	15	287	23.91	72*	–	2	1	49.00	1-27	6
Laraman, A.W.	38	321	14.59	50*	–	1	44	27.68	6-42	9
Law, S.G.	341	10300	34.44	163	20	50	90	35.17	5-26	134
Leatherdale, D.A.	311	4862	21.90	80	–	21	170	23.10	5- 9	121
Lewis, J.	127	445	10.59	33*	–	–	157	28.19	5-23	23
Lewis, J.J.B.	220	4350	27.88	102	1	20	0	–	–	36
Lewry, J.D.	72	203	7.00	16*	–	–	92	27.83	4-29	13
Logan, R.J.	49	171	10.05	24	–	–	57	33.87	5-24	14
Loudon, A.G.R.	19	332	20.75	53	–	3	9	22.77	4-48	5
Louw, J.	47	650	19.69	72	–	3	76	21.59	5-27	5
Love, M.L.	133	3823	32.67	127*	4	17	0	–	–	56
Loye, M.B.	226	6692	34.67	124*	8	44	–	–	–	56
Lucas, D.S.	30	69	8.62	19*	–	–	41	29.24	4-27	3
Lumb, M.J.	72	1551	25.01	92	–	9	–	–	–	23
Lungley, T.	36	234	13.76	45	–	–	51	23.78	4-28	6
McGrath, A.	195	4749	31.03	109*	3	27	45	32.13	4-41	62
McLean, J.J.	2	0	0.00	0	–	–	–	–	–	1
McLean, N.A.M.	179	1312	13.52	50*	–	1	226	26.80	5-26	32
Maddy, D.L.	259	6174	29.40	151	6	37	153	28.21	4-16	92
Mahmood, S.I.	32	105	9.54	29	–	–	55	22.36	4-39	1
Malik, M.N.	33	44	8.80	11	–	–	29	38.13	4-42	5
Martin-Jenkins, R.S.C.	145	1280	13.33	68*	–	3	167	26.85	4-22	31
Mascarenhas, A.D.	151	2398	21.80	79	–	16	195	22.91	5-27	40
Mason, M.S.	53	129	7.58	25	–	–	67	26.77	4-34	10
Masters, D.D.	52	198	9.90	27	–	–	39	45.33	5-20	5
Maunders, J.K.	12	165	13.75	49	–	–	0	–	–	1
Maynard, M.P.	433	13506	36.80	151*	16	81	3	94.66	1-13	183/5
Middlebrook, J.D.	75	528	17.03	47	–	–	56	34.73	4-33	23
Miller, D.J.	1	1	1.00	1	–	–	0	–	–	–
Mohammad Akram	106	213	8.19	33	–	–	114	31.60	4-19	21
Mongia, D.	128	3434	34.34	159*	8	12	42	28.61	4-31	57
Montgomerie, R.R.	163	5013	35.30	129*	4	35	0	–	–	40
Moore, S.C.	20	574	33.76	93*	–	5	1	20.00	1- 1	4
Morgan, E.J.G.	3	13	–	13*	–	–	0	–	–	2

176

L-O	M	Runs	Avge	HS	100	50	Wkts	Avge	Best	Ct/St
Moss, J.	49	1010	25.89	104	1	7	41	33.48	5-47	15
Muchall, G.J.	37	830	28.62	87	–	4	1	137.00	1-15	11
Mullally, A.D.	304	529	6.96	38	–	–	359	27.67	6-38	44
Munday, M.K.	1	–	–	–	–	–	1	39.00	1-30	–
Muralitharan, M.	304	559	6.73	19	–	–	468	21.23	7-30	115
Murtagh, T.J.	32	180	13.84	28	–	–	37	35.72	4-31	6
Mushtaq Ahmed	338	1495	11.41	41	–	–	409	28.58	7-24	56
Mustard, P.	24	249	13.10	41	–	–	–	–	–	24/4
Nambiar, A.P.	1	0	0.00	0	–	–	–	–	–	–
Napier, G.R.	107	1329	17.72	79	–	7	107	21.56	6-29	28
Nash, D.C.	112	1321	20.64	67	–	5	–	–	–	88/15
Naved-ul-Hasan	49	774	26.68	70*	–	4	67	28.82	4-25	23
New, T.J.	3	9	3.00	6	–	–	–	–	–	–
Newby, O.J.	4	5	5.00	3*	–	–	5	40.20	2-37	1
Newman, S.A.	26	516	20.64	106	1	1	–	–	–	3
Nicholson, M.J.	26	125	11.36	25	–	–	30	21.76	3-34	7
Nixon, P.A.	305	4996	23.79	101	1	21	0	–	–	324/70
Noffke, A.A.	55	257	14.27	58	–	1	60	34.48	4-32	14
Noon, W.M.	121	778	13.89	46	–	–	–	–	–	89/28
O'Brien, N.J.	15	114	16.28	27*	–	–	–	–	–	11/4
Onions, G.	13	10	10.00	5	–	–	12	29.91	2-24	1
Ormond, J.	109	317	9.05	18*	–	–	138	25.68	4-12	23
Ostler, D.P.	275	7238	32.16	134*	3	50	1	14.00	1- 4	98
Palladino, A.P.	8	17	5.66	16	–	–	12	24.25	3-32	1
Panesar, M.S.	4	23	–	16*	–	–	6	18.00	5-20	1
Parsons, K.A.	205	4253	29.13	121	2	23	123	35.14	5-39	82
Parsons, M.	8	1	0.25	1*	–	–	8	41.50	3-70	2
Patel, M.M.	78	255	9.80	27*	–	–	78	31.98	3-22	23
Patel, S.R.	12	134	19.14	44	–	–	7	24.85	2-14	1
Pattison, I.	16	109	9.90	48*	–	–	8	49.75	3-45	7
Pearson, J.A.	3	7	2.33	7	–	–	1	29.00	1-29	1
Peng, N.	81	1962	25.81	121	3	9	–	–	–	18
Penney, T.L.	270	4788	29.01	90	–	19	1	21.00	1- 8	101/2
Peploe, C.T.	2	–	–	–	–	–	1	51.00	1-32	–
Peters, S.D.	113	1810	18.46	82	–	9	–	–	–	29
Pettini, M.L.	34	618	22.88	92*	–	4	–	–	–	8
Phillips, B.J.	60	417	15.44	44*	–	–	64	28.25	4-25	17
Phillips, T.J.	7	20	5.00	6	–	–	6	34.83	2-36	2
Pietersen, C.	17	38	12.66	14*	–	–	18	37.61	4-32	3
Pietersen, K.P.	90	2687	40.71	147	5	14	33	50.36	3-14	41
Pipe, D.J.	19	303	23.30	56	–	2	–	–	–	19/5
Piper, K.J.	236	970	14.26	38*	–	–	–	–	–	251/53
Plunkett, L.E.	92	1153	21	–	–	–	14	30.14	3-35	3
Pothas, N.	156	2911	36.84	101	1	16	–	–	–	145/31
Powell, M.J. (Gm)	139	3170	27.56	91*	–	16	1	26.00	1-26	46
Powell, M.J. (Wa)	92	1673	25.34	101*	1	5	25	29.08	5-40	43
Pratt, A.	82	988	20.58	86	–	4	–	–	–	89/24
Pratt, G.J.	63	1515	32.93	101*	1	11	–	–	–	28
Pretorius, D.	51	38	2.53	7*	–	–	85	21.89	4-31	8
Price, R.W.	57	227	10.31	35	–	–	46	41.45	4-29	8
Prior, M.J.	75	1197	19.95	119	1	6	–	–	–	49/8
Prittipaul, L.R.	59	538	13.12	61	–	1	23	38.69	3-11	18
Pyrah, R.M.	6	150	25.00	42	–	–	9	12.77	5-50	2
Ramprakash, M.R.	339	10753	38.96	147*	11	71	45	27.88	5-38	115
Read, C.M.W.	175	2619	25.67	119*	1	5	–	–	–	189/44
Rees, G.P.	2	17	8.60	15	–	–	–	–	–	–
Rees, T.M.	2	7	7.00	7*	–	–	–	–	–	2
Richardson, A.	44	66	7.33	18	–	–	42	34.14	5-35	10
Roberts, T.W.	39	956	25.15	131	2	4	0	–	–	9

L-O	M	Runs	Avge	HS	100	50	Wkts	Avge	Best	Ct/St
Robinson, D.D.J.	173	3940	26.26	137*	4	19	1	26.00	1- 7	44
Rudge, W.D.	2	4	4.00	3	–	–	0	–	–	–
Sadler, J.L.	32	451	17.34	88	–	1	–	–	–	4
Saggers, M.J.	92	243	9.00	34*	–	–	130	24.44	5-22	21
Sales, D.J.G.	168	4330	31.83	133*	2	30	0	–	–	74
Salisbury, I.D.K.	236	1470	13.48	59*	–	1	233	32.59	5-30	80
Sampson, P.J.	21	35	5.00	16	–	–	21	36.09	3-42	5
Sayers, J.J.	2	69	34.50	62	–	1	–	–	–	–
Scott, B.J.M.	22	93	11.62	42	–	–	–	–	–	24/9
Shafayat, B.M.	44	677	17.35	66	–	1	9	34.55	4-35	16/1
Shah, O.A.	183	4594	30.22	134	7	22	8	31.12	2- 2	61
Shantry, A.J.	3	25	8.33	15	–	–	7	10.71	5-37	1
Shaw, A.D.	85	759	15.48	48	–	–	–	–	–	59/17
Sheikh, M.A.	91	383	11.96	50*	–	1	95	29.28	4-17	14
Sheriyar, A.	116	148	8.70	19	–	–	127	28.67	4-18	7
Shoaib Akhtar	149	607	12.38	56	–	1	239	22.70	6-16	26
Shreck, C.E.	9	14	7.00	9	–	–	18	21.94	5-19	3
Sidebottom, R.J.	113	262	10.91	30*	–	–	111	31.86	6-40	23
Sillence, R.J.	7	102	17.00	82	–	1	10	13.60	4-35	1
Silverwood, C.E.W.	180	954	14.45	61	–	4	241	23.60	5-28	27
Singh, A.	104	2743	27.70	123	1	19	–	–	–	26
Smith, B.F.	316	8012	30.34	115	2	52	2	52.50	1- 2	104
Smith, E.T.	79	2158	30.82	122	2	15	–	–	–	12
Smith, G.C.	101	3802	40.88	117*	3	30	31	29.54	3-35	43
Smith, G.J.	116	159	7.22	17*	–	–	170	23.38	5-11	17
Smith, W.R.	6	41	8.20	16	–	–	–	–	–	1
Snape, J.N.	230	3209	23.59	104*	1	11	186	29.39	5-32	84
Snell, S.D.	1	3	3.00	3	–	–	–	–	–	1
Solanki, V.S.	237	5709	29.12	164*	9	30	13	37.15	2- 5	88
Spearman, C.M.	215	6165	29.78	153	6	39	0	–	–	70
Spendlove, B.L.	28	402	15.46	58	–	2	–	–	–	9
Stevens, D.I.	126	2946	26.78	133	3	17	12	35.75	2-15	55
Stiff, D.A.	1	–	–	–	–	–	1	27.00	1-27	–
Strauss, A.J.	113	3034	30.34	127	3	22	–	–	–	18
Streak, H.H.	260	3584	25.59	90*	–	13	326	29.10	5-32	67
Stubbings, S.D.	70	1174	19.90	98*	–	4	–	–	–	8
Styris, S.B.	167	3473	29.68	141	3	21	178	28.93	6-25	65
Suppiah, A.V.	10	215	21.50	70	–	1	5	38.60	2-36	3
Sutcliffe, I.J.	111	3055	31.17	105*	4	19	–	–	–	25
Sutton, L.D.	87	1095	17.95	83	–	4	–	–	–	85/7
Swann, G.P.	126	1924	21.14	83	–	11	126	28.06	5-35	38
Taylor, B.V.	89	150	6.81	21*	–	–	123	23.47	5-28	16
Taylor, C.G.	90	1264	19.15	93	–	4	3	9.66	2- 5	30/1
Taylor, C.R.	4	57	19.00	28	–	–	–	–	–	–
Ten Doeschate, R.N.	2	–	–	–	–	–	2	53.50	1-39	–
Thomas, I.J.	40	1008	28.00	93	–	6	1	60.00	1-27	13
Thomas, S.D.	133	1197	15.96	71*	–	1	168	26.64	7-16	25
Thornicroft, N.D.	8	8	–	8*	–	–	11	24.63	5-42	1
Thorp, C.D.	10	16	16.00	12	–	–	14	30.14	4-46	2
Thorpe, G.P.	351	10650	39.73	145*	9	78	16	40.56	3-21	163
Tomlinson, J.A.	14	14	2.80	6	–	–	12	38.25	2-15	1
Tredwell, J.C.	63	590	15.12	71	–	2	52	34.21	3- 7	25
Tremlett, C.T.	57	261	11.34	38*	–	–	81	22.17	4-25	10
Trescothick, M.E.	237	7602	37.08	137	18	36	57	26.91	4-50	91
Trott, I.J.L.	55	1456	33.86	108*	1	10	5	23.80	2-32	19
Troughton, J.O.	56	1229	28.58	115*	2	5	14	19.92	4-23	15
Tudor, A.J.	66	414	12.93	56	–	1	97	22.90	4-26	18
Turk, N.R.K.	3	64	21.33	36	–	–	0	–	–	–
Turner, R.J.	227	3328	26.20	70	–	9	–	–	–	234/34

L-O	M	Runs	Avge	HS	100	50	Wkts	Avge	Best	Ct/St
Udal, S.D.	318	2192	15.43	78	–	8	355	30.54	5-43	103
Vaas, W.P.U.C.J.	279	1959	15.79	62*	–	3	359	25.70	8-19	58
Van Jaarsveld, M.	141	4455	40.87	123	6	29	8	41.37	1- 0	79
Vaughan, M.P.	234	5708	27.44	125*	2	33	69	31.24	4-22	72
Wagh, M A	68	1449	24.55	100*	1	8	25	34.48	4-35	12
Walker, M.J.	199	4480	28.35	117	3	25	23	26.21	4-24	51
Walker, N.G.E.	9	90	12.85	43	–	–	5	28.80	3-49	4
Wallace, M.A.	66	486	12.78	39	–	–	–	–	–	69/15
Ward, I.J.	148	3678	28.73	136	2	23	2	90.50	2-27	30
Warne, S.K.	266	1595	12.08	55	–	1	406	24.92	5-33	105
Warren, N.A.	4	2	1.00	2	–	–	3	50.00	3-34	2
Warren, R.J.	168	3256	25.24	100*	1	15	–	–	–	131/11
Watkins, R.E.	1	0	0.00	0	–	–	0	–	–	–
Weekes, P.N.	293	6467	29.39	143*	3	38	310	28.76	4-17	128
Welch, G.	196	2079	18.56	82	–	5	185	33.24	6-31	26
Weston, W.P.C.	169	3491	24.75	134	4	15	1	2.00	1- 2	39
Westwood, I.J.	4	78	19.50	55	–	1	2	69.50	1-28	1
Wharf, A.G.	98	737	15.04	72	–	1	109	30.99	6- 5	24
Whelan, C.D.	1	6	6.00	6	–	–	0	–	–	–
White, A.R.	5	69	23.00	44	–	–	3	45.66	3-43	1
White, C.	312	6203	26.06	148	3	24	317	25.73	5-19	91
White, R.A.	16	262	16.37	101	1	–	2	23.00	2-18	4
Wigley, D.H.	6	3	1.00	2	–	–	7	36.00	4-37	–
Windows, M.G.N.	202	4496	27.41	117	3	21	0	–	–	69
Wood, M.J. (Sm)	40	786	23.11	88*	–	5	–	–	–	8
Wood, M.J. (Y)	114	2594	28.50	160	4	12	3	22.00	3-45	41
Wright, C.J.C.	3	0	0.00	0	–	–	1	104.00	1-34	–
Wright, D.G.	54	484	18.61	55	–	2	62	29.91	4-23	14
Wright, L.J.	21	187	14.38	25*	–	–	12	48.83	4-12	2
Yardy, M.H.	60	881	19.57	88*	–	4	25	44.00	3-30	23

LIMITED-OVERS INTERNATIONALS
CAREER RECORDS

These records, complete to 14 February 2005, include all players registered for county cricket in 2005 at the time of going to press, plus those who have appeared in LOI matches since 12 July 2003 (the 2003 NatWest Series final). For reasons outlined in the Preface they exclude the Tsunami Appeal match between a World XI and an Asian XI at Melbourne in January 2005 and the NatWest Series match between West Indies and New Zealand at Southampton in 2004 which was abandoned without a ball bowled after the toss.

ENGLAND – BATTING AND FIELDING

	M	I	NO	HS	Runs	Avge	100	50	Ct/St
C.J.Adams	5	4	–	42	71	17.75	–	–	3
Kabir Ali	8	4	1	25	52	17.33	–	–	1
M.W.Alleyne	10	8	1	53	151	21.57	–	1	4
J.M.Anderson	39	13	5	11	41	5.12	–	–	8
G.J.Batty	6	4	1	3	4	1.33	–	–	4
I.R.Bell	8	7	1	75	189	31.50	–	2	2
M.P.Bicknell	7	6	2	31*	96	24.00	–	–	2
I.D.Blackwell	23	19	1	82	291	16.16	–	1	5
R.J.Blakey	3	2	–	25	25	12.50	–	–	2/1
A.D.Brown	16	16	–	118	354	22.12	1	1	6
D.R.Brown	9	8	4	21	99	24.75	–	–	1
A.R.Caddick	54	38	18	36	249	12.45	–	–	9
R.Clarke	17	10	–	37	99	9.90	–	–	11
P.D.Collingwood	70	63	16	100	1446	30.76	1	7	35

179

ENGLAND – BATTING AND FIELDING (continued)

	M	I	NO	HS	Runs	Avge	100	50	Ct/St
D.G.Cork	32	21	3	31*	180	10.00	–	–	6
J.P.Crawley	13	12	1	73	235	21.36	–	2	1/1
R.D.B.Croft	50	36	12	32	345	14.37	–	–	11
P.A.J.DeFreitas	103	66	23	67	690	16.04	–	1	26
M.A.Ealham	64	45	4	45	716	17.46	–	–	9
A.Flintoff	80	71	11	123	2111	35.18	3	13	28
J.S.Foster	11	6	3	13	41	13.66	–	–	13/7
P.J.Franks	1	1	–	4	4	4.00	–	–	1
A.F.Giles	54	31	11	41	334	16.70	–	–	20
D.Gough	147	82	36	45	527	11.45	–	–	24
A.P.Grayson	2	2	–	6	6	3.00	–	–	1
S.J.Harmison	25	11	6	13*	37	7.40	–	–	6
G.A.Hick	120	118	15	126*	3846	37.33	5	27	64
M.J.Hoggard	24	5	2	5	10	3.33	–	–	3
R.C.Irani	31	30	5	53	360	14.40	–	1	6
R.L.Johnson	10	4	1	10	16	5.33	–	–	4
G.O.Jones	23	19	4	80	403	26.86	–	2	29/1
S.P.Jones	2	–	–	–	–	–	–	–	–
R.W.T.Key	5	5	–	19	54	10.80	–	–	1
R.J.Kirtley	11	2	–	1	2	1.00	–	–	5
N.V.Knight	100	100	10	125*	3637	40.41	5	25	44
A.McGrath	14	12	2	52	166	16.60	–	1	4
D.L.Maddy	8	6	–	53	113	18.83	–	1	1
S.I.Mahmood	1	1	–	1	1	1.00	–	–	–
M.P.Maynard	14	12	1	41	156	14.18	–	–	4
A.D.Mullally	50	25	10	20	86	5.73	–	–	8
K.P.Pietersen	11	9	5	116	558	139.50	3	2	6
M.J.Prior	1	1	–	35	35	35.00	–	–	1
M.R.Ramprakash	18	18	4	51	376	26.85	–	1	8
C.M.W.Read	28	17	6	30*	239	21.72	–	–	36/2
I.D.K.Salisbury	4	2	1	5	7	7.00	–	–	1
O.A.Shah	15	15	2	62	283	21.76	–	2	6
R.J.Sidebottom	2	1	1	2*	2	–	–	–	–
C.E.W.Silverwood	7	4	–	12	17	4.25	–	–	4
J.N.Snape	10	7	3	38	118	29.50	–	–	5
V.S.Solanki	35	33	2	106	812	26.19	2	4	9
A.J.Strauss	29	28	5	100	762	33.13	1	4	7
G.P.Swann	1	–	–	–	–	–	–	–	–
G.P.Thorpe	82	77	13	89	2380	37.18	–	21	42
M.E.Trescothick	99	98	3	137	3469	36.51	8	19	41
J.O.Troughton	6	5	1	20	36	9.00	–	–	1
A.J.Tudor	3	2	1	6	9	9.00	–	–	1
S.D.Udal	10	6	4	11*	35	17.50	–	–	1
M.P.Vaughan	66	64	8	90*	1598	28.53	–	13	20
A.G.Wharf	13	5	3	9	19	9.50	–	–	1
C.White	51	41	5	57*	568	15.77	–	1	12

ENGLAND – BOWLING

	O	M	R	W	Avge	Best	4wI	R/Over
Kabir Ali	62.3	3	340	13	26.15	3-44	–	5.44
M.W.Alleyne	61	1	280	10	28.00	3-27	–	4.59
J.M.Anderson	317.1	31	1504	59	25.49	4-25	4	4.74
G.J.Batty	52	1	253	4	63.25	2-40	–	4.86
I.R.Bell	3.4	1	9	3	3.00	3-9	–	2.45
M.P.Bicknell	68.5	3	347	13	26.69	3-55	–	5.04
I.D.Blackwell	108	3	485	15	32.33	3-26	–	4.49
A.D.Brown	1	0	5	0	–	–	–	5.00
D.R.Brown	54	3	305	7	43.57	2-28	–	5.64
A.R.Caddick	489.3	66	1965	69	28.47	4-19	3	4.01
R.Clarke	67.2	3	351	10	35.10	2-28	–	5.21
P.D.Collingwood	230.3	4	1231	28	43.96	4-38	1	5.34

ENGLAND – BOWLING (continued)

	O	M	R	W	Avge	Best	4wI	R/Over
D.G.Cork	295.2	17	1368	41	33.36	3-27	–	4.63
R.D.B.Croft	411	25	1743	45	38.73	3-51	–	4.24
P.A.J.DeFreitas	952	113	3775	115	32.82	4-35	1	3.96
M.A.Ealham	537.5	32	2197	67	32.79	5-15	3	4.08
A.Flintoff	467.5	38	1966	82	23.97	4-14	3	4.20
P.J.Franks	9	0	48	0	–	–	–	5.33
A.F.Giles	409	15	1769	52	34.01	5-57	1	4.32
D.Gough	1318.1	118	5666	224	25.29	5-44	12	4.29
A.P.Grayson	15	0	60	3	20.00	3-40	–	4.00
S.J.Harmison	213.3	14	1031	33	31.24	4-22	1	4.82
G.A.Hick	206	6	1026	30	34.20	5-33	1	4.98
M.J.Hoggard	200.4	13	1034	32	32.31	5-49	1	5.15
R.C.Irani	213.5	5	989	24	41.20	5-26	2	4.62
R.L.Johnson	67	7	239	11	21.72	3-22	–	3.56
S.P.Jones	16	4	76	3	25.33	2-43	–	4.75
R.J.Kirtley	91.3	4	481	9	53.44	2-33	–	5.25
A.McGrath	38	2	175	4	43.75	1-13	–	4.60
S.I.Mahmood	7	0	56	0	–	–	–	8.00
A.D.Mullally	449.5	48	1728	63	27.42	4-18	2	3.84
K.P.Pietersen	2	0	22	0	–	–	–	11.00
M.R.Ramprakash	22	0	108	4	27.00	3-28	–	4.90
I.D.K.Salisbury	31	1	177	5	35.40	3-41	–	5.70
R.J.Sidebottom	14	0	84	2	42.00	1-42	–	6.00
C.E.W.Silverwood	51	0	244	6	40.66	3-43	–	4.78
J.N.Snape	88.1	2	403	13	31.00	3-43	–	4.57
A.J.Strauss	1	0	3	0	–	–	–	3.00
G.P.Swann	5	0	24	0	–	–	–	4.80
G.P.Thorpe	20	1	97	2	48.50	2-15	–	4.85
M.E.Trescothick	38.4	0	219	4	54.75	2-7	–	5.66
A.J.Tudor	21.1	1	136	4	34.00	2-30	–	6.42
S.D.Udal	95	4	371	8	46.37	2-37	–	3.90
M.P.Vaughan	103.4	2	516	12	43.00	4-22	1	4.97
A.G.Wharf	97.2	10	428	18	23.77	4-24	1	4.39
C.White	394	25	1725	65	26.53	5-21	2	4.37

AUSTRALIA – BATTING AND FIELDING

	M	I	NO	HS	Runs	Avge	100	50	Ct/St
M.G.Bevan	232	196	67	108*	6912	53.58	6	46	69
A.J.Bichel	67	36	13	64	471	20.47	–	1	19
N.W.Bracken	17	1	1	7*	7	–	–	–	5
M.J.Clarke	44	40	10	105*	1353	45.10	2	7	19
M.J.Di Venuto	9	9	–	89	241	26.77	–	2	1
M.T.G.Elliot	1	1	–	1	1	1.00	–	–	–
A.C.Gilchrist	203	197	7	172	6778	35.67	10	39	294/39
J.N.Gillespie	84	36	16	44*	274	13.70	–	–	8
B.J.Haddin	10	9	–	32	158	17.55	–	–	9/3
I.J.Harvey	73	51	11	48*	715	17.87	–	–	17
M.L.Hayden	107	103	11	146	3691	40.11	4	24	41
G.B.Hogg	57	37	17	71*	441	22.05	–	2	16
M.E.K.Hussey	1	1	1	17*	17	–	–	–	1
M.S.Kasprowicz	34	12	9	28*	71	23.66	–	–	8
S.M.Katich	11	9	2	76	172	24.57	–	1	4
S.G.Law	54	51	5	110	1237	26.89	1	7	12
B.Lee	99	43	15	51*	468	16.71	–	1	26
D.S.Lehmann	117	101	22	119	3078	38.96	4	17	26
G.D.McGrath	200	54	29	11	100	4.00	–	–	29
J.P.Maher	26	20	3	95	438	25.76	–	1	18
D.R.Martyn	166	143	44	144*	4126	41.67	5	26	54
R.T.Ponting	217	212	27	145	7606	41.11	15	42	87
A.Symonds	111	85	17	143*	2452	36.05	2	12	44
S.K.Warne	193	106	28	55	1016	13.02	–	1	80

	M	I	NO	HS	Runs	Avge	100	50	Ct/St
S.R.Watson	32	20	9	77*	341	31.00	–	1	10
B.A.Williams	25	6	4	13*	27	13.50	–	–	4

AUSTRALIA – BOWLING

	O	M	R	W	Avge	Best	4wI	R/Over
M.G.Bevan	327.4	4	1655	36	45.97	3-36	–	5.05
A.J.Bichel	542.5	28	2463	78	31.57	7-20	3	4.53
N.W.Bracken	142	18	552	28	19.71	4-29	1	3.88
M.J.Clarke	98.5	1	509	17	29.94	5-35	2	5.15
J.N.Gillespie	754.2	74	3103	130	23.86	5-22	6	4.11
I.J.Harvey	546.3	29	2577	85	30.31	4-16	4	4.71
M.L.Hayden	1	0	18	0	–	–	–	18.00
G.B.Hogg	446.1	17	1998	67	29.82	5-32	2	4.47
M.E.K.Hussey	3	0	15	0	–	–	–	5.00
M.S.Kasprowicz	286.5	19	1274	55	23.16	5-45	3	4.44
S.G.Law	134.3	3	635	12	52.91	2-22	–	4.72
B.Lee	837	64	3955	176	22.47	5-27	10	4.72
D.S.Lehmann	298.5	3	1445	52	27.78	4-7	1	4.83
G.D.McGrath	1749.4	234	6758	305	22.15	7-15	15	3.86
D.R.Martyn	132.2	2	704	12	58.66	2-21	–	5.32
R.T.Ponting	25	0	104	3	34.66	1-12	–	4.16
A.Symonds	619.1	19	3056	80	38.20	4-11	2	4.93
S.K.Warne	1766.4	110	7514	291	25.82	5-33	13	4.25
S.R.Watson	205.2	11	959	21	45.66	3-27	–	4.67
B.A.Williams	200.3	19	814	35	23.25	5-22	3	4.05

SOUTH AFRICA – BATTING AND FIELDING

	M	I	NO	HS	Runs	Avge	100	50	Ct/St
A.M.Bacher	10	10	–	45	187	18.70	–	–	3
D.M.Benkenstein	23	20	3	69	305	17.94	–	1	3
N.Boje	107	67	16	129	1403	27.50	2	4	30
M.V.Boucher	185	131	30	70	2458	24.33	–	15	258/12
A.C.Dawson	19	7	4	23*	69	23.00	–	–	2
A.B.de Villiers	4	4	–	20	47	11.75	–	–	3
H.H.Dippenaar	77	65	10	110*	2322	42.21	1	19	24
J.P.Duminy	5	5	–	22	29	5.80	–	–	2
H.H.Gibbs	163	162	11	153	5276	34.94	15	21	68
A.J.Hall	46	35	7	81	619	22.10	–	2	17
M.Hayward	21	5	1	4	12	3.00	–	–	4
C.W.Henderson	4	–	–	–	–	–	–	–	–
J.H.Kallis	210	201	36	139	7495	45.42	13	51	89
J.M.Kemp	21	13	2	80	276	25.09	–	2	9
L.Klusener	171	137	50	103*	3576	41.10	2	19	35
C.K.Langeveldt	9	2	–	3	5	2.50	–	–	–
J.A.Morkel	3	3	1	23*	40	20.00	–	–	–
A.Nel	29	6	4	3*	8	4.00	–	–	8
M.Ntini	110	26	14	42*	144	12.00	–	–	24
R.J.Peterson	21	8	1	36	91	13.00	–	–	3
S.M.Pollock	228	151	55	75	2336	24.33	–	9	89
N.Pothas	3	1	–	24	24	24.00	–	–	4/1
A.G.Prince	10	10	5	62*	282	56.40	–	1	4
J.A.Rudolph	34	28	5	81	911	39.60	–	5	8
G.C.Smith	63	62	3	115*	2305	39.06	2	15	24
M.van Jaarsveld	11	7	1	45	124	20.66	–	–	4

SOUTH AFRICA – BOWLING

	O	M	R	W	Avge	Best	4wI	R/Over
D.M.Benkenstein	10.5	0	44	4	11.00	3-5	–	4.06
N.Boje	699.5	18	3204	90	35.60	5-21	3	4.57
A.C.Dawson	150.1	11	715	21	34.04	4-49	1	4.76
J.P.Duminy	14	0	62	1	62.00	1-28	–	4.42
A.J.Hall	222.5	12	1003	32	31.34	3-32	–	4.50

SOUTH AFRICA – BOWLING (continued)

	O	M	R	W	Avge	Best	4wI	R/Over
M.Hayward	165.3	5	858	21	40.85	4-31	1	5.18
C.W.Henderson	36.1	2	132	7	18.85	4-17	1	3.64
J.H.Kallis	1274.3	59	6106	192	31.80	5-30	4	4.79
J.M.Kemp	101	5	488	17	28.70	3-20	–	4.83
L.Klusener	1222.4	48	5751	192	29.95	6-49	7	4.70
C.K.Langeveldt	63.2	2	257	13	19.76	4-21	1	4.05
J.A.Morkel	21	0	95	2	47.50	1-33	–	4.52
A.Nel	231	18	1126	35	32.17	4-39	1	4.87
M.Ntini	915	79	3983	170	23.42	5-31	7	4.35
R.J.Peterson	130	1	626	9	69.55	2-26	–	4.81
S.M.Pollock	1988.4	218	7452	313	23.80	6-35	15	3.74
J.A.Rudolph	4	0	26	0	–	–	–	6.50
G.C.Smith	43.2	0	280	4	70.00	1-24	–	6.46
M.van Jaarsveld	5.1	1	18	2	9.00	1-0	–	3.48

WEST INDIES – BATTING AND FIELDING

† Excluding match abandoned without a ball bowled after toss

	M	I	NO	HS	Runs	Avge	100	50	Ct/St
C.S.Baugh	6	6	2	29	68	17.00	–	–	2
T.L.Best	6	3	2	2	4	4.00	–	–	2
I.D.R.Bradshaw	22	9	2	34*	86	12.28	–	–	2
D.J.J.Bravo†	23	15	4	33*	152	13.81	–	–	9
C.O.Browne	38	24	6	36	278	15.44	–	–	53/9
S.Chanderpaul†	166	155	20	150	4945	36,62	3	33	52
P.T.Collins	28	10	5	10*	28	5.60	–	–	8
C.D.Collymore	56	21	9	13*	71	5.91	–	–	9
M.Dillon	108	51	20	21*	227	7.32	–	–	20
F.H.Edwards	4	1	1	4*	4	–	–	–	–
C.H.Gayle†	111	109	6	153*	3972	38.56	9	23	48
O.D.Gibson	15	11	1	52	141	14.10	–	1	3
R.O.Hinds	14	9	3	18*	101	16.83	–	–	2
W.W.Hinds	93	89	7	127*	2551	31.10	5	13	26
R.O.Hurley	9	4	–	6	13	3.25	–	–	5
R.D.Jacobs†	146	112	32	80*	1865	23.31	–	9	159/28
S.C.Joseph	9	7	1	28	87	14.50	–	–	3
R.D.King	50	23	14	12*	65	7.22	–	–	4
B.C.Lara†	249	243	26	169	9228	42.52	19	56	104
J.J.C.Lawson†	10	3	1	4	7	3.50	–	–	–
N.A.M.McLean	45	34	8	50*	431	12.07	–	1	7
X.M.Marshall	1	1	–	5	5	5.00	–	–	–
R.L.Powell†	104	96	16	124	2070	25.87	1	8	43
R.Rampaul	17	4	1	24	35	11.66	–	–	2
D.J.G.Sammy†	1	–	–	–	–	–	–	–	3
M.N.Samuels	57	54	8	108*	1448	31.47	1	10	17
R.R.Sarwan†	78	74	20	104*	2577	47.72	2	15	23
D.R.Smith†	19	15	1	62*	262	18.71	–	1	6
D.S.Smith†	6	6	1	44	129	25.80	–	1	3

WEST INDIES – BOWLING

	O	M	R	W	Avge	Best	4wI	R/Over
T.L.Best	43.2	2	204	10	20.40	4-35	1	4.70
I.D.R.Bradshaw	184	21	763	27	28.25	3-15	–	4.14
D.J.J.Bravo	158	6	818	27	30.29	3-26	–	5.17
S.Chanderpaul	119	0	617	14	44.07	3-18	–	5.18
P.T.Collins	243.5	18	1106	38	29.10	5-43	1	4.53
C.D.Collymore	457.1	28	1990	59	33.72	5-51	2	4.35
M.Dillon	913.2	67	4217	130	32.43	5-29	6	4.61
F.H.Edwards	30.5	1	125	12	10.41	6-22	1	4.05
C.H.Gayle	608.2	24	2834	95	29.83	5-46	4	4.65
O.D.Gibson	123.1	8	621	34	18.26	5-40	4	5.04
R.O.Hinds	68.1	0	353	6	58.83	2-19	–	5.17

WEST INDIES – BOWLING (continued)

LOI	O	M	R	W	Avge	Best	4wI	R/Over
W.W.Hinds	111.5	3	575	22	26.13	3-24	–	5.14
R.O.Hurley	63	2	313	5	62.60	1-25	–	4.96
R.D.King	433.5	41	1807	76	23.77	4-25	2	4.16
B.C.Lara	8.1	0	61	4	15.25	2-5	–	7.46
J.J.C.Lawson	74	4	377	15	25.13	4-57	1	5.09
N.A.M.McLean	353.2	18	1729	46	37.59	3-21	–	4.89
R.L.Powell	77.5	3	481	11	43.72	2-5	–	6.18
R.Rampaul	96.4	5	544	11	49.45	2-34	–	5.62
D.J.G.Sammy	6	0	19	1	19.00	1-19	–	3.16
M.N.Samuels	281	6	1414	35	40.40	3-25	–	5.03
R.R.Sarwan	56.4	1	336	7	48.00	3-31	–	5.92
D.R.Smith	52.2	2	266	6	44.33	3-24	–	5.08

NEW ZEALAND – BATTING AND FIELDING

† Excluding match abandoned without a ball bowled after toss

	M	I	NO	HS	Runs	Avge	100	50	Ct/St
A.R.Adams†	31	25	7	45	342	19.00	–	–	4
N.J.Astle†	187	184	11	145*	6030	34.85	14	35	72
I.G.Butler†	14	6	4	3	6	3.00	–	–	6
C.L.Cairns	198	179	22	115	4628	29.47	4	24	64
T.K.Canning	3	3	1	23*	36	18.00	–	–	1
C.D.Cumming	10	10	1	45*	138	15.33	–	–	4
S.P.Fleming†	228	220	19	134*	6539	32.53	6	38	110
J.E.C.Franklin	30	16	3	25*	116	8.92	–	–	9
P.G.Fulton	1	1	–	9	9	9.00	–	–	1
C.Z.Harris†	249	213	62	130	4379	29.00	1	16	96
P.A.Hitchcock	13	6	2	10	30	7.50	–	–	4
G.J.Hopkins†	4	1	–	0	0	0.00	–	–	8
R.A.Jones	5	5	–	63	168	33.60	–	1	–
B.B.McCullum	57	42	12	56*	617	20.56	–	2	75/3
C.D.McMillan†	156	147	13	105	3699	27.60	2	22	39
H.J.H.Marshall†	29	28	6	101*	833	37.86	1	8	8
M.J.Mason	5	1	1	13*	13	–	–	–	–
K.D.Mills	39	21	10	44*	177	16.09	–	–	10
C.J.Nevin	37	36	–	74	732	20.33	–	4	16/3
J.D.P.Oram	70	53	6	81	827	17.59	–	3	16
M.H.W.Papps	5	5	1	92*	204	51.00	–	2	–
M.S.Sinclair	43	42	2	118*	1165	29.12	2	7	14
C.M.Spearman	51	50	–	86	936	18.72	–	5	15
S.B.Styris†	94	81	12	141	1888	27.36	2	10	38
D.R.Tuffey†	72	37	18	20*	145	7.63	–	–	19
D.L.Vettori†	144	87	28	33	723	12.25	–	–	32
L.Vincent	62	60	8	60*	1133	21.78	–	4	23
M.D.J.Walker	3	1	–	10	10	10.00	–	–	2
K.P.Walmsley	2	–	–	–	–	–	–	–	–

NEW ZEALAND – BOWLING

	O	M	R	W	Avge	Best	4wI	R/Over
A.R.Adams	245.4	12	1261	44	28.65	5-22	3	5.13
N.J.Astle	735.3	28	3412	95	35.91	4-43	1	4.63
I.G.Butler	98.5	1	558	14	39.85	3-41	–	5.64
C.L.Cairns	1252.2	77	5910	187	31.60	5-42	4	4.71
T.K.Canning	24	1	123	4	30.75	2-30	–	5.12
S.P.Fleming	4.5	0	28	1	28.00	1-8	–	5.79
J.E.C.Franklin	217	11	1127	29	38.86	5-42	1	5.19
C.Z.Harris	1777.5	81	7613	203	37.50	5-42	3	4.28
P.A.Hitchcock	85	5	412	12	34.33	3-30	–	4.84
C.D.McMillan	235.3	6	1256	37	33.94	3-20	–	5.33
M.J.Mason	49	3	260	4	65.00	2-35	–	5.30
K.D.Mills	305.5	24	1392	47	29.61	4-14	1	4.55
J.D.P.Oram	535.5	52	2372	83	28.57	5-26	3	4.42

NEW ZEALAND – BOWLING (continued)

	O	M	R	W	Avge	Best	4wI	R/Over
C.M.Spearman	0.3	0	6	0	–	–	–	12.00
S.B.Styris	589.3	31	2780	91	30.54	6-25	3	4.71
D.R.Tuffey	560.2	60	2548	89	28.62	4-24	2	4.54
D.L.Vettori	1070.5	45	4603	134	34.35	5-30	4	4.29
L.Vincent	0.2	0	3	0	–	–	–	9.00
M.D.J.Walker	22	0	119	4	29.75	4-49	1	5.40
K.P.Walmsley	20	0	117	2	58.50	1-53	–	5.85

INDIA – BATTING AND FIELDING

	M	I	NO	HS	Runs	Avge	100	50	Ct/St
A.B.Agarkar	134	85	26	95	1058	17.93	–	3	41
H.K.Badani	40	36	10	100	867	33.34	1	4	13
S.V.Bahutule	8	4	1	11	23	7.66	–	–	3
L.Balaji	24	12	4	21*	95	11.87	–	–	8
S.B.Bangar	15	15	2	57*	180	13.84	–	1	4
A.Bhandari	2	1	1	0*	0	–	–	–	–
M.S.Dhoni	3	3	1	12	19	9.50	–	–	4/2
R.Dravid	245	224	27	153	7750	39.34	9	56	150/14
S.C.Ganguly	266	257	20	183	9914	41.83	22	59	93
R.S.Gavaskar	11	10	2	54	151	18.87	–	1	5
Harbhajan Singh	93	49	13	46	417	11.58	–	–	27
Joginder Sharma	3	2	2	29*	34	–	–	–	3
M.Kaif	81	69	16	111*	1734	32.71	1	10	40
K.D.Karthik	2	1	–	1	1	1.00	–	–	4/1
M.Kartik	17	9	4	32*	80	16.00	–	–	5
Z.Khan	89	46	18	34*	336	12.00	–	–	20
A.Kumble	259	128	44	26	886	10.54	–	–	83
V.V.S.Laxman	83	80	7	131	2309	31.63	6	10	39
D.Mongia	49	43	5	159*	1040	27.36	1	3	21
A.Nehra	55	20	12	24	71	8.87	–	–	7
P.A.Patel	14	10	1	28	132	14.66	–	–	12/3
I.K.Pathan	28	21	9	38	230	19.16	–	–	4
R.R.Powar	2	2	1	18*	32	32.00	–	–	–
A.M.Salvi	4	3	1	4*	4	2.00	–	–	2
V.Sehwag	106	103	6	130	3131	32.27	6	16	38
S.Sriram	8	7	1	57	81	13.50	–	1	1
S.R.Tendulkar	342	333	32	186*	13497	44.84	37	69	101
Yuvraj Singh	111	98	11	139	2598	29.86	2	17	41

INDIA – BOWLING

	O	M	R	W	Avge	Best	4wI	R/Over
A.B.Agarkar	1108.1	65	5652	203	27.84	6-42	9	5.10
H.K.Badani	30.3	0	149	3	49.66	1-7	–	4.88
S.V.Bahutule	49	0	283	2	141.50	1-31	–	5.77
L.Balaji	201.1	12	1097	30	36.56	4-48	1	5.45
S.B.Bangar	73.4	2	384	7	54.85	2-39	–	5.21
A.Bhandari	17.4	0	106	5	21.20	3-31	–	5.99
R.Dravid	31	1	170	4	42.50	2-43	–	5.48
S.C.Ganguly	677.1	27	3408	93	36.64	5-16	3	5.03
R.S.Gavaskar	12	0	74	1	74.00	1-56	–	6.16
Harbhajan Singh	827	49	3408	117	29.12	5-43	3	4.12
Joginder Sharma	21	3	99	1	99.00	1-28	–	4.71
M.Kartik	153	6	774	16	48.37	3-36	–	5.05
Z.Khan	730	43	3554	132	26.92	4-19	6	4.86
T.Kumaran	63	4	348	9	38.66	3-24	–	5.52
A.Kumble	2302.5	107	9854	321	30.69	6-12	10	4.27
V.V.S.Laxman	7	0	40	0	–	–	–	5.71
D.Mongia	55.3	1	290	8	36.25	3-31	–	5.22
A.Nehra	457	28	2151	63	34.14	6-23	2	4.70
I.K.Pathan	248.3	10	1240	47	26.38	4-24	1	4.98
R.R.Powar	10	0	52	0	–	–	–	5.20

INDIA – BOWLING (continued)

	O	M	R	W	Avge	Best	4wI	R/Over
A.M.Salvi	28.4	3	120	4	30.00	2-15	–	4.18
V.Sehwag	389.3	11	2041	51	40.01	3-25	–	5.24
S.Sriram	54	1	274	9	30.44	3-43	–	5.07
S.R.Tendulkar	1154.5	23	5818	132	44.07	5-32	5	5.03
Yuvraj Singh	219.5	9	1082	28	38.64	4-6	1	4.92

PAKISTAN – BATTING AND FIELDING

	M	I	NO	HS	Runs	Avge	100	50	Ct/St
Abdul Razzaq	183	158	40	112	3617	30.65	2	18	27
Azhar Mahmood	139	107	25	67	1492	18.19	–	3	37
Bazid Khan	2	2	–	12	12	6.00	–	–	1
Danish Kaneria	10	5	4	3*	4	4.00	–	–	–
Faisal Iqbal	17	15	2	100*	284	21.84	1	–	2
Iftikhar Anjum	8	4	4	19*	32	–	–	–	1
Imran Farhat	21	21	1	107	686	34.30	1	4	7
Imran Nazir	61	61	2	105*	1392	23.59	1	8	19
Inzamam-ul-Haq	336	312	44	137*	10631	39.66	10	78	101
Junaid Zia	4	2	1	2*	2	2.00	–	–	–
Kamran Akmal	20	15	2	124	350	26.92	1	–	15/2
Misbah-ul-Haq	12	11	2	50*	305	33.88	–	2	5
Mohammad Akram	23	9	7	7*	14	7.00	–	–	8
Mohammad Hafeez	28	28	–	69	494	17.64	–	3	13
Mohammad Khalil	3	1	1	0*	0	–	–	–	2
Mohammad Sami	66	33	18	23	195	13.00	–	–	16
Moin Khan	219	183	41	72*	3266	23.00	–	12	214/73
Mushtaq Ahmed	144	76	34	34*	399	9.50	–	–	30
Naved Latif	11	11	–	113	262	23.81	1	–	2
Naved-ul-Hasan	22	14	6	29	140	17.50	–	–	6
Rashid Latif	166	117	29	79	1709	19.42	–	3	182/38
Salim Elahi	48	47	4	135	1579	36.72	4	9	10
Salman Butt	13	13	1	108*	363	30.25	1	2	2
Saqlain Mushtaq	169	98	39	37*	709	12.01	–	–	40
Shabbir Ahmed	29	10	5	2	9	1.80	–	–	8
Shahid Afridi	199	190	9	109	4356	24.06	3	25	72
Shoaib Akhtar	120	57	29	43	296	10.57	–	–	15
Shoaib Malik	93	80	10	143	2224	31.77	4	11	34
Taufiq Umar	19	19	1	81*	447	24.83	–	3	9
Umar Gul	15	1	–	2	2	2.00	–	–	1
Yasir Hamid	46	46	1	127*	1707	37.93	3	9	9
Younis Khan	111	106	14	144	2914	31.67	1	20	57
Yousuf Youhana	189	179	27	141*	6414	42.19	11	40	42

PAKISTAN – BOWLING

	O	M	R	W	Avge	Best	4wI	R/Over
Abdul Razzaq	1338.4	78	6060	208	29.13	6-35	8	4.52
Azhar Mahmood	1024.4	57	4740	122	38.85	6-18	5	4.62
Bazid Khan	2	0	11	0	–	–	–	5.50
Danish Kaneria	90.2	9	382	9	42.44	3-31	–	4.22
Faisal Iqbal	3	0	33	0	–	–	–	11.00
Iftikhar Anjum	64	4	329	6	54.83	2-67	–	5.14
Imran Farhat	13.5	2	85	5	17.00	3-10	–	6.14
Imran Nazir	8.1	0	48	1	48.00	1-3	–	5.87
Inzamam-ul-Haq	9.4	1	64	3	21.33	1—	–	6.61
Junaid Zia	24.1	1	127	3	42.33	3-21	–	5.25
Mohammad Akram	164.5	6	790	19	41.57	2-28	–	4.79
Mohammad Hafeez	172	8	727	25	29.08	3-17	–	4.22
Mohammad Khalil	24	0	144	5	28.80	2-55	–	6.00
Mohammad Sami	544.3	32	2654	98	27.08	5-10	4	4.87
Mushtaq Ahmed	1257.1	51	5361	161	33.29	5-36	4	4.26
Naved Latif	8	0	51	0	–	–	–	6.37
Naved-ul-Hasan	183.1	6	1016	33	30.78	4-25	2	5.54

PAKISTAN – BOWLING (continued)

	O	M	R	W	Avge	Best	4wI	R/Over
Salim Elahi	1	0	10	0	–	–	–	10.00
Salman Butt	6	0	42	0	–	–	–	7.00
Saqlain Mushtaq	1461.4	65	6275	288	21.78	5-20	17	4.29
Shabbir Ahmed	247.2	23	1071	29	36.93	3-32	–	4.33
Shahid Afridi	1292.2	44	5946	163	36.47	5-11	3	4.60
Shoaib Akhtar	934.4	76	4287	186	23.04	6-16	7	4.58
Shoaib Malik	633.2	19	2715	80	33.93	4-19	1	4.28
Taufiq Umar	12	0	85	1	85.00	1-49	–	7.08
Umar Gul	112.2	7	519	19	27.31	5-17	1	4.62
Yasir Hamid	3	0	26	0	–	–	–	8.66
Younis Khan	15	0	99	1	99.00	1-24	–	6.60
Yousuf Youhana	0.1	0	1	0	–	–	–	6.00

SRI LANKA – BATTING AND FIELDING

	M	I	NO	HS	Runs	Avge	100	50	Ct/St
R.P.Arnold	128	111	29	103	2911	35.50	1	20	40
M.S.Atapattu	225	219	26	132*	7296	37.80	11	50	61
U.D.U.Chandana	133	101	13	89	1494	16.97	–	5	75
H.D.P.K.Dharmasena	141	87	33	69*	1222	22.62	–	4	34
T.M.Dilshan	52	43	13	53	864	28.80	–	2	29/1
C.R.D.Fernando	62	25	13	13*	84	7.00	–	–	11
K.A.D.M.Fernando	1	–	–	–	–	–	–	–	1
D.A.Gunawardana	59	59	1	132	1653	28.50	1	11	13
M.R.K.B.Herath	6	1	1	0*	0	–	–	–	3
W.S.Jayantha	17	17	2	74*	400	26.66	–	2	5
S.T.Jayasuriya	333	324	14	189	9896	31.92	18	57	105
D.P.M.D.Jayawardena	176	163	16	128	4436	30.17	6	21	88
R.S.Kaluwitharana	189	181	14	102*	3711	22.22	2	23	132/75
S.H.T.Kandamby	4	4	–	13	23	5.75	–	–	–
M.D.N.Kulasekera	6	3	2	4*	5	5.00	–	–	1
K.S.Lokuarachchi	12	10	2	28	91	11.37	–	–	2
M.F.Maharoof	17	9	3	38	101	16.83	–	–	1
S.L.Malinga	4	2	2	5*	6	–	–	–	–
M.Muralitharan	237	109	44	19	385	5.92	–	–	97
K.C.Sangakkara	123	111	16	103*	3180	33.47	3	19	107/31
W.P.U.C.J.Vaas	249	168	55	50*	1586	14.03	–	1	48
D.N.T.Zoysa	88	44	21	47*	332	14.43	–	–	12

SRI LANKA – BOWLING

	O	M	R	W	Avge	Best	4wI	R/Over
R.P.Arnold	334.4	8	1603	37	43.32	3-47	–	4.78
M.S.Atapattu	8.3	0	41	0	–	–	–	4.82
U.D.U.Chandana	920.3	18	4288	138	31.07	5-61	5	4.65
H.D.P.K.Dharmasena	1168.1	41	4998	138	36.21	4-37	1	4.27
T.M.Dilshan	103.1	1	498	10	49.80	4-52	1	4.82
C.R.D.Fernando	437.3	20	2247	81	27.74	4-48	1	5.14
K.A.D.M.Fernando	7	2	13	2	6.50	2-13	–	1.85
M.R.K.B.Herath	39	2	149	5	29.80	3-28	–	3.82
W.S.Jayantha	9.1	0	46	0	–	–	–	5.01
S.T.Jayasuriya	2031.4	35	9684	267	36.26	6-29	10	4.76
D.P.M.D.Jayawardena	91.4	1	518	7	74.00	2-56	–	5.65
M.D.N.Kulasekera	40	5	156	3	52.00	2-19	–	3.90
K.S.Lokuarachchi	91	4	383	14	27.35	3-37	–	4.20
M.F.Maharoof	106.2	7	474	17	27.88	3-3	–	4.45
S.L.Malinga	34	3	159	4	39.75	2-56	–	4.67
M.Muralitharan	2145.1	157	8102	366	22.13	7-30	18	3.77
W.P.U.C.J.Vaas	2036.3	212	8407	322	26.10	8-19	10	4.12
D.N.T.Zoysa	677.5	60	3006	103	29.18	5-26	3	4.43

ZIMBABWE – BATTING AND FIELDING

LOI	M	I	NO	HS	Runs	Avge	100	50	Ct/St
A.M.Blignaut	47	36	8	63*	533	19.03	–	4	10
G.B.Brent	48	33	14	24	202	10.63	–	–	10
S.V.Carlisle	108	104	8	121*	2676	27.87	3	9	39
E.Chigumbura	20	19	2	77	414	24.35	–	3	5
D.D.Ebrahim	82	76	6	121	1443	20.61	1	4	23
S.M.Ervine	42	34	7	100	698	25.85	1	2	5
G.M.Ewing	1	1	–	0	0	0.00	–	–	–
A.Flower	213	208	16	145	6786	35.34	4	55	141/32
G.W.Flower	219	212	18	142*	6536	33.69	6	40	86
T.J.Friend	51	39	5	91	548	16.11	–	3	17
M.W.Goodwin	71	70	3	112*	1818	27.13	2	8	20
T.R.Gripper	8	8	–	26	80	10.00	–	–	4
D.T.Hondo	56	29	12	17	127	7.47	–	–	15
N.B.Mahwire	3	2	2	8*	11	–	–	–	1
A.Maregwede	9	9	1	37	95	11.87	–	–	1
H.Masakadza	11	11	–	66	228	20.72	–	2	4
S.Matsikenyeri	42	40	2	73	600	15.78	–	2	13
C.B.Mpofu	8	5	3	3*	8	4.00	–	–	–
T.Mupariwa	5	5	1	12*	27	6.75	–	–	3
W.Mwayenga	3	2	–	1	1	0.50	–	–	2
M.L.Nkala	47	32	5	47	288	10.66	–	–	6
T.Panyangara	21	18	4	16*	81	5.78	–	–	3
R.W.Price	26	12	5	20*	90	12.85	–	–	1
E.C.Rainsford	5	5	1	5	13	3.25	–	–	–
B.G.Rogers	12	12	–	84	429	35.75	–	5	6
V.Sibanda	24	23	–	58	271	11.78	–	2	6
H.H.Streak	183	153	54	79*	2752	27.79	–	12	43
T.Taibu	76	63	15	96*	1252	26.08	–	6	66/7
B.R.M.Taylor	22	22	–	74	551	25.04	–	5	3
P.Utseya	19	16	6	31	116	11.60	–	–	4
M.A.Vermeulen	32	32	4	79	583	20.82	–	4	9
C.B.Wishart	89	81	8	172*	1716	23.50	2	5	26

ZIMBABWE – BOWLING

	O	M	R	W	Avge	Best	4wI	R/Over
A.M.Blignaut	343.1	10	1778	41	43.36	4-43	1	5.18
G.B.Brent	376.1	19	1914	50	38.28	4-53	1	5.08
E.Chigumbura	68.3	4	506	9	56.22	3-37	–	7.38
D.D.Ebrahim	0.5	0	11	0	–	–	–	13.20
S.M.Ervine	274.5	10	1561	41	38.07	3-29	–	5.67
G.M.Ewing	7	0	36	1	36.00	1-36	–	5.14
A.Flower	5	0	23	0	–	–	–	4.60
G.W.Flower	903.1	11	4187	104	40.25	4-32	2	4.63
T.J.Friend	321.4	13	1779	37	48.08	4-55	1	5.53
M.W.Goodwin	41.2	1	210	4	52.50	1-12	–	5.08
T.R.Gripper	20	5	76	2	38.00	2-28	–	3.80
D.T.Hondo	396.5	21	2171	61	35.59	4-37	3	5.47
N.B.Mahwire	10.4	3	65	1	65.00	1-35	–	6.09
H.Masakadza	1	0	4	0	–	–	–	4.00
S.Matsikenyeri	91	2	453	10	45.30	2-33	–	4.97
C.B.Mpofu	56.5	1	282	6	47.00	2-19	–	4.96
T.Mupariwa	46.3	1	247	8	30.87	2-44	–	5.31
W.Mwayenga	21	2	157	1	157.00	1-61	–	7.47
M.L.Nkala	259.5	8	1557	22	70.77	3-12	–	5.99
T.Panyangara	163.2	14	880	25	35.20	3-28	–	5.38
R.W.Price	221.2	9	917	15	61.13	2-16	–	4.14
E.C.Rainsford	42	1	185	4	46.25	2-29	–	4.40
B.G.Rogers	42	0	231	3	77.00	2-55	–	5.50
V.Sibanda	15	0	87	2	43.50	1-12	–	5.80
H.H.Streak	1532	109	6894	234	29.46	5-32	8	4.50
T.Taibu	14	1	61	2	30.50	2-42	–	4.35

ZIMBABWE – BOWLING (continued)

	O	M	R	W	Avge	Best	4wI	R/Over
B.R.M.Taylor	35	0	224	8	28.00	3-54	–	6.40
P.Utseya	142.5	6	534	8	66.75	2-33	–	3.73
C.B.Wishart	2	0	12	0	–	–	–	6.00

BANGLADESH – BATTING AND FIELDING

	M	I	NO	HS	Runs	Avge	100	50	Ct/St
Abdur Razzaq	6	6	2	21	39	9.75	–	–	–
Aftab Ahmed	13	13	1	81*	322	26.83	–	2	3
Alok Kapali	45	43	2	89*	818	19.95	–	4	17
Al Sahariar	29	29	1	62*	374	13.35	–	2	7
Enamul Haque II	3	2	1	4*	4	4.00	–	–	5
Faisal Hossain	4	4	–	17	35	8.75	–	–	2
Habibul Bashar	63	63	1	74	1201	19.37	–	9	11
Hannan Sarkar	20	20	–	61	383	19.15	–	3	8
Hasibul Hussain	32	26	6	21*	172	8.60	–	–	6
Jamal Ahmed	1	1	1	18*	18	–	–	–	1
Javed Omar	35	35	3	85*	726	22.68	–	6	7
Khaled Mahmud	72	69	3	50	939	14.22	–	1	16
Khaled Masud	93	86	18	54*	1357	19.95	–	6	64/24
Manjural Rana	18	17	5	63	284	23.66	–	1	4
Mashrafe Mortaza	18	17	3	39	188	13.42	–	–	6
Mohammed Ashraful	48	47	2	66	759	16.86	–	4	5
Mohammed Rafique	73	69	11	77	785	13.53	–	2	18
Moniruzzaman	2	2	–	1	1	0.50	–	–	–
Mushfiqur Rahman	28	25	3	49	360	16.36	–	–	6
Nafis Iqbal	14	14	–	58	282	20.14	–	2	1
Nazmul Hossain	10	8	5	6*	22	7.33	–	–	4
Rajin Saleh	31	31	–	82	710	22.90	–	5	7
Sanwar Hossain	27	27	2	52	290	11.60	–	1	11
Shahriar Hossain	20	19	–	95	362	19.05	–	2	5
Tapash Baisya	45	36	10	35*	282	10.84	–	–	6
Tareq Aziz	10	8	7	11*	26	26.00	–	–	4
Tushar Imran	24	23	–	65	403	17.52	–	2	3

BANGLADESH – BOWLING

	O	M	R	W	Avge	Best	4wI	R/Over
Abdur Razzaq	53	5	214	7	30.57	3-17	–	4.03
Aftab Ahmed	33	0	141	6	23.50	5-31	1	4.27
Alok Kapali	143.3	6	712	11	64.72	2-40	–	4.96
Enamul Haque II	30	1	129	4	32.25	2-37	–	4.30
Habibul Bashar	29.1	0	142	1	142.00	1-31	–	4.86
Hannan Sarkar	0.3	0	13	0	–	–	–	26.00
Hasibul Hussain	229.1	13	1338	29	46.13	4-56	1	5.83
Jamal Ahmed	4	1	28	0	–	–	–	7.00
Khaled Mahmud	538.5	30	2700	65	41.53	4-19	1	5.01
Manjural Rana	131.1	9	507	18	28.16	4-34	2	3.86
Mashrafe Mortaza	153.1	13	776	19	40.84	2-26	–	5.06
Mohammed Ashraful	50.2	1	305	8	38.12	3-26	–	6.06
Mohammed Rafique	605.2	34	2781	66	42.13	4-33	2	4.59
Mushfiqur Rahman	221.5	19	978	19	51.47	2-21	–	4.40
Nazmul Hossain	77.2	6	344	12	28.66	4-40	1	4.44
Rajin Saleh	66.2	1	333	9	37.00	3-48	–	5.02
Sanwar Hossain	63.5	1	327	10	32.70	3-49	–	5.12
Tapash Baisya	344.5	14	1856	49	37.87	4-16	2	5.38
Tareq Aziz	77.3	7	424	13	32.61	3-19	–	5.47

KENYA – BATTING AND FIELDING

	M	I	NO	HS	Runs	Avge	100	50	Ct/St
R.G.Aga	2	2	–	1	1	0.50	–	–	–
H.S.Modi	55	48	8	78*	984	24.60	–	5	8
K.O.Obuya	63	62	1	144	1445	23.68	2	8	27/14

KENYA – BATTING AND FIELDING (continued)

	M	I	NO	HS	Runs	Avge	100	50	Ct/St
T.M.Odoyo	63	60	7	53	1135	21.41	–	2	16
P.O.Ongondo	22	19	5	36	143	10.21	–	–	1
M.A.Ouma	2	2	–	49	72	36.00	–	–	–
B.J.Patel	24	18	2	44	319	19.93	–	–	6
M.L.Patel	1	1	–	0	0	0.00	–	–	–
A.O.Suji	44	33	7	67	317	12.19	–	1	13
M.A.Suji	61	49	22	16*	228	8.44	–	–	10
S.O.Tikolo	65	63	2	106*	1710	28.03	1	14	21

KENYA – BOWLING

	O	M	R	W	Avge	Best	4wI	R/Over
R.G.Aga	13	0	87	2	43.50	2-17	–	6.69
H.S.Modi	3.1	1	27	0	–	–	–	8.52
K.O.Obuya	1	0	5	0	–	–	–	5.00
T.M.Odoyo	456.2	33	2226	59	37.72	4-28	1	4.87
P.O.Ongondo	115	6	574	7	82.00	2-44	–	4.99
B.J.Patel	19.1	0	129	2	64.50	1-15	–	6.72
A.O.Suji	179.5	8	970	15	64.66	2-24	–	5.39
M.A.Suji	471	46	2060	43	47.90	4-24	1	4.37
S.O.Tikolo	283.5	6	1471	41	35.87	3-14	–	5.18

SCOTLAND – BATTING AND FIELDING

	M	I	NO	HS	Runs	Avge	100	50	Ct/St
J.A.R.Blain	5	5	1	9	15	3.75	–	–	1
G.M.Hamilton	5	5	1	76	217	54.25	–	2	1

SCOTLAND – BOWLING

	O	M	R	W	Avge	Best	4wI	R/Over
J.A.R.Blain	37.1	1	210	10	21.00	4-37	1	5.64
G.M.Hamilton	35.4	4	149	3	49.66	2-36	–	4.17

LEADING TEST AGGREGATES 2004

1000 RUNS

	M	I	NO	HS	Runs	Avge	100	50
J.L.Langer (A)	14	27	–	215	1481	54.85	5	4
D.R.Martyn (A)	14	26	2	161	1353	56.37	6	5
J.H.Kallis (SA)	11	21	5	162	1288	80.50	5	7
B.C.Lara (WI)	12	21	1	400*	1178	58.90	3	4
V.Sehwag (I)	12	19	1	309	1141	63.38	3	4
C.H.Gayle (WI)	12	22	1	141	1135	54.04	4	7
S.T.Jayasuriya (SL)	11	20	–	253	1130	56.50	4	3
M.L.Hayden (A)	14	27	1	132	1123	43.19	3	6
K.C.Sangakkara (SL)	11	20	–	270	1114	55.70	3	5
R.R.Sarwan (WI)	12	21	1	261*	1005	50.25	3	4
M.E.Trescothick (E)	13	26	3	132	1004	43.65	4	3

RECORD:

	M	I	NO	HS	Runs	Avge	100	50
I.V.A.Richards (WI)(1976)	11	19	–	291	1710	90.00	7	5

50 WICKETS

	M	O	R	W	Avge	Best	5wI	10wM
A.Kumble (I)	12	613.2	1838	74	24.83	8-141	6	2
S.K.Warne (A)	12	578.4	1685	70	24.07	6-125	5	2
S.J.Harmison (E)	13	526.5	1603	67	23.92	7- 12	3	–
J.N.Gillespie (A)	14	514.3	1369	55	24.89	5- 56	1	–

RECORD:

	M	O	R	W	Avge	Best	5wI	10wM
D.K.Lillee (A)(1981)	13	618.2	1781	85	20.95	7- 83	5	2

TEST CAREER RECORDS

These records, complete to 3 March 2005, contain all players registered for county cricket in 2005 at the time of going to press, plus those who have played Test cricket since 1 October 2003 (Test No. 1660 onwards).

ENGLAND – BATTING AND FIELDING

	M	I	NO	HS	Runs	Avge	100	50	Ct/St
C.J.Adams	5	8	–	31	104	13.00	–	–	6
U.Afzaal	3	6	1	54	83	16.60	–	1	–
K.Ali	1	2	–	9	10	5.00	–	–	–
J.M.Anderson	12	16	12	21*	68	17.00	–	–	4
G.J.Batty	5	8	1	38	144	20.57	–	–	2
I.R.Bell	1	1	–	70	70	70.00	–	1	2
M.P.Bicknell	4	7	–	15	45	6.42	–	–	2
R.J.Blakey	2	4	–	6	7	1.75	–	–	2
M.A.Butcher	71	131	7	173*	4288	34.58	8	23	61
A.R.Caddick	62	95	12	49*	861	10.37	–	–	21
R.Clarke	2	3	–	55	96	32.00	–	1	1
P.D.Collingwood	2	4	–	36	89	22.25	–	–	6
D.G.Cork	37	56	8	59	864	18.00	–	3	18
J.P.Crawley	37	61	9	156*	1800	34.61	4	9	29
R.D.B.Croft	21	34	8	37*	421	16.19	–	–	10
R.K.J.Dawson	7	13	3	19*	114	11.40	–	–	3
P.A.J.DeFreitas	44	68	5	88	934	14.82	–	4	14
M.A.Ealham	8	13	3	53*	210	21.00	–	2	4
A.Flintoff	45	72	3	167	2239	32.44	4	14	30
J.S.Foster	7	12	3	48	226	25.11	–	–	17/1
J.E.R.Gallian	3	6	–	28	74	12.33	–	–	1
A.F.Giles	45	63	9	52	1123	20.79	–	3	25
D.Gough	58	86	18	65	855	12.57	–	2	13
A.Habib	2	3	–	19	26	8.66	–	–	–
G.M.Hamilton	1	2	–	0	0	0.00	–	–	–
S.J.Harmison	28	37	11	42	287	11.03	–	–	3
W.K.Hegg	2	4	–	15	30	7.50	–	–	8
G.A.Hick	65	114	6	178	3383	31.32	6	18	90
M.J.Hoggard	38	50	20	38	274	9.13	–	–	16
R.C.Irani	3	5	–	41	86	17.20	–	–	2
R.L.Johnson	3	4	–	26	59	14.75	–	–	–
G.O.Jones	13	19	1	100	574	31.88	1	3	43/2
S.P.Jones	12	12	1	44	139	12.63	–	–	3
R.W.T.Key	15	26	1	221	775	31.00	1	3	11
R.J.Kirtley	4	7	1	12	32	5.33	–	–	3
N.V.Knight	17	30	–	113	719	23.96	1	4	26
A.McGrath	4	5	–	81	201	40.20	–	2	3
D.L.Maddy	3	4	–	24	46	11.50	–	–	4
M.P.Maynard	4	8	–	35	87	10.87	–	–	3
A.D.Mullally	19	27	4	24	127	5.52	–	–	6
J.Ormond	2	4	1	18	38	12.66	–	–	–
M.M.Patel	2	2	–	27	45	22.50	–	–	2
M.R.Ramprakash	52	92	6	154	2350	27.32	2	12	39
C.M.W.Read	11	16	3	38*	199	15.30	–	–	31/4
M.J.Saggers	3	3	–	1	1	0.33	–	–	1
I.D.K.Salisbury	15	25	3	50	368	16.72	–	1	5
R.J.Sidebottom	1	1	–	4	4	4.00	–	–	–
C.E.W.Silverwood	6	7	3	10	29	7.25	–	–	2
E.T.Smith	3	5	–	64	87	17.40	–	1	5
A.J.Strauss	12	24	2	147	1246	56.63	5	4	16
G.P.Thorpe	98	177	26	200*	6636	43.94	16	38	101
M.E.Trescothick	59	113	10	219	4430	43.00	10	24	69
A.J.Tudor	10	16	4	99*	229	19.08	–	1	3

	M	I	NO	HS	Runs	Avge	100	50	Ct/St
M.P.Vaughan	55	99	8	197	4023	44.20	13	12	34
I.J.Ward	5	9	1	39	129	16.12	–	–	1
C.White	30	50	7	121	1052	24.46	1	5	14

ENGLAND – BOWLING

	O	M	R	W	Avge	Best	5wI	10wM
C.J.Adams	20	5	59	1	59.00	1- 42	–	–
U.Afzaal	9	0	49	1	49.00	1- 49	–	–
K.Ali	36	5	136	5	27.20	3- 80	–	–
J.M.Anderson	339	70	1274	35	36.40	5- 73	2	–
G.J.Batty	217.2	32	689	10	68.90	3- 55	–	–
M.P.Bicknell	180	39	543	14	38.78	4- 84	–	–
M.A.Butcher	150.1	27	541	15	36.06	4- 42	–	–
A.R.Caddick	2259.4	501	6999	234	29.91	7- 46	13	1
R.Clarke	29	11	60	4	15.00	2- 7	–	–
P.D.Collingwood	16	3	37	0				
D.G.Cork	1279.4	264	3906	131	29.81	7- 43	5	–
R.D.B.Croft	769.5	195	1825	49	37.24	5- 95	1	–
R.K.J.Dawson	186	20	677	11	61.54	4-134	–	–
P.A.J.DeFreitas	1639.4	367	4700	140	33.57	7- 70	4	–
M.A.Ealham	176.4	43	488	17	28.70	4- 21	–	–
A.Flintoff	1317.5	299	3828	110	34.80	5- 58	1	–
J.E.R.Gallian	14	1	62	0				
A.F.Giles	1713	361	4719	127	37.15	5- 57	5	–
D.Gough	1970.1	370	6503	229	28.39	6- 42	9	–
G.M.Hamilton	15	1	63	0				
S.J.Harmison	1048.1	232	3182	111	28.66	7- 12	4	–
G.A.Hick	509.3	128	1306	23	56.78	4-126	–	–
M.J.Hoggard	1364.5	303	4472	143	31.27	7- 61	4	1
R.C.Irani	32	10	112	3	37.33	1- 22	–	–
R.L.Johnson	91.1	25	275	16	17.18	6- 33	2	–
S.P.Jones	333.1	51	1180	36	32.77	5- 57	1	–
R.J.Kirtley	179.5	50	561	19	29.52	6- 34	1	–
A.McGrath	17	1	56	4	14.00	3- 16	–	–
D.L.Maddy	14	1	40	0				
A.D.Mullally	754.1	214	1812	58	31.24	5-105	1	–
J.Ormond	62	12	185	2	92.50	1- 70	–	–
M.M.Patel	46	8	180	1	180.00	1-101	–	–
M.R.Ramprakash	149.1	16	477	4	119.25	1- 2	–	–
M.J.Saggers	82.1	20	247	7	35.28	2- 29	–	–
I.D.K.Salisbury	415.2	50	1539	20	76.95	4-163	–	–
R.J.Sidebottom	20	2	64	0				
C.E.W.Silverwood	138	27	444	11	40.36	5- 91	1	–
G.P.Thorpe	23	7	37	0				
M.E.Trescothick	50	6	155	1	155.00	1- 34	–	–
A.J.Tudor	252	51	963	28	34.39	5- 44	1	–
M.P.Vaughan	151	20	516	6	86.00	2- 71	–	–
C.White	659.5	119	2220	59	37.62	5- 32	3	–

AUSTRALIA – BATTING AND FIELDING

	M	I	NO	HS	Runs	Avge	100	50	Ct/St
A.J.Bichel	19	22	1	71	355	16.90	–	1	16
N.W.Bracken	3	3	1	6*	9	4.50	–	–	1
M.J.Clarke	9	14	1	151	631	48.53	2	2	12
M.T.G.Elliott	21	36	1	199	1172	33.48	3	4	14
A.C.Gilchrist	65	94	16	204*	4109	52.67	13	19	253/27
J.N.Gillespie	63	81	26	54*	891	16.20	–	2	20
N.M.Hauritz	1	2	–	15	15	7.50	–	–	1

	M	I	NO	HS	Runs	Avge	100	50	Ct/St
M.L.Hayden	64	112	10	380	5563	54.53	20	19	76
G.B.Hogg	4	5	1	17*	38	9.50	–	–	–
M.S.Kasprowicz	30	43	8	25	341	9.74	–	–	12
S.M.Katich	13	23	3	125	822	41.10	1	6	7
J.L.Langer	85	145	6	250	6401	46.05	21	24	55
S.G.Law	1	1	1	54*	54	–	–	1	1
B.Lee	37	36	6	62*	593	19.76	–	2	9
D.S.Lehmann	27	42	2	177	1798	44.95	5	10	11
M.L.Love	5	8	3	100*	233	46.60	1	1	7
S.C.G.MacGill	33	38	7	43	272	8.77	–	–	16
G.D.McGrath	106	118	42	61	556	7.31	–	1	33
D.R.Martyn	53	86	12	161	3712	50.16	11	21	25
M.J.Nicholson	1	2	–	9	14	7.00	–	–	–
R.T.Ponting	85	138	18	257	6657	55.47	21	26	101
A.Symonds	2	4	–	24	53	13.25	–	–	4
S.K.Warne	120	166	14	99	2465	16.21	–	9	106
S.R.Watson	1	1	–	31	31	31.00	–	–	1
S.R.Waugh	168	260	46	200	10927	51.06	32	50	112
B.A.Williams	4	6	3	10*	23	7.66	–	–	4

AUSTRALIA – BOWLING

	O	M	R	W	Avge	Best	5wI	10wM
A.J.Bichel	556	111	1870	58	32.24	5-60	1	–
N.W.Bracken	128	38	351	6	58.50	2-12	–	–
M.J.Clarke	10.2	0	37	6	6.16	6- 9	1	–
M.T.G.Elliott	2	1	4	0				
J.N.Gillespie	2155.2	586	6060	241	25.14	7-37	8	–
N.M.Hauritz	27	4	103	5	20.60	3-16	–	–
M.L.Hayden	9	0	40	0				
G.B.Hogg	129	25	452	9	50.22	2-40	–	–
M.S.Kasprowicz	962.2	214	2855	94	30.37	7-36	4	–
S.M.Katich	97.5	9	356	11	32.36	6-65	1	–
J.L.Langer	1	0	3	0				
S.G.Law	3	1	9	0				
B.Lee	1230	256	4402	139	31.66	5-47	4	–
D.S.Lehmann	162.2	36	412	15	27.46	3-42	–	–
S.C.G.MacGill	1454.5	300	4611	160	28.81	7-50	10	2
G.D.McGrath	4125.1	1242	10309	481	21.43	8-24	25	3
D.R.Martyn	58	15	168	2	84.00	1- 0	–	–
M.J.Nicholson	25	4	115	4	28.75	3-56	–	–
R.T.Ponting	75.5	19	205	4	51.25	1- 0	–	–
A.Symonds	24	4	85	1	85.00	1-68	–	–
S.K.Warne	5608	1545	14504	566	25.62	8-71	28	8
S.R.Watson	19	5	60	1	60.00	1-32	–	–
S.R.Waugh	1300.5	332	3445	92	37.44	5-28	3	–
B.A.Williams	142	43	406	9	45.11	4-53	–	–

SOUTH AFRICA – BATTING AND FIELDING

	M	I	NO	HS	Runs	Avge	100	50	Ct/St
H.D.Ackerman	4	8	–	57	161	20.12	–	1	1
P.R.Adams	45	55	15	35	360	9.00	–	–	29
H.M.Amla	3	6	–	25	62	10.33	–	–	2
N.Boje	29	43	6	85	874	23.62	–	3	10
M.V.Boucher	78	107	13	125	2877	30.60	4	18	285/13
Z.de Bruyn	3	5	1	83	155	38.75	–	1	–
A.B.de Villiers	5	10	1	109	362	40.22	1	2	13/1
H.H.Dippenaar	31	50	4	177*	1379	29.97	3	4	21
H.H.Gibbs	64	110	5	228	5053	48.12	14	18	50
A.J.Hall	14	22	3	163	557	29.31	1	2	12

	M	I	NO	HS	Runs	Avge	100	50	Ct/St
M.Hayward	16	17	8	14	66	7.33	–	–	4
C.W.Henderson	7	7	–	30	65	9.28	–	–	2
J.H.Kallis	87	147	24	189*	6833	55.55	20	34	84
G.Kirsten	101	176	15	275	7289	45.27	21	34	83
L.Klusener	49	69	11	174	1906	32.86	4	8	34
C.K.Langeveldt	1	1	1	5*	5	–	–	–	
N.D.McKenzie	41	65	4	120	2028	33.24	2	13	37
A.Nel	11	9	2	7	16	2.28	–	–	2
M.Ntini	54	58	17	32*	427	10.41	–	–	14
J.L.Ontong	2	4	1	32	57	19.00	–	–	1
R.J.Peterson	5	6	1	61	159	31.80	–	1	4
S.M.Pollock	92	131	31	111	3120	31.20	2	13	65
D.Pretorius	4	4	1	9	22	7.33	–	–	
J.A.Rudolph	23	41	4	222*	1487	40.18	4	7	14
G.C.Smith	33	58	4	277	2774	51.37	7	11	38
D.W.Steyn	3	5	3	8	25	12.50	–	–	1
D.J.Terbrugge	7	8	5	4*	16	5.33	–	–	4
T.L.Tsolekile	3	5	–	22	47	9.40	–	–	6
M.van Jaarsveld	9	15	2	73	397	30.53	–	3	11

SOUTH AFRICA – BOWLING

	O	M	R	W	Avge	Best	5wI	10wM
P.R.Adams	1475	340	4405	134	32.87	7-128	4	1
N.Boje	963.4	215	2737	78	35.08	5- 62	3	–
Z.de Bruyn	36	7	92	3	30.66	2- 32	–	–
A.J.Hall	349.1	69	1100	31	35.48	3- 1	–	–
M.Hayward	470.1	91	1609	54	29.79	5- 56	1	–
C.W.Henderson	327	79	928	22	42.18	4-116	–	–
J.H.Kallis	1949	531	5397	170	31.74	6- 54	4	–
G.Kirsten	58.1	19	142	2	71.00	1- 0	–	–
L.Klusener	1147.5	319	3033	80	37.91	8- 64	1	–
C.K.Langeveldt	33	7	96	5	19.20	5- 46	1	–
N.D.McKenzie	12	0	63	0				
A.Nel	397.1	102	1225	42	29.16	6- 81	2	–
M.Ntini	1900.2	448	5929	199	29.79	6- 66	7	1
J.L.Ontong	30.5	2	133	1	133.00	1- 79	–	–
R.J.Peterson	130.5	37	403	8	50.37	3- 46	–	–
S.M.Pollock	3505.2	1086	8195	374	21.91	7- 87	16	1
D.Pretorius	95	18	430	6	71.66	4-115	–	–
J.A.Rudolph	81	11	294	4	73.50	1- 1	–	–
G.C.Smith	103.5	17	337	5	67.40	1- 9	–	–
D.W.Steyn	100.2	16	416	8	52.00	2- 26	–	–
D.J.Terbrugge	168.4	44	517	20	25.85	5- 46	1	–
M.van Jaarsveld	7	0	28	0				

WEST INDIES – BATTING AND FIELDING

	M	I	NO	HS	Runs	Avge	100	50	Ct/St
O.A.C.Banks	8	12	4	50*	261	32.62	–	1	5
C.S.Baugh	5	10	–	68	196	19.60	–	1	4/1
T.L.Best	8	12	1	20*	82	7.45	–	–	1
D.J.J.Bravo	4	8	–	77	220	27.50	–	2	3
G.R.Breese	1	2	–	5	5	2.50	–	–	1
S.Chanderpaul	80	135	18	140	5192	44.37	11	32	31
P.T.Collins	27	41	7	24	229	6.73	–	–	4
C.D.Collymore	14	24	12	16*	124	10.33	–	–	1
M.Dillon	38	68	3	43	549	8.44	–	–	16
V.C.Drakes	12	20	2	67	386	21.44	–	1	2
F.H.Edwards	15	23	7	18	61	3.81	–	–	3
D.Ganga	30	53	–	117	1230	23.20	2	5	19

WEST INDIES – BATTING AND FIELDING (continued)

	M	I	NO	HS	Runs	Avge	100	50	Ct/St
C.H.Gayle	47	82	3	204	3035	38.41	6	18	55
O.D.Gibson	2	4	–	37	93	23.25	–	–	–
R.O.Hinds	7	13	1	84	290	24.16	–	2	3
W.W.Hinds	38	68	1	165	2142	31.97	4	12	30
R.D.Jacobs	65	112	21	118	2577	28.31	3	14	207/12
S.C.Joseph	2	4	–	45	85	21.25	–	–	1
B.C.Lara	112	197	6	400*	10094	52.84	26	46	147
J.J.C.Lawson	10	15	4	14	43	3.90	–	–	2
N.A.M.McLean	19	32	2	46	368	12.26	–	–	5
D.Mohammed	2	3	–	36	68	22.66	–	–	–
R.L.Powell	2	3	–	30	53	17.66	–	–	1
M.N.Samuels	19	33	3	104	874	29.13	1	6	9
A.Sanford	11	17	2	18*	72	4.80	–	–	4
R.R.Sarwan	50	89	6	261*	3401	40.97	6	21	35
D.R.Smith	6	8	1	105*	264	37.71	1	–	5
D.S.Smith	10	19	1	108	511	28.38	1	2	8
J.E.Taylor	3	4	1	9*	22	7.33	–	–	–

WEST INDIES – BOWLING

	O	M	R	W	Avge	Best	5wI	10wM
O.A.C.Banks	345.1	53	1179	23	51.26	4- 87	–	–
T.L.Best	203	26	700	16	43.75	3- 37	–	–
D.J.J.Bravo	128.4	25	419	16	26.18	6- 55	1	–
G.R.Breese	31.2	3	135	2	67.50	2-108	–	–
S.Chanderpaul	242	45	725	8	90.62	1- 2	–	–
P.T.Collins	969.1	176	3089	90	34.32	6- 53	3	–
C.D.Collymore	465	107	1356	37	36.64	7- 57	2	–
M.Dillon	1450.4	268	4398	131	33.57	5- 71	2	–
V.C.Drakes	436.1	65	1362	33	41.27	5- 93	1	–
F.H.Edwards	456.5	51	1831	39	46.94	5- 36	2	–
D.Ganga	26	2	82	0				
C.H.Gayle	372.5	79	944	23	41.04	5- 34	1	–
O.D.Gibson	78.4	9	275	3	91.66	2- 81	–	–
R.O.Hinds	108.2	23	267	4	66.75	2- 83	–	–
W.W.Hinds	135.1	27	473	14	33.78	3- 79	–	–
S.C.Joseph	2	0	8	0				
B.C.Lara	10	1	28	0				
J.J.C.Lawson	308.3	50	1157	39	29.66	7- 78	2	–
N.A.M.McLean	549.5	85	1873	44	42.56	3- 53	–	–
D.Mohammed	71	7	244	3	81.33	3-112	–	–
R.L.Powell	13	2	49	0				
M.N.Samuels	175	27	550	5	110.00	2- 49	–	–
A.Sanford	369.3	69	1316	30	43.86	4-132	–	–
R.R.Sarwan	246	31	793	20	39.65	4- 37	–	–
D.R.Smith	50	8	153	2	76.50	1- 30	–	–
J.E.Taylor	63.4	10	226	3	75.33	2- 38	–	–

NEW ZEALAND – BATTING AND FIELDING

	M	I	NO	HS	Runs	Avge	100	50	Ct/St
A.R.Adams	1	2	–	11	18	9.00	–	–	1
N.J.Astle	66	113	9	222	3906	37.55	9	19	60
S.E.Bond	10	10	5	17	53	10.60	–	–	4
I.G.Butler	8	10	2	26	76	9.50	–	–	4
C.L.Cairns	62	104	5	158	3320	33.53	5	22	14
S.P.Fleming	89	154	10	274*	5663	39.32	8	36	129
J.E.C.Franklin	6	7	1	23	64	10.66	–	–	3
R.G.Hart	11	19	3	57*	260	16.25	–	1	29/1
R.A.Jones	1	2	–	16	23	11.50	–	–	–
B.B.McCullum	10	17	2	143	571	38.06	1	4	24/2

	M	I	NO	HS	Runs	Avge	100	50	Ct/St
C.D.McMillan	53	88	10	142	3078	39.46	6	19	22
H.J.H.Marshall	2	2	1	69	109	109.00	–	1	–
C.S.Martin	18	24	10	7	28	2.00	–	–	5
M.J.Mason	1	2	–	3	3	1.50	–	–	–
K.D.Mills	2	4	1	29	41	13.66	–	–	1
J.D.P.Oram	17	29	6	126*	1002	43.56	2	4	12
M.H.W.Papps	4	8	1	86	172	24.57	–	2	5
M.H.Richardson	38	65	3	145	2776	44.77	4	19	26
M.S.Sinclair	25	42	5	214	1365	36.89	3	4	22
C.M.Spearman	19	37	2	112	922	26.34	1	3	21
S.B.Styris	19	33	2	170	1233	39.77	4	5	16
D.R.Tuffey	22	30	7	35	263	11.43	–	–	12
D.L.Vettori	59	85	13	137*	1482	20.58	1	8	29
L.Vincent	15	27	1	106	754	29.00	2	6	13
P.J.Wiseman	22	29	7	36	276	12.54	–	–	10

NEW ZEALAND – BOWLING

	O	M	R	W	Avge	Best	5wI	10wM
A.R.Adams	31.4	5	105	6	17.50	3-44	–	–
N.J.Astle	775.5	267	1712	36	47.55	2-22	–	–
S.E.Bond	301.3	64	1045	43	24.30	5-78	2	–
I.G.Butler	228	37	884	24	36.83	6-46	1	–
C.L.Cairns	1949.4	412	6410	218	29.40	7-27	13	1
J.E.C.Franklin	155	32	508	20	25.40	5-28	1	–
C.D.McMillan	417	101	1257	28	44.89	3-48	–	–
H.J.H.Marshall	1	0	4	0			–	–
C.S.Martin	572	127	2071	63	32.87	6-76	5	1
M.J.Mason	22	5	105	0			–	–
K.D.Mills	32	10	130	1	130.00	1-99	–	–
J.D.P.Oram	487.4	124	1269	35	36.25	4-41	–	–
M.H.Richardson	11	0	21	1	21.00	1-16	–	–
M.S.Sinclair	4	0	13	0			–	–
S.B.Styris	263.3	60	833	16	52.06	3-28	–	–
D.R.Tuffey	685	181	2057	66	31.16	6-54	2	–
D.L.Vettori	2483.2	635	6592	188	35.06	7-87	11	2
P.J.Wiseman	842.5	187	2611	59	44.25	5-82	2	–

INDIA – BATTING AND FIELDING

	M	I	NO	HS	Runs	Avge	100	50	Ct/St
A.B.Agarkar	22	35	4	109*	479	15.45	1	–	5
L.Balaji	5	4	–	11	15	3.75	–	–	–
A.Chopra	10	19	–	60	437	23.00	–	2	15
R.Dravid	86	146	18	270	7363	57.52	18	35	119
G.Gambhir	5	7	–	139	307	43.85	1	1	4
S.C.Ganguly	79	128	12	173	4901	42.25	11	25	53
Harbhajan Singh	43	60	11	66	695	14.18	–	2	19
M.Kaif	7	13	1	64	294	24.50	–	2	7
K.K.D.Karthik	5	6	–	46	97	16.16	–	–	17/2
M.Kartik	8	10	1	43	88	9.77	–	–	2
Z.Khan	37	48	12	75	441	12.25	–	1	10
A.Kumble	92	117	22	88	1550	16.31	–	3	40
V.V.S.Laxman	61	98	10	281	3795	43.12	7	20	70
A.Nehra	17	25	11	19	77	5.50	–	–	5
P.A.Patel	19	28	7	69	669	31.85	–	4	39/7
I.K.Pathan	10	11	1	55	211	21.10	–	1	4
V.Sehwag	31	50	1	309	2535	51.73	8	8	29
S.R.Tendulkar	120	193	21	248*	9879	57.43	34	38	75
Yuvraj Singh	6	10	2	112	302	37.75	1	1	8

TEST   INDIA – BOWLING

	O	M	R	W	Avge	Best	5wI	10wM
A.B.Agarkar	726.3	149	2473	53	46.66	6-41	1	–
L.Balaji	173	45	552	13	42.46	4-63	–	–
R.Dravid	20	4	39	1	39.00	1-18	–	–
S.C.Ganguly	379.2	81	1266	25	50.64	3-28	–	–
Harbhajan Singh	1946.3	416	5275	189	27.91	8-84	15	3
M.Kaif	3	0	4	0			–	–
M.Kartik	322	74	820	24	34.16	4-44	–	–
Z.Khan	1137.1	236	3677	101	36.40	5-29	3	–
A.Kumble	4835.5	1195	12371	444	27.86	10-74	28	6
V.V.S.Laxman	42	10	100	1	100.00	1-32	–	–
A.Nehra	574.3	122	1866	44	42.40	4-72	–	–
I.K.Pathan	358	92	1079	39	27.66	6-51	3	1
V.Sehwag	88.3	9	334	3	111.33	1-17	–	–
S.R.Tendulkar	510	74	1701	36	47.25	3-10	–	–
Yuvraj Singh	14	1	43	1	43.00	1-25	–	–

PAKISTAN – BATTING AND FIELDING

	M	I	NO	HS	Runs	Avge	100	50	Ct/St
Abdul Razzaq	32	52	6	134	1326	28.82	3	4	7
Asim Kamal	6	10	1	99	407	45.22	–	4	3
Azhar Mahmood	21	34	4	136	900	30.00	3	1	14
Danish Kaneria	23	30	15	15	81	5.40	–	–	6
Fazal-e-Akber	5	8	4	25	52	13.00	–	–	2
Imran Farhat	15	28	–	128	841	30.03	2	4	18
Inzamam-ul-Haq	97	160	16	329	7052	48.97	20	36	75
Kamran Akmal	10	17	–	56	276	16.23	–	1	28/7
Mohammad Akram	9	15	6	10*	24	2.66	–	–	4
Mohammad Asif	1	2	2	12*	12	–	–	–	1
Mohammad Khalil	1	2	–	5	5	2.50	–	–	–
Mohammad Sami	18	28	10	49	226	12.55	–	–	2
Moin Khan	69	104	8	137	2741	28.55	4	15	128/20
Mushtaq Ahmed	52	72	16	59	656	11.71	–	2	23
Naved-ul-Hasan	2	3	–	11	20	6.66	–	–	1
Riaz Afridi	1	1	–	9	9	9.00	–	–	–
Salman Butt	4	8	–	108	274	34.25	1	1	1
Saqlain Mushtaq	49	78	14	101*	927	14.48	1	2	15
Shabbir Ahmed	7	9	4	24*	82	16.40	–	–	3
Shahid Afridi	15	27	1	141	838	32.23	2	4	8
Shoaib Akhtar	36	54	10	37	360	8.18	–	–	9
Shoaib Malik	8	13	3	59	372	37.20	–	2	4
Taufiq Umar	22	40	2	135	1610	42.36	4	9	32
Umar Gul	5	6	–	14	27	4.50	–	–	1
Yasir Hamid	14	27	3	170	1023	42.62	2	6	8
Younis Khan	32	55	2	153	2077	39.18	6	10	35
Yousuf Youhana	56	93	8	204*	4035	47.47	12	21	50

PAKISTAN – BOWLING

	O	M	R	W	Avge	Best	5wI	10wM
Abdul Razzaq	785.5	161	2321	62	37.43	5- 35	1	–
Azhar Mahmood	502.3	109	1402	39	35.94	4- 50	–	–
Danish Kaneria	1031.5	207	3006	102	29.47	7- 77	8	2
Fazal-e-Akber	147	24	511	11	46.45	3- 85	–	–
Imran Farhat	38.1	3	182	3	60.66	2- 69	–	–
Inzamam-ul-Haq	1.3	0	8	0			–	–
Mohammad Akram	246.1	36	859	17	50.52	5-138	1	–
Mohammad Asif	18	3	88	0			–	–
Mohammad Khalil	25.2	0	97	0			–	–
Mohammad Sami	648.3	112	2233	48	46.52	5- 36	2	–
Mushtaq Ahmed	2088.4	406	6100	185	32.97	7- 56	10	3

LOI   **PAKISTAN – BOWLING (continued)**

	O	M	R	W	Avge	Best	5wI	10wM
Naved-ul-Hasan	70.5	9	270	6	45.00	3- 83	–	–
Riaz Afridi	31	10	87	2	43.50	2- 42	–	–
Saqlain Mushtaq	2345	538	6206	208	29.83	8-164	13	3
Shabbir Ahmed	317.5	76	841	33	25.48	5- 48	2	–
Shahid Afridi	250.5	45	776	21	36.95	5- 52	1	–
Shoaib Akhtar	1064.2	183	3568	144	24.77	6- 11	11	2
Shoaib Malik	130.1	23	417	8	52.12	4- 42	–	–
Taufiq Umar	11	2	36	0				
Umar Gul	182	31	614	25	24.56	5- 31	1	–
Yasir Hamid	1	0	5	0				
Younis Khan	37	7	139	1	139.00	1- 47	–	–
Yousuf Youhana	1	0	3	0				

SRI LANKA – BATTING AND FIELDING

	M	I	NO	HS	Runs	Avge	100	50	Ct/St
R.P.Arnold	44	69	4	123	1821	28.01	3	10	51
M.S.Atapattu	79	137	14	249	4873	39.61	15	13	51
U.D.U.Chandana	14	21	1	92	548	27.40	–	2	7
H.D.P.K.Dharmasena	31	51	7	62*	868	19.72	–	3	14
T.M.Dilshan	21	34	4	163*	951	31.70	3	2	29
C.R.D.Fernando	16	24	7	15	90	5.29	–	–	6
K.A.D.M.Fernando	2	3	1	51*	56	28.00	–	1	–
D.A.Gunawardena	4	8	–	43	143	17.87	–	–	1
M.R.K.B.Herath	7	10	1	33*	69	7.66	–	–	2
S.T.Jayasuriya	94	160	13	340	6388	43.45	14	29	69
D.P.M.D.Jayawardena	65	106	8	242	4738	48.34	12	22	89
H.A.P.W.Jayawardena	5	3	–	5	9	3.00	–	–	9/2
R.S.Kaluwitharana	49	78	4	132*	1933	26.12	3	9	93/26
K.S.Lokuarachchi	4	5	1	28*	94	23.50	–	–	1
M.F.Maharoof	4	5	2	40	54	18.00	–	–	1
L.S.Malinga	4	6	2	6*	7	1.75	–	–	4
J.Mubarak	4	8	–	48	167	20.87	–	–	6
M.Muralitharan	91	117	42	67	942	12.56	–	1	50
T.T.Samaraweera	24	34	7	142	1322	48.96	4	6	17
K.C.Sangakkara	44	73	4	270	3400	49.27	7	18	109/14
H.P.Tillekeratne	83	131	25	204*	4545	42.87	11	20	122/2
W.P.U.C.J.Vaas	82	118	22	74*	2028	21.12	–	8	23
D.N.T.Zoysa	30	40	6	28*	288	8.47	–	–	4

SRI LANKA – BOWLING

	O	M	R	W	Avge	Best	5wI	10wM
R.P.Arnold	222.2	45	598	11	54.36	3- 76	–	–
M.S.Atapattu	8	–	24	1	24.00	1- 9	–	–
U.D.U.Chandana	379.3	54	1303	35	37.22	6-179	3	1
H.D.P.K.Dharmasena	1156.3	263	2920	69	42.31	6- 72	3	–
T.M.Dilshan	51	17	113	5	22.60	2- 4	–	–
C.R.D.Fernando	414.2	55	1589	46	34.54	5- 42	2	–
K.A.D.M.Fernando	21	2	107	1	107.00	1- 29	–	–
M.R.K.B.Herath	293.2	61	870	24	36.25	4- 64	–	–
S.T.Jayasuriya	1177.5	278	2872	89	32.26	5- 34	2	–
D.P.M.D.Jayawardena	70.2	15	214	4	53.50	2- 32	–	–
K.S.Lokuarachchi	99	20	295	5	59.00	2- 47	–	–
M.F.Maharoof	85	20	278	5	55.60	2- 62	–	–
L.S.Malinga	105.3	13	432	15	28.80	4- 42	–	–
J.Mubarak	12	2	40	0				
M.Muralitharan	5187.3	1379	12165	532	22.86	9- 51	44	13
T.T.Samaraweera	213.1	36	665	14	47.50	4- 49	–	–
K.C.Sangakkara	1	0	4	0				
H.P.Tillekeratne	12.4	4	25	0				

LOI	SRI LANKA – BOWLING (continued)							
	O	M	R	W	Avge	Best	5wI	10wM
W.P.U.C.J.Vaas	3022	684	8045	269	29.90	7-71	9	2
D.N.T.Zoysa	737	160	2157	64	33.70	5-20	1	–

ZIMBABWE – BATTING AND FIELDING

	M	I	NO	HS	Runs	Avge	100	50	Ct/St
A.M.Blignaut	15	28	2	92	638	24.53	–	3	11
S.V.Carlisle	35	62	5	118	1584	27.78	2	8	31
E.Chigumbura	4	8	–	71	141	17.62	–	1	2
A.G.Cremer	2	4	–	2	3	0.75	–	–	2
D.D.Ebrahim	23	43	1	94	1060	25.23	–	9	15
S.M.Ervine	5	8	–	86	261	32.62	–	3	7
C.N.Evans	3	6	–	22	52	8.66	–	–	1
G.M.Ewing	2	4	–	71	74	18.50	–	1	1
A.Flower	63	112	19	232*	4794	51.54	12	27	151/9
G.W.Flower	67	123	6	201*	3457	29.54	6	15	43
T.J.Friend	13	19	4	81	447	29.80	–	3	2
M.W.Goodwin	19	37	4	166*	1414	42.84	3	8	10
T.R.Gripper	20	38	1	112	809	21.86	1	5	14
D.T.Hondo	9	15	6	19	83	9.22	–	–	5
N.B.Mahwire	6	9	3	8*	29	4.83	–	–	1
A.Maregwede	2	4	–	28	74	18.50	–	–	1
H.Masakadza	9	18	1	119	476	28.00	1	2	5
S.Matsikenyeri	6	12	1	57	309	28.09	–	2	7
C.B.Mpofu	2	4	2	5	6	3.00	–	–	–
T.Mupariwa	1	2	1	14	15	15.00	–	–	–
M.L.Nkala	10	15	2	47	187	14.38	–	–	4
T.Panyangara	3	6	2	40*	128	32.00	–	–	4
R.W.Price	18	30	7	36	224	9.73	–	–	3
B.G.Rogers	2	4	–	29	54	13.50	–	–	–
V.Sibanda	3	6	–	18	48	8.00	–	–	4
H.H.Streak	59	95	18	127*	1814	23.55	1	10	17
T.Taibu	18	34	2	153	996	31.12	1	6	38/4
B.R.M.Taylor	4	8	–	78	252	31.50	–	2	3
P.Utseya	1	2	–	45	45	22.50	–	–	2
M.A.Vermeulen	8	16	–	118	414	25.87	1	2	6
C.B.Wishart	25	46	1	114	1063	23.62	1	5	15

ZIMBABWE – BOWLING

	O	M	R	W	Avge	Best	5wI	10wM
A.M.Blignaut	467	98	1664	51	32.62	5- 73	3	–
E.Chigumbura	105.1	21	348	8	43.50	5- 54	1	–
A.G.Cremer	63.1	11	179	6	29.83	2- 32	–	–
S.M.Ervine	95	18	388	9	43.11	4-146	–	–
C.N.Evans	9	0	35	0				
G.M.Ewing	29	6	119	1	119.00	1- 27	–	–
A.Flower	0.3	0	4	0				
G.W.Flower	563	122	1537	25	61.48	4- 41	–	–
T.J.Friend	333.2	63	1090	25	43.60	5- 31	1	–
M.W.Goodwin	19.5	3	69	0				
T.R.Gripper	132.1	21	509	6	84.83	2- 91	–	–
D.T.Hondo	247.4	50	774	21	36.85	6- 59	1	–
N.B.Mahwire	110.5	20	492	6	82.00	3- 97	–	–
H.Masakadza	21	4	39	2	19.50	1- 9	–	–
S.Matsikenyeri	79.3	6	339	2	169.50	1- 58	–	–
C.B.Mpofu	74	17	213	5	42.60	4-109	–	–
T.Mupariwa	34	1	136	0				
M.L.Nkala	242	54	727	11	66.09	3- 82	–	–
T.Panyangara	89.1	21	286	8	35.75	3- 28	–	–
R.W.Price	855.5	198	2475	69	35.86	6- 73	5	1

LOI

ZIMBABWE – BOWLING (continued)

	O	M	R	W	Avge	Best	5wI	10wM
B.G.Rogers	3	0	17	0				
H.H.Streak	2123.1	570	5572	202	27.58	6-87	6	–
T.Taibu	8	1	27	1	27.00	1-27	–	–
B.R.M.Taylor	4	0	11	0				
P.Utseya	12	2	55	0				
M.A.Vermeulen	1	0	5	0				

BANGLADESH – BATTING AND FIELDING

	M	I	NO	HS	Runs	Avge	100	50	Ct/St
Aftab Ahmed	4	8	–	43	117	14.62	–	–	3
Alamgir Kabir	3	5	1	4	8	2.00	–	–	–
Alok Kapali	16	32	1	85	559	18.03	–	2	5
Enamul Haque II	5	8	6	9	13	6.50	–	–	1
Faisal Hossain	1	2	–	5	7	3.50	–	–	–
Habibul Bashar	34	67	1	113	2299	34.83	3	19	19
Hannan Sarkar	17	33	–	76	662	20.06	–	5	7
Javed Omar	27	54	1	119	1155	21.79	1	5	6
Khaled Mahmud	12	23	1	45	266	12.09	–	–	2
Khaled Masud	33	63	8	103*	1102	20.03	1	3	59/8
Manjural Islam	17	33	11	21	81	3.68	–	–	4
Manjural Rana	6	11	1	69	257	25.70	–	1	3
Mashrafe Mortaza	16	29	4	48	271	10.84	–	–	5
Mohammed Ashraful	25	49	3	158*	1161	25.23	2	6	6
Mohammed Rafique	18	34	5	111	685	23.62	1	2	6
Mushfiqur Rahman	10	19	2	46*	232	13.64	–	–	6
Nafis Iqbal	6	12	–	121	382	31.83	1	2	1
Nazmul Hossain	1	2	1	8*	8	8.00	–	–	–
Rajin Saleh	14	27	1	89	745	28.65	–	4	11
Shahriar Hossain	3	5	–	48	99	19.80	–	–	–/1
Talha Jubair	7	14	6	31	52	6.50	–	–	1
Tapash Baisya	20	38	6	66	366	11.43	–	2	6
Tareq Aziz	3	6	4	10*	22	11.00	–	–	1

BANGLADESH – BOWLING

	O	M	R	W	Avge	Best	5wI	10wM
Aftab Ahmed	4	0	14	0				
Alamgir Kabir	43.3	6	221	0				
Alok Kapali	180.5	15	697	6	116.16	3- 3	–	–
Enamul Haque II	229.2	52	643	24	26.79	7- 95	3	1
Habibul Bashar	39	1	195	0				
Javed Omar	1	0	12	0				
Khaled Mahmud	270	65	832	13	64.00	4- 37	–	–
Manjural Islam	495	103	1605	28	57.32	6- 81	1	–
Manjural Rana	124.5	19	401	5	80.20	3- 84	–	–
Mashrafe Mortaza	472.2	111	1452	43	33.76	4- 60	–	–
Mohammed Ashraful	126	7	550	8	68.75	2- 42	–	–
Mohammed Rafique	889.4	216	2196	67	32.77	6- 77	5	–
Mushfiqur Rahman	227.3	45	823	13	63.30	4- 65	–	–
Nazmul Hossain	25.5	4	114	2	57.00	2-114	–	–
Rajin Saleh	58	4	207	2	103.50	1- 9	–	–
Talha Jubair	181.4	21	771	14	55.07	3-135	–	–
Tapash Baisya	547.4	91	2057	36	57.13	4- 72	–	–
Tareq Aziz	60	7	261	1	261.00	1- 76	–	–

FIRST-CLASS CRICKET RECORDS

To the end of the 2004 season

TEAM RECORDS

HIGHEST INNINGS TOTALS

1107	Victoria v New South Wales	Melbourne	1926-27
1059	Victoria v Tasmania	Melbourne	1922-23
952-6d	Sri Lanka v India	Colombo	1997-98
951-7d	Sind v Baluchistan	Karachi	1973-74
944-6d	Hyderabad v Andhra	Secunderabad	1993-94
918	New South Wales v South Australia	Sydney	1900-01
912-8d	Holkar v Mysore	Indore	1945-46
910-6d	Railways v Dera Ismail Khan	Lahore	1964-65
903-7d	England v Australia	The Oval	1938
887	Yorkshire v Warwickshire	Birmingham	1896
863	Lancashire v Surrey	The Oval	1990
860-6d	Tamil Nadu v Goa	Panjim	1988-89

Excluding penalty runs in India, there have been 30 innings totals of 800 runs or more in first-class cricket. Tamil Nadu's total of 860-6d was boosted to 912 by 52 penalty runs.

HIGHEST SECOND INNINGS TOTAL

770	New South Wales v South Australia	Adelaide	1920-21

HIGHEST FOURTH INNINGS TOTAL

654-5	England v South Africa	Durban	1938-39

HIGHEST MATCH AGGREGATE

2376-37	Maharashtra v Bombay	Poona	1948-49

RECORD MARGIN OF VICTORY

Innings and 851 runs: Railways v Dera Ismail Khan Lahore 1964-65

MOST RUNS IN A DAY

721	Australians v Essex	Southend	1948

MOST HUNDREDS IN AN INNINGS

6	Holkar v Mysore	Indore	1945-46

LOWEST INNINGS TOTALS

12	†Oxford University v MCC and Ground	Oxford	1877
12	Northamptonshire v Gloucestershire	Gloucester	1907
13	Auckland v Canterbury	Auckland	1877-78
13	Nottinghamshire v Yorkshire	Nottingham	1901
14	Surrey v Essex	Chelmsford	1983
15	MCC v Surrey	Lord's	1839
15	†Victoria v MCC	Melbourne	1903-04
15	†Northamptonshire v Yorkshire	Northampton	1908
15	Hampshire v Warwickshire	Birmingham	1922

† *Batted one man short*

There have been 27 instances of a team being dismissed for under 20.

LOWEST MATCH AGGREGATE BY ONE TEAM

34 (16 and 18) Border v Natal   East London   1959-60

LOWEST COMPLETED MATCH AGGREGATE BY BOTH TEAMS

105   MCC v Australians   Lord's   1878

FEWEST RUNS IN AN UNINTERRUPTED DAY'S PLAY

95   Australia (80) v Pakistan (15-2)   Karachi   1956-57

TIED MATCHES

Before 1949 a match was considered to be tied if the scores were level after the fourth innings, even if the side batting last had wickets in hand when play ended. Law 22 was amended in 1948 and since then a match has been tied only when the scores are level after the fourth innings has been completed. There have been 56 tied first-class matches, five of which would not have qualified under the current law. The most recent are:

Warwickshire (446-7d & forfeit) v Essex (66-0d & 380)   Birmingham   2003
Worcestershire (262 & 247) v Zimbabweans (334 & 175)   Worcester   2003

BATTING RECORDS
HIGHEST INDIVIDUAL INNINGS

501*	B.C.Lara	Warwickshire v Durham	Birmingham	1994
499	Hanif Mohammed	Karachi v Bahawalpur	Karachi	1958-59
452*	D.G.Bradman	New South Wales v Queensland	Sydney	1929-30
443*	B.B.Nimbalkar	Maharashtra v Kathiawar	Poona	1948-49
437	W.H.Ponsford	Victoria v Queensland	Melbourne	1927-28
429	W.H.Ponsford	Victoria v Tasmania	Melbourne	1922-23
428	Aftab Baloch	Sind v Baluchistan	Karachi	1973-74
424	A.C.MacLaren	Lancashire v Somerset	Taunton	1895
405*	G.A.Hick	Worcestershire v Somerset	Taunton	1988
400*	B.C.Lara	West Indies v England	St John's	2003-04
394	Naved Latif	Sargodha v Gujranwala	Gujranwala	2000-01
385	B.Sutcliffe	Otago v Canterbury	Christchurch	1952-53
383	C.W.Gregory	New South Wales v Queensland	Brisbane	1906-07
380	M.L.Hayden	Australia v Zimbabwe	Perth	2003-04
377	S.V.Manjrekar	Bombay v Hyderabad	Bombay	1990-91
375	B.C.Lara	West Indies v England	St John's	1993-94
369	D.G.Bradman	South Australia v Tasmania	Adelaide	1935-36
366	N.H.Fairbrother	Lancashire v Surrey	The Oval	1990
366	M.V.Sridhar	Hyderabad v Andhra	Secunderabad	1993-94
365*	C.Hill	South Australia v NSW	Adelaide	1900-01
365*	G.St A.Sobers	West Indies v Pakistan	Kingston	1957-58
364	L.Hutton	England v Australia	The Oval	1938
359*	V.M.Merchant	Bombay v Maharashtra	Bombay	1943-44
359	R.B.Simpson	New South Wales v Queensland	Brisbane	1963-64
357*	R.Abel	Surrey v Somerset	The Oval	1899
357	D.G.Bradman	South Australia v Victoria	Melbourne	1935-36
356	B.A.Richards	South Australia v W Australia	Perth	1970-71
355*	G.R.Marsh	W Australia v S Australia	Perth	1989-90
355	B.Sutcliffe	Otago v Auckland	Dunedin	1949-50
353	V.V.S.Laxman	Hyderabad v Karnataka	Bangalore	1999-00
352	W.H.Ponsford	Victoria v New South Wales	Melbourne	1926-27
350	Rashid Israr	Habib Bank v National Bank	Lahore	1976-77

There have been 148 triple hundreds in first-class cricket, W.V.Raman (313) and Arjan Kripal Singh (302*) for Tamil Nadu v Goa at Panjim in 1988-89 providing the only instance of two batsmen scoring 300 in the same innings.

MOST HUNDREDS IN SUCCESSIVE INNINGS

6	C.B.Fry	Sussex and Rest of England		1901
6	D.G.Bradman	South Australia and D.G.Bradman's XI		1938-39
6	M.J.Procter	Rhodesia		1970-71

TWO DOUBLE HUNDREDS IN A MATCH

244	202*	A.E.Fagg	Kent v Essex	Colchester	1938

TRIPLE HUNDRED AND HUNDRED IN A MATCH

333	123	G.A.Gooch	England v India	Lord's	1990

DOUBLE HUNDRED AND HUNDRED IN A MATCH MOST TIMES

4	Zaheer Abbas	Gloucestershire	1976-81

TWO HUNDREDS IN A MATCH MOST TIMES

8	Zaheer Abbas	Gloucestershire and PIA	1976-82
7	W.R.Hammond	Gloucestershire, England and MCC	1927-45

MOST HUNDREDS IN A SEASON

18	D.C.S.Compton	1947	16	J.B.Hobbs	1925

100 HUNDREDS IN A CAREER

	Total		100th Hundred	
	Hundreds	Inns	Season	Inns
J.B.Hobbs	197	1315	1923	821
E.H.Hendren	170	1300	1928-29	740
W.R.Hammond	167	1005	1935	679
C.P.Mead	153	1340	1927	892
G.Boycott	151	1014	1977	645
H.Sutcliffe	149	1088	1932	700
F.E.Woolley	145	1532	1929	1031
L.Hutton	129	814	1951	619
G.A.Gooch	128	990	1992-93	820
G.A.Hick	126	777	1998	574
W.G.Grace	126	1493	1895	1113
D.C.S.Compton	123	839	1952	552
T.W.Graveney	122	1223	1964	940
D.G.Bradman	117	338	1947-48	295
I.V.A.Richards	114	796	1988-89	658
Zaheer Abbas	108	768	1982-83	658
A.Sandham	107	1000	1935	871
M.C.Cowdrey	107	1130	1973	1035
T.W.Hayward	104	1138	1913	1076
G.M.Turner	103	792	1982	779
J.H.Edrich	103	979	1977	945
L.E.G.Ames	102	951	1950	915
G.E.Tyldesley	102	961	1934	919
D.L.Amiss	102	1139	1986	1081

MOST 400s: 2 – B.C.Lara, W.H.Ponsford

MOST 300s or more: 6 – D.G.Bradman; 4 – W.R.Hammond, W.H.Ponsford

MOST 200s or more: 37 – D.G.Bradman; 36 – W.R.Hammond; 22 – E.H.Hendren

MOST RUNS IN A MONTH

1294 (avge 92.42)   L.Hutton   Yorkshire   June 1949

MOST RUNS IN A SEASON

Runs			I	NO	HS	Avge	100	Season
3816	D.C.S.Compton	Middlesex	50	8	246	90.85	18	1947
3539	W.J.Edrich	Middlesex	52	8	267*	80.43	12	1947
3518	T.W.Hayward	Surrey	61	8	219	66.37	13	1906

The feat of scoring 3000 runs in a season has been achieved 28 times, the most recent instance being by W.E.Alley (3019) in 1961. The highest aggregate in a season since 1969 is 2755 by S.J.Cook in 1991.

1000 RUNS IN A SEASON MOST TIMES

28   W.G.Grace (Gloucestershire), F.E.Woolley (Kent)

HIGHEST BATTING AVERAGE IN A SEASON

(Qualification: 12 innings)

Avge			I	NO	HS	Runs	100	Season
115.66	D.G.Bradman	Australians	26	5	278	2429	13	1938
104.66	D.R.Martyn	Australians	14	5	176*	942	5	2001
102.53	G.Boycott	Yorkshire	20	5	175*	1538	6	1979
102.00	W.A.Johnston	Australians	17	16	28*	102	–	1953
101.70	G.A.Gooch	Essex	30	3	333	2746	12	1990
100.12	G.Boycott	Yorkshire	30	5	233	2503	13	1971

FASTEST HUNDRED AGAINST AUTHENTIC BOWLING

35 min   P.G.H.Fender   Surrey v Northamptonshire   Northampton   1920

FASTEST DOUBLE HUNDRED

113 min   R.J.Shastri   Bombay v Baroda   Bombay   1984-85

FASTEST TRIPLE HUNDRED

181 min   D.C.S.Compton   MCC v NE Transvaal   Benoni   1948-49

MOST SIXES IN AN INNINGS

16   A.Symonds   Gloucestershire v Glamorgan   Abergavenny   1995

MOST SIXES IN A MATCH

20   A.Symonds   Gloucestershire v Glamorgan   Abergavenny   1995

MOST SIXES IN A SEASON

80   I.T.Botham   Somerset and England   1985

MOST FOURS IN AN INNINGS

72   B.C.Lara   Warwickshire v Durham   Birmingham   1994

MOST RUNS OFF ONE OVER

36   G.St A.Sobers   Nottinghamshire v Glamorgan   Swansea   1968
36   R.J.Shastri   Bombay v Baroda   Bombay   1984-85

Both batsmen hit for six all six balls of overs bowled by M.A.Nash and Tilak Raj respectively.

MOST RUNS IN A DAY

390*   B.C.Lara   Warwickshire v Durham   Birmingham   1994

There have been 19 instances of a batsman scoring 300 or more runs in a day.

LONGEST INNINGS

1015 min R.Nayyar (271)   Himachal Pradesh v Jammu & Kashmir Chamba   1999-00

HIGHEST PARTNERSHIPS FOR EACH WICKET

First Wicket

561	Waheed Mirza/Mansoor Akhtar	Karachi W v Quetta	Karachi	1976-77
555	P.Holmes/H.Sutcliffe	Yorkshire v Essex	Leyton	1932
554	J.T.Brown/J.Tunnicliffe	Yorkshire v Derbys	Chesterfield	1898

Second Wicket

576	S.T.Jayasuriya/R.S.Mahanama	Sri Lanka v India	Colombo (RPS)	1997-98
475	Zahir Alam/L.S.Rajput	Assam v Tripura	Gauhati	1991-92
465*	J.A.Jameson/R.B.Kanhai	Warwickshire v Glos	Birmingham	1974

Third Wicket

467	A.H.Jones/M.D.Crowe	N Zealand v Sri Lanka	Wellington	1990-91
456	Khalid Irtiza/Aslam Ali	United Bank v Multan	Karachi	1975-76
451	Mudassar Nazar/Javed Miandad	Pakistan v India	Hyderabad	1982-83
445	P.E.Whitelaw/W.N.Carson	Auckland v Otago	Dunedin	1936-37
438*	G.A.Hick/T.M.Moody	Worcestershire v Hants	Southampton	1997

Fourth Wicket

577	V.S.Hazare/Gul Mahomed	Baroda v Holkar	Baroda	1946-47
574*	C.L.Walcott/F.M.M.Worrell	Barbados v Trinidad	Port-of-Spain	1945-46
502*	F.M.M.Worrell/J.D.C.Goddard	Barbados v Trinidad	Bridgetown	1943-44
470	A.I.Kallicharran/G.W.Humpage	Warwickshire v Lancs	Southport	1982

Fifth Wicket

464*	M.E.Waugh/S.R.Waugh	NSW v W Australia	Perth	1990-91
405	S.G.Barnes/D.G.Bradman	Australia v England	Sydney	1946-47
401	M.B.Loye/D.Ripley	Northants v Glamorgan	Northampton	1998

Sixth Wicket

487*	G.A.Headley/C.C.Passailaigue	Jamaica v Tennyson's	Kingston	1931-32
428	W.W.Armstrong/M.A.Noble	Australians v Sussex	Hove	1902
411	R.M.Poore/E.G.Wynyard	Hampshire v Somerset	Taunton	1899

Seventh Wicket

460	Bhupinder Singh jr/P.Dharmani	Punjab v Delhi	Delhi	1994-95
347	D.St E.Atkinson/C.C.Depeiza	W Indies v Australia	Bridgetown	1954-55
344	K.S.Ranjitsinhji/W.Newham	Sussex v Essex	Leyton	1902

Eighth Wicket

433	V.T.Trumper/A.Sims	Australians v C'bury	Christchurch	1913-14
313	Wasim Akram/Saqlain Mushtaq	Pakistan v Zimbabwe	Sheikhupura	1996-97
292	R.Peel/Lord Hawke	Yorkshire v Warwicks	Birmingham	1896

Ninth Wicket

283	J.Chapman/A.Warren	Derbys v Warwicks	Blackwell	1910
268	J.B.Commins/N.Boje	SA 'A' v Mashonaland	Harare	1994-95
251	J.W.H.T.Douglas/S.N.Hare	Essex v Derbyshire	Leyton	1921

Tenth Wicket

307	A.F.Kippax/J.E.H.Hooker	NSW v Victoria	Melbourne	1928-29
249	C.T.Sarwate/S.N.Banerjee	Indians v Surrey	The Oval	1946
235	F.E.Woolley/A.Fielder	Kent v Worcs	Stourbridge	1909

35000 RUNS IN A CAREER

	Career	I	NO	HS	Runs	Avge	100
J.B.Hobbs	1905-34	1315	106	316*	61237	50.65	197
F.E.Woolley	1906-38	1532	85	305*	58969	40.75	145
E.H.Hendren	1907-38	1300	166	301*	57611	50.80	170
C.P.Mead	1905-36	1340	185	280*	55061	47.67	153
W.G.Grace	1865-1908	1493	105	344	54896	39.55	126
W.R.Hammond	1920-51	1005	104	336*	50551	56.10	167
H.Sutcliffe	1919-45	1088	123	313	50138	51.95	149
G.Boycott	1962-86	1014	162	261*	48426	56.83	151
T.W.Graveney	1948-71/72	1223	159	258	47793	44.91	122
G.A.Gooch	1973-2000	990	75	333	44846	49.01	128
T.W.Hayward	1893-1914	1138	96	315*	43551	41.79	104
D.L.Amiss	1960-87	1139	126	262*	43423	42.86	102
M.C.Cowdrey	1950-76	1130	134	307	42719	42.89	107
A.Sandham	1911-37/38	1000	79	325	41284	44.82	107
L.Hutton	1934-60	814	91	364	40140	55.51	129
M.J.K.Smith	1951-75	1091	139	204	39832	41.84	69
W.Rhodes	1898-1930	1528	237	267*	39802	30.83	58
J.H.Edrich	1956-78	979	104	310*	39790	45.47	103
R.E.S.Wyatt	1923-57	1141	157	232	39405	40.04	85
D.C.S.Compton	1936-64	839	88	300	38942	51.85	123
G.E.Tyldesley	1909-36	961	106	256*	38874	45.46	102
J.T.Tyldesley	1895-1923	994	62	295*	37897	40.60	86
K.W.R.Fletcher	1962-88	1167	170	228*	37665	37.77	63
G.A.Hick	1983/84-2004	777	76	405*	37505	53.50	126
C.G.Greenidge	1970-92	889	75	273*	37354	45.88	92
J.W.Hearne	1909-36	1025	116	285*	37252	40.98	96
L.E.G.Ames	1926-51	951	95	295	37248	43.51	102
D.Kenyon	1946-67	1159	59	259	37002	33.63	74
W.J.Edrich	1934-58	964	92	267*	36965	42.39	86
J.M.Parks	1949-76	1227	172	205*	36673	34.76	51
M.W.Gatting	1975-98	861	123	258	36549	49.52	94
D.Denton	1894-1920	1163	70	221	36479	33.37	69
G.H.Hirst	1891-1929	1215	151	341	36323	34.13	60
I.V.A.Richards	1971/72-93	796	63	322	36212	49.40	114
A.Jones	1957-83	1168	72	204*	36049	32.89	56
W.G.Quaife	1894-1928	1203	185	255*	36012	35.37	72
R.E.Marshall	1945/46-72	1053	59	228*	35725	35.94	68
G.Gunn	1902-32	1061	82	220	35208	35.96	62

BOWLING RECORDS

ALL TEN WICKETS IN AN INNINGS

This feat has been achieved 78 times in first-class matches (excluding 12-a-side fixtures).
Three Times: A.P.Freeman (1929, 1930, 1931)
Twice: V.E.Walker (1859, 1865); H.Verity (1931, 1932); J.C.Laker (1956)

Instances since 1945:

W.E.Hollies	Warwickshire v Notts	Birmingham	1946
J.M.Sims	East v West	Kingston on Thames	1948
J.K.R.Graveney	Gloucestershire v Derbyshire	Chesterfield	1949
T.E.Bailey	Essex v Lancashire	Clacton	1949
R.Berry	Lancashire v Worcestershire	Blackpool	1953
S.P.Gupte	President's XI v Combined XI	Bombay	1954-55
J.C.Laker	Surrey v Australians	The Oval	1956

K.Smales	Nottinghamshire v Glos	Stroud	1956
G.A.R.Lock	Surrey v Kent	Blackheath	1956
J.C.Laker	England v Australia	Manchester	1956
P.M.Chatterjee	Bengal v Assam	Jorhat	1956-57
J.D.Bannister	Warwicks v Combined Services	Birmingham (M & B)	1959
A.J.G.Pearson	Cambridge U v Leicestershire	Loughborough	1961
N.I.Thomson	Sussex v Warwickshire	Worthing	1964
P.J.Allan	Queensland v Victoria	Melbourne	1965-66
I.J.Brayshaw	Western Australia v Victoria	Perth	1967-68
Shahid Mahmood	Karachi Whites v Khairpur	Karachi	1969-70
E.E.Hemmings	International XI v W Indians	Kingston	1982-83
P.Sunderam	Rajasthan v Vidarbha	Jodhpur	1985-86
S.T.Jefferies	Western Province v OFS	Cape Town	1987-88
Imran Adil	Bahawalpur v Faisalabad	Faisalabad	1989-90
G.P.Wickremasinghe	Sinhalese v Kalutara	Colombo	1991-92
R.L.Johnson	Middlesex v Derbyshire	Derby	1994
Naeem Akhtar	Rawalpindi B v Peshawar	Peshawar	1995-96
A.Kumble	India v Pakistan	Delhi	1998-99
D.S.Mohanty	East Zone v South Zone	Agartala	2000-01

MOST WICKETS IN A MATCH

| 19 | J.C.Laker | England v Australia | Manchester | 1956 |

MOST WICKETS IN A SEASON

Wkts		Season	Matches	Overs	Mdns	Runs	Avge
304	A.P.Freeman	1928	37	1976.1	423	5489	18.05
298	A.P.Freeman	1933	33	2039	651	4549	15.26

The feat of taking 250 wickets in a season has been achieved on 12 occasions, the last instance being by A.P.Freeman in 1933. 200 or more wickets in a season have been taken on 59 occasions, the last being by G.A.R.Lock (212 wickets, average 12.02) in 1957.

The highest aggregates of wickets taken in a season since the reduction of County Championship matches in 1969 are as follows:

Wkts		Season	Matches	Overs	Mdns	Runs	Avge
134	M.D.Marshall	1982	22	822	225	2108	15.73
131	L.R.Gibbs	1971	23	1024.1	295	2475	18.89
125	F.D.Stephenson	1988	22	819.1	196	2289	18.31
121	R.D.Jackman	1980	23	746.2	220	1864	15.40

Since 1969 there have been 50 instances of bowlers taking 100 wickets in a season.

MOST HAT-TRICKS IN A CAREER

7	D.V.P.Wright
6	T.W.J.Goddard, C.W.L.Parker
5	S.Haigh, V.W.C.Jupp, A.E.G.Rhodes, F.A.Tarrant

2000 WICKETS IN A CAREER

	Career	Runs	Wkts	Avge	100w
W.Rhodes	1898-1930	69993	4187	16.71	23
A.P.Freeman	1914-36	69577	3776	18.42	17
C.W.L.Parker	1903-35	63817	3278	19.46	16
J.T.Hearne	1888-1923	54352	3061	17.75	15
T.W.J.Goddard	1922-52	59116	2979	19.84	16
W.G.Grace	1865-1908	51545	2876	17.92	10
A.S.Kennedy	1907-36	61034	2874	21.23	15
D.Shackleton	1948-69	53303	2857	18.65	20
G.A.R.Lock	1946-70/71	54709	2844	19.23	14

	Career	Runs	Wkts	Avge	100w
F.J.Titmus	1949-82	63313	**2830**	22.37	16
M.W.Tate	1912-37	50571	**2784**	18.16	13+1
G.H.Hirst	1891-1929	51282	**2739**	18.72	15
C.Blythe	1899-1914	42136	**2506**	16.81	14
D.L.Underwood	1963-87	49993	**2465**	20.28	10
W.E.Astill	1906-39	57783	**2431**	23.76	9
J.C.White	1909-37	43759	**2356**	18.57	14
W.E.Hollies	1932-57	48656	**2323**	20.94	14
F.S.Trueman	1949-69	42154	**2304**	18.29	12
J.B.Statham	1950-68	36999	**2260**	16.37	13
R.T.D.Perks	1930-55	53771	**2233**	24.07	16
J.Briggs	1879-1900	35431	**2221**	15.95	12
D.J.Shepherd	1950-72	47302	**2218**	21.32	12
E.G.Dennett	1903-26	42571	**2147**	19.82	12
T.Richardson	1892-1905	38794	**2104**	18.43	10
T.E.Bailey	1945-67	48170	**2082**	23.13	9
R.Illingworth	1951-83	42023	**2072**	20.28	10
F.E.Woolley	1906-38	41066	**2068**	19.85	8
N.Gifford	1960-88	48731	**2068**	23.56	4
G.Geary	1912-38	41339	**2063**	20.03	11
D.V.P.Wright	1932-57	49307	**2056**	23.98	10
J.A.Newman	1906-30	51111	**2032**	25.15	9
A.Shaw	1864-97	24580	**2026**+1	12.12	9
S.Haigh	1895-1913	32091	**2012**	15.94	11

ALL-ROUND RECORDS

THE 'DOUBLE'

3000 runs and 100 wickets: J.H.Parks (1937)
2000 runs and 200 wickets: G.H.Hirst (1906)
2000 runs and 100 wickets: F.E.Woolley (4), J.W.Hearne (3), W.G.Grace (2), G.H.Hirst (2), W.Rhodes (2), T.E.Bailey, D.E.Davies, G.L.Jessop, V.W.C.Jupp, J.Langridge, F.A.Tarrant, C.L.Townsend, L.F.Townsend
1000 runs and 200 wickets: M.W.Tate (3), A.E.Trott (2), A.S.Kennedy

Most Doubles: 16 – W.Rhodes; 14 – G.H.Hirst; 10 – V.W.C.Jupp

Double in Debut Season: D.B.Close (1949) – aged 18, the youngest to achieve this feat.

The feat of scoring 1000 runs and taking 100 wickets in a season has been achieved on 305 occasions, R.J.Hadlee (1984) and F.D.Stephenson (1988) being the only players to complete the 'double' since the reduction of County Championship matches in 1969.

WICKET-KEEPING RECORDS

EIGHT DISMISSALS IN AN INNINGS

9	(8ct, 1st)	Tahir Rashid	Habib Bank v PACO	Gujranwala	1992-93
9	(7ct, 2st)	W.R.James	Matabeleland v Mashonaland CD	Bulawayo	1995-96
8	(8ct)	A.T.W.Grout	Queensland v W Australia	Brisbane	1959-60
8	(8ct)	D.E.East	Essex v Somerset	Taunton	1985
8	(8ct)	S.A.Marsh	Kent v Middlesex	Lord's	1991
8	(6ct, 2st)	T.J.Zoehrer	Australians v Surrey	The Oval	1993
8	(7ct, 1st)	D.S.Berry	Victoria v South Australia	Melbourne	1996-97
8	(7ct, 1st)	Y.S.S.Mendis	Bloomfield v Kurungela Youth	Colombo	2000-01
8	(7ct, 1st)	S.Nath	Assam v Tripura (*on debut*)	Gauhati	2001-02
8	(8ct)	J.N.Batty	Surrey v Kent	The Oval	2004

TWELVE DISMISSALS IN A MATCH

13	(11ct, 2st)	W.R.James	Matabeleland v Mashonaland CD	Bulawayo	1995-96
12	(8ct, 4st)	E.Pooley	Surrey v Sussex	The Oval	1868
12	(9ct, 3st)	D.Tallon	Queensland v NSW	Sydney	1938-39
12	(9ct, 3st)	H.B.Taber	NSW v South Australia	Adelaide	1968-69

MOST DISMISSALS IN A SEASON

128 (79ct, 49st) L.E.G.Ames   1929

1000 DISMISSALS IN A CAREER

	Career	Dismissals	Ct	St
R.W.Taylor	1960-88	**1649**	1473	176
J.T.Murray	1952-75	**1527**	1270	257
H.Strudwick	1902-27	**1497**	1242	255
A.P.E.Knott	1964-85	**1344**	1211	133
R.C.Russell	1981-2004	**1320**	1192	128
F.H.Huish	1895-1914	**1310**	933	377
B.Taylor	1949-73	**1294**	1083	211
S.J.Rhodes	1981-2004	**1263**	1139	124
D.Hunter	1889-1909	**1253**	906	347
H.R.Butt	1890-1912	**1228**	953	275
J.H.Board	1891-1914/15	**1207**	852	355
H.Elliott	1920-47	**1206**	904	302
J.M.Parks	1949-76	**1181**	1088	93
R.Booth	1951-70	**1126**	948	178
L.E.G.Ames	1926-51	**1121**	703	418
D.L.Bairstow	1970-90	**1099**	961	138
G.Duckworth	1923-47	**1096**	753	343
H.W.Stephenson	1948-64	**1082**	748	334
J.G.Binks	1955-75	**1071**	895	176
T.G.Evans	1939-69	**1066**	816	250
A.Long	1960-80	**1046**	922	124
G.O.Dawkes	1937-61	**1043**	895	148
R.W.Tolchard	1965-83	**1037**	912	125
W.L.Cornford	1921-47	**1017**	675	342

FIELDING RECORDS

MOST CATCHES IN AN INNINGS

7	M.J.Stewart	Surrey v Northamptonshire	Northampton	1957
7	A.S.Brown	Gloucestershire v Nottinghamshire	Nottingham	1966

MOST CATCHES IN A MATCH

10	W.R.Hammond	Gloucestershire v Surrey	Cheltenham	1928

MOST CATCHES IN A SEASON

78	W.R.Hammond	1928	77	M.J.Stewart	1957

750 CATCHES IN A CAREER

1018	F.E.Woolley	1906-38	784	J.G.Langridge	1928-55
887	W.G.Grace	1865-1908	764	W.Rhodes	1898-1930
830	G.A.R.Lock	1946-70/71	758	C.A.Milton	1948-74
819	W.R.Hammond	1920-51	754	E.H.Hendren	1907-38
813	D.B.Close	1949-86			

LIMITED-OVERS INTERNATIONALS RESULTS

1970-71 to 13 February 2005

For reasons outlined in the Preface these records exclude the Tsunami Appeal match between a World XI and an Asian XI at Melbourne in January 2005, and the NatWest Series match between West Indies and New Zealand at Southampton in 2004 abandoned without a ball bowled after the toss.

Opponents		Matches	Won																				Tied	NR
			E	A	SA	WI	NZ	I	P	SL	Z	B	C	EA	H	K	N	SC	UAE	HK	USA		
England	Australia	78	32	44	–	–	–	–	–	–	–	–	–	–	–	–	–	–	–	–	–	1	1
	South Africa	34	11	–	21	–	–	–	–	–	–	–	–	–	–	–	–	–	–	–	–	1	1
	West Indies	70	29	–	–	37	–	–	–	–	–	–	–	–	–	–	–	–	–	–	–	–	4
	New Zealand	54	25	–	–	–	25	–	–	–	–	–	–	–	–	–	–	–	–	–	–	1	3
	India	51	25	–	–	–	–	24	–	–	–	–	–	–	–	–	–	–	–	–	–	–	2
	Pakistan	53	31	–	–	–	–	–	21	–	–	–	–	–	–	–	–	–	–	–	–	–	1
	Sri Lanka	32	19	–	–	–	–	–	–	13	–	–	–	–	–	–	–	–	–	–	–	–	–
	Zimbabwe	30	21	–	–	–	–	–	–	–	8	–	–	–	–	–	–	–	–	–	–	–	1
	Bangladesh	4	4	–	–	–	–	–	–	–	–	0	–	–	–	–	–	–	–	–	–	–	–
	Canada	1	1	–	–	–	–	–	–	–	–	–	0	–	–	–	–	–	–	–	–	–	–
	East Africa	1	1	–	–	–	–	–	–	–	–	–	–	0	–	–	–	–	–	–	–	–	–
	Holland	2	2	–	–	–	–	–	–	–	–	–	–	–	0	–	–	–	–	–	–	–	–
	Kenya	1	1	–	–	–	–	–	–	–	–	–	–	–	–	0	–	–	–	–	–	–	–
	Namibia	1	1	–	–	–	–	–	–	–	–	–	–	–	–	–	0	–	–	–	–	–	–
	U A Emirates	1	1	–	–	–	–	–	–	–	–	–	–	–	–	–	–	–	0	–	–	–	–
Australia	South Africa	56	–	29	24	–	–	–	–	–	–	–	–	–	–	–	–	–	–	–	–	–	3
	West Indies	108	–	49	–	55	–	–	–	–	–	–	–	–	–	–	–	–	–	–	–	2	2
	New Zealand	92	–	63	–	–	26	–	–	–	–	–	–	–	–	–	–	–	–	–	–	–	3
	India	80	–	49	–	–	–	27	–	–	–	–	–	–	–	–	–	–	–	–	–	–	4
	Pakistan	74	–	43	–	–	–	–	27	–	–	–	–	–	–	–	–	–	–	–	–	1	3
	Sri Lanka	55	–	36	–	–	–	–	–	17	–	–	–	–	–	–	–	–	–	–	–	–	2
	Zimbabwe	27	–	25	–	–	–	–	–	–	1	–	–	–	–	–	–	–	–	–	–	–	1
	Bangladesh	6	–	6	–	–	–	–	–	–	–	0	–	–	–	–	–	–	–	–	–	–	–
	Canada	1	–	1	–	–	–	–	–	–	–	–	0	–	–	–	–	–	–	–	–	–	–
	Holland	1	–	1	–	–	–	–	–	–	–	–	–	–	0	–	–	–	–	–	–	–	–
	Kenya	4	–	4	–	–	–	–	–	–	–	–	–	–	–	0	–	–	–	–	–	–	–
	Namibia	1	–	1	–	–	–	–	–	–	–	–	–	–	–	–	0	–	–	–	–	–	–
	Scotland	1	–	1	–	–	–	–	–	–	–	–	–	–	–	–	–	0	–	–	–	–	–
	USA	1	–	1	–	–	–	–	–	–	–	–	–	–	–	–	–	–	–	–	0	–	–
S Africa	West Indies	33	–	–	21	11	–	–	–	–	–	–	–	–	–	–	–	–	–	–	–	–	1
	N Zealand	40	–	–	23	–	14	–	–	–	–	–	–	–	–	–	–	–	–	–	–	–	3
	India	46	–	–	28	–	–	16	–	–	–	–	–	–	–	–	–	–	–	–	–	–	2
	Pakistan	41	–	–	28	–	–	–	13	–	–	–	–	–	–	–	–	–	–	–	–	–	–
	Sri Lanka	39	–	–	18	–	–	–	–	19	–	–	–	–	–	–	–	–	–	–	–	1	1
	Zimbabwe	18	–	–	15	–	–	–	–	–	2	–	–	–	–	–	–	–	–	–	–	–	1
	Bangladesh	7	–	–	7	–	–	–	–	–	–	0	–	–	–	–	–	–	–	–	–	–	–
	Canada	1	–	–	1	–	–	–	–	–	–	–	0	–	–	–	–	–	–	–	–	–	–
	Holland	1	–	–	1	–	–	–	–	–	–	–	–	–	0	–	–	–	–	–	–	–	–
	Kenya	8	–	–	8	–	–	–	–	–	–	–	–	–	–	0	–	–	–	–	–	–	–
	U A Emirates	1	–	–	1	–	–	–	–	–	–	–	–	–	–	–	–	–	0	–	–	–	–
W Indies	New Zealand	39	–	–	–	22	13	–	–	–	–	–	–	–	–	–	–	–	–	–	–	–	4
	India	76	–	–	–	46	–	28	–	–	–	–	–	–	–	–	–	–	–	–	–	1	1
	Pakistan	102	–	–	–	62	–	–	38	–	–	–	–	–	–	–	–	–	–	–	–	2	–
	Sri Lanka	39	–	–	–	23	–	–	–	15	–	–	–	–	–	–	–	–	–	–	–	–	1
	Zimbabwe	24	–	–	–	17	–	–	–	–	7	–	–	–	–	–	–	–	–	–	–	–	–
	Bangladesh	11	–	–	–	9	–	–	–	–	–	0	–	–	–	–	–	–	–	–	–	–	2
	Canada	1	–	–	–	1	–	–	–	–	–	–	0	–	–	–	–	–	–	–	–	–	–
	Kenya	6	–	–	–	5	–	–	–	–	–	–	–	–	–	1	–	–	–	–	–	–	–
	Scotland	1	–	–	–	1	–	–	–	–	–	–	–	–	–	–	–	0	–	–	–	–	–
N Zealand	India	72	–	–	–	–	33	35	–	–	–	–	–	–	–	–	–	–	–	–	–	–	4
	Pakistan	77	–	–	–	–	28	–	47	–	–	–	–	–	–	–	–	–	–	–	–	1	1
	Sri Lanka	56	–	–	–	–	29	–	–	24	–	–	–	–	–	–	–	–	–	–	–	1	2
	Zimbabwe	26	–	–	–	–	17	–	–	–	7	–	–	–	–	–	–	–	–	–	–	1	1
	Bangladesh	7	–	–	–	–	7	–	–	–	–	0	–	–	–	–	–	–	–	–	–	–	–
	Canada	1	–	–	–	–	1	–	–	–	–	–	0	–	–	–	–	–	–	–	–	–	–
	East Africa	1	–	–	–	–	1	–	–	–	–	–	–	0	–	–	–	–	–	–	–	–	–

Team	Opponents	Matches	E	A	SA	WI	NZ	I	P	SL	Z	B	C	EA	H	K	N	SC	UAE	HK	USA	Tied	NR
	Holland	1	-	-	-	-	1	-	-	-	-	-	-	-	0	-	-	-	-	-	-	-	-
	Scotland	1	-	-	-	-	1	-	-	-	-	-	-	-	-	-	-	0	-	-	-	-	-
	U A Emirates	1	-	-	-	-	1	-	-	-	-	-	-	-	-	-	-	-	0	-	-	-	-
	USA	1	-	-	-	-	1	-	-	-	-	-	-	-	-	-	-	-	-	-	0	-	-
India	Pakistan	95	-	-	-	-	-	33	58	-	-	-	-	-	-	-	-	-	-	-	-	-	4
	Sri Lanka	79	-	-	-	-	-	41	-	31	-	-	-	-	-	-	-	-	-	-	-	-	7
	Zimbabwe	47	-	-	-	-	-	37	-	-	8	-	-	-	-	-	-	-	-	-	-	2	-
	Bangladesh	14	-	-	-	-	-	13	-	-	-	1	-	-	-	-	-	-	-	-	-	-	-
	East Africa	1	-	-	-	-	-	1	-	-	-	-	-	0	-	-	-	-	-	-	-	-	-
	Holland	1	-	-	-	-	-	1	-	-	-	-	-	-	0	-	-	-	-	-	-	-	-
	Kenya	13	-	-	-	-	-	11	-	-	-	-	-	-	-	2	-	-	-	-	-	-	-
	Namibia	1	-	-	-	-	-	1	-	-	-	-	-	-	-	-	0	-	-	-	-	-	-
	U A Emirates	2	-	-	-	-	-	2	-	-	-	-	-	-	-	-	-	-	0	-	-	-	-
Pakistan	Sri Lanka	103	-	-	-	-	-	-	62	38	-	-	-	-	-	-	-	-	-	-	-	1	2
	Zimbabwe	34	-	-	-	-	-	-	30	-	2	-	-	-	-	-	-	-	-	-	-	1	1
	Bangladesh	18	-	-	-	-	-	-	17	-	-	1	-	-	-	-	-	-	-	-	-	-	-
	Canada	1	-	-	-	-	-	-	1	-	-	-	0	-	-	-	-	-	-	-	-	-	-
	Holland	3	-	-	-	-	-	-	3	-	-	-	-	-	0	-	-	-	-	-	-	-	-
	Kenya	5	-	-	-	-	-	-	5	-	-	-	-	-	-	0	-	-	-	-	-	-	-
	Namibia	1	-	-	-	-	-	-	1	-	-	-	-	-	-	-	0	-	-	-	-	-	-
	Scotland	1	-	-	-	-	-	-	1	-	-	-	-	-	-	-	-	0	-	-	-	-	-
	U A Emirates	2	-	-	-	-	-	-	2	-	-	-	-	-	-	-	-	-	0	-	-	-	-
	Hong Kong	1	-	-	-	-	-	-	1	-	-	-	-	-	-	-	-	-	-	0	-	-	-
Sri Lanka	Zimbabwe	36	-	-	-	-	-	-	-	29	6	-	-	-	-	-	-	-	-	-	-	-	1
	Bangladesh	11	-	-	-	-	-	-	-	11	-	0	-	-	-	-	-	-	-	-	-	-	-
	Canada	1	-	-	-	-	-	-	-	1	-	-	0	-	-	-	-	-	-	-	-	-	-
	Holland	1	-	-	-	-	-	-	-	1	-	-	-	-	0	-	-	-	-	-	-	-	-
	Kenya	5	-	-	-	-	-	-	-	4	-	-	-	-	-	1	-	-	-	-	-	-	-
	UAE	1	-	-	-	-	-	-	-	1	-	-	-	-	-	-	-	-	0	-	-	-	-
Zimbabwe	Bangladesh	18	-	-	-	-	-	-	-	-	14	4	-	-	-	-	-	-	-	-	-	-	-
	Holland	1	-	-	-	-	-	-	-	-	1	-	-	-	0	-	-	-	-	-	-	-	-
	Kenya	16	-	-	-	-	-	-	-	-	13	-	-	-	-	1	-	-	-	-	-	-	2
	Namibia	1	-	-	-	-	-	-	-	-	1	-	-	-	-	-	0	-	-	-	-	-	-
Bangladesh	Canada	1	-	-	-	-	-	-	-	-	-	0	1	-	-	-	-	-	-	-	-	-	-
	Kenya	7	-	-	-	-	-	-	-	-	-	1	-	-	-	6	-	-	-	-	-	-	-
	Scotland	1	-	-	-	-	-	-	-	-	-	1	-	-	-	-	-	0	-	-	-	-	-
	Hong Kong	1	-	-	-	-	-	-	-	-	-	1	-	-	-	-	-	-	-	0	-	-	-
Kenya	Canada	1	-	-	-	-	-	-	-	-	-	-	1	-	-	0	-	-	-	-	-	-	-
Holland	U A Emirates	1	-	-	-	-	-	-	-	-	-	-	-	-	0	-	-	-	1	-	-	-	-
	Namibia	1	-	-	-	-	-	-	-	-	-	-	-	-	1	-	0	-	-	-	-	-	-
		2224	204	353	196	289	198	270	327	204	70	9	1	0	1	12	0	0	0	1	0	20	69

MERIT TABLE OF ALL L-O INTERNATIONALS
1970-71 to 13 February 2005

	Matches	Won	Lost	Tied	No Result	% Won (exc NR)
Australia	585	353	209	7	16	62.03
South Africa	325	196	115	5	9	62.02
West Indies	510	289	201	5	15	58.38
Pakistan	611	327	266	6	12	54.59
England	413	204	193	3	13	51.00
India	578	270	281	3	24	48.73
Sri Lanka	458	204	235	3	16	46.15
New Zealand	469	198	246	4	21	44.19
Zimbabwe	278	70	196	4	8	25.92
Kenya	66	12	52	–	2	18.75
Bangladesh	106	9	95	–	2	8.65
Associate Members	49	3	46	–	–	6.12

TEAM RECORDS
HIGHEST TOTALS

398-5	(50 overs)	Sri Lanka v Kenya	Kandy	1995-96
376-2	(50 overs)	India v New Zealand	Hyderabad, India	1999-00
373-6	(50 overs)	India v Sri Lanka	Taunton	1999
371-9	(50 overs)	Pakistan v Sri Lanka	Nairobi	1996-97
363-3	(50 overs)	South Africa v Zimbabwe	Bulawayo	2001-02
363-7	(55 overs)	England v Pakistan	Nottingham	1992
360-4	(50 overs)	West Indies v Sri Lanka	Karachi	1987-88
359-2	(50 overs)	Australia v India	Johannesburg	2002-03
359-5	(50 overs)	Australia v India	Sydney	2003-04
354-3	(50 overs)	South Africa v Kenya	Cape Town	2001-02
353-5	(50 overs)	India v New Zealand	Hyderabad, India	2003-04
351-3	(50 overs)	India v Kenya	Paarl	2001-02

The highest for New Zealand is 349-9 (v India, Rajkot, 1999-00), for Zimbabwe 340-2 (v Namibia, Harare, 2002-03), for Bangladesh 272-8 (v Z, Bulawayo, 2000-01), and for Kenya 347-3 (v B, Nairobi, 1997-98).

HIGHEST TOTALS BATTING SECOND

WINNING:	330-7	(49.1 overs)	Australia v South Africa	Port Elizabeth	2001-02
LOSING:	344-8	(50.0 overs)	Pakistan v India	Karachi	2003-04

HIGHEST MATCH AGGREGATE

693-15	(100.0 overs)	India (349-7) v Pakistan (344-8)	Karachi	2003-04

LARGEST RUNS MARGINS OF VICTORY

256 runs	Australia beat Namibia	Potschefstroom	2002-03
245 runs	Sri Lanka beat India	Sharjah	2000-01
233 runs	Pakistan v Bangladesh	Dhaka	1999-00
232 runs	Australia beat Sri Lanka	Adelaide	1984-85
224 runs	Australia beat Pakistan	Nairobi	2002
217 runs	Pakistan beat Sri Lanka	Sharjah	2001-02
210 runs	New Zealand beat USA	The Oval	2004
209 runs	South Africa beat West Indies	Cape Town	2003-04
208 runs	South Africa beat Kenya	Cape Town	2001-02
208 runs	Australia beat India	Sydney	2003-04
206 runs	New Zealand beat Australia	Adelaide	1985-86
206 runs	Sri Lanka beat Holland	Colombo (RPS)	2002-03
202 runs	England beat India	Lord's	1975
202 runs	South Africa beat Kenya	Nairobi	1996-97
202 runs	Zimbabwe beat Kenya	Dhaka	1998-99
200 runs	India beat Bangladesh	Dhaka	2002-03

LOWEST TOTALS (Excluding reduced innings)

35	18.0 overs)	Zimbabwe v Sri Lanka	Harare	2003-04
36	(18.4 overs)	Canada v Sri Lanka	Paarl	2002-03
38	(15.4 overs)	Zimbabwe v Sri Lanka	Colombo (SSC)	2001-02
43	(19.5 overs)	Pakistan v West Indies	Cape Town	1992-93
45	(40.3 overs)	Canada v England	Manchester	1979
45	(14.0 overs)	Namibia v Australia	Potschefstroom	2002-03
54	(26.3 overs)	India v Sri Lanka	Sharjah	2000-01
54	(23.2 overs)	West Indies v South Africa	Cape Town	2003-04
55	(28.3 overs)	Sri Lanka v West Indies	Sharjah	1986-87
63	(25.5 overs)	India v Australia	Sydney	1980-81
64	(35.5 overs)	New Zealand v Pakistan	Sharjah	1985-86
65	(24.0 overs)	USA v Australia	Southampton	2004
68	(31.3 overs)	Scotland v West Indies	Leicester	1999
69	(28.0 overs)	South Africa v Australia	Sydney	1993-94
70	(25.2 overs)	Australia v England	Birmingham	1977
70	(26.3 overs)	Australia v New Zealand	Adelaide	1985-86

The lowest for England is 86 (v A, Manchester, 2001), for Bangladesh 76 (v SL, Colombo (SSC), 2002, and v I, Dhaka, 2002-03), and for Kenya 84 (v A, Nairobi, 2002).

LOWEST MATCH AGGREGATES

73-11	(23.2 overs)	Canada (36) v Sri Lanka (37-1)	Paarl	2002-03
75-11	(27.2 overs)	Zimbabwe (35) v Sri Lanka (40-1)	Harare	2003-04
78-11	(20.0 overs)	Zimbabwe (38) v Sri Lanka (40-1)	Colombo (SSC)	2001-02

BATTING RECORDS
HIGHEST INDIVIDUAL INNINGS

194	Saeed Anwar	Pakistan v India	Madras	1996-97
189*	I.V.A.Richards	West Indies v England	Manchester	1984
189	S.T.Jayasuriya	Sri Lanka v India	Sharjah	2000-01
188*	G.Kirsten	South Africa v UAE	Rawalpindi	1995-96
186*	S.R.Tendulkar	India v New Zealand	Hyderabad	1999-00
183	S.C.Ganguly	India v Sri Lanka	Taunton	1999
181	I.V.A.Richards	West Indies v Sri Lanka	Karachi	1987-88
175*	Kapil Dev	India v Zimbabwe	Tunbridge Wells	1983
173	M.E.Waugh	Australia v West Indies	Melbourne	2000-01
172*	C.B.Wishart	Zimbabwe v Namibia	Harare	2002-03
172	A.C.Gilchrist	Australia v Zimbabwe	Hobart	2003-04
171*	G.M.Turner	New Zealand v East Africa	Birmingham	1975
169*	D.J.Callaghan	South Africa v New Zealand	Pretoria	1994-95
169	B.C.Lara	West Indies v Sri Lanka	Sharjah	1995-96
167*	R.A.Smith	England v Australia	Birmingham	1993
161	A.C.Hudson	South Africa v Holland	Rawalpindi	1995-96
159*	D.Mongia	India v Zimbabwe	Gauhati	2001-02
158	D.I.Gower	England v New Zealand	Brisbane	1982-83
156	B.C.Lara	West Indies v Pakistan	Adelaide	2004-05
154	A.C.Gilchrist	Australia v Sri Lanka	Melbourne	1998-99
153*	I.V.A.Richards	West Indies v Australia	Melbourne	1979-80
153*	M.Azharuddin	India v Zimbabwe	Cuttack	1997-98
153*	S.C.Ganguly	India v New Zealand	Gwalior	1999-00
153*	C.H.Gayle	West Indies v Zimbabwe	Bulawayo	2003-04
153	B.C.Lara	West Indies v Pakistan	Sharjah	1993-94
153	R.Dravid	India v New Zealand	Hyderabad	1999-00
153	H.H.Gibbs	South Africa v Bangladesh	Potchefstroom	2002-03
152*	D.L.Haynes	West Indies v India	Georgetown	1988-89
152*	C.H.Gayle	West Indies v South Africa	Johannesburg	2003-04
152	C.H.Gayle	West Indies v Kenya	Nairobi	2001-02
152	S.R.Tendulkar	India v Namibia	Pietermaritzburg	2002-03
151*	S.T.Jayasuriya	Sri Lanka v India	Bombay	1996-97
150	S.Chanderpaul	West Indies v South Africa	East London	1998-99

The highest for Bangladesh is 101 by Mehrab Hossain (v Z, Dhaka, 1998-99), and for Kenya 144 by K.O.Obuya (v B, Nairobi, 1997-98).

HUNDRED ON DEBUT

D.L.Amiss	103	England v Australia	Manchester	1972
D.L.Haynes	148	West Indies v Australia	St John's	1977-78
A.Flower	115*	Zimbabwe v Sri Lanka	New Plymouth	1991-92
Salim Elahi	102*	Pakistan v Sri Lanka	Gujranwala	1995-96

Shahid Afridi scored 102 for P v SL, Nairobi, 1996-97, in his second match having not batted in his first.

Fastest 100	37 balls	Shahid Afridi (102)	P v SL	Nairobi	1996-97
Fastest 50	17 balls	S.T.Jayasuriya (76)	SL v P	Singapore	1995-96

CARRYING BAT THROUGH INNINGS (SIDE ALL OUT)

G.W.Flower	84*	Zimbabwe (205) v England	Sydney	1994-95
Saeed Anwar	103*	Pakistan (219) v Zimbabwe	Harare	1994-95
N.V.Knight	125*	England (246) v Pakistan	Nottingham	1996
R.D.Jacobs	49*	West Indies (110) v Australia	Manchester	1999
D.R.Martyn	116*	Australia (191) v New Zealand	Auckland	1999-00
H.H.Gibbs	59*	South Africa (101) v Pakistan	Sharjah	1999-00
A.J.Stewart	100*	England (192) v West Indies	Nottingham	2000
Javed Omar	33*	Bangladesh (103) v Zimbabwe	Harare	2000-01

5000 RUNS IN A CAREER

		LOI	I	NO	HS	Runs	Avge	100	50
S.R.Tendulkar	I	342	333	32	186*	13497	44.84	37	69
Inzamam-ul-Haq	P	336	312	44	137*	10631	39.66	10	78
S.C.Ganguly	I	266	257	20	183	9914	41.83	22	59
S.T.Jayasuriya	SL	333	324	14	189	9896	31.92	18	57
M.Azharuddin	I	334	308	54	153*	9378	36.92	7	58
P.A.de Silva	SL	308	296	30	145	9284	34.90	11	64
B.C.Lara	WI	249	243	26	169	9228	42.52	19	56
Saeed Anwar	P	247	244	19	194	8823	39.21	20	43
D.L.Haynes	WI	238	237	28	152*	8648	41.37	17	57
M.E.Waugh	A	244	236	20	173	8500	39.35	18	50
R.Dravid	I	245	224	27	153	7750	39.34	9	56
R.T.Ponting	A	217	212	27	145	7606	41.11	15	42
S.R.Waugh	A	325	288	58	120*	7569	32.90	3	45
J.H.Kallis	SA	210	201	36	139	7495	45.42	13	51
A.Ranatunga	SL	269	255	47	131*	7454	35.83	4	49
Javed Miandad	P	233	218	41	119*	7381	41.70	8	50
M.S.Atapattu	SL	225	219	26	132*	7296	37.80	11	50
Salim Malik	P	283	256	38	102	7171	32.89	5	47
M.G.Bevan	A	232	196	67	108*	6912	53.58	6	46
G.Kirsten	SA	185	185	19	188*	6798	40.95	13	45
A.Flower	Z	213	208	16	145	6786	35.34	4	55
A.C.Gilchrist	A	203	197	7	172	6778	35.67	10	39
I.V.A.Richards	WI	187	167	24	189*	6721	47.00	11	45
Ijaz Ahmed	P	250	232	29	139*	6564	32.33	10	37
S.P.Fleming	NZ	228	220	19	134*	6539	32.53	6	38
G.W.Flower	Z	219	212	18	142*	6536	33.69	6	40
A.R.Border	A	273	252	39	127*	6524	30.62	3	39
Yousuf Youhana	P	189	179	27	141*	6414	42.19	11	40
R.B.Richardson	WI	224	217	30	122	6248	33.41	5	44
D.M.Jones	A	164	161	25	145	6068	44.61	7	46
N.J.Astle	NZ	187	184	11	145*	6030	34.85	14	35
D.C.Boon	A	181	177	16	122	5964	37.04	5	37
J.N.Rhodes	SA	245	220	51	121	5935	35.11	2	33
Ramiz Raja	P	198	197	15	119*	5841	32.09	9	31
C.L.Hooper	WI	227	206	43	113*	5761	35.34	7	29
W.J.Cronje	SA	188	175	31	112	5565	38.64	2	39
A.Jadeja	I	196	179	36	119	5359	37.47	6	30
H.H.Gibbs	SA	163	162	11	153	5276	34.94	15	21
A.D.R.Campbell	Z	188	184	14	131*	5185	30.50	7	30
R.S.Mahanama	SL	213	198	23	119*	5162	29.49	4	35
C.G.Greenidge	WI	128	127	13	133*	5134	45.03	11	31

The most for England is 4677 in 162 innings by A.J.Stewart, for Bangladesh 1357 (86) by Khaled Masud, and for Kenya 1710 (65) by S.O.Tikolo.

15 HUNDREDS

		Inns	100	E	A	SA	WI	NZ	I	P	SL	Z	B	K	N
S.R.Tendulkar	I	333	37	1	7	3	2	4	–	3	7	5	–	4	1
S.C.Ganguly	I	257	22	1	1	3	–	3	–	2	4	3	1	3	1
Saeed Anwar	P	244	20	–	1	–	2	4	4	–	7	2	–	–	–
B.C.Lara	WI	243	19	1	3	3	–	2	–	5	2	1	1	1	–
M.E.Waugh	A	236	18	1	–	2	3	3	3	1	1	3	–	1	–
S.T.Jayasuriya	SL	324	18	2	1	–	4	5	3	–	1	2	–	–	–
D.L.Haynes	WI	237	17	2	6	–	–	2	2	4	1	–	–	–	–
H.H.Gibbs	SA	162	15	–	2	–	4	1	2	1	1	1	1	1	1
R.T.Ponting	A	212	15	2	–	4	1	4	1	1	3	1	1	–	–

The most for England is 8 by G.A.Gooch (122 innings) and 8 by M.E.Trescothick (98), for New Zealand 14 by N.J.Astle (184), for Zimbabwe 7 by A.D.R.Campbell (184), for Bangladesh 1 by Mehrab Hossain (18), and for Kenya 2 by K.O.Obuya (62).

214

HIGHEST PARTNERSHIP FOR EACH WICKET

1st 258	S.C.Ganguly/S.R.Tendulkar	India v Kenya	Paarl	2001-02
2nd 331	S.R.Tendulkar/R.Dravid	India v New Zealand	Hyderabad (Ind)	1999-00
3rd 237*	R.Dravid/S.R.Tendulkar	India v Kenya	Bristol	1999
4th 275*	M.Azharuddin/A.Jadeja	India v Zimbabwe	Cuttack	1997-98
5th 223	M.Azharuddin/A.Jadeja	India v Sri Lanka	Colombo (RPS)	1997-98
6th 161	M.O.Odumbe/A.V.Vadher	Kenya v Sri Lanka	Southampton	1999
7th 130	A.Flower/H.H.Streak	Zimbabwe v England	Harare	2001-02
8th 119	P.R.Reiffel/S.K.Warne	Australia v South Africa	Port Elizabeth	1993-94
9th 126*	Kapil Dev/S.M.H.Kirmani	India v Zimbabwe	Tunbridge Wells	1983
10th 106*	I.V.A.Richards/M.A.Holding	West Indies v England	Manchester	1984

BOWLING RECORDS
SIX WICKETS IN AN INNINGS

8-19	W.P.U.C.J.Vaas	Sri Lanka v Zimbabwe	Colombo (SSC)	2001-02
7-15	G.D.McGrath	Australia v Namibia	Potschefstroom	2002-03
7-20	A.J.Bichel	Australia v England	Port Elizabeth	2002-03
7-30	M.Muralitharan	Sri Lanka v India	Sharjah	2000-01
7-36	Waqar Younis	Pakistan v England	Leeds	2001
7-37	Aqib Javed	Pakistan v India	Sharjah	1991-92
7-51	W.W.Davis	West Indies v Australia	Leeds	1983
6-12	A.Kumble	India v West Indies	Calcutta	1993-94
6-14	G.J.Gilmour	Australia v England	Leeds	1975
6-14	Imran Khan	Pakistan v India	Sharjah	1984-85
6-15	C.E.H.Croft	West Indies v England	Kingstown	1980-81
6-16	Shoaib Akhtar	Pakistan v New Zealand	Karachi	2001-02
6-18	Azhar Mahmood	Pakistan v West Indies	Sharjah	1999-00
6-19	H.K.Olonga	Zimbabwe v England	Cape Town	1999-00
6-20	B.C.Strang	Zimbabwe v Bangladesh	Nairobi	1997-98
6-22	F.H.Edwards	West Indies v Zimbabwe	Harare	2003-04
6-23	A.A.Donald	South Africa v Kenya	Nairobi	1996-97
6-23	A.Nehra	India v England	Durban	2002-03
6-23	S.E.Bond	New Zealand v Australia	Port Elizabeth	2002-03
6-25	S.B.Styris	New Zealand v West Indies	Port-of-Spain	2002
6-25	W.P.U.C.J.Vaas	Sri Lanka v Bangladesh	Pietermaritzburg	2002-03
6-26	Waqar Younis	Pakistan v Sri Lanka	Sharjah	1989-90
6-28	H.K.Olonga	Zimbabwe v Kenya	Bulawayo	2002-03
6-29	B.P.Patterson	West Indies v India	Nagpur	1987-88
6-29	S.T.Jayasuriya	Sri Lanka v England	Moratuwa	1992-93
6-30	Waqar Younis	Pakistan v New Zealand	Auckland	1993-94
6-35	S.M.Pollock	South Africa v West Indies	East London	1998-99
6-35	Abdul Razzaq	Pakistan v Bangladesh	Dhaka	2001-02
6-39	K.H.MacLeay	Australia v India	Nottingham	1983
6-41	I.V.A.Richards	West Indies v India	Delhi	1989-90
6-42	A.B.Agarkar	India v Australia	Melbourne	2003-04
6-44	Waqar Younis	Pakistan v New Zealand	Sharjah	1996-97
6-49	L.Klusener	South Africa v Sri Lanka	Lahore	1997-98
6-50	A.H.Gray	West Indies v Australia	Port-of-Spain	1990-91
6-59	Waqar Younis	Pakistan v Australia	Nottingham	2001

The best for England is 5-15 by M.A.Ealham (v Z, Kimberley, 1999-00), for Bangladesh 5-31 by Aftab Ahmed (v NZ, Dhaka, 2004-05), and for Kenya 5-24 by C.O.Obuya (v SL, Nairobi, 2002-03).

150 WICKETS IN A CAREER

		LOI	Balls	R	W	Avge	Best	4w	R/Over
Wasim Akram	P	356	18186	11812	**502**	23.52	5-15	23	3.89
Waqar Younis	P	262	12698	9919	**416**	23.84	7-36	27	4.68
M.Muralitharan	SL	237	12871	8102	**366**	22.13	7-30	18	3.77
W.P.U.C.J.Vaas	SL	249	12219	8407	**322**	26.10	8-19	10	4.12
A.Kumble	I	259	13817	9854	**321**	30.69	6-12	10	4.27
J.Srinath	I	229	11935	8847	**315**	28.08	5-23	10	4.44
S.M.Pollock	SA	228	11932	7452	**313**	23.80	6-35	15	3.74
G.D.McGrath	A	200	10498	6758	**305**	22.15	7-15	15	3.86
S.K.Warne	A	193	10600	7514	**291**	25.82	5-33	13	4.25

		LOI	Balls	R	W	Avge	Best	4w	R/Over
Saqlain Mushtaq	P	169	8770	6275	288	21.78	5-20	17	4.29
A.A.Donald	SA	164	8561	5926	272	21.78	6-23	13	4.15
S.T.Jayasuriya	SL	333	12190	9684	267	36.26	6-29	10	4.76
Kapil Dev	I	225	11202	6945	253	27.45	5-43	4	3.72
H.H.Streak	Z	183	9192	6894	234	29.46	5-32	8	4.50
C.A.Walsh	WI	205	10822	6915	227	30.46	5- 1	7	3.83
C.E.L.Ambrose	WI	176	9353	5430	225	24.13	5-17	10	3.48
D.Gough	E	147	7909	5666	224	25.29	5-44	12	4.29
Abdul Razzaq	P	183	8032	6060	208	29.13	6-35	8	4.52
C.J.McDermott	A	138	7460	5018	203	24.71	5-44	5	4.03
C.Z.Harris	NZ	249	10667	7613	203	37.50	5-42	3	4.28
A.B.Agarkar	I	134	6649	5652	203	27.84	6-42	9	5.10
B.K.V.Prasad	I	161	8129	6332	196	32.30	5-27	4	4.67
S.R.Waugh	A	325	8883	6764	195	34.68	4-33	3	4.56
C.L.Hooper	WI	227	9573	6957	193	36.04	4-34	3	4.36
L.Klusener	SA	171	7336	5751	192	29.95	6-49	7	4.70
J.H.Kallis	SA	210	7647	6106	192	31.80	5-30	4	4.79
C.L.Cairns	NZ	198	7514	5910	187	31.60	5-42	4	4.71
Shoaib Akhtar	P	120	5608	4287	186	23.04	6-16	7	4.58
Aqib Javed	P	163	8012	5721	182	31.43	7-37	6	4.28
Imran Khan	P	175	7462	4845	182	26.62	6-14	4	3.90
B.Lee	A	99	5022	3955	176	22.47	5-27	10	4.72
M.Ntini	SA	110	5490	3983	170	23.42	5-31	7	4.35
Shahid Afridi	P	199	7754	5946	163	36.47	5-11	3	4.60
Mushtaq Ahmed	P	144	7543	5361	161	33.29	5-36	4	4.26
R.J.Hadlee	NZ	115	6182	3407	158	21.56	5-25	6	3.31
M.Prabhakar	I	130	6360	4534	157	28.87	5-33	6	4.27
M.D.Marshall	WI	136	7175	4233	157	26.96	4-18	6	3.54

The most for Bangladesh is 66 by Mohammad Rafique (73 LOI), and for Kenya 59 (63) by T.M.Odoyo.

HAT-TRICKS

Jalaluddin	Pakistan v Australia	Hyderabad	1982-83
B.A.Reid	Australia v New Zealand	Sydney	1985-86
C.Sharma	India v New Zealand	Nagpur	1987-88
Wasim Akram	Pakistan v West Indies	Sharjah	1989-90
Wasim Akram	Pakistan v Australia	Sharjah	1989-90
Kapil Dev	India v Sri Lanka	Calcutta	1990-91
Aqib Javed	Pakistan v India	Sharjah	1991-92
D.K.Morrison	New Zealand v India	Napier	1993-94
Waqar Younis	Pakistan v New Zealand	East London	1994-95
Saqlain Mushtaq	Pakistan v Zimbabwe	Peshawar	1996-97
E.A.Brandes	Zimbabwe v England	Harare	1996-97
A.M.Stuart	Australia v Pakistan	Melbourne	1996-97
Saqlain Mushtaq	Pakistan v Zimbabwe	The Oval	1999
W.P.U.C.J Vaas	Sri Lanka v Zimbabwe	Colombo (SSC)	2001-02
Mohammad Sami	Pakistan v West Indies	Sharjah	2001-02
W.P.U.C.J Vaas[1]	Sri Lanka v Bangladesh	Pietermaritzburg	2002-03
B.Lee	Australia v Kenya	Durban	2002-03
J.M.Anderson	England v Pakistan	The Oval	2003
S.J.Harmison	England v India	Nottingham	2004

[1] The first three balls of the match. Took four wickets in opening over (W W W 4 wide W 0).

WICKET-KEEPING RECORDS
SIX DISMISSALS IN AN INNINGS

6	(6ct)	A.C.Gilchrist	Australia v South Africa	Cape Town	1999-00
6	(6ct)	A.J.Stewart	England v Zimbabwe	Manchester	2000
6	(5ct/1st)	R.D.Jacobs	West Indies v Sri Lanka	Colombo (RPS)	2001-02
6	(5ct/1st)	A.C.Gilchrist	Australia v England	Sydney	2002-03
6	(6ct)	A.C.Gilchrist	Australia v Namibia	Potchefstroom	2002-03
6	(6ct)	A.C.Gilchrist	Australia v Sri Lanka	Colombo (RPS)	2003-04

100 DISMISSALS IN A CAREER

Total				LOI	Ct	St
333‡	A.C.Gilchrist	Australia		198	294	39
287‡	Moin Khan	Pakistan		211	214	73
270	M.V.Boucher	South Africa		185	258	12
233	I.A.Healy	Australia		168	194	39
220‡	Rashid Latif	Pakistan		164	182	38
207‡	R.S.Kaluwitharana	Sri Lanka		187	132	75
204‡	P.J.L.Dujon	West Indies		167	183	21
187	R.D.Jacobs	West Indies		146	159	28
165	D.J.Richardson	South Africa		122	148	17
165†‡	A.Flower	Zimbabwe		185	133	32
163†‡	A.J.Stewart	England		138	148	15
154‡	N.R.Mongia	India		139	110	44
136††	A.C.Parore	New Zealand		148	111	25
124	R.W.Marsh	Australia		92	120	4
119†‡	K.C.Sangakkara	Sri Lanka		80	88	31
103	Salim Yousuf	Pakistan		86	81	22

The most for Bangladesh is 88 by Khaled Masud (92 LOI), and for Kenya 40 by K.O.Obuya (45).
† Excluding catches taken in the field. ‡ Excluding matches when not wicket-keeper.

FIELDING RECORDS
FIVE CATCHES IN AN INNINGS

5	J.N.Rhodes	South Africa v West Indies	Bombay	1993-94

100 CATCHES IN A CAREER

Total			LOI
156	M.Azharuddin	India	334
127	A.R.Border	Australia	273
120	C.L.Hooper	West Indies	227
111	S.R.Waugh	Australia	325
110	S.P.Fleming	New Zealand	228
109	R.S.Mahanama	Sri Lanka	213
108	M.E.Waugh	Australia	244
105	J.N.Rhodes	South Africa	245
105	S.T.Jayasuriya	Sri Lanka	333
104	B.C.Lara	West Indies	249
101	I.V.A.Richards	West Indies	187
101	Inzamam-ul-Haq	Pakistan	336
101	S.R.Tendulkar	India	342

The most for England is 64 by G.A.Hick (120 LOI), for Zimbabwe 86 by GW Flower (219), for Bangladesh 18 by Mohammad Rafique (73), and for Kenya 21 by S.O.Tikolo (65).

ALL-ROUND RECORDS
50 RUNS AND 5 WICKETS IN A MATCH

I.V.A.Richards	119	5-41	West Indies v New Zealand	Dunedin	1986-87
K.Srikkanth	70	5-27	India v New Zealand	Vishakhapatnam	1988-89
M.E.Waugh	57	5-24	Australia v West Indies	Melbourne	1992-93
L.Klusener	54	6-49	South Africa v Sri Lanka	Lahore	1997-98
Abdul Razzaq	70*	5-48	Pakistan v India	Hobart	1999-00
G.A.Hick	80	5-33	England v Zimbabwe	Harare	1999-00
Shahid Afridi	61	5-40	Pakistan v England	Lahore	2000-01
S.C.Ganguly	71*	5-34	India v Zimbabwe	Kanpur	2000-01
S.B.Styris	*	6-25	New Zealand v West Indies	Port-of-Spain	2002
R.C.Irani	53	5-26	England v India	The Oval	2002
C.H.Gayle	60	5-46	West Indies v Australia	St George's	2002-03

1000 RUNS AND 100 WICKETS

England	I.T.Botham (2113/145)
Australia	S.P.O'Donnell (1242/108); S.K.Warne (1016/291); S.R.Waugh (7569/195)
South Africa	W.J.Cronje (5565/114); J.H.Kallis (7495/192); L.Klusener (3576/192); S.M.Pollock (2336/313)
West Indies	C.L.Hooper (5761/193); I.V.A.Richards (6721/118)
New Zealand	C.L.Cairns (4628/187); R.J.Hadlee (1751/158); C.Z.Harris (4379/203)
India	A.B.Agarkar (1058/203); Kapil Dev (3782/253); M.Prabhakar (1858/157); R.J.Shastri (3108/129); S.R.Tendulkar (13497/132)
Pakistan	Abdul Razzaq (3617/208); Azhar Mahmood (1492/122); Imran Khan (3709/182); Mudassar Nazar (2654/111); Shahid Afridi (4356/163); Wasim Akram 3717/502)
Sri Lanka	U.D.U.Chandana (1494/138); P.A.de Silva (9284/106); H.D.P.K.Dharmasena (1222/138); S.T.Jayasuriya (9896/267); W.P.U.C.J.Vaas (1586/322)
Zimbabwe	G.W.Flower (6536/104); H.H.Streak (2752/234)

APPEARANCE RECORDS

250 MATCHES

356	Wasim Akram	Pakistan		283	Salim Malik	Pakistan
342	S.R.Tendulkar	India		273	A.R.Border	Australia
336	Inzamam-ul-Haq	Pakistan		269	A.Ranatunga	Sri Lanka
334	M.Azharuddin	India		266	S.C.Ganguly	India
333	S.T.Jayasuriya	Sri Lanka		262	Waqar Younis	Pakistan
325	S.R.Waugh	Australia		259	A.Kumble	India
308	P.A.de Silva	Sri Lanka		250	Ijaz Ahmed	Pakistan

The most for England is 170 by A.J.Stewart, for South Africa 245 by J.N.Rhodes, for West Indies 249 by B.C.Lara, for New Zealand 249 by C.Z.Harris, for Zimbabwe 219 by G.W.Flower, for Bangladesh 93 by Khaled Masud, and for Kenya 65 by S.O.Tikolo. The most consecutive appearances is 172 by A.Flower for Zimbabwe (Feb 1992-Apr 2001).

100 MATCHES AS CAPTAIN

LOI			W	L	T	NR	% Won (exc NR)
193	A.Ranatunga	Sri Lanka	89	95	1	8	48.10
178	A.R.Border	Australia	107	67	1	3	61.14
174	M.Azharuddin	India	90	76	2	6	53.57
168	S.P.Fleming	New Zealand	75	82	1	10	47.46
139	Imran Khan	Pakistan	75	59	-1	4	55.55
138	W.J.Cronje	South Africa	99	35	1	3	73.33
137	S.C.Ganguly	India	71	61	–	5	53.78
118	S.T.Jayasuriya	Sri Lanka	66	47	2	3	57.39
109	Wasim Akram	Pakistan	66	41	2	–	60.55
108	I.V.A.Richards	West Indies	68	36	–	4	65.38
106	S.R.Waugh	Australia	67	35	3	1	63.80

The most for England is 56 by N.Hussain, for Zimbabwe 86 by A.D.R.Campbell, for Bangladesh 24 by Khaled Masud, and for Kenya 24 by S.O.Tikolo.

100 LOI UMPIRING APPEARANCES

164	D.R.Shepherd	England	Jun 1983	to	Sep 2004
131	S.A.Bucknor	Jamaica	Mar 1989	to	Feb 2005
132	R.E.Koertzen	South Africa	Dec 1992	to	Feb 2005
108	D.B.Hair	Australia	Dec 1991	to	Dec 2004
107	D.L.Orchard	South Africa	Dec 1994	to	Dec 2003
100	R.S.Dunne	New Zealand	Feb 1989	to	Feb 2002

WOMEN'S TEST CRICKET RECORDS

1934-35 to 10 April 2005

RESULTS SUMMARY

	Opponents	Tests	Won by									Drawn
			E	A	NZ	SA	WI	I	P	SL	Ire	
England	Australia	40	6	10	–	–	–	–	–	–	–	24
	New Zealand	23	6	–	0	–	–	–	–	–	–	17
	South Africa	6	2	–	–	0	–	–	–	–	–	4
	West Indies	3	2	–	–	–	0	–	–	–	–	1
	India	9	1	–	–	–	–	0	–	–	–	8
Australia	New Zealand	13	–	4	1	–	–	–	–	–	–	8
	West Indies	2	–	0	–	–	0	–	–	–	–	2
	India	8	–	3	–	–	–	0	–	–	–	5
New Zealand	South Africa	3	–	–	1	0	–	–	–	–	–	2
	India	6	–	–	0	–	–	0	–	–	–	6
South Africa	India	1	–	–	–	0	–	1	–	–	–	–
West Indies	India	6	–	–	–	–	1	1	–	–	–	4
	Pakistan	1	–	–	–	–	0	–	0	–	–	1
Pakistan	Sri Lanka	1	–	–	–	–	–	–	0	1	–	–
	Ireland	1	–	–	–	–	–	–	0	–	1	–
		123	**17**	**17**	**2**	**0**	**1**	**2**	**0**	**1**	**1**	**82**

	Tests	Won	Lost	Drawn	Toss Won
England	81	17	10	54	49
Australia	63	17	7	39	20
New Zealand	45	2	10	33	21
South Africa	10	–	4	6	6
West Indies	12	1	3	8	6†
India	30	2	5	23	14†
Pakistan	3	–	2	1	1
Sri Lanka	1	1	–	–	1
Ireland	1	1	–	–	1

† *Results of tosses in five of the six India v West Indies Tests in 1976-77 are not known*

TEAM RECORDS
HIGHEST INNINGS TOTALS

569-6d	Australia v England	Guildford	1998
525	Australia v India	Ahmedabad	1983-84
517-8	New Zealand v England	Scarborough	1996
503-5d	England v New Zealand	Christchurch	1934-35
497	England v South Africa	Shenley	2003
467	India v England	Taunton	2002
455	England v South Africa	Taunton	2003
440	West Indies v Pakistan	Karachi	2003-04
427-4d	Australia v England	Worcester	1998
426-7d	Pakistan v West Indies	Karachi	2003-04
426-9d	India v England	Blackpool	1986
414	England v New Zealand	Scarborough	1996
414	England v Australia	Guildford	1998
404-9d	India v South Africa	Paarl	2001-02
403-8d	New Zealand v India	Nelson	1994-95

The highest totals for countries not included above are:

316	South Africa v England	Shenley	2003
193-3d	Ireland v Pakistan	Dublin	2000

LOWEST INNINGS TOTALS

35	England v Australia	Melbourne	1957-58
38	Australia v England	Melbourne	1957-58
44	New Zealand v England	Christchurch	1934-35
47	Australia v England	Brisbane	1934-35
53	Pakistan v Ireland	Dublin	2000

The lowest innings totals for countries not included above are:

67	West Indies v England	Canterbury	1979
89	South Africa v New Zealand	Durban	1971-72
65	India v West Indies	Jammu	1976-77

BATTING RECORDS
1000 RUNS IN TESTS

			M	I	NO	HS	Avge	100	50
1935	J.A.Brittin	England	27	44	5	167	49.61	5	11
1594	R.Heyhoe-Flint	England	22	38	3	179	45.54	3	10
1301	D.A.Hockley	New Zealand	19	29	4	126*	52.04	4	7
1164	C.A.Hodges	England	18	31	2	158*	40.13	2	6
1110	S.Agarwal	India	13	23	1	190	50.45	4	4
1078	E.Bakewell	England	12	22	4	124	59.88	4	7
1007	M.E.Maclagan	England	14	25	1	119	41.95	2	6

HIGHEST INDIVIDUAL INNINGS ‡ *On debut*

242	Kiran Baluch	P v WI	Karachi	2003-04
214	M.Raj	I v E	Taunton	2002
209*	K.L.Rolton	A v E	Leeds	2001
204	K.E.Flavell	NZ v E	Scarborough	1996
204‡	M.A.J.Goszko	A v E	Shenley	2001
200	J.Broadbent	A v E	Guildford	1998
193	D.A.Annetts	A v E	Collingham	1987
190	S.Agarwal	I v E	Worcester	1986
189	E.A.Snowball	E v NZ	Christchurch	1934-35
179	R.Heyhoe-Flint	E v A	The Oval	1976
177	S.C.Taylor	E v SA	Shenley	2003
176*	K.L.Rolton	A v E	Worcester	1998
167	J.A.Brittin	E v A	Harrogate	1998
161*	E.C.Drumm	E v A	Christchurch	1994-95
160	B.A.Daniels	E v NZ	Scarborough	1996
158*	C.A.Hodges	E v NZ	Canterbury	1984
155*	P.F.McKelvey	NZ v E	Wellington	1968-69

5 HUNDREDS

							Opponents					
		M	I	E	A	NZ	SA	WI	IND	P	SL	IRE
5	J.A.Brittin (E)	27	44	–	3	1	–	–	1	–	–	–

HIGHEST PARTNERSHIP FOR EACH WICKET

1st	241	Kiran Baluch/Sajjida Shah	P v WI	Karachi	2003-04
2nd	235	E.A.Snowball/M.E.Hide	E v NZ	Christchurch	1934-35
3rd	309	L.A.Reeler/D.A.Annetts	A v E	Collingham	1987
4th	253	K.L.Rolton/L.C.Broadfoot	A v E	Leeds	2001
5th	138	J.Logtenberg/C.van der Westhuizen	SA v E	Shenley	2003
6th	132	B.A.Daniels/K.M.Leng	E v NZ	Scarborough	1996
7th	157	M.Raj/J.Goswami	I v E	Taunton	2002
8th	181	S.J.Griffiths/D.L.Wilson	A v NZ	Auckland	1989-90
9th	107	B.Botha/M.Payne	SA v NZ	Cape Town	1971-72
10th	78	E.Barker/H.Hegarty	E v A	Adelaide	1957-58
	78	S.Gupta/S.Chakraborty	I v A	Lucknow	1983-84

BOWLING RECORDS
50 WICKETS IN TESTS

Wkts			M	Balls	Runs	Avge	Best	5wI	10wM
77	M.B.Duggan	E	17	3734	1039	13.49	7- 6	5	–
68	E.R.Wilson	A	11	2885	803	11.80	7- 7	4	2
63	D.F.Edulji	I	20	5098†	1624	25.77	6- 64	1	–
60	M.E.Maclagan	E	14	3432	935	15.58	7- 10	3	–
57	R.H.Thompson	A	16	4304	1040	18.24	5- 33	1	–
56	S.Kulkarni	I	18	3320	1599	28.55	6- 99	5	–
55	J.Lord	NZ	15	3108	1049	19.07	6-119	4	1
50	E.Bakewell	E	12	2697	831	16.62	7- 61	3	1

† *Excludes balls bowled in Sixth Test v West Indies 1976-77*

TEN WICKETS IN A TEST

13-226	Shaiza Khan	P v WI	Karachi	2003-04
11- 16	E.R.Wilson	A v E	Melbourne	1957-58
11- 63	J.Greenwood	E v WI	Canterbury	1979
11-107	L.C.Pearson	E v A	Sydney	2002-03
10- 65	E.R.Wilson	A v NZ	Wellington	1947-48
10- 75	E.Bakewell	E v WI	Birmingham	1979
10-107	K.Price	A v I	Lucknow	1983-84
10-118	D.A.Gordon	A v E	Melbourne	1968-69
10-137	J.Lord	NZ v A	Melbourne	1978-79

SEVEN WICKETS IN AN INNINGS

8-53	N.David	I v E	Jamshedpur	1995-96
7- 6	M.B.Duggan	E v A	Melbourne	1957-58
7- 7	E.R.Wilson	A v E.	Melbourne	1957-58
7-10	M.E.Maclagan	E v A	Brisbane	1934-35
7-18	A.Palmer	A v E	Brisbane	1934-35
7-24	L.Johnston	A v NZ	Melbourne	1971-72
7-34	G.E.McConway	E v I	Worcester	1986
7-41	J.Burley	NZ v E	The Oval	1966
7-51	L.C.Pearson	E v A	Sydney	2002-03
7-59	Shaiza Khan	P v WI	Karachi	2003-04
7-61	E.Bakewell	E v WI	Birmingham	1979

HAT-TRICKS

E.R.Wilson	Australia v England	Melbourne	1957-58
Shaiza Khan	Pakistan v West Indies	Karachi	2003-04

WICKET-KEEPING, FIELDING AND APPEARANCE RECORDS
25 DISMISSALS IN TESTS

Total			Tests	Ct	St
58	C.Matthews	Australia	20	46	12
36	S.A.Hodges	England	11	19	17
28	B.Brentnall	New Zealand	10	16	12
26	J.Smit	England	16	24	2

EIGHT DISMISSALS IN A TEST

9 (8ct, 1 st)	C.Matthews	A v I	Adelaide	1990-91
8 (6ct, 2st)	L.Nye	E v NZ	New Plymouth	1991-92

SIX DISMISSALS IN AN INNINGS

8 (6ct, 2st)	L.Nye	E v NZ	New Plymouth	1991-92
6 (2ct, 4st)	B.Brentnall	NZ v SA	Johannesburg	1971-72

20 CATCHES IN THE FIELD IN TESTS

Total			Tests
25	C.A.Hodges	England	18
21	S.Shah	India	20
20	L.A.Fullston	Australia	12

25 TEST MATCH APPEARANCES

27	J.A.Brittin	England	1979-98

TEST MATCHES RESULTS SUMMARY

Matches completed before 3 March 2005

	Opponents	Tests	Won by										Tied	Drawn
			E	A	SA	WI	NZ	I	P	SL	Z	B		
England	Australia	306	95	125	–	–	–	–	–	–	–	–	–	86
	South Africa	130	54	–	26	–	–	–	–	–	–	–	–	50
	West Indies	134	38	–	–	52	–	–	–	–	–	–	–	44
	New Zealand	88	41	–	–	–	7	–	–	–	–	–	–	40
	India	91	33	–	–	–	–	16	–	–	–	–	–	42
	Pakistan	60	16	–	–	–	–	–	10	–	–	–	–	34
	Sri Lanka	15	7	–	–	–	–	–	–	4	–	–	–	4
	Zimbabwe	6	3	–	–	–	–	–	–	–	0	–	–	3
	Bangladesh	2	2	–	–	–	–	–	–	–	–	0	–	–
Australia	South Africa	71	–	39	15	–	–	–	–	–	–	–	–	17
	West Indies	99	–	45	–	32	–	–	–	–	–	–	1	21
	New Zealand	43	–	20	–	–	7	–	–	–	–	–	–	16
	India	68	–	32	–	–	–	15	–	–	–	–	1	20
	Pakistan	52	–	24	–	–	–	–	11	–	–	–	–	17
	Sri Lanka	18	–	11	–	–	–	–	–	1	–	–	–	6
	Zimbabwe	3	–	3	–	–	–	–	–	–	0	–	–	–
	Bangladesh	2	–	2	–	–	–	–	–	–	–	0	–	–
South Africa	West Indies	15	–	–	10	2	–	–	–	–	–	–	–	3
	New Zealand	30	–	–	16	–	4	–	–	–	–	–	–	10
	India	16	–	–	7	–	–	3	–	–	–	–	–	6
	Pakistan	11	–	–	5	–	–	–	2	–	–	–	–	4
	Sri Lanka	15	–	–	8	–	–	–	–	2	–	–	–	5
	Zimbabwe	5	–	–	4	–	–	–	–	–	0	–	–	1
	Bangladesh	4	–	–	4	–	–	–	–	–	–	0	–	–
West Indies	New Zealand	32	–	–	–	10	7	–	–	–	–	–	–	15
	India	78	–	–	–	30	–	10	–	–	–	–	–	38
	Pakistan	39	–	–	–	13	–	–	12	–	–	–	–	14
	Sri Lanka	8	–	–	–	2	–	–	–	3	–	–	–	3
	Zimbabwe	6	–	–	–	4	–	–	–	–	–	–	–	2
	Bangladesh	4	–	–	–	3	–	–	–	–	–	0	–	1
New Zealand	India	44	–	–	–	–	9	14	–	–	–	–	–	21
	Pakistan	45	–	–	–	–	6	–	21	–	–	–	–	18
	Sri Lanka	20	–	–	–	–	7	–	–	4	–	–	–	9
	Zimbabwe	11	–	–	–	–	5	–	–	–	0	–	–	6
	Bangladesh	4	–	–	–	–	4	–	–	–	–	0	–	–
India	Pakistan	50	–	–	–	–	–	7	10	–	–	–	–	33
	Sri Lanka	23	–	–	–	–	–	8	–	3	–	–	–	12
	Zimbabwe	9	–	–	–	–	–	5	–	–	2	–	–	2
	Bangladesh	3	–	–	–	–	–	3	–	–	–	0	–	–
Pakistan	Sri Lanka	30	–	–	–	–	–	–	14	7	–	–	–	9
	Zimbabwe	14	–	–	–	–	–	–	8	–	2	–	–	4
	Bangladesh	6	–	–	–	–	–	–	6	–	–	0	–	–
Sri Lanka	Zimbabwe	15	–	–	–	–	–	–	–	10	0	–	–	5
	Bangladesh	3	–	–	–	–	–	–	–	3	–	0	–	–
Zimbabwe	Bangladesh	8	–	–	–	–	–	–	–	–	4	1	–	3
		1736	289	301	95	148	56	81	94	37	8	1	2	624

	Tests	Won	Lost	Drawn	Tied	Toss Won
England	832	289	240	303	–	398
Australia	662	301	176	183	2	335
South Africa	297	95	106	96	–	140
West Indies	415	148	125	141	1	220
New Zealand	317	56	126	135	–	162
India	382	81	126	174	1	194
Pakistan	307	94	80	133	–	144
Sri Lanka	147	37	57	53	–	80
Zimbabwe	77	8	43	26	–	45
Bangladesh	36	1	31	4	–	18

TEST CRICKET RECORDS
To 3 March 2005

TEAM RECORDS

HIGHEST INNINGS TOTALS

952-6d	Sri Lanka v India	Colombo (RPS)	1997-98
903-7d	England v Australia	The Oval	1938
849	England v West Indies	Kingston	1929-30
790-3d	West Indies v Pakistan	Kingston	1957-58
758-8d	Australia v West Indies	Kingston	1954-55
751-5d	West Indies v England	St John's	2003-04
735-6d	Australia v Zimbabwe	Perth	2003-04
729-6d	Australia v England	Lord's	1930
713-3d	Sri Lanka v Zimbabwe	Bulawayo	2003-04
708	Pakistan v England	The Oval	1987
705-7d	India v Australia	Sydney	2003-04
701	Australia v England	The Oval	1934
699-5	Pakistan v India	Lahore	1989-90
695	Australia v England	The Oval	1930
692-8d	West Indies v England	The Oval	1995
687-8d	West Indies v England	The Oval	1976
682-6d	South Africa v England	Lord's	2003
681-8d	West Indies v England	Port-of-Spain	1953-54
676-7	India v Sri Lanka	Kanpur	1986-87
675-5d	India v Pakistan	Multan	2003-04
674-6	Pakistan v India	Faisalabad	1984-85
674	Australia v India	Adelaide	1947-48
671-4	New Zealand v Sri Lanka	Wellington	1990-91
668	Australia v West Indies	Bridgetown	1954-55
660-5d	West Indies v New Zealand	Wellington	1994-95
659-8d	Australia v England	Sydney	1946-47
658-8d	England v Australia	Nottingham	1938
658-9d	South Africa v West Indies	Durban	2003-04
657-7d	India v Australia	Calcutta	2000-01
657-8d	Pakistan v West Indies	Bridgetown	1957-58
656-8d	Australia v England	Manchester	1964
654-5	England v South Africa	Durban	1938-39
653-4d	England v India	Lord's	1990
653-4d	Australia v England	Leeds	1993
652-7d	England v India	Madras	1984-85
652-7d	Australia v South Africa	Johannesburg	2001-02
652-8d	West Indies v England	Lord's	1973
652	Pakistan v India	Faisalabad	1982-83
650-6d	Australia v West Indies	Bridgetown	1964-65

223

The highest for Zimbabwe is 563-9d (v WI, Harare, 2001), and for Bangladesh 488 (v Z, Chittagong, 2004-05).

LOWEST INNINGS TOTALS

26	New Zealand v England	Auckland	1954-55
30	South Africa v England	Port Elizabeth	1895-96
30	South Africa v England	Birmingham	1924
35	South Africa v England	Cape Town	1898-99
36	Australia v England	Birmingham	1902
36	South Africa v Australia	Melbourne	1931-32
42	Australia v England	Sydney	1887-88
42	New Zealand v Australia	Wellington	1945-46
42	India v England	Lord's	1974
43	South Africa v England	Cape Town	1888-89
44	Australia v England	The Oval	1896
45	England v Australia	Sydney	1886-87
45	South Africa v Australia	Melbourne	1931-32
46	England v West Indies	Port-of-Spain	1993-94
47	South Africa v England	Cape Town	1888-89
47	New Zealand v England	Lord's	1958
47	West Indies v England	Kingston	2003-04

The lowest for Pakistan is 53 (v A, Sharjah, 2002-03), for Sri Lanka 71 (v P, Kandy, 1994-95), for Zimbabwe 63 (v WI, Port-of-Spain, 1999-00), and for Bangladesh 87 (v WI, Dhaka, 2002-03).

BATTING RECORDS
4000 RUNS IN A TEST CAREER

Runs			M	I	NO	HS	Avge	100	50
11174	A.R.Border	A	156	265	44	205	50.56	27	63
10927	S.R.Waugh	A	168	260	46	200	51.06	32	50
10122	S.M.Gavaskar	I	125	214	16	236*	51.12	34	45
10094	B.C.Lara	WI	112	197	6	400*	52.84	26	46
9879	S.R.Tendulkar	I	120	193	21	248*	57.43	34	38
8900	G.A.Gooch	E	118	215	6	333	42.58	20	46
8832	Javed Miandad	P	124	189	21	280*	52.57	23	43
8540	I.V.A.Richards	WI	121	182	12	291	50.23	24	45
8463	A.J.Stewart	E	133	235	21	190	39.54	15	45
8231	D.I.Gower	E	117	204	18	215	44.25	18	39
8114	G.Boycott	E	108	193	23	246*	47.72	22	42
8032	G.St A.Sobers	WI	93	160	21	365*	57.78	26	30
8029	M.E.Waugh	A	128	209	17	153*	41.81	20	47
7728	M.A.Atherton	E	115	212	7	185*	37.70	16	46
7624	M.C.Cowdrey	E	114	188	15	182	44.06	22	38
7558	C.G.Greenidge	WI	108	185	16	226	44.72	19	34
7525	M.A.Taylor	A	104	186	13	334*	43.49	19	40
7515	C.H.Lloyd	WI	110	175	14	242*	46.67	19	39
7487	D.L.Haynes	WI	116	202	25	184	42.29	18	39
7422	D.C.Boon	A	107	190	20	200	43.65	21	32
7363	R.Dravid	I	86	146	18	270	57.52	18	35
7289	G.Kirsten	SA	101	176	15	275	45.27	21	34
7249	W.R.Hammond	E	85	140	16	336*	58.45	22	24
7110	G.S.Chappell	A	87	151	19	247*	53.86	24	31
7052	Inzamam-ul-Haq	P	97	160	16	329	48.97	20	36
6996	D.G.Bradman	A	52	80	10	334	99.94	29	13
6971	L.Hutton	E	79	138	15	364	56.67	19	33

Runs		M	I	NO	HS	Avge	100	50
6868	D.B.Vengsarkar	I	116	185	22	166	42.13	17	35
6833	J.H.Kallis	SA	87	147	24	189*	55.55	20	34
6806	K.F.Barrington	E	82	131	15	256	58.67	20	35
6657	R.T.Ponting	A	85	138	18	257	55.47	21	26
6636	G.P.Thorpe	E	98	177	26	200*	43.94	16	38
6401	J.L.Langer	A	85	145	6	250	46.05	21	24
6388	S.T.Jayasuriya	SL	94	160	13	340	43.45	14	29
6361	P.A.de Silva	SL	93	159	11	267	42.97	20	22
6227	R.B.Kanhai	WI	79	137	6	256	47.53	15	28
6215	M.Azharuddin	I	99	147	9	199	45.03	22	21
6149	R.N.Harvey	A	79	137	10	205	48.41	21	24
6080	G.R.Viswanath	I	91	155	10	222	41.93	14	35
5949	R.B.Richardson	WI	86	146	12	194	44.39	16	27
5807	D.C.S.Compton	E	78	131	15	278	50.06	17	28
5768	Salim Malik	P	103	154	22	237	43.69	15	29
5764	N.Hussain	E	96	171	16	207	37.19	14	33
5762	C.L.Hooper	WI	102	173	15	233	36.46	13	27
5663	S.P.Fleming	NZ	89	154	10	274*	39.32	8	36
5563	M.L.Hayden	A	64	112	10	380	54.53	20	19
5444	M.D.Crowe	NZ	77	131	11	299	45.36	17	18
5410	J.B.Hobbs	E	61	102	7	211	56.94	15	28
5357	K.D.Walters	A	74	125	14	250	48.26	15	33
5345	I.M.Chappell	A	75	136	10	196	42.42	14	26
5334	J.G.Wright	NZ	82	148	7	185	37.82	12	23
5312	M.J.Slater	A	74	131	7	219	42.84	14	21
5248	Kapil Dev	I	131	184	15	163	31.05	8	27
5234	W.M.Lawry	A	67	123	12	210	47.15	13	27
5200	I.T.Botham	E	102	161	6	208	33.54	14	22
5192	S.Chanderpaul	WI	80	135	18	140	44.37	11	32
5138	J.H.Edrich	E	77	127	9	310*	43.54	12	24
5105	A.Ranatunga	SL	93	155	12	135*	35.69	4	38
5062	Zaheer Abbas	P	78	124	11	274	44.79	12	20
5053	H.H.Gibbs	SA	64	110	5	228	48.12	14	18
4901	S.C.Ganguly	I	79	128	12	173	42.25	11	25
4882	T.W.Graveney	E	79	123	13	258	44.38	11	20
4873	M.S.Atapattu	SL	79	137	14	249	39.61	15	13
4869	R.B.Simpson	A	62	111	7	311	46.81	10	27
4794	A.Flower	Z	63	112	19	232*	51.54	12	27
4738	D.P.M.D.Jayawardena	SL	65	106	8	242	48.34	12	22
4737	I.R.Redpath	A	66	120	11	171	43.45	8	31
4656	A.J.Lamb	E	79	139	10	142	36.09	14	18
4555	H.Sutcliffe	E	54	84	9	194	60.73	16	23
4554	D.J.Cullinan	SA	70	115	12	275*	44.21	14	20
4545	H.P.Tillekeratne	SL	83	131	25	204	42.87	11	20
4537	P.B.H.May	E	66	106	9	285*	46.77	13	22
4502	E.R.Dexter	E	62	102	8	205	47.89	9	27
4455	E.de C.Weekes	WI	48	81	5	207	58.61	15	19
4430	M.E.Trescothick	E	59	113	10	219	43.00	10	24
4415	K.J.Hughes	A	70	124	6	213	37.41	9	22
4409	M.W.Gatting	E	79	138	14	207	35.55	10	21
4399	A.I.Kallicharran	WI	66	109	10	187	44.43	12	21
4389	A.P.E.Knott	E	95	149	15	135	32.75	5	30
4378	M.Amarnath	I	69	113	10	138	42.50	11	24
4356	I.A.Healy	A	119	182	23	161*	27.39	4	22
4334	R.C.Fredericks	WI	59	109	7	169	42.49	8	26
4288	M.A.Butcher	E	71	131	7	173*	34.58	8	23

Runs			M	I	NO	HS	Avge	100	50
4236	R.A.Smith	E	62	112	15	175	43.67	9	28
4114	Mudassar Nazar	P	76	116	8	231	38.09	10	17
4109	A.C.Gilchrist	A	65	94	16	204*	52.67	13	19
4052	Saeed Anwar	P	55	91	2	188*	45.52	11	25
4035	Yousuf Youhana	P	56	93	8	204*	47.47	12	21
4023	M.P.Vaughan	E	55	99	8	197	44.20	13	12

The most for Bangladesh is 2299 by Habibul Bashar (67 innings).

750 RUNS IN A SERIES

Runs			Series	M	I	NO	HS	Avge	100	50
974	D.G.Bradman	A v E	1930	5	7	–	334	139.14	4	–
905	W.R.Hammond	E v A	1928-29	5	9	1	251	113.12	4	–
839	M.A.Taylor	A v E	1989	6	11	1	219	83.90	2	5
834	R.N.Harvey	A v SA	1952-53	5	9	–	205	92.66	4	3
829	I.V.A.Richards	WI v E	1976	4	7	–	291	118.42	3	2
827	C.L.Walcott	WI v A	1954-55	5	10	–	155	82.70	5	2
824	G.St A.Sobers	WI v P	1957-58	5	8	2	365*	137.33	3	3
810	D.G.Bradman	A v E	1936-37	5	9	–	270	90.00	3	1
806	D.G.Bradman	A v SA	1931-32	5	5	1	299*	201.50	4	–
798	B.C.Lara	WI v E	1993-94	5	8	–	375	99.75	2	2
779	E.de C.Weekes	WI v I	1948-49	5	7	–	194	111.28	4	2
774	S.M.Gavaskar	I v WI	1970-71	4	8	3	220	154.80	4	3
765	B.C.Lara	WI v A	1995	6	10	1	179	85.00	3	3
761	Mudassar Nazar	P v I	1982-83	6	8	2	231	126.83	4	1
758	D.G.Bradman	A v E	1934	5	8	–	304	94.75	2	1
753	D.C.S.Compton	E v SA	1947	5	8	–	208	94.12	4	2
752	G.A.Gooch	E v I	1990	3	6	–	333	125.33	3	2

HIGHEST INDIVIDUAL INNINGS

400*	B.C.Lara	WI v E	St John's	2003-04
380	M.L.Hayden	A v Z	Perth	2003-04
375	B.C.Lara	WI v E	St John's	1993-94
365*	G.St A.Sobers	WI v P	Kingston	1957-58
364	L.Hutton	E v A	The Oval	1938
340	S.T.Jayasuriya	SL v I	Colombo (RPS)	1997-98
337	Hanif Mohammed	P v WI	Bridgetown	1957-58
336*	W.R.Hammond	E v NZ	Auckland	1932-33
334*	M.A.Taylor	A v P	Peshawar	1998-99
334	D.G.Bradman	A v E	Leeds	1930
333	G.A.Gooch	E v I	Lord's	1990
329	Inzamam-ul-Haq	P v NZ	Lahore	2001-02
325	A.Sandham	E v WI	Kingston	1929-30
311	R.B.Simpson	A v E	Manchester	1964
310*	J.H.Edrich	E v NZ	Leeds	1965
309	V.Sehwag	I v P	Multan	2003-04
307	R.M.Cowper	A v E	Melbourne	1965-66
304	D.G.Bradman	A v E	Leeds	1934
302	L.G.Rowe	WI v E	Bridgetown	1973-74
299*	D.G.Bradman	A v SA	Adelaide	1931-32
299	M.D.Crowe	NZ v SL	Wellington	1990-91
291	I.V.A.Richards	WI v E	The Oval	1976
287	R.E.Foster	E v A	Sydney	1903-04
285*	P.B.H.May	E v WI	Birmingham	1957
281	V.V.S.Laxman	I v A	Calcutta	2000-01
280*	Javed Miandad	P v I	Hyderabad	1982-83

278	D.C.S.Compton	E v P	Nottingham	1954
277	B.C.Lara	WI v A	Sydney	1992-93
277	G.C.Smith	SA v E	Birmingham	2003
275*	D.J.Cullinan	SA v NZ	Auckland	1998-99
275	G.Kirsten	SA v E	Durban	1999-00
274*	S.P.Fleming	NZ v SL	Colombo (SSC)	2002-03
274	R.G.Pollock	SA v A	Durban	1969-70
274	Zaheer Abbas	P v E	Birmingham	1971
271	Javed Miandad	P v NZ	Auckland	1988-89
270*	G.A.Headley	WI v E	Kingston	1934-35
270	D.G.Bradman	A v E	Melbourne	1936-37
270	R.Dravid	I v P	Rawalpindi	2003-04
270	K.C.Sangakkara	SL v Z	Bulawayo	2003-04
268	G.N.Yallop	A v P	Melbourne	1983-84
267*	B.A.Young	NZ v SL	Dunedin	1996-97
267	P.A.de Silva	SL v NZ	Wellington	1990-91
266	W.H.Ponsford	A v E	The Oval	1934
266	D.L.Houghton	Z v SL	Bulawayo	1994-95
262*	D.L.Amiss	E v WI	Kingston	1973-74
261*	R.R.Sarwan	WI v B	Kingston	2004
261	F.M.M.Worrell	WI v E	Nottingham	1950
260	C.C.Hunte	WI v P	Kingston	1957-58
260	Javed Miandad	P v E	The Oval	1987
259	G.M.Turner	NZ v WI	Georgetown	1971-72
259	G.C.Smith	SA v E	Lord's	2003
258	T.W.Graveney	E v WI	Nottingham	1957
258	S.M.Nurse	WI v NZ	Christchurch	1968-69
257*	Wasim Akram	P v Z	Sheikhupura	1996-97
257	R.T.Ponting	A v I	Melbourne	2003-04
256	R.B.Kanhai	WI v I	Calcutta	1958-59
256	K.F.Barrington	E v A	Manchester	1964
255*	D.J.McGlew	SA v NZ	Wellington	1952-53
254	D.G.Bradman	A v E	Lord's	1930
253	S.T.Jayasuriya	SL v P	Faisalabad	2004-05
251	W.R.Hammond	E v A	Sydney	1928-29
250	K.D.Walters	A v NZ	Christchurch	1976-77
250	S.F.A.F.Bacchus	WI v I	Kanpur	1978-79
250	J.L.Langer	A v E	Melbourne	2002-03

The highest for Bangladesh is 158* by Mohammad Ashraful (v I, Chittagong, 2004-05).

20 HUNDREDS

			200	Inn	E	A	SA	WI	NZ	I	P	SL	Z	B
34	S.R.Tendulkar	I	4	193	6	7	3	3	3	–	2	6	3	1
34	S.M.Gavaskar	I	4	214	4	8	–	13	2	–	5	2	–	–
32	S.R.Waugh	A	1	260	10	–	2	7	2	2	3	3	1	2
29	D.G.Bradman	A	12	80	19	–	4	2	–	4	–	–	–	–
27	A.R.Border	A	2	265	8	–	–	3	5	4	6	1	–	–
26	G.St A.Sobers	WI	2	160	10	4	–	–	1	8	3	–	–	–
26	B.C.Lara	WI	7	197	7	8	2	–	1	1	–	5	1	1
24	G.S.Chappell	A	4	151	9	–	–	5	3	1	6	–	–	–
24	I.V.A.Richards	WI	3	182	8	5	–	–	1	8	2	–	–	–
23	Javed Miandad	P	6	189	2	6	–	2	7	5	–	1	–	–
22	W.R.Hammond	E	7	140	–	9	6	1	4	2	–	–	–	–
22	M.Azharuddin	I	–	147	6	2	4	–	2	–	3	5	–	–
22	M.C.Cowdrey	E	–	188	–	5	3	6	2	3	3	–	–	–

| | | | | | | | | Opponents | | | | | |
			200	Inn	E	A	SA	WI	NZ	I	P	SL	Z	B
22	G.Boycott	E	1	193	–	7	1	5	2	4	3	–	–	
21	R.N.Harvey	A	2	137	6	–	8	3	–	4	–	–	–	
21	R.T.Ponting	A	4	138	4	–	2	4	1	4	4	1	–	–
21	J.L.Langer	A	3	145	3	–	2	3	4	3	4	2	–	–
21	G.Kirsten	SA	3	176	5	2	–	3	2	3	2	1	1	2
21	D.C.Boon	A	1	190	7	–	3	3	6	1	1	–	–	
20	M.L.Hayden	A	2	112	3	–	4	3	1	3	1	3	2	–
20	K.F.Barrington	E	1	131	–	5	2	3	3	3	4	–	–	
20	J.H.Kallis	SA	–	147	5	1	–	5	3	1	1	–	3	1
20	P.A.de Silva	SL	2	159	2	1	–	–	2	5	8	–	1	1
20	Inzamam-ul-Haq	P	2	160	3	1	–	3	3	1	–	5	2	2
20	M.E.Waugh	A	–	209	6	–	4	4	1	1	3	1	–	
20	G.A.Gooch	A	2	215	–	4	–	5	4	5	1	1		

The most for New Zealand is 17 by M.D.Crowe (131 innings), for Zimbabwe 12 by A.Flower (112), and for Bangladesh 3 by Habibul Bashar (67).

The most double hundreds by batsmen not included above is 6 by M.S.Atapattu (15 hundreds for Sri Lanka), 5 by R.Dravid (18 for India), 4 by L.Hutton (19 for England), 4 by C.G.Greenidge (19 for West Indies) and 4 by Zaheer Abbas (12 for Pakistan).

HIGHEST PARTNERSHIP FOR EACH WICKET

1st	413	V.Mankad/Pankaj Roy	I v NZ	Madras	1955-56
2nd	576	S.T.Jayasuriya/R.S.Mahanama	SL v I	Colombo (RPS)	1997-98
3rd	467	A.H.Jones/M.D.Crowe	NZ v SL	Wellington	1990-91
4th	411	P.B.H.May/M.C.Cowdrey	E v WI	Birmingham	1957
5th	405	S.G.Barnes/D.G.Bradman	A v E	Sydney	1946-47
6th	346	J.H.W.Fingleton/D.G.Bradman	A v E	Melbourne	1936-37
7th	347	D.St E.Atkinson/C.C.Depeiza	WI v A	Bridgetown	1954-55
8th	313	Wasim Akram/Saqlain Mushtaq	P v Z	Sheikhupura	1996-97
9th	195	M.V.Boucher/P.L.Symcox	SA v P	Johannesburg	1997-98
10th	151	B.F.Hastings/R.O.Collinge	NZ v P	Auckland	1972-73
	151	Azhar Mahmood/Mushtaq Ahmed	P v SA	Rawalpindi	1997-98

BOWLING RECORDS

200 WICKETS IN TESTS

Wkts			M	Balls	Runs	Avge	5 wI	10 wM
566	S.K.Warne	A	120	33648	14504	25.62	28	8
532	M.Muralitharan	SL	91	31125	12165	22.86	44	13
519	C.A.Walsh	WI	132	30019	12688	24.45	22	3
481	G.D.McGrath	A	106	24751	10309	21.43	25	3
444	A.Kumble	I	92	29015	12371	27.86	28	6
434	Kapil Dev	I	131	27740	12867	29.64	23	2
431	R.J.Hadlee	NZ	86	21918	9612	22.29	36	9
414	Wasim Akram	P	104	22627	9779	23.62	25	5
405	C.E.L.Ambrose	WI	98	22104	8500	20.98	22	3
383	I.T.Botham	E	102	21815	10878	28.40	27	4
376	M.D.Marshall	WI	81	17584	7876	20.94	22	4
374	S.M.Pollock	SA	92	21032	8195	21.91	16	1
373	Waqar Younis	P	87	16224	8788	23.56	22	5
362	Imran Khan	P	88	19458	8258	22.81	23	6
355	D.K.Lillee	A	70	18467	8493	23.92	23	7
330	A.A.Donald	SA	72	15519	7344	22.25	20	3
325	R.G.D.Willis	E	90	17357	8190	25.20	16	–
309	L.R.Gibbs	WI	79	27115	8989	29.09	18	2

Wkts			M	Balls	Runs	Avge	5 wI	10 wM
307	F.S.Trueman	E	67	15178	6625	21.57	17	3
297	D.L.Underwood	E	86	21862	7674	25.83	17	6
291	C.J.McDermott	A	71	16586	8332	28.63	14	2
269	W.P.U.C.J.Vaas	SL	82	18132	8045	29.90	9	2
266	B.S.Bedi	I	67	21364	7637	28.71	14	1
259	J.Garner	WI	58	13169	5433	20.97	7	–
252	J.B.Statham	E	70	16056	6261	24.84	9	1
249	M.A.Holding	WI	60	12680	5898	23.68	13	2
248	R.Benaud	A	63	19108	6704	27.03	16	1
246	G.D.McKenzie	A	60	17681	7328	29.78	16	3
242	B.S.Chandrasekhar	I	58	15963	7199	29.74	16	2
241	J.N.Gillespie	A	63	12932	6060	25.14	8	–
236	A.V.Bedser	E	51	15918	5876	24.89	15	5
236	Abdul Qadir	P	67	17126	7742	32.80	15	5
236	J.Srinath	I	67	15104	7196	30.49	10	1
235	G.St A.Sobers	WI	93	21599	7999	34.03	6	–
234	A.R.Caddick	E	62	13558	6999	29.91	13	1
229	D.Gough	E	58	11821	6503	28.39	9	–
228	R.R.Lindwall	A	61	13650	5251	23.03	12	–
218	C.L.Cairns	NZ	62	11698	6410	29.40	13	1
216	C.V.Grimmett	A	37	14513	5231	24.21	21	7
212	M.G.Hughes	A	53	12285	6017	28.38	7	1
208	Saqlain Mushtaq	P	49	14070	6206	29.83	13	3
202	A.M.E.Roberts	WI	47	11136	5174	25.61	11	2
202	J.A.Snow	E	49	12021	5387	26.66	8	1
202	H.H.Streak	Z	59	12739	5572	27.58	6	–
200	J.R.Thomson	A	51	10535	5601	28.00	8	–

The most for Bangladesh is 67 in 18 Tests by Mohammad Rafique.

35 WICKETS IN A SERIES

Wkts			Series	M	Balls	Runs	Avge	5 wI	10 wM
49	S.F.Barnes	E v SA	1913-14	4	1356	536	10.93	7	3
46	J.C.Laker	E v A	1956	5	1703	442	9.60	4	2
44	C.V.Grimmett	A v SA	1935-36	5	2077	642	14.59	5	3
42	T.M.Alderman	A v E	1981	6	1950	893	21.26	4	–
41	R.M.Hogg	A v E	1978-79	6	1740	527	12.85	5	2
41	T.M.Alderman	A v E	1989	6	1616	712	17.36	6	1
40	Imran Khan	P v I	1982-83	6	1339	558	13.95	4	2
39	A.V.Bedser	E v A	1953	5	1591	682	17.48	5	1
39	D.K.Lillee	A v E	1981	6	1870	870	22.30	2	1
38	M.W.Tate	E v A	1924-25	5	2528	881	23.18	5	1
37	W.J.Whitty	A v SA	1910-11	5	1395	632	17.08	2	–
37	H.J.Tayfield	SA v E	1956-57	5	2280	636	17.18	4	1
36	A.E.E.Vogler	SA v E	1909-10	5	1349	783	21.75	4	1
36	A.A.Mailey	A v E	1920-21	5	1465	946	26.27	4	2
36	G.D.McGrath	A v E	1997	6	1499	701	19.47	2	–
35	G.A.Lohmann	E v SA	1895-96	3	520	203	5.80	4	2
35	B.S.Chandrasekhar	I v E	1972-73	5	1747	662	18.91	4	–
35	M.D.Marshall	WI v E	1988	5	1219	443	12.65	3	1

The most for New Zealand is 33 by R.J.Hadlee (3 Tests v A, 1985-86), for Sri Lanka 30 by M.Muralitharan (3 Tests v Z, 2001-02), for Zimbabwe 22 by H.H.Streak (3 Tests v P, 1994-95), and for Bangladesh 18 by Enamul Haque II (2 Tests v Z, 2004-05).

15 WICKETS IN A TEST († *On debut*)

19- 90	J.C.Laker	E v A	Manchester	1956
17-159	S.F.Barnes	E v SA	Johannesburg	1913-14
16-136†	N.D.Hirwani	I v WI	Madras	1987-88
16-137†	R.A.L.Massie	A v E	Lord's	1972
16-220	M.Muralitharan	SL v E	The Oval	1998
15- 28	J.Briggs	E v SA	Cape Town	1888-89
15- 45	G.A.Lohmann	E v SA	Port Elizabeth	1895-96
15- 99	C.Blythe	E v SA	Leeds	1907
15-104	H.Verity	E v A	Lord's	1934
15-123	R.J.Hadlee	NZ v A	Brisbane	1985-86
15-124	W.Rhodes	E v A	Melbourne	1903-04
15-217	Harbhajan Singh	I v A	Madras	2000-01

The best analysis for South Africa is 13-165 by H.J.Tayfield (v A, Melbourne, 1952-53), for West Indies 14-149 by M.A.Holding (v E, The Oval, 1976), for Pakistan 14-116 by Imran Khan (v SL, Lahore, 1981-82), for Zimbabwe 11-257 by A.G.Huckle (v NZ, Bulawayo, 1997-98), and for Bangladesh 12-200 by Enamul Haque II (v Z, Dhaka, 2004-05).

NINE WICKETS IN AN INNINGS

10- 53	J.C.Laker	E v A	Manchester	1956
10- 74	A.Kumble	I v P	Delhi	1998-99
9- 28	G.A.Lohmann	E v SA	Johannesburg	1895-96
9- 37	J.C.Laker	E v A	Manchester	1956
9- 51	M.Muralitharan	SL v Z	Kandy	2001-02
9- 52	R.J.Hadlee	NZ v A	Brisbane	1985-86
9- 56	Abdul Qadir	P v E	Lahore	1987-88
9- 57	D.E.Malcolm	E v SA	The Oval	1994
9- 65	M.Muralitharan	SL v E	The Oval	1998
9- 69	J.M.Patel	I v A	Kanpur	1959-60
9- 83	Kapil Dev	I v WI	Ahmedabad	1983-84
9- 86	Sarfraz Nawaz	P v A	Melbourne	1978-79
9- 95	J.M.Noreiga	WI v I	Port-of-Spain	1970-71
9-102	S.P.Gupte	I v WI	Kanpur	1958-59
9-103	S.F.Barnes	E v SA	Johannesburg	1913-14
9-113	H.J.Tayfield	SA v E	Johannesburg	1956-57
9-121	A.A.Mailey	A v E	Melbourne	1920-21

The best analysis for Zimbabwe is 8-109 by P.A.Strang (v NZ, Bulawayo, 2000-01), and for Bangladesh 7-95 by Enamul Haque II (v Z, Dhaka, 2004-05).

HAT-TRICKS

F.R.Spofforth	Australia v England	Melbourne	1878-79
W.Bates	England v Australia	Melbourne	1882-83
J.Briggs	England v Australia	Sydney	1891-92
G.A.Lohmann	England v South Africa	Port Elizabeth	1895-96
J.T.Hearne	England v Australia	Leeds	1899
H.Trumble	Australia v England	Melbourne	1901-02
H.Trumble	Australia v England	Melbourne	1903-04
T.J.Matthews (2)[2]	Australia v South Africa	Manchester	1912
M.J.C.Allom[1]	England v New Zealand	Christchurch	1929-30
T.W.J.Goddard	England v South Africa	Johannesburg	1938-39
P.J.Loader	England v West Indies	Leeds	1957
L.F.Kline	Australia v South Africa	Cape Town	1957-58
W.W.Hall	West Indies v Pakistan	Lahore	1958-59
G.M.Griffin	South Africa v England	Lord's	1960
L.R.Gibbs	West Indies v Australia	Adelaide	1960-61
P.J.Petherick[1]	New Zealand v Pakistan	Lahore	1976-77
C.A.Walsh[3]	West Indies v Australia	Brisbane	1988-89

M.G.Hughes[3]	Australia v West Indies	Perth	1988-89
D.W.Fleming[1]	Australia v Pakistan	Rawalpindi	1994-95
S.K.Warne	Australia v England	Melbourne	1994-95
D.G.Cork	England v West Indies	Manchester	1995
D.Gough	England v Australia	Sydney	1998-99
Wasim Akram[4]	Pakistan v Sri Lanka	Lahore	1998-99
Wasim Akram[4]	Pakistan v Sri Lanka	Dhaka	1998-99
D.N.T.Zoysa[5]	Sri Lanka v Zimbabwe	Harare	1999-00
Abdul Razzaq	Pakistan v Sri Lanka	Galle	2000-01
G.D.McGrath	Australia v West Indies	Perth	2000-01
Harbhajan Singh	India v Australia	Calcutta	2000-01
Mohammad Sami	Pakistan v Sri Lanka	Lahore	2001-02
J.J.C.Lawson	West Indies v Australia	Bridgetown	2002-03
Alok Kapali	Bangladesh v Pakistan	Peshawar	2003
A.M.Blignaut	Zimbabwe v Bangladesh	Harare	2003-04
M.J.Hoggard	England v West Indies	Bridgetown	2003-04
J.E.C.Franklin	New Zealand v Bangladesh	Dhaka	2004-05

[1] On debut. [2] Hat-trick in each innings. [3] Involving both innings. [4] In successive Tests.
[5] His first 3 balls (second over of the match).

WICKET-KEEPING RECORDS
100 DISMISSALS IN TESTS†

Total			Tests	Ct	St
395	I.A.Healy	Australia	119	366	29
355	R.W.Marsh	Australia	96	343	12
298	M.V.Boucher	South Africa	78	285	13
280	A.C.Gilchrist	Australia	65	253	27
270†	P.J.L.Dujon	West Indies	79	265	5
269	A.P.E.Knott	England	95	250	19
241†	A.J.Stewart	England	82	227	14
228	Wasim Bari	Pakistan	81	201	27
219	R.D.Jacobs	West Indies	65	207	12
219	T.G.Evans	England	91	173	46
201†	A.C.Parore	New Zealand	67	194	7
198	S.M.H.Kirmani	India	88	160	38
189	D.L.Murray	West Indies	62	181	8
187	A.T.W.Grout	Australia	51	163	24
176	I.D.S.Smith	New Zealand	63	168	8
174	R.W.Taylor	England	57	167	7
165	R.C.Russell	England	54	153	12
152	D.J.Richardson	South Africa	42	150	2
151†	A.Flower	Zimbabwe	55	142	9
147†	Moin Khan	Pakistan	66	127	20
141	J.H.B.Waite	South Africa	49	124	17
130	Rashid Latif	Pakistan	37	119	11
130	K.S.More	India	49	110	20
130	W.A.S.Oldfield	Australia	54	78	52
119	R.S.Kaluwitharana	Sri Lanka	49	93	26
112†	J.M.Parks	England	43	101	11
107	N.R.Mongia	India	44	99	8
106†	K.C.Sangakkara	Sri Lanka	31	92	14
104	Salim Yousuf	Pakistan	32	91	13
101†	J.R.Murray	West Indies	31	98	3

The most for Bangladesh is 67 (59 ct, 8 st) by Khaled Masud in 33 Tests.
† Excluding catches taken in the field

25 DISMISSALS IN A SERIES

28	R.W.Marsh	Australia v England	1982-83
27 (inc 2st)	R.C.Russell	England v South Africa	1995-96
27 (inc 2st)	I.A.Healy	Australia v England (6 Tests)	1997
26 (inc 3st)	J.H.B.Waite	South Africa v New Zealand	1961-62
26	R.W.Marsh	Australia v West Indies (6 Tests)	1975-76
26 (inc 5st)	I.A.Healy	Australia v England (6 Tests)	1993
26 (inc 1st)	M.V.Boucher	South Africa v England	1998
26 (inc 2st)	A.C.Gilchrist	Australia v England	2001
25 (inc 2st)	I.A.Healy	Australia v England	1994-95
25 (inc 2st)	A.C.Gilchrist	Australia v England	2002-03

TEN DISMISSALS IN A TEST

11	R.C.Russell	England v South Africa	Johannesburg	1995-96
10	R.W.Taylor	England v India	Bombay	1979-80
10	A.C.Gilchrist	Australia v New Zealand	Hamilton	1999-00

SEVEN DISMISSALS IN AN INNINGS

7	Wasim Bari	Pakistan v New Zealand	Auckland	1978-79
7	R.W.Taylor	England v India	Bombay	1979-80
7	I.D.S.Smith	New Zealand v Sri Lanka	Hamilton	1990-91
7	R.D.Jacobs	West Indies v Australia	Melbourne	2000-01

FIVE STUMPINGS IN AN INNINGS

5	K.S.More	India v West Indies	Madras	1987-88

FIELDING RECORDS

100 CATCHES IN TESTS

Total			Tests	Total			Tests
181	M.E.Waugh	Australia	128	112	S.R.Waugh	Australia	168
157	M.A.Taylor	Australia	104	110	R.B.Simpson	Australia	62
156	A.R.Border	Australia	156	110	W.R.Hammond	England	85
147	B.C.Lara	West Indies	112	109	G.St A.Sobers	West Indies	93
129	S.P.Fleming	New Zealand	89	108	S.M.Gavaskar	India	125
122	G.S.Chappell	Australia	87	106	S.K.Warne	Australia	120
122	I.V.A.Richards	West Indies	121	105	I.M.Chappell	Australia	75
120	I.T.Botham	England	102	105	M.Azharuddin	India	99
120	M.C.Cowdrey	England	114	103	G.A.Gooch	England	118
119	R.Dravid	India	86	101	R.T.Ponting	Australia	85
115	C.L.Hooper	West Indies	102	101	G.P.Thorpe	England	98

The most for South Africa is 84 by J.H.Kallis (87 Tests), for Pakistan 93 by Javed Miandad (124), for Sri Lanka 90 by H.P.Tillekeratne (72), for Zimbabwe 60 by A.D.R.Campbell (60) and for Bangladesh 19 by Habibul Bashar (34).

15 CATCHES IN A SERIES

15	J.M.Gregory	Australia v England	1920-21

SEVEN CATCHES IN A TEST

7	G.S.Chappell	Australia v England	Perth	1974-75
7	Yajurvindra Singh	India v England	Bangalore	1976-77
7	H.P.Tillekeratne	Sri Lanka v New Zealand	Colombo (SSC)	1992-93
7	S.P.Fleming	New Zealand v Zimbabwe	Harare	1997-98
7	M.L.Hayden	Australia v Sri Lanka	Galle	2003-04

FIVE CATCHES IN AN INNINGS

5	V.Y.Richardson	Australia v South Africa	Durban	1935-36
5	Yajurvindra Singh	India v England	Bangalore	1976-77
5	M.Azharuddin	India v Pakistan	Karachi	1989-90
5	K.Srikkanth	India v Australia	Perth	1991-92
5	S.P.Fleming	New Zealand v Zimbabwe	Harare	1997-98

APPEARANCE RECORDS
100 TEST MATCH APPEARANCES

168	S.R.Waugh	Australia		116	D.B.Vengsarkar	India
156	A.R.Border	Australia		115	M.A.Atherton	England
133	A.J.Stewart	England		114	M.C.Cowdrey	England
132	C.A.Walsh	West Indies		112	B.C.Lara	West Indies
131	Kapil Dev	India		110	C.H.Lloyd	West Indies
128	M.E.Waugh	Australia		108	G.Boycott	England
125	S.M.Gavaskar	India		108	C.G.Greenidge	West Indies
124	Javed Miandad	Pakistan		107	D.C.Boon	Australia
121	I.V.A.Richards	West Indies		106	G.D.McGrath	Australia
120	S.R.Tendulkar	India		104	M.A.Taylor	Australia
120	S.K.Warne	Australia		104	Wasim Akram	Pakistan
119	I.A.Healy	Australia		103	Salim Malik	Pakistan
118	G.A.Gooch	England		102	I.T.Botham	England
117	D.I.Gower	England		102	C.L.Hooper	West Indies
116	D.L.Haynes	West Indies		101	G.Kirsten	South Africa

The most for New Zealand is 89 by S.P.Fleming, for Sri Lanka 94 by S.T.Jayasuriya, for Zimbabwe 67 by G.W.Flower, and for Bangladesh 34 by Habibul Bashar.

100 CONSECUTIVE TEST APPEARANCES

153	A.R.Border	Australia	March 1979 to March 1994
107	M.E.Waugh	Australia	June 1993 to October 2002
106	S.M.Gavaskar	India	January 1975 to February 1987

50 TESTS AS CAPTAIN

93	A.R.Border	Australia		54	M.A.Atherton	England
74	C.H.Lloyd	West Indies		53	W.J.Cronje	South Africa
65	S.P.Fleming	New Zealand		50	I.V.A.Richards	West Indies
57	S.R.Waugh	Australia		50	M.A.Taylor	Australia
56	A.Ranatunga	Sri Lanka				

The most for India is 47 by M.Azharuddin and S.M.Gavaskar, for Pakistan 48 by Imran Khan, for Zimbabwe 21 by A.D.R.Campbell and H.H.Streak, and for Bangladesh 12 by Khaled Masud.

50 TEST UMPIRING APPEARANCES

99	S.A.Bucknor	(Jamaica)	April 1989 to January 2005
86	D.R.Shepherd	(England)	August 1985 to January 2005
73	S.Venkataraghavan	(India)	January 1993 to January 2004
66	H.D.Bird	(England)	July 1973 to June 1996
59	R.E.Koertzen	(South Africa)	December 1992 to December 2004
58	D.B.Hair	(Australia)	January 1992 to December 2004

TEST MATCH SCORES AND SERIES AVERAGES
BANGLADESH v ZIMBABWE (1st Test)

At Harare Sports Club on 19, 20, 21, 22, 23 February 2004.
Toss: Zimbabwe. Result: **ZIMBABWE** won by 183 runs.
Debuts: Bangladesh – Manjural Rana.

ZIMBABWE

D.D.Ebrahim	st Masud b Rafique	65	c Sarkar b Baisya		31
T.R.Gripper	c Habibul b Baisya	0	c Masud b Manjural Islam		5
S.V.Carlisle	c and b Baisya	58	run out		33
G.W.Flower	c Sarkar b Rafique	5	c Masud b Baisya		3
†T.Taibu	lbw b Rafique	59	c Habibul b Rafique		58
S.M.Ervine	c Sarkar b Baisya	86	c Baisya b Manjural Rana		74
*H.H.Streak	c Masud b Mushfiqur	68			
A.M.Blignaut	st Masud b Rafique	7	(7) b Manjural Rana		32
G.M.Ewing	c Masud b Mushfiqur	71	(8) c Masud b Rafique		1
R.W.Price	c Saleh b Mushfiqur	9	(9) not out		1
D.T.Hondo	not out	0			
Extras	(B 1, LB 7, W 3, NB 2)	13	(LB 2, W 2)		4
Total		**441**	(8 wickets declared)		**242**

BANGLADESH

Hannan Sarkar	lbw b Streak	4	lbw Blignaut		10
Shahriar Hossain	lbw b Hondo	48	lbw b Hondo		1
Tapash Baisya	c Taibu b Streak	4	(9) lbw b Price		2
*Habibul Bashar	c Taibu b Blignaut	0	(3) lbw b Hondo		0
Rajin Saleh	b Price	49	(4) st Taibu b Price		47
Mohammad Ashraful	b Streak	98	(5) c sub (T.J.Friend) b Blignaut		0
Mushfiqur Rahman	b Streak	44	(6) c Taibu b Blignaut		0
Manjural Rana	not out	35	(7) c Gripper b Price		31
†Khaled Masud	c Taibu b Hondo	6	(8) st Taibu b Price		61
Mohammad Rafique	c Ervine b Hondo	3	c and b Ewing		5
Manjural Islam	c Taibu b Blignaut	5	not out		1
Extras	(B 1, LB 11, W 8, NB 15)	35	(B 5, LB 1, NB 5)		11
Total		**331**			**169**

BANGLADESH	O	M	R	W		O	M	R	W
Manjural Islam	28	8	69	0	(2)	12	4	24	1
Tapash Baisya	36	6	133	3	(1)	16	1	65	2
Mushfiqur Rahman	24.2	8	75	3		9	0	49	0
Mohammad Rafique	57	11	121	4		20	3	62	2
Manjural Rana	13	4	26	0		7.2	0	40	2
Mohammad Ashraful	2	1	9	0					

ZIMBABWE	O	M	R	W		O	M	R	W
Streak	26.2	11	44	4					
Blignaut	22.4	6	73	2	(1)	4	1	12	3
Ervine	12	2	52	0		12	3	34	0
Hondo	19.4	5	49	3	(2)	12	3	24	2
Price	25	4	79	1	(4)	20.5	3	61	4
Ewing	7	2	19	0	(5)	8	3	27	1
Gripper	3	2	3	0	(6)	1	0	5	0

FALL OF WICKETS

	Z	B	Z	B
Wkt	1st	1st	2nd	2nd
1st	0	13	12	12
2nd	107	34	50	14
3rd	130	35	54	14
4th	133	77	90	14
5th	258	162	180	14
6th	299	259	232	81
7th	306	265	234	110
8th	412	278	242	112
9th	433	288	–	123
10th	441	331	–	169

Umpires: N.A.Mallender (*England*) (2) and D.L.Orchard (*South Africa*) (41).
Referee: Wasim Raja (*Pakistan*) (14).   **Test No. 1683/5 (B27/Z72)**

BANGLADESH v ZIMBABWE (2nd Test)

At Queens Sports Club, Bulawayo, on 26 (*no play*), 27 (*no play*), 28, 29 February
(*no play*), 1 March 2004.
Toss: Zimbabwe. Result: **MATCH DRAWN.**
Debuts: None.

BANGLADESH

Hannan Sarkar	b Ervine	25
Shahriar Hossain	c Taibu b Ervine	31
*Habibul Bashar	c Friend b Streak	4
Rajin Saleh	c Ervine b Hondo	6
Mohammad Ashraful	c Carlisle b Friend	1
Manjural Rana	c Taibu b Price	39
Mushfiqur Rahman	lbw b Hondo	0
†Khaled Masud	lbw b Ervine	9
Tapash Baisya	c Flower b Price	2
Mohammad Rafique	not out	26
Alamgir Kabir	c Ebrahim b Price	3
Extras	(LB 4, W 6, NB 12)	22
Total		**168**

ZIMBABWE

D.D.Ebrahim	c Sarkar b Baisya	2
T.R.Gripper	c Masud b Baisya	65
S.V.Carlisle	not out	103
G.W.Flower	not out	37
†T.Taibu		
S.M.Ervine		
*H.H.Streak		
T.J.Friend		
N.B.Mahwire		
R.W.Price		
D.T.Hondo		
Extras	(NB 3)	3
Total	(2 wickets)	**210**

ZIMBABWE	O	M	R	W
Streak	15	9	19	1
Hondo	18	5	25	2
Ervine	15	4	44	3
Mahwire	10	2	36	0
Friend	9	2	20	1
Price	8.5	2	20	3

BANGLADESH	O	M	R	W
Tapash Baisya	15	3	43	2
Alamgir Kabir	8	1	39	0
Mushfiqur Rahman	10	1	36	0
Mohammad Rafique	20	7	53	0
Manjural Rana	6	0	33	0
Mohammad Ashraful	1.2	0	6	0

FALL OF WICKETS

	B	Z
Wkt	1st	1st
1st	64	5
2nd	73	134
3rd	73	–
4th	81	–
5th	87	–
6th	89	–
7th	126	–
8th	137	–
9th	144	–
10th	168	–

Umpires: N.A.Mallender (*England*) (3) and D.L.Orchard (*South Africa*) (42).
Referee: Wasim Raja (*Pakistan*) (15).   **Test No. 1684/6 (B28/Z73)**

SRI LANKA v AUSTRALIA (1st Test)

At Galle International Stadium on 8, 9, 10, 11, 12 March 2004.
Toss: Australia. Result: **AUSTRALIA** won by 197 runs.
Debuts: Australia – A.Symonds.

AUSTRALIA

Batsman		R		R
J.L.Langer	c Sangakkara b Dharmasena	12	lbw b Jayasuriya	32
M.L.Hayden	c Chandana b Muralitharan	41	c Jayawardena b Muralitharan	130
*R.T.Ponting	st Sangakkara b Chandana	21	run out	28
D.R.Martyn	c Jayawardena b Dharmasena	42	c sub (‡) b Muralitharan	110
D.S.Lehmann	b Muralitharan	39	c and b Muralitharan	129
A.Symonds	c Jayawardena b Muralitharan	24	st Sangakkara b Muralitharan	0
†A.C.Gilchrist	c Dharmasena b Muralitharan	4	lbw b Chandana	0
S.K.Warne	c Sangakkara b Vaas	23	st Sangakkara b Muralitharan	11
J.N.Gillespie	not out	4	not out	24
M.S.Kasprowicz	b Muralitharan	1	not out	3
S.C.G.MacGill	lbw b Muralitharan	0		
Extras	(B 3, LB 6)	9	(B 15, LB 28, NB 2)	45
Total		**220**	(8 wickets declared)	**512**

SRI LANKA

Batsman		R		R
M.S.Atapattu	b Gillespie	47	c Hayden b Warne	16
S.T.Jayasuriya	lbw b Warne	35	(5) c Hayden b MacGill	5
†K.C.Sangakkara	c and b Kasprowicz	22	(2) lbw b Kasprowicz	7
D.P.M.D.Jayawardena	c Hayden b Symonds	68	(3) c Hayden b Warne	21
T.M.Dilshan	c Langer b Kasprowicz	104	(4) lbw b Warne	6
*H.P.Tillekeratne	lbw b Warne	33	c Symonds b Warne	25
T.T.Samaraweera	not out	36	b MacGill	15
U.D.U.Chandana	c Gilchrist b Warne	27	c Langer b MacGill	43
W.P.U.C.J.Vaas	c Hayden b MacGill	0	not out	10
H.D.P.K.Dharmasena	c Hayden b Warne	6	c Hayden b Warne	0
M.Muralitharan	c and b Warne	0	st Gilchrist b MacGill	0
Extras	(B 2, NB 1)	3	(B 4, W 1, NB 1)	6
Total		**381**		**154**

SRI LANKA	O	M	R	W		O	M	R	W
Vaas	12	2	39	1		27	3	67	0
Dharmasena	20	4	52	2		24	1	100	1
Muralitharan	21.3	5	59	6		56	9	153	5
Chandana	14	1	59	1	(6)	24.3	2	102	1
Jayasuriya	1	0	2	0		14.3	2	38	1
Dilshan					(4)	6	3	9	0

AUSTRALIA	O	M	R	W		O	M	R	W
Gillespie	28	9	61	1	(2)	9	2	20	0
Kasprowicz	23	3	56	2	(3)	5	1	13	1
Warne	42.4	9	116	5	(1)	15	5	43	5
Symonds	19	3	68	1					
MacGill	22	4	69	1	(4)	16.2	2	74	4
Lehmann	2	0	9	0					

FALL OF WICKETS				
	A	SL	A	SL
Wkt	1st	1st	2nd	2nd
1st	31	53	91	14
2nd	62	92	175	41
3rd	76	123	245	49
4th	148	198	451	56
5th	153	298	480	56
6th	163	323	498	89
7th	215	369	498	119
8th	219	372	498	153
9th	220	381	–	153
10th	220	381	–	154

‡ K.S.Lokuarachchi

Umpires: R.E.Koertzen (*South Africa*) (47) and D.R.Shepherd (*England*) (79).
Referee: B.C.Broad (*England*) (3).   **Test No. 1685/14 (SL137/A649)**

SRI LANKA v AUSTRALIA (2nd Test)

At Asgiriya Stadium, Kandy, on 16, 17, 18, 19, 20 March 2004.
Toss: Australia. Result: **AUSTRALIA** won by 27 runs.
Debuts: None.

AUSTRALIA

J.L.Langer	lbw b Zoysa	3		c Sangakkara b Zoysa	9
M.L.Hayden	lbw b Muralitharan	54		c and b Vaas	5
*R.T.Ponting	lbw b Vaas	10	(6)	c Sangakkara b Vaas	27
D.R.Martyn	lbw b Muralitharan	1		st Sangakkara b Muralitharan	161
D.S.Lehmann	b Zoysa	8		lbw b Vaas	21
A.Symonds	c Tillekeratne b Zoysa	6	(7)	lbw b Muralitharan	23
†A.C.Gilchrist	c Sangakkara b Zoysa	0	(3)	lbw b Muralitharan	144
S.K.Warne	c Muralitharan b Vaas	18		c Zoysa b Muralitharan	6
J.N.Gillespie	c Jayawardena b Muralitharan	8		c Atapattu b Muralitharan	11
M.S.Kasprowicz	b Muralitharan	0		c Jayawardena b Zoysa	8
S.C.G.MacGill	not out	8		not out	17
Extras	(B 1, LB 3)	4		(B 2, LB 7, NB 1)	10
Total		**120**			**442**

SRI LANKA

M.S.Atapattu	c Gilchrist b Kasprowicz	9		lbw b Gillespie	8
S.T.Jayasuriya	lbw b Kasprowicz	1		c Gilchrist b Gillespie	131
D.A.Gunawardena	lbw b Kasprowicz	13		lbw b Kasprowicz	9
†K.C.Sangakkara	c Symonds b Gillespie	5		c and b Warne	29
D.P.M.D.Jayawardena	c Symonds b Warne	17		c Gilchrist b Gillespie	13
*H.P.Tillekeratne	c Gilchrist b Warne	16	(7)	c Ponting b Warne	7
T.M.Dilshan	lbw b Warne	0		b Warne	43
W.P.U.C.J.Vaas	not out	68		c Langer b Warne	45
D.N.T.Zoysa	c Gilchrist b Kasprowicz	4	(10)	c Gilchrist b Gillespie	0
K.S.Lokuarachchi	c Kasprowicz b Warne	15	(9)	lbw b Warne	16
M.Muralitharan	c Symonds b Warne	43		not out	4
Extras	(B 8, LB 9, NB 3)	20		(B 4, LB 14, NB 1)	19
Total		**211**			**324**

SRI LANKA	O	M	R	W		O	M	R	W	FALL OF WICKETS				
Vaas	11.2	5	14	2		33	6	103	3		A	SL	A	SL
Zoysa	16	3	54	4	(3)	33	11	102	2	*Wkt*	*1st*	*1st*	*2nd*	*2nd*
Muralitharan	15	4	48	4	(2)	50.3	8	173	5	1st	25	6	11	17
Lokuarachchi						12	2	33	0	2nd	47	34	26	36
Jayasuriya						5	0	16	0	3rd	50	39	226	98
Dilshan						1	0	6	0	4th	60	49	255	174
										5th	84	67	304	218
AUSTRALIA										6th	84	67	360	239
Gillespie	12	4	25	1	(2)	20	1	76	4	7th	86	88	376	272
Kasprowicz	24	5	83	4	(1)	17	1	55	1	8th	100	111	393	319
Warne	20.1	3	65	5		21.1	2	90	5	9th	106	132	408	320
Symonds	2	1	1	0		3	0	16	0	10th	120	211	442	324
MacGill	5	1	20	0		12	0	69	0					

Umpires: S.A.Bucknor (*West Indies*) (87) and D.L.Orchard (*South Africa*) (43).
Referee: B.C.Broad (*England*) (4).   Test No. 1686/15 (SL138/A650)

237

SRI LANKA v AUSTRALIA (3rd Test)

At Sinhalese Sports Club, Colombo, on 24, 25, 26, 27, 28 March 2004.
Toss: Australia. Result: **AUSTRALIA** won by 121 runs.
Debuts: None.

AUSTRALIA

J.L.Langer	c Dilshan b Vaas	19		b Vaas	166
M.L.Hayden	c sub (UDU Chandana) b Samaraweera	25		lbw b Vaas	28
*R.T.Ponting	c Muralitharan b Vaas	92		c Samaraweera b Herath	20
D.R.Martyn	c Sangakkara b Vaas	14	(5)	lbw b Herath	5
D.S.Lehmann	c Jayasuriya b Muralitharan	153	(6)	c Sangakkara b Muralitharan	1
S.M.Katich	c and b Muralitharan	14	(7)	lbw b Muralitharan	86
†A.C.Gilchrist	c Jayasuriya b Muralitharan	22	(8)	not out	31
S.K.Warne	lbw b Muralitharan	32	(9)	c Samaraweera b Herath	0
J.N.Gillespie	c Tillekeratne b Muralitharan	0	(4)	c Jayawardena b Muralitharan	1
M.S.Kasprowicz	b Jayasuriya	4		run out	2
B.A.Williams	not out	0		c and b Herath	3
Extras	(B 13, LB 9, NB 4)	26		(B 11, LB 11, W 4, NB 6)	32
Total		**401**			**375**

SRI LANKA

M.S.Atapattu	b Kasprowicz	118		b Kasprowicz	14
S.T.Jayasuriya	c Gillespie b Lehmann	71		c Katich b Lehmann	51
†K.C.Sangakkara	c Gilchrist b Lehmann	22	(5)	b Warne	27
D.P.M.D.Jayawardena	c Gilchrist b Gillespie	2		c Gilchrist b Lehmann	37
T.M.Dilshan	b Gillespie	0	(6)	c Martyn b Warne	31
*H.P.Tillekeratne	not out	74	(7)	lbw b Gillespie	17
T.T.Samaraweera	c Gilchrist b Gillespie	41	(3)	st Gilchrist b Lehmann	53
W.P.U.C.J.Vaas	b Warne	24		lbw b Warne	9
D.N.T.Zoysa	st Gilchrist b Lehmann	3		b Warne	1
M.R.K.B.Herath	c Martyn b Warne	3		lbw b Kasprowicz	0
M.Muralitharan	c Warne b Kasprowicz	8		not out	0
Extras	(B 4, LB 7, W 1, NB 2)	14		(B 4, LB 1, W 1, NB 2)	8
Total		**407**			**248**

SRI LANKA	O	M	R	W		O	M	R	W
Vaas	26	3	93	3		21	3	61	2
Zoysa	3.3	1	23	0		12	0	54	0
Samaraweera	14.3	1	38	1	(5)	15	4	40	0
Muralitharan	37.1	6	123	5	(3)	29	5	93	3
Herath	23	5	75	0	(4)	24.2	1	92	4
Jayasuriya	11	1	27	1		4	0	13	0
Dilshan						1	1	0	0

AUSTRALIA	O	M	R	W		O	M	R	W
Gillespie	23	3	96	4		18	6	38	1
Kasprowicz	22.1	5	58	2		16.4	5	37	2
Williams	19	5	48	0	(4)	5	0	19	0
Warne	36	7	115	2	(3)	33	11	92	4
Lehmann	19	2	50	3		17	2	42	3
Katich	8	0	29	0		4	1	15	0

	FALL OF WICKETS			
	A	SL	A	SL
Wkt	1st	1st	2nd	2nd
1st	43	134	40	45
2nd	60	175	79	92
3rd	96	240	80	156
4th	217	240	89	181
5th	244	256	98	191
6th	299	327	316	232
7th	376	378	341	245
8th	380	381	346	247
9th	387	390	368	248
10th	401	407	375	248

Umpires: S.A.Bucknor (*West Indies*) (88) and D.L.Orchard (*South Africa*) (44).
Referee: B.C.Broad (*England*) (5).   **Test No. 1687/16 (SL139/A651)**

NEW ZEALAND v SOUTH AFRICA (1st Test)

At Seddon Park, Hamilton, on 10, 11, 12, 13, 14 March 2004.
Toss: South Africa. Result: **MATCH DRAWN**
Debuts: New Zealand – B.B.McCullum, M.H.W.Papps.

SOUTH AFRICA

*G.C.Smith	c Oram b Vettori	25		c McCullum b Tuffey	5
H.H.Gibbs	c Styris b Vettori	40		c McCullum b Wiseman	47
J.A.Rudolph	c McCullum b Styris	72		b Cairns	0
J.H.Kallis	c Tuffey b Oram	92		not out	150
G.Kirsten	c Papps b Vettori	137	(6)	not out	34
P.R.Adams	b Oram	7			
N.D.McKenzie	lbw b Vettori	10	(5)	c Richardson b Wiseman	52
†M.V.Boucher	lbw b Styris	22			
S.M.Pollock	run out	10			
M.Ntini	run out	21			
A.Nel	not out	4			
Extras	(B 1, LB 5, W 1, NB 12)	19		(B 12, LB 5, NB 8)	25
Total		**459**		(4 wickets declared)	**313**

NEW ZEALAND

M.H.Richardson	lbw b Pollock	4			
M.H.W.Papps	lbw b Kallis	59	(1)	c Boucher b Nel	12
*S.P.Fleming	lbw b Adams	27			
S.B.Styris	b Pollock	74	(3)	not out	3
C.D.McMillan	lbw b Kallis	19			
C.L.Cairns	c Boucher b Ntini	28			
J.D.P.Oram	not out	119			
†B.B.McCullum	c Boucher b Kallis	57	(2)	not out	19
D.L.Vettori	b Adams	53			
P.J.Wiseman	b Pollock	36			
D.R.Tuffey	c Boucher b Pollock	0			
Extras	(B 12, LB 11, NB 10)	33		(LB 1, W 1, NB 3)	5
Total		**509**		(1 wicket)	**39**

NEW ZEALAND	O	M	R	W	O	M	R	W
Tuffey	26	11	62	0	15	3	28	1
Oram	27	7	76	2	15	4	29	0
Cairns	18	2	52	0	15	3	48	1
Vettori	39.2	13	158	4	34	11	79	0
Wiseman	12	1	54	0	19	4	68	2
Styris	16	4	46	2	13	4	29	0
McMillan	1	0	5	0	5.1	0	15	0

SOUTH AFRICA	O	M	R	W	O	M	R	W
Pollock	30.4	4	98	4	4	2	5	0
Ntini	29	9	74	1	4	0	15	0
Kallis	26	7	71	3				
Nel	27	8	91	0	(3) 4	0	15	1
Adams	45	11	118	2	(4) 1	1	2	0
Rudolph	5	0	20	0				
Smith	2	0	14	0				
McKenzie					(5) 1	0	1	0

FALL OF WICKETS

	SA	NZ	SA	NZ
Wkt	1st	1st	2nd	2nd
1st	51	20	15	34
2nd	79	75	16	–
3rd	211	127	108	–
4th	271	172	215	–
5th	281	223	–	–
6th	305	225	–	–
7th	364	309	–	–
8th	379	422	–	–
9th	415	509	–	–
10th	459	509	–	–

Umpires: S.J.Davis (*Australia*) (7) and R.B.Tiffin (*Zimbabwe*) (38).
Referee: C.H.Lloyd (*West Indies*) (31).   **Test No. 1688/28 (NZ308/SA286)**

NEW ZEALAND v SOUTH AFRICA (2nd Test)

At Eden Park, Auckland, on 18, 19, 20, 21, 22 March 2004.
Toss: New Zealand. Result: **NEW ZEALAND** won by nine wickets.
Debuts: None.

SOUTH AFRICA

*G.C.Smith	lbw b Martin	88	b Martin	0
H.H.Gibbs	b Cairns	80	lbw b Oram	61
J.A.Rudolph	c Papps b Martin	17	not out	154
J.H.Kallis	c McCullum b Martin	40	lbw b McMillan	71
G.Kirsten	b Oram	1	lbw b Martin	1
N.D.McKenzie	c Papps b Martin	27	c Papps b Martin	0
†M.V.Boucher	c McMillan b Martin	4	c Fleming b Martin	10
S.M.Pollock	b Tuffey	10	c Fleming b Martin	10
N.Boje	not out	12	c McCullum b Cairns	24
M.Ntini	c McCullum b Martin	0	c McMillan b Cairns	6
D.J.Terbrugge	lbw b Oram	0	c sub (J.A.H.Marshall) b Cairns	2
Extras	(LB 13, W 1, NB 3)	17	(B 6, LB 1, NB 3)	10
Total		**296**		**349**

NEW ZEALAND

M.H.Richardson	c Gibbs b Kallis	45	(2) c Boje b Ntini	10
M.H.W.Papps	c Boje b Pollock	0	(1) not out	8
*S.P.Fleming	c Kallis b Ntini	4	not out	31
S.B.Styris	c Pollock b Boje	170		
C.D.McMillan	b Pollock	82		
†B.B.McCullum	b Ntini	13		
C.L.Cairns	c Kallis b Smith	158		
J.D.P.Oram	b Ntini	90		
D.L.Vettori	not out	4		
D.R.Tuffey	b Pollock	13		
C.S.Martin	b Pollock	0		
Extras	(LB 10, NB 6)	16	(NB 4)	4
Total		**595**	(1 wicket)	**53**

NEW ZEALAND	O	M	R	W		O	M	R	W
Tuffey	24	7	41	1	(3)	4	1	13	0
Martin	31	7	76	6	(1)	23	5	104	5
Oram	28.3	6	60	2	(2)	27	13	47	1
Cairns	21	6	54	1		13.3	1	63	3
Styris	14	5	37	0	(6)	13	5	39	0
Vettori	5	1	15	0	(5)	24	4	73	0
McMillan						4	1	3	1

SOUTH AFRICA	O	M	R	W		O	M	R	W
Pollock	32.5	6	113	4		5	1	16	0
Ntini	36	7	110	3		5	0	31	1
Terbrugge	22	4	93	0					
Kallis	23	1	108	1					
Boje	22	2	108	1	(3)	0.2	0	6	0
McKenzie	2	0	8	0					
Rudolph	6	0	26	0					
Smith	5	0	19	1					

FALL OF WICKETS

	SA	NZ	SA	NZ
Wkt	1st	1st	2nd	2nd
1st	177	5	0	20
2nd	177	12	103	–
3rd	225	137	249	–
4th	236	285	250	–
5th	240	314	250	–
6th	246	349	272	–
7th	273	574	290	–
8th	289	578	327	–
9th	289	595	337	–
10th	296	595	349	–

Umpires: Alim Dar (*Pakistan*) (5) and E.A.R. de Silva (*Sri Lanka*) (29).
Referee: C.H.Lloyd (*West Indies*) (32).   **Test No. 1689/29 (NZ309/SA287)**

NEW ZEALAND v SOUTH AFRICA (3rd Test)

At Basin Reserve, Wellington, on 26, 27, 28, 29, 30 March 2004.
Toss: South Africa. Result: **SOUTH AFRICA** won by six wickets.
Debuts: New Zealand – M.J.Mason.

NEW ZEALAND

M.H.Richardson	c Boucher b Kallis	14	(2)	c Smith b Boje	37
M.H.W.Papps	lbw b Ntini	7	(1)	lbw b Pollock	0
*S.P.Fleming	c Pollock b Boje	30		c Boucher b Nel	9
M.S.Sinclair	lbw b Boje	74		lbw b Pollock	21
S.B.Styris	b Boje	1		c and b Nel	73
†B.B.McCullum	lbw b Pollock	55		b Boje	3
C.L.Cairns	b Pollock	69		c Van Jaarsveld b Boje	41
J.D.P.Oram	st Boucher b Boje	34		lbw b Boje	40
D.L.Vettori	c Boucher b Pollock	0		c Van Jaarsveld b Ntini	9
M.J.Mason	c Van Jaarsveld b Nel	3		run out	0
C.S.Martin	not out	1		not out	1
Extras	(B 2, LB 1, W 1, NB 5)	9		(B 1, LB 9, W 3, NB 5)	18
Total		**297**			**252**

SOUTH AFRICA

*G.C.Smith	b Cairns	47		not out	125
H.H.Gibbs	c sub (J.A.H.Marshall) b Martin	77		c Fleming b Martin	16
J.A.Rudolph	not out	93		b Martin	0
G.Kirsten	c McCullum b Martin	1	(5)	lbw b Styris	76
M.van Jaarsveld	c Oram b Martin	59	(6)	not out	13
J.H.Kallis	c McCullum b Martin	0	(4)	lbw b Oram	1
†M.V.Boucher	c Papps b Martin	0			
S.M.Pollock	c Fleming b Oram	5			
N.Boje	b Cairns	25			
M.Ntini	c McCullum b Cairns	4			
A.Nel	c Oram b Cairns	0			
Extras	(LB 1, NB 4)	5		(LB 2, NB 1)	3
Total		**316**		**(4 wickets)**	**234**

SOUTH AFRICA	O	M	R	W		O	M	R	W
Pollock	29	2	85	3		22	10	65	2
Ntini	21	6	63	1		20	6	50	1
Kallis	7	5	4	1					
Nel	27	9	77	1	(3)	21	5	58	2
Boje	20	2	65	4	(4)	33.2	7	69	4
NEW ZEALAND									
Martin	20	6	55	5		18.2	2	65	2
Mason	16	4	73	0		6	1	32	0
Oram	11	3	21	1		11	3	23	1
Vettori	26	6	76	0	(5)	18	2	53	0
Cairns	16.5	2	60	4	(4)	10	2	19	0
Styris	10	4	30	0		9	1	40	1

FALL OF WICKETS

	NZ	SA	NZ	SA
Wkt	1st	1st	2nd	2nd
1st	23	103	1	29
2nd	23	130	42	31
3rd	90	136	73	36
4th	97	251	107	207
5th	163	265	111	–
6th	248	265	198	–
7th	257	270	201	–
8th	257	304	220	–
9th	264	308	224	–
10th	297	316	252	–

Umpires: Alim Dar (*Pakistan*) (6) and E.A.R.de Silva (*Sri Lanka*) (30).
Referee: C.H.Lloyd (*West Indies*) (33).   **Test No. 1690/30 (SA288/NZ310)**

WEST INDIES v ENGLAND (1st Test)

At Sabina Park, Kingston, Jamaica, on 11, 12, 13, 14, March 2004.
Toss: West Indies. Result: **ENGLAND** won by ten wickets.
Debuts: None.

WEST INDIES

C.H.Gayle	b Harmison	5		c Thorpe b Harmison	9
D.S.Smith	st Read b Giles	108		c and b Hoggard	12
R.R.Sarwan	lbw b Hoggard	0		lbw b Harmison	0
*B.C.Lara	c Flintoff b Jones	23	(5)	c Flintoff b Hoggard	0
S.Chanderpaul	b Hoggard	7	(4)	b Harmison	0
R.O.Hinds	c Butcher b Giles	84		c Read b Jones	3
†R.D.Jacobs	c Vaughan b Jones	38		c Hussain b Harmison	15
T.L.Best	lbw b Harmison	20		c Read b Harmison	0
A.Sanford	c Trescothick b Flintoff	1		c Trescothick b Harmison	1
C.D.Collymore	not out	3		not out	2
F.H.Edwards	c Flintoff b Hoggard	1		c Trescothick b Harmison	0
Extras	(LB 6, W 1, NB 14)	21		(LB 4, NB 1)	5
Total		**311**			**47**

ENGLAND

M.E.Trescothick	b Edwards	7		not out	6
*M.P.Vaughan	c Lara b Edwards	15		not out	11
M.A.Butcher	c Jacobs b Edwards	58			
N.Hussain	c sub (D.E.Bernard) b Best	58			
G.P.Thorpe	c Sanford b Best	19			
A.Flintoff	c Hinds b Sarwan	46			
†C.M.W.Read	c Hinds b Best	20			
A.F.Giles	b Sanford	27			
M.J.Hoggard	not out	9			
S.P.Jones	c Sanford b Hinds	7			
S.J.Harmison	run out	13			
Extras	(B 7, LB 28, W 7, NB 18)	60		(B 1, NB 2)	3
Total		**339**		(0 wickets)	**20**

ENGLAND	O	M	R	W		O	M	R	W	FALL OF WICKETS				
											WI	E	WI	E
Hoggard	18.4	3	68	3		9	2	21	2					
Harmison	21	6	61	2		12.3	8	12	7	*Wkt*	*1st*	*1st*	*2nd*	*2nd*
Flintoff	16	3	45	1						1st	17	28	13	–
Jones	18	2	62	2	(3)	4	1	10	0	2nd	22	33	13	–
Giles	12	0	67	2						3rd	73	152	15	–
Vaughan	1	0	2	0						4th	101	194	16	–
										5th	223	209	21	–
WEST INDIES										6th	281	268	41	–
Collymore	26	7	55	0						7th	289	278	41	–
Edwards	19.3	4	72	3						8th	300	313	43	–
Best	19	1	57	3	(1)	1.3	0	8	0	9th	307	325	43	–
Sanford	22	1	90	1						10th	311	339	47	–
Hinds	11.5	2	18	1	(2)	1	0	11	0					
Gayle	1	0	6	0										
Sarwan	4	1	6	1										

Umpires: B.F.Bowden (*New Zealand*) (12) and D.J.Harper (*Australia*) (38).
Referee: M.J.Procter (*South Africa*) (21). **Test No. 1691/127 (WI406/E817)**

WEST INDIES v ENGLAND (2nd Test)

At Queen's Park Oval, Port-of-Spain, Trinidad, on 19, 20, 21, 22, 23 March 2004.
Toss: West Indies. Result: **ENGLAND** won by seven wickets.
Debuts: None.

WEST INDIES

C.H.Gayle	c Read b Harmison	62		b Jones		16
D.S.Smith	lbw b Harmison	35		c Hoggard b Jones		17
R.R.Sarwan	c Flintoff b Harmison	21		lbw b Jones		13
*B.C.Lara	c Giles b Harmison	0	(6)	lbw b Harmison		8
S.Chanderpaul	c Read b Jones	2		c Hussain b Flintoff		42
D.R.Smith	c Hussain b Harmison	16	(7)	c sub (P.D.Collingwood) b Flintoff		14
†R.D.Jacobs	run out	40	(4)	c Flintoff b Jones		70
T.L.Best	c Read b Hoggard	1		lbw b Hoggard		2
A.Sanford	run out	1		c Trescothick b Hoggard		1
P.T.Collins	b Harmison	10		b Jones		7
C.D.Collymore	not out	3		not out		0
Extras	(LB 7, W 6, NB 4)	17		(B 1, LB 3, W 5, NB 10)		19
Total		**208**				**209**

ENGLAND

M.E.Trescothick	c Sanford b Best	1		b Best		4
*M.P.Vaughan	lbw b Collins	0		lbw b Sanford		23
M.A.Butcher	c Jacobs b Best	61		not out		46
N.Hussain	b Best	58		c Jacobs b Sanford		5
G.P.Thorpe	c Gayle b Collins	90		not out		13
A.Flintoff	c and b D.R.Smith	23				
†C.M.W.Read	lbw b Collins	3				
A.F.Giles	c D.S.Smith b Collins	37				
M.J.Hoggard	not out	0				
S.P.Jones	b Gayle	1				
S.J.Harmison	b Gayle	0				
Extras	(B 5, LB 20, W 3, NB 17)	45		(B 4, LB 3, NB 1)		8
Total		**319**		(3 wickets)		**99**

ENGLAND	O	M	R	W		O	M	R	W
Hoggard	15	3	38	1		16	5	48	2
Harmison	20.1	5	61	6		16	5	40	1
Flintoff	10	3	38	0	(4)	12	1	27	2
Giles	3	0	20	0	(5)	7	1	29	0
Jones	12	2	44	1	(3)	15	2	57	5
Trescothick						1	0	4	0

WEST INDIES	O	M	R	W		O	M	R	W
Collins	29	8	71	4	(2)	4	0	25	0
Best	28	5	71	3	(1)	4	0	27	1
Sanford	26	6	60	0		4	1	32	2
Collymore	24	7	39	0		3	1	8	0
D.R.Smith	9	0	30	1					
Gayle	16.5	6	20	2					
Sarwan	1	0	3	0					

FALL OF WICKETS

	WI	E	WI	E
Wkt	1st	1st	2nd	2nd
1st	100	2	34	8
2nd	110	8	45	59
3rd	110	128	56	71
4th	113	186	158	–
5th	142	218	171	–
6th	143	230	194	–
7th	148	315	195	–
8th	165	318	200	–
9th	202	319	205	–
10th	208	319	209	–

Umpires: B.F.Bowden (*New Zealand*) (13) and D.J.Harper (*Australia*) (39).
Referee: M.J.Procter (*South Africa*) (22). **Test No. 1692/128 (WI407/E818)**

WEST INDIES v ENGLAND (3rd Test)

At Kensington Oval, Bridgetown, Barbados, on 1, 2, 3 April 2004.
Toss: England. Result: **ENGLAND** won by eight wickets.
Debuts: None.

WEST INDIES

C.H.Gayle	lbw b Hoggard	6	b Harmison		15
D.Ganga	lbw b Harmison	11	c Thorpe b Hoggard		11
*B.C.Lara	c Butcher b Flintoff	36	c Vaughan b Harmison		33
R.R.Sarwan	c Flintoff b Harmison	63	c Giles b Hoggard		5
S.Chanderpaul	c Thorpe b Flintoff	50	lbw b Hoggard		0
R.O.Hinds	c Jones b Harmison	5	c Flintoff b Hoggard		0
†R.D.Jacobs	c sub (P.D.Collingwood) b Flintoff	6	c Butcher b Flintoff		1
T.L.Best	c Butcher b Flintoff	17	c Trescothick b Flintoff		12
P.T.Collins	c Trescothick b Jones	7	run out		1
C.D.Collymore	not out	1	not out		6
F.H.Edwards	c Read b Flintoff	0	c Hussain b Harmison		2
Extras	(LB 14, W 1, NB 7)	22	(LB 5, NB 3)		8
Total		**224**			**94**

ENGLAND

M.E.Trescothick	b Edwards	2	c Jacobs b Collymore		42
*M.P.Vaughan	c Jacobs b Edwards	17	c Jacobs b Collymore		32
M.A.Butcher	c Gayle b Edwards	5	not out		13
N.Hussain	b Collymore	17	not out		0
G.P.Thorpe	not out	119			
A.Flintoff	c Collymore b Best	15			
†C.M.W.Read	lbw b Edwards	13			
A.F.Giles	c sub (A.N.Mayers) b Collins	11			
M.J.Hoggard	lbw b Collins	0			
S.P.Jones	c Sarwan b Best	4			
S.J.Harmison	b Collins	3			
Extras	(LB 5, W 3, NB 12)	20	(LB 3, W 1, NB 2)		6
Total		**226**	(2 wickets)		**93**

ENGLAND	O	M	R	W		O	M	R	W	FALL OF WICKETS				
											WI	E	WI	E
Hoggard	16	5	34	1		14	4	35	4	Wkt	1st	1st	2nd	2nd
Harmison	18	6	42	3		15.1	5	34	3	1st	6	8	19	57
Flintoff	16.2	2	58	5		13	4	20	2	2nd	20	24	34	91
Jones	16	1	55	1						3rd	88	33	45	–
Giles	9	1	21	0						4th	167	65	45	–
										5th	179	90	45	–
WEST INDIES										6th	197	119	48	–
Edwards	20	4	70	4		6	0	32	0	7th	198	147	80	–
Collins	23	6	60	3	(4)	4	0	16	0	8th	208	155	81	–
Collymore	16	3	26	1		7	2	24	2	9th	224	187	85	–
Hinds	4	1	7	0						10th	224	226	94	–
Best	14	4	26	2	(2)	3	0	18	0					
Gayle	13	3	32	0										

Umpires: D.B.Hair (*Australia*) (52) and R.E.Koertzen (*South Africa*) (48).
Referee: M.J.Procter (*South Africa*) (23).   **Test No. 1693/129 (WI408/E819)**

WEST INDIES v ENGLAND (4th Test)

At Recreation Ground, St John's, Antigua, on 10, 11, 12, 13, 14 April 2004.
Toss: West Indies. Result: **MATCH DRAWN**.
Debuts: England – G.O.Jones.

WEST INDIES

C.H.Gayle	c and b Batty	69
D.Ganga	lbw b Flintoff	10
*B.C.Lara	not out	400
R.R.Sarwan	c Trescothick b Harmison	90
R.L.Powell	c Hussain b S.P.Jones	23
R.O.Hinds	c and b Batty	36
†R.D.Jacobs	not out	107
T.L.Best		
P.T.Collins		
C.D.Collymore		
F.H.Edwards		
Extras	(B 4, LB 5, W 2, NB 5)	16
Total	**(5 wickets declared)**	**751**

ENGLAND

M.E.Trescothick	c Jacobs b Best	16	c Sarwan b Edwards	88
*M.P.Vaughan	c Jacobs b Collins	7	c Jacobs b Sarwan	140
M.A.Butcher	b Collins	52	c Gayle b Hinds	61
N.Hussain	b Best	3	b Hinds	56
G.P.Thorpe	c Collins b Edwards	10	not out	23
A.Flintoff	not out	102	c Lara b Sarwan	14
†G.O.Jones	b Edwards	38	not out	10
G.J.Batty	c Gayle b Collins	8		
M.J.Hoggard	c Jacobs b Collins	1		
S.P.Jones	lbw b Hinds	11		
S.J.Harmison	b Best	5		
Extras	(B 1, LB 5, W 4, NB 22)	32	(B 4, LB 7, W 3, NB 16)	30
Total		**285**	**(5 wickets)**	**422**

ENGLAND	O	M	R	W		O	M	R	W
Hoggard	18	2	82	0					
Harmison	37	6	92	1					
Flintoff	35	8	109	1					
S.P.Jones	29	0	146	1					
Batty	52	4	185	2					
Vaughan	13	0	60	0					
Trescothick	18	3	68	0					

WEST INDIES	O	M	R	W		O	M	R	W
Collins	26	4	76	4	(8)	8	2	34	0
Edwards	18	3	70	2		20	2	81	1
Collymore	19	5	45	0		18	3	58	0
Best	10.3	3	37	3	(1)	16	1	57	0
Hinds	17.3	7	29	1		38	8	83	2
Sarwan	7	0	18	0	(7)	12	2	26	2
Gayle	1	0	4	0	(6)	17	6	36	0
Powell					(4)	8	0	36	0

FALL OF WICKETS

	WI	E	E
Wkt	1st	1st	2nd
1st	33	8	182
2nd	98	45	274
3rd	330	54	366
4th	380	98	387
5th	469	98	408
6th	–	182	–
7th	–	205	–
8th	–	229	–
9th	–	283	–
10th	–	285	–

Umpires: Alim Dar (*Pakistan*) (7) and D.B.Hair (*Australia*) (53).
Referees: M.J.Procter (*South Africa*) (24) first three days and J.J.Crowe (*New Zealand*) (1) last two days.   **Test No. 1694/130 (WI409/E820)**

WEST INDIES v ENGLAND 2003-04

WEST INDIES – BATTING AND FIELDING

	M	I	NO	HS	Runs	Avge	100	50	Ct/St
B.C.Lara	4	7	1	400*	500	83.33	1	–	2
R.D.Jacobs	4	7	1	107*	277	46.16	1	1	10
D.S.Smith	2	4	–	108	172	43.00	1	–	4
R.R.Sarwan	4	7	–	90	192	27.42	–	2	2
C.H.Gayle	4	7	–	69	182	26.00	–	2	4
R.O.Hinds	3	5	–	84	128	25.60	–	1	2
S.Chanderpaul	3	6	–	50	101	16.83	–	1	–
C.D.Collymore	4	6	6	6*	15	–	–	–	1
D.Ganga	2	3	–	11	32	10.66	–	–	–
T.L.Best	4	6	–	20	52	8.66	–	–	–
P.T.Collins	3	4	–	10	25	6.25	–	–	1
A.Sanford	2	4	–	1	4	1.00	–	–	3
F.H.Edwards	3	4	–	2	3	0.75	–	–	–

Played in one Test: R.L.Powell 23; D.R.Smith 16, 14 (1 ct).

WEST INDIES – BOWLING

	O	M	R	W	Avge	Best	5wI	10wM
R.R.Sarwan	24	3	53	3	17.66	2-26	–	–
T.L.Best	96	14	301	12	25.08	3-37	–	–
P.T.Collins	94	20	282	11	25.63	4-71	–	–
F.H.Edwards	83.3	12	325	10	32.50	4-70	–	–
R.O.Hinds	72.2	18	148	4	37.00	2-83	–	–
C.H.Gayle	48.5	15	98	2	49.00	2-20	–	–
A.Sanford	52	8	182	3	60.66	2-32	–	–
C.D.Collymore	113	28	255	3	85.00	2-24	–	–

Also bowled: R.L.Powell 8-0-36-0; D.R.Smith 9-0-30-1.

ENGLAND – BATTING AND FIELDING

	M	I	NO	HS	Runs	Avge	100	50	Ct/St
G.P.Thorpe	4	6	3	119*	274	91.33	1	1	3
M.A.Butcher	4	7	2	61	296	59.20	–	4	4
A.Flintoff	4	5	1	102*	200	50.00	1	–	7
M.P.Vaughan	4	8	1	140	245	35.00	1	–	2
N.Hussain	4	7	1	58	197	32.83	–	3	5
A.F.Giles	3	3	–	37	75	25.00	–	–	2
M.E.Trescothick	4	8	1	88	166	23.71	–	1	7
C.M.W.Read	3	3	–	20	36	12.00	–	–	6/1
S.P.Jones	4	4	–	11	23	5.75	–	–	1
S.J.Harmison	4	4	–	13	21	5.25	–	–	–
M.J.Hoggard	4	4	2	9*	10	5.00	–	–	2

Played in one Test: G.J.Batty 8 (2 ct); G.O.Jones 38, 10*.

ENGLAND – BOWLING

	O	M	R	W	Avge	Best	5wI	10wM
S.J.Harmison	139.5	41	342	23	14.86	7- 12	2	–
M.J.Hoggard	106.4	24	326	13	25.07	4- 35	–	–
A.Flintoff	102.2	21	297	11	27.00	5- 58	1	–
S.P.Jones	94	8	374	11	34.00	5- 57	1	–
A.F.Giles	31	2	137	2	68.50	2- 67	–	–
G.J.Batty	52	4	185	2	92.50	2-185	–	–

Also bowled: M.E.Trescothick 19-3-72.0; M.P.Vaughan 14-0-62-0.

PAKISTAN v INDIA (1st Test)

At Multan Cricket Stadium on 28, 29, 30, 31 March, 1 April 2004.
Toss: India. Result: **INDIA** won by an innings and 52 runs.
Debuts: None.

INDIA

A.Chopra	c Farhat b Saqlain	42
V.Sehwag	c Taufiq b Sami	309
*R.Dravid	c Hamid b Sami	6
S.R.Tendulkar	not out	194
V.V.S.Laxman	run out	29
Yuvraj Singh	c and b Farhat	59
†P.A.Patel		
A.Kumble		
Z.Khan		
L.Balaji		
I.K.Pathan		
Extras	(B 8, LB 20, W 1, NB 7)	36
Total	(5 wickets declared)	**675**

PAKISTAN

Imran Farhat	lbw b Balaji	38	c Patel b Kumble		24
Taufiq Umar	c Dravid b Pathan	23	lbw b Kumble		9
Yasir Hamid	c Patel b Pathan	91	c Sehwag b Yuvraj		23
*Inzamam-ul-Haq	c Chopra b Kumble	77	run out		0
Yousuf Youhana	c Patel b Khan	35	c Dravid b Pathan		112
Abdul Razzaq	c Patel b Pathan	47	c Chopra b Kumble		22
†Moin Khan	b Tendulkar	17	lbw b Pathan		5
Saqlain Mushtaq	c Khan b Pathan	5	(9) lbw b Kumble		0
Mohammad Sami	b Kumble	15	(8) lbw b Kumble		0
Shoaib Akhtar	c and b Tendulkar	0	c Laxman b Kumble		4
Shabbir Ahmed	not out	19	not out		0
Extras	(B 4, LB 26, NB 10)	40	(B 4, LB 5, W 1, NB 2, Pen 5)		17
Total		**407**			**216**

PAKISTAN	O	M	R	W		O	M	R	W
Shoaib Akhtar	32	4	119	0					
Mohammad Sami	34	4	110	2					
Shabbir Ahmed	31	6	122	0					
Saqlain Mushtaq	43	4	204	1					
Abdul Razzaq	15	3	61	0					
Imran Farhat	6.5	0	31	1					

INDIA	O	M	R	W		O	M	R	W
Khan	23	6	76	1					
Pathan	28	5	100	4	(1)	21	12	26	2
Kumble	39.3	12	100	2		30	10	72	6
Balaji	20	4	54	1	(2)	11	3	48	0
Sehwag	2	0	11	0	(4)	3	0	8	0
Tendulkar	14	1	36	2		6	2	23	0
Yuvraj Singh					(5)	6	1	25	1

FALL OF WICKETS

Wkt	1st	1st	2nd
		I	P	P
1st	160	58	33
2nd	173	73	44
3rd	509	233	44
4th	565	243	75
5th	675	321	106
6th	–	364	113
7th	–	364	124
8th	–	371	136
9th	–	371	206
10th	–	407	216

Umpires: D.R.Shepherd (*England*) (80) and S.J.A.Taufel (*Australia*) (12).
Referee: R.S.Madugalle (*Sri Lanka*) (59). **Test No. 1695/48 (P300/I372)**

PAKISTAN v INDIA (2nd Test)

At Gaddafi Stadium, Lahore, on 5, 6, 7, 8 April 2004.
Toss: India. Result: **PAKISTAN** won by nine wickets.
Debuts: None.

INDIA

Batsman	Dismissal 1		Dismissal 2	
A.Chopra	lbw b Sami	4	lbw b Akhtar	5
V.Sehwag	c Akmal b Gul	39	c Akmal b Akhtar	90
*R.Dravid	c Inzamam b Gul	33	run out	0
S.R.Tendulkar	lbw b Gul	2	lbw b Sami	8
V.V.S.Laxman	c Taufiq b Gul	11	b Gul	13
Yuvraj Singh	c Farhat b Kaneria	112	c Akmal b Sami	12
†P.A.Patel	lbw b Gul	0	not out	62
A.B.Agarkar	c Akmal b Akhtar	2	(9) c Taufiq b Kaneria	36
I.K.Pathan	c and b Kaneria	49	(8) c Taufiq b Akhtar	0
L.Balaji	c Akmal b Sami	0	(11) lbw b Kaneria	0
A.Kumble	not out	6	(10) st Akmal b Kaneria	0
Extras	(B 6, LB 8, W 6, NB 9)	29	(LB 8, W 1, NB 6)	15
Total		**287**		**241**

PAKISTAN

Batsman	Dismissal 1		Dismissal 2	
Imran Farhat	c Patel b Balaji	101	c Yuvraj b Balaji	9
Taufiq Umar	b Balaji	24	not out	14
Yasir Hamid	c Dravid b Agarkar	19	not out	16
*Inzamam-ul-Haq	lbw b Pathan	118		
Yousuf Youhana	c Patel b Balaji	72		
Asim Kamal	c Patel b Kumble	73		
†Kamran Akmal	lbw Pathan	5		
Mohammad Sami	b Pathan	2		
Shoaib Akhtar	c Yuvraj b Kumble	19		
Umar Gul	hit wicket b Tendulkar	14		
Danish Kaneria	not out	0		
Extras	(B 4, LB 18, W 4, NB 16)	42	(NB 1)	1
Total		**489**	(1 wicket)	**40**

PAKISTAN	O	M	R	W	O	M	R	W
Shoaib Akhtar	16	1	69	1	17	4	62	3
Mohammad Sami	23	1	117	2	26	6	92	2
Umar Gul	12	2	31	5	13	1	65	1
Danish Kaneria	13.1	1	56	2	6.4	2	14	3
INDIA								
Pathan	44	14	107	3	4	0	25	0
Balaji	33	11	81	3	3	0	15	1
Agarkar	23	5	80	1				
Kumble	44.1	5	146	2				
Tendulkar	12	1	38	1				
Yuvraj Singh	3	0	7	0				
Sehwag	1	0	8	0				

FALL OF WICKETS

Wkt	1st	1st	2nd	2nd
	I	P	I	P
1st	5	47	15	15
2nd	69	95	15	–
3rd	75	205	43	–
4th	94	356	88	–
5th	125	366	105	–
6th	127	379	160	–
7th	147	386	160	–
8th	264	432	235	–
9th	265	470	241	–
10th	287	489	241	–

Umpires: S.A.Bucknor (*West Indies*) (89) and S.J.A.Taufel (*Australia*) (13).
Referee: R.S.Madugalle (*Sri Lanka*) (60).   **Test No. 1696/49 (P301/I373)**

PAKISTAN v INDIA (3rd Test)

At Rawalpindi Cricket Stadium on 13, 14, 15, 16 April 2004.
Toss: India. Result: **INDIA** won by an innings and 131 runs.
Debuts: None.

PAKISTAN

Imran Farhat	lbw b Nehra	16		c Sehwag b Balaji	3
Taufiq Umar	lbw b Balaji	9		lbw b Pathan	13
Yasir Hamid	c Laxman b Pathan	26		c Patel b Nehra	20
*Inzamam-ul-Haq	c Patel b Nehra	15	(5)	c Patel b Balaji	9
Yousuf Youhana	b Pathan	13	(6)	c and b Kumble	48
Asim Kamal	lbw b Balaji	21	(7)	not out	60
†Kamran Akmal	c Laxman b Balaji	17	(4)	b Balaji	23
Mohammad Sami	run out	49		c Dravid b Kumble	0
Shoaib Akhtar	b Balaji	0		c Nehra b Kumble	28
Fazal-e-Akbar	lbw b Kumble	25		c Pathan b Kumble	12
Danish Kaneria	not out	4		c Ganguly b Tendulkar	0
Extras	(B 14, LB 5, W 7, NB 3)	29		(B 5, LB 11, W 2, NB 11)	29
Total		**224**			**245**

INDIA

V.Sehwag	c Hamid b Akhtar	0
†P.A.Patel	c Kamran b Fazal	69
R.Dravid	b Farhat	270
S.R.Tendulkar	c Akmal b Akhtar	1
V.V.S.Laxman	b Akhtar	71
*S.C.Ganguly	run out	77
Yuvraj Singh	lbw b Sami	47
I.K.Pathan	c Fazal b Kaneria	15
A.Kumble	st Akmal b Kaneria	9
L.Balaji	c sub (Shoaib Malik) b Farhat	11
A.Nehra	not out	1
Extras	(B 11, LB 12, W 6)	29
Total		**600**

INDIA	O	M	R	W		O	M	R	W
Pathan	22	7	49	2		15	6	35	1
Balaji	19	4	63	4		20	2	108	3
Nehra	21	4	60	2	(4)	6	2	20	1
Ganguly	2	0	9	0	(5)	4	0	18	0
Kumble	8.5	2	24	1	(3)	8	2	47	4
Tendulkar						1	0	1	1

PAKISTAN	O	M	R	W
Shoaib Akhtar	21.2	7	47	3
Fazal-e-Akbar	40.4	3	162	1
Danish Kaneria	62	4	178	2
Mohammad Sami	40	11	116	1
Imran Farhat	12.2	1	69	2
Yasir Hamid	1	0	5	0

FALL OF WICKETS

	P	I	P
Wkt	1st	1st	2nd
1st	34	0	30
2nd	34	129	34
3rd	77	130	64
4th	77	261	90
5th	110	392	94
6th	120	490	175
7th	137	537	179
8th	137	572	221
9th	207	593	244
10th	224	600	245

Umpires: R.E.Koertzen (*South Africa*) (49) and D.R.Shepherd (*England*) (81).
Referee: R.S.Madugalle (*Sri Lanka*) (61). **Test No. 1697/50 (P302/I374)**

ZIMBABWE v SRI LANKA (1st Test)

At Harare Sports Club on 6, 7, 8 May 2004.
Toss: Sri Lanka. Result: **SRI LANKA** won by an innings and 240 runs.
Debuts: Zimbabwe – E.Chigumbura, A.Maregwede, T.Panyangara, B.R.M.Taylor,
P.Utseya; Sri Lanka – M.F.Maharoof.

ZIMBABWE

S.Matsikenyeri	c DPMD Jayawardena b Zoysa	10	c DPMD Jayawardena b Zoysa	11
B.R.M.Taylor	c and b Maharoof	19	c Muralitharan b Vaas	4
D.D.Ebrahim	lbw b Zoysa	1	c HAPW Jayawardena b Zoysa	2
*†T.Taibu	c DPMD Jayawardena b Muralitharan	40	lbw b Zoysa	0
E.Chigumbura	c Muralitharan b Zoysa	14	c HAPW Jayawardena b Zoysa	0
A.Maregwede	lbw b Muralitharan	0	c and b Muralitharan	22
M.L.Nkala	lbw b Muralitharan	2	c DPMD Jayawardena b Muralitharan	24
P.Utseya	b Muralitharan	45	b Maharoof	0
N.B.Mahwire	b Muralitharan	0	c DPMD Jayawardena b Zoysa	2
D.T.Hondo	b Muralitharan	19	not out	15
T.Panyangara	not out	32	c DPMD Jayawardena b Jayasuriya	18
Extras	(B 4, LB 6, NB 7)	17	(LB 2, NB 2)	4
Total		**199**		**102**

SRI LANKA

*M.S.Atapattu	b Hondo	170
S.T.Jayasuriya	c Hondo b Taibu	157
K.C.Sangakkara	c#Taibu b Matsikenyeri	11
D.P.M.D.Jayawardena	c Utseya b Chigumbura	37
T.M.Dilshan	c Utseya b Mahwire	10
T.T.Samaraweera	c Taibu b Panyangara	6
†H.A.P.W.Jayawardena	b Panyangara	4
W.P.U.C.J.Vaas	c Matsikenyeri b Mahwire	28
M.F.Maharoof	lbw b Mahwire	40
D.N.T.Zoysa	not out	28
M.Muralitharan	c Maregwede b Panyangara	26
Extras	(B 2, LB 13, W 3, NB 6)	24
Total		**541**

SRI LANKA	O	M	R	W		O	M	R	W
Vaas	19	6	39	0		8	2	24	1
Zoysa	17	6	53	2		9.5	2	20	5
Maharoof	10	3	45	1	(4)	4	0	18	1
Muralitharan	24.2	10	45	6	(3)	9.1	1	37	2
Jayasuriya	1	0	7	0		1	0	1	1

ZIMBABWE	O	M	R	W
Hondo	27	6	103	1
Panyangara	26.1	2	101	3
Mahwire	18	1	97	3
Nkala	7	1	41	0
Utseya	12	2	55	0
Matsikenyeri	15	2	58	1
Taibu	8	1	27	1
Chigumbura	12	2	44	1

FALL OF WICKETS			
	Z	SL	Z
Wkt	1st	1st	2nd
1st	30	281	13
2nd	32	312	15
3rd	35	369	17
4th	57	387	17
5th	69	399	18
6th	85	403	63
7th	118	414	64
8th	118	457	64
9th	149	496	72
10th	199	541	102

Not as wkt-kpr.

Umpires: B.F.Bowden (*New Zealand*) (14) and R.E.Koertzen (*South Africa*) (50).
Referee: M.J.Procter (*South Africa*) (25).   Test No. 1698/14 (Z74/SL140)

250

ZIMBABWE v SRI LANKA (2nd Test)

At Queens Sports Club, Bulawayo, on 14, 15, 16, 17 May 2004.
Toss: Sri Lanka. Result: **SRI LANKA** won by an innings and 254 runs.
Debuts: Zimbabwe – T.Mupariwa.

ZIMBABWE

S.Matsikenyeri	run out	45	c HAPW Jayawardena b Zoysa		14
B.R.M.Taylor	c HAPW Jayawardena b Vaas	5	c DPMD Jayawardena b Muralitharan		61
M.A.Vermeulen	c Muralitharan b Vaas	0	c Muralitharan b Zoysa		6
D.D.Ebrahim	c Dilshan b Maharoof	70	c Atapattu b Jayasuriya		42
*†T.Taibu	c Samaraweera b Maharoof	27	c Dilshan b Muralitharan		0
A.Maregwede	run out	24	lbw b Vaas		28
E.Chigumbura	c DPMD Jayawardena b Vaas	0	lbw b Muralitharan		12
M.L.Nkala	c Sangakkara b Muralitharan	19	c Dilshan b Vaas		0
T.Panyangara	c Vaas b Zoysa	11	not out		40
T.Mupariwa	not out	1	c Vaas b Jayasuriya		14
D.T.Hondo	b Muralitharan	11	c Atapattu b Muralitharan		3
Extras	(LB 2, W 3, NB 10)	15	(LB 7, W 1, NB 3)		11
Total		**228**			**231**

SRI LANKA

*M.S.Atapattu	c Taibu b Chigumbura	249
S.T.Jayasuriya	c Taibu b Nkala	48
K.C.Sangakkara	c Taibu b Panyangara	270
D.P.M.D.Jayawardena	not out	100
T.T.Samaraweera	not out	32
T.M.Dilshan		
†H.A.P.W.Jayawardena		
W.P.U.C.J.Vaas		
M.F.Maharoof		
D.N.T.Zoysa		
M.Muralitharan		
Extras	(LB 5, W 4, NB 5)	14
Total	(3 wickets declared)	**713**

SRI LANKA	O	M	R	W		O	M	R	W
Vaas	19	8	41	3		18	6	53	2
Zoysa	14	0	50	1		13	4	27	2
Maharoof	16	2	62	2	(4)	6	0	32	0
Muralitharan	22	3	58	2	(3)	28.1	6	79	4
Jayasuriya	4	0	15	0		10	0	33	2

ZIMBABWE	O	M	R	W
Hondo	29	5	116	0
Panyangara	25	4	120	1
Mupariwa	34	1	136	0
Nkala	32	3	111	1
Chigumbura	21	2	108	1
Matsikenyeri	23.3	1	112	0
Vermeulen	1	0	5	0

FALL OF WICKETS

	Z	SL	Z
Wkt	1st	1st	2nd
1st	24	100	22
2nd	31	538	40
3rd	82	627	125
4th	134	–	127
5th	176	–	143
6th	176	–	173
7th	193	–	173
8th	211	–	173
9th	216	–	204
10th	228	–	231

Umpires: B.F.Bowden (*New Zealand*) (15) and R.E.Koertzen (*South Africa*) (51).
Referee: M.J.Procter (*South Africa*) (26).　　　**Test No. 1699/15 (Z75/SL141)**

ENGLAND v NEW ZEALAND (1st Test)

At Lord's, London, on 20, 21, 22, 23, 24 May 2004.
Toss: New Zealand. Result: **ENGLAND** won by seven wickets.
Debuts: England – A.J.Strauss.

NEW ZEALAND

Batsman	Dismissal 1	Runs		Dismissal 2	Runs
M.H.Richardson	lbw b Harmison	93		c G.O.Jones b Harmison	101
*S.P.Fleming	c Strauss b S.P.Jones	34		c Hussain b Harmison	4
N.J.Astle	c G.O.Jones b Flintoff	64	(7)	c G.O.Jones b Harmison	49
S.B.Styris	c G.O.Jones b S.P.Jones	0		c Hussain b Giles	4
C.D.McMillan	lbw b Hoggard	6		c Hussain b Giles	0
J.D.P.Oram	c G.O.Jones b Harmison	67		run out	4
D.R.Tuffey	b Harmison	8	(10)	not out	14
C.L.Cairns	c Harmison b Flintoff	82		c Butcher b Giles	14
†B.B.McCullum	b S.P.Jones	5	(3)	c G.O.Jones b S.P.Jones	96
D.L.Vettori	b Harmison	2	(9)	c G.O.Jones b Harmison	5
C.S.Martin	not out	1		b Flintoff	7
Extras	(B 9, LB 6, W 2, NB 7)	24		(B 14, LB 16, NB 8)	38
Total		**386**			**336**

ENGLAND

Batsman	Dismissal 1	Runs		Dismissal 2	Runs
*M.E.Trescothick	c McCullum b Oram	86		c and b Tuffey	2
A.J.Strauss	c Richardson b Martin	112		run out	83
M.A.Butcher	c McCullum b Vettori	26		c Fleming b Martin	6
M.J.Hoggard	c McCullum b Oram	15			
N.Hussain	b Martin	34	(4)	not out	103
G.P.Thorpe	b Cairns	3	(5)	not out	51
A.Flintoff	c Richardson b Martin	63			
†G.O.Jones	c Oram b Styris	46			
A.F.Giles	c Oram b Styris	11			
S.P.Jones	b Martin	4			
S.J.Harmison	not out	0			
Extras	(B 4, LB 18, NB 19)	41		(B 7, LB 12, W 5, NB 13)	37
Total		**441**		(3 wickets)	**282**

ENGLAND	O	M	R	W		O	M	R	W
Hoggard	22	7	68	1	(3)	14	3	39	0
Harmison	31	7	126	4	(1)	29	8	76	4
Flintoff	21.4	7	63	2	(2)	16.1	5	40	1
S.P.Jones	23	8	82	3		23	5	64	1
Giles	5	0	32	0		39	8	87	3

NEW ZEALAND	O	M	R	W		O	M	R	W
Tuffey	26	4	98	0	(2)	10	3	32	1
Martin	27	6	94	3	(4)	18	2	75	1
Oram	30	8	76	2	(1)	15	4	39	0
Cairns	16	2	71	1	(6)	6	0	27	0
Vettori	21	1	69	2	(3)	25	5	53	0
Styris	4.3	0	11	2	(5)	13	5	37	0

FALL OF WICKETS

	NZ	E	NZ	E
Wkt	1st	1st	2nd	2nd
1st	58	190	7	18
2nd	161	239	180	35
3rd	162	254	187	143
4th	174	288	187	–
5th	280	297	203	–
6th	287	311	287	–
7th	324	416	290	–
8th	329	428	304	–
9th	338	441	310	–
10th	386	441	336	–

Umpires: D.B.Hair (*Australia*) (54) and R.E.Koertzen (*South Africa*) (52).
Referee: C.H.Lloyd (*West Indies*) (34). **Test No. 1700/86 (E821/NZ311)**

ENGLAND v NEW ZEALAND (2nd Test)

At Headingley, Leeds, on 3, 4, 5, 6, 7 June 2004.
Toss: England. Result: **ENGLAND** won by nine wickets.
Debuts: None.

NEW ZEALAND

M.H.Richardson	b Saggers	13		c Jones b Hoggard	40
M.H.W.Papps	lbw b Flintoff	86	(9)	c Vaughan b Harmison	0
*S.P.Fleming	c Vaughan b Harmison	97	(2)	c Strauss b Flintoff	11
N.J.Astle	c Butcher b Saggers	2		lbw b Hoggard	8
S.B.Styris	c Jones b Harmison	21		c Jones b Hoggard	19
J.D.P.Oram	c Thorpe b Flintoff	39	(7)	not out	36
C.L.Cairns	c Strauss b Harmison	41	(8)	lbw b Hoggard	10
†B.B.McCullum	b Hoggard	54	(3)	c Trescothick b Harmison	20
D.L.Vettori	b Harmison	35		absent hurt	–
D.R.Tuffey	lbw b Hoggard	0	(6)	c Jones b Harmison	7
C.S.Martin	not out	0	(10)	not out	0
Extras	(B 5, LB 14, W 2)	21		(B 4, LB 4, NB 2)	10
Total		**409**			**161**

ENGLAND

M.E.Trescothick	b Styris	132		not out	30
A.J.Strauss	c Tuffey b Vettori	62		c Astle b Tuffey	10
M.A.Butcher	lbw b Vettori	4		not out	5
*M.P.Vaughan	c Fleming b Styris	13			
G.P.Thorpe	b Martin	34			
A.Flintoff	c Martin b Styris	94			
†G.O.Jones	c Fleming b Cairns	100			
A.F.Giles	c Fleming b Martin	21			
M.J.Hoggard	c McCullum b Tuffey	4			
M.J.Saggers	c sub (S.E.Bond) b Cairns	0			
S.J.Harmison	not out	0			
Extras	(B 25, LB 21, W 3, NB 13)	62			
Total		**526**		(1 wicket)	**45**

ENGLAND	O	M	R	W	O	M	R	W		FALL OF WICKETS			
Hoggard	27	6	93	2	15	4	75	4			NZ	E	NZ	E
Harmison	36.2	8	74	4	16	5	57	3	*Wkt*	*1st*	*1st*	*2nd*	*2nd*
Flintoff	27	7	64	2	6	0	16	1	1st	33	153	39	18
Saggers	30	6	86	2	5	3	5	0	2nd	202	174	75	–
Trescothick	2	0	3	0					3rd	215	229	77	–
Giles	19	1	67	0					4th	215	240	84	–
Vaughan	2	0	3	0					5th	263	339	91	–
									6th	293	457	118	–
NEW ZEALAND									7th	355	491	144	–
Tuffey	26.1	7	88	1	(2)	4	0	28	1	8th	409	526	149	–
Martin	30	9	127	2	(1)	4	1	17	0	9th	409	526	161	–
Styris	27	5	88	3					10th	409	526	–	–
Cairns	27	6	94	2									
Vettori	23	2	83	2									
Styris													

Umpires: S.A.Bucknor (*West Indies*) (90) and S.J.A.Taufel (*Australia*) (14).
Referee: C.H.Lloyd (*West Indies*) (35). **Test No. 1701/87 (E822/NZ312)**

ENGLAND v NEW ZEALAND (3rd Test)

At Trent Bridge, Nottingham, on 10, 11, 12, 13 June 2004.
Toss: New Zealand. Result: **ENGLAND** won by four wickets.
Debuts: New Zealand – K.D.Mills.

NEW ZEALAND

M.H.Richardson	c Vaughan b Giles	73	lbw b Giles		49
*S.P.Fleming	c Thorpe b Flintoff	117	lbw b Flintoff		45
S.B.Styris	c sub (B.M.Shafayat) b Giles	108	(4) c Jones b Harmison		39
N.J.Astle	b Harmison	15	(5) lbw b Flintoff		0
C.D.McMillan	lbw b Harmison	0	(6) lbw b Harmison		30
J.D.P.Oram	c Strauss b Saggers	14	(8) c Flintoff b Harmison		0
C.L.Cairns	c Thorpe b Saggers	12	(9) b Giles		1
†B.B.McCullum	c Hoggard b Harmison	21	(3) c Flintoff b Giles		4
J.E.C.Franklin	not out	4	(7) c Jones b Flintoff		17
K.D.Mills	c Jones b Hoggard	0	c Harmison b Giles		8
C.S.Martin	c Vaughan b Hoggard	2	not out		0
Extras	(B 2, LB 14, NB 2)	18	(B 1, LB 21, NB 3)		25
Total		**384**			**218**

ENGLAND

M.E.Trescothick	c Styris b Franklin	63	c and b Franklin		9
A.J.Strauss	c McCullum b Cairns	0	lbw b Cairns		6
M.A.Butcher	c Styris b Franklin	5	lbw b Cairns		59
*M.P.Vaughan	lbw b Cairns	61	lbw b Cairns		10
G.P.Thorpe	c McCullum b Franklin	45	not out		104
A.Flintoff	lbw b Cairns	54	c sub (H.J.H.Marshall) b Cairns		5
M.J.Hoggard	c Styris b Franklin	5			
†G.O.Jones	lbw b Styris	22	(7) c Oram b Franklin		27
A.F.Giles	not out	45	(8) not out		36
M.J.Saggers	b Cairns	0			
S.J.Harmison	b Cairns	0			
Extras	(B 2, LB 5, NB 12)	19	(B 4, LB 16, NB 8)		28
Total		**319**	(6 wickets)		**284**

ENGLAND	O	M	R	W		O	M	R	W		FALL OF WICKETS				
Hoggard	28	6	85	2		6	2	25	0			NZ	E	NZ	E
Harmison	32	9	80	3		25	7	51	3		*Wkt*	*1st*	*1st*	*2nd*	*2nd*
Flintoff	14	2	48	1	(4)	20	3	60	3		1st	163	1	94	12
Saggers	22	5	80	2	(3)	6	2	14	0		2nd	225	18	106	16
Giles	27	6	70	2		24	6	46	4		3rd	272	128	126	46
Vaughan	1	0	5	0							4th	272	140	134	134
											5th	308	221	185	162
NEW ZEALAND											6th	331	244	198	214
Martin	1.5	0	1	0							7th	366	255	198	–
Cairns	23.3	5	79	5	(1)	25	2	108	4		8th	163	1	94	12
Franklin	26.1	4	104	4	(2)	17	2	59	2		8th	382	295	208	–
Mills	6	2	31	0							9th	382	301	210	–
Oram	15	0	47	0	(4)	14.3	1	50	0		10th	384	319	218	–
Styris	11	1	45	1	(5)	14	1	43	0						
McMillan	2	1	5	0											
Richardson					(3)	1	0	4	0						

Umpires: D.J.Harper (*Australia*) (41) and S.J.A.Taufel (*Australia*) (15).
Referee: C.H.Lloyd (*West Indies*) (36).   Test No. 1702/88 (E823/NZ313)

ENGLAND v NEW ZEALAND 2004

ENGLAND – BATTING AND FIELDING

	M	I	NO	HS	Runs	Avge	100	50	Ct/St
G.P.Thorpe	3	5	2	104*	237	79.00	1	1	3
M.E.Trescothick	3	6	1	132	322	64.40	1	2	1
A.F.Giles	3	4	2	45*	113	56.50	–	–	–
A.Flintoff	3	4	–	94	216	54.00	–	3	2
G.O.Jones	3	4	–	100	195	48.75	1	–	14
A.J.Strauss	3	6	–	112	273	45.50	1	2	4
M.P.Vaughan	2	3	–	61	84	28.00	–	1	4
M.A.Butcher	3	6	1	59	105	21.00	–	1	2
M.J.Hoggard	3	3	–	15	24	8.00	–	–	1
S.J.Harmison	3	3	2	0*	0	0.00	–	–	2
M.J.Saggers	2	2	–	0	0	0.00	–	–	–

Played in one Test: N.Hussain 34, 103* (3 ct); S.P.Jones 4.

ENGLAND – BOWLING

	O	M	R	W	Avge	Best	5wI	10wM
S.J.Harmison	169.2	44	464	21	22.09	4-74	–	–
A.Flintoff	104.5	24	291	10	29.10	3-60	–	–
A.F.Giles	114	21	302	9	33.55	4-46	–	–
S.P.Jones	46	13	146	4	36.50	3-82	–	–
M.J.Hoggard	109	28	385	9	42.77	4-75	–	–
M.J.Saggers	63	16	185	4	46.25	2-80	–	–

Also bowled: M.E.Trescothick 2-0-3-0; M.P.Vaughan 3-0-8-0.

NEW ZEALAND – BATTING AND FIELDING

	M	I	NO	HS	Runs	Avge	100	50	Ct/St
M.H.Richardson	3	6	–	101	369	61.50	1	2	2
S.P.Fleming	3	6	–	117	308	51.33	1	1	4
B.B.McCullum	3	6	–	96	200	33.33	–	2	6
J.D.P.Oram	3	6	1	67	160	32.00	–	1	3
S.B.Styris	3	6	–	108	191	31.83	1	–	3
C.L.Cairns	3	6	–	82	160	26.66	–	1	–
N.J.Astle	3	6	–	64	138	23.00	–	1	1
D.L.Vettori	2	3	–	35	42	14.00	–	–	–
D.R.Tuffey	2	4	1	14*	29	9.66	–	–	2
C.D.McMillan	2	4	–	30	36	9.00	–	–	–
C.S.Martin	3	6	3	7	10	3.33	–	–	1

Played in one Test: J.E.C.Franklin 4*, 17 (1 ct); K.D.Mills 0, 8; M.H.W.Papps 86, 0.

NEW ZEALAND – BOWLING

	O	M	R	W	Avge	Best	5wI	10wM
J.E.C.Franklin	43.1	6	163	6	27.16	4-104	–	–
C.L.Cairns	97.3	15	379	12	31.58	5- 79	1	–
S.B.Styris	69.3	12	224	6	37.33	3- 88	–	–
D.L.Vettori	69	8	205	4	51.25	2- 69	–	–
C.S.Martin	80.5	18	314	6	52.33	3- 94	–	–
D.R.Tuffey	66.1	14	246	3	82.00	1- 28	–	–
J.D.P.Oram	74.3	13	212	2	106.00	2- 76	–	–

Also bowled: C.D.McMillan 2-1-5-0; K.D.Mills 6-2-31-0; M.H.Richardson 1-0-4-0.

WEST INDIES v BANGLADESH (1st Test)

At Beausejour Stadium, Gros Islet, St Lucia, on 28, 29, 30, 31 May, 1 June 2004.
Toss: Bangladesh. Result: **MATCH DRAWN**.
Debuts: Bangladesh – Faisal Hossain, Tareq Aziz.

BANGLADESH

Hannan Sarkar	lbw b Collins	0	b Edwards		9
Javed Omar	c D.S.Smith b Collins	32	c Jacobs b Collins		7
*Habibul Bashar	c D.R.Smith b Lawson	113	b Best		25
Rajin Saleh	c Jacobs b Sarwan	26	lbw b Edwards		51
Mohammad Ashraful	lbw b Lawson	81	c and b Sarwan		1
Faisal Hossain	c Best b Collins	5	c Gayle b Sarwan		2
Mushfiqur Rahman	c Jacobs b Sarwan	1	lbw b Sarwan		0
†Khaled Masud	st Jacobs b Gayle	2	not out		103
Mohammad Rafique	b Collins	111	c Jacobs b Sarwan		29
Tapash Baisya	c and b Sarwan	9	c and b Gayle		26
Tareq Aziz	not out	6	not out		1
Extras	(LB 10, W 1, NB 19)	30	(LB 5, NB 12)		17
Total		**416**	**(9 wickets declared)**		**271**

WEST INDIES

D.S.Smith	run out	0	(2) not out		40
C.H.Gayle	c Habibul b Baisya	141	(1) not out		66
R.R.Sarwan	c Rafique b Baisya	40			
*B.C.Lara	c Masud b Mushfiqur	53			
S.Chanderpaul	c Masud b Rafique	7			
D.R.Smith	c Aziz b Rafique	42			
†R.D.Jacobs	not out	46			
T.L.Best	b Rafique	3			
P.T.Collins	c Habibul b Mushfiqur	4			
J.J.C.Lawson	c Sarkar b Mushfiqur	0			
F.H.Edwards	lbw b Mushfiqur	5			
Extras	(LB 3, NB 8)	11	(B 4, LB 1, NB 2)		7
Total		**352**	**(0 wickets)**		**113**

WEST INDIES	O	M	R	W		O	M	R	W
Collins	27.3	8	83	4		17	5	42	1
Edwards	21	2	78	0		19	1	61	2
Lawson	16	2	66	2		16	0	60	0
Best	20	4	64	0	(5)	13	1	33	1
D.R.Smith	4	1	5	0					
Gayle	24	3	51	1		19.2	7	33	1
Sarwan	23	7	59	3	(4)	20	9	37	4
Chanderpaul					(7)	1	1	0	0

BANGLADESH	O	M	R	W		O	M	R	W
Tapash Baisya	26	5	87	4		3	0	26	0
Tareq Aziz	23	3	95	0		6	1	31	0
Mushfiqur Rahman	25.4	8	65	4		6	0	25	0
Mohammad Rafique	36	12	90	3		5	1	7	0
Rajin Saleh	6	0	12	0					
Mohammad Ashraful					(5)	3	0	19	0

FALL OF WICKETS

	B	WI	B	WI
Wkt	1st	1st	2nd	2nd
1st	0	2	17	–
2nd	121	89	21	–
3rd	171	162	70	–
4th	227	183	73	–
5th	238	253	79	–
6th	241	312	79	–
7th	250	321	123	–
8th	337	336	179	–
9th	370	342	253	–
10th	416	352	–	–

Umpires: D.J.Harper (*Australia*) (40) and J.W.Lloyds (*England*) (1).
Referee: R.S.Mahanama (*Sri Lanka*) (1).   **Test No. 1703/3 (WI410/B29)**

WEST INDIES v BANGLADESH (2nd Test)

At Sabina Park, Kingston, Jamaica, on 4, 5, 6, 7 June 2004.
Toss: Bangladesh. Result: **WEST INDIES** won by an innings and 99 runs.
Debuts: None.

BANGLADESH

Hannan Sarkar	lbw b Collins	0	(2)	lbw b Collins	10
Javed Omar	c Jacobs b Edwards	20	(1)	c D.R.Smith b Best	5
*Habibul Bashar	c Banks b Collins	20		lbw b Collins	77
Rajin Saleh	c and b Banks	47		c D.R.Smith b Collins	0
Mohammad Ashraful	c Sarwan b Banks	16	(6)	c Lara b Sarwan	9
Manjural Rana	c Jacobs b Best	7	(5)	c Lara b Banks	35
Mushfiqur Rahman	st Jacobs b Banks	22		c D.R.Smith b Collins	0
†Khaled Masud	c Banks b Edwards	39		c Sarwan b Banks	0
Mohammad Rafique	c Collins b Banks	30		b Collins	2
Tapash Baisya	c D.S.Smith b Collins	48		c Sarwan b Collins	3
Tareq Aziz	not out	10		not out	5
Extras	(B 4, LB 7, W 2, NB 12)	25		(B 8, LB 6, W 8, NB 8)	30
Total		**284**			**176**

WEST INDIES

C.H.Gayle	c Masud b Aziz	14
D.S.Smith	run out	44
R.R.Sarwan	not out	261
*B.C.Lara	c Masud b Rafique	120
T.L.Best	c Masud b Baisya	4
S.Chanderpaul	not out	101
†R.D.Jacobs		
D.R.Smith		
P.T.Collins		
O.A.C.Banks		
F.H.Edwards		
Extras	(B 4, LB 5, W 1, NB 5)	15
Total	(4 wickets declared)	**559**

WEST INDIES	O	M	R	W		O	M	R	W
Collins	19	2	64	3		18	3	53	6
Edwards	20	5	66	2					
Best	20	4	53	1	(2)	10	0	32	1
Banks	31	5	87	4	(3)	13	2	40	2
Sarwan	2	2	0	0	(6)	3	1	9	1
D.R.Smith	3	1	3	0	(5)	5	1	19	0
Gayle					(4)	2	0	9	0

BANGLADESH	O	M	R	W
Tapash Baisya	25	5	99	1
Tareq Aziz	19	2	76	1
Mushfiqur Rahman	33	3	127	0
Mohammad Rafique	38	2	124	1
Manjural Rana	28	2	100	0
Mohammad Ashraful	1	1	0	0
Rajin Saleh	7	1	24	0

FALL OF WICKETS

	B	WI	B
Wkt	1st	1st	2nd
1st	0	26	16
2nd	37	109	24
3rd	54	288	34
4th	88	297	154
5th	97	–	154
6th	145	–	154
7th	152	–	155
8th	192	–	160
9th	238	–	164
10th	284	–	176

Umpires: R.E.Koertzen (*South Africa*) (53) and J.W.Lloyds (*England*) (2).
Referee: R.S.Mahanama (*Sri Lanka*) (2). **Test No. 1704/4 (WI1411/B30)**

AUSTRALIA v SRI LANKA (1st Test)

At Marrara Cricket Ground, Darwin, on 1, 2, 3 July 2004.
Toss: Sri Lanka. Result: **AUSTRALIA** won by 149 runs.
Debuts: Sri Lanka – S.L Malinga.

AUSTRALIA

Batsman	1st innings		2nd innings	
J.L.Langer	c Chandana b Samaraweera	30	c Sangakkara b Vaas	10
M.L.Hayden	c Jayasuriya b Vaas	37	c Sangakkara b Zoysa	2
M.T.G.Elliott	c Arnold b Vaas	1	c Dilshan b Vaas	0
D.R.Martyn	c Arnold b Jayasuriya	47	c Sangakkara b Malinga	7
D.S.Lehmann	lbw b Malinga	57	c Sangakkara b Malinga	51
S.M.Katich	c Sangakkara b Vaas	9	c Dilshan b Chandana	15
*†A.C.Gilchrist	c Sangakkara b Malinga	0	run out	80
S.K.Warne	run out	2	lbw b Malinga	1
J.N.Gillespie	lbw b Vaas	4	c Samaraweera b Chandana	16
M.S.Kasprowicz	not out	2	c and b Malinga	15
G.D.McGrath	c Samaraweera b Vaas	0	not out	0
Extras	(B 2, LB 6, W 2, NB 8)	18	(LB 3, NB 1)	4
Total		**207**		**201**

SRI LANKA

Batsman	1st innings		2nd innings	
*M.S.Atapattu	b McGrath	4	c Warne b Kasprowicz	10
S.T.Jayasuriya	lbw b McGrath	8	lbw b McGrath	16
†K.C.Sangakkara	lbw b Gillespie	2	run out	0
D.P.M.D.Jayawardena	c Langer b Gillespie	14	b McGrath	44
D.N.T.Zoysa	c Gilchrist b McGrath	12	(10) c Gilchrist b Kasprowicz	1
T.T.Samaraweera	c Gilchrist b McGrath	1	(5) c Gilchrist b Kasprowicz	32
T.M.Dilshan	not out	17	(6) c Gilchrist b Kasprowicz	14
R.P.Arnold	c Elliott b McGrath	6	(7) c Gilchrist b Kasprowicz	11
U.D.U.Chandana	c Gilchrist b Warne	14	(8) b Kasprowicz	5
W.P.U.C.J.Vaas	c Hayden b Warne	5	(9) not out	10
S.L.Malinga	c Gillespie b Warne	0	c Gilchrist b Kasprowicz	0
Extras	(LB 7, NB 7)	14	(LB 1, W 2, NB 4)	7
Total		**97**		**162**

SRI LANKA	O	M	R	W		O	M	R	W
Vaas	18.3	6	31	5		14	4	51	2
Malinga	14	3	50	2	(3)	15.1	3	42	4
Zoysa	13	4	24	0	(2)	16	3	57	1
Samaraweera	9	1	43	1					
Chandana	6	0	30	0		11	1	30	2
Jayasuriya	11	4	21	1	(4)	6	3	9	0
Arnold					(6)	1	0	9	0

FALL OF WICKETS				
	A	SL	A	SL
Wkt	1st	1st	2nd	2nd
1st	72	10	12	23
2nd	73	20	12	23
3rd	80	33	14	30
4th	177	47	64	109
5th	189	50	77	113
6th	189	51	114	132
7th	201	59	127	141
8th	202	85	154	152
9th	207	91	201	162
10th	207	97	201	162

AUSTRALIA	O	M	R	W	O	M	R	W
McGrath	15	4	37	5	16	9	24	2
Gillespie	13	4	18	2	13	2	37	0
Kasprowicz	7	1	15	0	17.4	3	39	7
Warne	6.5	1	20	3	19	2	61	0

Umpires: Alim Dar (*Pakistan*) (8) and B.F.Bowden (*New Zealand*) (16).
Referee: B.C.Broad (*England*) (6). **Test No. 1705/17 (A652/SL142)**

AUSTRALIA v SRI LANKA (2nd Test)

At Bundaberg Rum Stadium, Cairns, on 9, 10, 11, 12, 13 July 2004.
Toss: Sri Lanka. Result: **MATCH DRAWN**.
Debuts: None.

AUSTRALIA

J.L.Langer	c Jayawardena b Malinga	162	c Kaluwitharana b Zoysa		8
M.L.Hayden	c Jayasuriya b Samaraweera	117	b Chandana		132
*R.T.Ponting	c Atapattu b Malinga	22	c Jayasuriya b Zoysa		45
D.R.Martyn	lbw b Chandana	97	st Kaluwitharana b Chandana		52
D.S.Lehmann	c Sangakkara b Chandana	50	c Jayawardena b Chandana		21
S.M.Katich	b Chandana	1	st Kaluwitharana b Dilshan		1
*†A.C.Gilchrist	c Kaluwitharana b Malinga	35	b Dilshan		0
S.K.Warne	c Samaraweera b Chandana	2	c Samaraweera b Chandana		4
J.N.Gillespie	c Kaluwitharana b Malinga	1	st Kaluwitharana b Chandana		1
M.S.Kasprowicz	c Atapattu b Chandana	9	not out		3
G.D.McGrath	not out	0			
Extras	(B 7, LB 3, W 4, NB 7)	21	(LB 20, W 1, NB 4)		25
Total		**517**	(9 wickets declared)		**292**

SRI LANKA

*M.S.Atapattu	c Hayden b McGrath	133	c Warne b Gillespie		9
S.T.Jayasuriya	c Gilchrist b Gillespie	13	c Gilchrist b Warne		22
K.C.Sangakkara	c Gillespie b Warne	74	b Warne		66
D.P.M.D.Jayawardena	c and b Kasprowicz	43	c Gilchrist b McGrath		6
T.T.Samaraweera	c Ponting b Gillespie	70	run out		0
T.M.Dilshan	c Kasprowicz b Warne	35	c Warne b Gillespie		21
†R.S.Kaluwitharana	c Warne b McGrath	34	c Lehmann b Warne		14
U.D.U.Chandana	st Gilchrist b Warne	19	st Gilchrist b Warne		14
W.P.U.C.J.Vaas	c Ponting b Gillespie	2	not out		11
D.N.T.Zoysa	not out	0	not out		3
S.L.Malinga	run out	0			
Extras	(B 3, LB 10, W 2, NB 17)	32	(B 5, LB 3, NB 9)		17
Total		**455**	(8 wickets)		**183**

SRI LANKA	O	M	R	W		O	M	R	W		FALL OF WICKETS				
Vaas	27	2	102	0		13	3	52	0			A	SL	A	SL
Zoysa	19	5	72	0		14	6	34	2		*Wkt*	*1st*	*1st*	*2nd*	*2nd*
Samaraweera	17	2	55	1	(4)	11	0	50	0		1st	255	18	10	15
Malinga	29.2	2	149	4	(3)	5	0	23	0		2nd	291	156	105	49
Chandana	26	2	109	5		18.4	1	101	5		3rd	392	280	195	58
Jayasuriya	6	0	20	0		3	0	8	0		4th	454	280	261	64
Dilshan						2	0	4	2		5th	462	345	284	107
											6th	469	420	284	136
AUSTRALIA											7th	474	445	288	159
McGrath	34	10	79	2		16	7	31	1		8th	476	455	288	174
Gillespie	37.4	6	116	3		18	6	39	2		9th	485	455	292	–
Kasprowicz	32	5	113	1	(4)	11	4	39	0		10th	517	455	–	–
Warne	38	7	129	3	(3)	37	14	70	4						
Lehmann	3	0	5	0		3	2	1	0						

Umpires: Alim Dar (*Pakistan*) (9) and B.F.Bowden (*New Zealand*) (17).
Referee: B.C.Broad (*England*) (7). **Test No. 1706/18 (A653/SL143)**

ENGLAND v WEST INDIES (1st Test)

At Lord's, London, on 22, 23, 24, 25, 26 July 2004.
Toss: West Indies. Result: **ENGLAND** won by 210 runs.
Debuts: West Indies – D.D.J.Bravo.

ENGLAND

M.E.Trescothick	c Sarwan b Best	16	b Collins		45
A.J.Strauss	c Jacobs b Banks	137	c Sarwan b Collins		35
R.W.T.Key	c Lara b Bravo	221	run out		15
*M.P.Vaughan	c Smith b Collins	103	not out		101
G.P.Thorpe	c Jacobs b Bravo	19	c and b Gayle		38
A.Flintoff	b Banks	6	c Jacobs b Collins		58
†G.O.Jones	c Jacobs b Collins	4			
A.F.Giles	c Smith b Collins	5			
M.J.Hoggard	not out	1			
S.P.Jones	lbw b Collins	4			
S.J.Harmison	b Bravo	4			
Extras	(B 2, LB 20, W 13, NB 13)	48	(B 3, LB 14, NB 16)		33
Total		**568**	**(5 wickets declared)**		**325**

WEST INDIES

C.H.Gayle	lbw b Giles	66	b Harmison		81
D.S.Smith	b Giles	45	lbw b Giles		6
R.R.Sarwan	lbw b Hoggard	1	lbw b Hoggard		4
*B.C.Lara	c G.O.Jones b Giles	11	b Giles		44
S.Chanderpaul	not out	128	not out		97
D.D.J.Bravo	c G.O.Jones b S.P.Jones	44	c and b Giles		10
†R.D.Jacobs	c G.O.Jones b Hoggard	32	c Thorpe b Hoggard		1
O.A.C.Banks	b Flintoff	45	b Harmison		0
T.L.Best	b Flintoff	0	st Jones b Giles		3
P.T.Collins	b Flintoff	0	st Jones b Giles		2
F.H.Edwards	b Giles	5	c Jones b Flintoff		2
Extras	(B 20, LB 11, W 5, NB 3)	39	(B 5, LB 9, NB 3)		17
Total		**416**			**267**

WEST INDIES	O	M	R	W		O	M	R	W
Collins	24	2	113	4	(2)	14.4	1	62	3
Best	21	1	104	1	(1)	3	1	14	0
Edwards	21	2	96	0	(4)	13	0	47	0
Bravo	24.4	5	74	3	(5)	7	0	28	0
Banks	22	3	131	2	(3)	26	1	92	0
Sarwan	9	0	28	0	(7)	4	0	20	0
Gayle					(6)	9	0	45	1
ENGLAND									
Hoggard	28	7	89	2		14	2	65	2
Harmison	21	6	72	0		21	2	78	2
S.P.Jones	17	3	70	1	(4)	8	3	29	0
Giles	40.4	5	129	4	(3)	35	9	81	5
Flintoff	10	4	25	3		1.3	1	9	1

FALL OF WICKETS

	E	WI	E	WI
Wkt	1st	1st	2nd	2nd
1st	29	118	86	24
2nd	320	119	104	35
3rd	485	127	117	102
4th	527	139	233	172
5th	534	264	325	194
6th	541	327	–	195
7th	551	399	–	200
8th	557	399	–	203
9th	563	401	–	247
10th	568	416	–	267

Umpires: D.J.Harper (*Australia*) (42) and R.E.Koertzen (*South Africa*) (54).
Referee: R.S.Madugalle (*Sri Lanka*) (62).　　　　**Test No. 1707/131 (E824/WI412)**

ENGLAND v WEST INDIES (2nd Test)

At Edgbaston, Birmingham, on 29, 30, 31 July, 1 August 2004.
Toss: England. Result: **ENGLAND** won by 256 runs.
Debuts: None.

ENGLAND

M.E.Trescothick	c Lara b Bravo	105	run out		107
A.J.Strauss	c Jacobs b Lawson	24	c Jacobs b Lawson		5
R.W.T.Key	c Lara b Collins	29	c Gayle b Lawson		4
*M.P.Vaughan	c and b Bravo	12	c Gayle b Lawson		3
G.P.Thorpe	c Jacobs b Collymore	61	st Jacobs b Gayle		54
A.Flintoff	lbw b Bravo	167	c Bravo b Gayle		20
†G.O.Jones	c Jacobs b Collymore	74	b Lawson		4
A.F.Giles	c Chanderpaul b Bravo	24	b Gayle		15
M.J.Hoggard	not out	15	c Smith b Gayle		6
J.M.Anderson	b Banks	2	(11) not out		8
S.J.Harmison	not out	31	(10) b Gayle		1
Extras	(LB 6, W 1, NB 15)	22	(B 8, LB 2, W 5, NB 6)		21
Total	(9 wickets declared)	**566**			**248**

WEST INDIES

C.H.Gayle	b Hoggard	7	c Strauss b Giles		82
D.S.Smith	c Giles b Hoggard	4	c Trescothick b Hoggard		11
R.R.Sarwan	b Flintoff	139	c Strauss b Giles		14
*B.C.Lara	c Thorpe b Flintoff	95	c Flintoff b Giles		13
S.Chanderpaul	c Key b Giles	45	lbw b Giles		43
D.J.J.Bravo	b Giles	13	b Giles		0
†R.D.Jacobs	c Trescothick b Hoggard	0	c Anderson b Hoggard		0
O.A.C.Banks	c Jones b Harmison	4	not out		25
P.T.Collins	c Flintoff b Giles	6	lbw b Hoggard		0
C.D.Collymore	lbw b Giles	2	b Anderson		10
J.J.C.Lawson	not out	0	b Anderson		2
Extras	(B 9, LB 5, W 1, NB 6)	21	(B 17, LB 4, NB 1)		22
Total		**336**			**222**

WEST INDIES	O	M	R	W		O	M	R	W
Collins	18	1	90	1		9	1	29	0
Collymore	30	6	126	2		9	2	33	0
Lawson	23	4	111	1		21	2	94	4
Bravo	24	6	76	4		6	1	28	0
Banks	27	3	108	1		5	1	20	0
Sarwan	12	0	49	0					
Gayle					(6)	15.1	4	34	5

ENGLAND	O	M	R	W		O	M	R	W
Hoggard	18	0	89	3		16	5	64	3
Harmison	14	1	64	1		5	1	29	0
Anderson	11	3	37	0	(5)	5.3	1	23	2
Giles	30.3	7	65	4		21	9	57	5
Flintoff	15	1	52	2	(3)	5	1	19	0
Vaughan	1	0	8	0		3	0	9	0
Trescothick	2	0	7	0					

FALL OF WICKETS

	E	WI	E	WI
Wkt	1st	1st	2nd	2nd
1st	77	5	24	15
2nd	125	12	37	54
3rd	150	221	52	101
4th	210	297	184	172
5th	262	323	195	172
6th	432	324	214	177
7th	478	324	226	177
8th	522	334	234	182
9th	525	336	239	210
10th	–	336	248	222

Umpires: D.B.Hair (*Australia*) (55) and S.J.A.Taufel (*Australia*) (16).
Referee: R.S.Madugalle (*Sri Lanka*) (63). **Test No. 1708/132 (E825/WI413)**

ENGLAND v WEST INDIES (3rd Test)

At Old Trafford, Manchester, on 12, 13 (*no play*), 14, 15, 16 August 2004.
Toss: West Indies. Result: **ENGLAND** won by seven wickets.
Debuts: West Indies – S.C.Joseph.

WEST INDIES

C.H.Gayle	c Strauss b Hoggard	5	c Hoggard b Giles		42
S.C.Joseph	c Thorpe b Harmison	45	c Vaughan b Flintoff		15
R.R.Sarwan	b Flintoff	40	c Trescothick b Harmison		60
*B.C.Lara	b Flintoff	0	c Strauss b Flintoff		7
S.Chanderpaul	c Jones b Hoggard	76	c Vaughan b Flintoff		2
D.J.J.Bravo	c Jones b Hoggard	77	c Flintoff b Giles		6
†C.S.Baugh	c Vaughan b Anderson	68	c sub (A.N.Bressington) b Harmison		3
D.Mohammed	c Strauss b Flintoff	23	c Key b Giles		9
P.T.Collins	retired hurt	19	b Harmison		8
C.D.Collymore	b Hoggard	5	not out		5
F.H.Edwards	not out	4	c Flintoff b Harmison		0
Extras	(B 9, LB 14, W 6, NB 4)	33	(B 2, LB 4, W 1, NB 1)		8
Total		**395**			**165**

ENGLAND

M.E.Trescothick	c Sarwan b Edwards	0	b Collymore		12
A.J.Strauss	b Bravo	90	c Chanderpaul b Collins		12
R.W.T.Key	b Collymore	6	not out		93
*M.P.Vaughan	b Bravo	12	c Lara b Gayle		33
G.P.Thorpe	c Lara b Bravo	114			
A.Flintoff	lbw b Bravo	7	(5) not out		57
M.J.Hoggard	c Sarwan b Collymore	23			
†G.O.Jones	b Bravo	12			
A.F.Giles	c and b Bravo	10			
S.J.Harmison	lbw b Collins	8			
J.M.Anderson	not out	1			
Extras	(B 10, LB 10, W 18, NB 9)	47	(B 7, LB 3, NB 14)		24
Total		**330**	(3 wickets)		**231**

ENGLAND	O	M	R	W		O	M	R	W
Hoggard	22	3	83	4		7	0	21	0
Harmison	26	5	94	1		13.4	3	44	4
Flintoff	20	5	79	3		12	1	26	3
Anderson	11.3	1	49	1	(5)	5	1	22	0
Giles	15	0	67	0	(4)	22	6	46	3
WEST INDIES									
Edwards	18	2	68	1		11	0	51	0
Collymore	26	6	66	2		16	7	33	1
Bravo	26	6	55	6	(4)	12	3	41	0
Joseph	2	0	8	0					
Gayle	4	1	7	0	(6)	8.4	0	32	1
Mohammed	26	2	77	0	(5)	6	0	25	0
Collins	10.2	1	29	1	(3)	8	2	24	1
Sarwan					(7)	4	0	15	0

FALL OF WICKETS

	WI	E	WI	E
Wkt	1st	1st	2nd	2nd
1st	10	0	41	15
2nd	85	13	88	27
3rd	97	40	95	111
4th	108	217	99	–
5th	265	227	110	–
6th	267	283	121	–
7th	308	310	146	–
8th	383	321	152	–
9th	395	322	161	–
10th	–	330	165	–

Umpires: Alim Dar (*Pakistan*) (10) and S.J.A.Taufel (*Australia*) (17).
Referee: R.S.Madugalle (*Sri Lanka*) (64).   **Test No. 1709/133 (E826/WI414)**

ENGLAND v WEST INDIES (4th Test)

At Kennington Oval, London, on 19, 20, 21 August 2004.
Toss: England. Result: **ENGLAND** won by 10 wickets.
Debuts: England – I.R.Bell.

ENGLAND

M.E.Trescothick	c Sarwan b Edwards	30	not out	4
A.J.Strauss	c Edwards b Lawson	14	not out	0
R.W.T.Key	c Baugh b Bravo	10		
*M.P.Vaughan	c Lara b Bravo	66		
I.R.Bell	c Baugh b Lawson	70		
A.Flintoff	c Lawson b Edwards	72		
†G.O.Jones	c Sarwan b Collymore	22		
A.F.Giles	c Lara b Bravo	52		
M.J.Hoggard	c Joseph b Lawson	38		
S.J.Harmison	not out	36		
J.M.Anderson	b Gayle	12		
Extras	(B 5, LB 21, W 5, NB 17)	48		
Total		**470**	(0 wickets)	**4**

WEST INDIES

C.H.Gayle	c Jones b Harmison	12	c Flintoff b Anderson	105
S.C.Joseph	c Giles b Harmison	9	c Jones b Harmison	16
R.R.Sarwan	c Strauss b Flintoff	2	c Bell b Harmison	7
*B.C.Lara	c Bell b Harmison	79	c Trescothick b Anderson	15
S.Chanderpaul	c Key b Hoggard	14	(6) c Jones b Giles	32
D.J.J.Bravo	c Jones b Harmison	16	(5) lbw b Hoggard	54
†C.S.Baugh	c Strauss b Harmison	6	(8) c Jones b Harmison	34
C.D.Collymore	c Trescothick b Harmison	4	(9) c Jones b Anderson	7
F.H.Edwards	run out	0	(10) b Anderson	2
J.J.C.Lawson	not out	3	(11) not out	4
D.R.Smith	absent injured	–	(7) c Anderson b Flintoff	28
Extras	(LB 7)	7	(B 1, LB 12, NB 1)	14
Total		**152**		**318**

WEST INDIES	O	M	R	W		O	M	R	W
Edwards	19	4	64	2		0.3	0	4	0
Collymore	23	8	58	1					
Lawson	24	4	115	3					
Bravo	29	4	117	3					
Smith	14	4	50	0					
Gayle	7.2	2	18	1					
Sarwan	7	0	22	0					
ENGLAND									
Hoggard	9	2	31	1		12	5	50	1
Harmison	13	1	46	6		18	1	75	3
Flintoff	8	1	32	1	(4)	17	3	64	1
Anderson	6.5	0	36	0	(5)	15.2	2	52	4
Giles					(3)	22	5	64	1

FALL OF WICKETS

	E	WI	E	
Wkt	1st	1st	2nd	2nd
1st	51	19	73	–
2nd	64	22	81	–
3rd	64	26	126	–
4th	210	54	155	–
5th	236	101	237	–
6th	313	118	265	–
7th	321	136	285	–
8th	408	149	312	–
9th	410	152	314	–
10th	470	–	318	–

Umpires: D.B.Hair (*Australia*) (56) and R.E.Koertzen (*South Africa*) (55).
Referee: R.S.Madugalle (*Sri Lanka*) (65).   Test No. 1710/134 (**E827/WI415**)

ENGLAND v WEST INDIES 2004

ENGLAND – BATTING AND FIELDING

	M	I	NO	HS	Runs	Avge	100	50	Ct/St
A.Flintoff	4	7	1	167	387	64.50	1	3	5
R.W.T.Key	4	7	1	221	378	63.00	1	1	3
G.P.Thorpe	3	5	–	114	286	57.20	1	2	3
M.P.Vaughan	4	7	1	103	330	55.00	2	1	3
M.E.Trescothick	4	8	1	107	319	45.57	2	–	4
A.J.Strauss	4	8	1	137	317	45.28	1	1	7
M.J.Hoggard	4	5	2	38	83	27.66	–	–	1
S.J.Harmison	4	5	2	36*	80	26.66	–	–	–
G.O.Jones	4	5	–	74	116	23.20	–	1	14/2
A.F.Giles	4	5	–	52	106	21.20	–	1	3
J.M.Anderson	3	4	2	12	23	11.50	–	–	2

Played in one Test: I.R.Bell 70 (2 ct); S.P.Jones 4.

ENGLAND – BOWLING

	O	M	R	W	Avge	Best	5wI	10wM
A.Flintoff	88.3	17	297	14	21.21	3-25	–	–
A.F.Giles	186.1	41	509	22	23.13	5-57	2	–
S.J.Harmison	131.4	20	502	17	29.52	6-46	1	–
M.J.Hoggard	126	24	492	16	30.75	4-83	–	–
J.M.Anderson	55.1	8	219	7	31.28	4-52	–	–

Also bowled: S.P.Jones 25-6-99-1; M.E.Trescothick 2-0-7-0; M.P.Vaughan 4-0-17-0.

WEST INDIES – BATTING AND FIELDING

	M	I	NO	HS	Runs	Avge	100	50	Ct/St
S.Chanderpaul	4	8	2	128*	437	72.83	1	2	2
C.H.Gayle	4	8	–	105	400	50.00	1	3	3
R.R.Sarwan	4	8	–	139	267	33.37	1	1	6
B.C.Lara	4	8	–	95	264	33.00	–	2	7
C.S.Baugh	2	4	–	68	111	27.75	–	1	2
D.J.J.Bravo	4	8	–	77	220	27.50	–	2	3
O.A.C.Banks	2	4	1	45	74	24.66	–	–	–
S.C.Joseph	2	4	–	45	85	21.25	–	–	1
D.S.Smith	2	4	–	45	66	16.50	–	–	3
J.J.C.Lawson	2	4	3	4*	9	9.00	–	–	1
R.D.Jacobs	2	4	–	32	33	8.25	–	–	8/1
P.T.Collins	3	6	1	19*	35	7.00	–	–	–
C.D.Collymore	3	6	1	10	33	6.60	–	–	–
F.H.Edwards	3	6	1	5	13	2.60	–	–	1

Played in one Test: T.L.Best 0, 3; D.Mohammed 23, 9; D.R.Smith 28.

WEST INDIES – BOWLING

	O	M	R	W	Avge	Best	5wI	10wM
C.H.Gayle	44.1	7	136	8	17.00	5- 34	1	–
D.J.J.Bravo	128.4	25	419	16	26.18	6- 55	1	–
P.T.Collins	84	8	347	10	34.70	4-113	–	–
J.J.C.Lawson	68	10	320	8	40.00	4- 94	–	–
C.D.Collymore	104	29	316	6	52.66	2- 66	–	–
F.H.Edwards	82.3	8	330	3	110.00	2- 64	–	–
O.A.C.Banks	80	8	351	3	117.00	2-131	–	–

Also bowled: T.L.Best 24-2-118-1; S.C.Joseph 2-0-8-0; D.Mohammed 32-2-102-0; R.R.Sarwan 36-0-134-0; D.R.Smith 14-4-50-0.

SRI LANKA v SOUTH AFRICA (1st Test)

At Galle International Stadium on 4, 5, 6, 7, 8 August 2004.
Toss: Sri Lanka. Result: **MATCH DRAWN**.
Debuts: None.

SRI LANKA

*M.S.Atapattu	c Boucher b Pollock	9	lbw b Klusener		25
S.T.Jayasuriya	c Klusener b Pollock	12	c Boucher b Pollock		74
K.C.Sangakkara	c Boucher b Boje	58	c Hayward b Boje		13
D.P.M.D.Jayawardena	lbw b Hayward	237	c Rudolph b Boje		5
T.T.Samaraweera	lbw b Pollock	13	b Klusener		19
T.M.Dilshan	b Hayward	25	lbw b Pollock		1
†R.S.Kaluwitharana	b Pollock	33	c Pollock b Boje		19
U.D.U.Chandana	b Ntini	5	c Dippenaar b Boje		29
W.P.U.C.J.Vaas	c Hayward b Boje	69	not out		13
M.F.Maharoof	not out	6	(11) not out		3
M.Muralitharan	b Hayward	0	(10) c Dippenaar b Boje		2
Extras	(B 8, LB 3, W 2, NB 6)	19	(B 4, LB 1, W 2, NB 4)		11
Total		**486**	(9 wickets declared)		**214**

SOUTH AFRICA

H.H.Dippenaar	run out	46	(2) c Jayawardena b Muralitharan		11
M.van Jaarsveld	c Samaraweera b Muralitharan	37	(3) lbw b Dilshan		29
J.A.Rudolph	c Kaluwitharana b Muralitharan	102	(5) not out		27
J.H.Kallis	c Sangakkara b Muralitharan	59	not out		52
*G.C.Smith	lbw b Jayasuriya	23	(1) b Chandana		74
†M.V.Boucher	c Kaluwitharana b Jayasuriya	6			
S.M.Pollock	c Sangakkara b Vaas	25			
L.Klusener	c Jayawardena b Dilshan	2			
N.Boje	c Kaluwitharana b Vaas	31			
M.Ntini	c Chandana b Muralitharan	10			
M.Hayward	not out	2			
Extras	(B 14, LB 8, W 1, NB 10)	33	(B 1, LB 4, W 2, NB 3)		10
Total		**376**	(3 wickets)		**203**

SOUTH AFRICA	O	M	R	W		O	M	R	W
Pollock	23	5	48	4		12	2	19	2
Ntini	20	1	61	1	(4)	5	0	19	0
Hayward	16.4	0	81	3	(2)	6	1	21	0
Kallis	16	3	52	0	(6)	8	1	22	0
Klusener	19	0	69	0	(3)	14	2	40	2
Boje	42	3	148	2	(5)	22	0	88	5
Rudolph	9	2	16	0					
SRI LANKA									
Vaas	25	10	50	2		10	3	20	0
Maharoof	19	9	42	0	(4)	5	2	4	0
Muralitharan	46.4	9	130	4	(5)	20	5	37	1
Chandana	18	0	68	0	(6)	18	1	60	1
Jayasuriya	25	9	40	2	(3)	17	7	30	0
Dilshan	6	0	24	1	(3)	16	5	30	1
Samaraweera						3	0	13	0
Sangakkara						1	0	4	0

FALL OF WICKETS

	SL	SA	SL	SA
Wkt	1st	1st	2nd	2nd
1st	13	84	62	34
2nd	22	96	89	98
3rd	108	168	103	135
4th	145	213	140	–
5th	189	225	142	–
6th	274	287	166	–
7th	279	295	172	–
8th	449	348	199	–
9th	486	363	209	–
10th	486	376	–	–

Umpires: D.J.Harper (*Australia*) (43) and D.R.Shepherd (*England*) (82).
Referee: C.H.Lloyd (*West Indies*) (37). **Test No. 1711/14 (SL144/SA289)**

SRI LANKA v SOUTH AFRICA (2nd Test)

At Sinhalese Sports Club, Colombo on 11, 12, 13, 14, 15 August 2004.
Toss: Sri Lanka. Result: **SRI LANKA** won by 313 runs.
Debuts: None.

SRI LANKA

*M.S.Atapattu	c Boucher b Pollock	4	b Rudolph		72
S.T. Jayasuriya	lbw b Boje	43	st Boucher b Boje		19
K.C. Sangakkara	c Kallis b Pollock	232	c Ntini b Kallis		64
D.P.M.D.Jayawardena	b Ntini	82	c Boucher b Kallis		3
W.P.U.C.J.Vaas	c Van Jaarsveld b Pollock	10			
T.T.Samaraweera	c Ntini b Kallis	21	(5) not out		21
T.M.Dilshan	c Kallis b Pollock	3	(6) not out		23
†R.S.Kaluwitharana	c Boucher b Hayward	7			
U.D.U.Chandana	st Boucher b Boje	40			
M.R.K.B.Herath	b Ntini	7			
S.L.Malinga	not out	6			
Extras	(LB 6, W 1, NB 8)	15	(B 6, LB 1, W 2)		9
Total		**470**	(4 wickets declared)		**211**

SOUTH AFRICA

*G.C.Smith	c and b Jayasuriya	65	c Samaraweera b Malinga		17
H.H.Gibbs	lbw b Vaas	0	c Samaraweera b Malinga		4
M.van Jaarsveld	c Sangakkara b Jayasuriya	51	b Vaas		2
N.Boje	b Jayasuriya	0	(9) lbw b Vaas		16
J.H.Kallis	b Jayasuriya	13	(4) c Dilshan b Vaas		3
J.A.Rudolph	c Kaluwitharana b Malinga	6	(5) c Malinga b Vaas		1
H.H.Dippenaar	c Dilshan b Herath	25	(6) not out		59
†M.V.Boucher	not out	10	(7) c Kaluwitharana b Vaas		51
S.M.Pollock	lbw b Herath	1	(8) c Atapattu b Dilshan		3
M.Ntini	b Herath	0	c Kaluwitharana b Vaas		0
M.Hayward	b Jayasuriya	1	c and b Malinga		1
Extras	(B 1, LB 8, NB 8)	17	(B 6, LB 3, W 1, NB 12)		22
Total		**189**			**179**

SOUTH AFRICA	O	M	R	W		O	M	R	W
Pollock	30	8	81	4		8	0	46	0
Ntini	33	6	108	2		4	0	19	0
Hayward	17	4	75	1	(4)	3	1	15	0
Kallis	17	6	54	1	(6)	6	4	6	2
Boje	34.3	5	102	2	(3)	23	6	81	1
Rudolph	4	0	16	0	(7)	7	2	22	1
Van Jaarsveld	7	0	28	0					
Smith					(5)	4	0	15	0
SRI LANKA									
Vaas	7	3	10	1		18	8	29	6
Malinga	13	1	51	1		13	1	54	3
Herath	25	6	60	3	(4)	8	5	13	0
Chandana	6	0	21	0	(5)	7	1	26	0
Dilshan	4	1	4	0	(6)	12	6	26	1
Jayasuriya	14.1	4	34	5	(3)	12	6	22	0

FALL OF WICKETS

	SL	SA	SL	SA
Wkt	1st	1st	2nd	2nd
1st	4	1	46	4
2nd	99	109	142	18
3rd	291	109	149	24
4th	316	140	179	36
5th	392	141	–	36
6th	399	166	–	137
7th	416	186	–	140
8th	418	188	–	163
9th	437	188	–	163
10th	470	189	–	179

Umpires: B.F.Bowden (*New Zealand*) (18) and S.A.Bucknor (*West Indies*) (91).
Referee: C.H.Lloyd (*West Indies*) (38).   Test No. 1712/15 (*SL145/SA290*)

INDIA v AUSTRALIA (1st Test)

At Chinnaswamy Stadium, Bangalore, on 6, 7, 8, 9, 10 October 2004.
Toss: Australia. Result: **AUSTRALIA** won by 217 runs.
Debuts: Australia – M.J.Clarke.

AUSTRALIA

J.L.Langer	b Pathan	52	lbw Pathan		0
M.L.Hayden	c Yuvraj b Harbhajan	26	run out		30
S.M.Katich	b Kumble	81	c Dravid b Kumble		39
D.R.Martyn	c Chopra b Kumble	3	c sub (M.Kaif) b Harbhajan		45
D.S.Lehmann	c Dravid b Kumble	17	c Chopra b Harbhajan		14
M.J.Clarke	c Patel b Khan	151	c Chopra b Harbhajan		17
*†A.C.Gilchrist	c and b Harbhajan	104	c Chopra b Kumble		26
S.K.Warne	c Dravid b Harbhajan	1	c Yuvraj b Harbhajan		31
J.N.Gillespie	not out	7	c Yuvraj b Harbhajan		8
M.S.Kasprowicz	c Yuvraj b Harbhajan	3	c Dravid b Harbhajan		8
G.D.McGrath	lbw b Harbhajan	0	not out		3
Extras	(B 5, LB 15, W 1, NB 8)	29	(B 2, LB 1, W 1, NB 3)		7
Total		**474**			**228**

INDIA

A.Chopra	lbw b McGrath	0	lbw b Gillespie		5
V.Sehwag	c Langer b Kasprowicz	39	lbw b McGrath		0
R.Dravid	b McGrath	0	lbw b Kasprowicz		60
*S.C.Ganguly	c Gilchrist b Kasprowicz	45	run out		5
V.V.S.Laxman	b Warne	31	lbw b Warne		3
Yuvraj Singh	c Gilchrist b McGrath	46	c Gilchrist b McGrath		27
†P.A.Patel	b Gillespie	46	lbw b Warne		4
I.K.Pathan	c Gilchrist b Warne	45	c Gilchrist b Gillespie		55
A.Kumble	b Gillespie	26	b Kasprowicz		2
Harbhajan Singh	c Lehmann b McGrath	8	c McGrath b Gillespie		42
Z.Khan	not out	0	not out		22
Extras	(B 5, LB 2, W 5, NB 3)	15	(B 6, LB 5, NB 3)		14
Total		**246**			**239**

INDIA	O	M	R	W	O	M	R	W
Pathan	21	6	62	1	12	2	38	1
Khan	22	2	60	1	13	1	45	0
Harbhajan Singh	41	7	146	5	30.1	5	78	6
Kumble	39	4	157	3	23	4	64	2
Sehwag	5	0	26	0				
Yuvraj Singh	2	0	3	0				

AUSTRALIA	O	M	R	W		O	M	R	W
McGrath	25	8	55	4		20	10	39	2
Gillespie	16.2	4	63	2		14.4	4	33	3
Warne	28	4	78	2	(4)	32	8	115	2
Kasprowicz	20	4	43	2	(3)	14	7	23	2
Lehmann						6	3	14	0
Clarke						1	0	4	0

FALL OF WICKETS

	A	I	A	I
Wkt	1st	1st	2nd	2nd
1st	50	0	0	1
2nd	124	4	65	7
3rd	129	87	86	12
4th	149	98	104	19
5th	256	116	146	81
6th	423	136	167	86
7th	427	196	204	118
8th	471	227	216	125
9th	474	244	217	214
10th	474	246	228	239

Umpires: B.F.Bowden (*New Zealand*) (19) and S.A.Bucknor (*Australia*) (92).
Referee: R.S.Madugalle (*Sri Lanka*) (66).   **Test No. 1713/65 (I375/A654)**

INDIA v AUSTRALIA (2nd Test)

At M.A.Chidambaram Stadium, Chepauk, Madras, on 14, 15, 16, 17, 18 (*no play*)
October 2004.
Toss: Australia. Result: **MATCH DRAWN.**
Debuts: None.

AUSTRALIA

J.L.Langer	c Dravid b Harbhajan	71		c Dravid b Kumble	19
M.L.Hayden	c Laxman b Harbhajan	58		c Laxman b Kumble	39
S.M.Katich	not out	36	(4)	lbw b Khan	9
D.R.Martyn	c Yuvraj b Kumble	26	(5)	c Dravid b Harbhajan	104
D.S.Lehmann	c Patel b Kumble	0	(8)	c Patel b Kumble	31
M.J.Clarke	lbw b Kumble	5	(7)	not out	39
*†A.C.Gilchrist	c Yuvraj b Kumble	3	(3)	b Kumble	49
S.K.Warne	c and b Kumble	4	(9)	c Kaif b Kumble	0
J.N.Gillespie	c Kaif b Kumble	5	(6)	c Dravid b Harbhajan	26
M.S.Kasprowicz	c Laxman b Kumble	4		lbw b Kumble	5
G.D.McGrath	run out	2		b Harbhajan	2
Extras	(B 7, LB 4, W 1, NB 4, Pen 5)	21		(B 19, LB 15, W 3, NB 4, Pen 5)	46
Total		**235**			**369**

INDIA

Yuvraj Singh	c Gilchrist b Warne	8	not out	7
V.Sehwag	c Clarke b Warne	155	not out	12
I.K.Pathan	c Hayden b Warne	14		
R.Dravid	b Kasprowicz	26		
*S.C.Ganguly	c Gilchrist b Gillespie	9		
V.V.S. Laxman	b Gillespie	4		
M.Kaif	run out	64		
†P.A.Patel	c Gilchrist b Warne	54		
A.Kumble	b Warne	20		
Harbhajan Singh	c and b Warne	5		
Z.Khan	not out	0		
Extras	(B 6, LB 3, W 2, NB 6)	17		
Total		**376**	(0 wickets)	**19**

INDIA	O	M	R	W	O	M	R	W		FALL OF WICKETS			
Pathan	12	3	29	0	12	3	39	0			A	I	A	I
Khan	11	2	44	0	22	6	36	1	Wkt	1st	1st	2nd	2nd
Harbhajan Singh	29	2	90	2	46.5	12	108	3	1st	136	28	53	–
Kumble	17.3	4	48	7	47	8	133	6	2nd	136	83	76	–
Sehwag	2	1	8	0	1	0	5	0	3rd	189	178	121	–
Yuvraj Singh					2	0	7	0	4th	191	203	145	–
Ganguly					3	1	2	0	5th	204	213	284	–
									6th	210	233	285	–
AUSTRALIA									7th	216	335	347	–
McGrath	25	4	74	0	2	0	18	0	8th	224	369	347	–
Gillespie	35	8	70	2	1	0	1	0	9th	228	372	364	–
Warne	42.3	5	125	6					10th	235	376	369	–
Kasprowicz	25	5	65	1									
Lehmann	5	0	26	0									
Katich	2	0	7	0									

Umpires: R.E.Koertzen (*South Africa*) (56) and D.R.Shepherd (*England*) (83).
Referee: R.S.Madugalle (*Sri Lanka*) (67).   **Test No. 1714/66 (I376/A655)**

INDIA v AUSTRALIA (3rd Test)

At Vidarbha C.A. Ground, Nagpur, on 26, 27, 28, 29 October 2004.
Toss: Australia. Result: **AUSTRALIA** won by 342 runs.
Debuts: None.

AUSTRALIA

J.L.Langer	c Dravid b Khan	44		c Laxman b Kartik	30
M.L.Hayden	c Patel b Khan	23		b Khan	9
S.M.Katich	c Chopra b Kumble	4		lbw b Kartik	99
D.R.Martyn	c Agarkar b Kumble	114		c Patel b Khan	97
D.S.Lehmann	c Dravid b Kartik	70			
M.J.Clarke	c Patel b Khan	91	(5)	c Kaif b Kumble	73
*†A.C.Gilchrist	c and b Kartik	2	(6)	not out	3
S.K.Warne	st Patel b Kartik	2			
J.N.Gillespie	lbw b Khan	9			
M.S.Kasprowicz	c Patel b Agarkar	0			
G.D.McGrath	not out	11			
Extras	(B 6, LB 13, W 1, NB 8)	28		(B 1, LB 15, W 2)	18
Total		**398**		(5 wickets declared)	**329**

INDIA

A .Chopra	c Warne b Gillespie	9		b Gillespie	1
V.Sehwag	c Gilchrist b McGrath	22		c Clarke b Warne	58
*R.Dravid	c Warne b McGrath	21		b Gillespie	2
S.R Tendulkar	lbw b Gillespie	8		c Martyn b McGrath	2
V.V.S. Laxman	c Clarke b Warne	13		c McGrath b Kasprowicz	2
M.Kaif	c Warne b McGrath	55		c Gilchrist b Kasprowicz	7
†P.A.Patel	c Hayden b Warne	20		c Gilchrist b Gillespie	32
A.B.Agarkar	c Clarke b Gillespie	15		not out	44
A.Kumble	not out	7		b Gillespie	2
M.Kartik	c Clarke b Gillespie	3		c Gilchrist b McGrath	22
Z.Khan	b Gillespie	0		c Martyn b Warne	25
Extras	(LB 10, W 1, NB 1)	12		(LB 2, NB 1)	3
Total		**185**			**200**

INDIA	O	M	R	W		O	M	R	W		FALL OF WICKETS			
												A	I	A	I
Agarkar	23	2	99	1	(2)	21	7	68	0						
Khan	26.2	6	95	4	(1)	21.1	5	64	2		Wkt	1st	1st	2nd	2nd
Kumble	25	6	99	2		21	1	89	1		1st	67	31	19	1
Kartik	20	1	57	3	(5)	26	5	74	2		2nd	79	34	99	9
Tendulkar	6	1	29	0	(4)	8	1	12	0		3rd	86	49	171	20
Sehwag						1	0	6	0		4th	234	75	319	29
											5th	314	103	329	37
AUSTRALIA											6th	323	150	–	102
McGrath	25	13	27	3		16	1	79	2		7th	337	173	–	114
Gillespie	22.5	8	56	5		16	7	24	4		8th	376	178	–	122
Kasprowicz	21	4	45	0		7	1	39	2		9th	377	181	–	148
Warne	23	8	47	2		14.3	2	56	2		10th	398	185	–	200

Umpires: Alim Dar (*Pakistan*) (11) and D.R.Shepherd (*England*) (84).
Referee: R.S.Madugalle (*Sri Lanka*) (68).　　　　**Test No. 1715/67 (I377/A656)**

INDIA v AUSTRALIA (4th Test)

At Wankhede Stadium, Bombay, on 3, 4, 5 November 2004.
Toss: India. Result: **INDIA** won by 13 runs.
Debuts: India – G.Gambhir, K.D. Karthik; Australia – N.M.Hauritz

INDIA

G .Gambhir	lbw b Gillespie	3		c Clarke b McGrath	1
V.Sehwag	b McGrath	8		lbw b McGrath	5
*R.Dravid	not out	31	(5)	c Gilchrist b Clarke	27
S.R Tendulkar	c Gilchrist b Gillespie	5		c Clarke b Hauritz	55
V.V.S. Laxman	c Gilchrist b Gillespie	1	(3)	c and b Hauritz	69
M.Kaif	lbw b Gillespie	2		lbw b Clarke	25
†K.D.Karthik	b Kasprowicz	10		c Ponting b Clarke	4
A.Kumble	c Ponting b Hauritz	16		not out	13
Harbhajan Singh	c Katich b Hauritz	14		c Hayden b Clarke	0
M.Kartik	c Gilchrist b Hauritz	0		b Clarke	2
Z.Khan	b Kasprowicz	0		lbw b Clarke	0
Extras	(B 6, LB 7, NB 1)	14		(B 4)	4
Total		**104**			**205**

AUSTRALIA

J.L.Langer	c Dravid b Khan	12		c Karthik b Khan	0
M.L.Hayden	c Kaif b Kartik	35		b Harbhajan	24
*R.T.Ponting	lbw b Kumble	11		c Laxman b Kartik	12
D.R.Martyn	b Kartik	55		lbw b Kartik	0
S.M.Katich	c Kaif b Kumble	7		c Dravid b Harbhajan	1
M.J.Clarke	st Karthik b Kumble	17		b Kartik	7
†A.C.Gilchrist	c Kaif b Kartik	26		c Tendulkar b Harbhajan	5
J.N.Gillespie	c Kaif b Kumble	2		not out	9
N.M.Hauritz	c Harbhajan b Kumble	0		lbw b Kumble	15
M.S.Kasprowicz	c Kumble b Kartik	19		c Dravid b Harbhajan	7
G.D.McGrath	not out	9		c Laxman b Harbhajan	0
Extras	(B 2, LB 4, NB 4)	10		(B 8, LB 5)	13
Total		**203**			**93**

AUSTRALIA	O	M	R	W		O	M	R	W
McGrath	16	9	35	1	(3)	12	6	29	2
Gillespie	12	2	29	4	(1)	15	1	47	0
Kasprowicz	8.3	3	11	2	(4)	13	5	29	0
Hauritz	5	0	16	3	(2)	22	4	87	2
Clarke						6.2	0	9	6
INDIA									
Khan	6	0	10	1		2	0	14	1
Harbhajan Singh	21	4	53	0		10.5	2	29	5
Kumble	19	0	90	5	(4)	6	3	5	1
Kartik	15.3	1	44	4	(3)	12	3	32	3

FALL OF WICKETS

	I	A	I	A
Wkt	1st	1st	2nd	2nd
1st	11	17	5	0
2nd	11	37	14	24
3rd	29	81	105	24
4th	31	101	153	33
5th	33	121	182	48
6th	46	157	188	48
7th	68	167	195	58
8th	100	171	195	78
9th	102	184	199	93
10th	104	203	205	93

Umpires: Alim Dar (*Pakistan*) (12) and R.E.Koertzen (*South Africa*) (57).
Referee: R.S.Madugalle (*Sri Lanka*) (69).   **Test No. 1716/67 (I378/A657)**

BANGLADESH v NEW ZEALAND (1st Test)

At Bangabandhu National Stadium, Dhaka, on 19, 20, 21, 22 October 2004.
Toss: Bangladesh. Result: **NEW ZEALAND** won by an innings and 99 runs.
Debuts: Bangladesh – Nafis Iqbal.

BANGLADESH

Hannan Sarkar	c Fleming b Oram	0	(3) c and b Vettori		1
Javed Omar	b Franklin	1	c McCullum b Vettori		14
Nafis Iqbal	c McCullum b Oram	1	(1) run out		49
Rajin Saleh	c Oram b Franklin	41	c McCullum b Vettori		0
Mohammad Ashraful	c Astle b Vettori	67	c Styris b Vettori		26
Alok Kapali	c McCullum b Vettori	14	c McCullum b Wiseman		0
*†Khaled Masud	not out	23	c Styris b Wiseman		2
Manjural Rana	c McCullum b Franklin	16	c Richardson b Vettori		1
Mohammad Rafique	c Styris b Franklin	0	c Fleming b Wiseman		24
Tapash Baisya	b Franklin	0	(11) not out		0
Tareq Aziz	c Astle b Oram	0	(10) lbw b Vettori		0
Extras	(LB 7, W 1, NB 6)	14	(B 6, NB 3)		9
Total		**177**			**126**

NEW ZEALAND

M.H.Richardson	c Masud b Rafique	15
M.S Sinclair	lbw b Rafique	76
*S.P.Fleming	c Masud b Manjural	29
S.B.Styris	c Saleh b Manjural	2
N.J.Astle	c Manjural b Rafique	11
J.D.P.Oram	c Manjural b Rafique	23
†B.B.McCullum	c Kapali b Rafique	143
D.L.Vettori	c Nafis b Manjural	23
J.E.C.Franklin	c Saleh b Baisya	23
P.J.Wiseman	b Rafique	28
I.G.Butler	not out	15
Extras	(B 3, LB 5, W 4, NB 2)	14
Total		**402**

NEW ZEALAND	O	M	R	W		O	M	R	W
Oram	22.5	9	36	3		7	4	6	0
Franklin	17	7	28	5		5	1	14	0
Styris	2	1	4	0					
Butler	12	3	34	0	(3)	4	1	8	0
Vettori	29	15	26	2	(4)	22	13	28	6
Wiseman	16	5	42	0	(5)	16.5	1	64	3

BANGLADESH	O	M	R	W
Tapash Baisya	28	4	112	1
Tareq Aziz	12	1	59	0
Mohammad Rafique	59.1	18	122	6
Manjural Rana	42	12	84	3
Rajin Saleh	1	0	4	0
Alok Kapali	2	0	6	0
Mohammad Ashraful	1	0	7	0

FALL OF WICKETS

	B	NZ	B
Wkt	1st	1st	2nd
1st	0	34	27
2nd	5	97	33
3rd	5	99	41
4th	120	122	87
5th	124	139	88
6th	136	223	92
7th	165	294	101
8th	165	351	112
9th	165	371	122
10th	177	402	126

Umpires: M.R.Benson (*England*) (1) and D.J.Harper (*Australia*) (44).
Referee: A.G.Hurst (*Australia*) (1).   Test No. 1717/3 (B31/NZ314)

BANGLADESH v NEW ZEALAND (2nd Test)

At M.A.Aziz Stadium, Chittagong, on 26, 27, 28, 29 October 2004.
Toss: New Zealand. Result: **NEW ZEALAND** won by an innings and 101 runs.
Debuts: Bangladesh – Aftab Ahmed.

NEW ZEALAND

M.H.Richardson	c Mushfiqur b Enamul	28
M.S Sinclair	b Rafique	23
*S.P.Fleming	c Mushfiqur b Saleh	202
S.B.Styris	c and b Rafique	89
N.J.Astle	lbw b Rafique	39
H.J.H.Marshall	c Baisya b Enamul	69
J.D.P.Oram	not out	38
†B.B.McCullum	not out	17
D.L.Vettori		
J.E.C.Franklin		
P.J.Wiseman		
Extras	(B 9, LB 11, W 2, NB 18)	40
Total	(6 wickets declared)	**545**

BANGLADESH

Nafis Iqbal	c Styris b Vettori	13	b Wiseman		9
Javed Omar	c Sinclair b Wiseman	58	c and b Franklin		1
Aftab Ahmed	lbw b Vettori	20	b Vettori		28
Rajin Saleh	c Sinclair b Wiseman	2	c Sinclair b Vettori		35
Mohammad Ashraful	c Astle b Wiseman	0	c Styris b Vettori		0
Alok Kapali	c Fleming b Vettori	13	c Astle b Wiseman		13
*†Khaled Masud	lbw b Vettori	18	b Oram		51
Mushfiqur Rahman	c McCullum b Franklin	15	b Vettori		20
Mohammad Rafique	c Wiseman b Vettori	32	c Sinclair b Vettori		31
Tapash Baisya	c Sinclair b Vettori	0	st McCullum b Vettori		66
Enamul Haque II	not out	0	not out		0
Extras	(B 4, LB 2, W 2, NB 3)	11	(B 4, LB 3, W 1)		8
Total		**182**			**262**

BANGLADESH	O	M	R	W	O	M	R	W
Tapash Baisya	17	0	82	0				
Mushfiqur Rahman	15	1	68	0				
Mohammad Rafique	55	12	130	3				
Enamul Haque	42	4	142	2				
Rajin Saleh	19	0	81	1				
Mohammad Ashraful	1	0	5	0				
Alok Kapali	3	0	17	0				

NEW ZEALAND	O	M	R	W	O	M	R	W
Oram	5	0	20	0	10	4	33	1
Franklin	5	0	17	1	8	3	16	1
Vettori	32.2	12	70	6	(4) 28.2	9	100	6
Wiseman	27	5	68	3	(3) 24	4	106	2
Astle	2	1	1	0				

FALL OF WICKETS

	NZ	B	B
Wkt	1st	1st	2nd
1st	49	34	9
2nd	61	66	25
3rd	265	82	47
4th	364	82	51
5th	447	108	74
6th	517	128	123
7th	–	142	161
8th	–	181	183
9th	–	182	217
10th	–	182	262

Umpires: M.R.Benson (*England*) (2) and D.J.Harper (*Australia*) (45).
Referee: A.G.Hurst (*Australia*) (2).   **Test No. 1718/4 (B32/NZ315)**

PAKISTAN v SRI LANKA (1st Test)

At Iqbal Stadium, Faisalabad, on 20, 21, 22, 23 24 October 2004.
Toss: Sri Lanka. Result: **SRI LANKA** won by 201 runs.
Debuts: None

SRI LANKA

*M.S.Atapattu	lbw b Akhtar	0	lbw b Akhtar		0
S.T.Jayasuriya	c Kamal b Sami	38	lbw b Kaneria		253
K.C.Sangakkara	c Farhat b Akhtar	2	c Moin b Akhtar		59
D.P.M.D.Jayawardena	c Moin b Sami	0	c Moin b Kaneria		57
T.T.Samaraweera	c Sami b Akhtar	100	run out		21
J.Mubarak	c Inzamam b Sami	34	c Moin b Akhtar		0
†R.S.Kaluwitharana	c and b Kaneria	4	c sub (Naved-ul-Hassan) b Kaneria		1
W.P.U.C.J.Vaas	c Youhana b Akhtar	22	b Malik		4
M.R.K.B.Herath	not out	33	lbw b Kaneria		5
C.R.D.Fernando	b Akhtar	0	run out		1
S.L.Malinga	b Sami	1	not out		0
Extras	(LB 3, NB 6)	9	(B 12, LB 5, W 3, NB 12, PEN 5)		37
Total		**243**			**438**

PAKISTAN

Yasir Hamid	c Mubarak b Fernando	58	lbw b Fernando		17
Imran Farhat	c Mubarak b Malinga	11	lbw b Fernando		53
Asim Kamal	c Jayawardena b Fernando	17	b Fernando		1
*Inzamam-ul-Haq	c Malinga b Herath	32	b Fernando		3
Yousuf Youhana	c Kaluwitharana b Herath	17	lbw b Herath		44
Shoaib Malik	run out	48	c and b Herath		59
Abdul Razzaq	c Jayawardena b Vaas	39	lbw b Herath		0
†Moin Khan	b Jayasuriya	5	c Kaluwitharana b Vaas		1
Mohammad Sami	not out	5	run out		6
Shoaib Akhtar	lbw b Herath	9	st Kaluwitharana b Herath		12
Danish Kaneria	run out	1	not out		0
Extras	(B 6, LB 4, NB 12)	22	(B 4, LB 1, W 6, NB 9)		20
Total		**264**			**216**

PAKISTAN	O	M	R	W	O	M	R	W
Shoaib Akhtar	19	3	60	5	25	1	115	3
Mohammad Sami	21.4	5	71	4	12	1	48	0
Abdul Razzaq	15	5	33	0	22	7	78	0
Danish Kaneria	18	3	53	1	38.2	4	117	4
Shoaib Malik	8	1	23	0	12	1	58	1

SRI LANKA	O	M	R	W	O	M	R	W
Vaas	26	5	62	1	16	4	54	1
Malinga	10	1	50	1	6	2	13	0
Fernando	16	0	65	2	(4) 20	4	77	4
Herath	27.1	6	68	3	(3) 32.2	10	64	4
Samaraweera	1	0	5	0				
Jayasuriya	4	1	4	1	(5) 4	2	2	0
Mubarak					(6) 1	0	1	0

FALL OF WICKETS

	SL	P	SL	P
Wkt	1st	1st	2nd	2nd
1st	0	28	0	59
2nd	6	94	98	65
3rd	9	109	216	86
4th	77	134	309	91
5th	142	188	314	154
6th	147	227	319	158
7th	180	246	330	159
8th	237	248	337	187
9th	242	262	438	215
10th	243	264	438	216

Umpires: B.F.Bowden (*New Zealand*) (20) and S.A.Bucknor (*West Indies*) (93).
Referee: J.J.Crowe (*New Zealand*) (2).   Test No. 1719/29 (P303/SL146)

PAKISTAN v SRI LANKA (2nd Test)

At National Stadium, Karachi, on 28, 29, 30, 31 October, 1 November 2004.
Toss: Pakistan. Result: **PAKISTAN** won by six wickets.
Debuts: Pakistan – Naved-ul-Hasan, Riaz Afridi.

SRI LANKA

S.T.Jayasuriya	lbw b Kaneria	26	c Malik b Kaneria		107
*M.S.Atapattu	c Younis b Kaneria	44	c Hamid b Kaneria		25
†K.C.Sangakkara	c Kaneria b Riaz	13	c Akmal b Naved		138
D.P.M.D.Jayawardena	c Inzamam b Riaz	16	c Hamid b Kaneria		32
T.T.Samaraweera	c Farhat b Razzaq	13	c Younis b Kaneria		22
J.Mubarak	c Hamid b Razzaq	13	c Farhat b Kaneria		2
R.S.Kaluwitharana	c Akmal b Kaneria	54	b Kaneria		7
W.P.U.C.J.Vaas	c Farhat b Razzaq	7	not out		32
M.F.Maharoof	c Akmal b Razzaq	2	b Kaneria		3
M.R.K.B.Herath	c Akmal b Razzaq	12	c and b Naved		6
C.R.D.Fernando	not out	0	c Akmal b Naved		4
Extras	(B 4, LB 3, W 1)	8	(B 9, LB 7, NB 12)		28
Total		**208**			**406**

PAKISTAN

Yasir Hamid	c Sangakkara b Maharoof	3	c Atapattu b Herath		15
Imran Farhat	lbw b Vaas	72	c Jayawardena b Vaas		19
Younis Khan	c Samaraweera b Herath	124	c Atapattu b Vaas		14
*Inzamam-ul-Haq	c Jayawardena b Vaas	117			
Riaz Afridi	b Vaas	9			
Yousuf Youhana	c Sangakkara b Fernando	46	(4) lbw b Herath		1
Shoaib Malik	lbw b Fernando	44	(5) not out		53
Abdul Razzaq	c Fernando b Jayasuriya	16	(6) not out		35
†Kamran Akmal	c Jayawardena b Herath	15			
Naved-ul-Hassan	b Fernando	11			
Danish Kaneria	not out	5			
Extras	(LB 9, NB 7)	16	(LB 1, NB 1)		2
Total		**478**	(4 wickets)		**139**

PAKISTAN	O	M	R	W	O	M	R	W		FALL OF WICKETS			
Naved-ul Hasan	17	2	52	0	24.5	4	83	3			SL	P	SL	P
Riaz Afridi	19	7	42	2	12	3	45	0		*Wkt*	*1st*	*1st*	*2nd*	*2nd*
Abdul Razzaq	23.1	9	35	5	29	8	99	0		1st	66	13	117	31
Danish Kaneria	23	3	72	3	60	20	118	7		2nd	79	135	170	43
Shoaib Malik					16	5	45	0		3rd	97	284	253	47
										4th	106	298	333	57
SRI LANKA										5th	126	372	351	–
Vaas	33	5	106	3	14	0	45	2		6th	140	387	359	–
Maharoof	23	4	62	1	2	0	13	0		7th	158	437	360	–
Fernando	22.1	1	96	3	(5) 3	0	11	0		8th	164	462	364	–
Herath	33	3	125	2	(3) 15	2	63	2		9th	208	464	387	–
Mubarak	9	2	33	0						10th	208	478	406	–
Jayasuriya	11	3	35	1	(4) 3	1	6	0						
Samaraweera	6	0	12	0										

Umpires: B.F.Bowden (*New Zealand*) (21) and S.A.Bucknor (*West Indies*) (94).
Asad Rauf deputised for Bowden on the third day after lunch.
Referee: J.J.Crowe (*New Zealand*) (3). **Test No. 1720/30 (P304/SL147)**

274

AUSTRALIA v NEW ZEALAND (1st Test)

At Woolloongabba, Brisbane, on 18, 19, 20, 21 November 2004.
Toss: New Zealand. Result: **AUSTRALIA** won by an innings and 156 runs.
Debuts: None.

NEW ZEALAND

M.H.Richardson	c Ponting b Kasprowicz	19	c Gilchrist b McGrath	4
M.S.Sinclair	c Ponting b Gillespie	69	lbw b McGrath	0
*S.P.Fleming	c Warne b Kasprowicz	0	c Langer b McGrath	11
S.B.Styris	c Gilchrist b Kasprowicz	27	lbw b Warne	7
N.J.Astle	run out	19	c Warne b Kasprowicz	17
C.D.McMillan	c Gilchrist b Warne	23	lbw b Gillespie	9
J.D.P.Oram	not out	126	c Hayden b Warne	8
†B.B.McCullum	st Gilchrist b Warne	10	c Gilchrist b Gillespie	8
D.L.Vettori	c Warne b Kasprowicz	21	c Hayden b Warne	2
K.D.Mills	c Hayden b Warne	29	not out	4
C.S.Martin	c Ponting b Warne	0	lbw b Warne	0
Extras	(B 1, LB 2, W 3, NB 4)	10	(LB 2, NB 4)	6
Total		**353**		**76**

AUSTRALIA

J.L.Langer	lbw b Vettori	34
M.L. Hayden	lbw b Mills	8
*R.T.Ponting	c Astle b Martin	51
D.R.Martyn	c McMillan b Martin	70
D.S.Lehmann	c McCullum b Vettori	8
M.J.Clarke	b Vettori	141
†A.C.Gilchrist	c Styris b Martin	126
S.K.Warne	lbw b Vettori	10
J.N.Gillespie	not out	54
M.S.Kasprowicz	c Mills b Martin	5
G.D.McGrath	c Astle b Martin	61
Extras	(B1, LB 7, W 1, NB 8)	17
Total		**585**

AUSTRALIA	O	M	R	W	O	M	R	W
McGrath	27	4	67	0	8	1	19	3
Gillespie	29	7	84	1	10	5	19	2
Kasprowicz	28	5	90	4	8	2	21	1
Warne	29.3	3	97	4	10.2	3	15	4
Lehmann	4	0	12	0				

NEW ZEALAND	O	M	R	W
Martin	39.5	7	152	5
Mills	26	8	99	1
Styris	8	1	33	0
Oram	25	4	116	0
Vettori	50	9	154	4
McMillan	5	1	23	0

FALL OF WICKETS

Wkt	NZ 1st	A 1st	NZ 2nd
1st	26	16	6
2nd	26	85	7
3rd	77	109	19
4th	138	128	42
5th	138	222	44
6th	180	438	55
7th	206	450	69
8th	264	464	72
9th	317	471	72
10th	353	585	76

Umpires: Alim Dar (*Pakistan*) (13) and S.A.Bucknor (*West Indies*) (95).
Referee: M.J.Procter (*South Africa*) (27).   **Test No. 1721/42 (A658/NZ316)**

AUSTRALIA v NEW ZEALAND (2nd Test)

At Adelaide Oval on 26, 27, 28, 29, 30 November 2004.
Toss: Australia. Result: **AUSTRALIA** won by 213 runs.
Debuts: None.

AUSTRALIA

J.L.Langer	c Oram b Vettori	215	lbw b Wiseman		46
M.L.Hayden	c and b Wiseman	70	c McCullum b Vettori		54
*R.T.Ponting	st McCullum b Vettori	68	not out		26
D.R.Martyn	c Fleming b Wiseman	7	not out		6
D.S.Lehmann	b Wiseman	81			
M.J.Clarke	lbw b Vettori	7			
†A.C.Gilchrist	c and b Vettori	50			
S.K.Warne	not out	53			
J.N.Gillespie	c Richardson b Vettori	12			
M.S.Kasprowicz					
G.D.McGrath					
Extras	(B 4, LB 4, NB 4)	12	(LB 6, NB 1)		7
Total	(8 wickets declared)	**575**	(2 wickets declared)		**139**

NEW ZEALAND

M.H.Richardson	b Kasprowicz	9		c Langer b Kasprowicz		16
M.S.Sinclair	c Warne b Gillespie	0		lbw b Gillespie		2
*S.P.Fleming	c Gilchrist b McGrath	83		b McGrath		3
P.J.Wiseman	lbw b Kasprowicz	11	(10)	not out		15
N.J.Astle	c Langer b McGrath	52		c Langer b Lehmann		38
J.D.P.Oram	c Gilchrist b Gillespie	12		c Gilchrist b McCullum		40
†B.B.McCullum	lbw b Gillespie	10		lbw b Gillespie		36
D.L.Vettori	lbw b McGrath	20		c Gillespie b Lehmann		59
J.E.C.Franklin	lbw b Warne	7		c Gilchrist b Kasprowicz		13
S.B.Styris	c Clarke b McGrath	28	(4)	c Clarke b Warne		8
C.S.Martin	not out	2		c Ponting b Warne		2
Extras	(B 3, LB 5, NB 9)	17		(B 1, LB 12, NB 5)		18
Total		251				250

NEW ZEALAND	O	M	R	W		O	M	R	W
Martin	27	4	118	0		6	1	11	0
Franklin	17	2	102	0	(3)	5	0	18	0
Oram	24	7	55	0	(2)	5	1	17	0
Vettori	55.2	10	152	5	(5)	18	2	35	1
Wiseman	32	7	140	3	(4)	22	3	52	1
AUSTRALIA									
McGrath	20.1	3	66	4		12	2	32	2
Gillespie	19	4	37	3		5	5	41	2
Warne	28	5	65	1	(4)	27.3	6	79	2
Kasprowicz	16	3	66	2	(3)	14	4	39	2
Lehmann	5	2	9	0		13	0	46	2

FALL OF WICKETS

	A	NZ	A	NZ
Wkt	1st	1st	2nd	2nd
1st	137	2	93	11
2nd	240	44	119	18
3rd	261	80	–	34
4th	445	153	–	34
5th	457	178	–	97
6th	465	183	–	150
7th	543	190	–	160
8th	575	213	–	206
9th	–	242	–	243
10th	–	251	–	250

Umpires: S.A.Bucknor (*West Indies*) (96) and D.R.Shepherd (*England*) (85).
Referee: M.J.Procter (*South Africa*) (28).   **Test No. 1722/43 (A659/NZ317)**

INDIA v SOUTH AFRICA (1st Test)

At Green Park, Kanpur, on 20, 21, 22, 23, 24 November 2004.
Toss: South Africa. Result: **MATCH DRAWN**.
Debuts: South Africa – Z.de Bruyn, T.L. Tsolekile.

SOUTH AFRICA

*G.C.Smith	b Kumble	37	c Gambhir b Kartik		47
A.J.Hall	b Kumble	163	c Karthik b Harbhajan		26
M.van Jaarsveld	lbw b Kumble	2	lbw b Kartik		13
J.H.Kallis	lbw b Kumble	37	not out		28
J.A.Rudolph	b Kumble	0	c Karthik b Harbhajan		2
H.H.Dippenaar	c Karthik b Ganguly	48	not out		31
Z.de Bruyn	c Dravid b Harbhajan	83			
S.M.Pollock	not out	44			
†T.L.Tsolekile	lbw b Kumble	9			
R.J.Peterson	b Harbhajan	34			
M.Ntini					
Extras	(B 9, LB 22, W 1, NB 16, PEN 5)	53	(B 12, LB 5, NB 5)		22
Total	(9 wickets declared)	**510**	(4 wickets)		**169**

INDIA

V.Sehwag	lbw b Hall	164
G.Gambhir	c Tsolekile b Pollock	96
R.Dravid	c Tsolekile b Ntini	54
S.R.Tendulkar	b Hall	3
*S.C.Ganguly	c Peterson b De Bruyn	57
V.V.S.Laxman	b Ntini	9
†K.D.Karthik	lbw b Pollock	1
A.Kumble	c Tsolekile b Ntini	9
Harbhajan Singh	c Dippenaar b Peterson	17
Z.Khan	b Hall	30
M.Kartik	not out	0
Extras	(B10, LB 9, NB 7)	26
Total		**466**

INDIA	O	M	R	W		O	M	R	W
Khan	29	7	59	0		8	2	26	0
Ganguly	12	2	45	1					
Kumble	54	13	131	6	(2)	21	8	52	0
Harbhajan Singh	44.4	9	127	2	(3)	16	5	39	2
Kartik	42	12	76	0	(4)	14	6	17	2
Tendulkar	9	0	36	0	(5)	5	0	18	0

SOUTH AFRICA	O	M	R	W
Pollock	38	11	100	2
Ntini	39	0	135	3
Peterson	21	2	90	1
Hall	25.4	7	93	3
De Bruyn	11	3	29	1

FALL OF WICKETS

	SA	I	SA
Wkt	1st	1st	2nd
1st	61	218	67
2nd	69	294	100
3rd	154	298	110
4th	154	394	115
5th	241	407	–
6th	385	408	–
7th	445	419	–
8th	467	420	–
9th	510	456	–
10th	–	466	–

Umpires: D.J.Harper (*Australia*) (46) and S.J.A.Taufel (*Australia*) (18).
Referee: J.J.Crowe (*New Zealand*) (4). **Test No. 1723/15 (I379/SA291)**

INDIA v SOUTH AFRICA (2nd Test)

At Eden Gardens, Calcutta, on 28, 29, 30 November, 1, 2 December 2004.
Toss: South Africa. Result: **INDIA** won by eight wickets.
Debuts: South Africa – H.M.Amla.

SOUTH AFRICA

*G.C.Smith	c Karthik b Pathan	0	c Laxman b Harbhajan	71
A.J.Hall	c Karthik b Khan	7	c Karthik b Harbhajan	21
J.A.Rudolph	b Khan	61	lbw b Harbhajan	3
J.H.Kallis	b Ganguly	121	c and b Harbhajan	55
H.M.Amla	b Pathan	24	c Laxman b Harbhajan	2
H.H.Dippenaar	c Karthik b Pathan	1	c Sehwag b Kumble	2
Z.de Bruyn	c Karthik b Khan	15	not out	32
S.M.Pollock	c Dravid b Kumble	18	c Gambhir b Harbhajan	6
J.L.Ontong	not out	16	c Karthik b Harbhajan	0
†T.L.Tsolekile	c and b Harbhajan	15	b Kumble	1
M.Ntini	c Pathan b Harbhajan	0	c Dravid b Kumble	12
Extras	(LB 17, NB 10)	27	(B 12, LB 2, NB 3)	17
Total		**305**		**222**

INDIA

V.Sehwag	c Smith b Ntini	88	c Smith b Ntini	10
G.Gambhir	lbw b Pollock	7	lbw b Rudolph	26
R.Dravid	b Hall	80	not out	47
S.R.Tendulkar	b De Bruyn	20	not out	32
*S.C.Ganguly	lbw b De Bruyn	40		
V.V.S.Laxman	c Ontong b Ntini	38		
†K.D.Karthik	lbw b Pollock	46		
I.K.Pathan	c Smith b Ntini	24		
A.Kumble	c Kallis b Ntini	8		
Harbhajan Singh	c Dippenaar b Ontong	14		
Z.Khan	not out	11		
Extras	(LB 19, W 6, NB 10)	35	(LB 1, NB 4)	5
Total		**411**	(2 wickets)	**120**

INDIA	O	M	R	W	O	M	R	W
Pathan	31	7	72	3	5	1	17	0
Khan	27	7	64	3	5	0	22	0
Kumble	30	6	76	1	34.4	7	82	3
Ganguly	9	3	14	1				
Harbhajan Singh	21.3	6	54	2	(4) 30	3	87	7
Tendulkar	3	0	8	0				

SOUTH AFRICA	O	M	R	W	O	M	R	W
Pollock	45	13	101	2	7	1	22	0
Ntini	44	9	112	4	· 4	0	11	1
Ontong	18.1	1	79	1	10.4	1	44	0
Hall	27	5	68	1	(6) 3	2	2	0
De Bruyn	16	3	32	2				
Rudolph					(4) 8	1	24	1
Smith					(5) 7	1	16	0

FALL OF WICKETS				
	SA	I	SA	I
Wkt	1st	1st	2nd	2nd
1st	0	17	77	15
2nd	21	144	81	60
3rd	130	189	126	–
4th	176	238	138	–
5th	182	267	147	–
6th	230	308	183	–
7th	261	366	193	–
8th	273	382	193	–
9th	305	387	194	–
10th	305	411	222	–

Umpires: D.J.Harper (*Australia*) (47) and S.J.A.Taufel (*Australia*) (19).
Referee: J.J.Crowe (*New Zealand*) (5). **Test No. 1724/16 (I380/SA292)**

BANGLADESH v INDIA (1st Test)

At Bangabandhu National Stadium, Dhaka, on 10, 11, 12, 13 December 2004.
Toss: India. Result: **INDIA** won by an innings and 140 runs.
Debuts: None.

BANGLADESH

Javed Omar	lbw b Pathan	4	lbw b Pathan		4
Nafis Iqbal	lbw b Pathan	20	lbw b Kumble		54
*Habibul Bashar	c Tendulkar b Khan	8	c Khan b Pathan		12
Rajin Saleh	lbw b Pathan	0	lbw b Pathan		0
Mohammad Ashraful	not out	60	lbw b Pathan		0
†Khaled Masud	c Karthik b Khan	8	c Karthik b Pathan		5
Manjural Rana	c Karthik b Pathan	24	c Karthik b Khan		69
Mushfiqur Rahman	lbw b Pathan	0	c Dravid b Harbhajan		6
Mohammad Rafique	lbw b Kumble	47	c Sehwag b Kumble		11
Tapash Baisya	c Dravid b Kumble	0	c Tendulkar b Pathan		29
Mashrafe Mortaza	run out	7	not out		0
Extras	(LB 4, NB 2)	6	(LB 5, W 2, NB 5)		12
Total		**184**			**202**

INDIA

G.Gambhir	run out	35
V.Sehwag	lbw b Baisya	13
R.Dravid	b Mortaza	0
S.R.Tendulkar	not out	248
*S.C.Ganguly	b Baisya	71
V.V.S.Laxman	lbw b Rafique	32
†K.D.Karthik	c Mortaza b Mushfiqur	25
I.K.Pathan	c Mushfiqur b Rafique	5
A.Kumble	b Mortaza	1
Harbhajan Singh	c Habibul b Mushfiqur	8
Z.Khan	st Masud b Ashraful	75
Extras	(B 2, LB 11)	13
Total		**526**

INDIA	O	M	R	W		O	M	R	W
Pathan	16	5	45	3		15	5	51	6
Khan	15	2	51	2		13.2	2	60	1
Ganguly	4	2	16	0					
Kumble	13.5	2	45	2	(3)	13	4	42	2
Harbhajan Singh	9	1	23	0	(4)	12	3	44	1

BANGLADESH	O	M	R	W
Tapash Baisya	29	4	114	2
Mashrafe Mortaza	31	8	125	2
Mushfiqur Rahman	24	4	104	2
Mohammad Rafique	40	9	113	2
Manjural Rana	12	1	55	0
Mohammad Ashraful	0.4	0	2	1

FALL OF WICKETS

	B	I	B
Wkt	1st	1st	2nd
1st	8	19	4
2nd	29	24	24
3rd	29	68	24
4th	35	232	24
5th	50	291	36
6th	106	339	100
7th	106	348	117
8th	171	368	133
9th	171	393	202
10th	184	526	202

Umpires: Alim Dar (*Pakistan*) (14) and J.W.Lloyds (*England*) (3).
Referee: B.C.Broad (*England*) (8). Test No. 1725/2 (B33/I381)

BANGLADESH v INDIA (2nd Test)

At M.A.Aziz Stadium, Chittagong, on 17, 18, 19, 20 December 2004.
Toss: India. Result: **INDIA** won by an innings and 83 runs.
Debuts: Bangladesh – Nazmul Hossain.

INDIA

V.Sehwag	c Habibul b Mortaza	10
G.Gambhir	b Nazmul	139
R.Dravid	c Masud b Mortaza	160
S.R.Tendulkar	lbw b Mortaza	36
*S.C.Ganguly	c Jubair b Rafique	88
V.V.S.Laxman	c and b Rafique	9
†K.D.Karthik	c Masud b Rafique	11
I.K.Pathan	c Masud b Rafique	4
A.Kumble	st Masud b Ashraful	23
Harbhajan Singh	c Manjural b Nazmul	47
Z.Khan	not out	0
Extras	(B 5, LB 4, W 2, NB 2)	13
Total		**540**

BANGLADESH

Nafis Iqbal	c Gambhir b Harbhajan	31		lbw b Pathan	0
Javed Omar	c Dravid b Kumble	10		c Karthik b Pathan	6
Mashrafe Mortaza	lbw b Kumble	4	(9)	c Harbhajan b Tendulkar	6
*Habibul Bashar	st Karthik b Kumble	22	(3)	lbw b Pathan	17
Mohammad Ashraful	not out	158	(6)	lbw b Kumble	3
Aftab Ahmed	lbw b Kumble	43	(4)	c Karthik b Pathan	4
Manjural Rana	lbw b Khan	0		c Gambhir b Kumble	0
†Khaled Masud	c Karthik b Khan	22		c Dravid b Harbhajan	0
Mohammad Rafique	c Dravid b Pathan	4	(5)	c Sehwag b Pathan	22
Talha Jubair	b Pathan	0	(11)	c Pathan b Harbhajan	31
Nazmul Hossain	run out	0	(10)	not out	8
Extras	(B 17, LB 8, W 3, NB 11)	39		(B 9, LB 7, W 7, NB 4)	27
Total		**333**			**124**

BANGLADESH	O	M	R	W		O	M	R	W		FALL OF WICKETS			
Mashrafe Mortaza	26	5	60	3								I	B	B
Nazmul Hossain	25.5	4	114	2							*Wkt*	*1st*	*1st*	*2nd*
Talha Jubair	19	1	95	0							1st	14	48	0
Mohammad Rafique	50	2	156	4							2nd	273	54	30
Manjural Rana	16.3	0	63	0							3rd	334	54	34
Aftab Ahmed	4	0	14	0							4th	371	124	75
Mohammad Ashraful	7	0	29	1							5th	384	239	76
											6th	402	240	77
INDIA											7th	412	300	78
Pathan	23	7	86	2		9	2	32	5		8th	465	312	80
Khan	18	3	76	2		6	1	28	0		9th	540	312	84
Kumble	26	9	55	4		4	2	2	2		10th	540	333	124
Harbhajan Singh	22	5	79	1		4.4	0	19	2					
Tendulkar	2	0	12	0		3	0	27	1					

Umpires: Alim Dar (*Pakistan*) (15) and M.R.Benson (*England*) (3).
Referee: B.C.Broad (*England*) (9). **Test No. 1726/3 (B34/I382)**

AUSTRALIA v PAKISTAN (1st Test)

At W.A.C.A Ground, Perth on 16, 17, 18, 19 December 2004.
Toss: Pakistan. Result: **AUSTRALIA** won by 491 runs.
Debuts: Pakistan – Mohammad Khalil.

AUSTRALIA

J.L.Langer	c Younis b Sami	191	b Abdul Razzaq		97
M.L.Hayden	lbw b Akhtar	4	b Akhtar		10
*R.T.Ponting	b Sami	25	st Akmal b Kaneria		98
D.R.Martyn	c Akmal b Sami	1	not out		100
D.S.Lehmann	b Akhtar	12	b Kaneria		5
M.J.Clarke	c Inzamam b Akhtar	1	c Inzamam b Sami		27
†A.C.Gilchrist	b Razzaq	69	not out		0
S.K.Warne	c Youhana b Razzaq	12			
J.N.Gillespie	c Akmal b Akhtar	24			
M.S.Kasprowicz	lbw b Akhtar	4			
G.D.McGrath	not out	8			
Extras	(B 1, LB 14, W 5, NB 10)	30	(LB 15, W 2, NB 7)		24
Total		**381**	(5 wickets declared)		**361**

PAKISTAN

Salman Butt	c Gilchrist b Kasprowicz	17	c Hayden b McGrath		9
Imran Farhat	c Gilchrist b Gillespie	18	lbw b McGrath		1
Younis Khan	c Gillespie b Warne	42	c Warne b McGrath		17
*Inzamam-ul-Haq	b Kasprowicz	1	(6) c Gilchrist b McGrath		0
Yousuf Youhana	c Gilchrist b Kasprowicz	1	(4) c Gilchrist b McGrath		27
Abdul Razzaq	b Warne	21	(5) c Gilchrist b McGrath		1
†Kamran Akmal	b Kasprowicz	2	c Clarke b McGrath		0
Mohammad Sami	c Clarke b Kasprowicz	29	b Kasprowicz		2
Mohammad Khalil	b Warne	0	(10) c and b Kasprowicz		5
Shoaib Akhtar	c Warne b McGrath	27	(9) c Lehmann b McGrath		1
Danish Kaneria	not out	6	not out		0
Extras	(B 1, LB 3, W 7, NB 4)	15	(LB 7, W 2)		9
Total		**179**			**72**

PAKISTAN	O	M	R	W	O	M	R	W
Shoaib Akhtar	22	1	99	5	6.3	1	22	1
Mohammad Sami	25.5	3	104	3	14	1	55	1
Mohammad Khalil	16	0	59	0	9.2	0	38	0
Abdul Razzaq	12	0	55	2 (4)	12.3	1	48	1
Danish Kaneria	15	2	49	0	32	3	130	2
Imran Farhat					11	0	53	0

AUSTRALIA	O	M	R	W	O	M	R	W
McGrath	19	7	44	1	16	8	24	8
Gillespie	14	2	43	1	12	3	37	0
Kasprowicz	16.3	6	30	5	3.3	2	4	2
Warne	21	9	38	3				
Lehmann	4	2	5	0				
Ponting	3	1	15	0				

FALL OF WICKETS

	A	P	A	P
Wkt	1st	1st	2nd	2nd
1st	6	32	28	5
2nd	56	45	191	34
3rd	58	55	271	43
4th	71	60	281	49
5th	78	108	360	49
6th	230	110	–	61
7th	253	110	–	64
8th	333	111	–	66
9th	362	171	–	72
10th	381	179	–	72

Umpires: B.F.Bowden (*New Zealand*) (22) and R.E.Koertzen (*South Africa*) (58).
Referee: R.S.Madugalle (*Sri Lanka*) (70).   **Test No. 1727/50 (A660/P305)**

AUSTRALIA v PAKISTAN (2nd Test)

At Melbourne Cricket Ground on 26, 27, 28, 29 December 2004.
Toss: Pakistan. Result: **AUSTRALIA** won by nine wickets
Debuts: None.

PAKISTAN

Salman Butt	run out	70	c Kasprowicz b McGrath		0
Imran Farhat	c Ponting b Kasprowicz	20	c Martyn b Gillespie		5
Yasir Hamid	lbw b Gillespie	2	c Gilchrist b McGrath		23
Younis Khan	c Gilchrist b Gillespie	87	c Hayden b Kasprowicz		23
*Yousuf Youhana	st Gilchrist b Warne	111	c Ponting b Warne		12
Shoaib Malik	c Ponting b Gillespie	6	c Gillespie b Warne		41
Abdul Razzaq	not out	4	(8) c Gilchrist b McGrath		19
†Kamran Akmal	c Gilchrist b McGrath	24	(9) lbw b Warne		0
Mohammad Sami	lbw b Warne	12	(7) lbw b Gillespie		11
Shoaib Akhtar	st Gilchrist b Warne	0	b McGrath		14
Danish Kaneria	run out	0	not out		9
Extras	(LB 4, W 1)	5	(B 4, LB 1, NB 1)		6
Total		**341**			**163**

AUSTRALIA

J.L.Langer	c Farhat b Kaneria	50	c Kamran b Sami		5
M.L.Hayden	c Malik b Akhtar	9	not out		56
*R.T.Ponting	c Malik b Akhtar	7	not out		62
D.R.Martyn	lbw b Kaneria	142			
D.S.Lehmann	c Hamid b Akhtar	11			
M.J.Clarke	c Akhtar b Kaneria	20			
†A.C.Gilchrist	c Sami b Kaneria	48			
S.K.Warne	c and b Akhtar	10			
J.N.Gillespie	not out	50			
M.S.Kasprowicz	c sub (Naved-ul-Hasan) b Akhtar	4			
G.D.McGrath	lbw b Kaneria	1			
Extras	(B 1, LB 2, W 5, NB 19)	27	(LB 2, NB 2)		4
Total		**379**	(1 wicket)		**127**

AUSTRALIA	O	M	R	W	O	M	R	W	FALL OF WICKETS				
										P	A	P	A
McGrath	28	12	54	1	11.2	1	35	4	Wkt	1st	1st	2nd	2nd
Gillespie	26	7	77	3	12	7	15	2	1st	85	13	0	11
Kasprowicz	20	6	66	1	16	3	42	1	2nd	93	32	13	–
Warne	28.3	2	103	3	25	7	66	3	3rd	94	122	35	–
Clarke	3	0	24	0					4th	286	135	60	–
Lehmann	2	0	13	0					5th	298	171	68	–
									6th	301	230	98	–
PAKISTAN									7th	326	254	101	–
Shoaib Akhtar	27	4	109	5	7	0	35	0	8th	341	347	140	–
Mohammad Sami	23	2	102	0	5	0	22	1	9th	341	368	140	–
Abdul Razzaq	7	0	27	0					10th	341	379	163	–
Danish Kaneria	39.3	5	125	5	(3) 10.5	1	52	0					
Imran Farhat	3	0	13	0	(4) 5	2	16	0					

Umpires: R.E.Koertzen (*South Africa*) (59) and J.W.Lloyds (*England*) (4).
Referee: R.S.Madugalle (*Sri Lanka*) (71). **Test No. 1728/51 (A661/P306)**

AUSTRALIA v PAKISTAN (3rd Test)

At Sydney Cricket Ground on 2, 3, 4, 5 January 2005.
Toss: Pakistan. Result: **AUSTRALIA** won by nine wickets
Debuts: Australia – S.R.Watson; Pakistan – Mohammad Asif.

PAKISTAN

Salman Butt	c Gilchrist b McGrath	108	c Warne b MacGill	21
Yasir Hamid	c Clarke b Warne	58	lbw b Warne	63
Younis Khan	c McGrath b MacGill	46	lbw b Watson	44
*Yousuf Youhana	c Warne b MacGill	8	b MacGill	30
Asim Kamal	c Gillespie b MacGill	10	c Ponting b Gillespie	87
Shahid Afridi	c McGrath b MacGill	12	run out	46
†Kamran Akmal	c Warne b McGrath	47	c Hayden b Warne	4
Naved-ul-Hasan	lbw b McGrath	0	lbw b Warne	9
Shoaib Akhtar	b McGrath	0	c Martyn b Warne	0
Danish Kaneria	c Gilchrist b MacGill	3	b MacGill	0
Mohammad Asif	not out	0	not out	12
Extras	(B 6, LB 2, W 1, NB 3)	12	(B 4, LB 3, NB 2)	9
Total		**304**		**325**

AUSTRALIA

J.L.Langer	b Naved	13	b Kaneria	34
M.L.Hayden	b Kaneria	26	not out	23
*R.T.Ponting	b Naved	207	not out	4
D.R.Martyn	st Akmal b Kaneria	67		
M.J.Clarke	st Akmal b Kaneria	35		
†A.C.Gilchrist	st Akmal b Kaneria	113		
S.R.Watson	c Younis b Kaneria	31		
S.K.Warne	c Younis b Kaneria	16		
J.N.Gillespie	lbw b Naved	0		
G.D.McGrath	c Youhana b Kaneria	9		
S.G.MacGill	not out	9		
Extras	(B 6, LB 13, W 3, NB 20)	42	(NB 1)	1
Total		**568**	(1 wicket)	**62**

AUSTRALIA	O	M	R	W		O	M	R	W
McGrath	16.4	5	50	4		16	2	53	0
Gillespie	14	3	47	0		13.2	2	39	2
Watson	10	3	28	0	(5)	9	2	32	1
Warne	24	4	84	1	(3)	26	2	111	4
MacGill	22	4	87	5	(4)	25	3	83	3
PAKISTAN									
Shoaib Akhtar	15	2	69	0					
Naved-ul-Hasan	26	3	107	3	(1)	3	0	28	0
Mohammad Asif	16	3	72	0	(2)	2	0	16	0
Danish Kaneria	49.3	7	188	7	(3)	2.3	0	16	1
Shahid Afridi	27	3	113	0	(4)	2	0	2	0

FALL OF WICKETS				
	P	A	P	A
Wkt	1st	1st	2nd	2nd
1st	102	26	46	58
2nd	193	83	104	–
3rd	209	257	164	–
4th	241	318	164	–
5th	241	471	238	–
6th	261	529	243	–
7th	261	535	261	–
8th	261	537	269	–
9th	280	556	270	–
10th	304	568	325	–

Umpires: B.F.Bowden (*New Zealand*) (23) and D.R.Shepherd (*England*) (86).
Referee: R.S.Madugalle (*Sri Lanka*) (72). **Test No. 1729/52 (A662/P307)**

SOUTH AFRICA v ENGLAND (1st Test)

At St George's Park, Port Elizabeth, on 17, 18, 19, 20, 21 December 2004.
Toss: South Africa. Result: **ENGLAND** won by seven wickets.
Debuts: South Africa – A.B.de Villiers, D.W.Steyn.

SOUTH AFRICA

*G.C.Smith	c Strauss b Hoggard	0	(2)	c S.P.Jones b Flintoff	55
A.B.de Villiers	lbw b Flintoff	28	(1)	c and b Hoggard	14
J.A.Rudolph	c G.O.Jones b Flintoff	93		c Trescothick b Giles	28
J.H.Kallis	b Harmison	0		lbw b S.P.Jones	61
H.H.Dippenaar	c Trescothick b S.P.Jones	110		b Giles	10
Z.de Bruyn	b Flintoff	6		c Trescothick b Flintoff	19
S.M.Pollock	c Trescothick b Hoggard	31		c G.O.Jones b S.P.Jones	0
A.J.Hall	b Hoggard	6		run out	17
†T.L.Tsolekile	c Flintoff b Giles	22		b S.P.Jones	0
M.Ntini	not out	2		lbw b S.P.Jones	4
D.W.Steyn	c Strauss b Giles	8		not out	2
Extras	(LB 13, W 4, NB 14)	31		(B 4, LB 3, W 1, NB 6, PEN 5)	19
Total		**337**			**229**

ENGLAND

M.E.Trescothick	b Steyn	47		c Tsolekile b Pollock	0
A.J.Strauss	c De Villiers b Pollock	126		not out	94
M.A.Butcher	c Tsolekile b Ntini	79		c Smith b Ntini	0
*M.P.Vaughan	c Smith b Hall	10		b Steyn	15
G.P.Thorpe	b Smith	4		not out	31
A.Flintoff	c Rudolph b Ntini	35			
†G.O.Jones	c Dippenaar b Ntini	2			
A.F.Giles	c Hall b Pollock	26			
M.J.Hoggard	c Tsolekile b Hall	0			
S.P.Jones	c and b Steyn	24			
S.J.Harmison	not out	15			
Extras	(LB 21, W 1, NB 35)	57		(LB 3, NB 2)	5
Total		**425**		(3 wickets)	**145**

ENGLAND	O	M	R	W		O	M	R	W
Hoggard	20	4	56	3		12	2	38	1
Harmison	25	2	88	1		14	1	54	0
S.P.Jones	16	4	39	1	(5)	13.1	3	39	4
Flintoff	22	4	72	3		15	2	47	2
Giles	27.4	8	69	2	(3)	15	2	39	2
SOUTH AFRICA									
Pollock	32	14	61	2		11	2	36	1
Ntini	28	6	75	3		6.4	1	24	1
Steyn	25.5	2	117	2	(4)	6	1	29	1
Hall	22	1	95	2	(3)	9	1	14	0
De Bruyn	9	1	31	0					
Smith	10	3	25	1	(5)	8	0	39	0

FALL OF WICKETS

Wkt	SA 1st	E 1st	SA 2nd	E 2nd
1st	0	152	26	0
2nd	63	238	64	11
3rd	66	249	152	50
4th	178	267	168	–
5th	192	346	201	–
6th	253	353	201	–
7th	261	353	217	–
8th	324	358	218	–
9th	327	394	224	–
10th	337	425	229	–

Umpires: D.B.Hair (*Australia*) (57) and S.J.A.Taufel (*Australia*) (20).
Referee: C.H.Lloyd (West Indies) (39).   **Test No. 1730/126 (SA293/E828)**

SOUTH AFRICA v ENGLAND (2nd Test)

At Kingsmead, Durban, on 26, 27, 28, 29, 30 December 2004.
Toss: South Africa. Result: **MATCH DRAWN**.
Debuts: None.

ENGLAND

M.E.Trescothick	c De Villiers b Ntini	18	c De Villiers b Pollock	132
A.J.Strauss	c Ntini b Boje	25	c Van Jaarsveld b Ntini	136
M.A.Butcher	b Steyn	5	c Van Jaarsveld b Kallis	13
*M.P.Vaughan	lbw b Ntini	18	c De Villiers b Ntini	10
G.P.Thorpe	lbw b Pollock	1	not out	118
A.Flintoff	c Amla b Pollock	0	c De Villiers b Smith	60
†G.O.Jones	c Rudolph b Ntini	24	c Ntini b Boje	73
A.F.Giles	c Rudolph b Steyn	10	c De Villiers b Steyn	0
M.J.Hoggard	not out	6		
S.P.Jones	b Pollock	21		
S.J.Harmison	b Pollock	0		
Extras	(LB 9, NB 2)	11	(B 3, LB 8, W 2, NB 15)	28
Total		**139**	(7 wickets declared)	**570**

SOUTH AFRICA

*G.C.Smith	c Flintoff b Harmison	9	lbw b Hoggard	5
H.H.Gibbs	b Hoggard	15	c Giles b Harmison	36
J.A.Rudolph	c Thorpe b Harmison	32	(4) c Strauss b Giles	61
J.H.Kallis	c sub (‡) b Hoggard	162	(5) c G.O.Jones b Harmison	10
M.van Jaarsveld	b Flintoff	1	(6) c Trescothick b Hoggard	49
H.M.Amla	c G.O.Jones b Harmison	1	(7) lbw b S.P.Jones	0
†A.B.de Villiers	c Thorpe b S.P.Jones	14	(8) not out	52
S.M.Pollock	c G.O.Jones b Vaughan	43	(9) run out	35
N.Boje	c sub (‡) b Hoggard	15	(3) c Thorpe b Flintoff	10
M.Ntini	c S.P.Jones b Flintoff	22	not out	16
D.W.Steyn	not out	7		
Extras	(LB 7, NB 4)	11	(B 8, LB 4, W 1, NB 3)	16
Total		**332**	(8 wickets)	**290**

SOUTH AFRICA	O	M	R	W		O	M	R	W
Pollock	15.1	7	32	4		36	16	79	1
Ntini	13	2	41	3		37	4	111	2
Steyn	13	4	26	2		25.3	2	122	1
Kallis	7	4	10	0	(5)	25	4	57	1
Boje	9	2	21	1	(4)	44	5	163	1
Smith						5	1	27	1
ENGLAND									
Hoggard	23	8	58	3		19	3	58	2
Harmison	28	3	91	3		19	4	62	2
Flintoff	23	5	66	2		14	5	38	1
S.P.Jones	18	1	81	1		14	4	36	1
Vaughan	10	2	29	1	(6)	1	1	0	0
Giles					(5)	19	1	84	1

FALL OF WICKETS				
	E	SA	E	SA
Wkt	1st	1st	2nd	2nd
1st	21	17	273	12
2nd	32	48	293	33
3rd	53	70	306	87
4th	62	80	314	103
5th	64	90	428	172
6th	80	118	560	173
7th	93	205	570	183
8th	113	243	–	268
9th	139	293	–	–
10th	139	332	–	–

‡ P.D.Collingwood

Umpires: D.B.Hair (*Australia*) (58) and S.J.A.Taufel (*Australia*) (21).
Referee: C.H.Lloyd (West Indies) (40). **Test No. 1732/128 (SA295/E830)**

SOUTH AFRICA v ENGLAND (3rd Test)

At Newlands, Cape Town, on 2, 3, 4, 5, 6 January 2005.
Toss: South Africa. Result: **SOUTH AFRICA** won by 196 runs.
Debuts: South Africa – C.K.Langeveldt.

SOUTH AFRICA

*G.C.Smith	c Trescothick b Giles	74	lbw b Hoggard		2
H.H.Gibbs	b Hoggard	4	c G.O.Jones b Flintoff		24
J.A.Rudolph	c G.O.Jones b S.P.Jones	26	c Key b S.P.Jones		23
J.H.Kallis	c G.O.Jones b Flintoff	149	run out		66
H.H.Dippenaar	b Giles	29	c Vaughan b Flintoff		44
H.M.Amla	lbw b Hoggard	25	(7) c G.O.Jones b S.P.Jones		10
†A.B.de Villiers	b Giles	21	(8) c Giles b Harmison		10
S.M.Pollock	c G.O.Jones b Flintoff	4	(9) not out		3
N.Boje	c G.O.Jones b Flintoff	76	(6) run out		4
M.Ntini	c Vaughan b Flintoff	0	not out		0
C.K.Langeveldt	not out	5			
Extras	(B 4, LB 15, W 3, NB 6)	36	(B 7, LB 12, W 10, NB 7)		36
Total		**441**	(8 wickets declared)		**222**

ENGLAND

M.E.Trescothick	c Gibbs b Ntini	28	c Amla b Pollock		0
A.J.Strauss	b Ntini	45	lbw b Boje		39
R.W.T.Key	c De Villiers b Pollock	0	st De Villiers b Boje		41
*M.P.Vaughan	c De Villiers b Langeveldt	11	c Rudolph b Ntini		20
G.P.Thorpe	c Rudolph b Langeveldt	12	c De Villiers b Pollock		26
M.J.Hoggard	c Smith b Ntini	1	(9) not out		7
A.Flintoff	c Gibbs b Ntini	12	(6) c De Villiers b Pollock		20
†G.O.Jones	c Smith b Langeveldt	13	(7) c Kallis b Boje		38
A.F.Giles	not out	31	(8) c Kallis b Boje		25
S.P.Jones	b Langeveldt	0	c Kallis b Pollock		19
S.J.Harmison	c Smith b Langeveldt	0	c Dippenaar b Ntini		42
Extras	(B 4, LB 6)	10	(B 6, LB 3, W 6, NB 12)		27
Total		**163**			**304**

ENGLAND	O	M	R	W		O	M	R	W	FALL OF WICKETS				
Hoggard	32	7	87	2		10	0	46	1		SA	E	SA	E
Harmison	26	6	82	0		19	3	55	1	*Wkt*	*1st*	*1st*	*2nd*	*2nd*
Flintoff	31.1	7	79	4		18	1	46	2	1st	9	52	2	0
S.P.Jones	18	0	69	1	(5)	9.3	4	15	2	2nd	70	55	62	68
Giles	35	3	105	3	(4)	13	2	41	0	3rd	145	70	101	103
										4th	213	95	184	105
SOUTH AFRICA										5th	261	97	190	146
Pollock	17	5	36	1		31	11	65	4	6th	308	109	203	158
Ntini	19	6	50	4		24.4	6	49	2	7th	313	128	215	220
Langeveldt	16	4	46	5		17	3	50	0	8th	417	141	219	225
Boje	4	1	15	0		34	13	71	4	9th	417	149	–	253
Kallis	2	1	6	0		15	4	49	0	10th	441	163	–	304
Smith						2	0	11	0					

Umpires: S.A.Bucknor (West Indies) (97) and D.J.Harper (*Australia*) (48).
Referee: C.H.Lloyd (West Indies) (41).   Test No. 1731/127 (SA294/E829)

SOUTH AFRICA v ENGLAND (4th Test)

At The Wanderers, Johannesburg, on 13, 14, 15, 16, 17 January 2005.
Toss: England. Result: **ENGLAND** won by 77 runs.
Debuts: None.

ENGLAND

M.E.Trescothick	c Boucher b Steyn	16		c Boucher b Ntini	180
A.J.Strauss	c Kallis b Pollock	147		c De Villiers b Ntini	0
R.W.T.Key	c Smith b Ntini	83		c Kallis b Ntini	19
*M.P.Vaughan	not out	82		c Boucher b Pollock	54
G.P.Thorpe	c Dippenaar b Ntini	0		c and b Kallis	1
M.J.Hoggard	c De Villiers b Ntini	5	(9)	c Boucher b Kallis	0
A.Flintoff	c Smith b Ntini	2	(6)	c Boucher b Pollock	7
†G.O.Jones	c Smith b Pollock	2	(7)	c De Villiers b Pollock	13
A.F.Giles	c Gibbs b Steyn	26	(8)	c Gibbs b Kallis	31
S.J.Harmison	not out	30		not out	3
J.M.Anderson					
Extras	(LB 13, NB 5)	18		(LB 7, W 6, NB 11)	24
Total	(8 wickets declared)	**411**		(9 wickets declared)	**332**

SOUTH AFRICA

*G.C.Smith	lbw b Hoggard	29	(8)	not out	67
H.H.Gibbs	c Hoggard b Anderson	161		lbw b Giles	98
J.A.Rudolph	c Giles b Hoggard	4		b Hoggard	2
J.H.Kallis	b Hoggard	33		c Trescothick b Hoggard	0
H.H.Dippenaar	c Trescothick b Flintoff	0		c Giles b Hoggard	14
A.B.de Villiers	c Giles b Hoggard	19	(1)	lbw b Hoggard	3
†M.V.Boucher	c Strauss b Anderson	64	(6)	c Jones b Hoggard	0
S.M.Pollock	lbw b Hoggard	0	(9)	c Jones b Flintoff	4
N.Boje	run out	48	(7)	c and b Hoggard	18
M.Ntini	b Giles	26		lbw b Flintoff	13
D.W.Steyn	not out	0		c Jones b Hoggard	8
Extras	(B 9, LB 11, W 6, NB 9)	35		(B 2, LB 5, W 1, NB 12)	20
Total		**419**			**247**

SOUTH AFRICA	O	M	R	W		O	M	R	W
Pollock	33	12	81	2		19	2	74	3
Ntini	34	8	111	4		20.1	2	62	3
Steyn	21	7	75	2	(4)	9	0	47	0
Kallis	22	2	79	0	(3)	21	5	93	3
Boje	14	2	52	0		12	0	49	0
ENGLAND									
Hoggard	34	2	144	5		18.3	5	61	7
Harmison	12.5	4	25	0		14	1	64	0
Anderson	28	3	117	2		6	1	32	0
Flintoff	30.1	8	77	1	(3)	16	2	59	2
Giles	8.1	0	25	1		5	0	24	1
Trescothick	5	1	11	0					

FALL OF WICKETS

	E	SA	E	SA
Wkt	1st	1st	2nd	2nd
1st	45	64	2	10
2nd	227	75	51	18
3rd	262	138	175	18
4th	263	149	176	86
5th	273	184	186	86
6th	275	304	222	118
7th	278	306	272	163
8th	329	358	274	172
9th	–	399	332	216
10th	–	419	–	247

Umpires: Alim Dar (*Pakistan*) (16) and S.A.Bucknor (*West Indies*) (98).
Referee: C.H.Lloyd (West Indies) (42).   **Test No. 1733/129 (SA296/E831)**

SOUTH AFRICA v ENGLAND (5th Test)

At Centurion Park, (Verwoerdburg), Pretoria, on 21 (*no play*), 22, 23, 24, 25 January 2005.
Toss: England. Result: **MATCH DRAWN**.
Debuts: None.

SOUTH AFRICA

A.B.de Villiers	lbw b Giles	92	c Hoggard b S.P.Jones		109
H.H.Gibbs	c G.O.Jones b Flintoff	14	c G.O.Jones b Flintoff		4
J.A.Rudolph	c Key b Hoggard	33	(6) b Harmison		2
J.H.Kallis	b Flintoff	8	not out		136
*G.C.Smith	c Trescothick b Flintoff	25	c sub (‡) b Harmison		3
†M.V.Boucher	c Trescothick b S.P.Jones	25	(7) c Trescothick b Hoggard		6
S.M.Pollock	b Flintoff	0			
N.Boje	c Thorpe b S.P.Jones	9			
A.J.Hall	c Strauss b S.P.Jones	11	(3) b Flintoff		9
M.Ntini	c Hoggard b S.P.Jones	6			
A.Nel	not out	1			
Extras	(LB 1, W3, NB 19)	23	(B 2, LB 14, W 2, NB 9)		27
Total		**247**	(6 wickets declared)		**296**

ENGLAND

M.E.Trescothick	run out	20	b Ntini		7
A.J.Strauss	c Boucher b Nel	44	c Kallis b Ntini		0
R.W.T.Key	c Boucher b Pollock	13	lbw b Pollock		9
*M.P.Vaughan	c Rudolph b Pollock	0	not out		26
G.P.Thorpe	b Nel	86	c Gibbs b Ntini		8
A.Flintoff	c Boucher b Hall	77	not out		14
†G.O.Jones	c Smith b Nel	50			
A.F.Giles	b Nel	39			
M.J.Hoggard	c Kallis b Nel	1			
S.P.Jones	not out	0			
S.J.Harmison	lbw b Nel	6			
Extras	(B 1, LB 22, W 8, NB 4)	35	(LB 7, NB 2)		9
Total		**359**	(4 wickets)		**73**

ENGLAND	O	M	R	W		O	M	R	W	FALL OF WICKETS				
Hoggard	18	4	64	1		14	2	51	1		SA	E	SA	E
Harmison	17	2	79	0	(5)	16	2	59	2	*Wkt*	*1st*	*1st*	*2nd*	*2nd*
Flintoff	19	6	44	4	(2)	13	2	46	2	1st	27	27	17	0
S.P.Jones	15.3	1	47	4		19	2	74	1	2nd	114	29	29	16
Giles	6	1	12	1	(3)	11	1	50	0	3rd	144	29	256	20
										4th	187	114	267	45
SOUTH AFRICA										5th	200	255	277	–
Pollock	21	11	30	2	(3)	7	3	9	1	6th	200	257	296	–
Ntini	28	8	92	0	(1)	11	6	12	3	7th	222	335	—	–
Nel	29	7	81	6	(1)	12	5	24	0	8th	237	351	—	–
Hall	16	3	58	1	(5)	5.2	2	9	0	9th	245	352	—	–
Boje	19	7	59	0	(6)	1	1	0	0	10th	247	359	—	–
Kallis	2	0	5	0	(7)	2	0	4	0					
Smith	8	2	11	0	(4)	3	1	8	0	‡ P.D.Collingwood				

Umpires: Alim Dar (*Pakistan*) (17) and S.A.Bucknor (*West Indies*) (99).
Referee: C.H.Lloyd (West Indies) (43).   **Test No. 1734/130 (SA297/E832)**

SOUTH AFRICA v ENGLAND 2004-05
SOUTH AFRICA – BATTING AND FIELDING

	M	I	NO	HS	Runs	Avge	100	50	Ct/St
J.H.Kallis	5	10	1	162	625	69.44	3	2	8
H.H.Gibbs	4	8	–	161	356	44.50	1	1	5
A.B.de Villiers	5	10	1	109	362	40.22	1	2	13/1
H.H.Dippenaar	3	6	–	110	207	34.50	1	–	3
J.A.Rudolph	5	10	–	93	304	30.40	–	2	6
G.C.Smith	5	10	1	74	269	29.88	–	3	9
N.Boje	4	7	–	76	180	25.71	–	1	–
M.V.Boucher	2	4	–	64	95	23.75	–	1	8
S.M.Pollock	5	9	1	43	120	15.00	–	–	–
M.Ntini	5	9	3	26	89	14.83	–	–	2
D.W.Steyn	3	5	3	8	25	12.50	–	–	1
A.J.Hall	2	4	–	17	43	10.75	–	–	1
H.M.Amla	2	4	–	25	36	9.00	–	–	1

Played in one Test: Z.de Bruyn 6, 19; C.K.Langeveldt 5*; A.Nel 1*; T.L.Tsolekile 22, 0 (3 ct); M.van Jaarsveld 1, 49 (2 ct).

SOUTH AFRICA – BOWLING

	O	M	R	W	Avge	Best	5wI	10wM
A.Nel	41	12	105	6	17.50	6-81	1	–
C.K.Langeveldt	33	7	96	5	19.20	5-46	1	–
S.M.Pollock	222.1	83	503	21	23.95	4-32	–	–
M.Ntini	221.3	49	627	25	25.08	4-50	–	–
D.W.Steyn	100.2	16	416	8	52.00	2-26	–	–
A.J.Hall	52.2	7	176	3	58.66	2-95	–	–
G.C.Smith	36	7	121	2	60.50	1-25	–	–
N.Boje	137	31	430	6	71.66	4-71	–	–
J.H.Kallis	96	20	303	4	75.75	3-93	–	–

Also bowled: Z.de Bruyn 9-1-31-0.

ENGLAND – BATTING AND FIELDING

	M	I	NO	HS	Runs	Avge	100	50	Ct/St
A.J.Strauss	5	10	1	147	656	72.88	3	1	5
M.E.Trescothick	5	10	–	180	448	44.80	2	–	11
G.P.Thorpe	5	10	2	118*	287	35.87	1	1	4
M.P.Vaughan	5	10	2	82*	246	30.75	–	2	2
A.Flintoff	5	9	1	77	227	28.37	–	2	2
G.O.Jones	5	8	–	73	215	26.87	–	2	16
A.F.Giles	5	8	1	39	188	26.85	–	–	5
R.W.T.Key	3	6	–	83	153	25.50	–	1	2
M.A.Butcher	2	4	–	79	97	24.25	–	1	–
S.J.Harmison	5	7	3	42	96	24.00	–	–	–
S.P.Jones	4	5	1	24	64	16.00	–	–	2
M.J.Hoggard	5	7	2	7*	20	4.00	–	–	5

Played in one Test: J.M.Anderson did not bat.

ENGLAND – BOWLING

	O	M	R	W	Avge	Best	5wI	10wM
A.Flintoff	201.2	42	574	23	24.95	4- 44	–	–
M.J.Hoggard	200.3	37	663	26	25.50	7- 61	2	1
S.P.Jones	123.1	21	400	15	26.66	4- 39	–	–
A.F.Giles	139.5	18	449	11	40.81	3-105	–	–
S.J.Harmison	190.5	28	659	9	73.22	3- 91	–	–

Also bowled: J.M.Anderson 34-4-149-2; M.E.Trescothick 5-1-11-0; M.P.Vaughan 11-3-29-1.

BANGLADESH v ZIMBABWE (1st Test)

At M.A.Aziz Stadium, Chittagong, on 6, 7, 8, 9, 10 January 2005.
Toss: Bangladesh. Result: **BANGLADESH** won by 226 runs.
Debuts: Zimbabwe – A.G.Cremer, C.B.Mpofu, B.G.Rogers.

BANGLADESH

Javed Omar	c Taibu b Chigambura	33	(7)	c Masakadza b Chigumbura	15
Nafis Iqbal	c Sibanda b Nkala	56		c Taylor b Hondo	0
*Habibul Bashar	c Taibu b Mpofu	94		c Masakadza b Chigumbura	55
Mohammad Ashraful	c Masakadza b Nkala	19		c Taibu b Mpofu	22
Rajin Saleh	c and b Matsikenyeri	89	(1)	c and b Hondo	26
Aftab Ahmed	lbw b Mpofu	6	(5)	c Cremer b Chigumbura	11
†Khaled Masud	c Nkala b Cremer	49	(6)	c Cremer b Hondo	23
Mohammad Rafique	c Taibu b Mpofu	69		not out	14
Mashrafe Mortaza	c Sibanda b Cremer	48		c Hondo b Chigumbura	19
Tapash Baisya	b Mpofu	6		c Sibanda b Chigumbura	1
Enamul Haque II	not out	0			
Extras	(B 7, LB 3, W 6, NB 3)	19		(B 1, LB 8, NB 4, PEN 5)	18
Total		**488**		(9 wickets declared)	**204**

ZIMBABWE

S. Matsikenyeri	c Habibul b Baisya	28		b Haque	20
B.G.Rogers	run out	5		c sub (Manjural Rana) b Baisya	0
V.Sibanda	lbw b Rafique	12		lbw b Baisya	0
H.Masakadza	b Mortaza	29		c and b Haque	56
A.G.Cremer	lbw b Rafique	0	(9)	c Saleh b Haque	2
B.R.M.Taylor	lbw b Mortaza	39	(5)	lbw b Haque	44
*†T.Taibu	lbw b Rafique	92	(6)	c Aftab b Haque	0
E.Chigumbura	c Masud b Rafique	71	(7)	c Masud b Mortaza	10
M.L.Nkala	c Masud b Rafique	23	(8)	b Mortaza	5
D.T.Hondo	c Masud b Mortaza	1		not out	6
C.B.Mpofu	not out	0		c Ashraful b Haque	5
Extras	(B 1, LB 1, W 1, NB 9)	12		(LB 1, W 1, NB 4)	6
Total		**312**			**154**

ZIMBABWE	O	M	R	W		O	M	R	W
Mpofu	29	3	109	4		12	1	47	1
Hondo	27	6	70	0		17	0	61	3
Chigumbura	28	6	79	1		16.1	3	54	5
Nkala	26	10	50	2					
Cremer	16.3	1	86	2					
Matsikenyeri	23	3	84	1	(4)	6	0	28	0

BANGLADESH	O	M	R	W		O	M	R	W
Mashrafe Mortaza	31	12	59	3		17	4	45	2
Tapash Baisya	24	5	87	1		10	6	20	2
Mohammad Rafique	41.4	19	65	5	(4)	15	6	43	0
Enamul Haque	26	9	55	0	(3)	22.2	5	45	6
Mohammad Ashraful	5	0	19	0					
Rajin Saleh	4	0	25	0					

FALL OF WICKETS

	B	Z	B	Z
Wkt	1st	1st	2nd	2nd
1st	91	31	7	2
2nd	93	48	47	2
3rd	153	59	83	42
4th	272	59	114	112
5th	283	86	145	115
6th	341	152	156	126
7th	410	271	176	138
8th	472	308	202	143
9th	480	312	204	145
10th	488	312	–	154

Umpires: Asad Rauf (*Pakistan*) (1) and T.H.Wijewardene (*Sri Lanka*) (4).
Referee: R.S.Mahanama (*Sri Lanka*) (3).　　　　Test No. 1735/7 (B35/Z76)

BANGLADESH v ZIMBABWE (2nd Test)

At Bangabandhu National Stadium, Dhaka, on 14, 15, 16, 17, 18 January 2005.
Toss: Zimbabwe. Result: **MATCH DRAWN**.
Debuts: None.

ZIMBABWE

S. Matsikenyeri	b Haque	51	lbw b Mortaza		14
B.G.Rogers	b Haque	29	b Mortaza		20
D.D Ebrahim	lbw b Haque	12	lbw b Mortaza		1
H.Masakadza	c Aftab b Baisya	43	c Saleh b Rafique		1
B.R.M.Taylor	lbw b Haque	2	b Haque		78
*†T.Taibu	not out	85	c Baisya b Haque		153
E.Chigumbura	c Ashraful b Baisya	34	c Masud b Ashraful		0
T.Panyangara	c Masud b Mortaza	21	st Masud b Haque		6
A.G.Cremer	b Haque	1	lbw b Haque		6
D.T.Hondo	b Haque	9	c Aftab b Haque		3
C.B.Mpofu	c Ashraful b Haque	0	not out		1
Extras	(B 4, LB 6, NB 1)	11	(LB 2, NB 7)		9
Total		**298**			**286**

BANGLADESH

Javed Omar	c Taibu b Hondo	34	c Taylor b Cremer		43
Nafis Iqbal	c Taibu b Hondo	28	c Taylor b Panyangara		121
*Habibul Bashar	b Hondo	10	c Masakadza b Panyangara		2
Mohammad Ashraful	lbw b Hondo	5	c Ebrahim b Cremer		3
Rajin Saleh	c Masakadza b Cremer	24	not out		56
Aftab Ahmed	c Matsikenyeri b Hondo	0	c Taibu b Panyangara		5
†Khaled Masud	b Hondo	0	not out		28
Mohammad Rafique	c Ebrahim b Masakadza	56			
Mashrafe Mortaza	c Chigambura b Panyangara	26			
Tapash Baisya	c Chigambura b Cremer	13			
Enamul Haque II	not out	3			
Extras	(LB 7, NB 5)	12	(B 13, LB 6, NB 8)		27
Total		**211**	(5 wickets)		**285**

BANGLADESH	O	M	R	W		O	M	R	W
Tapash Baisya	22	7	67	2	(2)	13.2	2	50	0
Mashrafe Mortaza	23	5	69	1	(1)	19.4	7	51	3
Mohammad Rafique	38	14	57	0		24	9	56	1
Enamul Haque II	35	9	95	7		37	8	105	5
Mohammad Ashraful						9	2	22	1

ZIMBABWE	O	M	R	W		O	M	R	W
Panyangara	17	5	37	1		21	10	28	3
Mpofu	11	3	28	0		22	10	29	0
Hondo	22	7	59	6		21	7	37	0
Chigumbura	9	1	32	0		19	7	31	0
Cremer	12.4	1	32	2		34	9	61	2
Masakadza	7	1	16	1	(7)	10	3	11	0
Matsikenyeri					(6)	8	0	41	0
Taylor						4	0	11	0
Rogers						3	0	17	0

FALL OF WICKETS

	Z	B	Z	B
Wkt	1st	1st	2nd	2nd
1st	65	58	30	133
2nd	96	71	36	148
3rd	107	84	37	153
4th	111	85	37	196
5th	171	103	187	206
6th	221	107	196	–
7th	257	132	212	–
8th	262	168	218	–
9th	298	203	285	–
10th	298	211	286	–

Umpires: Nadim Ghauri (*Pakistan*) (1) and M.G.Silva (*Sri Lanka*) (3).
Referee: R.S.Mahanama (*Sri Lanka*) (4).

Test No. 1736/8 (B36/Z77)

TEST MATCH CHAMPIONSHIP SCHEDULE
Months indicate the start of a series

2005	Apr	West Indies host South Africa
		India host Pakistan
		India host Bangladesh
	May	England host Bangladesh
		West Indies host Pakistan
	Jun	England host Australia
	Jul	Sri Lanka host West Indies
	Sep	Zimbabwe host New Zealand
	Oct	Australia host West Indies
		South Africa host New Zealand
		Zimbabwe host India
	Nov	India host Sri Lanka
		Pakistan host England
	Dec	Australia host South Africa
		New Zealand host Zimbabwe
		New Zealand host Australia

2006	Jan	Australia host Sri Lanka
		Pakistan host India
	Feb	New Zealand host West Indies
		India host England
		South Africa host Australia
		Sri Lanka host Bangladesh
	Mar	Sri Lanka host Pakistan
	Apr	West Indies host India
		Bangladesh host Australia
	May	England host Sri Lanka
		West Indies host Zimbabwe
	Jun	England host Pakistan
	Aug	Zimbabwe host South Africa
	Sep	Zimbabwe host Australia
	Oct	Pakistan host Zimbabwe
		Bangladesh host India
		Sri Lanka host South Africa
	Nov	Australia host England
		Australia host New Zealand
	Dec	Pakistan host West Indies
		South Africa host India
		New Zealand host Bangladesh

2007	Jan	Australia host New Zealand
	Feb	Bangladesh host England
		New Zealand host India
		South Africa host Pakistan
		Sri Lanka host Zimbabwe
		West Indies host Australia
	Apr	*World Cup in West Indies*
	May	England host West Indies
	Jun	England host India
	Aug	Sri Lanka host New Zealand
	Sep	Zimbabwe host Pakistan
	Oct	India host Zimbabwe
		Bangladesh host New Zealand
		Pakistan host South Africa
		Sri Lanka host England
	Nov	Australia host Sri Lanka
	Dec	Australia host India
		New Zealand host Sri Lanka
		South Africa host West Indies
		Zimbabwe host Bangladesh

2008	Feb	India host West Indies
		New Zealand host England
		Bangladesh host Sri Lanka
		Pakistan host Australia
		South Africa host Zimbabwe
	Mar	Bangladesh host South Africa
	Apr	West Indies host New Zealand
	May	England host Zimbabwe
		West Indies host Sri Lanka
	Jun	England host South Africa
	Jul	Sri Lanka host India
	Sep	Sri Lanka host Australia
		Zimbabwe host West Indies
	Oct	India host South Africa
		Pakistan host New Zealand
	Nov	Australia host Pakistan
		West Indies host Bangladesh
	Dec	Australia host West Indies
		New Zealand host Pakistan
		South Africa host England
		Zimbabwe host Sri Lanka

2009	Jan	South Africa host India
		Bangladesh host Zimbabwe
		Australia host Pakistan
	Feb	New Zealand host Australia
		West Indies host England
	Mar	India host Pakistan
	Apr	West Indies host Zimbabwe
		South Africa host Bangladesh
	May	England host New Zealand
	Jun	England host Australia
	Jul	Sri Lanka host West Indies
	Sep	Pakistan host Bangladesh
	Oct	India host New Zealand
		South Africa host Sri Lanka
		Zimbabwe host England
		Bangladesh host West Indies
	Nov	Australia host Zimbabwe
		Pakistan host England
	Dec	Australia host South Africa
		India host Sri Lanka
		New Zealand host West Indies

2010	Jan	Australia host Zimbabwe
		Bangladesh host Pakistan
	Feb	New Zealand host Zimbabwe
		Pakistan host Sri Lanka
		South Africa host Australia
	Mar	West Indies host India
	Apr	West Indies host Pakistan
	May	England host Bangladesh
	Jun	England host West Indies
	Aug	Sri Lanka host Pakistan
	Sep	Zimbabwe host New Zealand
		Australia host Bangladesh
	Oct	India host Australia
		South Africa host New Zealand
	Nov	Australia host England
		Pakistan host Zimbabwe
		Bangladesh host West Indies
	Dec	New Zealand host Sri Lanka
		South Africa host Pakistan
		India host Bangladesh

SECOND XI FIXTURES 2005

No symbol	Second XI Championship	3 days
*	Second XI Championship	4 days
†	Second XI Trophy	1 day

APRIL

Tue 19	High Wycombe	MCC YC v Yorkshire
Wed 20	Belper Meadows	Derbys v Northants
Tue 26	Leeds	Yorks v Durham
Wed 27	Moseley	Warwicks v Glam
	Lady Bay SC	Notts v Lancs

MAY

Mon 2	Derby	Derbys v Lancs
Wed 4	Bristol	Glos v Glam
Tue 10	New Rover CC	Yorks v Northants
Wed 11	Sutton	Surrey v Sussex
	Nottingham (TB)	Notts v Glos
	Southampton	Hants v Warwicks
Tue 17	Uxbridge (Vine L)	MCC YC v Surrey
Wed 18	Coventry/N Warwick	Warwicks v Lancs
	Leicester	Leics v Derbys
Mon 23	Lady Bay SC	Notts v Durham
Tue 24	The Oval	Surrey v Glam
Wed 25	Walmley	Warwicks v Hants
	Taunton	Somerset v Surrey
Tue 31	Belper Meadows	Derbys v Surrey

JUNE

Wed 1	Cheltenham C	Glos v MCC YC
	Blackpool	Lancs v Northants
	Billericay	Essex v Glamorgan
	Worksop CC	Notts v Warwicks
Thu 2	Southampton	†Hants v Sussex
Tue 7	Wimbledon	Surrey v Hants
	Manchester (OT)	*Lancs v Yorks
Wed 8	Dunstall CC	Derbys v Leics
	Knowle & Dorridge	Warwicks v Glos
	Radlett	MCC YC v Essex
Thu 9	North Perrott	†Somerset v Glam
Mon 13	Longhirst	Durham v MCC YC
Tue 14	Lady Bay SC	Notts v Leics
	Neath	†Glam v Warwicks
Wed 15	Stowe S	Northants v Surrey
	Hove	Sussex v Hants
Fri 17	Wellbeck Colliery CC	†Notts v Minor C
Mon 20	Harborne	†Warwicks v Glos
	Stamford Bridge	†Yorks v Lancs
Tue 21	Southampton	†Hants v Surrey
	Hartlepool	†Durham v Lancs
	Belper Meadows	†Derbys v Leics
Wed 22	Cheltenham CC	†Glos v Worcs
Thu 23	Usk	†Glam v Worcs
	Milton Keynes	†Northants v Notts

	Todmorden	†Yorks v Leics
Fri 24	High Wycombe	†MCC YC v Hants
	Southport	†Lancs v Yorks
Mon 27	Wormsley	†MCC YC v Sussex
	Worksop C	†Notts v Middx
	Seaton Carew	†Durham v Derbys
	Normandy	†Surrey v Hants
	Bristol WI CC	†Glos v Warwicks
Tue 28	Cardiff	†Glam v Somerset
	Tonbridge S	†Kent v Hants
	York	†Yorks v Derbys
Wed 29	Lydney	†Glos v Glam
	Kenilworth Wardens	†Warwicks v Worcs
	Sunderland	†Durham v Leics
Thu 30	Ealing	†Middx v Minor C
	Stirlands CC	†Sussex v Kent
	Uxbridge (Vine L)	†MCC YC v Surrey
	Glossop	†Derbys v Lancs
	Sunderland	†Durham v Yorks
	Taunton	†Somerset v Glos

JULY

Fri 1	Southampton	†Hants v Kent
	Hinckley	†Leics v Lancs
	Kidderminster	†Worcs v Somerset
	Notts Unity	†Notts v Essex
	Northampton	†Northants v Minor C
Mon 4	Unsworth	†Lancs v Durham
	Barnt Green	†Worcs v Glos
	Maidstone	†Kent v Sussex
	Wickford	†Essex v Middx
	Cheam	†Surrey v MCC YC
	Denby	†Derbys v Yorks
Tue 5	Cheam	†Surrey v Sussex
	Bristol WI CC	†Glos v Somerset
	Nelson	†Lancs v Leics
Wed 6	Northampton	†Northants v Essex
	Ombersley	†Worcs v Warwicks
Thu 7	Leicester	†Leics v Durham
	Cardiff	†Glam v Glos
	Winchmore Hill	†Middx v Northants
	Chester (Boughton H)	†Lancs v Derbys
	Milton Keynes	†Minor C v Notts
	Canterbury	†Kent v Surrey
	Horsham	†Sussex v MCC YC
Fri 8	Old Hill	†Worcs v Glam
	Uxbridge	†Middx v Notts
	Walmley	†Warwicks v Somerset

	Sandiacre CC	†Derbys v Durham	
	Leicester	†Leics v Yorks	
	Southampton	†Hants v MCC YC	
	Milton Keynes	†Minor C v Essex	
Mon 11	Billericay	†Essex v Notts	
	Northampton	†Northants v Middx	
	Hinckley	†Leics v Derbys	
	Stamford Bridge	†Yorks v Durham	
	Banstead	†Surrey v Kent	
Tue 12	Beckenham	†Kent v MCC YC	
	Panteg	Glam v Worcs	
	Southampton	Hants v Glos	
Wed 13	Milton Keynes	†MCC YC v Middx	
	Lady Bay SC	Notts v Surrey	
	Chesterfield	Derbys v Yorks	
	Taunton	†Somerset v Warwicks	
	Bishop's Stortford	†Essex v Northants	
	Middleton (*tbc*)	Lancs v Leics	
Thu 14	Milton Keynes	†Minor C v Northants	
	Uxbridge (Vine L)	†MCC YC v Kent	
	Shenley	†Middx v Essex	
Mon 18	Horsham	†Sussex v Hants	
Tue 19	Coggleshall	Essex v Hants	
	Whitgift S	Surrey v Yorks	
	Papplewick & Linby CC	†Notts v Northants	
Wed 20	Taunton	†Somerset v Worcs	
	Maidstone	Kent v Middx	
	S Northumberland	Durham v Notts	
	Liverpool	Lancs v Derbys	
Thu 21	Dorridge	†Warwicks v Glam	
Fri 22	Horsham	†Sussex v Surrey	
	Coggleshall	†Essex v Minor C	
Tue 26	Northern	Lancs v Durham	
	Stamford Bridge	Yorks v Worcs	
	Stowe S	Northants v Leics	
Wed 27	Worksop C	Notts v Derbys	
	Purley	Surrey v Kent	
	Eastbourne	Sussex v MCC YC	
	North Perrott	Somerset v Warwicks	
	Chelmsford	Essex v Middx	

AUGUST

Tue 2	High Wycombe	MCC YC v Hants
	Cardiff	Glam v Somerset

Wed 3	Stirlands CC	Sussex v Surrey	
	Bristol	Glos v Lancs	
	Hinckley	Leics v Kent	
	Lady Bay SC	Notts v Northants	
Mon 8 (9)	tba	†Trophy Semi-Finals	
Wed 10	Uxbridge (Vine L)	Middx v Sussex	
	Dunstall CC	Derbys v Warwicks	
	Leeds	Yorks v Notts	
	Milton Keynes	Northants v Durham	
	Leicester	Leics v Worcs	
	Billericay	Essex v MCC YC	
Mon 15	Radlett	MCC YC v Northants	
Tue 16	Barnt Green	Worcs v Lancs	
	Bournemouth	Hants v Middx	
	Hove	Sussex v Yorks	
	Hatherley & Reddings	Glos v Somerset	
Wed 17	Hinckley	Leics v Durham	
	Guildford	Surrey v Essex	
	Denby	Derbys v Notts	
Mon 22	Chester-le-St	Durham v Yorks	
	Brighton & Hove	Sussex v Glos	
	Derby	Derbys v Essex	
Tue 23	Ombersley	*Worcs v Warwicks	
	Uxbridge	Middx v MCC YC	
	Southampton	Hants v Surrey	
Wed 24	Taunton	Somerset v Lancs	
	Northampton	Northants v Kent	
Mon 29	Manchester (OT)	*Lancs v Notts	
Tue 30	Kidderminster	Worcs v Glos	
Wed 31	Panteg	Glam v Hants	
	Beckenham	Kent v Derbys	
	Southgate	Middx v Surrey	
	Halstead	Essex v Northants	

SEPTEMBER

Mon 5 (6)	tba	†Trophy Final
Tue 6	Cardiff	Glam v Yorks
Wed 7	Southampton	Hants v Sussex
	Kenilworth Wardens	Warwicks v Leics
	Canterbury	Kent v Essex
Tue 13	Hinckley	Leics v Notts
	Hove	Sussex v Somerset
	Leeds	Yorks v Lancs

MINOR COUNTIES 2005
CHAMPIONSHIP FIXTURES

(* Noon start 1st day)

MAY

29-31	Dunstable	Beds v Cambs
	Bournemouth (DP)	Dorset v Devon
	*Banbury	Oxon v Wilts
	Bury St Edmunds	Suffolk v Herts

JUNE

5-7	Falkland CC	Berks v Cornwall
	Kington	Herefords v Cheshire
	*Sleaford	Lincs v Staffs
	Jesmond	Northumb v Norfolk
	*Colwyn Bay	Wales v Salop
6-8	Barrow	Cumb v Bucks
19-21	Luton Town	Beds v Suffolk
	*Beaconsfield	Bucks v Staffs
	*March	Cambs v Lincs
	Keswick	Cumb v Northumb
	*Bishop's Stortford	Herts v Norfolk
	Challow & Childrey	Oxon v Devon
	*Bridgnorth	Salop v Herefords
	Swansea	Wales v Berks
	Salisbury (S Wilts)	Wilts v Dorset

JULY

3-5	*Finchampstead	Berks v Wilts
	Gerrards Cross	Bucks v Cambs
	Camborne	Cornwall v Wales
	Bovey Tracey	Devon v Cheshire
	Colwall	Herefords v Dorset
	Hertford	Herts v Cumb
	Jesmond	Northumb v Lincs
	*Longton	Staffs v Beds
	Shrewsbury	Salop v Oxon
17-19	*Bedford (Mod S)	Beds v Lincs
	Cambridge (Fenner's)	Cambs v Northumb

	Truro	Cornwall v Herefords
	Exmouth	Devon v Salop
	Chesterton	Oxon v Berks
	Stone	Staffs v Herts
	*Ipswich (Ransome's)	Suffolk v Bucks
	Abergavenny	Wales v Dorset
	Trowbridge	Wilts v Cheshire
24-26	Norwich (MP)	Norfolk v Cumb
31-Aug 2	Norwich (MP)	Norfolk v Suffolk

AUGUST

7-9	*Nantwich	Cheshire v Oxon
	Torquay	Devon v Berks
	Bournemouth (DP)	Dorset v Cornwall
	Kingsland (Luct'ns)	Herefords v Wales
	Long Marston	Herts v Cambs
	Grantham	Lincs v Bucks
	*Norwich (MP)	Norfolk v Beds
	Whitchurch	Salop v Wilts
	Walsall	Staffs v Northumb
	Mildenhall	Suffolk v Cumb
21-23	Slough	Bucks v Norfolk
	*Reading	Berks v Herefords
	*March	Cambs v Staffs
	*Chester (BH)	Cheshire v Wales
	*St Austell	Cornwall v Salop
	Netherfield	Cumb v Beds
	Bournemouth (DP)	Dorset v Oxon
	Cleethorpes	Lincs v Herts
	Jesmond	Northumb v Suffolk
	Corsham	Wilts v Devon

SEPTEMBER

11-13	(tba – E Div)	CHAMPIONSHIP FINAL

MCCA TROPHY FIXTURES

FIRST ROUND – MAY 15

1	March	Cambs v Suffolk
2	Finchampstead	Berks v Lincs
3	Bournemouth (DP)	Dorset v Cornwall
4	Colwall	Herefords v Salop

SECOND ROUND – JUNE 12

5	Jesmond	Northumb v Winner # 1
6	Nantwich	Cheshire v Wales
7	Leek	Staffs v Herts
8	Kingsland/Oswestry	Winner # 4 v Beds
9	Bournemouth (DP)/tba	Winner # 3 v Devon
10	Norwich (MP)	Norfolk v Winner # 2
11	Sedbergh S	Cumb v Oxon

12	Beaconsfield	Bucks v Wilts

QUARTER-FINALS – JULY 10

13	Ascott Park/Westbury	Winner # 12 v Winner # 6
14	Bournemouth (DP)/tba	Winner # 9 v Winner # 11
15	Norwich (MP)/ tba	Winner # 10 v Winner # 8
16	Jesmond/ tba	Winner # 5 v Winner # 7

SEMI-FINALS – JULY 24 (Reserve July 25)

17	(tba)	Winner # 13 v Winner # 14
18	(tba)	Winner # 15 v Winner # 16

FINAL – AUGUST 22 (Probably no reserve day)

19	Lord's

PRINCIPAL FIXTURES 2005

Fri 8 – Mon 11 April

FCF	Lord's	MCC v Warwickshire

Sat 9 – Mon 11 April

	Cardiff	Glamorgan v Cardiff UCCE
	Northampton	Northants v Brad/Leeds UCCE
FCF	Taunton	Somerset v Durham UCCE
FCF	Hove	Sussex v Loughboro' UCCE
FCF	Cambridge	Cambridge UCCE v Essex
FCF	Oxford	Oxford UCCE v Glos

Wed 13 – Sat 16 April

CC2	Derby	Derbyshire v Worcs
CC2	Chelmsford	Essex v Yorkshire
CC1	Southampton	Hampshire v Glos
CC2	Manchester	Lancashire v Somerset
CC2	Leicester	Leics v Durham
CC1	The Oval	Surrey v Sussex
CC1	Birmingham	Warwks v Glamorgan

Wed 13 – Fri 15 April

	Canterbury	Kent v Cardiff UCCE
FCF	Nottingham	Notts v Loughboro' UCCE

Sun 17 April

NL2	Derby	Derbyshire v Kent
NL1	Southampton	Hampshire v Essex
NL1	Manchester	Lancashire v Glamorgan
NL2	Leicester	Leics v Durham
NL1	Northampton	Northants v Worcs
NL1	Nottingham	Notts v Middlesex
NL2	The Oval	Surrey v Yorkshire
NL2	Birmingham	Warwks v Somerset

Wed 20 – Sat 23 April

CC2	Chester-le-St	Durham v Worcs
CC1	Canterbury	Kent v Warwks
CC1	Lord's	Middlesex v Notts
CC2	Northampton	Northants v Leics
CC1	Hove	Sussex v Hampshire
CC2	Leeds	Yorkshire v Somerset

Wed 20 – Fri 22 April

	The Oval	Surrey v Brad/Leeds UCCE
FCF	Oxford	Oxford UCCE v Derbyshire

Fri 22 April

NL1	Cardiff	Glamorgan v Essex

Sun 24 April

NL2	Chester-le-St	Durham v Surrey
NL1	Bristol	Glos v Northants
NL2	Canterbury	Kent v Leics
NL1	Lord's	Middlesex v Lancashire
NL2	Hove	Sussex v Derbyshire
NL2	Leeds	Yorkshire v Somerset

Wed 27 – Sat 30 April

CC2	Derby	Derbyshire v Northants
CC1	Cardiff	Glamorgan v Surrey
CC1	Bristol	Glos v Kent
CC1	Nottingham	Notts v Sussex
CC2	Taunton	Somerset v Essex
CC1	Birmingham	Warwks v Middlesex
CC2	Worcester	Worcs v Lancashire

Wed 27 – Fri 29 April

	Southampton	Hampshire v Cardiff UCCE
FCF	Leicester	Leics v Durham UCCE

Sun 1 May

NL1	Manchester	Lancashire v Notts
NL1	Lord's	Middlesex v Worcs
NL1	Northampton	Northants v Hampshire
NL2	Taunton	Somerset v Leics
NL2	Birmingham	Warwks v Kent
NL2	Leeds	Yorkshire v Sussex
NL2	Edinburgh	Scotland v Durham

Mon 2 May

NL2	Chester-le-St	Durham v Sussex
NL1	Southampton	Hampshire v Glos
NL1	Nottingham	Notts v Glamorgan
NL2	Taunton	Somerset v Surrey

Tue 3 May (*Reserve 4 May*)

CGT		Round 1
	Reading	Berkshire v Glos
	Wormsley	Bucks v Lancashire
	Brondby	Denmark v Northants
	Exmouth	Devon v Essex
	Rotterdam	Holland v Warwks
	Belfast (CS)	Ireland v Yorkshire
	Jesmond	Northumb v Middlesex
	Salisbury	Wiltshire v Kent

Wed 4 May (*Reserve 5 May*)

CGT		Round 1

	Luton	Beds v Sussex
	Chester-le-St	Durham v Derbyshire
	Leicester	Leics v Somerset
	Edinburgh	Scotland v Worcs
	Whitchurch	Shropshire v Hampshire
	Leek	Staffs v Surrey
	Bury St Eds	Suffolk v Glamorgan
	Swansea	Wales MC v Notts

Fri 6 – Mon 9 May

CC2	Chester-le-St	Durham v Somerset
CC2	Chelmsford	Essex v Leics
CC1	Cardiff	Glamorgan v Glos
CC1	Southampton	Hampshire v Middlesex
CC2	Manchester	Lancashire v Derbyshire
CC1	The Oval	Surrey v Notts
CC2	Leeds	Yorkshire v Northants

Sun 8 – Tue 10 May

FCF	Kidderminster	Worcs v Loughboro' UCCE

Sun 8 May

NL2	Horsham	Sussex v Warwks
NL2	Edinburgh	Scotland v Kent

Tue 10 – Fri 13 May

CC1	Horsham	Sussex v Warwks

Tue 10 – Thu 12 May

FCF	Cambridge	Brit U v Bangladeshis

Wed 11 – Sat 14 May

CC1	Canterbury	Kent v Hampshire
CC2	Manchester	Lancashire v Durham
CC2	Leicester	Leics v Yorkshire
CC1	Lord's	Middlesex v Glos
CC2	Northampton	Northants v Essex
CC1	The Oval	Surrey v Glamorgan
CC2	Worcester	Worcs v Derbyshire

Wed 11 May

NL2	Edinburgh	Scotland v Somerset

Sun 15 – Tue 17 May

FCF	Hove	Sussex v Bangladeshis

Sun 15 May

NL2	Chester-le-St	Durham v Yorkshire
NL1	Chelmsford	Essex v Glamorgan
NL1	Manchester	Lancashire v Northants
NL2	Leicester	Leics v Surrey
NL1	Lord's	Middlesex v Hampshire
NL1	Worcester	Worcs v Notts

Tue 17 May (*Reserve 18 May*)

CGT	Round 2	
		Berkshire/Glos v Staffs/Surrey
		Bucks/Lancashire v Devon/Essex
		Durham/Derbyshire v Wiltshire/Kent
		Holland/Warwks v Leics/Somerset
		Ireland/Yorkshire v Scotland/Worcs

		Northumb/Middlesex v Denmark/Northants
		Suffolk/Glamorgan v Shropshire/Hampshire

Wed 18 May (*Reserve 19 May*)

CGT	Round 2	
		Beds/Sussex v Wales MC/Notts

Fri 20 – Mon 23 May

CC2	Chester-le-St	Durham v Yorkshire
CC2	Chelmsford	Essex v Worcs
CC1	Southampton	Hampshire v Glamorgan
CC1	Nottingham	Notts v Kent
CC2	Taunton	Somerset v Lancashire

Fri 20 – Sun 22 May

FCF	Northampton	Northants v Bangladeshis

Fri 20 May

NL2	F Derby	Derbyshire v Warwks
NL2	Edinburgh	Scotland v Surrey

Sat 21 – Mon 23 May

FCF	Cambridge	Cambridge UCCE v Warwks

Sun 22 May

NL1	Bristol	Glos v Middlesex

Wed 25 – Sat 28 May

CC1	Bristol	Glos v Notts
CC1	Tunbridge W	Kent v Surrey
CC2	Northampton	Northants v Somerset
CC1	Hove	Sussex v Middlesex
CC1	Stratford	Warwks v Hampshire
CC2	Leeds	Yorkshire v Essex

Wed 25 – Fri 27 May

FCF	Durham	Durham UCCE v Durham
FCF	Oxford	Oxford UCCE v Lancashire

Thu 26 – Sun 29 May

CC2	Derby	Derbyshire v Leics

Thu 26 – Mon 30 May

TM1	Lord's	England v Bangladesh

Fri 27 May

NL1	F Cardiff	Glamorgan v Worcs

Sun 29 May

NL2	Tunbridge W	Kent v Durham
NL2	Birmingham	Warwks v Scotland

Mon 30 May

NL2	F Derby	Derbyshire v Leics
NL1	Bristol	Glos v Lancashire
NL1	Southampton	Hampshire v Northants
NL1	Nottingham	Notts v Essex
NL2	Taunton	Somerset v Sussex
NL2	The Oval	Surrey v Durham
NL1	Worcester	Worcs v Middlesex
NL2	Leeds	Yorkshire v Scotland

Wed 1 – Sat 4 June

CC2	Chelmsford	Essex v Derbyshire
CC1	Swansea	Glamorgan v Sussex
CC1	Maidstone	Kent v Glos
CC2	Manchester	Lancashire v Northants
CC2	Oakham S	Leics v Somerset
CC1	Nottingham	Notts v Hampshire
CC1	Whitgift S	Surrey v Warwks
CC2	Worcester	Worcs v Durham

Wed 1 – Fri 3 June

	Leeds	Yorkshire v Brad/Leeds UCCE
FCF	Cambridge	Cambridge UCCE v Middlesex

Fri 3 – Tue 7 June

TM2	Chester-le-St	England v Bangladesh

Sun 5 June

NL1	Swansea	Glamorgan v Notts
NL2	Maidstone	Kent v Derbyshire
NL1	Manchester	Lancashire v Hampshire
NL2	Oakham S	Leics v Somerset
NL1	Lord's	Middlesex v Essex
NL2	Whitgift S	Surrey v Warwks

Wed 8 – Sat 11 June

CC1	Cardiff	Glamorgan v Kent
CC1	Lord's	Middlesex v Surrey
CC2	Bath	Somerset v Worcs
CC2	Leeds	Yorkshire v Lancashire

Thu 9 – Sun 12 June

CC2	Chester-le-St	Durham v Essex

Fri 10 – Mon 13 June

CC1	Gloucester	Glos v Warwks

Fri 10 June

	^FDerby	Derbyshire v Bangladeshis
NL2	Edinburgh	Scotland v Sussex

Sat 11 June

	Southampton	Hampshire v England XI
	Leicester	Leics v Australians

Sun 12 June

NL2	Leicester	Leics v Yorkshire
NL1	Northampton	Northants v Middlesex
NL1	Nottingham	Notts v Lancashire
NL2	Bath	Somerset v Kent
	Worcester	Worcs v Bangladeshis

Mon 13 June

(T20)	Southampton	England v Australia
NL2	Chester-le-St	Durham v Derbyshire

Wed 15 – Sat 18 June

CC2	Derby	Derbyshire v Lancashire
CC1	Southampton	Hampshire v Surrey
CC2	Leicester	Leics v Worcs
CC1	Southgate	Middlesex v Glamorgan

CC2	Northampton	Northants v Durham
CC1	Arundel	Sussex v Notts
CC1	Birmingham	Warwks v Kent

Wed 15 June

	Taunton	Somerset v Australians

Thu 16 June

LOI	The Oval	England v Bangladesh

Fri 17 June

NL1	^FChelmsford	Essex v Glos
NL2	Taunton	Somerset v Scotland
	Lord's	Cambridge U v Oxford U

Sat 18 June

LOI	Cardiff	Australia v Bangladesh

Sun 19 June

LOI	Bristol	England v Australia
NL2	Derby	Derbyshire v Scotland
NL1	Southampton	Hampshire v Glamorgan
NL1	Southgate	Middlesex v Notts
NL1	Stowe S	Northants v Glos
NL2	Arundel	Sussex v Durham
NL2	Birmingham	Warwks v Leics
NL1	Worcester	Worcs v Essex

Mon 20 June

NL2	Leicester	Leics v Scotland

Tue 21 June

LOI	Nottingham	England v Bangladesh

Wed 22 June

T20	Derby	Derbyshire v Durham
T20	^FCardiff	Glamorgan v Somerset
T20	Southampton	Hampshire v Middlesex
T20	Beckenham	Kent v Surrey
T20	Leicester	Leics v Notts
T20	Milton Keynes	Northants v Glos
T20	^FHove	Sussex v Essex
T20	Worcester	Worcs v Warwks
T20	Leeds	Yorkshire v Lancashire

Thu 23 June

LOI	^FChester-le-St	England v Australia
T20	Taunton	Somerset v Worcs
T20	Lord's	Middlesex v Surrey

Fri 24 June

T20	Derby	Derbyshire v Leics
T20	^FChelmsford	Essex v Kent
T20	Bristol	Glos v Glamorgan
T20	Southampton	Hampshire v Sussex
T20	Northampton	Northants v Warwks
T20	Nottingham	Notts v Lancashire

Sat 25 June

LOI	Manchester	Australia v Bangladesh
T20	Swansea	Glamorgan v Warwks

298

| T20 | Beckenham | Kent v Middlesex |
| T20 | The Oval | Surrey v Hampshire |

Sun 26 June

LOI	Leeds	England v Bangladesh
T20	Chelmsford	Essex v Sussex
T20	Bristol	Glos v Worcs
T20	Nottingham	Notts v Yorkshire
T20	Leicester	Leics v Durham

Mon 27 June

T20	Southampton	Hampshire v Kent
T20	Manchester	Lancashire v Leics
T20	Taunton	Somerset v Glamorgan
T20	Worcester	Worcs v Northants

Tue 28 June

LOI	Birmingham	England v Australia
T20	Chester-le-St	Durham v Notts
T20	Bristol	Glos v Warwks
T20	Southampton	Hampshire v Essex
T20	The Oval	Surrey v Middlesex
T20	Leeds	Yorkshire v Derbyshire

Tue 28 June – Fri 1 July

| FCF | Cambridge | Cambridge U v Oxford U |

Wed 29 June

T20	ᶠChelmsford	Essex v Hampshire
T20	Manchester	Lancashire v Derbyshire
T20	Uxbridge	Middlesex v Kent
T20	Northampton	Northants v Somerset
T20	ᶠHove	Sussex v Surrey

Thu 30 June

LOI	Canterbury	Australia v Bangladesh
T20	Nottingham	Notts v Leics
T20	Birmingham	Warwks v Glamorgan
T20	Leeds	Yorkshire v Durham

Fri 1 July

T20	Chester-le-St	Durham v Leics
T20	ᶠCardiff	Glamorgan v Northants
T20	Bristol	Glos v Somerset
T20	Manchester	Lancashire v Yorkshire
T20	Southgate	Middlesex v Essex
T20	Nottingham	Notts v Derbyshire
T20	The Oval	Surrey v Kent
T20	ᶠHove	Sussex v Hampshire
T20	Birmingham	Warwks v Worcs

Sat 2 July (†Reserve 3 July)

LOI	†Lord's	NatWest Series Final
T20	Taunton	Somerset v Northants
T20	Worcester	Worcs v Glos

Sun 3 July

| T20 | Manchester | Lancashire v Durham |
| T20 | Leeds | Yorkshire v Notts |

Mon 4 July

T20	Derby	Derbyshire v Lancashire
T20	Chester-le-St	Durham v Yorkshire
T20	ᶠHove	Sussex v Middlesex
T20	Birmingham	Warwks v Somerset

Tue 5 July

T20	ᶠChelmsford	Essex v Surrey
T20	ᶠCardiff	Glamorgan v Glos
T20	Canterbury	Kent v Sussex
T20	Leicester	Leics v Derbyshire
T20	Northampton	Northants v Worcs

Wed 6 July

T20	Derby	Derbyshire v Notts
T20	Chester-le-St	Durham v Lancashire
T20	Canterbury	Kent v Essex
T20	Leicester	Leics v Yorkshire
T20	Richmond	Middlesex v Hampshire
T20	Taunton	Somerset v Glos
T20	The Oval	Surrey v Sussex
T20	Birmingham	Warwks v Northants
T20	Worcester	Worcs v Glamorgan

Thu 7 July

| LOI | Leeds | England v Australia |

Fri 8 – Mon 11 July

CC2	Chester-le-St	Durham v Lancashire
CC1	Bristol	Glos v Surrey
CC1	Southgate	Middlesex v Hampshire
CC1	Nottingham	Notts v Glamorgan
CC2	Taunton	Somerset v Leics
CC2	Worcester	Worcs v Yorkshire

Fri 8 July

| NL1 | ᶠChelmsford | Essex v Northants |
| NL2 | ᶠHove | Sussex v Kent |

Sat 9 July

| NL2 | Birmingham | Warwks v Derbyshire |

Sun 10 July

| LOI | Lord's | England v Australia |

Sun 10 – Wed 13 July

| CC1 | Canterbury | Kent v Sussex |
| CC2 | Chelmsford | Essex v Northants |

Tue 12 July

| LOI | Oval | England v Australia |

Wed 13 July

| NL2 | ᶠLeeds | Yorkshire v Surrey |

Fri 15 and Sat 16 July (Reserve 16/17 July)

| CGT | | Quarter-Finals |

Fri 15 July

| | tba | Sx/Le/Sm v Australians |

299

Sun 17 July
NL2	Chester-le-St	Durham v Warwks
NL1	Southgate	Middlesex v Glos
NL1	Northampton	Northants v Lancashire
NL1	Nottingham	Notts v Hampshire
NL2	The Oval	Surrey v Derbyshire
NL1	Worcester	Worcs v Glamorgan

Mon 18 July
T20		Quarter-Finals
	Oxford	Brit U v Bangladesh A

Tue 19 July
NL1	F Manchester	Lancashire v Essex

Wed 20 – Sat 23 July
CC1	Southampton	Hampshire v Sussex
CC2	Northampton	Northants v Worcs
CC1	Guildford	Surrey v Kent
CC1	Birmingham	Warwks v Notts
CC2	Scarborough	Yorkshire v Leics

Wed 20 – Fri 22 July
FCF	Bristol	Glos v Bangladesh A

Wed 20 July
NL2	F Derby	Derbyshire v Durham
NL1	F Cardiff	Glamorgan v Middlesex

Thu 21 – Mon 25 July
TM1	Lord's	England v Australia

Thu 21 – Sun 24 July
CC2	Derby	Derbyshire v Durham
CC1	Cardiff	Glamorgan v Middlesex
CC2	Manchester	Lancashire v Essex

Sun 24 July
	Southampton	Hampshire v Bangladesh A
NL1	Bristol	Glos v Worcs
NL2	Canterbury	Kent v Somerset
NL1	Nottingham	Notts v Northants
NL2	Guildford	Surrey v Sussex
NL2	Scarborough	Yorkshire v Warwks
NL2	Edinburgh	Scotland v Leics

Tue 26 – Fri 29 July
CC2	Leicester	Leics v Essex
CC1	Nottingham	Notts v Surrey
CC2	Taunton	Somerset v Durham
CC1	Hove	Sussex v Glos
CC2	Leeds	Yorkshire v Derbyshire

Tue 26 – Thu 28 July
FCF	Abergavenny	Glamorgan v Bangladesh A

Tue 26 July
NL1	F Southampton	Hampshire v Worcs

Wed 27 July
NL2	F Canterbury	Kent v Warwks

Sat 30 July
T20	Oval	Semi-Finals/F Final

Sat 30 July – Mon 1 August
FCF	tba	Wo/Gm /Gs/Nh v Australians

Sun 31 July
NL2	Leicester	Leics v Warwks
NL2	Leeds	Yorkshire v Kent

Mon 1 August
	Liverpool	Lancashire v Bangladesh A
NL2	F Hove	Sussex v Somerset

Tue 2 August
NL1	F Worcester	Worcs v Northants

Wed 3 – Sat 6 August
CC2	Southend	Essex v Durham
CC1	Cheltenham	Glos v Hampshire
CC1	Canterbury	Kent v Glamorgan
CC2	Leicester	Leics v Lancashire
CC1	Lord's	Middlesex v Warwks
CC1	Hove	Sussex v Surrey

Wed 3 – Fri 5 August
	Leeds	Yorkshire v Bangladesh A

Wed 3 August
NL2	F Derby	Derbyshire v Somerset

Thu 4 – Mon 8 August
TM2	Birmingham	England v Australia

Thu 4 – Sun 7 August
CC2	Derby	Derbyshire v Somerset
CC2	Worcester	Worcs v Northants

Sun 7 August
	Chester-le-St	Durham v Bangladesh A
NL1	Southend	Essex v Middlesex
NL1	Cheltenham	Glos v Hampshire
NL2	Canterbury	Kent v Surrey
NL2	Hove	Sussex v Leics
NL2	Edinburgh	Scotland v Yorkshire

Tue 9 August
NL1	Cheltenham	Glos v Notts
NL2	F Oval	Surrey v Leics

Wed 10 – Sat 13 August
CC1	Colwyn Bay	Glamorgan v Warwks
CC1	Cheltenham	Glos v Sussex
CC2	Northampton	Northants v Derbyshire
CC1	Nottingham	Notts v Middlesex
CC2	Taunton	Somerset v Yorkshire

Wed 10 – Fri 12 August
	The Oval	Surrey v Bangladesh A

Wed 10 August
NL1	F Southampton	Hampshire v Lancashire

300

Thu 11 – Mon 15 August
TM3 Manchester England v Australia

Fri 12 – Mon 15 August
CC2 Chester-le-St Durham v Leics
CC1 Southampton Hampshire v Kent

Sun 14 – Wed 17 August
CC1 Nottingham Notts v Warwks

Sun 14 August
NL2 Derby Derbyshire v Sussex
NL1 Colwyn Bay Glamorgan v Lancashire
NL1 Cheltenham Glos v Essex
NL2 Taunton Somerset v Yorkshire

Mon 15 August
NL1 Lord's Middlesex v Northants

Tue 16 – Fri 19 August
CC2 Derby Derbyshire v Essex
CC2 Manchester Lancashire v Yorkshire
CC1 Lord's Middlesex v Sussex
CC1 The Oval Surrey v Glos
CC2 Worcester Worcs v Somerset

Tue 16 – Thu 18 August
FCF Canterbury Kent v Bangladesh A

Tue 16 August
NL2 Chester-le-St Durham v Leics

Wed 17 August
NL1 F Northampton Northants v Glamorgan

Thu 18 August
Edinburgh Scotland v Australians

Sat 20 – Sun 21 August
tba Nh/Mx v Australians

Sat 20 August (*Reserve 21 August*)
CGT tba Semi-Finals

Sun 21 August
NL1 Manchester Lancashire v Glos
NL2 Leicester Leics v Sussex
NL2 Taunton Somerset v Durham
NL2 Birmingham Warwks v Yorkshire
NL1 Worcester Worcs v Hampshire

Mon 22 August
NL1 F Chelmsford Essex v Notts
NL2 F The Oval Surrey v Kent

Tue 23 August
NL1 F Cardiff Glamorgan v Glos
NL2 F Birmingham Warwks v Sussex

Wed 24 – Sat 27 August
CC2 Colchester Essex v Somerset
CC1 Canterbury Kent v Middlesex
CC2 Leicester Leics v Northants
CC1 The Oval Surrey v Hampshire

CC2 Scarborough Yorkshire v Durham

Wed 24 August
NL1 F Manchester Lancashire v Worcs

Thu 25 – Mon 29 August
TM4 Nottingham England v Australia

Thu 25 – Sun 28 August
CC1 Bristol Glos v Glamorgan
CC1 Birmingham Warwks v Sussex
CC2 Blackpool Lancashire v Worcs

Fri 26 August
NL2 Edinburgh Scotland v Derbyshire

Sun 28 August
NL2 Chester-le-St Durham v Scotland
NL1 Colchester Essex v Hampshire
NL1 Northampton Northants v Notts
NL2 The Oval Surrey v Somerset
NL2 Scarborough Yorkshire v Derbyshire

Tue 30 August – Fri 2 September
CC2 Chester-le-St Durham v Derbyshire
CC1 Cardiff Glamorgan v Notts
CC1 Bristol Glos v Middlesex
CC1 Southampton Hampshire v Warwks
CC2 Northampton Northants v Lancs
CC2 Worcester Worcs v Leics

Tue 30 August
NL2 F Canterbury Kent v Yorkshire
NL2 Hove Sussex v Scotland

Tue 31 August
NL2 F Hove Sussex v Leics

Thu 1 September
NL2 Canterbury Kent v Scotland

Sat 3 – Sun 4 September
tba Ex/Sx/Nt v Australians

Sat 3 September (*Reserve Sun 4 September*)
CGT Lord's Final

Sun 4 September
NL2 Derby Derbyshire v Surrey
NL2 Chester-le-St Durham v Kent
NL1 Cardiff Glamorgan v Northants
NL1 Southampton Hampshire v Middlesex
NL1 Worcester Worcs v Glos
NL2 Leeds Yorkshire v Leics

Mon 5 – Thu 8 September
CC1 Nottingham Notts v Glos

Mon 5 September
NL2 F Taunton Somerset v Wa

Tue 6 September
NL2 F Leicester Leics v Derbyshire

Wed 7 – Sat 10 September
CC1	Lord's	Middlesex v Kent
CC2	Taunton	Somerset v Northants
CC1	Hove	Sussex v Glamorgan
CC2	Leeds	Yorkshire v Worcs

Wed 7 September
| NL1 | FChelmsford | Essex v Lancashire |

Thu 8 – Mon 12 September
| TM5 | The Oval | England v Australia |

Thu 8 – Sun 11 September
| CC2 | Leicester | Leics v Derbyshire |

Fri 9 – Mon 12 September
| CC2 | Chelmsford | Essex v Lancashire |

Fri 9 September
| NL1 | FNottingham | Notts v Glos |

Sat 10 – Tue 13 September
| CC1 | Birmingham | Warwks v Surrey |

Sun 11 September
NL1	Lord's	Middlesex v Glamorgan
NL1	Nottingham	Notts v Worcs
NL2	Leeds	Yorkshire v Durham

Tue 13 September
| NL1 | FCardiff | Glamorgan v Hampshire |

Wed 14 – Sat 17 September
| CC1 | Canterbury | Kent v Notts |
| CC2 | Chester-le-St | Durham v Northants |

Wed 14 September
| NL2 | FDerby | Derbyshire v Yorkshire |

| NL2 | FBirmingham | Warwks v Surrey |

Thu 15 – Sun 18 September
| CC1 | Cardiff | Glamorgan v Hampshire |

Fri 16 – Mon 19 September
| CC2 | Derby | Derbyshire v Yorkshire |

Sun 18 September
NL2	Chester-le-St	Durham v Somerset
NL1	Chelmsford	Essex v Worcs
NL2	Canterbury	Kent v Sussex
NL1	Manchester	Lancashire v Middlesex
NL2	Edinburgh	Scotland v Warwks

Wed 21 – Sat 24 September
CC1	Southampton	Hampshire v Notts
CC2	Manchester	Lancashire v Leics
CC2	Northampton	Northants v Yorkshire
CC2	Taunton	Somerset v Derbyshire
CC1	The Oval	Surrey v Middlesex
CC1	Hove	Sussex v Kent
CC1	Birmingham	Warwks v Glos
CC2	Worcester	Worcs v Essex

Sun 25 September
NL1	Bristol	Glos v Glamorgan
NL1	Southampton	Hampshire v Notts
NL2	Leicester	Leics v Kent
NL1	Northampton	Northants v Essex
NL2	Taunton	Somerset v Derbyshire
NL2	The Oval	Surrey v Scotland
NL2	Hove	Sussex v Yorkshire
NL2	Birmingham	Warwks v Durham
NL1	Worcester	Worcs v Lancs

UNDER-19 CRICKET

LIMITED-OVERS INTERNATIONALS
England v Sri Lanka
LOI	Worcester	Tue 26 July
LOI	Manchester	Thu 28 July
LOI	Manchester	Thu 29 July

TEST MATCH SERIES
England v Sri Lanka
TM1	Shenley	Wed 3 – Sat 6 August
TM2	Scarborough	Tue 9 – Fri 12 August
TM3	Leeds	Mon 15 – Thu 18 August

WOMEN'S CRICKET

WOMEN'S TEST MATCH
England v Australia
| TM1 | Hove | Tue 9 – Fri 12 August |
| TM2 | Worcester | Wed 24 – Sat 27 August |

WOMEN'S LIMITED-OVERS
England v Australia
| LOI | Cheltenham | Mon 15 August |

LOI	Kidderminster	Fri 19 August
LOI	Stratford	Sun 21 August
LOI	Taunton	Tue 30 August
LOI	Taunton	Thu 1 September
T20	Taunton	Fri 2 September

FIELDING CHART

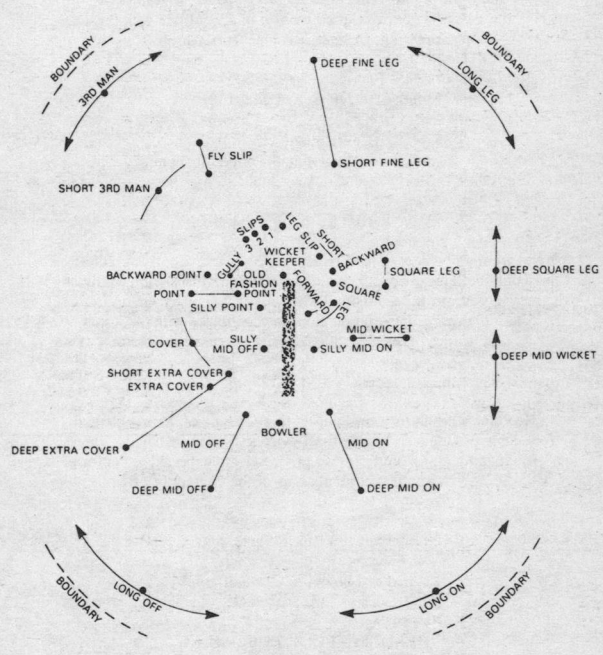

First published in 2005
by HEADLINE BOOK PUBLISHING

Cover photographs:
(*Front*) Steve Harmison © Popperfoto.com;
(*Back*) The Ashes © Marylebone Cricket Club, London/Bridgeman Art Library

10 9 8 7 6 5 4 3 2 1

ISBN 0 7553 1298 8

Headline's policy is to use papers that are natural, renewable and
recyclable products and made from wood grown in sustainable forests.
The logging and manufacturing processes are expected to conform
to the environmental regulations of the country of origin.

Typeset in Times by
Letterpart Limited, Reigate, Surrey

Printed and bound in Great Britain by
Clays Ltd, St Ives plc

HEADLINE BOOK PUBLISHING
A division of Hodder Headline
338 Euston Road
London NW1 3BH

www.headline.co.uk
www.hodderheadline.com